American Musicological Society
Music Library Association Reprint Series

Dover Publications, Inc., New York, in cooperation with the American Musicological Society and the Music Library Association, has undertaken to bring back into print a select list of scholarly musical works long unavailable to the researcher, student, and performer. A distinguished Committee representing both these professional organizations has been appointed to plan and supervise the series, which will include facsimile editions of indispensable historical, theoretical and bibliographical studies as well as important collections of music and translations of basic texts. To make the reprints more useful and to bring them up to date, new introductions, supplementary indexes and bibliographies, etc., will be prepared by qualified specialists.

Sir John Hawkins, *A General History of the Science and Practice of Music*
W. H., A. F., and A. E. Hill, *Antonio Stradivari, His Life and Work*
Curt Sachs, *Real-Lexikon der Musikinstrumente,* new revised, enlarged edition
The Complete Works of Franz Schubert (19 volumes), the Breitkopf & Härtel Critical Edition of 1884-1897 *(Franz Schubert's Werke. Kritisch durchgesehene Gesammtausgabe.)*
Charles Read Baskervill, *The Elizabethan Jig and Related Song Drama*
George Ashdown Audsley, *The Art of Organ-Building,* corrected edition
Emanuel Winternitz, *Musical Autographs from Monteverdi to Hindemith,* corrected edition
William Chappell, *Popular Music of the Olden Time,* 1859 edition
F. T. Arnold, *The Art of Accompaniment from a Thorough-Bass as Practised in the 17th and 18th Centuries*
The Breitkopf Thematic Catalogue, 1762-1787, with new introduction and indexes by B. S. Brook
Otto Kinkeldey, *Orgel und Klavier in der Musik des 16. Jahrhunderts*
Andreas Ornithoparcus, *Musice active micrologus,* together with John Dowland's translation, *A. O. his Micrologus, or Introduction, Containing the Art of Singing*
O. G. T. Sonneck, *Early Concert-life in America (1731-1800)*
Giambattista Mancini, *Practical Reflections on the Figurative Art of Singing* (translated by Pietro Buzzi)
Denis Stevens, *Thomas Tomkins, 1572-1656*
Thoinot Arbeau, *Orchesography* (translated by Mary Stewart Evans)
Edmond vander Straeten, *La Musique aux Pays-Bas avant le XIXe siècle*
Frits Noske, *La Mélodie française de Berlioz à Duparc* (translated by Rita Benton)
Board of Music Trade, *Complete Catalogue of Sheet Music and Musical Works* (1870)

THE ART OF ORGAN-BUILDING.

VOLUME FIRST.

G. A. Audsley

THE ART

OF

ORGAN-BUILDING

A COMPREHENSIVE HISTORICAL, THEORETICAL, AND PRACTICAL TREATISE

ON THE

TONAL APPOINTMENT AND MECHANICAL CONSTRUCTION OF CONCERT-ROOM, CHURCH, AND CHAMBER ORGANS

PROFUSELY ILLUSTRATED

BY

GEORGE ASHDOWN AUDSLEY, LL.D.

ARCHITECT

AUTHOR OF "THE ORNAMENTAL ARTS OF JAPAN," "THE PRACTICAL DECORATOR" AND AUTHOR AND JOINT-AUTHOR OF NUMEROUS WORKS ON ARCHITECTURE AND ART

VOLUME FIRST

DOVER PUBLICATIONS, INC., NEW YORK

Published in Canada by General Publishing Company, Ltd., 30 Lesmill Road, Don Mills, Toronto, Ontario.

Published in the United Kingdom by Constable and Company, Ltd., 10 Orange Street, London WC 2.

This Dover edition, first published in 1965, is an unabridged and corrected republication of the work first published by Dodd, Mead, and Company, New York, in 1905.

International Standard Book Number: 0-486-21314-5

Manufactured in the United States of America
Dover Publications, Inc.
180 Varick Street
New York, N. Y. 10014

PROEM

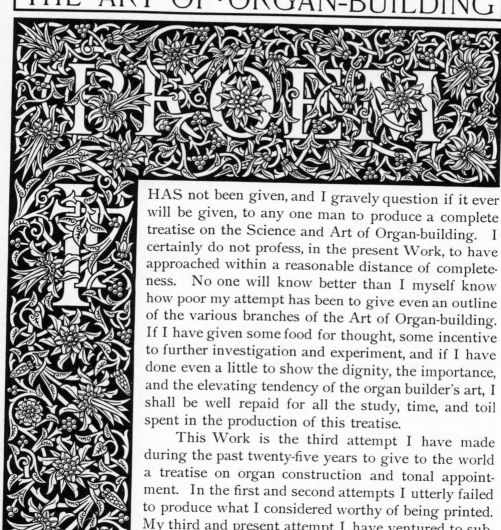

IT HAS not been given, and I gravely question if it ever will be given, to any one man to produce a complete treatise on the Science and Art of Organ-building. I certainly do not profess, in the present Work, to have approached within a reasonable distance of completeness. No one will know better than I myself know how poor my attempt has been to give even an outline of the various branches of the Art of Organ-building. If I have given some food for thought, some incentive to further investigation and experiment, and if I have done even a little to show the dignity, the importance, and the elevating tendency of the organ builder's art, I shall be well repaid for all the study, time, and toil spent in the production of this treatise.

This Work is the third attempt I have made during the past twenty-five years to give to the world a treatise on organ construction and tonal appointment. In the first and second attempts I utterly failed to produce what I considered worthy of being printed. My third and present attempt I have ventured to submit to the organ-loving world, in the hopes of its proving a stimulus to some greater pen and pencil than mine. The Work has been a labor of love. It has been a source of enjoyment during the hours that could be stolen from an exacting profession, and the hours that could reasonably be added to those of each professional day. Such being the case, I can well ask the indulgence of the exacting critic, and the kind consideration of the learned reader.

In the opening Chapter a very faint outline of the History of the inception and development of the Organ is given. This Chapter is merely an introduction to the general subject of the treatise, and lays no claim to either originality or intrinsic value. This Chapter is supplemented by the brief historical notes which open certain subsequent Chapters, and which may be found interesting to the student of organ-building. An exhaustive History of the Organ has yet to be written, for nothing approaching it has appeared in any work in any language.

I have contributed a few new Chapters to the literature of the Organ, with the view of directing more attention to the tonal branch of organ appointment; and the very newness of these Chapters must be their excuse for all imperfections and shortcomings.

An attempt has been made to improve the popular and somewhat unsatisfactory English nomenclature of the Organ. With this aim I have abandoned the use of such common terms as sound-board, flue pipe, super-octave coupler, and others which are either incorrect or objectionable when applied to organ work. And for the first time, so far as my knowledge extends, in the literature of the Organ, a systematic attempt is made to give the names of the numerous organ stops in the different languages orthographically correct: and coupled with this essay, I have offered some suggestions for the formation of a systematic stop nomenclature, to do away with, if possible, the heterogeneous system, or want of system, which at present obtains in the stop-labeling of English and American Organs, not to speak of the flagrant inaccuracies which one sees on the draw-stop labels or name-plates, indicative of either carelessness or want of knowledge.

With the kind co-operation of Mr. Hermann Smith, of London, a gentleman who has gained a distinguished position as an investigator in matters relating to sound-production in musical instruments, I am able to lay before my readers a reasonable theory of the production of sound in organ pipes—a theory widely different from those which have been propounded in the several learned works on acoustics. These theories are fully commented on in the Chapter on Acoustical Matters connected with Organ Pipes.

There has appeared during late years a disposition on the part of English and American organ builders, and others interested in organ matters, to underrate the value, from a tonal point of view, of the compound harmonic-corroborating stops. Some causes have obviously led to this view being held or expressed which it is unnecessary to go into here; but I enter a firm protest in my Chapter on the Compound Stops of the Organ against the abandonment of such important factors in tone-production; and I commend the contents of that Chapter—the logical supplement to the preceding Chapter on the Tonal Structure of the Organ—to the careful consideration of all true lovers of the Organ. More attention has been paid to the tonal appointment of Concert-room, Church, and Chamber instruments than has been considered necessary by any of the writers on the Organ up to the present time: but as the Organ has an extremely complex musical structure, in which science and art are intimately combined, more study, taste, and skill should be devoted to its development than is necessary in any other branch of organ construction. It is this belief that has induced me to devote so many pages to matters connected with the sound-producing and tone-controlling portions of the Organ, in which are presented the series of illustrations which go beyond everything of the kind to be found in all works on the Organ, hitherto issued, put together.

I trust that my descriptions of the several mechanical systems and appliances which have been and are being used in organ construction, aided by the fairly comprehensive series of illustrations, will be found intelligible by the student of the art of organ-building and the general reader, to whom my treatise is specially addressed. Much of interest and value has necessarily been omitted, partly through want of space, and partly through the want of co-operation on the part of certain organ builders who did not desire to have methods on which they lay great store submitted to public criticism. Perhaps, in some cases, this reserve was a wise one; but whether the builders gain anything by it or not is open to question. It is proper to add that in several cases I have had to depend for information on Patent Specifications, or on my own investigations, receiving no direct assistance from the patentees whose names have been mentioned.

Among all the Chapters contained in the Second Volume, that devoted to the Electro-pneumatic Action is certainly the most incomplete. Realizing the tentative state of that branch of organ construction at this time, I have simply aimed at giving a brief historical résumé and a bare outline of the principles on which all the better class of electro-pneumatic organ actions are constructed. It must be left to an abler pen than mine, and to a time when such actions leave nothing to be desired, to produce an exhaustive treatise on the subject.

In the more important works on organ-building in the English language large and valuable collections of Specifications of existing Organs are given; and numerous interesting Specifications are also to be found in the several well-known German and French works. Such being the case, I have considered it only necessary to append such Specifications to the present treatise as have been directly referred to in the text. By doing so I have been able to give ample space to the more important branches of my subject.

My sincere acknowledgments are due to all the distinguished inventors and builders who have freely given me valuable information and drawings relating to their mechanical systems and appliances: but as the names of these inventors and builders are properly recorded in the text of this treatise, it is unnecessary to repeat them here. It is, however, both a pleasure and a duty on my part to acknowledge their kind assistance and courtesy, and tender them my hearty thanks in this Proem.

In connection with the illustrations which appear in the First Volume, I have to express my best thanks to Mr. Arthur George Hill, B. A., F. S. A., Organ Builder, of London, for his kind permission to reproduce a selection of the drawings which adorn his magnificent and valuable work, "The Organ-cases and Organs of the Middle Ages and the Renaissance." My thanks are also due to the Rev. Père Delattre, Director of the Musée Lavigerie de Saint-Louis de Carthage, for his kindness in furnishing the photographs of the ancient terra cotta model of a Hydraulic Organ, from which I have been able to obtain the interesting engravings given in Plate I.

It is with much pleasure I acknowledge the encouragement I have received from Mr. F. E. Robertson, C. E., of London, during my arduous task, and his valuable help in the preparation of pipe-scales. I also gladly acknowledge the assistance I have received from Mr. Gustave Frese, of New York, in matters connected with the foreign nomenclature of organ stops; and from Professor Gabriel Bédart, of Lille, France, for much interesting information.

I have also received great encouragement during my long and exacting labors from several kind friends, some of whom, including the late Mr. A. J. Hipkins, F. S. A., are no longer alive. To those still living, and especially to Mr. John Rogers, of Nottingham, I am greatly indebted.

GEORGE ASHDOWN AUDSLEY.

NEW YORK, OCTOBER, 1905.

CONTENTS

VOLUME I

VOLUME II

THE ART OF ORGAN-BUILDING.

VOLUME FIRST.

THE ORGAN

" *The Organ is in truth the grandest, the most daring, the most magnificent of all instruments invented by human genius. It is a whole orchestra in itself. It can express anything in response to a skilled touch. Surely it is in some sort a pedestal on which the soul poises for a flight forth into space, essaying on her course to draw picture after picture in an endless series, to paint human life, to cross the Infinite that separates heaven from earth? And the longer a dreamer listens to those giant harmonies, the better he realizes that nothing save this hundred-voiced choir on earth can fill all the space between kneeling men and a God hidden by the blinding light of the sanctuary. The music is the one interpreter strong enough to bear up the prayers of humanity to heaven, prayer in its omnipotent moods, prayer tinged by the melancholy of many different natures, colored by meditative ecstasy, upspringing with the impulse of repentance—blended with the myriad fancies of every creed. Yes. In those long vaulted aisles the melodies inspired by the sense of things divine are blent with a grandeur unknown before, are decked with new glory and might. Out of the dim daylight, and the deep silence broken by the chanting of the choir in response to the thunder of the Organ, a veil is woven for God, and the brightness of His attributes shines through it.*"

HONORÉ DE BALZAC

CHAPTER I.

THE ORGAN HISTORICALLY CONSIDERED.

IN the estimation of the general reader and the student of the art of organ-building a work like the present would, in all probability, be considered incomplete without some particulars relating to the origin and development of the Organ. The subject has, however, been discussed in so many other works that it is only necessary to pass what has been gathered from numerous sources in hurried review in these pages.

At the outset it must be clearly understood that the Organ, even in the crudest and simplest form with which we are acquainted, cannot be said to have been *invented.* The modern Organ is an evolution from what may be called, by way of comparison, a musical moneron—in other words, from the first single hollow reed pipe or whistle sounded by the breath of man. In the natural order of things the discovery would quickly follow that reeds or whistles of different dimensions yielded musical sounds of different pitches. The imaginative mind can easily follow the slow application of this discovery, until the syrinx, or so called "Pipe of Pan," formed of a number of hollow reeds of different lengths, stopped at one end, and bound together, and yielding, when blown across their open ends, a more or less regular series of musical sounds, became the first mouth organ and the germ from which the modern Organ has grown, through a thousand progressive stages, to its present lofty position as the King of Instruments, and one of the greatest achievements of human ingenuity and skill.

There is no doubt that in Greece the syrinx was of a very high antiquity, its invention being ascribed to Pan, the god of pastures and forests. In the Museo Nazionale, at Naples, is an ancient sculpture representing Pan teaching Apollo to play the syrinx. Tradition explains the double name given to this primitive instrument by the following legend:

Syrinx, a lovely water-nymph of Arcadia, daughter of Ladon the river-god, was beloved by Pan, but she did not reciprocate his passion. To escape from his importunities, the fair nymph fled from him and besought the aid of her sisters, who immediately changed her into a reed. Pan, still infatuated, possessed himself of the reed, and cut it into seven, or according to some versions nine, pieces, joined them side by side in gradually decreasing lengths, and formed the musical instrument bearing the name of his beloved. Henceforth Pan was seldom seen without it. In Greek and Roman art the syrinx has at all times been the chief attribute of Pan and the Satyrs.

FIG. I.

The syrinx is mentioned several times in Homer's Iliad and in the Hymn to Mercury. Theocritus, a Greek pastoral poet of Syracuse, who flourished in the third century B. C., gives a version of the above legend in one of those curious poems which were known as *Idyllia figurata*, because they pictured an object by means of the number, disposition, and varied length of the lines. The *Idyllia figurata* in question represents a syrinx by an arrangement of twenty lines, each succeeding pair of lines forming a reed. In this case the instrument is supposed to have ten reeds.

The syrinx was formed of reeds differing in number according to the time and place of construction; seven and nine appear to have been most frequently adopted, but a greater number was sometimes used. Virgil tells us that seven pipes of different lengths were employed:—"Est mihi disparibus septem compacta cicutis Fistula." (Virgil, Ecl. II, 37.) He also tells us that wax was first used, by Pan, to join the reeds together:—"Pan primus calamos cera conjungere plures

Instituit." (Virgil, Ecl. II, 32.) Tibullus likewise mentions the use of wax, and speaks of the arrangement of the reeds:—"Fistula cui semper decrescit arundinis ordo Nam calamis cera jungitur usque minor." (Tibullus, lib. II, 5, 31.) The accompanying illustration, Fig. I, taken from an Etruscan bas-relief, shows the syrinx of antiquity in its most complete form, comprising nine tubes. Kathleen Schlesinger, in her interesting paper on the "Origin of the Organs of the Ancients,"* remarks:—"The syrinx is evidently of the highest antiquity and its invention must have followed closely on the discovery of the single reed. The principle on which the syrinx works is practically that of the stopped pipe of the present day. Reeds were first used for the purpose—those growing on the shores of Lake Orchomenus being very greatly esteemed by the Greeks—later horn, ivory, bone, wood, and metal were all used to make the pipes. We must not imagine that these various materials were adopted to vary the tone of the instrument, it has been practically demonstrated in our day that material has very little influence on timbre; but it was rather for the sake of durability, and because in some countries reeds were not available. These pipes composing the syrinx were stopped at one end, . . . giving a note nearly an octave lower than that produced by an open pipe of equal length. The breath was blown horizontally across the open end, impinging with force against the sharp inner edge, and setting the whole column of air in vibration. Many of the ancient Egyptian flutes were sounded in a similar manner."

From the simple syrinx, constructed, as has been said, of tubes closed at one end, and made to emit musical sounds of different pitches by air forced across their open ends, an important step was made toward the inception of the true organ pipe, by the discovery that similar sounds could be produced by blowing across a hole perforated in the side of a tube in the neighborhood of its closed end. Probably the next step was the invention of a fixed mouth-piece, whereby the direct action of the lips was done away with, and the wind stream was properly directed so as to at all times produce the desired musical sound. When this was accomplished the true whistle was created—the precursor of the organ labial pipe, which is simply a perfected whistle. The invention of the first musical instrument in which the sound was produced by means of a vibrating tongue or split reed was doubtless long after that of the mouthed pipe or whistle.

We have been alluding to extremely remote times. The representations of long flutes and reed pipes have been found in Egyptian paintings and sculptures, showing that the invention of such musical instruments is of the highest antiquity. Specimens of these instruments have been found in Egyptian tombs, and are now to be seen in different museums in Europe. The following remarks by William Chappell cannot but be interesting:

"It was the custom of the Egyptians, in the early dynasties of the empire, to deposit a musical pipe by the side of the body of a deceased person, and, together with the pipe, a long straw of barley. The pipes were played upon by short

* "Researches into the Origin of the Organs of the Ancients."—*Sammelband der Internationalen Musikgesellschaft*, Jahrgang 2, Heft 2, 1901.

pieces of barley-straw, which were cut partly through, to perhaps a fourth of the diameter, and then, by turning the blade of the knife flat, and passing it upwards towards the mouth end, a strip of an inch or more in length was raised, to serve as a beating reed, like the hautboy reed, and thus to sound the pipe. The principle is the same as the old shepherds' pipe, and as shepherds are no longer as musical as in former days, boys bred in the country have taken up the art. One of the pipes in the British Museum has still the cut piece of straw with which it had been played within it, and a similar piece is to be found within a pipe in the Museum of Egyptian Antiquities at Turin. Entire straws which were thus deposited are preserved in the Museum at Leyden, and in the Salt Collection at the British Museum. . . . . We learn from these pipes that the early Egyptians understood the principle of the bagpipe drone, and that of the old English Recorder, alluded to by Shakespeare in 'Hamlet' and in 'A Midsummer Night's Dream.' Also that they played music in the *pentaphonic* or Scotch scale, as well as in the diatonic scale. One of the pipes in the collection at Turin required the piece of straw to be sunk three inches within the pipe to elicit any sound. This is the principle of the bagpipe drone, and that pipe could not have been played at any time by the lips directly upon the straw. The Recorder pipe is in the collection of the British Museum. It is a treble pipe of 10⅛ inches in length, and has four holes for musical notes, besides two round apertures, opposite to one another, and bored through the pipe, at within an inch of the mouth end. If those had remained open, there could have been no sound produced; but, by analogy with the English Recorder, they were covered with the thinnest bladder, such as that of a small fish, the object being to produce a slightly tremulous tone by the vibration of the bladder, making it more like the human voice than the pure and steady quality of an English flute, such as was blown at the end, or of a diapason pipe in an organ. This pipe is also remarkable for being on the *pentaphonic* or Scotch scale, and that the pitch should be precisely that of a modern harmonium, and the notes to correspond with the black keys upon a pianoforte.

The scale is 

The first note of this scale is produced by the whole length of the pipe.

"The next to be remarked upon is a tenor pipe in the British Museum of 8¾ inches in length, which has also four holes for notes.

The scale at the present pitch is 

"The last sharp is a puzzle. It may have been intended for G, but, if not, it was probably to give the leading note to a treble pipe. We find three pipers playing together with pipes so varied in length in the tomb of Tebhen of the 4th Dynasty of Egypt [probably about 2050 B. C.], that they must have been playing treble, tenor, and bass. It is this which suggests the idea of the F sharp being a leading note to another pipe, and further, because one of those at Turin has the first four notes only a tone lower, without any fifth note. It is the one with the bagpipe drone, 23⅜ inches in length, and has only three holes."

In continuation and elaboration of the same subject we return with pleasure to the able essay by Kathleen Schlesinger:

"Although the Egyptians used so many different kinds of flutes and pipes, and were familiar with the principle of the drone, we do not find the syrinx among the musical scenes depicted on the tombs, but it was known to the Chinese, to the Hebrews, and to the Greeks. A probable explanation of the absence of the syrinx in Egypt, is that the object of the Pandean-pipe being to provide a scale or sequence of sounds by means of columns of air of different lengths, the simplest means of attaining this end was to cut several reeds of the requisite sizes. The Egyptians, however, had discovered a still more ingenious method of obtaining columns of air of different lengths, which did not necessitate removing the lips from the embouchure of one pipe to the next; they found out the principle of shortening the column of air in any given open pipe by boring lateral holes in it, and of stopping these with the fingers in order to lengthen the column. This discovery, which may have caused the Egyptians to relegate the more primitive instrument to the shepherds and nomadic tribes, was a very important one for the history of wind instruments; and to the system of boring lateral holes in tubes or pipes we owe all the wood-wind and much of the brass in the modern orchestra. But although the priestly class of musicians in Egypt may have despised the syrinx, a time came when other nations valued it, and experimentalizing upon it in many directions gave us what by degrees developed into the lordly Organ. Henceforth the stopped pipe of the syrinx and the open pipe of the flute went their several ways, diverging more and more, until some there were who even forgot that their common ancestor was the primitive pipe. The musical instruments of China supply a very valuable link in the history of the Organ, and according to Chinese authorities their antiquity is such as to command attention next to those of Egypt; unfortunately, however, the difficulties of the language preclude any possibility of independent research in this field, and one can but repeat what others have said before, accepting Chinese reports and traditions with reserve."

Of all the instruments of antiquity which seem to foreshadow the Organ, the *cheng* of the Chinese holds the most noteworthy position. Respecting this interesting musical instrument, Engel writes: "This is one of the oldest instruments of the Chinese still in use, and may be regarded as the most ancient species of organ with which we are exactly acquainted. Formerly it was made with a long spout for a mouth-piece, which gave it the appearance of an old-fashioned coffee-pot. The *cheng* is also popular in Japan, and a similarly constructed instrument, though different in outward appearance, is the *heen* of Burmah and Siam. The Siamese call their *heen* 'The Laos organ,' which indicates that they consider it to have been originally derived by them from Laos. Moreover, there deserves to be noticed another Chinese instrument of this kind, simple in construction, which probably represents the *cheng* in its most primitive condition. It is to be found among the Meaou-tsze, or mountaineers, who are supposed to be the aboriginal inhabitants of China. They call it *sang*. This species has no bowl, or air-chest; it rather resembles the Pan-pipe, but is sounded by means of a common mouth-piece consisting of a tube, which is placed at a right angle across the pipes. The Chinese assert that the *cheng* was used in olden time in the religious rites performed in honor of Confucius. Tradescant Lay, in his account of the Chinese, calls it 'Jubal's organ,' and remarks, 'this seems to be the embryo of our multiform and magnificent organ.'" *

The *cheng* consists of a small wind-chest, usually in the shape of half an egg, formed of wood hollowed out, or from a gourd, and covered externally with lacquer, usually black. From its side projects a short tube or mouth-piece, against which the lips are pressed while supplying the instrument with compressed air. On the flat cover of the wind-chest are planted a number of slender bamboo tubes containing free reeds, or vibrating tongues, of metal. The tubes are of different lengths, and vary in number from seventeen to twenty-four. The *cheng* with seventeen tubes usually has thirteen which speak, the remaining four tubes serving as supports. The tubes are arranged in a circular fashion close to the edge of the wind-chest. Each speaking pipe has a small lateral hole near its lower end; and it sounds only when this hole is covered by a finger. The *cheng* has been tuned in different ways at different periods. While the thirteen tubes were commonly tuned to yield notes of the pentatonic scale, the ancient *cheng* was tuned according to the chromatic scale. Beyond the *cheng* no steps seem to have been taken by the Chinese toward the construction of an instrument of the organ class.

A considerable amount of discussion has obtained in certain quarters as to whether or not the Organ, in some primitive form, was known to the Jews in ancient times: but as absolutely nothing has been accomplished by this discussion it is unnecessary to dwell upon it here beyond the following brief remarks. Special attention has been paid to the Chaldee word *mashrokitha*, used by Daniel (580 B. C.), in his third chapter, in describing the music at the worship of the golden image that Nebuchadnezzar, the king, had set up. Athanasius Kircher, in his "Musurgia," written about the middle of the seventeenth century, gives a drawing of what he conceives the *mashrokitha* or *magraketha* of the Chaldee orchestra to have been. Of course, as we do not know his authority for this representation, we must look upon it as in all probability a work of his imagination. We give, in Fig. II., a rendering of Father Kircher's instrument. He describes the *magraketha*, from its supposed whistling sounds, as an instrument formed of several pipes, supported on a wooden box, and arranged in proper order according to their tones. He tells us that they are open at top, and closed below by a flexible skin, inclosed in a wooden chest, and inflated by means of a tube blown into by the mouth. The holes which admit the compressed air into the pipes are opened and closed by the action of the fingers. From his drawing it would seem that the instrument was furnished with small slides or levers for admitting the air to the pipes. With all due deference to

* "Catalogue of the Musical Instruments in the South Kensington Museum," by Carl Engel, London, 1874.

the opinion of this imaginative writer of the seventeenth century, we are convinced that no such instrument as he describes existed in the time of Daniel.

The facts that have been outlined in the preceding pages show at what an early date in the world's history the knowledge of the art of forming musical instruments from hollow reeds and straws was attained. So advanced were the ancient Egyptians and the early Greeks in the fabrication of such wind instruments that it is a matter of wonder that an instrument more closely resembling the Organ was not immediately conceived. It is possible that some isolated and tentative efforts may have been essayed of which no record has been made or preserved. Certain it is that at what date and by what people the first attempt was made to produce a compound instrument of the true organ class cannot now be known: but in imagination we can form some reasonable idea respecting the progressive stages which led to the first appearance of what may be considered an Organ in the true meaning of the term.

The steps or stages in the evolution of the primitive Organ were, in all probability, somewhat as follows: Possessed of the syrinx, the whistle with a fixed mouth-piece, and such reed pipes as the Egyptians in all likelihood invented, it naturally followed, in the course of time, that attempts should be made to associate several whistles or reed pipes together in such a manner as to render it easy to sound them singly or in groups, in rapid succession, by the breath of a single performer. To accomplish this it was only necessary to mount a series of pipes on a long and narrow box, or wind-chest, provided with a tube, through which the chest was charged with air from the mouth, and furnished with some simple means of controlling the admission of wind to the pipes. At this stage the instrument would resemble, in all essentials, the *magraketha* of Father Kircher (Fig. II). Some writers have suggested that before any mechanical means of

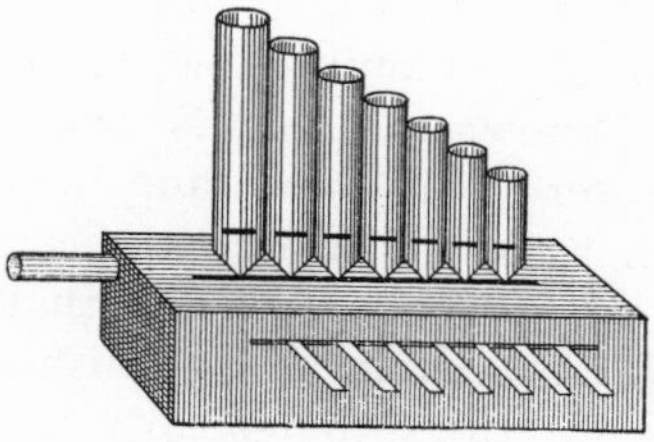

FIG. II.

controlling the admission of wind were adopted, the pipes that had to remain silent were simply stopped by the fingers: but this most inconvenient method, if it ever obtained, must soon have been abandoned in favor of a mechanical device which the inventive genius of the ancients was quite capable of supplying. That such an initial step was taken at some early date, unknown to us, there can be no reasonable doubt; and that it led, through the difficulty experienced in supplying the necessary amount of compressed air by the lungs of the player, to the next important step in the evolution of the Organ—namely, the addition of some artificial or mechanical means of collecting, storing, and compressing the air—is, we venture to think, also unquestionable. There appears to be good grounds for believing that the idea of supplying wind to the earliest form of the Organ by other means than directly from the mouth of the player was suggested by the primitive bagpipe. No record exists of the use of the bagpipe by the ancient Egyptians; but we have satisfactory evidence, from ancient paintings, that the bellows, in the form of a leather bag, was used in Egypt for blowing the smelting furnace so early as the fifteenth century before Christ.*

The bellows was also well known to the ancient Greeks. We are told that two inflated skins (*δύο φύσαι*) constituted a pair of bellows. These were furnished with valves adjusted to the natural apertures at one part for admitting the air, and a pipe inserted into another part for its emission. Such primitive bellows, probably placed between boards hinged together at one end, formed an essential piece of furniture in every forge and foundry. We find the bellows alluded to in the Iliad (1200–850 B. C.), in which there is a vivid description of the forge and bellows presided over by Vulcan. We read that when Thetis entered his forge she found the lame god hurrying from fire to fire blowing the "roaring bellows;" and as he ceased from his labors to offer hospitality to his visitor he moved the bellows away from the fires. So much for the primitive bellows.

The bagpipe was a common instrument in the pastoral districts of Greece at a very remote period, but the time of its invention is unknown. Numerous allusions are made to it by the classical authors. Aristophanes, who is believed to have lived between the years 450 and 380 B. C., in his play of "The Acharnians" (performed in 425 B. C.) uses the word *βομβαύλιον*, which has been translated "bumblebee pipers," and, by Blaydes, "droners on the bagpipes." The use of this word clearly shows that in Greece, at that early time, the bagpipe had the drone pipes, and that the instrument was so well known that the satirist did not consider it necessary to mention it by name.

Plato likewise alludes to the humming tone of the bagpipe, indicating that the instrument itself was well known to him. Notwithstanding the fact that both the bellows and the bagpipe were well known and in constant use so early as the fifth century before Christ, it was fully two centuries later before the Hydraulic Organ (*ὑδραυλικὸν ὀργάνον*) was invented. From that time the Organ, in what may be considered its true form, became an established fact; and from it starts the history and development of the grandest and most complex musical instrument fabricated by the hand of man. Further conjecture is unnecessary, for we can now enter on the historical period.

"According to an author quoted by Athenæus, the first organist was Ctesibius of Alexandra, who lived about B. C. 200. He evidently took the idea of his Organ from the syrinx or Pandean pipes, a musical instrument of the highest antiquity among the Greeks. His object being to employ a row of pipes of great

* Champollion, in his "Monuments de l'Égypte et de la Nubie," gives an illustration from a painting discovered in a tomb at Kourna, in which two men are depicted operating pairs of bellows, in the shape of bags, by alternately pressing them down with their feet, and drawing them up and inflating them by cords held in their hands.

size, and capable of emitting the most powerful as well as the softest sounds, he contrived the means of adapting keys with levers (ἀγκωνίσκοι), and with perforated sliders (πώματα), to open and shut the mouths of the pipes (γλωσσόκομα), a supply of wind being obtained, without intermission, by bellows, in which the pressure of water performed the same part which is fulfilled in the modern Organ by a weight. On this account the instrument invented by Ctesibius was called the Water-Organ (ὑδραυλικὸν ὀργάνον). Its pipes were partly of bronze and partly of reed. The number of its stops, and consequently of its rows of pipes, varied from one to eight, so that Tertullian describes it with reason as an exceedingly complicated instrument. It continued in use so late as the ninth century of our era: in the year 826, a Water-Organ was erected by a Venetian in the church of Aquisgranum, the modern Aix-la-Chapelle."*

Neron, the great Alexandrian mathematician who lived in the third century before Christ, has left us in his work on Pneumatics (preserved in a fragmentary state) a tolerably clear outline of the Organ of his time; but for what is practically a detailed description of the early Hydraulic Organ we must turn to the pages of the interesting work on Architecture by Marcus Vitruvius Pollio, who lived sometime in the first century before Christ. His work was probably written about the year 25 B. C. In the XIII. chapter of the Tenth Book, he says:

"I cannot omit a brief explanation, as clearly as I can give it, of the principles on which Hydraulic Organs are constructed. A base of framed wood-work is prepared, on which is placed a brazen box. On the base, right and left, uprights are fixed, with cross-pieces like those of a ladder, to keep them together; between which are inclosed brass barrels with movable pistons, perfectly round, having iron rods fixed in their centers, and covered with leather and wool, attached by pins to the levers. There are also, on the upper surface, holes about three inches diameter, in which, near the pin joint, are brazen dolphins with chains hanging from their mouths, which sustain the valves that descend below the holes of the barrels. Within the box, where the water is deposited, there is a species of inverted funnel, under which two collars [supporting pieces] about three inches high, answer the purpose of keeping it level, and preserving the assigned distance between the lips of the wind-chest [the funnel-shaped portion] and the bottom of the box. On the neck a chest, framed together, sustains the head of the instrument, which in Greek is called κανὼν μουσικὸς (canon musicus); upon which, lengthwise, are channels, four in number, if the instrument be tetrachordal, six if hexachordal, and eight if octachordal. In the channels are fixed [fitted] stops, that are connected with iron finger-boards; on pressing down which, the communication between the chest and the channels is opened. Along the channels is a range of holes corresponding with others on an upper table, called πίναξ in Greek. Between this table and the canon, rules are interposed, with corresponding holes, well oiled so that they may be easily pushed in and return; they are called *pleuritides*, and are for the purpose of stopping and opening the holes along the channels, which they do by passing backwards and forwards. These rules have iron jacks attached to them, and being united to the keys, when

* James Yates, in "Dictionary of Greek and Roman Antiquities," London, 1848.

those are touched they move the rules. Over the table are holes through which the wind passes into the pipes. Rings are fixed in the rules [?] for the reception of the feet of the organ pipes. From the barrels run pipes joined to the neck of the wind-chest, which communicate with the holes in the chest; in which pipes are closely fitted valves; these, when the chest is supplied with wind, serve to close their orifices, and prevent its escape. Thus, when the levers are raised, the pistons are depressed to the bottom of the barrels, and the dolphins, turning on their pivots, suffer the valves attached to them to descend, thus filling with air the cavities of the barrels. Lastly; the pistons in the barrels being alternately raised and depressed with a quick motion, cause the valves to stop the upper holes: the air, therefore, which is spent [which fills the barrels], escapes into the pipes, through which it passes into the wind-chest, and thence, by its neck, to the box. By the quick motion of the levers still compressing the air, it finds its way through the apertures of the stops, and fills the channels with wind. Hence, when the keys are touched by hand, they propel and repel the rules, alternately stopping and opening the holes, and producing a varied melody founded upon the rules of music. I have done my utmost to give a clear explanation of a complex machine. This has been no easy task, nor, perhaps, shall I be understood, except by those who are experienced in matters of this nature. Such, however, as comprehend but a little of what I have written, would, if they saw this instrument, be compelled to acknowledge the skill exhibited in its contrivance."*

Apparently clear as this description is, it has, in the absence of any diagram, given rise to much ingenious speculation. No one has been able to construct a satisfactory instrument in strict accordance with the descriptive text. The purely hydraulic portion presents great difficulties from a practical point of view. Dr. Burney, in his "History of Music," remarks: "Neither the description of the Hydraulic Organ in Vitruvius, nor the conjectures of his innumerable commentators, have put it in the power of the moderns either to imitate, or perfectly conceive the manner of its construction; and it still remains a doubt whether it was ever worthy of the praises which poets have bestowed upon it." From the text of Vitruvius we gather certain facts. It is clearly shown that means were provided for collecting and compressing the wind, the water in the brazen box having, doubtless, an important office in sustaining and equalizing to some extent the pressure of the wind in its passage from the blowing apparatus to the *canon musicus* and the pipes. We cannot imagine the hydraulic part of the instrument having any other office in the economy of the Organ; but the description gives no direct clue to the part played by the water. Considering the name given to this Organ, it is remarkable that so little stress is laid on its hydraulic arrangements. Means were also provided, apparently in a very complete form, for controlling the different ranks of pipes, and for enabling the performer to admit the wind into any pipe at pleasure. Some description of lever suitable for the hand or fingers was provided for each note, the moving of which opened the slider or "rule" under the pipe—"Hæ regulæ habent ferrea choragia fixa et juncta cum pinnis, quarum pinnarum tactus motiones efficit regularum." Gwilt

* Gwilt's translation of Vitruvius. London, 1860.

translates "*pinnis*" by the word "keys;" but it is most improbable that the Organ of Vitruvius' time had anything in the nature of finger keys. The invention of keys for the fingers is attributed to an age more than a thousand years later than that of Vitruvius. To the above we may add the following remarks from the pen of Dr. Rimbault:

"The mechanical operation of the *water-organ* is scarcely intelligible; this much, however, is certain, that the *hydraulicon* was provided with pipes and a wind-chest, and registered like the wind-organ. We must not suppose that the water directly produced the wind, but that it served merely to give the wind, by means of counterpressure, equality and power. Ctesibius' object was 'to employ a row of pipes of great size, and capable of emitting the most powerful as well as the softest sounds.' He is also said to have invented, or perfected, the perforated slide by which means he was enabled to open and shut the mouths of the pipes with greater facility."

The Organ as described by Vitruvius, with, perhaps some slight improvements, seems to have been held in high esteem by the Romans in the early years of the first century after Christ. As Yates remarks: "The Organ was well adapted to gratify the Roman people in the splendid entertainments provided for them by the emperors and other opulent persons. Nero was very curious about Organs, both in regard to their musical effect and their mechanism. A contorniate coin of this emperor, in the British Museum, [of which an illustration is

FIG. III.

given in Fig. III.] shows an Organ with a sprig of laurel on one side, and a man standing on the other, who may have been victorious in the exhibitions of the circus or the amphitheatre. It is probable that these medals were bestowed upon such victors, and that the Organ was impressed upon them on account of its introduction on such occasions. The general form of the Organ is also clearly exhibited in a poem by Publilius Porphyrius Optatianus, describing the instrument, and composed of verses so constructed as to show both the lower part which contained the bellows, the wind-chest which lay upon it, and over this, the row of 26 pipes. These are represented by 26 lines, which increase in length each by one letter, until the last line is twice as long as the first." The pipes are represented with the treble on the left and the bass or larger pipes toward the right—the reverse of the modern arrangement.* It is to be regretted that the representation on the contorniate coin gives us no idea of the mechanical part of the instrument. It looks like a portable Pneumatic Organ.

The Organ described by Heron, in his work "Pneumatika," differs in no essential point from that described by Vitruvius. It had, however, only a single stop or rank of pipes, while the later Organ of Vitruvius had four, six, or eight ranks of pipes, marking a decided advance in tonal appointment. Vitruvius does not tell us in what manner the "rules" (*pleuritides*) return when the levers actuating them are released by the hands of the performer, but Heron furnishes the necessary information. From his description, we gather that from the portion manipulated by the player an arm swings down, from the hinge, and is connected at its lower end with the corresponding slide or "rule." When the lever is depressed the slide is pushed in, and the holes which admit the wind into the corresponding pipe or pipes take their places opposite each other. When the lever is released the reverse action takes place, the slide being drawn out by a spring of horn, attached to the slide by a sinue.

According to the foregoing descriptions, we have to realize an instrument of considerable complexity, which comprised a piston blowing apparatus, an air reservoir in which a certain pressure was imparted to the condensed air, a draw-stop mechanism, a manual action by means of which the pipes were made to sound at the will of the player, and ranks of pipes extending to so many as eight, presenting a state of perfection scarcely reached a thousand years later. We can understand why the Organ of this early time was highly prized, and what induced Tertullian, the celebrated ecclesiastical writer (A. D. 150–230), to exclaim: "Behold the marvellous art of Archimedes, I allude to the Hydraulic Organ; so many members, so many parts, so many joints, so many sound conduits, so much tonal effect, so many combinations, so many pipes, and all at one touch." †

After the preceding somewhat lengthy dissertation on the Hydraulic Organs of Ctesibius, Heron, and Vitruvius, the reader, interested in the early history of the Organ, will probably glance with some interest at the accompanying diagrams, in which we have depicted what we conceive the general construction and disposition of the ancient Hydraulic Organ to have been in the first century of our era. Of course, no attempt has been made to draw the several parts to scale. The larger diagram is a Longitudinal Section through the center of the instru-

* E. de Coussemaker gives the following translation of the lines of the poem specially alluding to the Organ: "Ces vers sont la figure de l'instrument sur lequel on peut faire entendre des chants variés, et dont les sons puissants s'échappent de tuyaux d'airain, creux, arrondis, et dont la longueur s'accroît régulièrement, *calamis crescentibus*. Au-dessous des tuyaux sont placées les touches au moyen desquelles la main de l'artiste, ouvrant ou fermant à son gré les conduits du vent, enfante une mélodie agréable et bien rhythmée. L'eau, placée au-dessous de ces tuyaux, et agitée par la pression de l'air que produisent le travail et les efforts de plusieurs jeunes gens, donne les sons nécessaires et assortis à la musique. Au moindre mouvement, les touches, ouvrant les soupapes, peuvent exprimer aussitôt des chants rapides et animés, ou une mélodie calme et simple, ou bien encore, par la puissance du rhythme et de la mélodie, répandre au loin la terreur."—"Annales Archéologiques," vol. iii, p. 275.

† "Specta portentuosum, Archimedis munificitium organum hydraulicum dico, tot membra, tot partes, tot compagines, tot itinera vocum, tot compendia sonorum, tot commercia modorum, tot acies tibiarum et una moles omnia."—Tertullian de anima, Cap. XIV.

ment; while the smaller diagram is a Transverse Section through the front portion of the wind-chest, showing the manual appliance by means of which the performer sounded the pipe-work.

In the Longitudinal Section, A is the base of framed wood-work on which all parts of the instrument are supported. B is the vessel constructed of brass, closed at bottom, so as to hold water, and open to the atmosphere at top. Within this vessel is fixed the conical or funnel-shaped wind reservoir C, the lower edge of

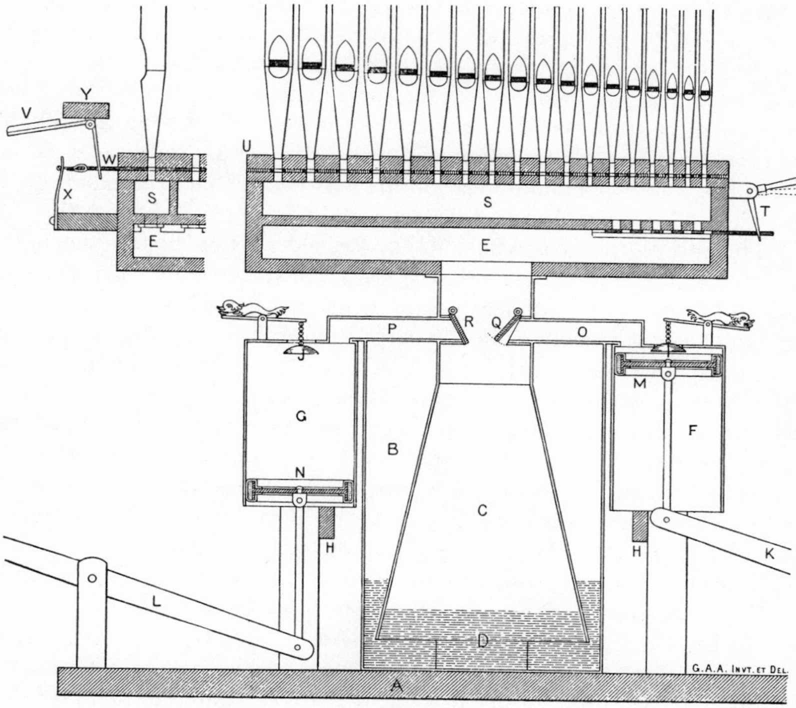

Fig. IV.

which is supported a few inches above the bottom of the vessel, and is immersed in water, as indicated at D. The upper portion or neck of this wind reservoir opens into the lower chamber, E, of the wind-chest (κανὼν μουσικὸς). On the right and left of the brazen vessel are placed the air-pumps F and G, supported by the uprights and cross-pieces H. These air-pumps are cylindrical and carefully formed of brass, entirely open at bottom, and closed at top, with the exception of a central orifice, about three inches in diameter, and the opening for the pipe which connects each pump with the wind reservoir. The pumps are fitted with the pistons M and N, made of brass, and having their broad rims covered with leather well padded with wool, so as to allow them to move easily and practically air-tight. To the center of the pistons are pivoted rods which connect them with the blowing levers K and L. Suspended within the air-pumps, and directly under their central orifices, are the valves I and J, attached by chains to small rocking levers, weighted, ornamentally, with small brazen dolphins, as indicated. From the tops of the air-pumps the pipes O and P conduct the wind, forced by the pistons, into the wind reservoir. These pipes are furnished with the flap-valves Q and R, which allow the compressed air to enter the reservoir, but prevent its escape. We have now to describe the wind-chest. E is the lower chamber directly communicating with the wind reservoir C. S is one of the channels which conduct the wind to the different ranks of pipes planted on the wind-chest. At T is shown a contrivance by means of which the wind is admitted into the stop-channel S. The external bent lever moves an internal slide which opens or closes a series of holes in the bottom of the stop-channel. As the ancient writers are far from clear respecting the draw-stop action,* we have ventured to imagine a probable one, similar to that described for the manual action. In our diagram the slide is drawn outward and the holes of communication are closed. When the handle is pressed down, as indicated by the dotted lines, the slide is pushed in and the holes are opened. The top of the wind-chest, U, is formed of two boards, between which are transverse bearers and sliders (*pleuritides*), constructed in a manner similar to the draw-stop action of the modern slider wind-chest. These bearers and sliders are shown, in transverse section, in the larger diagram; and the longitudinal section of the front portion of a slider is shown at W, in the smaller diagram. The manual action, by means of which the slider is pushed in, and subsequently withdrawn, on the removal of the hand or finger, by means of a spring, is shown in the smaller diagram. The hand of the performer, pressing down the bent lever at V, pushes the slider W inward and opens the holes from the stop channels S to the pipes. On removing his hand, the horn spring X, attached to the slider by a sinue, instantly draws the slider outward, and returns the lever V to its original position against the under surface of the bearer Y, to which it is hinged. Each stop comprises eighteen pipes which answer to the following notes: G. A. B♭. B♮. C. D. E♭. E. F. F♯. G. A♭. A. B♭. B♮. C. D. E. The operation of the Hydraulic Organ, as here represented, is very simple. The piston N is shown at the extreme limit of its downward stroke; and the cylinder G is filled with air drawn in through the orifice of the hanging valve J. The other piston M is shown at the extreme limit of its upward stroke. It has allowed the valve I to close its orifice, and has pressed the air in the cylinder F, that was above the piston, through the conduit O and the open valve Q into the wind reservoir C. The air in the reservoir, being considerably condensed, presses against the surface of the water within the reservoir and lowers its level, in the manner indicated at D. The amount of condensation in the wind contained in the reservoir C is regulated by the difference between the levels of the water in the reservoir and in the vessel B. This regulation is, however, not constant, for as the difference between the levels is increased the degree of condensation, or the "weight of the wind," is also increased. In the Hydraulic Organ, therefore, a

* "Singulis autem canalibus singula epistomia sunt inclusa, manubriis ferreis collocata: quæ manubria cum torquentur, ex arca patefaciunt nares in canales."—M. Vitruvii Pollionis Architectura.

PLATE I

steady wind was never possible, however carefully the air-pumps were operated. The instant the suction ceases in the cylinder G, and the piston N starts to ascend, the valve J is lifted, by the weight of the brass dolphin, and closes its orifice, and the valve R is pressed open by the condensed air rushing from the cylinder through the conduit P. On the other hand, the instant the piston M commences to descend, the valve Q closes, and the suction within the cylinder F instantly opens the valve I, and allows the external air to fill the cylinder above the descending piston. Accordingly the alternate action of the two air-pumps keeps the wind reservoir charged with compressed air. The action connected with the wind-chest has already been described.

In the preparation of our diagrams of the Hydraulic Organ, we have been greatly assisted by the photographs, presented to us by the Rev. Père Delattre, Director of the Musée Lavigerie de Saint-Louis de Carthage, and which are reproduced in Plate I. These photographs are taken from a terra cotta model of a Hydraulic Organ, found at Carthage, and attributed by experts in antique pottery to the first or second century of our era. The model unquestionably represents, in a rude but fairly correct manner, the Organ described by Vitruvius. On the front of the wind-chest, or the opposite side to that at which the player stands, is inscribed the name of the artist who executed the model—POSSESSORIS. The model clearly shows the hydraulic vessel, flanked by the two cylindrical air-pumps and their supports, and surmounted by the wind-chest (*κανὼν μουσικὸς*), planted, in front, with nineteen pipes. On a ledge, at what we may consider the rear of the instrument, stood the figure of the organist; but, unfortunately, only its legs and lower part of its garment remain. The organist was evidently represented standing at what we may call the manual clavier of the Organ. This clavier appears occupying a position (similar to that indicated in Fig. IV.) elevated above the sliders (*pleuritides*). The free ends of the sliders appear, immediately under the pipes, in the front of the Organ. No parts of the manual action are represented, as it was impossible to execute minute or detached work in terra cotta. It would appear from the manner in which the air-pumps are supported that their pistons were operated from above; and in all probability the two curious holes at the ends of the wind-chest, in front, had blowing handles inserted into them. There are, it would seem, three ranks of pipes, although the indications of the second and third are extremely unsatisfactory.* This terra cotta is an object of the greatest interest to the student of the art of organ-building, being a veritable landmark in the history of the King of Instruments.

Although no additional information has been handed down respecting the construction of Hydraulic Organs, it seems certain that they were made and used up

*Mr. A. J. Hipkins, F. S. A., has kindly sent us the following notes: "The compass of the Hydraulic Organ, following an anonymous treatise on music—'Anonymi Scriptio de Musica'—published by Bellermann (Berlin 1841) would be for eighteen keys: G . A . B♭. B♮ . c^1. d^1. $e♭^1$. e^1. f^1. $f♯^1$. g^1. $a♭^1$. a^1. $b♭^1$. $b♮^1$. c^2. d^2. e^2, or an octave lower. The place of the *nineteenth* key is uncertain. The anonymous writer tells us 'players on the water-organ' (the quotation is from 'The Modes of Ancient Greek Music,' by D. B. Monro, Oxford 1894) 'use only six modes (*τρόποι* here meaning octave scales like our descending minor), viz.: Hyper-lydian, Hyper-ionian, Lydian, Phrygian, Hypo-lydian, Hypo-phrygian.' But these six would require twenty-one notes: for with only eighteen we have to leave out the highest scale—the Hyper-lydian—which would have completed the second octave."

to a comparatively late period. In the Chronicle of William of Malmesbury we find, in the portion which alludes to Pope Silvester II., who died in the year 1003, mention made of a Hydraulic Organ, the construction of which was due to his scientific knowledge and skill. This instrument, which was placed in the Church of Reims, is stated to have been in existence in the year 1125, and is described as being sounded by "air escaping in a surprising manner by the force of heated water." This, in truth, seems to have been a Hydraulic Organ, for, as Mason says, the word *ventus* used by the Chronicler evidently meant steam, because the sound was produced by means of heated water.* The original passage is as follows: "Aquæ calefactæ violentia ventus emergens implet concavitatem barbiti, et per multiforatiles transitus æneæ fistulæ modulatos clamores emittunt."

There seems to be no reasonable doubt that purely Pneumatic Organs were constructed and used at the same time as the later Hydraulicons; for it was found that the action of water was at all times most unsatisfactory. In the following Greek enigmatical epigram, attributed to the Emperor Julian (the Apostate), who died in A. D. 363, allusion is certainly made to a Pneumatic Organ:

Ἀλλοίην ὁρόω δονάκων φύσιν· ἦπου ἀπ' ἄλλης
Χαλκείης τάχα μᾶλλον ἀνεβλάστησαν ἀρούρης,
Ἄγριοι, οὐδ' ἀνέμοισιν ὑφ' ἡμετέροις δονέονται,
Ἀλλ' ὑπὸ ταυρείης προθορῶν σπήλυγγος ἀήτης,
Νέρθεν ἐϋτρήτων καλάμων ὑπὸ ῥίξαν ὁδεύει.
Καί τις ἀνὴρ ἀγέρωχος ἔχων θοὰ δάκτυλα χειρὸς,
Ἵσταται ἀμφαφόων κανόνας συμφράδμονας αὐλῶν·
Οἱ δ' ἁπαλὸν σκιρτῶντες, ἀποθλίβουσιν ἀοιδήν.

Burney, in his "History of Music," gives the following translation of these lines: "I see reeds of a new species, the growth of another and a brazen soil, such as are not agitated by our winds, but by a blast that rushes from a leathern cavern beneath their roots; while a robust mortal, running with swift fingers over the concordant keys [*κανόνας*], makes them, as they smoothly dance, emit melodious sounds."†

From the words just quoted, it is quite evident that the instrument alluded to was an Organ blown by a bellows made of stout leather, probably in the form of a large bag pressed between boards, the upper one of which was weighted or pressed down by the blower standing upon it. It may have been an entire bull's hide, tied

* "Essays Historical and Critical, on English Church Music." York, 1795.

† Rimbault takes exception to this translation, and gives the following as a *literal* one: "I see a species of reeds: surely from another and a brazen soil have they sprung—rude. Nor are they agitated by our winds, but a blast rushing forth from a cavern of bull's hide makes its way from below the root of reeds with many openings; and a highly-gifted man, with nimble fingers handles the yielding rods of the pipes, while they, softly bounding, press out a sound." Exception is taken to the rendering of the word *κανόνας* (*canonas*) as *keys*, and he translates it *rods*—a distinction without a difference, we venture to think, seeing that they are operated upon by "swift," or "nimble," fingers, and that they "smoothly dance," or "softly bound," under the action of the "nimble fingers." Keys, in the likeness of the modern clavier, they certainly were not; but that they were in the form of balanced or pivoted levers, easily manipulated, is surely implied by dancing or "softly bounding" motions imparted to them by the fingers of the "highly-gifted" performer. We have shown that the early Hydraulic Organ had pivoted levers, or what were equivalent to keys.

and stitched, and made airtight in the seams. From the expressions used we may arrive at the conclusion that the instrument had a considerable number of pipes of brass, and that each one was furnished with a valve controlled by a rod, lever, or key, easily depressed by the "nimble fingers" of the "highly-gifted" performer. In any event this somewhat poetical description of a Pneumatic Organ is of the highest value in the early history of the instrument.

Saint Augustine (A. D. 354–430), in his Commentary on the LVI. Psalm, alludes to the Pneumatic Organ in the following words: "Organa dicuntur omnia instrumenta musicorum. *Non solum illud organum dicitur, quod grande est et inflatur follibus*, sed etiam quidquid aptatur ad cantilenam et corporeum est quo instrumento utitur qui cantat, organum dicitur;" which may be translated thus: "All instruments of music are designated by the word organs. The term is not confined to the instrument of large dimensions in which the air is furnished by bellows; but is employed to designate any instrument on which the musician performs a melody."

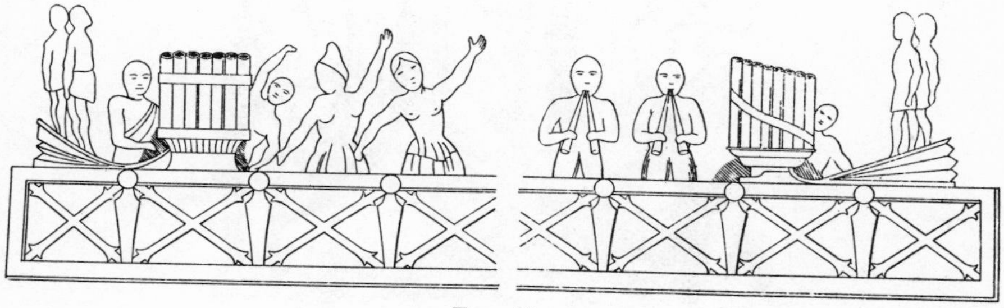

FIG. V.

The earliest known representation of a Pneumatic Organ is that found on the obelisk erected at Constantinople by Theodosius the Great (A. D. 346–395). The sculpture, which is of considerable length, contains the representation of two small Organs, formed of pipes planted on wind-chests, and supplied with wind from detached bellows, of the diagonal form, on the upper-boards of which men are standing. Between the Organs are ranged ten figures, three of which are represented as performing on the *tibia pares*, while the rest are apparently singing and gesticulating. The accompanying illustration, Fig. V., is an outline sketch showing the two Organs of this early and rude work of art. Each Organ has a performer who is seated behind it, in the neighborhood of the bellows. It will be observed that in one case the pipes are represented of different lengths, while in the other they are represented of equal lengths. In all probability such irregularity did not obtain in the original sculpture; but is due to the carelessness of the artist who made the first drawing from the actual work; and which drawing has subsequently been copied and handed down without any attempt at correction.*

*E. de Coussemaker, alluding to the sculpture, says: "Les deux orgues placés à droite et à gauche de la scène nous montrent cet instrument dans son état presque d'enfance. Les soufflets dont ils sont munis ressem-

Another rude representation of a Pneumatic Organ of the fourth century is to be seen in an interesting sculpture of the Gallo-Romaine period, preserved in the Museum at Arles, France. The accompanying illustration, Fig. VI., has been drawn from this early work of art. It shows a wind-chest, supported on a wind reservoir, and planted with eleven pipes, unless the two end features are intended as supports, between which is the pipe-stay. Two figures are represented in the act of blowing. The blowing apparatus is merely expressed, without any attempt

FIG. VI.

at detail.* While this sculpture is commonly accepted to represent a Pneumatic Organ, it may, with equal propriety, be pronounced to represent a Hydraulicon.

Cassiodorus (A. D. 468-560), in his Commentary on the CL. Psalm, says: "Organum itaque est quasi turris quædam diversis fistulis fabricata, quibus flatu follium vox copiosissima destinatur; et ut eam modulatio decora componat, linguis

blent à des soufflets de forge ; ils sont mis en mouvement par deux hommes qui, par le poids de leur corps, paraissent les faire monter et descendre. Cette manière de souffler ne peut se concevoir qu'en suppôsant deux soufflets pour chaque souffleur; ce qui en donne quatre pour chaque orgue. L'orgue de droite a huit tuyaux, celui de gauche n'en a que sept. Ces tuyaux sont tenus ensemble par un simple lien, semblable à celui de la syrinx. Il est facile de voir que les tuyaux de l'orgue de droite sont plus minces que ceux de l'orgue de gauche; les sons du premier étaient donc plus aigus que ceux du second. Cela semble démontrer qu'il y avait deux sortes d'orgues: un orgue grave et un orgue aigu. Les tuyaux sont placés sur une espèce de sommier dans lequel on faisait entrer l'air par les soufflets ; cet air se transmettait ensuite et se distribuait dans chaque tuyau séparément, selon la volonté de l'exécutant, au moyen de certaines touches qu'on n'aperçoit pas ici à cause de la position de l'instrument."—"Annales Archéologiques," vol. iii, p. 277.

* Mr. J. Matthews, in "A Handbook of the Organ," speaks of the objects the figures hold as "tubes," which are blown into by the mouth for the purpose of supplying wind to the pipes. The relative size of the Organ surely condemns this idea. Had they been intended for tubes, the figures would certainly have been represented blowing into them, and not merely holding them as levers.

quibusdam ligneis ab interiori parte construitur, quas disciplinabiliter magistrorum digiti reprimentis, grandisonam efficiunt et suavissimam cantilenam." This may be translated: "The Organ is as a tower, constructed of divers pipes, which blown by the wind of the bellows produces a very full sound; and that a proper modulation may be rendered practicable, it is provided with certain wooden tongues internally, which, skilfully pressed by the fingers of the performer, produce very grand and melodious music."

From the above it is clearly demonstrated that the Pneumatic Organ was well known in the latter part of the fourth century; and was becoming recognized as an important musical instrument in the fifth century, when Cassiodorus wrote. It is highly probable that it would have entirely superseded the Hydraulic Organ had means been readily found for regulating and imparting a uniform pressure to the wind from the bellows. It was centuries later before this wind regulating was successfully accomplished.

For a considerable time after the invention of the Organ, in both its hydraulic and pneumatic forms, it seems to have been used exclusively in places of amusement. When and where it was introduced into the service of the Church is not clearly decided. According to Bishop Julianus, the Organ was used in public worship in Spain in the middle of the fifth century. Platina, in his "Lives of the Popes," says that it was first used in the Church by Pope Vitalianus (A. D. 657-672). The Organ is stated to have been used in an English church about the year 640. It is probable, however, that it was occasionally used in public worship at an earlier date than the middle of the fifth century. St. Ambrosius, Archbishop of Milan (A. D. 374-397), encouraged the use of instrumental music, and it is only reasonable to suppose that his attention was specially directed to so important an instrument as the Organ. The history of the Organ during the early centuries of our era is, however, so unsatisfactory that it may be passed over without great loss to the student.

Pepin, King of the Franks, and father of Charlemagne (A. D. 752-768), in his great zeal for the Church of Rome, whose ritual he was the active means of establishing in France, sent to the Byzantine Emperor Constantinus, V., surnamed Compronymus (A. D. 741-775), an urgent request to be furnished with an Organ fit for the service of the Church; the art of organ-building and, indeed, the instrument itself being then unknown in France. This request was complied with about the year 757, by the Byzantine Emperor sending him, as an offering to his church, in charge of a special embassy, headed by a Roman Bishop named Stephanus, a "great Organ with leaden pipes."* This instrument was placed, we are told, with great pomp and ceremony, in the Church of Saint Corneille, at Compiègne. This Organ is generally believed to have been of the hydraulic class in favor at the time.

About the year 812 Charlemagne had an Organ constructed for his church at Aix-la-Chapelle, after the model of his father's Organ at Compiègne; but in this

* "Constantinus ad Pipinum proficisci jubet legatos, quorum princeps Stephanus Episcopus Romanus. Munera imperatoris, quæ a legatis deferebantur, erant instrumentum musices maximum, res adhuc Germanis et Gallis incognitum, Organum appellant."—Gfr. *Aventini* "Annales Bavariæ."

instance the instrument seems to have been purely pneumatic. Apparently alluding to this Organ, Walafrid Strabo writes:

"Dulce melos tantum vanas deludere mentes
Coepit, ut una suis decedens sensibus ipsam
Foemina perdiderit vocum dulcedine vitam."

This must indeed have been a wonderful instrument, for Strabo, in these lines, assures us that its dulcet tone caused the death of a female. This statement must, however, be accepted with caution. Rimbault says: "It also appears that an Organ, constructed by an Arabian named Giafar, was sent to Charlemagne by the renowned 'Commander of the Faithful,' the Caliph Haroun Alraschid." Later, or about the year 820, a Priest at Venice constructed an Organ for Louis le Débonnaire, King of France, which was erected in Aix-la-Chapelle. Theophilus, Emperor of the East (A. D. 829–842), a great lover and patron of the arts, caused two large Organs to be constructed by Byzantine artists, the pipes and other portions of which were richly gilded, and the cases embellished with gold and precious stones.

The erection of the Organs at Compiègne and Aix-la-Chapelle was sufficient to give an impulse to French artists; and, accordingly, we find that before the close of the ninth century the building of Organs became an established industry in France and Germany, and the finest instruments were fabricated there. Pope John, VIII. (A. D. 872–882), in a letter to Bishop Anno, of Friesingen, acknowledges this fact in requesting him to send him an Organ and an organist to teach the art of playing it to Roman students. A passage in his letter is as follows: "Precamur ut optimum organum cum artifice, qui hoc moderari, et facere ad omnem modulationis efficaciam possit, ad instructionem musicæ disciplinæ nobis aut deferas, aut mittas." (Sandini. "Vit. Pont.") About this time Bavarian organ builders were invited to practice their art in Italian cities. The first Organ of any great size was constructed in Munich.

England does not seem to have been much behind France and Germany, for we learn that fair Organs, with pipes of copper mounted in gilded frames, were constructed there. During the reign of Edgar (A. D. 957–975), St. Dunstan, Primate of England, erected, as we are told by William of Malmesbury, an Organ in Abingdon Abbey, which must have been one of the most perfect instruments fabricated up to that time. Thus speaks this historian: "Ideo in multis locis munificus, quæ tunc in Anglia magni miraculi essent, decusque et ingenium conferentis ostenderent, offerre credo. Itaque signa sono et mole præstantia, et organo ubi per æreas fistulas musicis mensuris elaboratas, 'dudum conceptas follis vomit anxius auras.' Ibi hoc distichon laminis æreis impressit:

"Organo de Sancto Præsul Dunstanus Aldhelmo;
Perdat hic æternum qui vult hinc tollere regnum."*

St. Dunstan also had an Organ erected in the church of the Abbey of Glastonbury; and it is probable that other Organs were constructed under his patronage, and placed in English churches.

* "Music of the Anglo-Saxons," Wackerbarth, p. 19.

In the "Acta Sanctorum Ordinis Benedict," the following passage occurs: "Triginta præterea libras ad fabricandum cupreos organorum calamos erogavit, qui in alveo suo, super unam cochlearum denso ordine foraminibus insidentes, et diebus festis follium spiramento fortiore pulsati, prædulcem melodiam et clangorem longius resonantem ediderunt." This alludes to an Organ presented to the Convent of Ramsey by Earl Elwin, sometime in the tenth century. It may be thus translated: "Moreover he paid out thirty pounds for the construction of copper pipes for the Organ, each of which, in the case, rested on one of the concave perforations, located close together; and which on festal days, being played with a powerful bellows, gave forth an exquisite melody and a far resounding clang."

An important Pneumatic Organ was erected in the Monastic Church of Winchester in the time of Bishop Ethelwold (A. D. 963–980), as we are told by the contemporary Chronicler Wolstan in his poetic life of that great ecclesiastic. The passage in the poem describing the Organ is as follows:

"Talia et auxistis hic organa qualia nunquam
Cernuntur, gemino constabilita solo.
Bisseni supra sociantur ordine folles,
Inferiusque jacent quatuor atque decem.
Flatibus alternis spiracula maxima reddunt
Quos agitant validi septuaginta viri;
Brachia versantes, multo et sudore madentes,
Certatimque suos quisque movet socios,
Viribus ut totis impellant flamina sursum
Rugiat et pleno capsa referta sinu
Sola quadringentas quæ sustinet ordine musas
Quas manus organici temperat ingenii.
Has aperit clausas, iterumque has claudit apertas
Exigit ut varii certa camæna soni.
Considuntque duo concordi pectore fratres,
Et regit alphabetum rector uterque suum.
Suntque quaterdenis occulta foramina linguis,
Inque suo retinet ordine quæque decem:
Huc aliæ currunt, illuc aliæque recurrunt
Servantes modulis singula puncta suis;
Et feriunt jubilum septem discrimina vocum
Permixto lyrici carmine semitoni:
Inque modum tonitrus vox ferrea verberat aures,
Præter ut hunc solum nil capiat sonitum.
Concrepat in tantum sonus hinc illincque resultans,
Quisque manu patulas claudat ut auriculas,
Haudquaquam sufferre valens propiando rugitum,
Quem reddunt varii concrepitando soni:
Musarumque melos auditur ubique per urbem,
Et peragrat totam fama volans patriam.
Hoc decus Ecclesiæ vovit tua cura Tonanti,
Clavigeri inque sacri struxit honore Petri."

Wackerbarth, in his "Music of the Anglo-Saxons", gives the following translation:

"Such Organs as you have built are seen nowhere, fabricated on a double ground. Twice six bellows above are ranged in a row, and fourteen lie below. These, by alternate blasts, supply an immense quantity of wind, and are worked by seventy strong men, labouring with their arms, covered with perspiration, each inciting his companions to drive the wind up with all his strength, that the full-bosomed box may speak with its four hundred pipes which the hand of the organist governs. Some when closed he opens, others when open he closes, as the individual nature of the varied sound requires. Two brethern (religious) of concordant spirit sit at the instrument, and each manages his own alphabet. There are, moreover, hidden holes in the forty tongues, and each has ten (pipes) in their due order. Some are conducted hither, others thither, each preserving the proper point (or situation) for its own note. They strike the seven differences of joyous sounds, adding the music of the lyric semitone. Like thunder the iron tones batter the ear, so that it may receive no sound but that alone. To such an amount does it reverberate, echoing in every direction, that every one stops with his hand his gaping ears, being in no wise able to draw near and bear the sound, which so many combinations produce. The music is heard throughout the town, and the flying fame thereof is gone out over the whole country. This honorable church has your care dedicated to the Ruler of the Thunder, and built up in honor of the key-bearing St. Peter."

This description is apparently full and clear, yet it has given rise to considerable discussion, and is in some matters perplexing, especially so in that of the seventy strong men required to actuate the twenty-six bellows with which the Organ was furnished. Rimbault makes two suggestions deserving of consideration. He says: "The brethern of Winchester were a rich and a large body, and the writer [Wolstan] probably meant that it was the office of seventy inferior monks, at different periods, to succeed each other in this labour. Or probably *seventy* may be a corruption of the text for seven." The Organ required two persons to play it, who sat at the instrument, each one managing his "own alphabet," or, in other words, the set of slides or levers which admitted the wind into the pipes of his department. From the text it would seem that there were forty such slides or levers connected with the "forty tongues" or valves of the "full-bosomed box," or wind-chest, each of which commanded ten pipes, making four hundred in all. It is difficult to accept Rimbault's very dogmatic statement. "It is clear," he says, "that the compass did not exceed ten notes, 'and for each note forty pipes,' which make up the number of *four hundred*." Surely it did not require "two brethern of concordant spirit," each managing "his own alphabet," to perform on ten notes. Again, it is much more likely that there were two departments of twenty notes each, having ten pipes to each note, than only one department of ten notes, with forty pipes to each note, as Rimbault opines. Wackerbarth is of the opinion that there was one department with a compass of three and a half octaves, and a key-board with semitones, the ten ranks of pipes being governed by registers, forming stops in the modern manner. The key-board was not invented at the time this Organ was built; but his argument in favor of forty notes has a better foundation than Rimbault's in favor of only ten. Let all this be as it may, it is evident that an Organ of four hundred pipes, blown by twenty-six bellows, the sound of which could be "heard throughout the town," must have been a wonderful instrument in its day.

Seidel tells us that "at the end of the tenth century, Germany was already in possession of a small number of Organs; for Prætorius, in his 'Syntagma Musicum,' relates, that in 944 there were Organs at Erfurt, Magdeburg, and Halberstadt. About this time Pope Sylvester II. (who died at Mayence in 1003) is said to have made considerable improvements on the Hydraulic Organ, which had, up to this time, maintained its ground. In the eleventh century an Organ with sixteen keys [levers?] was built for the Cathedral of Magdeburg. From this time," continues Seidel, alluding to Germany in particular, "we have no sufficient accounts on the progress of organ-building. Either such undertakings were suspended on account of the wars, or the zeal in this direction was cooled down and checked by some fanatics, who deemed the use of Organs in churches profane."

A most important treatise on the art of organ-building has been handed down to us in the work by Theophilus, "De Diversis Artibus," written about the end of the eleventh century. The English translation of this work, by Robert Hendrie, was published in 1847; and as it is a work rarely met with, we transcribe the chapters of the Third Book relating to organ construction.

THEOPHILUS UPON VARIOUS ARTS.

BOOK III.—CHAPTER LXXXI.

OF ORGANS.—The manufacturer of organs should first possess the knowledge of the measure, how the grave and sharp and treble pipes should be meted out; he may then make for himself a long and thick iron to the size which he wishes the pipes to possess; this must be round, filed and polished with great care, thicker at one extremity and slightly diminished, so that it can be placed in another curved iron, by which it is encompassed, after the fashion of the wood in which the auger is revolved, and at the other extremity let it be slender, according to the size of the lower end of the pipe which should be placed on the bellows. Then pure and very sound copper is thinned, so that the impression of the nail may appear on the other side. When this has been marked out and cut according to the size of the iron for the longer pipes, which are called grave, an opening is made according to the precept of the lesson, into which the valve should be placed, and it is rasped round a little to the size of the rod, and tin is anointed over it with the soldering iron, and it is rasped upon one edge of the length inside, and outside, upon the other edge, and it is tinned over thinly. Which tinnings, before the newly made lines are scraped, are slightly anointed, the copper being warmed with resin of the fir, that the tin may the more easily adhere. Which being done this copper is folded around the iron and is strongly bound round with an iron wire moderately thick, so that the tinned lines may agree with each other. This wire should be first carried through a very small hole which is at the thin extremity of the iron and be twisted twice round in it, and so be carried down revolving to the other extremity, and be there similarly fastened. Then with its joinings agreeing together and carefully fastened, it is placed with its ligature, as with the iron, before the furnace upon the glowing embers, and the boy sitting and slightly blowing, in the left hand is held a thin wood, at the split top of which a small cloth with resin is fixed, and in the right can be held a long piece of tin beaten thin, so that directly the pipe has become hot he can anoint the join with the rag filled with resin, and the tin applied may liquify, and he must carefully solder the join together. Which being done, the pipe cold, the iron is placed in the instrument prepared like that of a turner, and the curved iron being placed on, and wire loosened, one (hand) can revolve the curved iron, the other, both hands being provided with gloves, can hold the pipe firmly, so that the iron may be carried round and the pipe remain still, until it appear elegant to the eyes, as if turned. The iron being then taken out, the pipe is struck slightly with the hammer near the opening, above and below, so that this round shape may depress almost to the center for a space of two fingers; the valve [*plectrum*] may be made from copper somewhat thicker, like a half wheel, and be soldered over about the round part, as the pipe above, and be so placed in the lower part of the opening that its edge may stand equally under it, nor protrude below or above. He can have also a soldering iron of the same breadth and roundness as is the valve. With this, heated, he can place small particles of tin upon the valve, and a little resin, and can carefully pass over the hot iron that he may not move the valve, but that the tin being melted it may so adhere that no wind can come out in its circumference, unless only into the upper opening. Which being done he can bring it to his mouth and blow at first slightly, then more, and then strongly; and according to what he discerns by hearing, he can arrange the sound, so that if he wish it strong, the opening is made wider; if slighter, however, it is made narrower. In this order all the pipes are made; he can make the measure of each, from the valve upwards, according to the rule inculcated, but from the valve below, all will be of one measure and of the same thickness.*

CHAPTER LXXXII.

OF THE ORGAN ERECTION.—In the manufacture of the construction, upon which the pipes are to stand, see whether you intend to have it of wood or copper. If of wood, procure for yourself two pieces of wood of the plane tree, very dry, two feet and a half in length, and in breadth rather more than one; one four, the other two fingers thick, which must not be knotty, but without blemish. Which being carefully joined together, in the lower part of the thicker wood a square hole must be made in the center, four fingers in breadth, and about which, borders must be left of the same wood of one finger in breadth and height, in which the bellows can be placed. In the upper part of the side, however, small hollows are made, through which the wind can arrive at the pipes. But the other part of the wood, which should also be uppermost, is measured out inside equally, where seven or eight small openings are disposed, in which the stops are carefully joined, so that they may have an easy means of being drawn out or restored, so however, that no air can come out between the joins.

In the upper part, however, cut small openings opposite the lower ones, which may be rather wider, in which may be joined so many pieces of wood, so that between these and the larger, the openings of the wood may remain empty through which the wind can mount to the pipes; for in these same pieces of wood openings should be made in which the pipes are to be made fast. The openings in which the stops are fitted in the front part should increase, like slanting windows, through which these stops are introduced and removed.

In the hinder part, under the end of these stops, holes are made equally wide and long of the size of two fingers, through which the wind can ascend from the lower to the upper parts, so that when the stops are pressed upon them these holes may be stopped by them;

* In this series of directions one may follow with ease the somewhat troublesome process of making the copper pipes used in the ancient Organs. Some confusion may arise, however, from the rather unfortunate translation of the original word "*plectrum*" by the word "valve." This doubtless is due to Mr. Hendrie's little knowledge of organ construction. The word used by Theophilus should have been rendered by the technical term "languid," or "language." By the directions to make only one iron rod on which to form the copper, and by the closing remarks of the Chapter, it would seem that the pipes were made all of the same diameter, and only varied in length from the languid upward.

when, however, they are withdrawn they may again lie open. In those pieces of wood which are joined upon the stops openings are made, carefully and in order, according to the number of the pipes of every tone, in which these pipes are placed, so that they may stand firmly and receive the wind from the lower parts. But in the handles of the stops letters are marked, according to the rise and fall of the sound, by which it can be known which tone it may be. In each one of the stops single slender holes are made, half of the little finger in length, in the front part, near the handles, lengthwise, in which single copper headed nails may be placed, which may pass through the small windows in the middle, by means of which these stops are drawn from the upper side of the construction down to the lower, and the heads of the nails appear above, so that when the stops are withdrawn from the sounding instruments, they cannot be quite extracted. These things being thus arranged, these two pieces of wood, which perfect the organ house, are joined together with cheese-glue; then those parts which are joined over the stops, in which the holes exist, are also pared round carefully, and scraped.*

CHAPTER LXXXIII.

OF THE BELLOWS.—In making the wind-chamber, join together two pieces of wood of the plane tree, in the above mode, of one foot in length, one of which may be a palm thick, the other three fingers, and let them be round at one end, like a shield, and there a foot and a half wide, at the other end blunt, a palm in breadth. When these have been carefully fitted together, cut, in the round front in the thicker wood, the openings which you wish, according to the number of the bellows, and in the blunt end one, which must be larger. Then cut, from each opening, a hollow leading to the larger opening, through which the wind may have way to the working bellows; and you will thus glue these woods together with the cheese-glue, and you will bind them round with a linen cloth, new and strong, which you anoint with the same casein glue that it may adhere: you also make strong iron bindings tinned over within and without, that they may not become disunited from the woodwork, these you will fix on with long nails, headed and tinned, so that between two openings a binding may exist, which may include each wood from the upper to the lower side. Then procure for yourself a curved piece of oak wood, sound and strong, which must have at one end, from the curve, the length of one foot, in the other of two, which you will pierce in each end with a large auger, with which the middle portions are pierced in the wheels of ploughs. But because the openings cannot meet together, on account of the curve, make for yourself an iron which may have a round head, like an egg, and a long thin stem, which is fitted with a handle, and let it be slightly curved, near the head, with which, made hot, you burn the holes curved inside, until they meet together in an even manner. Which being done, cut this wood in a square manner, set so that it be one palm wide in each side, to the size of the wind-chamber in the blunt part. After these things join this wood on the longer part, to the lower opening of the organ construction, so that a projection may be cut to the same wood a thumb in length, which can be placed, or forced into this opening, and that the join be so subtle that no wind can escape from it. You join on in the same manner the other end to the bellows, and will fasten this wood with cheese-glue, and will wrap round the whole wood, with the join, with cloth, to which you also fix a wide piece of copper which may also compass the edge of each wood. These things being thus completed, should you wish to establish the organ beyond the masonry of the wall, so that noth-

* In this Chapter the construction of a simple wind-chest is described; and it is quite evident that nothing in the form of a key-board, as we now understand the term, appeared in the Organ of Theophilus. It would appear that the pipes were controlled by small sliding pieces of wood, in which the necessary perforations were made to allow the passage of the wind to the pipes, when drawn out. We have given Hendrie's translation verbatim; but had he been conversant with organ-building there is little doubt that he would have given a clearer rendering of the original text.

ing may appear beneath the cloister, unless the erection alone with the pipes, and that the bellows may extend from the other side, you must so turn the construction that the stops may be drawn out towards the bellows, and an arch may be made in the wall itself in which the chanter can sit, whose seat is so adapted that he can keep his feet above the bellows. There is also a square opening in the middle of the arch through the masonry, through which the construction with the pipes is laid out; and upon the neck of the bellows which is in the wall, beneath, the opening is made firm with stones, it is supported at its junction, and is rested upon two long iron nails evenly fixed in the wall; to this opening a wooden window hangs, which, when shut, is defended by a lock and key, that no stranger coming unawares be able to learn what may be contained in it. Outside also, above the organ, a thick drapery, extended inside with wood like a dome, for warding off the dust, can hang by a rope from the ceiling, which rope arranged with art around a wheel above the ceiling itself, is drawn whilst the organ is sounding, and thus raises the roof, and the chant being finished, it is lowered upon the organ. This dome also has a spire, made from the same cloth, extended by four pieces of wood in shape of a triangle, at the top of which a small wooden ball can stand, to which the rope cleaves. The bellows, and the instrument upon which they may lie, arrange at your pleasure according to the situation of the spot.

CHAPTER LXXXIV.

OF THE COPPER CONSTRUCTION AND ITS BELLOWS.—Dispose the length and width of the case according to the number of the pipes, and make a mould in beaten clay, and being dry cut it to whatever size you may wish, and cover it with wax carefully thinned, between two rods equally thick, with the round wood. Then cut the openings of the stops in this wax, and the hole below through which the wind can enter; the air-holes with the funnel being added, cover altogether with the same clay, and again, and a third time. And when the mould has become dry, cast in the same manner as the form of the censer above mentioned [in a previous chapter]. You will also fashion the bellows in clay, the wind-issues proceeding everywhere below in the similitude of the roots of a tree, and meeting at the top in one opening. Which, when disposed in rule you have cut with a knife, cover with wax and act as above. And when you have cast the case, you join, inside, at the height of one finger from the bottom, a beaten copper plate, in an even manner under the openings of the stops, that these stops may rest upon it, so that they can be smoothly drawn forth and returned; and lining these stops with thin clay, you pour over the rest of the case some melted lead everywhere, over these stops up to the top. This being done, you cast out this lead and will carefully mark the openings of the pipes in the stops; then you will most carefully perforate in this lead with a thin iron or with a bore. Then you make the issues for the wind under the stops; you introduce these stops singly in their places, and you replace the lead and you fit them to the construction by beating with the hammer, so that no wind can issue, unless through the openings in which the pipes are placed. When the wind-case has been cast and filed, and the pipe of each air-issue fitted to its conductor, it should be joined together and firmly soldered below to the organ construction, so that the wind may find its access freely, and can in nowise issue through the other joints. This also is to be carefully provided, that a thin piece of copper may hang down before the opening of its pipe, which can close the access of the air-hole, so that when by the breathing of the bellows this copper is displaced, it may rise, and the wind may freely issue; and when the bellows is raised, so that it may recover air through its own ventilator, this copper can quite close its mouth and not permit the wind which it emitted to return.

Here ends all that Theophilus tells us on the matters pertaining to organ-building, as practiced in his day. Unfortunately he leaves us in doubt respecting several details with which we would like to be acquainted. He neglects to state the compass of his Organ — a detail of great interest in the history of the instrument — and he gives absolutely no information respecting the form and construction of the bellows. It is probable, however, that the organ bellows did not differ materially from that used by the blacksmith at the forge, the formation of which is given by Theophilus in Chapter IV.

As a supplement to the above treatise by the artist monk, we have in the eleventh century manuscript known as the "Psalter of Eadwine," preserved in the Library of Trinity College, Cambridge, a most interesting drawing of a large Pneumatic Organ—large in all respects save in the number and proportions of its pipes. A copy of this is given in the accompanying illustration, Fig. VII. One cannot look at this drawing without being struck with the absence of all reasonable proportion between the wind-collecting and sound-producing portions of the instrument. Engel pertinently remarks: "The instrument has ten pipes,— or

FIG. VII.

perhaps fourteen, as four of them appear to be double pipes. It requires four men exerting all their power to produce the necessary wind, and two men to play the instrument. Moreover, both players are depicted also busily engaged in directing the blowers about the proper supply of wind. Six men and only fourteen pipes! It must be admitted that since the twelfth [eleventh] century some progress has been made, at all events, in the construction of the Organ." It is quite impossible to form any idea, from the drawing, respecting the kind of bellows used; but that it required considerable labor to actuate them is evident. It is difficult to divine the nature and office of the three circular, hooped vessels, unless that they are reservoirs for the compressed air. As no method of regulating the pressure of the air was then invented for the purely Pneumatic Organ, the greatest care was necessary in the blowing; hence the evident anxiety portrayed on the part of the performers.

Mr. C. A. Edwards, in his "Organs and Organ-Building," gives a drawing, very similar to that in the Psalter of Eadwine, said to be an accurate copy of one in the Utrecht Psalter, a manuscript of much earlier date than that in Cambridge. The drawing is extremely rude, but the blowing arrangements are shown in such a manner as to give some idea of the apparatus used. The bellows, four in number, are either circular vessels or cylinders fitted with pistons and valves, as in the ancient Hydraulic Organ; or constructions of wood and leather, of a round form, the lower discs of which are linked to the blowing levers. There are two hooped vessels directly under the wind-chest which are evidently reservoirs for the storage of the wind. Nothwithstanding the several points of difference, it is commonly believed that the drawing in the Eadwine Psalter is a copy from that in the Utrecht manuscript. Mr. Edwards also gives a drawing of a smaller Organ, which appears over the CLI. Psalm in the latter Psalter. The blowing mechanism here is similar to that depicted in the larger drawing, which appears over the CL. Psalm.

In the quotation from Seidel, previously given, mention is made of an Organ with "sixteen keys" having been constructed in the eleventh century for the Cathedral of Magdeburg. We have suggested the use of the term levers instead of keys, because, in their large dimensions, peculiar disposition, and the great force necessary to depress them, they partook more of the nature of levers than keys, as we understand the latter term. This, however, is a matter of but slight importance. Prætorius, in his "Theatrum Instrumentorum seu Sciagraphia," published at Wolfenbüttel in 1620, gives a drawing of large levers or keys, which he entitles: "Gross Magdeburgisch Clavier."* We gravely question if this represents the clavier of the Organ said to have been built in the eleventh century. Seidel remarks: "The keys at this time were about an ell long, three inches wide (some say even five or seven inches), and an inch and a half deep. Their mechanism was so clumsy and heavy, that the player had to beat them down about one foot deep [?] with his fists; whence the expression 'organ-beater.' Instead of our present action, strings and ropes were used. There was no such thing as a regularly progressing harmony, because the player could beat down but one key at a time." On other pertinent matters, the same authority says: "Alike deficient was the mechanism of the bellows. They being very small at the time, every Organ had to be provided with a number of them. We certainly must wonder at the perseverance of our ancestors, when we read in the old documents and chronicles that the larger Organs of this time had frequently twenty and more bellows. Prætorius, in his 'Syntagma Musicum,' says, that the Organ in Halberstadt had twenty and the one in Magdeburg twenty-four bellows. The bellows had each several folds, like those of smiths, and were unprovided with weights. There was no such thing as measuring or proportioning the wind, and, consequently, the wind became unequal, and the tone alternately feebler and stronger. Nor was there a pure or correct tuning of the Organ."

There is great difficulty in tracing, in anything approaching a satisfactory manner, the development of the Organ in the eleventh and two following centuries. The treatise of Theophilus certainly gives us an outline idea of the Organ of the eleventh century, but leaves us in the dark on many interesting points.

* An outline reproduction (full size) of this interesting drawing is given in our Chapter on the Manual Claviers.

Illustrations in which the Organ appears are extremely rare in the manuscripts of this century. Seidel says, probably alluding to German work: "In the twelfth century the number of keys was increased; and after this every key received two or three additional pipes, which sounded either the fifth and octave, or the third and tenth. By this addition the Organ was made a Mixture; which it remained until the idea was conceived of partitioning the whole lot of stops, and giving the MIXTURE register a separate slide." The thirteenth century appears to have seen little, if anything, of importance in the development of the art of organ-building, for it received a decided check by both the Latin and Greek Churches declaring against the use of the Organ in public worship. In the latter Church it has never been reintroduced; while in the Latin Church the Organ was soon restored to its former position as a dignified aid to the services of the altar. As Mr. Edwards correctly remarks: "This little opposition was the very impulse that was required to further the art. Controversy produced notoriety, and we find the Organ at last asserting itself in such a manner that in a few years every monastery possessed a small instrument, termed a 'Regal,' to lead the voices, and from this period the Organ has steadily progressed."

On entering the fourteenth century we approach the epoch which saw immense strides made in the development of the Organ on true musical lines. In this century every church of importance had one or more Organs, generally of a portable form, so that they could be easily moved to different parts of the edifice as the services required. Seidel tells us: "In the fourteenth century Organs were more universally adopted. A Venetian patrician, Marinus Sanutus, a zealous promoter of Christianity, caused, in 1312, an Organ to be built for the Church of St. Raphael: the builder was a German. From this we see that already the Germans had a reputation as organ builders, which extended far beyond the frontiers of their fatherland; and we shall see that the later inventions and improvements in organ-building almost solely came from the Germans." Even allowing for Seidel's natural leanings and his national pride, this statement must, in the main, be accepted as accurate. Until the nineteenth century Germany led the world in the art and science of organ construction. He continues: "The Organ mentioned above found so many admirers in Venice, that the builder received the honorable surname of 'Torcellus' (Organs, at that time, being called '*Torcelli*' in Italy). Monks and the Clergy—the assiduous preservers and promoters of learning and the arts during the Middle Ages—not only interested themselves greatly in the erection and decoration of Organs in their churches, but frequently employed themselves in organ-building and playing: so we must reckon them among the most ardent promoters of this art. In 1350, an Organ was built by a monk, at Thorn, with twenty-two keys. In this century improvements were made in the clumsy and heavy keyboard. The keys were made smaller and neater, and their number was increased both upward and downward, extending over two and sometimes three octaves: besides, a lesser fall was given to them, so that they could now be pressed down with the fingers, instead of with the fists. To the diatonic tones, which were hitherto exclusively used, were now added the chromatic tones C sharp, D sharp, etc."

Representations of Organs of this period are very few in number. One of the more important representations is to be found in a miniature in a Latin Psalter of the fourteenth century, preserved in the Bibliothèque nationale, at Paris. An outline drawing of this instrument is given in Fig. VIII. While it is extremely interesting as showing the form of the unweighted hand-bellows and the manner of operating them, it is to be regretted that the keyboard is not shown. Judging from the ranks of pipes, the instrument in all probability had seventeen keys—two pipes, at the interval of a fifth apart, sounding on each key. The position of the drone pipe, at the extreme right of the performer, and adjoining the smallest pipes of the series, is noteworthy. We have not found a similar disposition in any other representation of a mediæval Organ. This is doubtless a correct representation of the larger kind of Church Organ produced in the fourteenth century; and as it could not be readily moved from place to place it was known as a "Positive," to distinguish it from the smaller kind of Organ then in use called the "Portative" or "Regal."

FIG. VIII.

As Rimbault states: "The first monastic and conventual Organs were very small, being merely used to play the melody of the plain song with the voices. These Organs were called *Regals*. The term *regal* or *rigol* appears to have come from the Italian *Rigabello*. Sir Henry Spelman tells us 'that in the Church of St. Raphael, at Venice, the figure of a certain musical instrument, called a *Rigabello*, was to be seen; it was wont to be used in churches before Organs came into vogue. Another instrument, called *Turcello* [or *Torcello*], succeeded the *rigabello*, the use of which was introduced at Venice by a German.' This passage clearly shows the word *regal* to be a corruption or contraction of *rigabello*." We are, however, inclined to question this conclusion; holding the opinion that the name *regal* was given to the early mediæval Portative because it was looked upon as the regal instrument of its time, just as the Organ to-day is acknowledged as the "king of instruments;" or, perhaps, because it was, in its great rarity, first introduced in royal households or in royal pageants.

Portatives or Regals of various kinds were in common use in the latter part of the fourteenth and during the whole of the fifteenth century; and representations of those of the latter epoch are frequently to be seen in the miniatures of illuminated manuscripts, paintings, and engravings, and more rarely in sculptures.* In a beautiful miniature, in a Breviary of the fifteenth century, preserved in the Bibliothèque de l'Arsenal, at Paris, representing King René and his court of music, we see a female figure playing a Portative which rests on her knees. It has eleven pipes and flat, diatonic keys. It is used in concert with five other musical instruments. In another fine miniature, in a Breviary of the same period, preserved in the Bibliothèque de Bourgogne, at Brussels, representing the Tree of Jessé, we find one of the kings playing a Portative of two ranks of pipes, supported on his knees, also in concert with several other instruments.

Portatives, as all existing representations indicate, were small instruments easily carried by a single person, and, accordingly, were frequently used in pro-

Fig. IX.

cessions of both a religious and secular character. We are told by a writer in "Rees's Encyclopedia," that "the Regal, in all Roman Catholic countries, is a portable Organ used in processions, carried by one person and played upon by another." This may in rare instances have been the case, but we are inclined to question the statement, for in no instance have we seen a Regal depicted as being carried and played by different persons. In Fig. IX. is shown a Portative carried and played at the same time by a single person. It is supported by a cord which passes over the left shoulder of the angel. It is blown by his left hand and performed on by his right.

* Carl Engel remarks: "Of the little portable Organ, known as the *regal* or *regals*, often tastefully shaped and embellished, some interesting sculptured representations are still extant in the old ecclesiastical edifices of England and Scotland. There is, for instance, in Beverley Minster a figure of a man playing on a single regal, or a regal provided with only one set of pipes; and in Melrose Abbey, the figure of an angel holding in his arms a double regal, the pipes of which are in two sets. The regal generally had keys like those of the Organ, but smaller. To avoid misapprehension, it is necessary to mention that the name *regal* (or *regals*, *rigols*) was also applied to an instrument of percussion with sonorous slabs of wood."

The peculiar form of the keys which rise from the sloping desk of the wind-chest should be noticed. This illustration is taken from a painting by Melozzo da Forli (A. D. 1438–1494), in the National Gallery, London, and is doubtless a correct representation of a Portative of the latter part of the fifteenth century—such an instrument as the artist was familiar with. In this example the bellows is of the size of the lower portion or wind-chest of the instrument, and is attached directly to the bottom of the same. This arrangement was doubtless convenient for the player. It is certainly unique so far as our observation of mediæval representations extends.

The more usual form of the fifteenth century Portative is given in the accompanying illustration, Fig. X., which is reproduced from a drawing in a manuscript copy of the "Miroir historial," of Vincent de Beauvais, preserved in the Bibliothèque nationale, at Paris. It is extremely simple in its construction. It comprises a small wind-chest, placed between two standards, and planted with two ranks of eight pipes each; a clavier of eight flat, diatonic keys; and a single bellows in the shape of the ordinary domestic article. This form of bellows, which is operated by hand and without the aid of weights, seems to have been common in connection with mediæval Organs of all sizes.

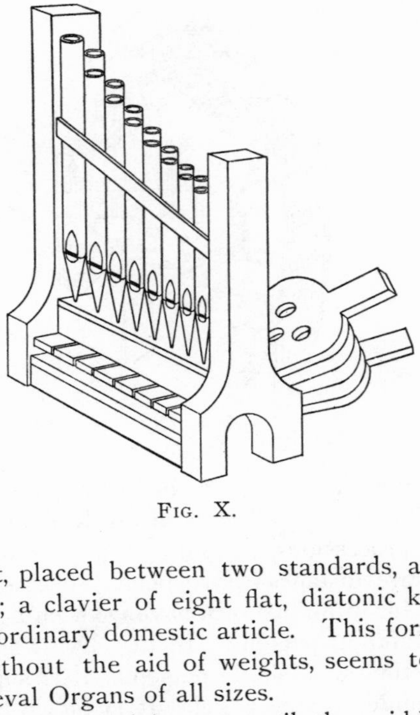

FIG. X.

Portatives or Regals continued in use until the middle of the eighteenth century, and were very common during the sixteenth and seventeenth centuries. This is proved by the numerous notices respecting them in old documents. For instance, in the inventory of the musical instruments that belonged to Henry the Eighth, taken in 1547, we find mention made of "thirteen pair of single Regalls," and "five pair of double Regalls." The term "single" is used to distinguish the instrument with one keyboard, from the double Regal which was furnished with two keyboards, commanding two distinct tonal divisions. The term "pair" has no relation to the number of keyboards, or to the tonal divisions of the instrument, notwithstanding the fact that certain authorities believe it has. The Organ with two keyboards was, in olden time, properly called a "double Organ," or "double Regal." Mr. Albert Way, in "Promptorium Parvulorum" (Camden Society publication), remarks: "It appears that the usual term 'a pair of Organs' has reference to the double bellows, whereby continuous sound was produced." He overlooked the fact that the term "pair" was applied to other musical instruments that had no bellows. Douce, an authority quoted by Way, tells us that a pair of Organs means an instrument "formed with a double row of pipes." This is, of course, incorrect; for the term was applied, as in the inventory above mentioned, to both single and double Regals. Pepys, in his "Diary," describing his visit to Hackney Church, on April 20th, 1667, says: "That which I went chiefly to see was the young ladies of the schools, whereof there is a great store, very pretty; and also the Organ, which is handsome, and tunes the psalm and plays with the people; which is mighty pretty, and makes me mighty earnest to have a pair at our church, I having almost a mind to give them a pair if they would settle a maintenance on them for it." The use of the singular "it" is significant. Rimbault says: "Some authorities tell us that 'a pair of Organs' meant an Organ with two stops. But this could not have been the case; as, in Henry the Eighth's Household Book, we read of 'a payer of Virginalls with *four* stoppes.' The truth is, that 'a pair of Organs' meant simply an Organ *with more pipes than one*. . . . Jonson, Heywood, and other of the older poets, always use the term *pair* in the sense of an aggregate, and as synonymous with *set*: thus we have 'a *pair* of chessmen,' 'a *pair* of beads,' 'a *pair* of cards,' 'a *pair* of Organs,' &c. When speaking of a *flight* of stairs, we often say a *pair* of stairs. Therefore this ancient form of expression, although obsolete in most cases, is still in *use* at the present day."

While we have no direct authority for believing that the names *Regal* and *Portative* were used to designate Organs dissimilar in form or size, during the centuries named, we are disposed to confine the former name to those smaller Organs which were carried in processions, and performed upon while being so carried. In the accounts connected with a pageant that was conducted at Coventry in the year 1556, the following entry appears:

> "Payed to James Hewet for playing of his Regols in the payggeant, viij*d*."

The name *portative*, derived from the Latin word *portare*—"to carry," may well be applied to those Organs which, while they were portable, could not be carried by a single person and played while being carried. The smaller Organs used in churches, and which were carried from chapel to chapel as the services required, were, strictly speaking, Portatives. We meet with the term in this sense, in the will of Richard Fitz-James, Bishop of London (1522):

> "Item, I will that my payre of Portatives, being in my chapels in the palace of London, mine Organs, also being and standing in my chapels within my three manors of

Fulham, Hadham, and Wykeham, shall stand there still and remain to my successor, next Bishop of London, that they may be used there to the honor and service of God."

At the same time we admit that the small instruments carried and played by a single person are correctly called Portatives. It is somewhat difficult to define the line which divides the Portative from the larger and more complete Organ called the Positive. One would feel disposed to confine the latter name to such early Organs as were of sufficient dimensions to be practically stationary, or which required the services of two or more persons to move them.

Rimbault says: "In contradistinction to the Portative, we have the *Positive* Organ, from the Latin word *ponere*—'to set down.' This instrument was provided with a keyboard of full compass, and was of course played upon with both hands." In the series of engravings, entitled the Triumph of the Emperor Maximilian, drawn in the year 1516 by Hans Burgmair, is one showing the court organist, Paul Hofhaimer, performing on a Positive. The Organ is supported on a table placed on a car in the procession. His assistant blows the bellows behind the instrument. In the descriptive matter, accompanying the engravings, it is remarked: "In the car is a Regal and a Positif; Paul Hofhaimer, master organist, plays the latter instrument." The Regal is portrayed in the engraving, behind the master organist.

An accurate representation of a small Positive, of the latter part of the fifteenth century, has been preserved to us in the engraving, by the celebrated artist Israël van Mecken, of which a facsimile is given in Fig. XI. It depicts a German organist in the act of performing on the instrument placed on a table. It will be observed that the keys are small, being depressed by the tips of the fingers. Divisions marked on certain keys would indicate the presence of chromatic notes: and the appearance of the ends of four sliders, projecting from the end of the case, would indicate that the Positive had four stops, although the general form of the instrument hardly favors that assumption. The wind is supplied by two bellows which are properly weighted, showing a decided advance over the earlier forms which were pressed down by the hands of the blower. The organist's wife attends to the blowing, and she has only to raise the top-boards, which carry the weights, alternately and then allow the bellows to empty themselves. Here we see the inception of the weighted diagonal bellows which were used exclusively by German organ builders up to a very recent date. For instance, in the large Organ erected in 1862 by E. Schulze, of Paulinzelle, in the Parish Church of Doncaster, England, diagonal bellows, weighted and regulated, were alone introduced.

In the "Theatrum Instrumentorum" of Prætorius, published in 1620, is an interior view of a large bellows-chamber. Here are shown two rows of diagonal bellows, which deliver their wind into a long wind-trunk running between them. Each of the twenty bellows indicated in the engraving seems, in comparison with the size of the men who are blowing, to be about five feet in length and two feet in width at its larger end. On the upper-board of each is a sort of shoe, apparently made of wood and stout leather, into which the blower places his foot while he moves the upper-board and inflates or collapses the bellows. Each blower controls two bellows, raising and depressing their upper-boards alternately. While doing so he supports himself by firmly grasping a horizontal rod which extends over the front end of the bellows, at the height of about five feet six inches. The action is extremely awkward, and calculated to produce, in the absence of

FIG. XI.

any contrivance to regulate the pressure of the wind, evidently not invented at the time, a most irregular supply to the pipe-work of the Organ. The blower simply raised the upper-board of one bellows by the muscular force of one leg, while he collapsed the other bellows by the weight of his body. In the engraving, two men are represented in the act of blowing; but it is evident that to operate the twenty bellows at one time ten men would be required.

In another engraving, Fig. XII., entitled "Music Personified," in "Margarita Philosophica Nova," published in 1508, we find another instructive representation of a small Positive, of the first years of the sixteenth century. It appears to have

Fig. XII.

a clavier of twenty-two notes, in which three black keys are introduced, indicating the presence of certain chromatic notes in the scale. There are also twenty-two pipes, which show that the instrument had only one stop. A very small weighted bellows appears, but no blower is introduced.

Prætorius, in the first plate of his "Theatrum Instrumentorum," gives an illustration of a Positive, of a very unusual and tasteful design, which was constructed, in all probability, in the latter half of the sixteenth century. An outline reproduction of this illustration is given in Fig. XIII. The design of the instrument presents certain novel treatments, the most striking of which is the grouping of the labial pipes on the top of the case. The tonal appointment is stated to have comprised three stops, of 2 feet, $1\frac{1}{3}$ feet, and 1 foot respectively. The projecting ends of the sliders which commanded these stops are shown at the end of the case. From the extended compass of the clavier, and the few pipes grouped above, we presume that two of the stops were formed of small reeds, inclosed within the case, in the manner common in the table Regals of the sixteenth century.

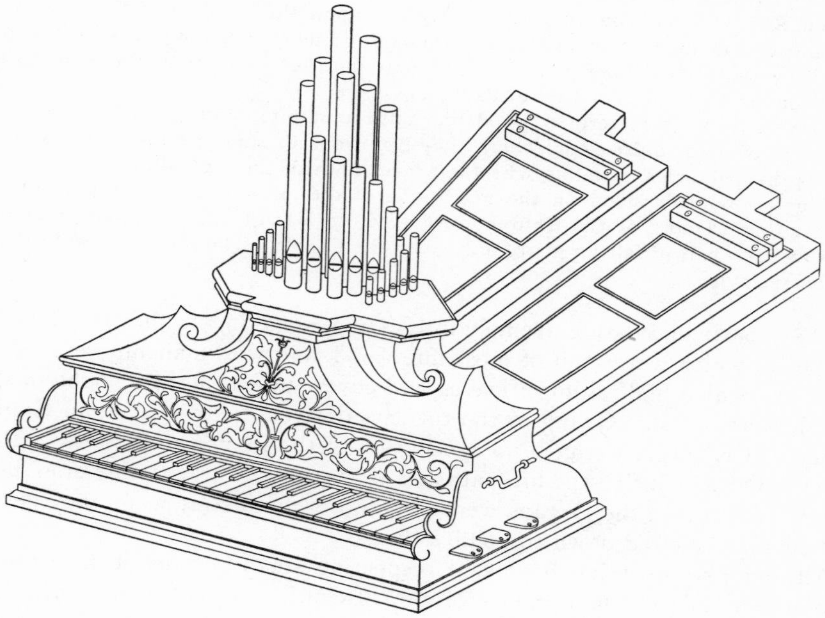

FIG. XIII.

The Organ was designed to stand upon a table while being played, in the same manner as that shown in the engraving by Israël van Mecken, Fig. XI. The bellows of ample dimensions, shown extending behind the case, were inflated alternately, and then allowed to deliver their wind under the pressure of their weighted top-boards. The form and decoration of the case are of considerable elegance, and clearly show the artistic care and skill expended on Organs during this period.

In documents of the fifteenth century and early part of the sixteenth, we find portable Organs alluded to; and the practice which then obtained of moving them from church to church also spoken of. In the Records of York, under the year 1485, is this entry:

"To John Hewe for repairing the Organ at the altar of B. V. M., in the Cathedral Church, and for carrying the same to the House of the Minorite Brethern, and for bringing back the same to the Cathedral Church, 13*s.* 9*d.*"

Again, in old documents, information is given respecting the practice of having several Organs in Cathedrals and Abbey Churches. One example of this practice will be sufficient for our present purpose. In the "Ancient Rites and Monuments of the Monastical and Cathedral Church of Durham," published by Davis in 1672, the following passage occurs:

"There were three pair of Organs belonging to the said quire, for maintenance of God's service, and the better celebrating thereof. One of the fairest pair of the three stood over the quire door, only opened and play'd upon on principal feasts, the pipes being all of most fine wood, and workmanship very fair, partly gilt upon the inside, and the outside of the leaves and covers up to the top, with branches, and flowers finely gilt, with the name of JESUS gilt with gold. There were but two pair more of them in all England of the same making; one in York, and another in Paul's.

"Also there was a lantern of wood like unto a pulpit, standing and adjoining to the wood-organs over the quire door, where they had wont to sing the nine lessons, in the old time, on principal dayes, standing with their faces towards the high altar.

"The second pair stood on the north side of the quire, being never play'd upon, but when the four Doctors of the Church were read, viz., Augustine, Ambrose, Gregory, and Jerome, being a pair of fair large organs, called the *Cryers*. The third pair were daily used at ordinary service."

These particulars are extremely interesting, speaking as they do of an Organ, the pipes of which were "all of most fine wood, and workmanship very fair;" and the case of which had folding "leaves and covers up to the top," richly decorated with colors and gold. Owing to the ruthless destruction of Organs in England in the time of Cromwell, we have no conception of the immense richness of England in Church Organs during the fifteenth and sixteenth centuries. The more beautiful and richly decorated the Organs were, the more completely were they destroyed, and their pipes melted down to make bullets.

Although so much has been said respecting small Organs, it must not be understood that all the instruments of the fifteenth and sixteenth centuries were Regals, Portatives, and Positives of a portable size. Probably there were few Organs of important dimensions constructed in England during these centuries; but in Germany the Organ had made considerable progress. On this subject German authorities are unanimous.

After describing the state of the Organ in Germany in the thirteenth century, Töpfer says: "The Organ remained in this condition up to the fourteenth century; when the desire to impart varying degrees of power to the organ-tone caused the employment of more than one wind-chest, and a varied pipe appointment which could be played upon by turns. The oldest example of this kind was the Organ erected in the Cathedral of Halberstadt in 1361; which had three claviers, two treble and one bass, with a separate wind-chest for each. The tone series had been increased to twenty-four by the insertion of seven semitones. About this time, or a little later, a beginning was made through the insertion of double rows of ventils—one behind the other—to divide the pipe-work into separate registers; one row of ventils being actuated directly by the keys, while the other row was actuated simultaneously, at will, by means of a coupling device. . . . Thus the PRINCIPAL stops, the OCTAVES, and the QUINTS, could be singled out from the aggregate of pipes and placed on a separate wind-chest, while the MIXTURE remained on its own chest with its separate and separable wind supply.

"The invention of the Pedal falls into the end of the fifteenth century. Heretofore all harmony in singing as well as on the Organ consisted in a progression of Octaves and Fifths and their doublings; the Organ did not play tones, but whole chords, and its playing required the use of one key at a time. However, after the foundation stops had been separated from the compound ones, and after musical taste had progressed far enough to form chords with changing intervals, the old Organ keyboard no longer fulfilled its purpose, and it then received the form it has retained to this day, except that the keys had a greater width—a fifth then occupying the space now embracing a whole octave. It is readily seen that for three- or four-part playing the fingers no longer sufficed, hence the need of the Pedal.

"As early as the end of the fifteenth century, then, the Organ had assumed a form, no essentials of which have been changed during the subsequent centuries; namely, with a plurality of keyboards and wind-chests, the arrangement of the stop action, and the Pedal.

"The sixteenth century brought the addition of the Rückpositiv [Back-Positive], a small transportable Organ, the kind commonly used in liturgic ceremonies. This was located at the back of the organist, being connected with a keyboard in the principal Organ by means of trackers running under his feet. This Positive developed later into an independent division, planned at the same time with the chief Organ and connected with it once for all. This arrangement of the Rückpositiv obtained into the nineteenth century, especially in France, but has recently fallen into complete desuetude. Another innovation of the sixteenth century was the introduction of characteristic stops. So long as the Organ had only ranks of MIXTURES, all the pipes had PRINCIPAL scales, for any others would have been useless. But now, interest in varying degrees of power, and variety in tonal character having been aroused, stopped pipes were added to the PRINCIPALS; SPITZFLÖTEN were constructed; and the Regal—the harmonium of the sixteenth century—furnished the reed stops which were now incorporated in the Organ. The tone compass was extended to four complete octaves, and a pitch, hitherto totally wanting, was fixed."

With reference to the state of organ-building in Germany in the fifteenth century, Seidel gives the following interesting particulars: "In 1426, the Abbé Conrad Winkler had an Organ built for the Church of St. Ulrich, at Augsburg. Germany, in general, was well off at this time with regard to Organs; for there were large ones at Solmansweiler, in Suabia, and at Nürnberg, Breslau, and Nördlingen. The invention of the Pedal, in 1470–71, by a German, named Bernhard, organist to the Doge of Venice, made it now possible to play complete harmonies upon the Organ. From this important invention, by which the Organ gained its principal grandeur and fulness, dates a new era in organ-building. The eight pedal keys, however, had at first no separate pipes, but were connected with the deeper pipes of the manual. All these old works had either a short or broken octave, as we still see [1844] in old churches in rural districts, and in some convents. In 1475 Conrad Rotenbürger built an Organ for the Church of the Bare-

FIG. XIV.

footed Friars, at Nürnberg, with upper keys of ivory and under keys of ebony; and in 1493 he built a still larger one, having more keys, for the Cathedral of Bamberg. According to some other account, the Organ at Bamberg was built in 1475, and enlarged in 1493. The Organ in the Cathedral of Erfurt was built, in 1483, by Castendorfer, of Breslau, who also built one, in 1490, for the Church of St. Ulrich, at Augsburg; the cost of which latter instrument was 107 florins.

The great Organ in the Collegiate Church of St. Blaise, at Brunswick, was built in 1499 by Henry Cranz. Before the end of the fifteenth century the first large Organs stood in the Cathedral of Strasbourg, the Cathedral of Halberstadt, and in the two churches at Augsburg. All of them, as might be expected, were provided with pedal keys."

Through the courtesy of Mr. Arthur George Hill, B. A., we are able to give reproductions of two drawings of fifteenth century organ-cases from his valuable work—"The Organ-Cases and Organs of the Middle Ages and the Renaissance." The first, Fig. XIV., shows the case of the Organ in the Church of St. George, at Nördlingen, alluded to by Seidel.

Speaking of this interesting work, Mr. Hill remarks: "The instrument stands in a beautiful Gothic gallery at the west end of the church, and both the gallery and organ-case are decorated with paintings on panel. The Organ was built in the year 1466 by the celebrated Stephan Castendorfer, of Breslau, who, besides being a noted organ builder, enjoyed a considerable reputation as an organist. The archives of the place show that there were two paid organists at Nördlingen in 1412, and in that same year it is recorded that an Organ was built for the Convent of the Barefooted Friars.

"Although the main structure of the case of which we give a drawing is the work of Castendorfer, yet the paintings which enrich it are of a much later date, and by a signature which is appended to one of the subjects they are shown to have been executed by Johann Simon Metzger about the year 1605. As is shown by the drawing, these paintings cover the whole surface of the doors or shutters of the Organ, which, for the sake of the pictures, are represented closed. . . . The cornices of the towers are richly moulded, and the friezes are beautifully carved, as are also the pipe shades of the little Organ below."

The second reproduction, Fig. XV., is from Mr. Hill's admirable drawing of the Organ in the Marienkirche, at Dortmund. This remarkable case conveys a clear idea of the labor and artistic skill expended upon the important Organs of the period. Mr. Hill remarks: "This fine work dates from about the year 1480, and is exceedingly elaborate. . . . The case presents the somewhat unusual Gothic features of semi-circular towers, which are treated in a beautiful manner. The way these latter are corbelled out on groined brackets is strikingly good. As is usual in all old cases up to a certain date, the sides hang over considerably beyond the base, and are here supported by brackets, richly ornamented with intersecting cusps in the true German fashion."

Seidel, a recognized authority on matters connected with early organ-building in Germany, appears to have been unable to obtain particulars respecting the compass and tonal contents of the instruments mentioned in the passage we have quoted. With respect to the Organ built by Castendorfer, in 1490, for the Church of St. Ulrich, it is evident that it must, notwithstanding the high value of money in Germany at the time, have been a small instrument according to our modern ideas, and, indeed, in comparison to many other Organs of the same period. Rimbault gives no special information on the subject. A considerable amount of interesting information may, however, be gathered from the following extract from

Mr. A. J. Hipkins' Third Cantor Lecture, delivered before the Society of Arts, London, February 9, 1891. Alluding to the representation of a Portative, which

FIG. XV.

exists in an altar-piece in the Cistercian Monastery of Nuestra Señora de Piedra, Aragon, dated 1390, this learned authority says:

"Here is shown a Portatif with three rows of pipes and balanced white natural keys, with one square chromatic key let in. Assuming that the treble of the instrument terminates at A, which occurs in fifteenth century Positive Organs, and recognizing the necessity in the plain song of a B flat for transposition, we cannot be wrong in regarding this square key as that note. If there is another B flat an octave lower, which according to Guido's scale was likely to be the case, the hand of the player covers it. Virdung, in 1511, figures a diatonic keyboard with two B flats, but this drawing is not altogether to be relied upon as an exact representation. There were such keyboards, no doubt, only of an older fashion. Fra Angelico, who was painting in the first half of the fifteenth century, represents Portatifs with diatonic keyboards, and, in one important instance, a dubious indication of incidental upper keys. I think, however, it is proved that full chromatic keyboards were in contemporary use with diatonic ones, including B flat, which was reckoned a diatonic note in the fourteenth and fifteenth centuries.

"With regard to the keyboards of large Church Organs, I cannot do better than briefly summarize the information on them, supplied by Prætorius in the second volume, 'De Organographia,' of his great work entitled 'Syntagma Musicum,' and published at Wolffenbüttel, A. D. 1618; it was completed by the 'Theatrum Instrumentorum seu Sciagraphia,' that is to say, the illustrative plates, A. D. 1620. I will pass by what he says about the earliest Organs in churches, because he is not speaking from personal knowledge, to start with the famous old Halberstadt Organ with which he was familiar. This Organ was built, according to inscriptions upon it, in A. D. 1361, and renovated in A. D. 1495. Whatever happened in this renovation, we shall find that the manual keyboards and compass of the keys were undisturbed, and that probably the pedal keyboard was original, but as to this doubt may be allowed. The compass of the two highest keyboards was the same, and exactly that of the ancient Greek scale of fourteen natural notes, extending from B natural in the bass clef, 'hypate hypaton,' to A in the treble clef, 'nete hyperbolæon.' Thus proving that the Church Organ keyboard was a scholastic conception in the first instance, and we shall find it, although afterwards only partially, for some time adhered to, and with Pythagorean, which was a non-harmonic tuning. The fifteenth natural key in that conception was the B flat near middle C, which belonged to the conjunct tetrachord, 'trite synnemenon.' But the necessities of the transposition of the plain song to accommodate voices, for which we have the authority of Arnold Schlick, who published his book in the same year as Virdung, A. D. 1511, had brought about the intercalation of the chromatic keys or 'ficti' as they were then called—feigned notes—and consequently the restricted compass of the Halberstadt Organ was, I have no doubt about it, originally chromatic. The lowest manual was a bass keyboard from an approximately 32 foot B natural, to 16 foot C. The highest was for the MIXTURE, various pipes of different but related pitches sounding together when a key was put down, without any attempt to sort them into various registers. In fact, the first essay in this direction is here seen, in the speaking pipes in the front of the Organ, the 'PRINCIPAL,' as it was called, being on the scond or intermediate keyboard apart from the MIXTURE, and on the third or bass manual connected with the large deep bass pipes in the side towers. This PRINCIPAL was a four-foot stop, the measure of an English PRINCIPAL of the present day, and it is curious that this old German tradition has really been maintained in England while it has not in Germany, where the eight-foot foundation register is now the PRINCIPAL. We call the eight-foot foundation stops DIAPASONS; that is to say, octaves below our PRINCIPAL, diapason being the Greek equivalent for octave. I can hardly accept the explanation which derives this name from an organ builder's rule, inasmuch as, though called diapason, his rule would serve to measure any pipe in any register. I believe the deep, third keyboard pipes were originally used for drones, and to keep such notes continually sounding was how pedals first came into use. We call a drone now a pedal point, and composers use it, especially for the tonic or dominant, with great effect. The Halberstadt pedals were for bass notes to the MIXTURE, and were mixture notes themselves, although without the highest rows of pipes. We may consider the pipes in the side towers were also upon the pedals, but as to this the text is not clear. If the usually received statement, that pedals were invented by Bernhard, organist to the Doge of Venice, in A. D. 1470, then the Halberstadt pedals were no older than the renovation; but, I think, we may safely follow the suggestion of Prætorius that pedals had been long in use in Germany, and were only introduced by Bernhard at that date into Italy. They were not generally adopted in other parts of Italy, or in England either, until the present century. The compass of the Halberstadt pedals was only an octave: B natural, C, C sharp, D, D sharp, E, F, F sharp, G, G sharp, A, and B flat. We learn from Schlick that B flat had been the highest pedal key, and some inconvenience had been caused to organists by changing this note to B natural.

"Now, the Halberstadt keys were very wide: on the two upper keyboards, four inches from center to center of each key, with chromatic keys two inches wide, placed two and a half inches above the diatonic. The keys of the two discant manuals were rounded, but in the bass keyboard they were square. I am indebted to Dr. Hopkins for these measurements, which are given in his valuable article upon the Organ in Sir George Grove's dictionary, and, I presume, are founded upon Prætorius's text and drawings. There could be, with this keyboard, no question of stretching an octave with the extended hand, or even more than a major third, and, what we call fingering, was entirely out of the question. The organist used the side of his clenched hand to depress the keys.

"I will now briefly show, from Prætorius, the gradual upward extension of compass, but, for a long while, the B natural in the bass clef remained the starting note, according, as I have said, to the old Greek scale. It would appear that the pitch of the renovated Halberstadt Organ was about a tone above our medium pitch of C, 528 double vibrations a second; but the pre-Reformation B natural was a fourth higher than this Halberstadt pitch, as was the case in the old Magdeburg Organ, which was still remaining in Prætorius's time. We have seen that the Halberstadt Organ had no higher key than the old Greek A in the treble clef. Prætorius describes the keyboard of the Church Organ of St. Egidius, at Brunswick, the date of which was A. D. 1456, as permitting the stretch of a fifth, instead of a major third, as at Halberstadt. He gives a drawing, but, unfortunately, not the compass of the Brunswick keyboard; but he does of another Organ of the same period, that of St. Salvator, at Vienna. In this the manual compass extended to C in the treble clef; the pedals as at Halberstadt. An undated Organ at Minden, with keys 2½ inches wide, according to Prætorius's own measurement, had the same compass, pedal and manual, as this Viennese Organ. The next quoted by him was the Organ of St. Sebald, at Nürnberg. Here the pedals went down to the lower A of the bass clef, the 'Greek proslambanomenos,' with B flat also added, but the manual kept to the normal B natural, ascending, however, to treble clef D. Another by the same builder, Heinrich Traxdorff, was in the Church of our Lady, at Nürnberg, without pedals, and only ascending in the manual to the Halberstadt A, but he introduced the octave register in the St. Sebald Organ, and presumably in this, in addition to the already separated PRINCIPAL; the MIXTURE remaining as the Hintersatz or Back Organ. A further extension was made by Krebs and Mülner in the Organ at Mildenberg, where the manual was advanced to the higher F of the treble clef; the lowest bass key still remaining B natural but the pedal starting from A, and thence to the A above, a chromatic octave. We are now nearing the period of a great change in the organ keyboard, when Conrad Rotenbürger built, about A. D. 1475, the great Organ at Bamberg, with similar compass, but to change it eighteen years later, that is, in A. D. 1493, to the 'long measure' in the bass, for the pedals, F, G, A, B flat, and then from B natural, chromatically, to the B flat above the bass clef, altogether an octave and a fourth; and for the manuals from the same F below the bass clef, to A above the treble, three octaves and a third. The width of the keys was gradually being lessened until, when Cranz, in A. D. 1499, built the great Organ of St. Blaise, at Brunswick, the octave was only the width of nine keys of Prætorius's time, when the octave had come to be comfortably grasped, as it has remained ever since, by an average hand. . . .

"From the end of the fifteenth century the drone bass notes, as tonics or dominants to an octave system, appear to have got the better of the scholastic tetrachordal idea of the scale. Where the long measure, as it may be called, to the low F was not carried out on the keyboard, it was, in fact, as far as possible by substitution of pipes. The B natural key served no longer for that note, but for the G below it; the C sharp key doing duty for A; and the D sharp, when not retained for E flat, for B natural; but as this was hardly a drone note, E flat was often preferred. This was the short measure—for 300 years the well-known 'short octave.' In Italy the short octave has remained quite up to the present time, but generally with E for the apparently lowest key, which really sounds C, as F sharp sounds D, and G sharp E; neither of these chromatics being good drone notes. Long drone pipes may be observed in pictures in which are represented the old Portatifs, or processional Organs, as in the Orcagna altar-piece and the Spanish fourteenth century miniature I have mentioned. I can give many examples. And, in the Cecilia panel by the Van Eycks, painted for the Church of St. Bavon, Ghent, but now at Berlin, a Positive or small Chapel Organ is painted in the most realistic manner, and the lowest note, D, has a special key situated below the keyboard at the left-hand side, while above this key there is a latch, the only possible use for which could have been to fix a drone. Perhaps the deep drones came later into large Church Organs on account of the greater cost of the deep bass pipes."

The particulars given in the above extract are of the highest value and interest to the student of the art of organ-building, and are not to be found in any work on the Organ hitherto published in the English language. To add further interest to Mr. Hipkins' remarks respecting the Organ painted by the Van Eycks, we give on the following page, Fig. XVI., an outline sketch of the Cecilia panel. The white and black keys of the chromatic keyboard and the lower drone key are distinctly shown. This painting was executed in the early part of the fifteenth century.

Respecting the size of the more important Church Organs of the fifteenth and sixteenth centuries we have some additional information of interest. Sponsel, in his "Orgelhistorie," published in 1771, tells us that the Organ in the Church of St. Laurence, at Nürnberg, built by Leonard Marca, in 1479, contained one thousand one hundred pipes in the Great Organ, and four hundred and fifty-four in the Positive Organ. The largest pipe in the instrument is stated to have been thirty-nine feet in length, doubtless including its foot.*

The Organ in the Church of St. Sebald, at Nürnberg, built by Heinrich Traxdorff in 1444, cost the then large sum of 1,150 florins, proving it to have been quite a large instrument.

As has already been said, it is probable that, although small Organs were chiefly used in the English churches during the fifteenth century, instruments of considerable importance were in a few instances constructed. Documentary information is, however, very limited on this subject. It is recorded that Abbot Whethamstead, of St. Alban's, about the year 1450, gave to his Abbey Church a "pair of Organs" which cost *fifty pounds*, an immense sum at that time. We are assured that no other Organ comparable to this in size, tone, and excellence of construction, was to be found in any of the Monasteries in England. While we have no proof of the fact, we may reasonably presume that this important instru-

*A reproduction of an old engraving, showing this and the later Organ, in the Church of St. Laurence, Nürnberg, is given in the First Volume of Mr. Hill's work, "The Organ-Cases and Organs of the Middle Ages and Renaissance."

ment was made in England. It seems, however, that Organs were, about the close of the fifteenth century and the beginning of the sixteenth century, import-

Fig. XVI.

ed from the Continent. In the parish accounts of Louth, of about the year 1500, mention is made of a "pair of Flemish Organs," suitable for erection on the rood-loft of the church, which cost 13 pounds, 6 shillings, and 8 pence. At this period the Flemish had attained considerable skill in organ-building, a skill which they long retained.

It seems almost certain that prior to the fifteenth century all Organs made in England were the work of monks or priests. Who the first lay or professional organ builder in England was will probably never be settled for want of documentary evidence. The first in any way noteworthy name is that of William Wotton, of Oxford, who, about the year 1489, built an Organ for Merton College, and another for Magdalen Chapel. We find in a document of this period (published by the Roxburghe Club), mention made of an organ builder who was in all probability a layman. The following entry appears under the year 1482:

"Item, the xxi. day of March, my Lord payd Robert Borton of Stowmarket, the organ maker, for mendyng of organys, vij^{s}"

This is followed by an entry in which a priest is mentioned in connection with the payment for "a lok [probably a lock] for the orgyns." In the parish accounts of St. Mary's Church, Sandwich, both a priest and a monk are spoken of as organ builders:

"1462.	To a Priest for amending of the organys . .	iiij *d.*
"	To a Priest that playth at organys	iiij *d.*
1521.	Payd Winsborough the Monke of Crists Church for mendyng the grete organys .	iij *s.* iv *d.*"

During the sixteenth century nothing of great importance, beyond an interesting Indenture, seems to have been recorded that has been spared to our time. The names of Chamberlyn (1509), Duddyngton (1519), Perrott (1526), and White (1531), appear, however, as organ builders. Another, named Robart, is recorded as letting Organs out on hire by the year. This builder lived in the last quarter of the century.

So far as the history of the Organ is concerned the most important of the above names is that of Duddyngton, because the discovery of the Indenture between him and the churchwardens of Allhallows', Barking, for the building of "a payer of Organs for the foresed church," under the date of July 29, 1519, furnished Dr. E. J. Hopkins material for some valuable remarks in his able and instructive lecture, "On the Progress of Organ-Building in England," delivered before the College of Organists. So instructive are his remarks that we give them here:

"Duddyngton's contract furnishes us with several interesting particulars: from it we learn the important fact that the compass of the sixteenth century English Organ was 'double C Fa-ut;' that is to say, it was of CC or 8 feet downward range, and therefore corresponded in that respect precisely with the manual compass of the English and Continental instruments of the present day. The expression 'xxvij playne keyes' I take to mean that number of keys on a 'plane' or level:—in common language, that number of so-called naturals, the requisite number of short keys probably being understood. This would give the compass, if the scale were *unbroken*, as from CC to a^{3} in alt; and, if broken, that is to say, having the CC pipes planted on the *apparently* EE key, a range corresponding exactly with the short octave CC four octave compass, still occasionally to be met with in some of the old German Organs. The Allhallows' Organ evidently had but one manual, and the English Organs of the period appear never to have had more; the expression 'payer of organs' in Duddyngton's contract having no reference whatever to the number of the manuals, but being used in a totally different sense. No complete specification is presented by the various old documents under consideration, but the names of two stops are mentioned, and in a manner that clearly shows that they were applied precisely as in the present day. Thus we find the word 'pryncipale' used to indicate the octave sounding stop, and 'diapason' to distinguish the unison."

Turning our attention to Continental countries, we find that the art of organ-building was not confined to Germany and Flanders, although, as has been shown, the Germans were the true pioneers in all great developments. In France important Organs were constructed during the fifteenth and sixteenth centuries, as is proved by the fine cases which still remain of these periods. In Amiens Cathedral the case of an Organ which was constructed about the year 1430 still remains to prove the great size of the original instrument. Sometime in the fifteenth century an imposing Organ was erected in the Cathedral of Chartres, much of the original case of which still remains to indicate its importance. Two magnificent examples of the early years of the sixteenth century are to be found in the Cathedral of Perpignan (Pyrénées-Orientales) and the Church of Hombleux (Somme). Illustrations of both these are given in Viollet-le-Duc's "Dictionnaire Raisonné de L'Architecture Française," from which we transcribe the following interesting notes:

"On désigne ainsi les armatures en charpente et menuiserie qui servent à renfermer les orgues des églises. Jusqu'au XVe siècle, il ne paraît pas que les grandes orgues fussent en usage. On ne se servait guère que d'instruments de dimensions médiocres, et qui pouvaient être renfermés dans des meubles posés dans les chœurs, sur les jubés, ou sur des tribunes plus ou moins vastes destinées à contenir non-seulement les orgues, mais encore des chantres et musiciens. Ce n'est que vers la fin du XVe siècle et au commencement du XVIe que l'on eut l'idée de donner aux orgues des dimensions inusitées jusqu'alors, ayant une grande puissance de son et exigeant, pour les renfermer, des charpentes colossales. Les buffets d'orgues les plus anciens que nous connaissions ne remontent pas au delà des dernières années du XVe siècle; et ces orgues ne sont rien auprès des instruments monstrueux que l'on fabrique depuis le XVIIe siècle. Cependant, dès le XIVe siècle, certaines orgues étaient déjà composées des mêmes éléments que celles de nos jours: claviers superposés et pouvant se réunir, tuyaux d'étain en montre, trois soufflets, jeux de mutation; et ce qui doit être noté ici particulièrement, ces orgues avaient un *positif* placé derrière l'organiste, et dans lequel on avait mis des flûtes dont l'effet est signalé comme très-agréable.

"M. Félix Clément, à qui nous devons des renseignements précieux sur l'ancienne musique et sur les orgues, nous fait connaître qu'il a trouvé, dans les archives de Toulouse, un document fort curieux sur la donation faite à une confrérie, par Bernard de Rosergio, archevêque de Toulouse, d'un orgue, à la date de 1463. Il résulte de cette pièce que cinq orgues furent placées sur le jubé dans l'ordre suivant: un grand orgue s'élevait au milieu-derrière un petit orgue disposé comme l'est actuellement le positif; un autre orgue, de petite dimension, était placé du haut au grand buffet et surmonté d'un ange; à droite et à gauche du jubé se trouvaient deux autres orgues, dont deux confréries étaient autorisées à se servir, tandis que l'usage des trois premières était exclusivement réservé aux chanoines et au chapitre de la cathédrale. Les cinq instruments pouvaient, du reste, résonner ensemble à la volonté de l'archevêque.

"Au XVe siècle, on parle, pour la première fois, d'orgues de seize et même de trente-deux pieds; les buffets durent donc prendre, dès cette époque, des dimensions monumentales.

"Au XVIe siècle, tous les jeux de l'orgue actuel étaient en usage et formaient un ensemble de quinze cents à deux mille tuyaux. L' orgue qui passe pour le plus ancien en France est celui de Soliès-Ville dans le Var. Celui de la cathédrale de Perpignan date des premières années du XVIe siècle; nous en donnons [Fig. XVII.] la montre. Le buffet se ferme au moyen de deux grands volets couverts de peintures représentant l' Adoration des Mages, le baptême de Notre-Seigneur et les quatre Évangélistes. Un positif, placé à la fin

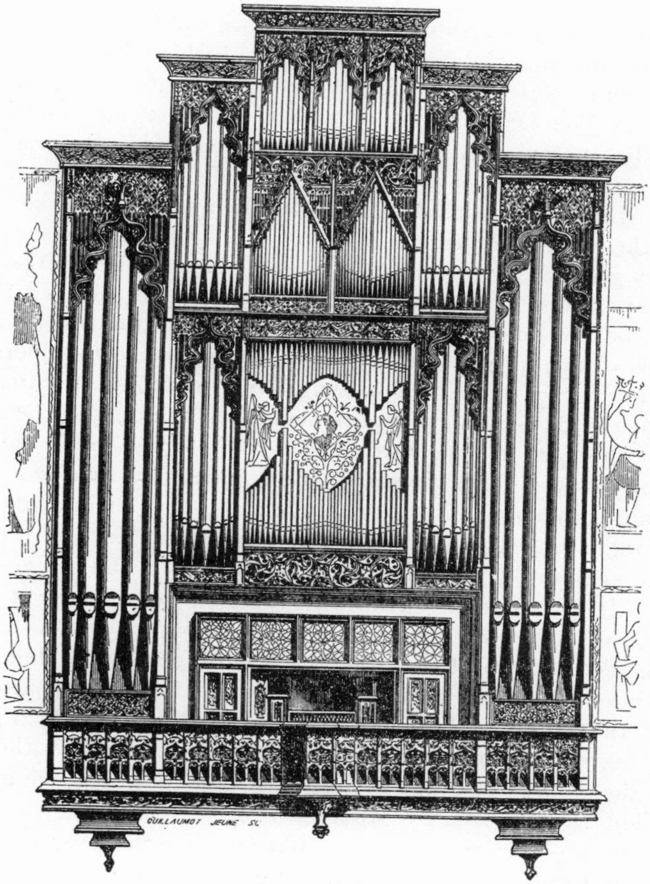

FIG. XVII.

du XVIe siècle, est venu défigurer la partie inférieure de la montre; le dessin que nous donnons ici le suppose enlevé. Le positif n'est pas, d'ailleurs, indispensable dans les grandes orgues. Lorsque le facteur peut disposer son mécanisme sur une tribune assez spacieuse pour placer ses sommiers dans le corps principal du buffet, le positif n'est plus qu'une décoration qui cache l'organiste aux regards de la foule. . . . Le buffet de la cathédrale de Perpignan est bien exécuté, en beau bois de chêne, et sa construction, comme on peut le voir, établie sur un seul plan, est fort simple; elle ne se compose que de montants et de traverses avec panneaux à jour. Presque tous les tuyaux de montre sont utilisés. L'organiste, placé derrière la balustrade, au centre, touchait les claviers disposés dans le renfoncement inférieur; la soufflerie est établie par derrière dans un réduit.

"On va voir le buffet et la tribune des orgues de l'église d'Hombleux* (Picardie) qui date du commencement du XVIe siècle. Ici, l'instrument est porté par des encorbellements, la partie inférieure n'ayant guère que la largeur nécessaire aux claviers et aux registres. Nous citerons encore les buffets d'orgues de la cathédrale de Strasbourg, des églises de Gonesse, de Moret près Fontainebleau, de Clamecy, de Saint-Bertrand de Comminges, de la cathédrale de Chartres, qui datent de la fin du XVe siècle et du XVIe."

These notes go far to show the importance the Organ assumed in France during the fifteenth and sixteenth centuries, and which naturally led up to the great developments which have placed French organ-building in the position it now occupies. The Organ in the Church of Gonesse, mentioned by Viollet-le-Duc, is certainly a noteworthy work. It was constructed in the year 1508, and the design of its case is in an early Renaissance style. A drawing of this Organ is given by Mr. Hill in his valuable work. In his notes he remarks: "The entire woodwork of the main organ-case is illuminated in gold and colors, and the whole presents a very gorgeous appearance. The scale-shaped tiles of the three cupolas [which surmount the central and two lateral, square features of the front] are decorated in blue and gold, and blue is used generally for friezes and for the recessed portions of the upright shafts, gold being applied to the fillets and to some of the lower carving. The pierced carving over the pipes is colored red, and red is also used for the turned finials on the summit of the case. The most remarkable features of this case are the three curiously designed pipes which occupy the center positions in the three towers. These pipes are enriched by a series of metal bands and ornaments which are attached to the main cylinder, and which have been wrought into elegant and striking shapes. Each of these three large pipes has been elaborately decorated in gold and colors, and some of the patterns are very beautifully designed. The lower portion of the case is enriched with carved panels, the subjects being a series of medallions such as is a common form of Renaissance decoration. These sculptured heads are illuminated in color. The extreme width of the front is about fourteen feet." These particulars convey some idea of the art expended on the adornment of the Organ in the opening years of the sixteenth century. Drawings of the Organs in the Cathedral of Chartres and the Church of Saint-Bertrand de Comminges, which are also alluded to by Viollet-le-Duc, are given by Mr. Hill.

In Spain, organ-building appears to have made great progress from the fourteenth century onward. The case of an Organ constructed in the last quarter of the fourteenth century has been preserved in the old Cathedral of Salamanca. This was quite an important instrument in its time. A still more important Organ was erected, in 1413, in the Cathedral of Zaragoza;† and about seven years later another representative instrument was placed in the Church of San Pablo, in the same city. In the sixteenth century several large Organs were constructed for Spanish cathedrals and churches. About the middle of this century the large

*A reproduction of this engraving is given in our Chapter on the External Design of the Organ.—Fig. XXVI.

†An illustration of this Organ is given in the Chapter on the External Design of the Organ.—Fig. XXV.

Organ in the Cathedral of Barcelona was constructed. Externally it presents a fine specimen of early Spanish Renaissance art. We are permitted to give, in the accompanying illustration, Fig. XVIII., a reproduction of Mr. A. G. Hill's

Fig. XVIII.

spirited drawing of this noteworthy Organ. A still more magnificent instrument was erected, in the year 1563, in the Cathedral of Tarragona. The Organ was designed by Canon Amigó, of Tortosa, and is a superb work of sixteenth-century

Spanish Renaissance.* Mr. Hill says: "The Organ possesses three manuals, and a short octave of pedals. The following are the stops:

"On the right-hand side:

TROMPETILLA.	VOX HUMANA.
FLAUTA.	CORNETILLA.
TROMPETA REAL TIPLE.	BAJONES.
CLARIN.	NAZARDO EN 17.
CORNETA.	NAZARDO EN 15.
CARCANARDA.	OCTAVA.
FLAUTADO EN 14.	OBOE.
FLAUTADO DE 28.	TROMPETTA CONTRAS.

"On the left-hand side:

PAJARILLOS.	CORNO INGLES.
FAGOTE.	OCTAVA.
BORDON.	TROMPETA REAL BAJO.
CLARIN EN 15.	TROMPETA REAL.
DULZAIANA.	TROMPETA MAGNA.
LLENO SIMBALO.	LLENO CORONA.
LLENO EN 15.	FLAUTADO.
CARA DE 28.	CARA DE 14.
ORLOS.	LLENO EN 15.
NAZARDO EN 12.	FLAUTO CONICA.
NAZARDO EN 15.	BORDON."

It will be interesting to the reader to compare the tonal appointment of this representative Spanish Organ, of the sixteenth century, with the tonal appointment of an equally representative German instrument, constructed by Julius Antonius, in 1585, for the Church of St. Martin, at Danzig. The following specification of this Organ is according to Prætorius ("Syntagma Musicum," p. 161):

OBERWERK.

1.	PRINZIPAL, . .	16 Fuss.	7.	OFFENFLÖT oder VIOL,	3 Fuss.
2.	HOHLFLÖT, . .	16 "	8.	SPILLPFEIFE, . . .	4 "
3.	QUINTADENA, .	16 "	9.	VIOL.	
4.	SPILLPFEIFE, . .	8 "	10.	SEDECIMA.	
5.	OKTAV, ...	8 "	11.	RAUSCHQUINT.	
6.	QUINTADENA, .	8 "	12.	ZIMBEL, dreifach 144 Pfeifen.	
	(Von diesen Stimmen hatte jede 48 Pfeifen).		13.	MIXTUR, vierundzwanzigfach 1152 Pfeifen.	

RÜCKPOSITIV.

1.	PRINZIPAL.		6.	KLEINE BLOCKFLÖT,	4 Fuss.
2.	HOHLFLÖT, . .	8 Fuss.	7.	GEMSHORN.	
3.	SPILLPFEIFE, . .	8 "	8.	SEDECIMA.	
4.	OKTAV, . . .	4 "	9.	FLÖTE.	
5.	OFFENFLÖT, . .	4 "	10.	WALDFLÖT.	

*An illustration and description of this Organ are given in the Chapter on the External Design of the Organ. —Fig. XXIV.

11. Rauschquint.
12. Nasatt.
13. Zimbel, 144 Pfeifen.
14. Mixtur, 220 Pfeifen.
15. Trommel, . . . 8 Fuss.
16. Krumbhorn, . . 8 "
17. Zinken, . . . 4 "
18. Schallmeyen, . 4 "

Brust—oder Vorpostiv.

1. Gedackt-Stimme, 8 Fuss.
2. Gedackt, . . . 4 "
3. Prinzipal, . . 4 "
4. Quintadena, . . 4 "
5. Zimbel.
6. Dunecken, . . 2 Fuss.
7. Regal, singend, . 8 "
8. Zinken, ... 4 "

Pedal zum Oberwerk. (43 Noten).

1. Gross-Unterbass, 32 Fuss.
2. Unterbass, . . 16 "
3. Posaunenbass, . 16 Fuss.
4. Trommete, . . 8 "

Pedal auf beiden Seiten.

1. Flöte oder Oktav, 8 Fuss.
2. Gedackt, . . . 8 "
3. Quintadena, . . 4 "
4. Superoktav, . . 2 "
5. Nachthorn.
6. Rauschquint.
7. Bauernpfeife.
8. Zimbel, 144 Pfeifen.
9. Mixtur, 220 Pfeifen.
10. Spitz oder Kornett.
11. Trommeten oder Schallmeyen.
12. Krummhörner.

From this list it will be seen that a considerable range of varied tonal effects were possible in the Organ of the sixteenth century: and it is interesting to observe the regard paid to tradition in its tonal appointment. The Mixture-Organ of the earlier centuries is in this instrument represented by the overwhelming amount of compound work. In the "Oberwerk" there are no fewer than twenty-seven ranks in the Zimbel and Mixtur, with an aggregate of 1,296 pipes; in the "Rückpositiv" there are eight ranks, with an aggregate of 364 pipes; and in the Pedal there are eight ranks, with an aggregate of 364 pipes. In all, forty-three ranks, with a total of 2,024 pipes. In this calculation the Zimbel in the "Vorpositiv" is not included, which in all probability comprised 144 pipes. This would bring the total number of Mixture pipes up to 2,168. The range of Pedal department is very remarkable.

Commenting on this noteworthy scheme, Töpfer remarks: "To the above Specification must be added three Tremolants and a Bass-drum: that is, a contrivance by which two pipes, with powerful tone pulsations [beats], produce a rumbling noise. This Organ can be said to be not only a precursor, but the very type, of the present Organ. For it already has all the chief departments of an Organ. It has the Principal-choir, Gedackt-choir, Flute-choir, and Reed-work, as well as Mixture-work. Only the Gambas are still absent. On the other hand it bears an equally strong resemblance to the Mixture-Organ, as shown by the twenty-four rank Mixture—an Organ in itself. Besides, the other parts have the character of a spread-out Mixture: they have plenty of Quints and upper and lower Octaves, but a scarcity of 8 feet stops. And this is a character not wholly discarded by the Organ up to the present [in Germany in the middle of the nineteenth century]—it still retains certain mediæval traits."

Of the art of organ-building in Italy during the earlier centuries of the Middle Ages little of an authentic nature is known. It seems likely that the earlier instruments, of any importance, placed in Italian churches were of German manufacture. One noteworthy instance is on record, under the date 1312, of a German Organ being erected, through the instrumentality of Marinus Sanutus, a patrician of Venice, in the Church of St. Raphael in that city. During the fifteenth and sixteenth centuries the art of organ-building made great strides in Italy, as in all the other countries of Europe where it was encouraged. The continual communication between all Catholic countries and Italy, especially in ecclesiastical matters, naturally led to the introduction of foreign inventions in organ construction, and, in all probability, of foreign organ builders. It has already been mentioned that the invention of the pedal clavier has been attributed to a German named Bernhard, organist to the Doge of Venice, in the year 1470; but, as Mr. Hipkins has justly remarked, it is safe to look upon Bernhard as simply the introducer of the pedals; for, as Prætorius has argued, they were doubtless used in Germany at a much earlier date. It is quite certain that all the important stops, known in Germany, including those of 32 feet and 16 feet pitch, were introduced in the larger Italian Organs during the fifteenth century. During this period the Organs in the Cathedrals of Milan, Mantua, Cremona, Bergamo, Como, and Brescia were constructed by Bartolommeo Antegnati, of Brescia, the most renowned Italian organ builder of the time. The family of Antegnati continued for several generations to practice the art of organ-building, and many important instruments were erected throughout Italy by its members. In the year 1471 the Organ in the Basilica of San Petronio, at Bologna, was erected by a celebrated Italian builder. Mr. Hill gives a drawing of the imposing exterior of this instrument, accompanied by interesting notes from which we derive the following information:

"The Organ is of extreme interest, and one of the finest examples of mediæval Italian art. It is the work of Maestro Lorenzo di Giacomo da Prato, son of Giacomo da Prato, and was begun in the year 1470. In May of that year the authorities of the city determined to erect an Organ in their basilica which should be worthy of the church upon which so much art and labor had been expended. For this purpose letters were sent to Maestro Lorenzo requiring him to come to Bologna. In the fabric rolls of S. Petronio the following entry occurs: '1470. *Die secunda Junii Ant. pred. det Maestro Laurentio Jacobi di Prato organiste lib. quinque et sol. duodecim gt. pro resto expensarum illi promissarum veniendo et redeundo a Civitate Senarum ad Civitatem Bononiæ.*' It appears from the archives that Lorenzo accepted this invitation and arrived at Bologna within a few weeks, and the Organ is stated to have been nearly completed in 1471, the following year. 'Lorenzo di Giacomo da Prato fa (fecit) l'organo di San Petronio di Bologna nel 1471.' (MSS. Strozzi, p. 271.)

"The organ builder worked during this time in the church itself, and not in his factory; and this was the custom of most craftsmen in the olden times. The *Fabriceria* (or committee of works connected with the fabric), moreover, supplied him with the wood, lead, tin, and other materials necessary for his craft, which seems to have been customary at the time. In illustration of this we quote from the contract for building the Organ in Santa Maria del Fiore, at Florence—'*quod Expensis Operæ fieri faciant unum lastronum in cava Frasinariæ pro liquidando te eiciendo cannones dictorum organorum super eo.*' This refers to a period c. 1450.

"In 1475 the Organ was dedicated, as it appears from the work '*La Musica in San Petronio*' by Gaspari, who was *bibliothecarius musicalis* of the church. The instrument is referred to as '*istud stupendum organum quod etiam nunc videri potest ad latus sacristiæ.*' . . . The original Organ consisted chiefly of metal flue stops, beginning with *Principalis*, 24 ft.; with which were associated the *Octava; Decimaquinta; Decimanona; Vigesima seconda; Vigesima sexta; Vigesima nona;* and other series corresponding to the modern MIXTURE stop, the ranks of which could be used separately, as is usual in Italian instruments. There was also a *Flauto*, or flute, which seems to have been the invention of that period. The 24 ft. diapason was divided, the bass part being played by the pedal keys, and the upper part from the manual. . . . It seems that the *Flauto* stop mentioned as having been put into the Organ at S. Petronio by Lorenzo, was also inserted into the instruments at Lucca [built for the Churches of St. Martin and St. Michael, in 1480, by Domenico, son of Lorenzo], and was regarded as a new register at the time. This was in reality a soft toned stop, called originally *Fiffaro*, and in later times *Tremolanti*, and *Voce-umana;* and to-day known as *Unda Maris.*"

In the opening years of the sixteenth century several important Organs were constructed for Italian churches. In the year 1500 a fine instrument was erected in the Chapel of the Palazzo Pubblico, at Siena, the case of which was designed by Baldassare Peruzzi, who also designed the Organs in the Duomo, and in the Ospedale della Scala in the same city. As this Organ presents, externally, several interesting features, we give, with Mr. Hill's permission, a reproduction of his drawing of the case, Fig. XIX. The treatment is dignified and highly characteristic of the somewhat eclectic style which obtained in Tuscany at the close of the fifteenth century. The introduction of pipes of their actual speaking lengths is noteworthy, and highly to be commended on artistic and tonal grounds. The entire case is richly decorated with colors and gold. About ten years later, another beautiful Organ was erected in the Church of Sta. Maria della Scala, Siena.* This has all the displayed pipes of the true speaking lengths, and which terminate clear of the arches within which they are placed.

About the middle of the sixteenth century a somewhat remarkable departure from the ordinary works of the time was essayed by an organ builder named Vincenzo Columbi, who constructed, for the distinguished organist Nicolo Vicentino, an instrument with one hundred and twenty-six keys; to which the name "Archiorgano" was given, to distinguish it from the Organ of ordinary compass. The keys were so arranged as to facilitate playing in three different ways—diatonic, chromatic, and enharmonic. About the year 1590, Luca Blasi of Perugia built a large Organ for the Cathedral of Orvieto. This instrument, somewhat

*A reproduction of the drawing of this case in Mr. Hill's work is given in the Chapter on the External Design of the Organ.—Fig. XXXII.

altered and added to, still remains, occupying a high gallery in the north transept. The same builder reconstructed, in the year 1599, the Organ in the Church

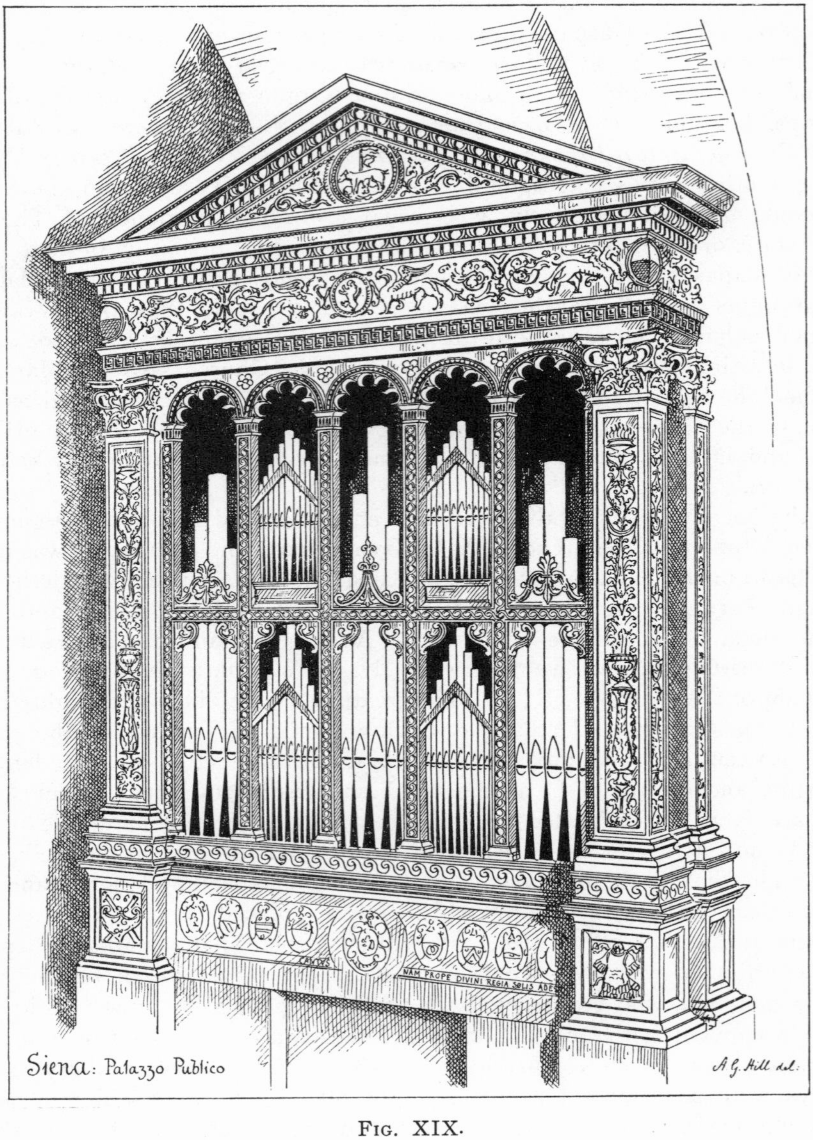

Fig. XIX.

of St. John Lateran, Rome, which had been erected by Vincenzo Columbi, whose notable invention, the "Archiorgano," has already been mentioned.

We have reviewed in the briefest, and in a necessarily imperfect, manner the evolution of the Organ from its inception to the point of development which may reasonably be accepted as representing its first important period. Although its progress toward perfection was still gradual, both in its mechanical and tonal departments, such strides were made during the seventeenth century all over Western Europe as guarantee our accepting that century as the true commencement of a new epoch in the art — that in which, owing to the conservative character of the organ-building world, we are still working. Respecting the Organs and organ builders of the seventeenth, eighteenth, and nineteenth centuries, our notes must, in the limited space at our disposal, be of the most sketchy character.

Before treating directly of organ-building in Germany, during the centuries named, we desire, through the able pen of the musical historian Dr. Burney, to show the high respect in which the art was held — a respect which naturally led to a noble emulation among builders and a satisfactory development in their works. In his "History of Music," Dr. Burney says:

"Great Organs and great organists seem, for more than two centuries, to have been the natural growth of Germany. The Organ which is still subsisting in St. Martin's Church, at Groningen, in North Holland, and of which some of the stops are composed of the sweetest toned pipes I ever heard, was partly made by the celebrated Rudolph Agricola, the elder [a learned Priest, born 1442, died 1485]. And, from that time to the present, the number of organ builders whose names are well known to the lovers of that noble instrument, in Germany, is hardly credible in any other country. But, to show my English readers what a serious concern the erection of an Organ is in that part of the world, I shall close my account of the progress of music in Germany, during the sixteenth century, by relating the manner in which the magistrates of Groningen contracted with David Beck, of Halberstadt, to construct an Organ for the Castle Church of that city.

"In the year 1592, articles were drawn up between the magistrates and organ builder, in which it was agreed by the former, that, for an instrument, the contents of which were minutely described, a certain sum stipulated should be paid to the latter upon its completion, provided it was approved, after trial and examination by such organists as they should nominate for that purpose. The instrument, in its construction, employed the builder four years; and, in 1596, the most eminent organists of Germany being invited, the names of all those who signed the certificate of approbation, to the amount of fifty-three in number, are recorded in a book called 'Organum Gruningense Redivivum,' published by Andrew Werckmeister, 1705."

During this century considerable attention was paid to the mechanical department of the Organ; and the construction of the bellows was much improved, so as to allow their being made larger, and more regular and satisfactory in their action. Up to this time no provision had been made to secure a correct and uniform pressure of the organ wind, although the necessity for some sort of regulation had been felt ever since the Pneumatic Organ was introduced. An important step was now made by an organ builder of Wettin, named Förner, who invented the *anemometer*, by the aid of which the weight or pressure of the wind could be at all times determined and adjusted. It recorded all unsteadiness caused by imperfect blowing arrangements; and determined the amount of weight that had to be placed upon the bellows. The cuniform or diagonal bellows were still used, and some of their obvious imperfections exercised the ingenuity of builders. The form, however, was radically wrong, and a perfectly steady wind was never secured by the old builders. About the year 1570, Hans Lobsinger, an organ builder of Nürnberg, had introduced, and probably invented, the bellows with a single fold, the ribs being of wood jointed or hinged with leather; and it was to overcome the unequal pressure which attended the collapsing of this style of bellows, clearly shown by the newly-invented anemometer, that the organ builders of the seventeenth and eighteenth centuries exercised their ingenuity.

Seidel tells us that during the seventeenth century German Organs were tuned to two different pitches; namely, a low pitch, known as the "chamber-pitch," which at that time was also the pitch of the orchestra; and a pitch a whole tone higher, called the "choir-pitch." The latter pitch was frequently adopted for the more important instruments, because it saved considerable expense in the metal pipe-work. All through this century the Organs were tuned according to the "unequal temperament," which confined the performer to sixteen keys, and rendered such keys as A flat major, B major, and E major, with the five remaining keys, altogether useless. This undesirable system of tuning received its death blow in the following century when several great musicians advocated its abandonment.

Considerable improvement in the tonal department of the Organ took place during this century; and several new stops were added to the list, chiefly Flute-toned and Reed stops. Ratz, an organ builder of Mühlhausen, is stated to be the inventor of the Vox Angelica: and the Vox Humana was introduced for the first time during this period. As greater regularity in the wind supply had been secured, and the means of determining its pressure invented, it is natural that attention would be quickly directed to a higher standard of voicing. In this all-important matter great progress was made by the German organ builders.

Numerous large and fine Organs were constructed in Germany during the seventeenth century. In the year 1625, Isaac Compenius, organ builder of Brunswick, erected a fine Organ in the Church of St. Maurice, at Halle. This has been replaced by a modern instrument, of forty stops, by Schulze. An important Organ was erected in the Cathedral of Merseburg in the year 1629, and underwent enlargement in 1698. It remained in its seventeenth-century form until 1853, when, under the hands of Ladegast, it assumed its present dimensions with eighty-one speaking stops. In 1645 an Organ was built for the Church of Wesel, but by whom appears not to have been recorded. A view of this instrument is given in Hill's "Organ-Cases and Organs," representing an Organ of considerable importance and characteristic design. In the same work is given a drawing of the large Organ in the Church of St. Nicholas, at Stralsund. This was one of the most imposing instruments of the century, having been built about the year 1660. Alluding to this Organ, Mr. Hill remarks: "The great Organ stands in a stone gallery at the western end of the church, and presents a front which is broken up into a multitude of compartments containing pipes of all sizes. The two great towers contain 16 ft. pipes, and are apparently supported from below by two large figures representing a man and woman. The central portion of the case is recessed back, and relieved in the center by a continuous series of V-shaped towers separated one from the other by bold cornices. . . . The date of this case is circa 1660, a time at which many great Organs were built in this part of Europe. The design is strongly Dutch in many respects, and is certainly very magnificent." Mr. Hill also gives an illustration of the truly magnificent Organ, erected in 1675, in the Ægidienkirche, at Lübeck, in which much of the original pipe-work remains. In describing this noble landmark of seventeenth-century organ-building, he says: "The Organ was erected in the year 1675, which date appears upon the case, and is in perfect preservation. It is an imposing structure, designed with powerful architectural feeling, and executed with much elaboration of detail. It is evident no pains nor expense has been spared to produce so fine a work, which ranks among the most notable examples of the church furniture of the period. The woodwork is of oak, without gilding or painting, and of a light color. The center case is a complete design of itself, and exhibits overhanging sides of a characteristic form; while the lateral towers are cleverly arranged to harmonize with the other portions, and bind them together as a whole. The gallery and *Positiv* are splendidly enriched, and the canted soffit or base of the Organ is admirably contrived."

The above description of this extremely elaborate and complicated design will be readily understood on reference to the illustration on the following page, Fig. XX., reproduced from Mr. Hill's drawing.

Although the Organs themselves are not now in their original state, the external treatments of these important examples give us a good idea of the advancement of the art of organ-building in the period under consideration. We may conclude this hasty review of German work of the period by particulars of the contents of the Organs erected by the Abbé Schnittker in the city of Hamburg. In 1686 he built the Organ for the Church of St. Nicholas, which unfortunately was destroyed by fire in 1842. This was a fine and representative instrument of four manuals and pedal, containing sixty-seven sounding stops, and displaying the highest development reached by the organ builders toward the close of the seventeenth century. Both Seidel and Hopkins give specifications of this instrument, as it was, we presume, at the time of its destruction. The exact condition in which Schnittker left it is not alluded to. The same celebrated builder constructed the Organ in the Church of St. Jacobi, at Hamburg, an instrument of four manuals and pedal. This appears to have been built some time before the St. Nicholas instrument. Dr. Hopkins remarks:

"The name of the builder of the above excellent Organ is held in great veneration in Germany; where his instruments are as highly prized for their stability, as they are justly celebrated for their dignified and impressive tone. The Abbé Schnittker resided at a place about thirty-six English miles from Hamburg, in the Hanoverian territories, in a house that has gone by the name of 'the organ builder's box' or villa ever since."

Comparing the old instruments in the Churches of St. Michael, St. Catherine, and St. Jacobi, all in Hamburg, with the works of certain contemporaneous builders in England, the same writer remarks: "The three fine instruments, just

Fig. XX.

noticed, form most interesting objects for examination to an English admirer of the Organ; not simply on account of the very distinct character in the tone of each, but because they so closely resemble in quality the Organs of three of the most celebrated builders of this country of past times; and they therefore picture to the hearer what the instruments of those builders would have been, had the art in England been in a more advanced state in their day. The Organ in the Church of St. Catherine, which is the oldest of the three [containing fifty-six speaking stops, distributed on four manuals and pedal], is strikingly like Harris's in tone; clear, ringing, and dashing in the MIXTURES. That in the Church of St. Jacobi calls to mind the instruments of Father Smith; resonant, solemn, and dignified; with somewhat less fire than that at St. Catherine's, but rather more fulness. The Organ at St. Michael's, the most recently constructed one of the three, is also the largest in scale; is less powerful than the others, but very musical and pleasing; and, in all these respects, forcibly calls to mind the excellent instruments of Green."

Seidel says: "In the course of the seventeenth and in the beginning of the eighteenth centuries great care was bestowed on, and money expended for, the external embellishment of the Organ. The whole case was ornamented with statues, heads of angels, vases, foliage, and even figures of animals. Sometimes the front pipes were gilded or painted. The lips of the pipes were formed like lions' jaws, and ornamental patterns were embossed on the pipes. To this paltry sort of artifice we should not object much, the less so, as in the course of time it was abolished as being useless and unsuitable. But people went farther, and threw away the money which might have been expended in a worthier manner, for the most insipid and absurd ornaments, degrading thereby—unknowingly perhaps—the sublime instrument to a raree-show. Among these ornaments the figures of angels played a very conspicuous part. Trumpets were placed in their hands, which, by some contrivance, they could move to or from their mouths. Carillons and kettledrums were handled by these angels. Not unfrequently there was in the midst of this heavenly host some larger angel, soaring above the others, and beating with his baton time for his heavenly orchestra. Under such circumstances the firmament could not be dispensed with. There were revolving suns and moons and moving stars which jingled—called cymbal stars. Even the host of the animal kingdom was summoned. . . . In praise of the later organ builders, however, we must say that they gradually abolished these absurd and detrimental things, and directed their attention to more important matters."

With the eighteenth century we enter upon a period of great activity and marked progress in German organ-building—a period which it is impossible to do justice to, in any direction, in this brief historical digest. In this century several organ builders, most eminent in their art, whose names will ever be bound up with the history of organ-building, lived and labored; and their works, in many instances, remain to this day as monuments to their skill and high attainments. Amidst all the more distinguished names, that of Gottfried Silbermann stands forth in well-deserved prominence as the greatest of Germany's eighteenth-century builders.

A representative list of a few noteworthy Organs and their distinguished builders will suffice to show the skill and enterprise which marked this century of organ-building. Speaking of the instruments constructed in Dresden by the great builder above named, Edward Holmes, in his "Ramble Among the Musicians of

Germany," published in 1828, says: "In glancing over the list of contents, the musical reader may please his imagination by fancying with what effect a piece of florid and artful counterpoint comes out of a German Organ, where the player sits with a flood of sound ready to the touch of his fingers, and store of thunder lying harmless at his feet. The thickness, depth, and independence of the Pedals, here vindicate supremely the poetical ascendancy of the fugue over every other class of musical composition; and in slow subjects, when the bass rolls in its ponderousness—there is no disputing it—it is like the fiat of the Omnipotent. As a matter of science, it is worthy of consideration how far the construction of our Organs [English] might be improved by uniting the sweet Cathedral quality of tone for which those of the Temple, Westminster Abbey, etc., are noted, with the magnificence of Silbermann. If there lived now in England a mechanic capable of associating the best points of the two, a perfect specimen of the kind would be the result." We have quoted this passage, from the pen of an able critic, writing at a time when German Organs stood supreme in the development and dignity of the pedal department, for the purpose of showing the proud position occupied by the instruments of the eighteenth century in Germany, and how truly they led the way toward the greatest achievements subsequently accomplished in other countries. There can be no disputing with Germany the honor of having created the Pedal Organ, and of having been far in advance of all the rest of Europe in this direction until very recent times. These are very important facts in connection with the History of the Organ.

In the year 1702 the organ builder Theussner constructed the large Organ for the Cathedral of Merseburg, containing 68 speaking stops, distributed over five manuals and pedal. This is stated to have been a noteworthy instrument when built. In the following year, Eugenius Casparini and his son, Adam Horatius, erected a fine Organ in the Church of SS. Peter and Paul, at Goerlitz. This instrument, according to Dr. Hopkins, contains 82 stops, 55 of which are through speaking stops. It has 3270 pipes, only 522 of which are of metal; the front, or exposed, 280 pipes being of polished tin, with the FFFF pipe of the Pedal Organ, 24 feet in length, occupying the most prominent position. It has three manuals and pedal, and is blown by twelve pairs of diagonal bellows. It is stated to have occupied six years in its construction. The same builder erected, in 1705, an Organ of 34 speaking stops, in the Church of St. Bernhardin, at Breslau. In the scheme of this comparatively small instrument we find a remarkable pedal department of 12 stops, the specification of which we give, in support of the remarks we have already made respecting the German treatment of this all-important department.

PEDAL ORGAN.

Major-Bass,	32 feet	Major-Quinte,	$10\frac{2}{3}$ feet
Posaune,	32 "	Doppelflöte,	8 "
Principal,	16 "	Quintatön,	8 "
Violon,	16 "	Violin,	8 "
Sub-Bass,	16 "	Trompette,	8 "
Posaune,	16 "	Super-Octave,	4 "

In 1707, an accomplished builder named Sterzing built the Organ in the Church at Eisenach, which contained 58 stops distributed over four manuals and pedal. We now come to the period of Germany's most artistic builder of the eighteenth century. In 1716, Silbermann erected his fine Organ, of 42 speaking stops, in the Cathedral of Strasbourg. The compass of the manuals is CC to $c^3 = 49$ notes, and of the pedals CCC to $C = 25$ notes. The instrument has three manuals. It contains 2242 pipes, and is blown by six bellows, each measuring 12 feet by 6 feet. The Gothic case in which this beautifully-toned Organ is placed was constructed about the year 1497, and has, very fortunately for art, been carefully preserved. In 1720, the same builder erected an Organ, of 32 speaking stops, in the Royal Church of the Evangelists, at Dresden, having two manuals and pedal. In 1740, Gottfried Silbermann built two fine Organs for Strasbourg: one in the Church of St. Thomas, with 36 speaking stops, distributed on three manuals and pedal; and the other in the Protestant Church, with 46 speaking stops, distributed on three manuals and pedal. Both these instruments are celebrated for the beautiful tones of their "MONTRES," 8 FT. (DIAPASONS), and their flute-toned stops—stops for which German voicers have always been celebrated, and which they can largely claim the credit of inventing and perfecting. In the middle of the century, Gottfried Silbermann had reached the zenith of his fame; and at this time he erected in the Cathedral of Freiberg, in Saxony, one of his largest and finest instruments. It contains 45 speaking stops, distributed on three manuals and pedal. The Pedal Organ is, on historical grounds, well worthy of record. It contains the following ten stops:

UNTERSATZ,	(wood)	- - 32 feet		OCTAVE,	(tin)	- - 8 feet
PRINCIPAL,	(tin)	- - 16 "		TROMPETTE,	(tin)	- - 8 "
OCTAVE,	(wood)	- - 16 "		SUPER-OCTAVE,	(tin)	- - 4 "
SUB-BASS,	(wood)	- - 16 "		CLAIRON,	(tin)	- - 4 "
BOMBARDE,	(tin)	- - 16 "		FOURNITURE,	(tin)	- - VI. ranks

Throughout this excellent instrument nothing is used for the pipe-work save English tin and wood, furnishing an object-lesson for all subsequent organ builders and those interested in organ construction. Both in the choice of materials and in the beauty and brilliance of his organ-tones, this renowned builder supported his name—Silverman. In 1750, he constructed the Organ for the Church of St. Sophia, at Dresden—a very fine instrument of 33 speaking stops on two manuals and pedal. The Pedal Organ, of six stops, is noteworthy as possessing four stops of 16 feet pitch, and a CORNET of VIII. ranks. Then, four years later, the magnificent Organ in the Royal Catholic Church, at Dresden, was completed, justly esteemed Silbermann's masterpiece. It was schemed and substantially constructed under his direction, but he did not live to see it finished in the church, his nephew and partner, John Daniel Silbermann, completing the work. The Organ contains 48 speaking stops, distributed on three manuals and pedal. The compass of the manuals is CC to d^3, and of the pedals CCC to C. The Great Organ, of 16 stops, has three stops of 16 feet pitch; while the Pedal Organ has one of 32 feet and only two of 16 feet. In comparison to the completeness of the three manual divisions, which have, respectively, sixteen, fourteen, and ten stops, the Pedal Organ of only eight stops seems insufficient, judged by the general practice of the German masters of the period.

In the year 1718, the Organ in the Church of Halberstadt was erected by Henry Herbst and his son. It contained 74 stops, and, according to Seidel, had three manuals in front and two on the sides, and pedal. This writer gives no specification of the instrument, nor does he inform us for what purpose the manual claviers were so peculiarly located. It may have been with the view of allowing two or three organists to perform at the same time. This instrument was completely rebuilt by J. F. Schulze in 1838. In 1722, an Organ was erected in the Church of St. Mary, at Berlin, by Joachim Wagner: and the same eminent builder erected, in 1725, the Organ in the Garrison Church, in Berlin. This latter instrument contains 49 speaking stops, distributed on three manuals and pedal. Dr. Hopkins gives the specification of this instrument in the Appendix to "The Organ." Seidel tells us that in the year 1724, Röder, of Berlin, built the Organ in the Church of St. Mary Magdalen, at Breslau, containing 55 stops [in its renovated state], distributed on three manuals and pedal. The GGGG pipe of the pedal MAJOR-BASS, 32 FT., stands in front. It is of polished tin, 25 feet in height and 12 inches in diameter, and weighs 375 pounds. This single pipe cost 300 florins. Dr. Hopkins gives the specification of this instrument as renovated by Engler in 1821. The original contents are not given by either writer. Röder also built a fine Organ for the Church of the Cross of Christ, at Hirschberg, in 1727. This has been renovated by Buckow, in 1830, and contains 63 stops, distributed on four manuals and pedal. The pedal department contains 16 stops, including two of 32 feet and five of 16 feet pitch; and it has VII. ranks of mixture-work. Here we find a thoroughly characteristic German treatment of this important department. In the year 1730 an Organ was erected in the Cathedral of Ulm, by Schmahl and Son, containing 45 stops on two manuals and pedal, and blown by 16 diagonal bellows. An idea of the size and dignity of this work can be gathered from the fact that it was contained in a case, of elaborate design, about 95 feet in height by 28 feet in width. This Organ has been destroyed. In the same year Trost, of Altenburg, erected in the Church of Walterhausen, a grand Organ of 50 speaking stops, with three manuals and pedal. The fine pedal department contains 14 stops, including one of 32 feet and five of 16 feet pitch. The GROSS-PRINCIPAL, 16 ft., is of English tin, and is mounted in front. The Great Organ contains three stops of 16 feet and seven of 8 feet pitch.

We now come, in the order of time, to one of the greatest achievements in the organ-building world of the eighteenth century. We allude to the magnificent Organ in the Church of the Benedictine Monastery, at Weingarten, in Suabia, a superb line engraving of which is given by Dom Bedos, in Plate LXXVII. of his great treatise. This landmark in the history of the art was constructed by Josephus Gabler, of Ravensburg, and completed on the 24th of June, 1750, after occupying several years in building. According to the specification given by Dom Bedos, and which is doubtless that of the instrument as originally constructed, it contained 66 stops and 6,666 pipes. Only ten stops are of wood; all the rest being of tin. The larger pipes of the pedal CONTRE-BASSE, 32 FT., are of polished tin, and occupy the most prominent position in the front of the instrument. The largest pipe is stated to measure about 16 inches in diameter. For further information respecting this remarkable instrument, see the specification and notes given by Dom Bedos, quoted in our collection of representative Specifications.

Limited space prevents our mentioning more than one other German Organ of the eighteenth century; and we select the grand Organ constructed by Hildebrandt for the Church of St. Michael, at Hamburg. This was completed shortly after 1762, when the present church was opened for service. The Organ contains 70 speaking stops, distributed in the four divisions on the three manuals, and in the pedal department. The Pedal is singularly full and complete, containing three stops of 32 feet and six of 16 feet pitch, five important reed stops, and a MIXTURE of X. ranks. There are on the manuals four stops of 16 feet and twenty-five of 8 feet pitch, and XLIV. ranks of mixture-work. Viewed externally, this Organ presents a most imposing appearance. The case is sixty feet in height and width, and has in its center the CCCC pipe of the pedal PRINCIPAL, which measures 35 feet 6 inches in height by 20 inches in diameter, and contains about 970 pounds of pure tin. As Dr. Hopkins says, the Organ is finely laid out inside, in four stories, to each of which free access is obtained by wide staircases. Passage-boards occur in abundance; and any pipe in this immense instrument can be got at without disturbing a second one.

Leaving the consideration of the art of organ-building in the nineteenth century for the concluding remarks of the present hurried historical survey, we may now glance at its condition in some other European countries during the seventeenth and eighteenth centuries.

During these centuries the Dutch builders seem to have ranked next to those of Germany in the excellence and importance of their works, although it must be admitted that great progress had been made by the Belgian builders. In the year 1673, the fine Organ in the Nieuwe Kerk, at Amsterdam, was constructed by J. Duyscher van Goor, of Dordrecht, a celebrated builder of the time. This instrument contains 44 speaking stops, distributed on three manuals and pedal. The compass of the former is CC to $d^3 = 51$ notes, and of the pedal department CCC to $D = 27$ notes; corresponding in these particulars with the most advanced German instruments of the same period. There is no stop of 32 feet pitch in the instrument, while there are two of 16 feet pitch in the Great Organ. The most noteworthy feature in the tonal scheme is the mixture-work. Here we find seven stops comprising no fewer than XXXIII. ranks. This is another proof of the great importance given to the compound, harmonic-corroborating stops by the early masters. It is now many years since we heard this Organ, but the impression still remains that the MIXTURES seemed too bright and powerful—a fault not confined to such early work. The Organ is externally a very imposing object, standing above the west door of the church. Mr. Hill gives a drawing of the case in his valuable Work; and remarks, in his brief description: "The composition consists of two classical orders, or tiers [not to be understood as signifying classical columns and their entablatures], the upper surmounted by a pediment. Though the details are late in style, yet the arrangement of the various groups of pipes is most excellent, the whole being greatly enhanced by the huge picturesque doors, or shutters, which can be folded over the instrument at pleasure. These are embellished with paintings on canvas, now dark with age. The Choir Organ is a miniature representation of the greater Organ above, and, with the exception of the figures and festoons, is well designed." Such an example as this illustrates the care taken by the old builders to protect their instruments from damp and dust; and what a contrast it presents to the open, starved, and miserable apologies for cases which people are content with in the present day. A little later, or about the year 1686, R. B. Druyschot, another noted builder, erected the Organ in the Old Church, at Amsterdam. This instrument contains 51 stops, distributed on three manuals and pedal, with the same compass as the preceding example. Here, again, we observe an almost overwhelming mass of mixture-work, comprising XLII. ranks in the eight compound stops, exclusive of the five mutation stops. According to Dr. Hopkins, the foundation stops of this instrument are *doubled*, greatly increasing the volume and solidity of its fundamental tone, and thereby permitting a larger use of the harmonic-corroborating stops. The pedal department, of ten stops, is generally lacking in gravity, when compared with that met with in German instruments of similar size. With these representative examples of the most advanced work in Holland during the seventeenth century, we may pass on to the consideration of the Organs which mark the art in the eighteenth. In the proper order of things, the Organ which first claims attention is the long-renowned instrument in the Cathedral of St. Bavon, at Haarlem. It is, perhaps, not too much to say that no Organ ever constructed has earned so world-wide a reputation as this; and as it still remains practically in the state it was left by its distinguished builder, it has the very greatest value and interest from a historical point of view. At the same time it is a truly noble work of art from every other point of view. It was constructed by Christian Müller, of Amsterdam, who commenced the work on the 23rd day of April, 1735, and completed it on the 13th day of September, 1738. The Organ stands on an elevated gallery at the end of the Cathedral, and, externally, it is most imposing. Considering the state of ornamental art at the time of its construction, it is singularly successful in its design. This can be realized from the accompanying illustration, Plate II. The specification of its contents will be found in our collection of representative Specifications. The Organ contains 60 speaking stops, distributed on the manuals and pedal, all of which, with the exception of certain compound stops, and the HAUTBOIS in the Great Organ, being complete stops. The PRESTANT, 16 FT., and the OCTAAV, 8 FT., in the Great; the PRESTANT, 8 FT., in the Choir; and the PRESTANT, 8 FT., in the Echo, have each two ranks of pipes in the treble octaves. This expedient was adopted by the builder with the view of overcoming the natural tendency toward weakness in the treble in all organ stops formed of single ranks of pipes. In four of the compound stops the ranks of pipes increase in number as they ascend the manual scale. Originally every stop in the Organ was of metal; all the front pipes, including the pedal SUB-PRINCIPAL, 32 FT., are of pure

English tin, burnished. The CCCC pipe, standing in one of the lateral towers, measures about 39 feet in length by 15 inches in diameter. The compass of the manual department is CC to d^3 = 51 notes, and of the pedal department CCC to D = 27 notes. The cost of the complete work amounted to about $58,000. The instrument is supplied with wind from twelve bellows, which measure each 9 feet by 5 feet.

Several other very important Organs mark the history of organ-building in Holland during this century; notably the Organ in the Church of St. John, at Gouda, constructed by Moreau, of Rotterdam, in the year 1736. This contains 51 speaking stops, distributed on three manuals and pedal. Its compass on the manuals is CC to d^3 = 51 notes, and on the pedals CCC to C = 25 notes. This instrument is noted for its many beautifully-toned stops and especially for its Vox Humana. It contains six stops of 16 feet pitch; and its seven compound stops contain XXXIV. ranks.

The progress of organ-building in the Netherlands and in Belgium, during the seventeenth and eighteenth centuries, differed little from that which obtained in Holland and North Germany. There was doubtless almost constant intercourse, during peaceful times, between the organ builders of all these countries; and, in some instances, instruments were erected in one country by builders belonging to another adjoining country. This appears to have been the case with the Organs in the Churches of St. Stephen, Nymegen, and St. John, at Bois le Duc. The history of the latter instrument, as given by Mr. Hill, from Hezenmans' Work on the Church, is interesting, and we gather from it the following particulars. In the year 1617, negotiations were opened between the church authorities and Matthew Langedul, organ builder to the Archduke Albert, at Brussels. This eminent builder undertook to build an Organ of the size decided upon for the sum of 8,800 florins. He, however, had immediately to throw up the contract, on being ordered by the Archduke to build an Organ for the King of Spain. "After an interval of indecision the town authorities put themselves into communication with various organ builders, from among which two, Florent Hocque, of Cologne, and Nicolas Nÿhoff, of Bois le Duc, where chosen. Eventually the former was selected as builder, and on the 15th of June, 1618, a contract was entered into with him to erect an Organ at a cost of 9,600 florins. The wars between Spain and the Low Countries now caused an interruption in the work; but a contemporary writer, Zÿlius, informs us that the instrument was in use before the year 1629. A notice in the archives of the church shows that Hocque was working upon the Organ in 1630, and on November 30th of that year the committee reported that 400 florins were due to him for the work that he had recently done, and that 800 florins remained to be held over till the Organ should be declared to be complete according to the original contract of 1618. In 1632 Hocque was requested to finish the work according to the schedule, and he employed a builder named Hans Goldfur, to whom the authorities objected, for they finally called in Galtys Germertsen and Germer Galtÿssen, father and son, who completed the whole in the following year. The instrument was then examined by the organists of Haarlem, Amsterdam, and Utrecht, who reported that it was perfect in all particulars.

"The magnificent case is the work of two artists: Francis Sÿmons, who had already executed much fine woodwork for the church; and George Schÿsler, sculptor, of Cologne."

It would be difficult to imagine anything grander, of its style and class, than this sumptuous case: it occupies almost the entire space of the western wall of the nave, rising to the height of about 100 feet from the floor, and spreading to the width of about 40 feet. It stands on a highly ornamental gallery of the same Renaissance style.*

The Organ contains 41 stops, distributed on three manuals and pedal. The specification is remarkable, showing one stop of 32 feet and three stops of 16 feet pitch in the Great Organ, while in the Pedal Organ there is no stop of 32 feet and only two of 16 feet pitch—PRESTANT and BOURDON.

While the fine Organ in the Church of St. Stephen, Nymegen, cannot be considered an example of local work, like the instrument just described it may be looked upon as representative of the taste of the time in the Netherlands. The instrument contains 53 speaking stops, distributed on three manuals and pedal. The compass of the manual divisions is CC to $f^3 = 54$ notes; and of the pedal department CCC to D = 27 notes. The PRESTANT and (Bass) TROMPETE in the Great, the BOURDON in the Choir, and the QUINTADENA in the Echo, are all of 16 feet pitch. The Pedal Organ of twelve stops, contains a PRINCIPAL, VIOLON, SUB-BASS, and BOMBARDE, of 16 feet pitch. There are seven compound stops in the manual divisions with an aggregate of XXIX. ranks of pipes. The instrument was built by König, of Cologne, in the year 1766.

The Organ in the Cathedral at Antwerp was constructed, in the year 1645, by a local builder named De la Haye. It contains forty-four stops distributed on three manuals and pedal: having a compass on the former from CC to $f^3 = 54$ notes; and on the latter from FFF to F = 25 notes. The Great Organ is singularly large and complete, containing eighteen stops, three of which are of 16 feet pitch. It has the unusual addition in the shape of a VOX HUMANA. In the year 1670, Terbrugen, of Antwerp, erected the Organ in the Church of St. Paul in that city. It was originally a large and effective instrument; but, having been "repaired and improved" in 1825, it is now difficult to trace its original scheme. It now contains 51 speaking stops, distributed on three manuals and pedal; the compass of the manuals being from CC to $f^3 = 54$ notes; and of the pedals from CCC to C = 25 notes. The Great Organ contains nineteen stops; and the Pedal Organ only seven stops—a weakness in the tonal appointment unusual in large instruments of this period. Other and later Organs constructed in Belgium are of no direct historical interest.

The history of the art of organ-building in France during the seventeenth and eighteenth centuries presents little that calls for special comment. The art certainly made considerable progress there, as it did in the neighboring countries already spoken of; and it certainly received considerable attention both in its theoretical and practical aspects in some influential quarters. This is unquestion-

* An illustration of this case, reproduced from Mr. A. G. Hill's beautiful drawing, is given in the Chapter on the External Design of the Organ.—Fig. XXIII.

ably evidenced by the publication, in 1766, under the auspices of the French Academy, of "L'Art du Facteur d'Orgues,"* by Dom Bedos de Celles, Benedictine of the Congregation of Saint-Maur. This Work is the largest and most complete treatise on the science and art of organ-building ever published. The plan of the Work is at once simple and exhaustive, so far as the art had developed in the middle of the eighteenth century; and the system of illustration, by fine and elaborate line-engravings, surpasses everything subsequently attempted in works on organ-building. The noble volumes lie open before us as we pen these remarks, and we turn their time-honored pages with a feeling of profound respect for the labors of the old Benedictine of Saint-Maur, and the engravers who aided them so artistically.

As "L'Art du Facteur d'Orgues" is of necessity a very rare book, to be found only in large collections of technical works, and is practically unknown to the great majority of English and American organ builders, a few words respecting its contents, chiefly from a historical point of view, may not be without interest and value here. The plates, one hundred and thirty-seven in number including thirty-six large folding ones, with their accompanying descriptions, clearly show the state of organ construction about the year 1766 in France and Germany. Respecting the mechanical portion of the Organ, we find the simplest action to have been used; namely, the tracker-action, in which backfalls, roller-boards, and roller-squares are largely introduced. The wind-chests were of the grooved, palleted, and slidered variety, which, with some slight modifications, has held its position in the art of organ-building up to the present day. The pedals were of the form known as "toe-pedals," with a compass of twenty-seven notes—CCC to D. The illustration on the following page, Fig. XXI. (from Plate XXXIII.) shows the form of the toe-pedals, and likewise the position of the manual claviers and the clumsy draw-stops of the period. The only large bellows illustrated, and, accordingly, the only kind then used, are of the diagonal form, with so many as five folds, permitting them to be expanded to a large extent.† Respecting the sound-producing portion of the Organ a few words will suffice. We find in the plates representations of the leading varieties of pipes now in use, labial and reed, but

* The "*Avertissement*" at the commencement of this Work is, historically considered, interesting:

"Il y a certains Arts très-difficiles à décrire non-seulement parce qu'ils tiennent à beaucoup d'autres, mais encore parce qu'ils ne se présente pas fréquemment des occasions de les pratiquer. Le Facteur d'Orgues est de ce genre; pour le bien traiter, il faut avoir des principes de Mathématiques, il faut être harmoniste, il faut connoître beaucoup d'Arts qui tous concourent à faire ce bel & grand instrument. Il importoit à la perfection de l'Histoire des Arts dont l'Académie s'occupe que celui-ci fût bien décrit: heureusement tous les talents nécessaires se sont trouvés réunis dans la personne de Dom Bedos, Religieux Bénédictin de la Congrégation de S. Maur; & plus heureusement encore ce savant Religieux charmé de concourir à la perfection de l'entreprise de l'Académie, a sur le champ acquiescé à l'invitation que l'Académie lui a faite d'entreprendre la description de l'Art du Facteur d'Orgues. Il a bien voulu en restraindre la théorie à ce qui étoit absolument nécessaire pour rendre clairement les opérations pratiques; & sachant qu'on doit traiter à part les différents Arts dont le Facteur d'Orgues emprunte des secours, il n'a pris de ces Arts que ce dont il avoit un besoin absolu. Notre célèbre Auteur a jugé à propos de diviser son Ouvrage en trois Parties qui paroîtront successivement; elles mériteront d'autant plus l'attention du Public que nous n'avons aucun Ouvrage qui ait traité de la facture de l'Orgue.

Signés, Duhamel du Monceau, & Grandjean de Fouchy, } *Commissaires de l'Académie.*

† We see, in connection with a Barrel-organ (Plate XCV.), and a Harpsichord with Organ attached (Plate CXXXV.), that a form of horizontal bellows with diagonal drop-feeders was known.

the range of tone color must have been very limited. The string-toned and LIEBLICHGEDECKT families of stops do not seem to have been known, or appreciated if known, by Dom Bedos. To some extent string-toned stops were used by German builders of his time, for in the specification he gives of the Organ at Weingarten stops called "VIOLONCHEL" and "GROSSE GAMBE" appear.

Numerous important Organs were erected in the cathedrals and parish churches of France during the seventeenth and eighteenth centuries; but we are not aware of any, of historical interest, remaining in the original state. It is

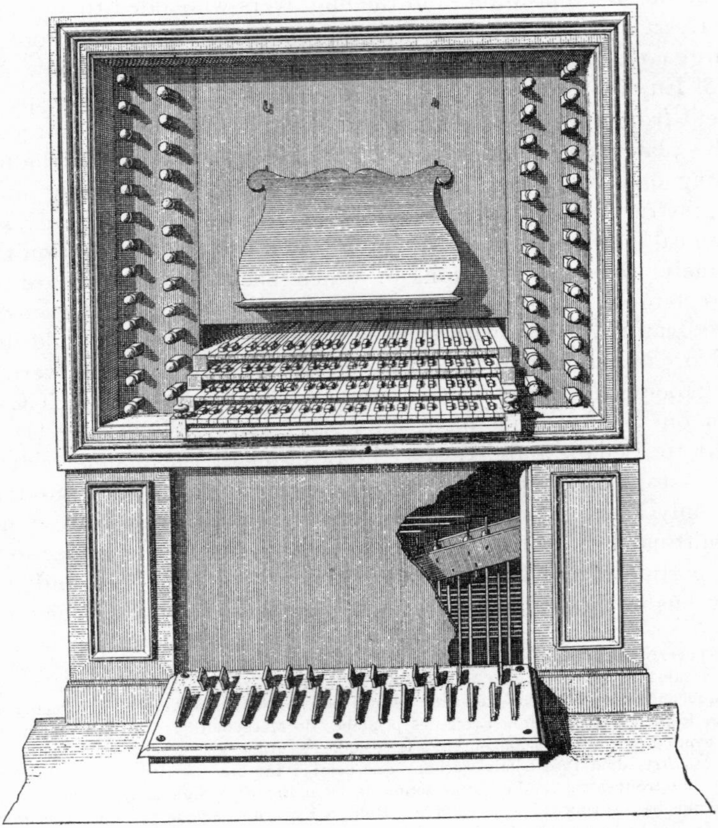

FIG. XXI.

true, however, as in the Church of Saint-Ouen, at Rouen, that cases made during these centuries still remain which convey some idea of the importance of the original instruments. Speaking of the Organ in Saint-Ouen, Dr. Hopkins says: "It had five manuals; a Pedal Organ of two octaves in compass; twelve pairs of bellows; and 49 sounding stops." This instrument was constructed in 1630.

Dom Bedos gives a fine design for a large Organ in the style of Louis XV.

which is highly characteristic of the art taste in France in the middle of the eighteenth century. We give, as a heading to the present Chapter, a reproduction of the "Buffet du Positif" belonging to this design.

Organ-building appears to have been in a satisfactory state in Spain and Italy during the seventeenth and eighteenth centuries. In Spain some important instruments were constructed. About the year 1650 a fine Organ was erected in the Cathedral of Tortosa, the case of which is illustrated in Mr. Hill's valuable Work. In regard to Italy, it would seem more correct to say that the appreciation for, rather than the practice of, the art of organ-building was in a satisfactory state; for several of the more important Organs erected in these centuries were the work of German or Flemish artists. An example is furnished by the Organ in the Church of Santa Maria di Carignano, at Genoa, which was constructed, in 1660, by William Hermann, a Flemish Jesuit, assisted by his countrymen, Johann Heid and Hans Dietrich. Hermann also built an Organ for the Cathedral of Como, and several other fine and important instruments in Italy. According to Mr. Hill, Hermann's Organ in Santa Maria consisted of a Great Organ of twenty-five speaking stops, a Choir of five stops, an Echo of six stops, and a pedal department of six stops, with ten accessory movements. The compass of the manuals was CCC short to c^3, and of the pedals CCC short to D.

We may now turn our attention to the condition of the art of organ-building in England during the centuries latterly under consideration. The earliest English builder of the seventeenth century of whom there is any reliable record is Thomas Dallam, of London. His accounts for organ work in King's College Chapel, Cambridge, are still preserved; extending from June 1605 to August 1606. The curious reader will find the items of these accounts given in Dr. Rimbault's "History of the Organ." From them it may be gathered that it was a practice, at that period, for organ builders, living at a distance, to transport their entire working establishments to the localities in which their instruments were to be erected, and there construct and finish them. The difficulties attending the carriage of large organ work to great distances doubtless favored the adoption of this practice. No specification of this Organ has been discovered, and the accounts throw no light on the subject. In the year 1613, as we learn from an entry in the archives of the Dean and Chapter of Worcester Cathedral, Thomas Dallam constructed an Organ in that grand building. The entry is as follows:

> "A. D. 1613.—All the materials and workmanship of the new double Organ in the Cathedral Church of Worcester to Thomas Dallam, organ-maker, came to £211."

Later on we find another Dallam, named Robert, as an organ builder of note. In the year 1632 this builder entered into an agreement with the Dean and Chapter of York Minster to construct an Organ for the Minster. The most interesting portion of this agreement, from a historical point, is that which enumerates the stops to be inserted. This portion we quote, as showing what was then considered sufficient for so grand and vast a cathedral as that of York:

> "The names and number of the stoppes or setts of pipes for the said Great Organ, to

be new made; every stopp containeinge fiftie-one pipes; the said Great Organ containeinge eight stoppes.

"Imprimis two open diapasons of tynn, to stand in sight, many of them to be chased, ...	lxxx *li.*
Item one diapason stopp of wood, ...	x *li.*
Item two principalls of tynn, ...	xxiiij *li.*
Itm one twelft to the diapason, ...	viij *li.*
Itm one small principall of tynn, ...	vi *li.*
Itm one recorder unison to the said principall, ...	vi *li.*
Itm one two and twentieth, ...	v *li.*
Itm the great sound-board with conveyances, windchestes, carryages, and conduits of lead, ...	xl *li.*
Itm a rowler board, carriages, and keys, ...	xx *li.*

"The names and number of stoppes of pipes for the Chaire Organ, every Stopp containeinge fifty-one pipes, the said Chaire Organ containeinge five stoppes.

"Imprimis one diapason of wood, ...	x *li.*
Itm one principall of tynn, to stand in sight, many of them to be chased, ...	xii *li.*
Itm one flute of wood, ...	xiij *li.*
Itm one small principall of tynn, ...	v *li.*
Itm one recorder of tynn, unison to the voice, ...	viij *li.*
Itm the sound-board, windchest, drawinge stoppes, conveyances, and conduits, ...	xxx *li.*
Itm the rowler board, carriages, and keys, ...	x *li.*
Itm the three bellowes with winde truncks, and iron workes and other thinges thereto, ...	x *li.*"

We have here an Organ of two manuals and no pedals, and only 14 speaking stops; of the simplest tonal structure, containing only a single mutation stop, the Twelfth. This was in all probability a representative English Organ of the period. Robert Dallam also built Organs for the Cathedral of Durham and St. Paul's, London, which are believed to have resembled the York instrument in size and general character. There were, doubtless, several other professional organ builders who worked contemporaneously with the Dallams, but their names and works have not been handed down.

With the year 1644 a bad time for Organs and organ builders was ushered in. On the 4th of January of that year an Ordinance was passed in the House of Lords, which has been described as an "Ordinance of the Lords and Commons assembled in Parliament, for the speedy demolishing of all organs, images, and all manner of superstitious monuments in the Cathedrals, and Collegiate or Parish Churches and Chapels, throughout the Kingdom of England and the Dominion of Wales; the better to accomplish the blessed reformation so happily begun, and to remove all offences and things illegal in the worship of God." Then followed, under an illogical and fanatical zeal, a ruthless destruction of Organs and other articles of church furniture throughout the land. Some Organs were purchased by private persons and, accordingly, preserved; others were saved from destruction by being removed by the church authorities; some few were overlooked by the armies of spoilers; and all the others were wholly or partially demolished. The crusade against Organs had begun before the passing of the above-mentioned Ordinance; for we see that in 1642, a Tract was published in London, entitled, "The Organ's Funerall, or the Quiristers Lamentation for the Abolishment of Superstition and Superstitious Ceremonies."

We see a curious picture of these unreasoning times, set forth in a book published in 1647, entitled "Mercurius Rusticus; the Country's Complaint recounting the sad Events of this Unparraleld Warr." Two or three extracts will be sufficient to show the mad temper of the despoilers. Of their doings at Westminster we read: "The soldiers of Westborne and Cæwoods' Companies were quartered in the Abbey Church, where they brake down the rayl about the Altar, and burnt it in the place where it stood: they brake down the Organs, and pawned the pipes at severall ale-houses for pots of ale." At Winchester Cathedral, the soldiers "entered the Church with colours flying and drums beating": they rode up through the body of the Church and Quire, until they came to the Altar, there they rudely pluck downe the table and brake the rayle, and afterwards carrying it to an ale-house, they set it on fire: . . . they threw downe the organs, and brake the Stories of the Old and New Testament, curiously cut out in carved work." Respecting the spoliation in Chichester Cathedral, we read: "They leave the destructive and spoyling part to be finished by the common soldiers, brake down the organs, and dashing the pipes with their pole-axes, scoffingly said, "*Harke how the organs goe.*" Their doings at Exeter Cathedral were still more disgusting and disgraceful: here "they brake down the organs, and taking two or three hundred pipes with them, in a most scornefull contemptuous manner, went up and downe the streets piping with them." In Gunton's "History of the Church of Peterborough," we read, after an allusion to the arrival of a foot regiment, under Colonel Hubbard, on the scene: "Some two days afterwards comes a regiment of horse, under Colonel Cromwell, a name as fatal to ministers as it had been to monasteries before. The next day after their arrival, early in the morning, these break open the church doors, pull down the organs, of which there were two pair. The greater pair, that stood upon a high loft over the entrance into the choir, was thence thrown down upon the ground, and there stamped and trampled on, and broke in pieces, with such a strange, furious, and frantick zeal, as cannot well be conceived, but by those who saw it."

So the ruthless destruction went on all over the land until the fairest works of the early English organ builders were swept out of existence. But, as we have said, all the Organs were not destroyed at this terrible time. We find in Evelyn's "Diary," under the year 1654, the following interesting entry:

> "Next we walked to Magdalen College [Oxford], where we saw the library and chapel, which was likewise in pontifical order, the altar only I think turned tablewise; and there was still the double Organ, which abominations (as now esteemed) were almost universally demolished; Mr. Gibbon, that famous musician, giving us a taste of his skill and talents on the instrument."

This instrument was subsequently transported, by Cromwell's order, to

Hampton Court Palace; and in the year 1660 it was restored to the College and reërected in the Chapel.

The Restoration, in 1660, stayed all further destruction of Church Organs, though it did not lead to the immediate construction of new instruments all over the country; indeed, it was not until about fifty or sixty years afterwards that Organs became common in the parish churches. It is reasonable to suppose that during the disturbed times organ-building was abandoned in England; and that immediately after the Restoration few workmen could be found capable of constructing important instruments. On this subject Dr. Burney says: "After the suppression of Cathedral Service and prohibition of the Liturgy, some of the ecclesiastical instruments had been sold to private persons, and others but partially destroyed; these being produced, were hastily repaired, and erected for present use. A sufficient number of workmen for the immediate supply of cathedrals and parish churches with Organs, not being found in our own country, it was thought expedient to invite foreign builders of known abilities to settle among us; and the premiums offered on this occasion brought over the two celebrated workmen, Smith and Harris."

These talented organ builders appear to have arrived in England immediately at the Restoration; and with their advent was inaugurated the first great period of English organ-building, for they brought with them the advanced systems of Germany and France. Bernard Schmidt was a native of Germany; while Renatus Harris, who came from France, was a member of an English family of organ-building renown. His grandfather was an organ builder who practiced his art in England with considerable success. We are indebted to the musical historian, Dr. Burney, who gives the following particulars respecting "Father Smith," as he was commonly called:

"Bernard Schmidt, as the Germans write the name, brought over with him from Germany, of which country he was a native, two nephews, Gerard and Bernard, his assistants; and to distinguish him from these, as well as to express the reverence due to his abilities, which placed him at the head of his profession, he was called Father Smith. The first Organ he was engaged to build for this country was for the Royal Chapel at Whitehall, which being hastily put together did not quite fulfil the expectations of those who were able to judge of its excellence. An Organ is so operose, complicated, and comprehensive a piece of mechanism, that to render it complete in tone, touch, variety, and power, exclusive of the external beauty and majesty of its form and appearance, is perhaps one of the greatest efforts of human ingenuity and contrivance.* It was probably from some such early failure that this admirable workman determined never to

* We note the worthy Doctor's high opinion of the simple organ construction of his day: and wonder what he would have said had he examined such instruments as are known in this year of grace, 1903, with their five manual claviers and complete pedal department; their ten thousand pipes; their several swell divisions; their complicated combination actions; their numerous couplers; their majestic reed-work; their delicate touch and instantaneous response to the flying finger; their overwhelming power and volume of tone; their almost endless changes and inexhaustible variety of tone-color; and their perfectly regulated wind supply, of numerous pressures from 1½ inches up to 30 inches, furnished by steam, water, or electric power. Of "external beauty," and "majesty of form and appearance," alas, we cannot boast, for they are almost unknown in modern Organs.

engage to build an Organ upon short notice, nor for such a price as would oblige him to deliver it in a state of less perfection than he wished. And I have been assured by Snetzler, and by the immediate descendants of those who have conversed with Father Smith, and seen him work, that he was so particularly careful in the choice of his wood, as never to use any that had the least knot or flaw in it; and so tender of his reputation, as never to waste his time in trying to mend a bad pipe, either of wood or metal, so that when he came to voice a pipe, if it had any radical defect, he instantly threw it away, and made another. This, in a great measure, accounts for the equality and sweetness of his stops, as well as the soundness of his pipes to this day."

Little else is known about Father Smith; and we are left without any definite knowledge of his birthplace or the date of his birth. His first Organ, that in Whitehall, must have been hurriedly constructed, for we learn from an entry in Pepys' Diary that it was in use in the Chapel in July, 1660. The entry runs:

"July 8, 1660. (Lord's day). To White Hall Chapel, where I got in with ease, by going before the Lord Chancellor with Mr. Kipps. Here I heard very good musique, the first time that ever I remember to have heard the Organs, and singing-men in surplices, in my life."

One is somewhat surprised that Pepys does not describe the Organs, in his favorite style, as "mighty pretty," and as making him "mighty earnest to have a pair" at his church. This desire, however, does not appear in his Diary until years later.

Father Smith soon became firmly established in business, and actively engaged in the construction of Organs. While employed on the Organ for Whitehall, he received the commission to build one for Westminster Abbey. This instrument, it is believed, he constructed before the close of 1660. Pepys evidently alludes to this Organ in his valuable and interesting Diary, under the date of November 4th, 1660: "Lord's day. I went to the Abbey, where the first time that ever I heard the Organs in a cathedral." Between this year and that of the famous contest between Renatus Harris and himself, concerning the Organ for the Temple Church, he is known to have built six Organs, including the Organs for Wells Cathedral, in 1664, for the Church of St. Margaret, Westminster, in 1675, and Christ Church Cathedral, Oxford, in 1680. These, and his other works of this period, have all been well spoken of. Smith was appointed organist of St. Margaret's in 1676.

We now come to the Smith and Harris contest, and cannot do better than introduce it in the language of Dr. Burney:

"About the latter end of King Charles the Second's reign, the Master of the Temple and the Benchers, being determined to have as complete an Organ erected in their church as possible, received proposals from both these eminent artists (*i. e.* Smith and Harris), backed by the recommendation of such an equal number of powerful friends and celebrated organists that they were unable to determine among themselves which to employ. They therefore told the candidates, if each of them would erect an Organ, in different parts of the church, they would retain that which, in the greatest number of excellences, should be allowed to deserve the preference. Smith and Harris agreeing to this proposal, in about eight or nine months each had, with the utmost exertion of his abilities, an instrument ready for trial. Dr. Tudway, living at that time, the intimate acquaintance of both, says that Dr. Blow and Purcell, then in their prime, performed on Father Smith's Organ, on appointed days, and displayed its excellence; and, till the other was heard, every one believed that this must be chosen."

Harris' turn now came, and he engaged the celebrated organist to Queen Catherine, Baptist Draghi, to display the beauties and resources of his instrument. Draghi's masterly touching of Harris' Organ at once brought it into favor, and opinion became divided, and continued divided all through the contest, which had a duration of several months. Burney adds:

"At length, Harris challenged Father Smith to make additional reed-stops in a given time; these were the VOX HUMANA, CREMORNE, the DOUBLE COURTEL, or DOUBLE BASSOON, and some others. The stops, which were newly invented, or at least new to English ears, gave great delight to the crowds who attended the trials; and the imitations were so exact and pleasing on both sides that it was difficult to determine who had best succeeded."

Now followed a sort of dispute between the Benchers of the Middle Temple and those of the Inner Temple, which has no special interest to the student of history, so it may be passed over here. The exact date on which the "battle of the Organs" terminated has not been decided, but it must have been about the beginning of 1688, for it was on the 21st of June in that year that the deed of sale between the Societies of the Middle and Inner Temple and Bernard Smith was completed. Of this deed it is only desirable to quote the schedule of stops, as showing what was considered an important instrument in England toward the close of the seventeenth century.

"SCHEDULE" OF THE TEMPLE ORGAN.

	"GREAT ORGAN.	PIPES	FOOTE TONE
1.	PRESTAND of Mettle,	61	12
2.	HOLFLUTE of Wood and Mettle,	61	12
3.	PRINCIPALL of Mettle,	61	06
4.	QUINTA of Mettle,	61	04
5.	SUPER OCTAVO,	61	03
6.	CORNETTE of Mettle,	112	02
7.	SESQUIALTERA of Mettle,	183	03
8.	GEDACKT of Wainescott,	61	06
9.	MIXTURE of Mettle,	226	03
10.	TRUMPETT of Mettle,	61	12
		948	
	"CHOIR ORGAN.		
11.	GEDACKT Wainescott,	61	12
12.	HOLFLUTE of Mettle,	61	06
13.	A SADT of Mettle,	61	06
14.	SPITTS FLUTE of Mettle,	61	03

15.	A VIOLL and VIOLIN of Mettle,	61	12
16.	VOICE HUMANE of Mettle,	61	12
		366	
	"ECCHOS.		
17.	GEDACKT of Wood,	61	06
18.	SUPER OCTAVO of Mettle,	61	03
19.	GEDACKT of Wood,	29	
20.	FLUTE of Mettle,	29	
21.	CORNETT of Mettle,	87	
22.	SESQUIALTERA,	105	
23.	TRUMPETT,	29	
		401	

"With 3 full setts of keys and quarter notes."

Father Smith entered into an agreement, on August 18th, 1683, with the Dean and Chapter of Durham Cathedral, in which we find the following interesting details respecting an Organ for that noble building:

"Imprimis. It is agreed by and between the said partys and the said Bernard Smith for himself, his executors, and administrators, doth hereby covenant, promise, and agree to and with the said Dean and Chapter and their successors by these presents that he the said Bernard Smith for and in consideration of the severall sums of money hereinafter mentioned shall and will before the first day of May which will be in the year of our Lord one thousand six hundred and eighty five, at his own proper cost and charges make and fitt up in the Organ loft of the said Cathedral Church of Durham, a good, perfect, laudable, and harmonious Great Organ and Choir Organ with a case of good sound and substantiall Oak wood, according to a draught or modell of an organ in parchment whereon or whereunto all the said partys have subscribed their names at or before the time of sealing and delivering of these presents.

"Item it is agreed by and between the said partys that the said Bernard Smith shall make in the said Great Organ these seventeen stops, viz.:

"Two OPEN DIAPASONS of Metall containing one hundred and eight pipes.
A STOP DIAPASON of Wood containing fifty four pipes.
A PRINCIPAL of Metall containing fifty four pipes.
A CORNET of Metall containing nynty six pipes.
A QUINTA of Metall containing fifty four pipes.
A SUPER OCTAVE of Metall containing fifty four pipes.
A HOLFLUIT of Wood containing fifty four pipes.
A BLOCK FLUTE of Metall containing fifty four pipes.
A small QUINT of Metall containing fifty four pipes.
A MIXTURE of three ranks of pipes of Metall containing one hundred and sixty two pipes.
A TRUMPETT of Metall containing fifty four pipes.

And in the Choir Organ five stops, viz.:

A PRINCIPAL of Metall in front containing fifty four pipes.
A STOP DIAPASON of Wood containing fifty four pipes.
A VOICE HUMAND of Metall containing fifty four pipes.
A HOLFLUIT of Wood containing fifty four pipes.
And a SUPER OCTAVE of Metall containing fifty four pipes.

"Item it is agreed by and between these partys that the said Great Organ shall have a back front towards the body or west end of the church which shall be in all things and respects like to the fore front both in pipes and carving. And all the pipes belonging to the two diapason stops shall speak at will in the said back front as in the fore."

For this Organ Bernard Smith received the sum of seven hundred pounds; and for the painting and gilding of the pipes of the two main fronts and the front of the Choir Organ, he received the additional sum of fifty pounds.

So admirably had Father Smith carried out the work connected with the Organs in the Temple Church and Durham Cathedral, and so great a reputation had he acquired for his skill and business probity, that he was selected to construct the Organ for St. Paul's Cathedral, then in course of erection under Sir Christopher Wren. A workshop was given him in the Cathedral, in which, after considerable and annoying delay, he executed the work required. The delay was caused by a contention arising between the Dean and Chapter and Sir Christopher Wren respecting the position of the Organ. The former wished to have it located at the west end of the choir, in an elevated position; while Wren insisted that, in such a place, it would ruin the internal effect of his building. He was unquestionably correct in his view; and the positions now occupied, on each side of the choir, at its western end, go to prove his opinion was sound. Wren wanted it placed on one side of the choir, within one of the arches. The all-powerful Dean and Chapter carried the day, and the architect had to design a central case, which he took good care to make as small as possible. Indeed, he made it so small that when Father Smith essayed to place his work in it he found three stops crowded out. When expostulated with on the subject, Sir Christopher positively declined to enlarge the case, saying that "the architectural proportions of the interior were already spoiled by the damned box of whistles." The Organ was opened at the Thanksgiving Service for the Peace of Ryswick, December 2nd, 1697. The construction of this important instrument created a great deal of jealousy and criticism, especially in the minds of Renatus Harris and his partisans. This is proved by a "Broadside," issued at the time, entitled "Queries about St. Paul's Organ," and of which a copy is preserved in the British Museum. This broadside, which was evidently written by Harris or some of his friends, consists of twelve questions, all of which aim at the disparagement of Smith's knowledge and skill as an organ builder. The origin of this attack on Smith is practically settled by the eighth and ninth questions, seeing that the Organ in the Church of St. Andrew, Undershaft, was built by Harris. The questions are:

"VIII. Whether there been't Organs in the City, lowder, sweeter, and of more variety than St. Paul's (which cost not one third of the Price) and particularly, whether Smith at the Temple has not out-done Smith of St. Paul's? And whether St. Andrew Undershaft has not out-done them both?

"IX. Whether the open Diapason of Metal that speaks on the lower set of keys at St. Andrew Undershaft, be not a Stop of extraordinary Use and Variety, and such as neither St. Paul's has, or can have?"*

*The complete text of this interesting broadside is given by Dr. Rimbault in "The Organ."

The last of the many important instruments built by this master was that of Trinity College, Cambridge. He died, in 1708, before the Organ was completely finished, and was succeeded in the work by his son-in-law, Christopher Schrider.

The distinguished works of Bernard Smith and those of his contemporary Renatus Harris, urged, in every succeeding instance, toward greater excellence by the intense spirit of rivalry that existed between their authors, laid the foundation of the modern school of organ-building in England—a school that, although slow in its progress, has surely been carried onward toward unquestioned supremacy, in several important directions, in the hands of worthy masters of the art.

Renatus Harris came of a family of organ builders, both his father and grandfather having followed the art. Dr. Burney tells us that "Smith had not been many months here [in England], before Harris [John] arrived from France, with his son René or Renatus, an ingenious and active young man, to whom he had confided all the secrets of his art. However, they met with but little encouragement at first, as Dallams and Smith had the chief business in the kingdom; but upon the decease of Dallams, who died while he was building an Organ for the old church at Greenwich, 1672, and of the elder Harris, who did not long survive him, the younger became a formidable rival to Smith." The grandfather of Renatus Harris practiced his art in England, as has been clearly proved by the "Registers of Magdalen College, Oxford," published by Dr. Bloxham, in which we are told that in the year 1672 Renatus Harris offered his services to repair the Organ in the College Chapel, "the rather because his grandfather made it at first, and he was sufficiently known to be as skilful an artist as any in England." Dr. Bloxham gives the agreement between Renatus Harris and the President and Fellows of Magdalen College, for the enlargement and repairs of his grandfather's Organ, for which he was to receive "One hundred and fifty pounds of lawful money of England." These repairs, etc., were executed in 1691.

The keen rivalry in matters of skill which existed between Harris and Smith is shown by two advertisements which appeared in the *Post Boy* of April 12th and 30th, 1698, quoted by Dr. E. F. Rimbault in his interesting Paper on "The Early English Organ Builders and their Works," read before the College of Organists, November 15, 1864. These advertisements are as follows:

"Whereas the Division of half a Note (upon an Organ) into 50 Gradual and distinguishable parts has been declar'd by Mr. Smith, as also by the generality of Masters to be impracticable: All Organists, Masters, and Artists of the Faculty, are together with the said Mr. Smith, invited to Mr. Harris's house in Wine Office Court, Fleet Street, on Easter Monday next at Two of the clock in the Afternoon, to hear and see the same demonstrated."

"Whereas the Division of half a Note (upon an Organ) into 50 Gradual and distinguishable parts, was performed by Mr. Harris on Easter Monday to the full satisfaction of the Persons of Quality and Masters that were present: And Whereas the said Mr. Harris intends a further division of half a Note, viz., into One Hundred parts (and this not mathematically, but purely by the Ear), all Masters and others of curious and Nice Ears are invited to the said Mr. Harris's house in Wine Office Court, Fleet Street, on the 10th day May, at Three of the clock in the afternoon, to hear and see the Performance, and to be informed (if any doubt) of its usefulness."

These curious advertisements are interesting only in so much that they show the misdirected ingenuity sometimes indulged in by the early organ builders, in their desire to improve the Organ, or to draw public attention toward their works. The skill displayed by Harris was in all probability provoked by the fame which had attended Father Smith's introduction of "quarter notes" in the Temple Church Organ. His invention, if such it may be called, does not appear to have gone beyond the demonstrations advertised; for so far as is known it was never applied in any practical form by himself or any subsequent organ builder.

The business and artistic career of Renatus Harris in England was decidedly a brilliant one, and organ-building in his hands made good progress. As in the case of Father Smith, Harris was a good musician, and his knowledge of the science of music aided him greatly in his practice of organ-building. He commenced his career sometime prior to the year 1665, and continued constructing Organs up to his death, which is believed to have taken place in the year 1715.

Renatus Harris built numerous Organs, including several of the first rank viewed from the standpoint of English organ-building in his day. It is known that he erected instruments in the Cathedrals of Gloucester, Worcester, Chichester, Winchester, Bristol, Hereford, Dublin, Ely, and Salisbury. The Organ in the last named cathedral appears, from the brief descriptions that have been handed down, to have been one of the most important instruments, if not the most important one, constructed in England in the early part of the eighteenth century. It is thus mentioned in "The Modern British Traveller," published in 1779: "The Organ, which is fixed over the entrance to the choir, is very large, being 20 feet broad, and 40 feet high to the top of its ornaments. It has 50 stops, which are 18 more than there are in the Organ of St. Paul's Cathedral in London." Some further particulars are given in notes appended to a large and rare engraving, by Francis Dewing, of the East Front of the instrument. From these we learn that the Organ had four claviers, "very large bellows" located within the body of the case, and "eleven stops of Echos" placed in its lower portion; and we are informed that "This Organ is a new contrivance, and on it may be more varietys express'd, than by all y[e] Organs in England, were their several excellencies united." After making all allowance for such an expression of approval, we may safely believe the Organ to have been a masterpiece at the time. It was built in the year 1710, when Harris was ripe with experience in all the methods of organ construction then practiced in England.

In addition to the Cathedral Organs mentioned, Renatus Harris built instruments of more or less importance in several London churches. The Organ he constructed in the year 1696, for the Church of St. Andrew, Undershaft, seems to have been one of the finest: it has been described in published works on London as "a most excellent and costly Organ," and as "a fine large Organ." It is understood to have cost about £1,500, a considerable sum for an English Organ at the time of its construction. This was the instrument mentioned in the eighth Query in the broadside previously quoted.

In the Chapter Book of St. Patrick's Cathedral, Dublin, is the following interesting entry:

"12th August, 1695. The Dean and Chapter agrees with Renatus Harris, of London, organ builder, to make and set up a Double Organ for the sum of £505. In the great organ —Open Diapason of metal, Stop Diapason of wood, Principal of metal, Nason of wood, a great 12th of metal, 15th of metal, a Cornet of metal. In the little organ—a Principal of metal, Stop Diapason of wood, 15th of metal, and a Nason of wood, being in all 13 stops, consisting of 800 pipes, sound-board, &c., &c."

This is indeed a humble scheme for a Cathedral Organ, and one that would not to-day be considered suitable for a small village church. It shows, however, that the old builders were sometimes paid a fair price for their work, although in this particular instance the expenses for traveling and carriage from London to Dublin must have been considerable. Six additional stops were added to the above scheme by Harris in 1697, for which he was paid £350.

Harris competed for the Temple Church Organ, as we have already pointed out; and although unsuccessful he suffered no loss of reputation, as Dr. Burney tells us. The instrument when removed from Temple Church was divided, part being erected in the Church of St. Andrew, Holborn, and part in Christ Church, Dublin. It is more than probable that Harris exerted all his powers to be appointed the builder of the Organ for St. Paul's Cathedral: and apparently, if one can judge from a notice which appeared in the London *Spectator* of December 3, 1712, he continued, after Smith had completed his instrument on the choir screen, to press a scheme on the Dean and Chapter for a grand west-end Organ. The notice alluded to is as follows:

"The ambition of this artificer [Renatus Harris] is to erect an Organ in St. Paul's Cathedral, over the west door, at the entrance into the body of the church, which in art and magnificence shall transcend any work of that kind ever before invented. The proposal [by Harris] in perspicuous language sets forth the honour and advantage such a performance would be to the British name, as well as that it would apply the power of sounds in a manner more amazingly forcible than perhaps has yet been known, and I am sure to an end much more worthy."

We have not been able to find any record of the "Proposal" alluded to; and this is to be regretted, because it would have thrown much additional light on the art of organ-building, in its highest development, in the opening years of the eighteenth century in England, and only four years prior to the construction of Silbermann's renowned Organ, of forty-two speaking stops, in Strasbourg Cathedral.

In a brief survey like the present, it is only necessary to note the works of the greater masters of organ-building in England: we may accordingly pass over those of the relations and pupils of Father Smith and Renatus Harris. The Jordans are the next names in the roll of fame, and deserve special recognition as the inventors of the Swell Organ, in the year 1712. As this subject is fully considered in our Chapter on The Swell in the Organ, it need not be pursued here. England was, in this most important feature of the Organ, about half a century in advance of all other organ-building countries; although her builders of to-day can lay no claim to preëminence either in the treatment or application of the swell. In Burney's Work entitled, "Present State of Music in France and Italy," published in 1771, the following passage occurs: "It is very extraordinary that the *swell*, which has been introduced into the English Organ more than fifty years, and which is so capable of expression and of pleasing effects that it may well be said to be the greatest and most important improvement that ever was made on any keyed instrument, should be utterly *unknown* in Italy; and now I am on the subject, I must observe that most of the Organs I have met with on the Continent seem to be inferior to ours by Father Smith, Byfield, or Snetzler, in everything but size!"

In a subsequent Work,* he informs us that he found the swell entirely unknown in Berlin; for none of the musical people he questioned in that city knew of any such contrivance worked by pedals: and speaking of the Organ in the Church of St. Michael, at Hamburg, built by Hildebrand in the year 1764, he remarks: "A swell has been *attempted* in this instrument, but with little effect; only three stops have been put into it, and the power of *crescendo* and *diminuendo* is so small with them, that if I had not been told there was a swell, I should not have discovered it." It is generally believed that in this instrument the swell was introduced for the first time on the Continent; just fifty-two years after its invention by the Jordans.

The Jordans built numerous Organs, including the instrument for the Chapel at Cannons, the Seat of the Duke of Chandos, rendered historical from the fact that it was performed upon by Handel; and that landmark in the history of organ-building, the Organ in the Church of St. Magnus the Martyr, London Bridge, in which the swell was for the first time introduced.† It does not appear that they built an Organ for any of the English cathedrals.

Several important Church Organs were constructed jointly by the Jordans and Byfield and Bridge, two organ firms of considerable reputation. The grandest instrument built by this coalition was that for the Parish Church of St. Nicholas, Great Yarmouth. This was constructed in the year 1733. It originally had three manual divisions: Great, Choir, and Swell. The Great and Choir had a compass from GGG to d^3, with the then usual omission of the GGG♯; and the Swell from tenor C to d^3. The Organ was blown by diagonal bellows, which were removed in 1844.

The most distinguished provincial builders at this period (first half of the eighteenth century) were Glyn and Parker, who, in partnership, carried on business at Salford, Manchester. They built an Organ for the noble Collegiate Church of Manchester in the year 1730; and the first instrument in the Chapel of the Foundling Hospital, London, in 1749. Handel opened the latter Organ; and it is believed that it was through his recommendation that the work was intrusted to Glyn and Parker, to the disappointment of the metropolitan builders.

About the year 1740 the art of organ-building in England was considerably improved, by the introduction of certain German methods and ideas, by John Snetzler, a native of Passau. He was about thirty years of age when he commenced business in London; and for upwards of forty years he prosecuted his art

* "Present State of Music in Germany, the Netherlands, and United Provinces," 1775.

† See the Chapter on The Swell in the Organ.

with satisfaction to his clients and honor and profit to himself. As in the case of Bernard Smith, Snetzler cannot be considered an English organ builder, notwithstanding the fact that all his important works were executed in England, and for English churches. Snetzler did an immense amount of work, but it is only necessary to mention two or three of his Organs in these brief notes. Dr. Burney evidently held his skill in the highest estimation; and the musical historian was one whose judgment could be depended upon. Snetzler constructed a fine Organ in the Church of St. Margaret, Lynn Regis, Norfolk, in the year 1754, under the direction of Dr. Burney, costing about £700. In this instrument he introduced, for the first time in England, the DOUBLE DIAPASON and the DULCIANA, stops which caused quite a sensation in musical quarters, and gained him a great reputation, backed up by Dr. Burney's expression of approval. It has not been learned whether Snetzler invented or merely introduced the DULCIANA. We have not been able to find any record of the contents of the Lynn Regis Organ, in a complete form, as originally inserted by Snetzler.

In the year 1769 Snetzler built a fine instrument for Beverley Minster; which was inaugurated by a grand performance of Oratorios on September 20th and 21st of that year. In 1774 he erected a representative Organ in the Church of St. Martin, Leicester, opened on the 21st of September with a performance of the Dettingen Te Deum and Jubilate. This Organ had twenty-two speaking stops, distributed in three manual divisions, but had no Pedal Organ, or pedals operating on the bass of the manual claviers. We give the original contents of this instrument as an example of the approved tonal structure of a Church Organ in the third quarter of the eighteenth century in England.

SNETZLER'S ORGAN IN THE CHURCH OF ST. MARTIN, LEICESTER.

GREAT ORGAN—GGG to e^3 (GGG♯ omitted).

1.	OPEN DIAPASON, Large,	12 feet.	6.	FIFTEENTH, . . .	3 feet.
2.	OPEN DIAPASON, Small,	12 "	7.	SESQUIALTERA, . .	IV. ranks.
3.	STOPPED DIAPASON, . .	12 "	8.	CORNET (Middle c^1),	V. "
4.	PRINCIPAL, ...	6 "	9.	TRUMPET, ...	12 feet.
5.	TWELFTH, ...	4 "	10.	CLARION, ...	6 "

CHOIR ORGAN—GGG to e^3 (GGG♯ omitted).

11.	OPEN DIAPASON . . . (stopped below CC)	12 feet.	14.	FLUTE, ...	6 feet.
12.	STOPPED DIAPASON, .	12 "	15.	FIFTEENTH, ...	3 "
13.	PRINCIPAL, ...	6 "	16.	BASSOON, ...	12 "

SWELL ORGAN—F to e^3 (36 Notes).

17.	OPEN DIAPASON, . .	8 feet.	20.	CORNET, ...	II. ranks.
18.	STOPPED DIAPASON, . .	8 "	21.	HAUTBOY, ...	8 feet.
19.	PRINCIPAL, ...	4 "	22.	TRUMPET, ...	8 "

It is somewhat remarkable that the DULCIANA does not find a place in this monotonous scheme, in which there are no fewer than four OPEN DIAPASONS, three

STOPPED DIAPASONS, three PRINCIPALS, and two TRUMPETS, without a single soft-toned stop to contrast with the uniform, assertive character of the stops in the three divisions; yet, just twenty years before, he introduced that beautiful and valuable stop in the notable Lynn Regis instrument.

Snetzler is generally credited with having introduced the pedal clavier in England; and the Organ in which it was first used is believed to be the one he built for the Lutheran Chapel, Savoy, London. We are not aware of the date of this noteworthy instrument.

Contemporaneous with Snetzler, from about the year 1775, flourished Samuel Green, an organ builder of high artistic skill and reputation. His instruments were characterized by a special class of voicing which distinguished them from the works of all the other builders of the eighteenth century. Green was born in 1740, or thirty years later than Snetzler, and commenced business under his own name sometime about the year 1770. In the *Gentleman's Magazine*, for June, 1814, a list is given of forty-nine buildings and places for which he constructed Organs. From this we learn that he placed instruments in the Cathedrals of Wells, Canterbury, Salisbury, Lichfield, Rochester, Bangor, and Cashel. Green was an artist both skilful and progressive in his work, always aiming at improvements in tone and mechanism. For refinement and sweetness of tone his Organs have probably never been surpassed. His reed stops were finer than any made by his contemporaries. His mechanical genius led him to greatly improve the construction of the swell-box, by furnishing it with small shutters or louvres moving on pivots, deriving the idea from a similar contrivance that had been introduced in certain harpsichords. His swell received the name "Venetian," probably from the resemblance of its moving portion to a Venetian shutter. In his Organ for the Chapel at Greenwich Hospital he introduced a Swell division with the unprecedented downward range to FF. This instrument was built in the year 1789. In the following year he boldly stepped ahead of all who had built Organs, by inclosing the Great Organ, of the instrument he constructed for St. George's Chapel, Windsor Castle, in a large Venetian swell. As we say elsewhere,* Green may be justly called the Father of the Swell Organ, in its approved treatment. In the *Christian Remembrancer*, of January, 1834, we find the following short notice of Samuel Green:

> "We possess more cathedral and collegiate Organs of this builder's construction than of any other; and, although patronized as he was by his Majesty George the Third, and long at the head of his profession, this admirable artist scarcely obtained a moderate competency. His zeal for the mechanical improvement of the Organ consumed much of his valuable time in experimental labors, which to him produced little or no emolument; and it is painful to know that a man so eminent in his profession should not, at his decease, be able to leave even a slender provision for his family."

As it has been our chief aim in these necessarily brief notes to trace, with the aid of such fragmentary and unsatisfactory materials as have been handed down to our time, the rise and progress of the art of organ-building, rather than the per-

* See Chapter on The Swell in the Organ.

sonal history of those who contributed to that progress, many organ builders have been left unmentioned whose works, good as they doubtless were, displayed no marked individuality or special development in their tonal appointment or mechanical appliances. At the close of the eighteenth century no English organ builder could lay claim to rank on an equality with Samuel Green; and, accordingly, with this very slight notice of his works we may close our survey of that period.

In the opening years of the nineteenth century we find the Organ, in every country where it was constructed, a very clumsy and insufficient instrument in all its mechanical features. The blowing arrangements, including the cumbersome and imperfect diagonal bellows, were of the most primitive description; the key action, especially in large instruments, was heavy in the extreme, and destructive of all delicacy of manipulation, indeed, in many cases, it was sufficient to tire the muscles of a blacksmith; and the draw-stop action was frequently of so extraordinary a character as to be beyond the unaided control of the organist, calling for the exertions of one or two able-bodied assistants during a performance of any consequence. We witnessed the gymnastic feats of two assistants during an organ recital in Holland, about thirty years ago, and have never forgotten them. The draw-stop handles, which appeared to have a draw of nearly nine inches, were pulled out by both hands, and driven in by the weight of the assistants' bodies, directed sidewise against them. The agility displayed by the organist's assistants on this occasion was as remarkable as it was ludicrous.

The tonal appointments of the Organ at the commencement of the century, although much in advance of the mechanical appliances, were, in comparison with their present condition, of a very monotonous character. For the first third of the century little progress of any noteworthy kind was made; but about the year 1835 a new era in the mechanical construction of the Organ commenced; and from that date a gradual improvement has attended the art of organ-building, the prominent builders of England and the United States leading with a series of ingenious inventions, all tending toward ultimate perfection in the mechanical portion of the instrument. During this period the sound-producing portion has also received considerable attention from the pipe maker and voicer. Numerous fine stops have been introduced, adding valuable voices to the tonal forces of the Organ; yet it must be acknowledged that more attention has been bestowed, during late years, on the mechanical than upon the purely musical departments of the instrument. It is to be hoped, however, that before the first decade of the twentieth century has run its course we shall see the tonal structure and stop apportionment of the Organ in a state that will leave little, if anything, to be desired.

As most of the following Chapters are more or less of a historical character, treating of the artistic and constructional matters connected with the development of the modern Organ, it is unnecessary for us to carry the present historical survey beyond the point it has now reached.

CHAPTER II.

THE POSITION OF THE ORGAN.

AS, in the proper order of things, the position which the Organ is to occupy should be carefully considered and wisely decided before the instrument is schemed, and its appointment and the disposition of its several parts become settled matters; so, in the present treatise, which is devoted to all important questions and details connected with the King of Instruments, we may appropriately open our dissertation with the consideration of the matters and questions which affect the Position of the Organ in Churches, Concert-rooms, and Dwelling-houses.

THE POSITION OF THE ORGAN IN CHURCHES.

The questions respecting the most desirable or correct position for the Organ in churches are of exceptional interest to all connected with church building and the ritual side of ecclesiastical matters. Much has been said and written on the subject, more especially in relation to the position of the Organ in English cathedrals and parish churches; but nothing like a definite conclusion, of general application, has been arrived at. At the present day, while there are in England ancient churches as left from Reformation times; restored churches which are supposed to represent their original state; and modern churches of all varieties of plan and internal proportions, how is it possible that anything in the nature of a rule of universal application can be formulated? Every ancient church, restored, or in its Reformation rags and tatters, claims to be considered independently; and the most favorable position to be occupied by the Organ will have to be dictated by the architectural arrangement and the disposition of the plan in each individual case. The question is rendered more difficult in connection with the ancient cathedrals and churches, from the fact that they were never designed for the reception of such large Organs as modern requirements have created and as are now deemed necessary. As regards modern churches, erected more or less closely on mediæval models, the problem, so far as the Anglican Church is concerned, is scarcely less difficult than in the case of the mediæval churches, for their architects, in their enthusiastic imitation of mediæval models, have practically ignored the claims, and overlooked the requirements, of the Organ of to-day.

We are free to admit that the question as to the best position for the Organ in an Anglican church is not one-sided; and it can hardly be expected to be solved by any one who looks upon it from one point of view only. An able authority, writing on this subject, recognizes the difficulties which beset the question, and summarizes them in the following terse words: "It is evident that there are several various and often conflicting interests to be consulted in the selection of a proper site for a Church Organ. There are first the interests of the clergy, who regard the matter, perhaps, from an ecclesiological point of view. Then there are the interests of the singers in the choir, who will view the question on its vocal side. Next we have the interest of the organist, who regards the position of the Organ from a comparatively instrumental aspect. After him comes the architect, who chiefly looks at the appearance of the case, and too frequently hates the Organ entirely, and would fain conceal as much of it as possible. Lastly, there is the organ builder, who knows how much better his instrument will sound with free space around it than when boxed up in a small chamber, and who feels that his reputation is more or less dependent on the decision as to locality to which those who have the management of the affair shall finally come. Here is, then, a fruitful source of quarrels and differences, of contentions and recriminations, of jealousies and revilings, of grumbling and discontent. It is really a matter of wonder that such occasions as the discussion of the position for a new Organ so often pass off as amicably and peacefully as we find they do."

The late Rev. Sir Frederick A. Gore Ouseley—the writer of the above paragraph—in enumerating the parties interested in the placing of the Church Organ, has omitted to mention the people of the congregation, who have to listen to the instrument on all occasions when it is legitimately used. He has, in short, overlooked the ritual aspect of the question, to which every other consideration should be subservient.

Before attempting to give any hints, more or less of a practical nature, concerning the placing of Organs in churches, it may be profitable to glance at what has already been done. In such a survey we shall probably find some positive, and it is certain we shall find much negative, teaching.

During the Middle Ages—the great church-building epoch, in which all the magnificent Romanesque and Gothic cathedrals and conventual and parish churches were erected throughout Western Europe—no difficulty beset the now vexed question of the proper position of the Organ; simply because the most important instruments then fabricated were so small, in comparison to the vast buildings in which they were placed, that they could be accommodated in any desirable situations, or moved from one place to another, as circumstances dictated. The smaller Organs were portable; and were not only moved about in the churches to which they belonged, but, on certain occasions, were transported from one church to another. In no instance with which we are acquainted does an early mediæval church present an original and specially constructed place for the reception of a stationary Organ. While we have little reliable information respecting the mediæval usage in the matter of the Organ, we may reasonably surmise that where the singers were, there the Organ would be also. This rational arrangement would conclusively point to some convenient position on either side of the choir or chancel; or, probably, in some isolated cases, to a central position eastward of the high altar. It is reasonable to suppose that in cathedrals and large conventual churches the principal Positive Organ was placed permanently in one or other of the above-named situations; while the small portable Organs—in many cases Regals or Portatives—were doubtless carried from chapel to chapel, either to give out the melody of the plain-song, or to in some way accompany the voices during the services at the respective altars.

When one ventures to argue that even the largest Church Organs constructed during the great church-building periods of the Middle Ages were, at the best, extremely primitive affairs, and limited to the last degree in musical resources, one is referred to that unknown quantity, the "monster Organ" of the Monastic Church of Winchester, as poetically described by Wolston the Deacon, who wrote in the middle of the tenth century. For this description we must refer the reader to the preceding Chapter: here we need only remark that it points to an instrument of extremely limited musical resources however complex and cumbersome its bellows arrangements may have been. Wolston, unfortunately, gives no hints as to where this Organ was placed in the church. In our historical notes we have given a quotation from the "Ancient Rites and Monuments of the Monastical and Cathedral Church of Durham," published in 1672. From this we learn that "there were three pair of Organs" belonging to the choir of the cathedral; and that "the fairest pair of the three" stood over the central door of the choir-screen, that is, in the middle of the rood-loft. From the brief description given it would appear that this was an instrument of considerable importance at the time; for we are told that "there were but two pair more of them in all England of the same making; one in York and another in Paul's." The other two "pair of Organs" evidently stood in lateral positions in the choir. In the accounts of the Parish Church of Louth, Lincolnshire, an entry appears of the purchase, about the year 1500, of a pair of Organs of Flemish manufacture, *suitable for erection in the rood-loft of that church.* From these records it will be seen that the central or choir-screen position was recognized at a comparatively early period in the history of the Organ in England. Bentham, in his "History of Ely Cathedral," gives an inventory in which are mentioned "two paer of Organs in the quyer," and "a paer of Organs in the Ladye Chaple." Storer, in his "English Cathedrals," informs us that, in the Cathedral of Worcester, the Chapel of St. Edmund had a pair of Organs; that another pair stood in the Chapel of St. George, while the great Organ was in the choir.

When we turn our attention to the Organ as it was placed in certain of the more important English cathedrals, we find evidences of conflicting opinions, which became more pronounced as the Organ became larger and correspondingly more difficult to place conveniently. The cathedral builders of the Middle Ages, as has already been said, never contemplated the possibility of such cumbersome instruments as later ingenuity and skill devised being introduced into their structures. There can be no reasonable doubt that, had the mediæval architects had such immense Organs to accommodate, they would, in their unvarying practical way of looking at things, and in their resourceful ingenuity and artistic skill, have devised and constructed proper places for their reception just where they were required by the musical services. While we gravely doubt whether they would have adopted any central position, we feel convinced that what they would have schemed specially for the accommodation of the Organ would have given the interiors of their buildings additional features of beauty and interest. The mediæval architects never ignored any article of utility; and had large Organs been known in the twelfth, thirteenth, and fourteenth centuries, we should, in all probability, find little diversity of opinion respecting their proper position in large mediæval churches to-day.

The first cathedral which naturally presents itself for consideration is the ancient one at Canterbury, as erected by Lanfranc (A. D. 1070-1089). Of this building we have a singularly precise account, by Gervase the monk. Quoting from this account,* Britton writes: "In the midst of the Church was a tower, like a center in the midst of a circumference, supported by very large pillars. . . . In the middle of the center tower was the altar of the Holy Cross. . . . The great center tower had a transept, called wings, both on the north and south side of it, and in the center of each was a strong pillar, which received the arch springing in three parts from the wall. The south transept had an Organ placed above the arch, and beneath it a portico, through which was an entrance to the east part of the Church." By the word *arch*, in the above quotation, it is quite clear that a *vault* is signified;† and this points to an elevated platform or gallery, on which the Organ was placed. Here, then, we have a south lateral and elevated position, contiguous to the high altar, clearly mentioned. After Lanfranc's death, his successor Anselm rebuilt and adorned the choir, giving the superintendence of the work to Prior Conrad. The operations were completed in 1114; and so magnificent was the result that it was known as "the glorious choir of Conrad." Gervase describes this choir, but he does not speak of an Organ. When this choir was burned, in 1174, the central tower and the transepts were practically uninjured; accordingly, it is probable that the gallery in the south transept remained the organ-loft until this part of the Cathedral was entirely rebuilt by Archbishop Sudbury (1376-1381). It is believed that subsequently an Organ was again placed in the south transept, on the large stone corbel which projected over the arch leading to the Chapel of St. Michael, in the south-east bay. Dart gives a view, in his Work,‡ in which an Organ is shown within the fourth arch on the north side of the choir. Later, an important instrument was placed on the choir-screen, as is

* Gervas, "Dorob. de Combust. et Repar. Dorob. Eccles." Edit. 1652.

† "Fornicem a parietibus prodeuntem, in tribus sui partibus suscipiebat." Gervas, *ibid.*

‡ "History and Antiquities of the Cathedral Church of Canterbury;" by the Rev. J. Dart. Folio, 1726.

shown in Britton's Work. This authority informs us that the Organ he shows (1821) was the instrument originally erected in Westminster Abbey for the Handel Commemoration, and subsequently moved to Canterbury. In 1842 the Organ was rebuilt and erected over the south aisle of the choir, the claviers being placed in the choir, on the decani side. We have enlarged somewhat on this interesting example, because it clearly shows that continual doubts obtained amongst those at the head of affairs as to the most favorable position for the Organ. The limited space at our disposal will prevent our making such extended remarks relating to any other Church and its Organs.

In the interior view of the old Gothic Cathedral of St. Paul, London, given by Dugdale in his Work on that structure, the Organ is shown on the north side of the choir, immediately over the stalls. Speaking of this instrument, Sir Frederick A. Gore Ouseley remarks: "It is not known for certain how long that Organ had been there, but it probably was one of the largest instruments of the period, and had, doubtless, been played upon by such worthies as Batten, Bevin, Tomkins, and Gibbons. It appears to have consisted of a Great Organ and a separate Choir, the former furnished with triptych shutters, as was usually the case with ancient organ-cases. This was one of the few Organs which survived the Great Rebellion, and only came to a sad end when the old Church perished in the Great Fire of London in 1666." Of the positions of any early Organs placed in the magnificent Minster at York, nothing is known; but there are good grounds for believing that the Organ which preceded the instrument constructed by Robert Dallam, in 1633, occupied a position on the choir-screen. When Charles the First visited the Minster in that year, and obtained information with reference to the Organ then in course of construction, he expressed a wish that it should not be erected on the choir-screen to the detriment of the grand view of the nave and choir. The result of this was that Dallam's instrument was placed on the north side of the choir. Later on, for some reason, this position was disapproved of. In 1690 Archbishop Lamplugh had the Organ removed, and erected in the central position on the choir-screen. King Charles certainly appears to have held very decided views on the proper position for the Organ, for he also ordered the instrument in the Cathedral of Winchester, which had been erected, at the Reformation, on the choir-screen, to be removed and placed on the north side of the choir. Dugdale, in his "Monasticon," gives an interior view of Lincoln Cathedral which shows an Organ rising above the north stalls of the choir. In an engraving of the interior of Durham Cathedral by Hollar, the large Organ, also of Reformation date, is depicted on the north side of the choir. Sandford, in his "Coronation of James II.," gives an interior view of Westminster Abbey, in which a small Organ is shown above the stalls on the north side of the choir. This was the instrument Purcell played upon. It was removed from the Abbey on the erection of the Organ, by Schreider & Jordan, in 1730, on the choir-screen. According to the MS. Archives of Worcester, the "Great Organ" in the Cathedral stood, prior to the year 1550, at one side (probably the north) of the choir. When the question arose as to the position of the Organ in the present Cathedral of St. Paul, London, Sir Christopher Wren naturally desired to follow precedent by placing it on the north side of his choir; this, however, did not agree with the views of the master of the position—the then Dean—who insisted on the central situation, on the choir-screen, being adopted.

From the above notes it seems obvious that before the Reformation the lateral choir position was the accepted one in English cathedrals, and was very seldom deviated from. The same rule obtained in college chapels and parish churches. Parker remarks: "They were formerly placed in various situations in churches, though probably seldom, before the Reformation, over the screen between the nave and the choir, as is now usual [1850] in our cathedrals and large churches."* Speaking of the Organs in the college chapels, Dr. Rimbault gives the following notes: "At New College, Oxford, the Organ given by William Port, in 1458, stood at the stall end of the 'north side of the choir,' near the vestry, supported by pillars. Previously to the year 1740, the Organ of Magdalen College, Oxford, stood on the 'south side of the choir.' The Organ of St. John's College, in the same university, built in 1660, was placed in a little ante-chapel 'on the north side of the choir.' It was in that situation in 1768, when Byfield erected an Organ on the present screen. Quaint old Thomas Fuller, speaking of the Cambridge Colleges, under the date 1633, adds: 'Now began the university to be much beautified in buildings; every College either casting its skin with the snake, or renewing it with the eagle. . . . But the greatest alteration was in their chapels, most of them being graced with the accession of Organs.' The Organ of Christ's College still remains on the south side of the choir; and tradition assigns similar situations for the instruments of King's College, St. John's College, etc. The same position, 'at the side of the choir,' is still retained in Winchester College, the Royal Chapels at St. James's and Hampton Court, and within memory it was so in Christ Church, Dublin."

Although the choir or chancel position was, in old times, the favored one, and we think wisely so, other situations, often dictated by special circumstances, were adopted. We may remark, however, that the west-end position never was a favorite one in England. The peculiar architectural treatment of the western portion of the mediæval churches, which involved the introduction of large west windows, in all probability prevented the erection of Organs there. It must not be understood, however, that Organs never occupied such a position in old times, for Mr. W. B. Gilbert, speaking of the Organ which Abbot Lyllyngton presented to the Abbey of Croyland sometime about the middle of the fifteenth century, says: "This instrument, which was described as the 'Great Organ,' was placed at the west entrance of the Abbey Church; a smaller one was situated in the choir, which latter Organ was carried on the shoulders of two porters, who conveyed it from London to Croyland. The only other instance in this country of an ancient Organ being placed over the west entrance is that of Beauchamp Chapel, at Warwick; and the contract—A. D. 1440—for that beautiful building expressly mentions 'an organ-loft ordained to stand over the west door of the Chappel.'"† The

* "Glossary of Architecture," Fifth edition, Vol. I., p. 332.

† "On the Musical Associations of Boston Church, Lincolnshire." Paper printed in *The Choir*, viii, 68.

archway and the small gallery over the projecting doorway, where an Organ was in all likelihood placed, still remain in the Chapel.

Before we direct attention to the positions occupied by modern Organs in ancient churches in England, and discuss the general question of the most desirable positions for the instrument in different churches and chapels, we may profitably extend our hasty survey to the more important churches in France, Germany, and other Continental countries.

We are not much better informed as regards the positions usually adopted for the Organs in the Romanesque and Gothic churches on the Continent, during the grand centuries of the Middle Ages, than we are with respect to the practice which obtained in England during the same periods. The art of organ-building was more advanced on the Continent than in England, and it is certain that comparatively large instruments were introduced there long before Organs of any great importance made their appearance in English churches. We are speaking more particularly of the eleventh and three following centuries. But, however this may be, there appears to be little doubt that so long as Organs remained of moderate dimensions, they either occupied a lateral position in the choir or a central position eastward of the high altar. It is also probable that they were carried or moved about to different parts of the church, as certain Organs in St. Peter's, at Rome, are at the present day.

In the fifteenth century, the art of organ-building had made great strides, and important instruments began to be introduced in churches, and appropriate positions sought for them. The great height of the larger Continental churches favored the elevation of the Organ, so, accordingly, we find the positions most frequently adopted for the Grand Organ to be an elevated gallery at the west end, or a gallery or so-called "tribune," specially designed for its reception, bracketed out from the walls, the triforium, the piers of the nave, or some other part of the church. Several instances of the bracketed treatment existed at the beginning of the sixteenth century, but comparatively few have been preserved to the present time, larger west-end Organs having been substituted. Noteworthy examples exist in the following buildings:

In the large Cathedral of Chartres (Eure-et-Loir), the Organ is in the nave, bracketed out at the level of the triforium, and carried upward nearly to the vaulting. It extends laterally, across one bay, and its towers occupy about a quarter of each of the adjoining bays. This Organ dates from the fifteenth century.

The Organ in the Church of La Ferté Bernard (Sarthe) is bracketed out above one of the main arches, its "tribune" having a Gothic *cul-de-lampe*. The whole of the work is of the early part of the sixteenth century.

In the Cathedral of Strasbourg (Bas-Rhin), the Organ is placed above the main arch in the second bay of the nave, on the north side. It is supported at the level of the triforium floor, below which hangs a beautiful Gothic *cul-de-lampe*. The case, which now incloses Silbermann's noted instrument, dates from 1497. This is probably the most noteworthy and beautiful example of the bracketed treatment which exists. In the Church of St. Sebaldus, at Nürnberg, the Organ is bracketed out, at a great height, from the west wall of the south transept.

There are two Organs in the Cathedral of Freiburg, in Breisgau, the older one of which dates from about 1520. This instrument is placed on the north side of the nave toward the west end, and is corbelled out from one of the main piers at a considerable height from the floor. The second Organ stands on the floor on the south side of the choir.

The Organ in the Church of San Bernardino, at Verona, is bracketed out in the north-eastern part of the nave. In the fine Church of Sta. Anastasia, at Verona, the Organ is placed, at a considerable elevation, on the north side of the north aisle. In the Church of San Salvatore, at Venice, the Organ is bracketed out on the north wall of the north aisle.

Turning now to the west-end position, a few typical examples may be given. As an early one, we may take the case of the Cathedral of Amiens. Here the Organ was placed in an elevated west-end gallery so early as the year 1429. Another instance, of about the same date, exists in the Church of Notre-Dame, at Argentan. A rather later example is to be found in the Church of St. George, at Nördlingen, Bavaria. Here the Organ is placed in a gallery at the west end.

In the Marienkirche, at Lübeck, a magnificent Organ stands in a west-end gallery elevated about forty feet from the floor of the nave. From this gallery the organ case towers to about the height of eighty feet, and, accordingly, to within a few feet of the apex of the vaulting. This work dates from the year 1504.

The celebrated Organ in the Church of St. Jan, at Bois le Duc (North Brabant), stands in a west-end gallery, and rises to the total height of about one hundred feet from the floor. This Organ was built in the year 1580, whilst its case is dated 1602. The Organs in the Churches of Caudebec, Normandy, and St. Nicholas, Stralsund, are situated on stone galleries at the west end.

The Grand Organs in the Cathedrals of Lucerne, Fribourg (Switzerland), Haarlem, Paris, Abbeville, and the great Abbey Church of Saint-Denis; and in the Churches of Saint-Sulpice, Saint-Eustache, Sainte-Clotilde, Saint-Germain des Prés, and the Madeleine, all occupy commanding west-end positions, elevated on galleries. In addition to the above, almost countless examples of west-end Organs in Continental churches might be given. We must remark here that we use the term *west end* in all cases for the sake of clearness; it denotes a position at the end of the nave furthest from the choir or sanctuary. It is necessary to note this, for several churches, as in the case of the Madeleine and Sainte-Clotilde, Paris, are not built east and west.

In the more important French churches two Organs are usually introduced; the Grand Organ occupying the elevated, west-end position, and the Choir Organ being placed in or immediately adjoining the choir. In the Gothic churches the Choir Organ generally occupies a lateral position in the choir; and this arrangement obtains in certain of the large modern churches built in other styles, as in the Church of the Trinité, Paris. In the Cathedral of Notre-Dame, in the same city, the Choir Organ is placed in the arch of the second bay on the north side of the choir, and is elevated high above the screen of the stalls. The console is placed in front of the stalls, on the floor of the choir. The following are particulars of several noteworthy arrangements found in French churches, ancient and modern.

In the Church of the Madeleine, Paris, the Choir Organ is placed in a central position, in the hemicycle, behind the high altar. The musical effect of both the Grand and Choir Organs in this noble church is highly satisfactory. In the Church of Saint-Germain des Prés, Paris, the Choir Organ occupies a central position in the apse, behind the high altar, the space between it and the back of the altar being used for the accommodation of a small orchestra. The Choir Organ in the Church of Saint-Sulpice is placed in the central arch of the apse, the large space between it and the back of the high altar being fitted up as a ritual choir. The apsidal space behind the high altar in the Church of Saint-Philippe du Roule, Paris, is treated in a somewhat similar way. The Choir Organ is of good size, and occupies the central arch; and has its console well advanced in front, with the space around it furnished with seats and desks for instrumentalists. Stalls extend round the hemicycle, on each side of the Organ. The Grand Organ is, as usual, placed in a gallery above the western entrance. In the Church of Saint-Vincent de Paul, the high altar is situated in the chord of the apse, and the large Choir Organ stands a short distance behind it. The choir stalls extend on each side of the Organ and altar, forming the ritual choir, semicircular in form. The Grand Organ is placed high at the west end, and is divided by an arch and window. The case is, however, properly treated so as to form one design. The console is placed midway between the divisions, the player facing that on the right, as one looks toward the Organ from the nave. In the fine modern Church of Saint-Augustin, Paris, the high altar occupies a central position under the dome, with the choir stalls forming a quadrant on each side. The circular formation of the ritual choir is continued behind the altar, and in the middle is placed the Choir Organ with a small space on each side for instrumentalists. The console is well advanced, being almost midway between the Organ and the altar. The whole arrangement is unique and good. The Grand Organ is in an elevated chamber at the west end. In the modern Gothic Church of Sainte-Clotilde, Paris, we meet with an unusual disposition of the Choir Organ. Here it is divided into two sections of equal size, and placed, in elevated positions, in the side arches of the apsidal sanctuary, in line with the steps to the high altar. The console is located at the end of the stalls on the left side as one faces the altar. The Organ is electro-pneumatic, and the bellows are placed immediately behind the high altar. This arrangement proves very satisfactory. In the Church of Saint-Jacques du Haut-Pas, Paris, the Choir Organ is divided and placed in two arches of the apse, behind the high altar, and immediately adjoining the choir stalls. The console is in the center, between the Organ and the back of the altar.

In the Abbey Church of Saint-Denis, the Choir Organ is placed in the first arch of the choir, on the north side, in a case which has no displayed pipes, and is played from a reversed console behind the front row of stalls. In the Church of Saint-Eustache, Paris, the Choir Organ is placed in the second bay of the choir aisle, on the south side, on a slightly raised platform which also accommodates an orchestra. The platform is inclosed within four pillars of the double aisle.

In the Cathedral of Bayeux (Calvados), the Grand Organ occupies an elevated gallery at the west end; and the Choir Organ is placed within the first arch of the choir, on the north side, elevated above the ornamental canopy-work of the stalls, and played from a reversed console located in advance of the second range of stalls below. In the Cathedral of Rouen (Seine-Inférieure), the Grand Organ occupies the usual elevated west-end position; and the Choir Organ stands under the arch of the second bay of the choir, on the north side, and is played from a reversed console placed in advance of the second range of stalls. In the Church of Saint-Maclou, Rouen, the Grand Organ, in a fine Renaissance case, stands in a western gallery, reached by a beautiful spiral staircase.* The Choir Organ is placed behind the stalls, under the first arch of the choir, on the south side, and played from direct claviers. The above examples practically cover all the treatments found in important French churches. The French properly designate the Grand Organ, occupying the elevated west-end position, "L'Orgue de Tribune;" and the smaller Choir Organ, wherever it may be placed, "L'Orgue d'Accompagnement."

In the Church of Saint-Jacques, Antwerp, the Grand Organ is placed on the massive rood-screen, divided into two sections, and played from a console between them. In the Cathedral of Bruges, the Organ stands in the center of the rood-screen, and rises to a considerable height.

The Organs in the Churches of Sta. Maria Nuova, Perugia; San Ambrogio, Genoa; and San Bartolommeo all' Isola, Rome, are all in west-end positions.

Organs occupying positions in the transepts are to be met with in Continental churches, as in the Cathedral of Le Mans (Sarthe), where the Grand Organ is placed in a very high gallery in the south transept; and in the Church of Saint-Vincent de Paul, at Marseille (Bouches du Rhône), where the Organ is divided into two sections of nearly equal dimensions, and placed, in elevated positions, opposite each other, in the shallow north and south transepts. They have separate consoles; but both sections can be played from one console, the connection being by an electric action.

In the Duomo of Mantua the Organ occupies the end of the south transept, while a singers' gallery is placed on the north transept. The Organ in the Church of San Francesco, at Ferrara, is erected in a gallery in the north transept. In the Cathedral of Genoa there is an Organ in each transept; and in the Church of Sta. Maria Assunta dei Gesuiti, at Venice, there are also two Organs, occupying recesses in the western sides of the transept. Notwithstanding the examples just given, what may be generally understood as the choir position appears to have been commonly favored in Italian churches. A few instances may be mentioned.

In the Cathedral of Milan two Organs are placed, opposite each other, above the screens on the north and south sides of the choir. These are imposing instruments, with large painted doors. In the Church of Sta. Maria delle Grazie, in the same city, two Organs occupy similar lateral positions in the choir. In the Cathedral of San Marco, at Venice; San Pietro, at Bologna; the Duomo of Cre-

* An illustration of this noteworthy organ-case is given in the Chapter on the External Design of the Organ.—Fig. XXXI.

mona; the Duomo of Rovigo; and in the Church of San Michele, at Pavia, there are two Organs in the choir. Numerous other instances might be given.

In the Church of San Antonio, at Padua, there is a large space before the high altar and under the lantern, called the presbytery, devoted to the service of the altar. This space is square, with screens on its north and south sides supporting galleries for orchestral performers. At the four corners, and partly inclosing the great piers of the lantern, are four large Organs. These instruments have a very striking effect to the eye; and when they are all played together, as we understand they sometimes are, their effect on the ear must be highly impressive. Two Organs are placed in recesses in the two eastern diagonal faces of the octagon under the dome of the Cathedral of Florence. These instruments are elevated some distance above the floor, and underneath each is a sacristy door.

In the Church of Sta. Maria Maggiore, at Florence, a species of choir is situated behind the high altar, and the Organ is placed in a gallery at its eastern end. In the Chiesa del Carmine, in the same city, a cruciform church with a square-ended choir behind the high altar, there are two Organs—one, of small dimensions, placed at the east end; and the other, an imposing instrument, situated at the west end.

In the Cathedral of Como there are two Organs which stand under the easternmost arches of the nave, one on each side, facing each other. The Organ in the Church of San Domenico, at Cremona, is placed on the north side of the nave; that in the Church of San Eustorgio, at Milan, occupies a gallery on the north side of the choir; and that in the Church of Sta. Maria del Carmine, at Pavia, is placed behind the high altar which stands under the choir arch. These notes, few and sketchy as they are, must suffice so far as Italian Organs are concerned; and we may now glance at the positions occupied by Organs in Spanish churches.

The position of the Organ varies in Spain as in all other countries; but that which is about equivalent to our lateral choir position appears to be preferred and adopted when circumstances permit. The arrangement of Spanish cathedrals and churches is somewhat different from that which obtains in France and Italy; and this peculiar arrangement naturally affects the position of the Organ or the Organs, for there are frequently two. In the eastern portion of the church is the *capilla mayor*, in which stands the high altar, and westward of this, and frequently at a considerable distance, is an inclosed space called the *coro*, usually occupying two or three bays, surrounded with stalls and having large desks for office books in the center. It is usually in a position adjacent to the coro that the Organ is placed.

In Burgos Cathedral, the coro extends three bays westward of the transepts; and a large Organ is placed in each of the central arches, on galleries above the highly raised back ranges of stalls. The instruments are of different dates and dissimilar in design. The claviers are separate and directly connected with the instruments. In Toledo Cathedral, the coro extends about two and a half bays westward of the transepts, and two large Organs stand, above the arcaded stall-work, in the two eastern arches, and as usual are dissimilar in design.

In the Cathedral of Zaragoza a magnificent Organ occupies an arch on the south side of the coro, rising above the stalls. This is a work of the early part of the fifteenth century, and is probably the finest specimen of its class in Spain.* In the Cathedral of Tarragona, the coro occupies two bays immediately westward of the crossing; and an immense Organ, which rises almost to the vaulted roof, occupies the north bay adjoining the transept.† In the Church of San Benito, at Valladolid, the coro is placed at the fourth bay from the east end; and the Organ, a large and effective instrument, is situated on its north side. In addition to this Grand Organ, there is another placed on the south side of a large western gallery which is fitted up as a second coro. In the Church of San Esteban, at Burgos, there is also a west-end gallery fitted up as a coro; and an Organ is placed on the north side, in the bay eastward of the gallery, and approached from the gallery floor. In the Church of San Antholin, Medina del Campo, the coro, which is near the west end of the nave, has a fine Organ above it on the south side. In the Cathedral of Barcelona, the coro occupies two bays westward of the transepts, while the Organ stands in an elevated gallery in the end of the north transept, at a distance of about sixty feet from the center of the coro.‡

Speaking about the Church of San Juan, at Perpignan, Street remarks, in his "Gothic Architecture in Spain": "The most striking feature in this cathedral is that very rare thing—a very fine mediæval Organ. It is corbelled out from the north wall of the nave, and is of great size and height. The pipes are arranged in traceried compartments at five different levels. . . . The width of its front is about twenty-five feet, its projection from the wall three feet six inches, and the organist sits in a gallery at its base." §

Even this brief and sketchy review of the positions of Organs in Continental churches, in conjunction with the few particulars given anent old English Organs, goes far to prove that at no time in the history of mediæval church architecture was there any special provision made for the reception of the stationary Organ, or any universally approved rule for its location.

In considering matters connected with the placing of modern Organs in both ancient and modern churches, we must recognize that no rule of general application can either be formulated or adopted. Not only do the architectural treatments and peculiar forms of churches affect the question of the proper position of the Organ in all cases, but a still more important factor obtains in the nature or form of the worship to which they are devoted. Churches may, in the first instance, be divided into three groups—those belonging to the Latin Church; those belonging to the Anglican Church; and those which belong to the several bodies which dissent from both these old Communions, in religious tenets and forms of worship. Churches may again be divided into two classes—First, those in which the musical services are liturgical and prescribed. Secondly, those in which instru-

* An illustration of this interesting mediæval Organ is given in the Chapter on the External Design of the Organ.—Fig. XXV.

† An illustration of this Organ is given in the Chapter on the External Design of the Organ.—Fig. XXIV.

‡ An illustration of this Organ is given in the Chapter on the Organ Historically Considered.—Fig. XVIII.

§ An illustration of this Organ is given in the Chapter on the Organ Historically Considered.—Fig. XVII.

mental music is of very recent introduction, and the music, generally, is of a purely congregational and voluntary character. The former of these classes embraces Roman Catholic and Anglo-Catholic churches, while the latter embraces the multitudinous forms of places of worship belonging to the numerous Sects outside these Communions. In churches of the former class, the positions of the Organ or Organs are properly dictated by the character of the musical services; but the positions so dictated cannot always be adopted, owing to peculiar or adverse architectural dispositions, such as are frequently met with in ancient churches, and too often in unskilfully planned modern ones. In the latter class, the positions of the Organ are not of so much importance. For congregational singing it is only necessary for the Organ to be well heard; and for that purpose it is best placed in some prominent and exposed position, either in front of, or behind, the congregation.

In Roman Catholic churches, in which the principal music is strictly and almost exclusively of a liturgical character, the position of the Organ is practically a settled matter. When one Organ only is introduced, it is almost invariably placed in a commanding west-end position, in a gallery which also accommodates the vocalists. We find this arrangement in the great majority of Roman Catholic churches in England and the United States. The musical services are generally well rendered, and the effect of the Organ is good. It is true the sounds come from behind the congregation; but as the music is liturgical, and interwoven, so to speak, with the holy offices of the sanctuary, on which the attention of the worshipers is concentrated, the ear is not unpleasantly conscious of the direction from which the musical sounds come.

The effect of the vocal and instrumental music in such a church as the Madeleine, at Paris, is of course much grander; for there the choir, the Accompanimental Organ, and the orchestra, are located in the large space behind the high altar. We have already given particulars respecting the placing of the Grand and Choir Organs in representative French cathedrals and churches; and it is only necessary to add that under the conditions which there obtain the music of the Catholic Church is rendered in the most correct and impressive manner. The Accompanimental or Choir Organ, when not of large dimensions, is commonly supplemented by the stringed and certain wind instruments of the orchestra, producing a rich and refined volume of sound which supports without impairing the vocal music.

There can be no question that in a Roman Catholic cathedral or large parish church the French arrangement is the best. It is the most correct, because the choir should always be in the vicinity of the sanctuary so that a feeling of oneness may pervade the services at the altar: and the effect of the Grand Organ in incidental music, in its commanding and unobstructed position, is effective in the extreme. While in the French churches the small Choir Organ is used to accompany the vocalists, in English and American Catholic churches the vocalists are invariably accompanied on the west-end Grand Organ, at least in all churches in which such an instrument exists.

There can be no question, so far as the positions of the Organs are concerned, that those adopted in the large French churches are both the most logical and the most desirable. It is universally admitted, we believe, among all authorities in matters of church music, that the Organ used to accompany the choir should be as close as possible to the choir, so that a perfect unity of musical effect may obtain, and the voices be properly sustained. As a correctly appointed Accompanimental Organ need not be a large or cumbersome instrument, there can be no difficulty in providing for its reception in the proper eastern position in new Catholic churches of important dimensions. A true Accompanimental Organ need never contain many speaking stops; but it is essential that its stops should be of the grandest kind art can produce. Dignity, purity, roundness, and fulness should pervade its tonal structure, and full powers of expression must be provided throughout. We have long wished some musical apostle would arise and preach to unthinking and unbelieving organists some such doctrine as this; for if it were acted upon there would be less difficulty in finding accommodation for the Organ, in proper positions, in churches of ordinary dimensions.

When the Accompanimental Organ is properly placed, there need be no hesitation in adopting the elevated west-end position for the Grand Organ. It must be conceded, on acoustical grounds, that there is no position in a properly constructed church better suited for an Organ used for the rendition of incidental music of a majestic and inspiring character. The great advantage of the west-end position, apart from the purely acoustical one, lies in the fact that the Organ can be correctly planned, and all its parts conveniently arranged, without necessitating an undesirable depth, and the placing of one important division of the instrument in front of another. One pleasing and desirable result of such an arrangement is that every stop in the instrument can be heard at its full value; and, accordingly, there is no need for strained voicing and the use of inordinate pressures of wind. On this subject we may refer our readers to the Chapter on the Church Organ. It is but right to mention that, except in very large and lofty churches, the elevated west-end position is not altogether free from objection. It has been frequently found that the alterations of temperature in the higher levels of churches filled with large congregations and lighted with gas, have so affected the different classes of the pipe-work in their Organs as to throw the whole very much out of tune, and to raise the pitch of the greater portion of their stops to a very undesirable extent. In very lofty churches in which gas is sparingly used, or where the lighting is electric, the matter is not so serious. In every case, however, it is desirable to keep all sound-producing portions of an elevated Organ on as nearly the same level as possible, and not to allow any pipe-work liable to be quickly affected by a rise of temperature to approach the roof or ceiling.

When a tower stands at the western end of the church, it is convenient to locate the wind-collecting portion of the Organ in a room therein; carrying the wind by trunks to the instrument in the west gallery. Blowing operations, whether carried on by manual labor or by some description of motor, are invariably attended by more or less noise, which is extremely unpleasant when heard in the church: accordingly, it is always desirable to have the feeders and receivers removed from the Organ, and placed where they will not be heard in action.

They can, of course, be located at a considerable distance from the Organ, so long as proper provision has been made for the conveyance of wind-trunks, of ample size, to the reservoirs in the interior of the Organ. It must be borne in mind that wherever the bellows-chamber may be located, it must be supplied with air from the interior of the church, or at the same temperature as the air in the neighborhood of the Organ. The best arrangement is to provide two wind-trunks—one to carry the air from the immediate vicinity of the Organ to the bellows-chamber, and the other to carry the wind from the bellows to the several reservoirs in the Organ. Other trunks will be required when winds of different pressures are used. All the accommodation required for the above should be provided by the architect, in planning the church, and not be entirely overlooked in the thoughtless manner it usually is.

When we approach the consideration of the proper position for the Organ in an Anglo-Catholic church, we find somewhat different requirements and conditions to obtain from those already touched upon. In the first place, it is neither considered necessary nor desirable, under ordinary circumstances, to have more than a single Organ in a church; but it is considered necessary, in ninety-nine cases out of a hundred, that the single instrument shall contain the tonal resources of a Grand and an Accompanimental Organ combined. We are compelled to admit that the English Church Organ, as it is usually schemed by ambitious organists and inartistic organ builders, partakes more of the Grand than of the legitimate Accompanimental type of instrument; and it accordingly loses much of its utility and dignity in the choral services of the Church, while it seriously complicates the question of its proper location and accommodation.

We may now glance at the several positions occupied by modern Organs in representative English cathedrals and churches; some of which have apparently been dictated by purely musical considerations; while others have evidently been decided by the desire to have immense instruments, notwithstanding the difficulty of finding proper accommodation for them in buildings which were never designed for the reception of such Organs.

The first position which naturally presents itself for consideration is that known as the central, or choir-screen, position, and one (although it is met with elsewhere) that may be accepted as strictly belonging to a cathedral. In such a building the regular congregation is accommodated in the choir proper—as in the Cathedrals of York, Gloucester, and Wells, and in Westminster Abbey—and accordingly there is no serious objection to the position of the Organ on the screen which closes in that portion of the building at its western end. Speaking of this position, the Rev. Sir Frederick A. Gore Ouseley says: "Probably the very best place for the Organ in all such cases is over the choir-screen, in the center of the building. It is, perhaps, not the very best place *architecturally*, inasmuch as it renders it impossible to gain an uninterrupted view of the interior of the cathedral from west to east. But, *musically* speaking, it is the best place, not only because the Organ has free space all round it, but also because it occupies a very favorable position for supporting and leading the singers. It is just a case where it is necessary to balance the conflicting claims of sight and sound, of architecture and music. And, therefore, speaking as a musician, and a lover of the cathedral service, I am inclined to advocate in all such cases the retention of the Organ on the rood-screen."

We have in Sir Christopher Wren's contention with the Dean and Chapter of St. Paul's Cathedral the decided views of an architect on the question. When the position to be occupied by the Organ in the new Cathedral was brought forward for consideration, Sir Christopher Wren expressed a strong desire to have it placed on one side of the choir—as the Organ was located in the ancient Gothic Cathedral of St. Paul—so that the entire length and the true proportions of his fine interior might be seen at one view. The Dean, taking the contrary stand, insisted on it being placed in the center, on the choir-screen. Sir Christopher, like most architects who have inartistic and self-opinionated clients, had to give way. He however designed a case too small to contain the Organ that Father Smith was commissioned to build; and when that was discovered, he objected to the case being enlarged, declaring that the beauty of his interior was "already spoilt by the damned box of whistles." In a "broadside" which appeared concerning Father Smith's Organ, and which no doubt emanated from his rival, Renatus Harris, the following remarkable paragraph appears:

> "Whether Sir Christopher Wren would not have been well pleas'd to have received such a Proposal from the Organ-builder of St. Paul's, as shou'd have erected an Organ, so as to have separated 20 Foot in the Middle, as low as Gallery, and thereby given a full and airy Prospect of the length of the Church, and Six Fronts with Towers as high as requisite?"

We have used the word *remarkable* with reference to the above paragraph, because it contains a suggestion for a *divided* Organ (certainly a novelty at the time the "broadside" was issued), arranged in much the same manner as the instrument is at the present day, with the difference that it has no screen under it. The Organ has, however, the "six fronts" spoken of in the paragraph. Between the time of its original occupation of the choir-screen and its present arrangement, as an elevated, divided Organ, it was placed within the middle arch on the north side of the choir; at first played from claviers placed below, and subsequently from those located in a gallery above the stalls.

On both architectural and musical grounds we object to the central or choir-screen position for an *undivided* Organ; but as such a position is never likely to be again adopted for an undivided instrument, it is unnecessary to discuss the matter farther.

The most noteworthy example of a *divided* Organ, occupying the choir-screen position, is that of Westminster Abbey. Here the choir-screen is very deep extending, east and west, an entire bay; and, accordingly, at each end rises one of the lofty arches of the nave, affording admirable accommodation for the several divisions of the Organ. In the arch at the north end of the screen are placed, in three stages, the Great Organ, the Solo Organ, and portion of the reed-work of the Pedal Organ. At this end, in a chamber formed in the screen, from the choir floor, are conveniently located the pipes of the Pedal CONTRA POSAUNE, 32 FT., and POSAUNE, 16 FT., with their tubes rising above the floor of the screen. In the arch at the south end are placed, in two stages, the Swell Organ and another portion of the Pedal Organ stops. Along the western part of the gallery are disposed, horizontally, the larger pipes of the Pedal DOUBLE OPEN DIAPASON, 32 FT., of wood. In the center of the screen, adjoining the above pipes, is located the Choir Organ of eleven stops. This is arranged so as not to rise above the top of the screen, by having its longer pipes mitered. The console is placed in nearly a central position, enabling the organist to hear all the divisions of the Organ perfectly and to command a good view of the church on both sides of the screen. Although he cannot hear the choir so clearly as could be wished, his position is as good as could be arranged on a lofty choir-screen. The tonal effect of the Organ is satisfactory, heard either from the choir or from the nave. The bellows-chamber is placed in the cloisters, at a considerable distance from the Organ. It is constructed below the level of the ground, and receives its air for the feeders from the neighborhood of the Organ, through the brick shaft in which is carried the iron wind-trunks for the supply of the instrument.

Speaking of the divided Organ in St. Paul's Cathedral, which is bracketed on the piers at the entrance to the choir, Mr. Somers Clarke makes the following pertinent remarks:* "St. Paul's Cathedral. This church has acoustic qualities which make it different from any other building in this country; but the position of the Organ, hanging in halves above the choir stalls, is such as would not be out of place in lofty churches of less magnitude than the Cathedral. Indeed, were there shallow recesses in which parts of the Organ could be placed, the scheme would be quite practicable.

"The organist sits on the north side, in the north half of the Organ, and about eighteen or twenty feet above the choir. I say, advisedly, *in* the Organ, for he is boxed in to an extraordinary degree, and, I think, a plumb-line dropped from the Great DIAPASONS overhead would almost fall behind him. From his place he hears the voices most perfectly. I should suppose that nothing could be better in this respect. He can hear the Swell and Choir Organs, which are on the south side of the church, very well, but the Great Organ is most imperfectly heard. The DIAPASONS, very much over-winded, as I venture to think, puff and whistle to the exclusion of all other sounds. The result is that, unwittingly, the voices are often completely drowned when the Great Organ is used, partly from the reason above given, but in part because there are not enough stops of a moderate power on the Great manual, which is forced up to fill the whole Cathedral, and has not wherewith to support the voices in *forte* passages.

"Supposing by a similar arrangement a divided and suspended Organ was placed in a lofty church, some fifty or sixty feet high, the Organ being fifteen or eighteen feet from the ground; would it be best to put the organist in the gallery with the Organ, or to place the console somewhere below? An Organ so placed would, in an ordinary church, serve the nave as well as it would the choir." We would answer the above question, by advising the console to be placed below, close to the choir stalls.

* "Further 'Notes' on the Organ: Suggested by Papers of Sir F. A. G. Ouseley and Mr. Audsley." By Somers Clarke, F. S. A. Proceedings of the Musical Association, London, 1889–90.

We may now glance at certain noteworthy examples of the divided Organ occupying lateral positions within the choir proper. In Salisbury Cathedral the sections stand under the second arches on the north and south of the choir, extending some distance into the lateral aisles. The front displayed pipes are bracketed out from the overhanging portions of the cases, and rise in advance of the arches. In Durham Cathedral the divided Organ occupies similar positions north and south of the choir. In both these buildings the organist, sitting on one side, commands both sections, the action being carried from one side to the other beneath the choir floor. The tonal effects of both these Organs are fairly satisfactory. In the Durham instrument, as in that of St. Paul's Cathedral, the DIAPASONS are voiced on wind of inordinate pressures, and, accordingly, refinement of tone is sacrificed for unmusical power. This dividing of the Organ, when its tonal forces are judiciously apportioned, is highly favorable for the accompaniment of antiphonal chanting. The importance of anything that can aid this mode of rendering the chants and services of the Church cannot well be overrated. As the Rev. Sir Frederick Gore Ouseley remarks: "It has always appeared to me that this answering of side to side, varied by the grand conjunction of the two semi-choruses in the full parts, constitute one of the greatest charms of a true English choral service. Moreover, it is a feature which we possess in common with the rest of Christendom—both in Roman Catholic countries and in those which belong to the Eastern Orthodox Communion, this antiphonal system universally prevails; and besides its present universality, it has the additional claim of extreme antiquity."

The conditions which are necessary for securing a satisfactory result in the case of a divided Organ are: First, that both its sections shall be so placed that their sounds will be perfectly unobstructed, and that their pipe-work will require no forcing or inordinate pressures of wind: Secondly, that the tonal forces shall be so apportioned in the two sections, that each section will become a properly balanced accompanimental instrument, having a suitable portion of the Pedal Organ stops to furnish appropriate basses for the manual stops and combinations: and, Thirdly, that the console shall be so located, with respect to both the sections of the instrument and the vocal choir, that the organist will at all times be able to realize exactly the effect of his accompaniments.

An attempt has been made to meet such conditions as these in the Church of All Saints, Margaret Street, London. The Organ is divided, and placed against the north and south walls of the short lateral aisles of the chancel, each section having free space on its three exposed sides. Although the aisles and the arches toward the chancel and nave are not large, there is little obstruction to the free egress of sound. The console is placed in advance of the section of the Organ in the north aisle, the organist sitting so as to have a fair view of his choir and also a view of a considerable portion of the church. The Church of All Saints is small; and it is but right to point out that the arrangement mentioned has not the favorable conditions which would attend it in a larger church designed to properly accommodate it.

Leaving the subject of divided Organs, as presented by English treatments, we naturally come to the consideration of undivided Organs occupying lateral positions in, or immediately adjoining, the choir or chancel. Innumerable examples of undivided Organs so placed are to be found in English churches and a few are to be met with in cathedrals. For an undivided Organ used for the accompaniment of a choir, there appears to be no better position than a lateral one immediately adjoining the choir stalls, with the console placed on the floor and forming part of the stall-work. The lateral choir position seems to have been the one most favored in England when the Organ assumed fair proportions. Instances of Organs having occupied this position in old times have already been given. The Rev. Sir Frederick Gore Ouseley correctly says: "There does not appear to have been any deviation from this practice before the time of the Restoration, except in a few special and isolated instances. Nor is the case different in the case of ordinary Parish churches, save in that it was not unusual in the sixteenth century to have small portable Organs which could be moved from one place to another. Probably there is no authenticated instance in England of an Organ either on the rood-loft or at the west end of a church before the Reformation."

In the Cathedrals of Ely, Hereford, Llandaff, St. Asaph, and Bangor, the Organ occupies the old position on one side of the choir. The treatment at Ely is effective and we believe satisfactory. The Organ is boldly bracketed out over the choir stalls, in the third bay of the choir, on the north side, and extends upward through the height of the triforium. The case is of elaborate design, and the displayed pipes are richly decorated: the whole forming a handsome feature in the beautiful choir.

When the transepts are within, or immediately adjoining, the ritual choir, no better place can be found for a large undivided Organ, for there the instrument will find ample space, and can be kept free on all sides if desired. In the fine modern Church of St. Bartholomew, at Armley, Yorkshire, the magnificent Organ stands in the north transept which is within the boundary of the ritual choir: and in the Church of St. Margaret, at Anfield, Liverpool, where the ritual choir also extends to the western arch of the central tower, the Organ stands in the north transept. In both these noteworthy modern churches, the Organs occupy favorable positions on the north side of their choirs, and immediately opposite the stalls. In the former instance, the Organ rises from an elevated gallery, in which the organist is seated; while in the latter instance, the Organ rises from the level of the choir floor, and the organist is seated immediately behind the choir stalls. The Organ wind-chests and pipe-work are well elevated, the instrument being about thirty-five feet in height.

In Chester Cathedral the Organ also stands under the north arch of the tower, and, accordingly, in the north transept; but the organist is still less favorably placed than in St. Bartholomew's. He is not only elevated in an organ gallery, but is placed some distance westward of his choir, the space in front of the Organ being seated for the congregation. Here we have an instance where in the placing of a large Organ there was practically no choice. Before the recent restoration of the Cathedral the old Organ occupied the central position on the choir-screen; but at the restoration the massive screen was removed, and a light, open screen of oak erected across the eastern arch of the tower. Generally speaking, the desire in recent times has been to open the choir as much as possible to the nave in those cathedrals which have undergone restoration; and, accordingly, few now have the Organ standing on the choir-screen, practically blocking up the choir arch, as already mentioned. In Chester Cathedral a small Choir Organ is placed over the central entrance to the choir, played from the claviers of the transept Organ.

We have hitherto been devoting attention to the several positions of the Organ in cathedrals and large churches; and it is now desirable to approach the problems presented by churches of much smaller dimensions, designed on simpler plans. It is just in such churches that the true difficulty of finding adequate accommodation, and a favorable position, for the modern Church Organ, in its usual overgrown condition, is met with. This difficulty does not generally lie in any uncertainty respecting the proper position for the Organ in an Anglo-Catholic church; but in finding the necessary accommodation for it in that position. This difficulty is in almost all cases caused either by the want of knowledge on the part of the architect of the church, or by the desire to place an Organ of unnecessary size in the building.

With regard to the proper position for the Organ, it may be safely said that where the singers are there the Organ must be also. All musical authorities will agree on this subject. The following apt remarks by Mr. Somers Clarke fall in line here: "What is a church built for? This I will try to answer, hoping that others will agree with me. It is built as a place in which divine worship is to be celebrated, and worship it must be remembered is not the same as prayer. A magnificent musical service, in a magnificent place, is the highest exemplification we can give of divine worship; and not only the clergy, but the people are interested in it, and assist in some way or other. . . . In arranging a church the ability to render magnificent worship should not therefore be impeded.

"There was a time when Organs and singers had migrated to the west end. When the body and often the galleries of the church were full of square pews, it really did not matter where the singers were situated, they were sure to have some one looking at them in their pride of place, as people faced all ways. We can recall the gallery, with its brown front made as it seemed of gingerbread, and covered with shiny treacle, a pallid clock-face in the middle, and over it a nice cosy red curtain to hide the organist, being a modest man. The select company of singers, not equally modest, did not require red curtains. The Organ rose behind, flanked by tiers of charity children. Magnificent worship was not got in this way. We seem to have agreed, notwithstanding many divisions of opinion on religious matters, that this was not nice; and on looking back it was found that it states in the prayer book: 'And the chancels shall remain as they have done in times past.' I cannot go into the whole question now, it is one of history; but I think you will find that in the 'times past' the chancel was the place where the music was rendered, and if not intended for the purposes for which we once more use it, it is difficult to understand why this part of the church was planned as it was. The more the subject is considered the more clear does it seem to me that historical continuity fixes us to the chancel.

"But let us now conceive ourselves to be members of the congregation. If we are to admit the propriety of ornate worship, why is not the eye as well as the ear to be studied? The very fact that we now aim—as did our forefathers—at building a dignified type of church, and also at decorating it very considerably, shows that the old prejudices are dying out, and that people do not now think well to have splendid drawing-rooms but bare churches. And, happily, ornament in a church is no longer considered a party badge. I contend that—at least to me as a member of the congregation with, as I hope, artistic instincts—a fairly large chancel, the choristers in it, and the music they perform therein, are all more dignified and impressive because the whole scene is before me, and there is complete unity in it. Break this up and you lose a great deal. I must not dwell longer on this side of the question; but I have said enough to show why, as I contend, the chancel is the right place for the choristers, and will, in ninety-nine cases out of a hundred, continue to be used as such. If the choristers are in the chancel the Organ must be near them. Sir Frederick A. G. Ouseley says, speaking of Organs in the west gallery: 'and indeed it *must* be there if the singers sit in the west gallery.' He evidently thought that the two must be together, and his statement applies as well to the chancel as it does to the west gallery."

It is only necessary for us to add that we are in perfect accord with the views above expressed: and we may presume that very few, who possess any knowledge of, and love for, a true Anglican choral service, will question the propriety of placing the vocal choir in the ritual choir or chancel, and locating the Organ in the most favorable position to properly accompany and support the voices. By such a consistent arrangement alone can the choral services of the Anglo-Catholic Church be devoutly and artistically rendered, to the edification of all who hear and join in them.

As the plans of churches vary considerably both in disposition of parts and in dimensions, it is, of course, impossible to give hard and fast rules or instructions respecting the location or accommodation for the Organ in or adjoining the ritual choir or chancel. In churches already built, the provisions made by their architects practically settle the question of location in almost every case; and we are compelled to say that, owing to the very general ignorance of the architectural profession on all matters pertaining to the Organ, very inadequate provisions are made and very unsuitable places are provided for the reception of the Organ in the great majority of modern churches.

It is only just to remark, however, that architects are sometimes blamed without valid reason; for when they have succeeded in providing ample accommodation and a proper position for Organs of sufficient size for their churches, they are condemned by those wiseacres who have been induced to order instruments out of all proportion to the places they occupy. Cramping, crowding, and a host of other evils attend such unreasonable proceedings; and the architects get blamed for faults they have not committed. It is, however, highly desirable that architects should study the Organ sufficiently to enable them to plan proper accommodation for the instruments to be placed in their churches. Even a rudimentary knowledge of the nature and construction of the Organ would go far to prevent mistakes being made. Why architects should give the Organ so little attention is a matter of surprise to all interested in church building, for it certainly is a most important piece of church furniture. It is quite as necessary that the Organ as that the altar or pulpit should be properly placed. Apart from this, it may, and indeed should, be made a most beautiful and effective feature in a church interior. All who neglect the Organ err seriously both on utilitarian and artistic grounds.

"The Organ can go anywhere; any sort of a place will do for the Organ!" are ideas which have been only too rife among church builders, and only too often acted upon when the slightest difficulty with regard to space has arisen, or when peculiarities of site have called for special ingenuity and care. We firmly believe some church architects have looked upon Organs as necessary evils—things with which they have nothing to do, except it be to take care that they are made as little of as possible, and kept well out of sight; unfortunately this may mean out of hearing also. As a rule, an Organ to be well *heard* must be well *seen*—every obstruction to sight will likewise be an obstruction to sound.

In churches built on a cruciform plan, and in which the ritual choir extends to the western arch of the tower or crossing, as in the Churches of St. Bartholomew, Armley, and St. Margaret, Anfield, already mentioned, there is no difficulty in placing, and finding accommodation for, the Organ in one or other of the transepts; but in churches in which there are no transepts, special provision must be made for the accommodation of the Organ, either in a choir or chancel aisle, or in a chamber opening on the choir or chancel. When there are spacious and lofty aisles, the Organ can be divided and placed in them, as in the Church of All Saints, Margaret Street, London; or it can be undivided and located in one of them; the console, in both cases, being placed close to, or forming part of, the choir stalls, and in such a position that the organist can perfectly realize the effect of his accompaniments and hear his choir distinctly. The position of the console is hardly secondary to the position of the Organ. What Mr. Somers Clarke has said on this subject is so apt that we give his words in preference to words of our own. He says:

"We all know that the Organ must have plenty of space about it, height above it, and must not in itself be crowded; but there are other points on which the opinion of experts would be of great value.

"One of these is the position of the keyboard with regard to the Organ and the choir. Custom, ruled to a great extent by expense, makes it usual to place the Organ on one side of the chancel and the organist close to the Organ. The organist cannot hear his choir very clearly. The half of the choir nearest to him sings away from him, the other half that sings toward him has the first-mentioned half intervening. He is generally so near the Organ that he cannot clearly hear how much or little noise he is making (and my experience is that to be on the safe side he generally makes too much); and lastly, having the Organ and voices so close at hand, he knows but little what the congregation is about.

"As far as the choir is concerned the rules of ample space, height, and width are as essential for the welfare of voices as of the Organ.

"What then would be the conditions of an ideal position for the organist?

"1. That he should hear his choir well.
2. That he should hear the Organ well.
3. That he should be able to see the choir well and also see the clergy who may be serving at the altar.
4. That he may hear the congregation at least fairly well.
5. That he shall have a tolerable sight of the nave of the church and thus be able to keep his eye on processions or other functions taking place therein.
6. We might add, that he should be able to use the Organ in connection with a side chapel."

The writer adds: "Where all these combinations are to be found I do not know. In a parish church of good size they would be difficult of accomplishment. They are not often approached in a church of the first magnitude."

It is absolutely impossible to give a rule of universal application for the position of the console, simply because the size, form, and internal arrangement of churches vary greatly; but the conditions just given will serve as guides, and are deserving of very careful consideration by architects and musical authorities, in the planning of new churches or the rearrangement of old ones.

When a church has neither transepts, opening on the ritual choir, nor choir or chancel aisles, it is obvious that the Organ, if it is to occupy a position adjoining the choir stalls, must either be erected in the chancel itself or in a chamber, constructed for its reception, open to the chancel and, in all possible cases, to the body of the church also, so that there will be the minimum obstruction to the passage of sound.

Owing to the ignorance or thoughtlessness of church architects in matters pertaining to the Organ, the very name *organ-chamber* has become an abomination to organ builders and all interested in church music. Mistakes have been made without number where there were no difficulties to encounter, and where properly proportioned and constructed organ-chambers could have been erected just as easily as insufficient ones. It is unnecessary to allude to existing examples of objectionable organ-chambers, "their name is legion"; for to do so would be practically to name the architects who are responsible for such thoughtless and imperfect work. Professional etiquette certainly forbids such a course. If the following conditions are observed in the planning and construction of the organ-chamber no serious objections can be advanced against its introduction; provided, however, the common mistake of having an Organ of too large dimensions is not made.

First, sufficient floor space must be provided to allow the Organ to stand without the slightest crowding of its parts, and with sufficient space behind and at the sides to give free egress to sound and easy access to all parts.

Secondly, ample height must be given for the Organ to stand at the most favorable elevation, and yet leave considerable space above everything for the free emission of the sound from all the divisions of its pipe-work.

Thirdly, two arches or openings of the largest possible dimensions should be provided; the one toward the choir or chancel being carried up to the full height of the ceiling of the chamber so that no sound may be locked in above the Organ. Whatever shape the arch or upper part of this main opening may be, it is desirable that the ceiling of the chamber should follow it closely, and, if possible, at the same level. The second opening, toward the body of the church, should also be as wide and lofty as circumstances will permit.

Fourthly, every precaution must be taken to prevent damp, and to secure an equable temperature within the chamber. The external walls should be built double, with an air cavity between. All the inclosing walls and the ceiling should be lined with narrow grooved and tongued pine boards, tightly jointed, securely nailed, and well varnished; or, they may be metal-lathed and well plastered, and subsequently oil painted and varnished.

When the architect has attended to all these important matters, it is incumbent on those who have the providing of the Organ to see that an instrument of proper size and arrangement is placed therein; and that its ornamental fronts or screens are not made so heavy and close as to check the free egress of the sound from the inclosed pipe-work. While it is true that the generality of organ-chambers are badly constructed affairs, and unsuitable for the reception of properly appointed Organs, it is equally true that when organ-chambers are of fair dimensions their efficiency is very frequently destroyed through having instruments of extravagant size literally crammed into them, until there is hardly room for a pipe to speak its proper note, or its sound to find its way into the church.

There is one other matter connected with a Church Organ occupying a chamber, on one side of the choir or chancel, provided with two arches, one toward the choir and the other toward the nave or nave aisle, which is deserving of notice. It is usual to dispose speaking pipes in both arches; and too frequently the stop or stops selected for the nave arch are of a loud and very assertive character. This arrangement may not seem objectionable to the organist and the other occupants of the choir stalls; but to the congregation seated in the neighborhood of the nave arch, the effect produced when the exposed pipes are speaking is most unpleasant, annihilating all the more delicate sounds of the instrument. To correct this, to as great an extent as possible, the softest and sweetest-toned pipes available should form the displayed ranks in the nave arch.

There is no fixed rule in ecclesiastical architecture for the position of the organ-chamber; but the northern side of the choir or chancel is usually preferred; and, indeed, it is to be recommended on account of the constant shade on that side of the church, which goes far to secure equality of temperature. When the chamber is on the southern side it is subjected to the direct rays of the sun during the hottest hours of the day, and, accordingly, is liable to become heated to a considerable degree. When, however, the chamber is properly constructed with thick and cavitied walls, lined with wood, and has no windows, and is covered with a wooden ceiling, kept some distance below the external roof, there is little objection to a southern aspect.

As the Organ is an instrument exceedingly sensitive to changes of temperature, every means should be adopted to prevent the external atmosphere from having direct action on its pipe-work. Windows in the walls directly adjoining the sound-producing portions of the instrument are to be avoided, because they create local currents of cold air in winter and warm air in summer, which throw the pipe-work out of tune. Should the architect, probably for external appearance, have inserted windows in undesirable positions, they should either be boarded over in the inside, or furnished with an inner screen of glass. But when there is a space of a few feet between the Organ and the windows no precautions, as above mentioned, are necessary. It is advisable to construct organ-chambers, especially when small, without windows.

There is one class of chamber, occasionally used for the Organ, which we condemn in an unqualified manner; we allude to that formed in the lower part of a tower occupying a position adjoining the chancel. The chamber in this case is not only usually small in internal dimensions, so far as floor space is concerned, but has the serious disadvantages of thick walls, massive piers, and narrow arches. The chamber may be lofty, but that only makes matters worse when the arch or arches are so contracted and dwarfed as to lock in the sound, which finds its way upward and there becomes confused and practically lost.

In designing a church which is to have a spacious chancel, the architect may well consider the advisability of providing for the Organ therein by constructing a chamber in the form of a shallow but sufficiently wide and lofty quasi-transept. Such an addition to the chancel can be made a beautiful architectural feature with its lofty arch rising to the roof. The Organ bracketed out overhead and artistically treated throughout, will add another element of richness and beauty. If this quasi-transept is properly designed and proportioned, and a suitable Organ is placed therein, there need only be the single arch toward the chancel. It is perhaps unnecessary to remark that two quasi-transepts may be introduced, opposite each other, for the reception of a divided organ.

Wherever the Organ is placed in a church, it is desirable, if not imperative, to have its main bellows and blowing apparatus or machinery located in a chamber so situated as to prevent any noise from them reaching the ears of persons in the church; care being taken to supply air to the bellows-chamber directly from the church, or at the same temperature as that in the church. This is a matter of great importance, for it will be impossible to keep an Organ in tune or in good condition if it is supplied with cold and damp air while it stands in a warm and dry church, and *vice versa*. When air from the neighborhood of the Organ is conveyed to the feeders and main receivers by a special tube, the feeders and receivers should be inclosed in a large box, or a tight casing of wood, into which the tube will deliver the air. Under no circumstances should air directly from the exterior of the building be admitted through doors, windows, or other openings, to the feeders. When a gas-engine is used for blowing purposes, every precaution must be taken to protect the feeders from the fumes which issue from it. Unless this is effectually done great injury will accrue to the Organ, and especially to its delicate reed stops. Unless it is compulsory, a gas-engine should never be used in connection with the Organ. Water-motors are of all blowing machinery the safest and most satisfactory; and next to them electric motors. In cases where manual blowing, or a silent water-motor, is to be used, the bellows-chamber may, except in very damp situations, be located immediately under the floor of the organ-chamber; and the main receiver may be placed above in the Organ itself. Under these circumstances, the necessary reservoirs for the winds of different pressures need only be small.

We have dwelt, to some length, on matters connected with the form and construction of the organ-chamber and its attendant bellows-chamber, for they are of great importance, and should be thoroughly understood by the architect who professes to be able to build a properly appointed church. All organ-chambers should be constructed on the same general principles, whether they form parts of churches, concert-rooms, or private music-rooms; that is, provided the conditions as to exposed walls and roofs are similar to those contemplated in our preceding remarks.

On the placing of Organs in situations outside the boundaries of the choir or chancel, and at different distances therefrom, little need be said. There can, however, be no question that as a musical instrument pure and simple, the Organ, as placed in certain English churches of late date, in Dissenting chapels in England, in auditoriums in the United States, and in numerous churches in Holland, Germany, and Switzerland, gains greatly in general tonal effect. When the Organ is looked at from this acoustical point of view, there can be no question that an elevated position at one end or the other of the building is highly favorable: and accomplished organists, who are prone to look upon churches, chapels, and auditoriums as places for containing Organs, and for accommodating large audiences to listen to their performances, will naturally favor an open and commanding end position, preferably one facing the congregation. A very noteworthy example of an Organ occupying the latter position is met with in Trinity Methodist Episcopal Church, at Denver, Colorado. At the end of this building, and facing the auditorium proper, is a recess measuring about 46 feet in width, 16 feet in depth, and 37 feet in height. This recess is defined, toward the auditorium, by an ornamental frame resembling the proscenium-arch of a theatre; and both walls and ceiling are flush with its inner edge, so as to present no obstruction to the egress of sound. The ceiling is coved at sides and back. Within this well-constructed recess or chamber is disposed the fine Organ, built by the late Frank Roosevelt, of New York, admirably planned, and with its screen of ornamental woodwork and metal and wood displayed pipes extending from side to side. The console is elevated 4 feet 6 inches above the auditorium floor level; and arranged, in tiers, on each side of it are about fifty chairs, providing accommodation for a chorus of about one hundred singers. The Great and Choir Organ wind-chests are elevated 12 feet 6 inches above the auditorium floor, whilst those of the Swell and Solo Organs are elevated 22 feet 9 inches. The main wind-chests of the Pedal Organ are at about the level of the manual claviers; and those on which the stops of

32 feet are planted rest upon the floor. Directly underneath the floor of the recess is the bellows-room, and underneath it again is the motor-room. Surely in this building is an Organ and a commanding position calculated to rejoice the most ambitious organist's heart. The only regret he can have is that there is no detached and reversed console.

The treatment just described has, on a much smaller scale and with certain modifications, been adopted in some Scotch churches and English Dissenting chapels; and there can be no doubt it is generally more successful, from a musical point of view, than any west-end treatment could be made; for in the latter position the sound reaches the ears of the congregation from behind, and the effect is not agreeable. It must be remembered that wherever the Organ is, there the choir or singers should be also.

Whatever argument on purely acoustical grounds may be advanced by the advocates of the west-end position, the fact remains that it is the worst position for the listeners who are not prepared to sit on the book-boards of the pews with their backs to the altar or pulpit. Who would enjoy, or think of listening to, an orchestral concert or an organ recital, in a concert-room, with his back turned toward the sources of sound?

Some musical authorities have suggested the east-end position, behind the altar, for the Organ in an Anglo-Catholic church; but such a situation could only be adopted under very special and unusual conditions of plan and architectural treatment, not likely to be found in existing churches. One example, however, is furnished by Handel's Organ, at Whitechurch. We cannot advance any sufficient argument in favor of this position either in ancient or modern Anglo-Catholic churches, and we feel convinced that no argument, however good it might be, would lead to its adoption. In a Roman Catholic church, such as the Madeleine, at Paris, in which there is a space eastward of, or behind, the high altar, occupied by the choir, the east-end position is perfectly proper for the Accompanimental Organ.

Having touched, probably at sufficient length, on the several positions of the Organ in churches, we may conclude this branch of our subject with a few remarks on the question of elevation.

The idea that, for a satisfactory acoustical result, the Organ should be placed at a considerable elevation is held by a large number of persons more or less expert in organ matters; but it is surely obvious that no rule for general adoption can be laid down or accepted in this direction. The dimensions, and especially the height, of the church will exercise an almost controlling influence in the question of elevation; while the acoustical peculiarities of the building will also demand consideration. In every Organ of proper construction, properly placed, the chief sound-producing divisions, excepting the pipe-work of the Pedal Organ, will be found at a level, or levels, considerably above that of the ears of the choir and congregation. Such being the case, it is questionable if much can be gained by increasing its elevation. It must be borne in mind that if the Organ is elevated a considerable distance above the floor of the church, to secure perfect unity of effect, the singers should be elevated along with it. Although it may not be so difficult or unpleasant to sing to the accompaniment of an Organ placed high and directly overhead, as it is to sing to that of an Organ at a distance in a horizontal direction, it cannot be said to be entirely satisfactory from any musical point of view. When the church is very lofty and is favorable acoustically, the elevation of the Organ, within reasonable limits, will in all probability be attended with good results: and, further, if the instrument is to be used for incidental music, and not for the ordinary accompaniment of the choral service, its elevation, as well as its position generally, may be decided by controlling architectural conditions or observed acoustical effects. There will be in this case another instrument provided for accompanimental purposes, situated in immediate proximity to the choir, as in the important French churches.

We may here enlarge on a matter already mentioned. In cathedrals and very large churches which, on account of their great internal height and immense cubical contents, are never subject to great or rapid changes of temperature, the elevation of the Organ is a matter of little importance so far as the welfare of the instrument itself is concerned; but in churches, chapels, and auditoriums, of moderate dimensions, that are lighted by gas and filled to their utmost capacity by their congregations, the elevation of the Organ is usually attended by serious drawbacks. When portions of the pipe-work are so high as to be in a superheated stratum of the air within the building, whilst the remaining portions are lower and, accordingly, in a much cooler stratum, it is impossible to have the entire instrument in tune or in a fit condition to be used throughout for accompaniment. In such buildings every endeavor should be made to keep all the divisions of the Organ in the lower and cooler stratum of the air, and as nearly as practicable on one level.

There are some persons who hold the opinion that an Organ may, with advantage to its tone, be partly or entirely placed below the level of the floor of the church. One instance of an eminent organ builder holding this opinion may be cited. During the Discussion which followed the reading of a Paper before the Royal College of Organists,* Mr. T. C. Lewis is reported to have said: "I have thought for years that placing an Organ below the level of the church would answer, as the tone of both flue and reed pipes is finer when heard from above; but I could not see my way, though, to the proper ventilation of an organ-chamber much below the surface." He subsequently added: "Decidedly the upper part of a pipe sounded the best." The former opinion held by Mr. Lewis does not seem to have been founded on personal experience. It was, in all probability, suggested by the practice which obtains in certain theatres of locating the orchestra under the level of the floor and out of sight: one noteworthy example being the Wagner Opera House, at Bayreuth. No fair comparison can, however, be instituted between an orchestra so placed, with ample and unobstructed space for the emission of sound, and a buried Organ, crowded and confined as it would necessarily have to be. Mr. Lewis supported his first opinion

* "The Organ, its Position and Treatment." Paper by Mr. Somers Clarke, read before the Royal College of Organists on June 17, 1879.

by a second one, the accuracy of which we beg to question. He stated that "decidedly the upper part of a pipe sounded best:" now, so far as reed pipes are concerned of course he was correct, for all their sounds issue from the tops or open ends of their resonant tubes; but with reference to labial ("flue") pipes he was decidedly in error. In the case of all classes of stopped or covered pipes, of course not a sound of any kind can possibly issue from their upper or closed parts; their tones are produced at their mouths only. In the case of open labial pipes a similar state of affairs exists; their tones are also generated at their mouths, and no sounds of any value issue from their open ends. As labial pipes form the more important portion of the tonal structure of every Organ, and especially of a Church Organ, it is evident that to bury them would be fatal to musical effect. If it is true that the Organ gains by being placed at a moderate elevation, with free space around it, it must be realized that it would suffer little short of total annihilation by being placed in a chamber sunk below the level of the church floor. The few advocates for this sunken position do not tell us where the organist is to be placed; how the expressive divisions of the Organ are to be treated; how damp and dust are to be prevented; and how numerous other difficulties are to be overcome. The practical man must attend to every question, and provide for every contingency affecting the Organ. We need not follow this matter any farther, for there is no likelihood of the sunken position ever being adopted in churches of any class. Here we may leave the general subject of the Position of the Organ in Churches.

THE POSITION OF THE ORGAN IN CONCERT-ROOMS.

The position of the Organ in properly planned and constructed concert-rooms does not admit of much variation: the most correct and effective situation is at one end of the longer axis of the room, and behind and slightly above the seats for the orchestra and chorus.

It is of the greatest importance that in designing a concert-room the architect should carefully consider the requirements of the Organ which is to be placed therein; and all details of size and disposition of parts should be discussed with the organ builder before the building is proceeded with. We have seen, with respect to the Church Organ, that there are several conditions which attend the satisfactory placing of an Organ in a church; and conditions of a similar nature obtain in connection with the correct location of an Organ in a concert-room. There is certainly less diversity of opinion anent the proper position for the Concert-room Organ; and less difficulty, under ordinary circumstances, of properly providing for its accommodation; accordingly there is little or no excuse for the architect when he fails to make adequate provision for its reception. Great blunders have been made by architects in the past; and unless they take more interest in the Organ and its proper accommodation than they appear to do at present, more mistakes will be made in the future. The concert-room in the Hall of the Liverpool Philharmonic Society is allowed to be, acoustically and architecturally, one of the finest in the world; yet the provision made for its Organ is simply ridiculous. The instrument has had to be crammed into a narrow, low and deep chamber, from which the muffled sounds from the buried pipe-work can only reach the room through the narrow chinks between the front pipes, which, along with the clumsy case-work, literally fill up the only opening of the chamber. The tonal effect may be described as that of a "bee in a bottle." In the fine concert-room in the Town Hall of Manchester, a building on which no expense was spared, the provision for the Organ is so inadequate that M. Cavaillé-Coll, in constructing the instrument, found it impossible to locate a sufficient Pedal Organ, and had to resort to a wholesale system of borrowing to secure any satisfactory musical effect in this department. Here, again, the architect did not pay proper attention to, or understand, the requirements of an important Organ.

In the Albert Hall, at Sheffield, the provision for the Organ is highly satisfactory, admitting the erection of an admirably disposed instrument of sixty-four speaking stops, including a 32-ft. Pedal Organ of twelve stops. The Organ is partly in a recess, which measures about 38 feet in width by 11 feet in depth, and which is carried up to the highest portion of the ceiling of the hall. The Organ is advanced into the hall, having a total depth of about 18 feet. The claviers are in an advanced and reversed console, placed on the level of the highest seats of the chorus. While this position is convenient for the pneumatic lever action of the Organ, it is certainly not the most desirable one.

The Concert Organs in the Royal Albert Hall, London; St. George's Hall, Liverpool; the Town Hall, Leeds; the Public Halls, Glasgow; and the Salle des Fêtes, Palais du Trocadéro, Paris, are all placed in practically exposed positions in which free egress of sound is secured. The Organ in the Centennial Hall, Sydney, N. S. W., is well placed in all save the location of its claviers. It occupies a space at the end of the hall, 85 feet wide, with an average depth of about 24 feet, and a height, from the platform to the highest point of its elliptical arch, of 46 feet 6 inches. The back wall and ceiling of the recess are elliptical—a form favorable for the reflection of sound. Next to an entirely exposed position, this is about the best treatment that could be devised; and it reflects great credit on the architect intrusted with the work.

The Organ in the Music Hall, Cincinnati, Ohio, originally occupied a highly favorable position, as may be seen from the following extract from the brochure describing the Organ, published in 1878: "It is seldom that the builder has the opportunity to place the Organ in a proper position. He is necessarily restricted in space, and is obliged inconveniently to crowd the mechanism [and the pipework] so as to confuse and obstruct the tone. A great Organ should be placed, as is an orchestra, with greater width than depth. The builders of the Cincinnati Organ were offered all the space they required, and they gladly took advantage of the opportunity to give every part of it all the room it needed." The dimensions of the concert-room and its Organ may be interesting to some of our readers. The room is 192 feet long, 112 feet wide, and 70 feet high. It is seated for four thousand, four hundred and twenty-eight persons. The Organ is 50 feet wide, 30 feet deep, and rises to the height of 60 feet. All who had a voice in the placing of the Organ in accordance with the above particulars deserve all honor for their just appreciation of the importance and requirements of so large an instrument. It is indeed seldom that an organ builder is offered all the space he requires. We regret to say that such an evidence of appreciation, on the one hand, and sound common sense, on the other, is extremely rare. It is most certainly not shown in the placing of the most important Concert-room Organ in the United States. Perhaps in no instance in the world to-day is there so serious a blunder as that evidenced in the placing of the immense Organ in the Auditorium, at Chicago. We comment at some length on this subject in our remarks appended to the Specification of this Organ; so need only add that to pack so large an instrument, out of sight, in a narrow and deep lateral chamber, and then block up the only opening with an obstructive and extremely ugly perforated screen, displays an ignorance respecting organ matters only equalled by the absence of the artistic sense shown in the surroundings. We find a similar mistake made in placing the Organ in a confined lateral chamber in the Concert-room of Carnegie Hall, New York. The Concert Organ in the Symphony Hall, Boston, Mass., is somewhat more favorably located. It occupies a recess or chamber extending entirely across the rear of the stage. This is about 50 feet wide and 12 feet deep. The lower portion of the screen is closed; and above it extends a monotonous range of pipes of one length. The whole commonplace composition is surmounted by a perforated cove which aids the egress of sound, which otherwise has to find its way, as best it can, between the closely planted front pipes.

We unhesitatingly say that nothing in the form of a confined chamber should ever be constructed for a Concert-room Organ, or, indeed, for any sound-producing part thereof. As the instrument is required for solo performances or recitals, and alone, or in conjunction with the orchestra, for the accompaniment of the more important choral works, its voice should be perfectly free, and every tonal effect and *nuance* it is capable of producing should be heard with distinctness and at its true value. Another most important fact must not be overlooked; namely, when the Organ is correctly placed, with free space around it, or on three sides of it, there will be no necessity to strain its voice by the use of inordinate pressures of wind, or undesirable scales in its pipe-work.

As has already been said, the proper position for the Organ is above and in the rear of the orchestra tiers or seats; but there it should not be unduly elevated, so as to place any of the more delicate portions of its pipe-work in the higher stratum of super-heated air. Of course the upper ends of the larger pipes of the 32-ft. and 16-ft. stops may have to rise to that stratum, but they will not be seriously affected. The correct method is to keep all the manual divisions of the instrument on one level, and that as low as practicable under controlling circumstances, and to spread the instrument laterally, with a view of giving all divisions a minimum depth. Beyond the external screen, with its mounted or displayed pipes, the several divisions should have no obstruction to the free flow of sound in front of them. The displayed pipes should in all cases be speaking ones; and the Open Diapasons of 16-ft. and 8-ft., and the softer-toned stops of the Pedal Organ, should certainly find salient positions, so as to assert themselves without loss of grandeur and purity of tone. Under such favorable circumstances an instrument of moderate dimensions will prove more effective and useful than a large Organ placed in a chamber or other confined situation. Of this there can be no question.

There is just one matter in connection with the Swell division of the Concert-room Organ, that is when there is only one inclosed division, which calls for attention here. A prevailing opinion obtains at the present time that a swell-box cannot be made too thick or impervious to sound; and this opinion has resulted in the conviction that the pipe-work of the Swell Organ may, with great advantage, be located in a chamber specially built to receive it, and which from its solid structure and peculiar position will prevent any sound reaching the concert-room save through the front, fitted with the usual system of shutters. It will be seen, in our remarks on the construction of the swell-box, that we dispute the necessity or the advantage of having it either very thick or to any extreme degree impervious to sound; and such being the case, it is unnecessary to add that we cannot approve of the adoption of the kind of swell-chamber just alluded to. Certainly no satisfactory musical result can attend its adoption.

Should, however, any special peculiarity of the plan of the concert-room, or the necessity to gain every foot of space for the accommodation of the Organ, favor the adoption of a swell-chamber, it would be advisable to construct it of the largest possible internal dimensions to allow of the introduction therein of a properly constructed, independent, swell-box, having a foot or two of free space all round its inclosed sides. Such a treatment would greatly improve the sonorousness and general musical character of the Swell Organ. The chamber should in all cases be smoothly plastered, oil painted, and varnished.

In connection with a properly planned concert-room there will be no difficulty in providing a convenient bellows-room underneath the Organ. This may either be formed in the space created by the raised orchestra and chorus seats, or, still lower, in the basement of the building. In either case, care must be taken to supply the feeders or wind-collecting apparatus with air drawn from the immediate neighborhood of the Organ, as recommended in the case of the Church Organ.

In providing for the reception of the Organ, the architect must construct an absolutely rigid foundation for all its parts. Under no circumstances should the supports be entirely of wood, or be in any way connected with the structural work of the orchestra or chorus seats. Brick piers or iron columns, rising from a solid foundation, and carrying steel beams, can alone be depended on as sufficient supports. Upon these, strong joists and a boarding (double) of about 3 inches thick should be laid to form the floor for the Organ.

Finally, with respect to the position of the claviers. We have no hesitation in saying that, with the exception of two or three electro-pneumatic instruments, not one of the great Concert-room Organs hitherto constructed has its claviers placed where they ought to be, or, in the more important instruments, in what may be considered a moderately favorable situation for the performer. Perched high above, and far away from the orchestra, and usually, on important occasions, with a hundred or more of voices between him and it, and probably half buried in a recess in the front of the Organ, with his back toward everything save the claviers, how is it possible for the organist to do his duty satisfactorily or with comfort to himself? When the ordinary tracker and pneumatic lever action was the best at the disposal of the organ builder, he was almost compelled to adopt the closest and most direct position for the claviers and their accessories: and then he assured the organist that everything possible had been done for his comfort; and that he must needs be content with his isolated perch, and to play with his back to the conductor, orchestra, chorus, and audience. We need not enlarge upon the inconvenience of all this. This imperfect arrangement is to be found in the monster Organ in the Town Hall, Sydney, New South Wales; and in the Organs of the Royal Albert Hall, London, the Philharmonic Hall and St. George's Hall, Liverpool, and the Music Hall, Cincinnati. In the Public Halls, Glasgow, and the Town Hall, Leeds, the Organs have their claviers somewhat better placed; being slightly in advance of the bodies of their respective instruments, but not reversed or detached. The Organs in the Albert Hall, Sheffield, the Town Hall, Manchester, and the Palais du Trocadéro, Paris, all constructed by Cavaillé-Coll, have their claviers placed in consoles, reversed, and detached from the main portions of the cases. This arrangement is a decided step in the right direction; but it does not go far enough to meet all requirements. The action used in these instruments is the ordinary tracker and pneumatic lever, and, probably, the builder did not feel himself at liberty to make a greater departure from the old-fashioned way of placing the claviers. Now, however, when the tubular-pneumatic and electro-pneumatic actions are available, it is to be hoped that the proper position of the console, and accordingly of the organist, will be recognized and adopted.

The correct position is immediately adjoining the platform on which the conductor stands; and here it should be reversed so as to place the organist facing the conductor, and within speaking distance. When permanently fixed, the console should be partly sunk below the level of the orchestra platform, so as to prevent its being an undesirable obstruction, and so as to allow a grand pianoforte to stand over it when necessary, and when the Organ is not used. When the electro-pneumatic action is adopted, the console may be made to rise and fall in its appointed place, carrying the organist's seat along with it. By this arrangement, the console may disappear entirely and be covered over when the Organ is not required, and a uniformly flat platform is necessary; it may be raised the desired height when required with the orchestra; and it may be elevated entirely above the platform for organ recitals. Under such favorable conditions, either in solo or accompanimental music, the organist has an opportunity of realizing the effects he is producing; and he is directly under the control of the conductor when choral works are being rendered with or without the aid of an orchestra.

The electro-pneumatic action also permits a portable console to be used, which can be placed, at will, in any position on the orchestra platform: the electric cable, in this case, must be carefully protected from damage. Movable consoles are provided for the Organs in the Auditorium, Chicago, the Symphony Hall, Boston, and the McEwan Hall, Edinburgh.

On the position of the Organ in small concert-rooms, in which there are no set arrangements for an orchestra, little need be said, for it will present little or no difficulty. The Organ, under all ordinary circumstances, should be elevated on a platform at one end of the room; and the console should be reversed and placed well in advance of the body of the instrument. The adoption of a reliable tubular-pneumatic action will meet all the demands in this case. The less reliable electro-pneumatic action should not be used when it can be avoided, for the action is, under ordinary conditions, uncertain, and after some time extremely treacherous.

THE POSITION OF THE ORGAN IN DWELLING-HOUSES.

While we may be able to give some hints, more or less worthy of consideration, respecting the placing of Chamber Organs in dwelling-houses, it must be acknowledged that it is impossible to lay down rules of universal application in the matter.

There are certain considerations connected with the Chamber Organ which materially affect the question of its locality and disposition. A Chamber Organ may be specially designed for any one of three purposes. First, simply as an instrument for home practice or tuition. Secondly, as an instrument of a more ambitious character, to be used for the rendition of organ music pure and simple, and without any reference to other instruments. Thirdly, as an Organ which, while it combines all the advantages to be claimed in the preceding classes, is more especially designed for accompanimental and concerted music, in conjunction with the Pianoforte, Violin, Violoncello, and other chamber instruments. The first type of Chamber Organ is certainly the least interesting; while the last may be accepted as the most interesting and desirable. This third type comprises all the good and useful features of the others, while it goes far beyond them in everything that makes an Organ a perfect musical instrument. This is the type considered in our Chapter on The Chamber Organ.

Little need be said respecting the position best suited for the small instrument designed for ordinary practice or tuition; for in very rare instances will any difficulties present themselves in the matter of space required for its accommodation; nor will there be any exacting demands on the acoustic properties of the room in which it is placed. That it should be placed in a locality where it can be kept perfectly dry and at a uniform temperature goes without saying. Such an Organ may be constructed as an independent piece of furniture, inclosed on all sides with case-work and displayed pipes; and in such a form it will, in almost all ordinary rooms, stand against a wall: or it may be specially designed to fit into, or fill, some recess existing in the room. Such an Organ will probably never exceed nine speaking stops—four on each manual and one on the pedals—while in nine cases out of ten it will be of smaller dimensions.

As it is generally most convenient to tune the Swell of such a small Organ from the back, so as to prevent the objectionable practice of removing the front louvres and stretching over the pipes of the Great Organ, it is desirable, when it is treated as an independent piece of furniture, to set it on rollers or broad wheels, so as to admit of its being moved easily from the wall. If the Organ is very heavy, its wheels should run on flat iron bars: the lengths of these, under the case, on which the Organ rests when against the wall, should be permanently screwed down to the floor of the room; whilst the additional lengths required when the Organ is to be run forward should be made adjustable, having some simple arrangement for temporary fixture to the front ends of the permanent rails and to the floor. The same remarks apply to the small Organ placed in a recess but not built into it in any way.

The strength and rigidity of the floor on which the Organ is placed are matters which, in ordinary dwelling-houses, must be carefully tested; and means must be taken to give the floor whatever additional support it may require. If the floor is over a cellar or room of little consequence, a beam laid underneath the joists on which the Organ stands, and held up by a couple of props, is generally all that is necessary.

The second type of Chamber Organ is the one hitherto chiefly affected by organ builders. As it is commonly met with in important houses, it presents no special features or treatments which separate it from the ordinary small-sized Church Organ. Such being the case, coupled with the fact that this type of Chamber Organ is practically confined to the rendition of the simpler class of organ music, it is evident that it may be placed in several different positions in a house with equal propriety.

Some difficulty will always be experienced in placing anything approaching a satisfactory instrument in a small house with low ceilings; but little difficulty will present itself in a good-sized house with ceilings over twelve feet in height. In the case of building a house, in which an Organ is to be placed, decidedly the best course to adopt is to carefully plan one of the reception-rooms, or construct some convenient part of the central hall, when there is one, for the reception of the instrument. The best of all places is, of course, a properly constructed music-room; and next to this is a drawing-room, or large reception-room, which can, without interfering with its beauty or convenience, be readily arranged for the accommodation of an Organ. In many houses the drawing-room opens, by sliding doors or through a large arch, into an ante-room or lesser drawing-room, and when this arrangement obtains the Organ may appropriately find a place in the latter. In very large houses or mansions, the central or inner hall, if spacious, may have the Organ erected in it. Here the instrument may be made a very artistic and attractive feature; and in all probability its tones will prove most effective, especially if there is sufficient resonance without echo. Resonance, within reasonable limits, greatly enhances the charm of the organ tones, whilst echo seriously mars them. These facts should be duly considered in deciding the locality for the instrument.

In providing space for the accommodation of an Organ of considerable size in a properly constructed music-room, several methods may be followed. A large chamber may be built out from one end, into which the Organ can be placed, either in an independent case, free from the walls on all sides, or so constructed as to practically fill the space, with an ornamental front of light case-work and displayed pipes. When the chamber is shallow, the Organ may be extended into the room and made a very beautiful object. There cannot be said to be any objection to an organ-chamber in a domestic music-room, because if properly proportioned it has no further effect than that of slightly subduing the tone of the inclosed pipe-work. It must not be understood that, in saying this, we advocate any muffling of the tones of the pipes; indeed, nothing is further from our thoughts. It is too often the case, however, that large Chamber Organs are packed into deep and narrow chambers or small rooms, and so closed in with heavy ornamental case-work toward the music-room, that little more than musical hummings can be heard, lifeless, and expressionless. We have known several expensive Chamber Organs that answer this description.

The Organ must be made a living presence, so to speak, in a room, or it will, to all intents and purposes, be a most disheartening and disappointing instrument. We have met with large Chamber Organs so badly treated that it was impossible to obtain any satisfactory range of tonal effects from them: they always seemed to be evading the efforts of the player; to be always in another room, which, in truth, they were.

As a properly appointed Chamber Organ has, or should have, at least two swell-boxes, and very few stops outside them, it must be obvious that the instrument cannot be too fully exposed toward the music-room to be generally effective: indeed, every expedient should be adopted to bring all the uninclosed pipes as much as possible toward the front or exposed sides; while the swell-boxes should have as little obstruction in front of their shutters as ingenuity can devise.

Another treatment may be adopted when space is not very restricted, and when the room is specially planned for the reception of an Organ. Let a shallow chamber be formed, of the entire width of the room, and sufficiently deep to accommodate one of the swell-boxes, with a conveniently wide passage-board in front of it, and at either side portions of the Pedal Organ stops: and let a wide and high opening be left in the partition opposite this swell-box, through which the sound will enter the room. Other openings of an ornamental character can be formed in the partition, on each side of the large central opening, should there be any fear of the tones of the pipes within the chamber being muffled. Then in front of the central opening, and in advance of the back swell-box and passage-board, let the ornamental portion of the Organ be placed, comprising the second swell-box, surrounded with the uninclosed and displayed pipes. This portion can project boldly into the room, and be flanked, along the partition, with tastefully decorated flats, or curved sweeps, of wood or metal pipes belonging to the Pedal Organ. Should an expressive division of the Pedal Organ be desired, it can conveniently be located in one end of the chamber, the shutters opening toward the back swell-box: an opening in the partition, toward the room, may also have swell shutters, giving an additional power of expression.

Yet another treatment may be followed which is more favorable to the tone of the Organ than that just described. This provides for the erection of the entire instrument in the room proper—that is, without anything in the nature of a chamber—its different swell-boxes and its larger pedal pipes being arranged along the end wall of the room; while the uninclosed open metal pipes of the Great Organ and the smaller pipes of the Pedal Organ are disposed along with light case-work in the form of an ornamental screen across the room. By this arrangement no obstruction can be said to obtain; and every pipe in the instrument will be equally well heard. The front or screen may be broken up into features in any artistic fashion; and most effective and tasteful results may be secured in countless different ways.

With respect to Chamber Organs of the most advanced and refined type, such as are treated of in our Chapter on the Chamber Organ, only one position is to be recommended; namely, a perfectly unconfined position in an apartment suitable for musical performances, and in which proper accommodation is provided for a grand Pianoforte, and for at least four performers on the stringed or other orchestral instruments. A specially planned music-room, or a very spacious reception-room, will meet all these demands, leaving ample space for an audience. The great value of the true Chamber Organ as the *focus* of the musical life of the home-circle—as the domestic orchestra—seems at present to be but imperfectly realized even among musical people and lovers of the Organ. This is probably due to the fact that the Chamber Organ, in its perfect and truly expressive form, is practically unknown at the present time. We know of several instances of Organs occupying positions in large rooms, in which are placed, or could be placed, grand Pianofortes; but we can remember only one instance in England, outside our own music-room, in which the two instruments were tuned in accord, with the view of accompanimental and concerted playing. It is not too much to affirm that the interest and utility of the Chamber Organ are multiplied four-fold by this common-sense mode of procedure.

It goes without saying that an Organ which is to be effectively used along with the Pianoforte, Violin, Violoncello, and other refined solo instruments, must itself be refined in every tone it produces, and, at the same time, be capable of every possible gradation of tone, every possible degree of expression. Such being the case, it is obvious that the instrument must be so placed that no obstruction can exist to the free emission of its sounds, however loud or however soft.

So much for the position of the sound-producing portions of the Chamber Organ. A few words may now be said respecting the positions of the claviers and the wind-collecting department of the instrument. In the case of Organs constructed with ordinary tracker actions it is advisable, if not imperative, that their claviers should be located as near to the wind-chests as practicable, so that all the mechanism connecting them may be as direct and simple as can be made. For a Chamber Organ of moderate dimensions, located under ordinary conditions, we are strongly in favor of a well made and delicately adjusted tracker-action for the manual claviers: and this points to a direct and attached position for the claviers. The relative position of the pedal clavier follows as a matter of course, whether its action be tracker or tubular-pneumatic. The latter is to be recommended on account of its noiselessness and simplicity.

When a tubular-pneumatic action is adopted for the entire Organ, the claviers may be placed in a detached console, located in any convenient position in the music-room. In this case provision must be made for the conveyance of the pneumatic tubes and any necessary mechanical connections underneath the floor of the room.

By the adoption of the most approved forms of tubular-pneumatic or electro-pneumatic actions, the console can be placed at the greatest distance from the Organ the music-room will permit of. As this console, with its pedal clavier and stool, must of necessity be a somewhat bulky affair, it might be well for the architect, in planning the room, to bear this in mind; and to provide a desirable place for the same where it will not occupy valuable floor space. We are inclined to favor an advanced position, either directly in the center or toward one side of the Organ, where the player can hear perfectly the effects he is producing. The electro-pneumatic action allows a movable console to be adopted when desired. Adjoining the console should be placed the Pianoforte and the seats for the other instrumentalists, so that the music may have a unity of effect when heard from all parts of the room.

It is always desirable and in most cases imperative that the main bellows and the attendant blowing machinery should be located in an apartment either underneath or adjoining that in which the Organ is placed. By this arrangement the Organ is left uncrowded in its lower part and all noise is prevented. The reservoirs which directly supply the wind-chests may either be located in the Organ or, along with the main bellows, elsewhere. Under any conditions, it is necessary to so arrange matters that wind of the same temperature as that in the music-room shall at all times be supplied to the sound-producing portion of the instrument. As a general rule, this is best secured by inclosing the feeders and main receiver in a large wooden box or chamber, into which, by means of a trunk, air from the music-room is admitted. As absolute silence is essential in connection with so delicately-toned an instrument as the true Chamber Organ, every expedient must be devised to prevent any sound from the motor or blowing engine reaching the music-room. Care taken in all matters connected with the placing of the Chamber Organ and its accessories will be amply repaid.

CHAPTER III.

EXTERNAL DESIGN OF THE ORGAN.

IN the present Chapter we do not attempt to give anything approaching a full dissertation on the subject of Organ-case designing; but, following the general scheme laid down for our treatise, we simply make a few remarks and give some practical hints, which may prove serviceable to those who, without experience in organ-building matters, may be called upon to try their artistic skill in such designing.

Different opinions obtain among architects and organ builders respecting the desirable character of the organ-case; some advocating a close-fitting and elaborately ornamented case, extending to as great a height as the nature and locality of the instrument will permit; and others maintaining that little, if any, case-work should be introduced above the level of the Great Organ wind-chest, only standards with stay-bars or pipe-rails of wood or iron being placed where necessary to support (or appear to support) the external or displayed pipe-work. There is something to be said in favor of both methods, widely apart as they are from an artistic point of view. The former, which may be called the architect's method, besides being amply supported by the early practice in all the organ-building countries, imparts great dignity and beauty to the Organ—correct design being understood—and protects its interior to a considerable extent from dust and atmospheric changes. The latter, which may be designated the modern organ builder's method, is much less expensive, less difficult to treat in the matter of design, and less obstructive to the sound of the Organ.

When the Organ is erected in some open space, as on an end gallery or on a choir or transept screen, it is desirable to protect its internal mechanism and pipe-work to as large an extent as practicable by case-work throughout its entire height: and it unquestionably gains much in appearance by this treatment, providing, of course, that the case-work is skilfully disposed in conjunction with the displayed pipes, and otherwise artistically designed. But when the Organ occupies a confined place, such as a chamber or recess, less case-work is generally advisable; and in specially confined spaces, standards with ornamental stay-bars or pierced tracery or pipe-shades, and a symmetrical arrangement of pipes, will produce a satisfactory design. In designs of the latter class, the monotonous flatness, combined with the introduction of large metal pipes alone, which ruins so many modern organ builders' essays, should be studiously avoided. Large pipes should in all cases be sparingly used, and then only in towers and other salient features.

There seems to be no question that in the designing of organ-cases, the middle course is both the most artistic and the most consistent one to follow; it is certainly the best so far as the general requirements of the instrument are concerned. On the one hand, it is scarcely to be desired that the contents, or sound-producing portion, of the Organ should be so boxed up with a heavy and close-fitting case that its tones are muffled; or, on the other hand, that it should be left so open and unprotected that every current of air can freely pass through its interior, carrying dust and fluff into its innermost recesses. On purely architectural and artistic grounds it is desirable to have something more than two or more square posts with poorly designed pieces of ironwork or wooden stay-bars between them—a class of treatment which the insatiable desire for cheapness and the dearth of artistic feeling have fostered of late years in England and America;—and it is likewise desirable to have something less cumbersome and obstructive than the style of case which was prevalent in England during the eighteenth century and the early years of the nineteenth.

It is to be regretted that so few Gothic cases have been preserved to our day, for, judging by the other specimens of mediæval woodwork that have been spared, they would have furnished valuable object lessons to the ecclesiastical architect and the designer of Church Organs. The few mediæval cases which have survived the ruthless hands of the religious fanatic and natural decay are so suggestive that one cannot help devoutly wishing that more had been spared for our edification. The organ-cases of the Renaissance, many fine examples of which remain on the Continent of Europe, furnish, notwithstanding their many undesirable features, some valuable suggestions to the designer of to-day, and accordingly should be carefully studied by him.

In whatever style the upper portion of the Organ is treated, the lower part, up to the level of the Great or principal wind-chests, should be encased in the usual way; namely, closed in on all exposed sides with strong framed and paneled work, to exclude dust, currents of damp air, and anything else injurious to the mechanism, bellows, and all portions of the interior below the wind-chests. Sliding or hinged doors must be provided in this lower case-work to give access to all parts of the interior. One thing is essential here, that is, to have every door, panel, joint, etc., perfectly tight and free from vibration. A rickety organ-case, badly constructed of thin material, that jars and trembles whenever a large pipe speaks, is a most irritating and objectionable article, spoiling the tone of the best pipe-work with its unmusical shake. Thoroughly seasoned wood of good substance, perfect workmanship, and felted joints in all movable pieces, will remove all liability to vibration or tremblings. Imperfect case-building is one of the evils which attend cheap, competitive organ-building.

No rules of universal application, with perhaps a single exception which will be given farther on, can be formulated for the designing of organ-cases; for no two instruments are exactly alike in dimensions, in disposition of parts, in their contents, or in their surroundings. But some hints of general application, in no way aspiring to the dignity of rules, may be given—hints which the architect should bear in mind while designing an organ-case.

It may safely be premised that no one can design a thoroughly satisfactory case for an Organ—in true sympathy with the conditions and disposition of the instrument proper—unless he has a knowledge of the construction and appointment of the Organ generally. It is, accordingly, greatly to be regretted that so few architects take any pains to acquire a knowledge of the nature, construction, and requirements of the Organ, but rest content to be directed by the taste, or want of taste, of the average organ builder. We hope that the present humble essay will prove sufficient to induce the architect who reads it to take a lively interest in the subject. The ecclesiastical architect should certainly give the Organ his best attention.

The style of the organ-case should in all possible instances be dictated by the style of architecture of the church or concert-room in which the instrument is to stand: and, although no attempt should be made to affect the outward semblance of such structures as a triumphal arch, the portico of a Classic temple, or the façade of a Gothic cathedral, care should be taken to design the case so that it will harmonize perfectly with its architectural surroundings, rather accentuating than rivaling them. An Organ should be treated in an independent manner, clearly showing what it is, and honestly displaying the imperative conditions which governed its design. It is a musical instrument with hard and fast requirements and limitations; not a piece of ornamental architecture or furniture only. The proportions and details of the case should be sufficiently important in themselves to give dignity to the instrument without being obstructive in any perceptible degree to its tone. The case-work should frame-in and support the decorative pipe-work in a perfectly consistent and artistic manner. The outline of the case should be carefully studied, and relief should be given both vertically and horizontally by projecting features; and straight, inclined, and curved lines should be artistically contrasted and combined: at the same time it must never be forgotten that all features and their treatments should be dictated by, or appear to grow out of, the requirements of the instrument. We know, from experience, the difficulties attending the designing of appropriate organ-cases—appropriate both for the instruments they enshrine and the positions they are to occupy—and recognize the impossibility of giving anything beyond suggestions, of general application, for their artistic treatment. The single rule we have alluded to—the golden rule in all branches of architectural designing—is this: *In all cases meritricious ornament must be avoided: and let construction be decorated rather than decoration be constructed.*

Beauty and true dignity are more certain to be secured by simplicity of treatment than by the most elaborate devices; indeed, over-elaboration is an indication of artistic weakness, while meritricious ornament is the "last resort of the destitute." How seriously some of the old organ-cases are injured by a disregard of these facts, must strike every cultivated student of architectural art who visits the churches in which they are still preserved. One instance, and certainly an extreme one, may be found in the Organ in the Cathedral of Saint-Sauveur, at Bruges.* But this case, with its objectionable and meaningless wings and disproportionate figures, is surely the last one in the world a designer, with a particle of taste, would think of imitating.

We have said that, in modern work, the style of architecture in which the organ-case is designed should in every possible instance be dictated by the style of the building in which it is to be placed; and in this it will be seen that our views differ somewhat from those expressed by Mr. A. G. Hill, in his important work on old Organ-cases. As he will in all probability be quoted as an authority on this architectural question, although he is not an architect, we feel called upon to pass a few remarks on his views in further support of our own, leaving the decision as to who has the best argument to the interested reader. Mr. Hill says, speaking of old cases:

"The present Gothic revival has practically done nothing towards promoting a more intimate knowledge of the true characteristics of these ancient works of art, for the modern Gothic case is nearly always the most miserable caricature of mediæval work, and as for Renaissance examples, they are almost invariably considered out of place in a Gothic church, and are thus never studied with a view to their being adopted as models for architects of the present day. But an opinion is here expressed that insomuch as *all* good architecture of these times is a copy of ancient work, it is not in the slightest degree incongruous to fit a church built on an early model with woodwork and other furniture designed after one of the later schools of art."

These are bold statements to make; and their author must not be surprised if they are boldly questioned. We agree, however, with his condemnation of the majority of modern organ-cases designed in the Gothic styles; but it is only fair, in condemning them, to recognize the adverse conditions under which they were created. Because the times are niggardly in matters of architectural art; and as, in nine cases out of ten, scarcely enough money is forthcoming to secure good materials and workmanship in the Organ proper; does it follow that modern architects of skill and long training, with a knowledge of the requirements of the Organ, cannot design beautiful cases in the Gothic or later styles? Indeed, several modern Gothic cases exist in England equal to any old work of the same class that is to be found elsewhere. Let high-class artistic work be called for, and the designers will be forthcoming. Architects will soon awake, as some few have already done, to the advisability of studying organ construction, so far, at all events, as it affects external treatment. Judging by all the old cases we are acquainted with, we do not think it would put our artistic architects to very much

* An illustration of this case is given in Hill's "Organ-cases and Organs of the Middle Ages and Renaissance." London, 1873.

trouble to produce organ-cases equal, if not superior, to the examples which at present exist in the Continental churches—superior in refinement of general treatment, and in the absence of the meritricious ornaments and the meaningless and incongruous features and excrescences which disfigure the greater number of old cases. Surely Mr. Hill, in his admiration of such Renaissance works, does not want us to reproduce them and give them a place in our Gothic churches.

He further remarks: "In what does the beauty of an old 'unrestored' English or Continental church consist? Some will answer, 'Assuredly in its architectural purity or magnificence, for we are unable to do such work now-a-days.' It is true that we have not the art of designing such buildings as were produced in Europe by the workmen of the period included between A. D. 1050 and A. D. 1700, but at the same time the great charm of most old churches does not simply depend upon the beauty and originality of their designs, but also largely upon the effect produced by the wonderful fittings and accessories which generations of Christian artists and faithful churchmen have given as offerings, and which remain as monuments of the artistic skill of the times that are past. And yet there is, unfortunately, a very large majority among the architects of to-day who think that everything in a church should be of the same style or 'period,' and who carry out this principle to such a terrible extent that they are not only unwilling to design 'late' fittings for an 'early' church, but even take upon themselves to remove the works of Renaissance times from an old church undergoing 'restoration' at their hands!"

Mr. Hill writes as an authority on church architecture and art, and yet he is an organ builder and not an architect. With regard to the charm which pervades ancient churches being largely due, outside their beautiful architecture, to the exquisite works of different artistic periods which may adorn them, there can be no question: but Mr. Hill might have gone deeper for the cause of the wondrous charm which appeals to the soul of the true church architect, and have realized the symbolism and the "sacramentality" which throw the mantle of mystic beauty over the temples of the great ages of Faith. While we are free to admire the ancient churches in their varied appointments; it seems safe to believe that a thirteenth-century church, complete with every appointment as left by the architects and artists of the time, would charm us more than those churches do, in which the architects of succeeding periods have replaced the original fittings by inventions of their own. There was a considerable amount of questionable "restoration" practiced by the architects of the Middle Ages, and still more by those of the Renaissance. Does Mr. Hill seriously advise, because the architects of to-day have not the art of designing such buildings as were produced in Europe by the workmen of the period between A. D. 1050 and 1700, and accordingly have to copy their architecture, that they should go still farther, and, in a fit of archæological affectation, absolutely reproduce the accidental quaintness and "charm" of certain old churches, by introducing in a church of the Early English period, stall-work of the Perpendicular style, and an organ-case copied from some Renaissance example teeming with debased ornamentation and exaggerated detail? Would he see no want of taste and no incongruity in such a mode of proceeding? If we design our churches in the Gothic styles, in the name of architectural proprieties, and artistic common-sense let us study to carry out each one consistently, for nothing can be gained by making them a jumble of styles. On the other hand, if we have to design a new organ-case for an ancient church, let us do our best to make it harmonize with the surrounding architecture: no plea can be advanced in favor of the adoption of an antagonistic style like the Renaissance, which no more belongs to our time than the Gothic. Would Mr. Hill recommend, for the sake of the "charm" of variety he alludes to, the insertion of an Early Gothic organ-case in a Renaissance building? Yet, from his point of view, why not?

Let us see what Mr. Hill says further on this subject, while condemning the practice, which has unfortunately obtained in certain instances, of removing old woodwork or furniture of late date from early Gothic buildings, and replacing it by new work designed after the style of the buildings. He says: "It follows, therefore, that it is most certainly wrong to remove an old Renaissance organ-case out of a church because the building and the woodwork were not executed at the same time, and it may be said with equal justice that a modern organ-case need not be designed so as to have an apparent synchronism with the architecture of its surroundings. We do not say that a case for a Classical building should be Gothic, but there is no reason why a Renaissance case should not be constructed for a Gothic church." This is certainly a curious argument, and one that smacks little of either logic or reason. The solution lies in the simple fact that he approves of the Renaissance styles, with their frittered and often incongruous ornamentations, and does not appreciate the consistency and severity of the pure and early Gothic styles.

We agree with Mr. Hill in the conservation of every fragment of really good work which has been handed down to our time; and, when circumstances admit, the work should be retained in its original position and use. But we entirely disagree with him as regards the introduction of new organ-cases designed in a style different to that of the architecture of the buildings to which they belong. There can be no necessity or excuse for such a practice as he advocates; for, with our present knowledge of mediæval architecture and art, there is no difficulty in designing Gothic organ-cases superior to anything recently designed or likely to be designed in the styles of the Renaissance, as represented by so many Organs of that period.

"Again," says Mr. Hill, "it is obviously wrong to attempt to design a thirteenth-century case for an Organ to be placed in a modern church built according to the rules of that delightful period, for we have hardly any information concerning the Organs of that time, and what little we know about them shows us that the instruments, being very small, had practically no cases at all." This is really no argument worth entertaining for a moment. The architects of to-day are called upon to design cases for large Organs to be placed in churches of very moderate dimensions, and they can quite as easily, if not more easily, do so in the styles of the churches as in any foreign style. But, on second thoughts, we may admit that a case in the Northern Renaissance style can be more easily designed than a really good Gothic one, judging from what are pronounced the most noteworthy examples of the former style extant. All that appears necessary to be done by the designer is to pile up as many incongruous features and architectural details as the size of the Organ or the height of the building will admit of; and to construct as much inappropriate ornamentation as people can be induced to pay for. Taste, refinement, and artistic restraint go for nothing, as a rule, in the designing of Renaissance organ-cases. At any rate, all the modern essays are miserable affairs; and this cannot be said of a great number of modern Gothic cases designed by distinguished English architects who have given the Organ some consideration. Mr. Hill continues: "The old workmen were consistent in such matters, and had no fears for 'style' when they erected the magnificent Organs which are such conspicuous features at the west-end of most Continental churches." He is right, they "*had no fears for style*," and more is the pity, seeing that their works are pointed to as models for imitation at the present time. "What could have a finer effect in the matter of an organ-case," says this writer, "than the noble structure which fills up the western extremity of the Church at Stralsund? This splendid piece of work dates, most probably, from the year 1660, and is thus devoid of any Gothic spirit, yet so far from being incongruous, the Organ contrasts most charmingly with its Gothic surroundings, the early and late work being mutually improved by the contrast." Now if we agree with Ruskin that the Gothic spirit embraces *Sacrifice*, *Truth*, *Power*, *Life*, *Memory*, and *Obedience*, we can realize how much the Stralsund organ-case must gain in being "*devoid of any Gothic spirit*." That it contrasts with its early Gothic surroundings under these circumstances must be obvious. We have, however, held, as an article of art faith, that *harmony* is a more beautiful and satisfactory element in the styles of architecture than *conflicting contrast*, but we may be wrong.

While we readily admit that the Stralsund organ-case is "devoid of any Gothic spirit," we freely acknowledge that as a work of its style and period it presents much that commends it to the attention of the modern designer. Through the courtesy of Mr. Hill we are able to give a reproduction of his drawing of this celebrated organ-case, Fig. XXII. The design is specially interesting on account of its clever combination of curves, the varied and highly suggestive arrangements and disposition of the numerous displayed pipes, and the lavish introduction of richly carved and pierced pipe-shades. There is, on the other hand, a want of proportion between the upper and lower features and details: and the manner in which the large flanking towers are supported, and finished above the main cornice, cannot be too strongly condemned from an art point of view—here we have an eloquent proof of the total absence of the Gothic spirit. The bald termination to the central division of the case is commonplace and ugly.

Speaking of the large organ-case in the Church of St. John, at Bois le Duc, in North Brabant, Mr. Hill says: "The wonderful organ-case at Bois le Duc dates from about 1602, and is no less than 100 feet high, and yet the Dean of that Cathedral informed a friend of the writer that he (the Dean) had been advised by 'an eminent English architect' to have the Organ removed, because it did not harmonize with the architecture of the church." The case is certainly a superb specimen of Renaissance work—a veritable storehouse of design in which almost every feature of the style is introduced. We cannot imagine who this "eminent

English architect" was, but, as he was evidently a Gothic architect, we can easily understand his being impressed with its incongruity. That he should advise its

Fig. XXII.

removal because it did not harmonize with the architecture of the church is certainly little to his credit, and indicative of anything but a catholic art-spirit. The case is unquestionably the grandest Renaissance work of its class in North-western

Fig. XXIII.

Europe, and, as a landmark in the history of architectural art and of organ-building, it would be as wrong to remove it from the Gothic church in which it stands, as it would be to erect such a design in a Gothic building at the present time.

We are glad to have the privilege of giving here a reproduction, on a small scale, of Mr. Hill's large and beautiful drawing of the Bois le Duc case, Fig. XXIII. The superiority of its design to that of the Stralsund case must be obvious to every one at all conversant with architectural art. The composition is very imposing, and the details of the strictly architectural features are very beautiful. The terminations of the lateral divisions are good and highly suggestive; but the manner in which the central portion is completed is not so satisfactory. The only noteworthy features in the displayed pipe-work are the inverted ranks in the four smaller compartments of the central portion of the case; this treatment is not to be recommended for adoption in modern designs. The design of the small Positive Organ is remarkably good in its style. The main case and that of the Positive are the work of two artists, Francis Sÿmons, wood-carver, and George Schÿsler, sculptor, of Cologne. The work dates between 1618 and 1633.

We have thus enlarged upon the desirability of harmony of style between so important a work as an organ-case and the building in which it is erected; and have freely commented on Mr. Hill's views in the opposite direction, because we consider the question one of great importance, from an art point of view, at the present time, when so many expensive Organs are being constructed, and so little attention is being bestowed on their external appearance. It is only natural that persons, who have no firmly-grounded art-principles of their own, should be led away by the warm advocacy of so distinguished an author in favor of a general imitation of his favorite Renaissance designs, but we desire to point out the inartistic results that would be certain to follow the blind adoption of any one style of art for organ-cases which have to stand in buildings of widely different styles of architecture. We have enough excuses at present from organ builders and designers for all shapes and styles of organ-cases, or for no cases at all; and further licence from one writing as an authority on the subject cannot fail to aggravate the existing evil. But while we feel bound to differ from the opinion expressed by Mr. Hill on the points alluded to, we desire to recognize the great service he has rendered both to the history and the art of organ-building by the publication of his two handsome volumes, forming the unique Work entitled "The Organ-cases and Organs of the Middle Ages and the Renaissance." Every lover of the Organ owes a debt of gratitude to Mr. Hill for his great labor of love; and in our case the debt is largely increased by his kind permission to reproduce several of his drawings in our pages.

We may now resume the main subject of the present Chapter. Classic organ-cases, or, in other words, cases appropriate for interiors in the Grecian and Roman styles of architecture, are, in their artistic treatment, the most difficult problems the designer has to solve. This is readily understood when one bears in mind that the only elements of design such styles furnish are of a severe, structural nature, such as the different orders of columns with their massive entablatures, pediments, square-headed openings, and semicircular arches—all features, if in any sense properly carried out, very much out of place in an organ-case, in which pipes occupy, or should occupy, the chief positions, and in which as little massive work as possible should obstruct the free egress of sound. An instance of a lamentable failure in this direction is presented in the case of the Organ in the Public Halls, at Glasgow. Here an attempt has been made to produce a Classic design by using the ordinary architectural features and details, as above enumerated, and by treating large pipes in a most unseemly fashion in certain parts of the front to meet the exigencies of the design. Here we see an Organ made subservient to a so-called Classic case; not a case designed in subservience to the conditions and requirements of the Organ as a musical instrument. French designers, who, as a rule, are credited with both ingenuity and taste, do not seem to have accomplished much in the direction of Classic organ-cases. If we take, as an example, the large and massive case of the Grand Organ in the Church of Saint-Sulpice, at Paris, we find another instance of failure. The design comprises a high, paneled base, surmounted by eight tall Corinthian columns supporting a massive horizontal entablature. Between the columns are monotonous ranges of large pipes the mouths of which form a horizontal line and the tops of which disappear behind the entablature. Between the columns and in advance of the pipes are large statues, some of which are holding musical instruments. Surmounting the central portion of the entablature is a large lyre flanked by two sprawling angels. The entire composition is commonplace and uninteresting in the extreme. Here the desire to make the Organ accord with the Roman style of the interior has been carried beyond the proper limit, and the result is unsatisfactory. A well-designed Renaissance case would have been much more suitable, and would not have seemed out of place in such a freely treated interior.

In the composition of a Classic case all the architectural features strictly belonging to heavy stone construction should be laid aside, and with them all their accepted rules and proportions, in favor of a common-sense selection and disposition of details, perfectly suitable for woodwork, and consistent with the requirements of the Organ as a musical instrument. Such a case can be made in true sympathy with the architecture of a Classic building, in strict keeping with the materials of which it is constructed, and quite appropriate to the office it fulfils; and it may be enriched or decorated with all the refinement of Greek or the elaboration of Roman art. To enable him to produce satisfactory designs of this description, the architect must grasp the true spirit of Classic art in all its branches, not slavishly copy its dry bones, until he can feel what a Greek or Roman artist would have done had he been called upon to design a large organ-case for one of his temples or a hall in one of his thermæ. It must be borne in mind that an Organ is a piece of furniture; and that under no ordinary circumstances can it be considered an integral part of a building. As a piece of furniture, therefore, it has as much right to be designed and disposed in strict conformity with its use and requirements as a table or a bedstead, an altar or a pulpit; and it would not be more ridiculous to design a table with Doric columns for its legs than to design an organ-case after the likeness of a temple portico or colonnade.

The architect who now essays to design a Classic organ-case would do well to study the beautiful bronze articles of Etruscan art and the numerous objects of domestic use found at Pompeii; and, so far as decoration is concerned, the keramic works of the Greeks and Etruscans. From these he will derive many valuable hints and much inspiration. The designer may also derive considerable help from the study of the more severe and refined examples of Renaissance treatment. For instance, as regards disposition of parts and architectural propriety, he may study with advantage the magnificent organ-case in the Cathedral of Tarragona. In Fig. XXIV. we give a reproduction of Mr. Hill's clever drawing of this important work. To this we may append his notes on the case. He says: "It is a very sumptuous work, and a magnificent example of sixteenth-century Spanish Renaissance. The arrangement of pediment, friezes, cornices, and pilasters, is very classical, even to the triglyphs in the lower frieze, such being characteristic of this period, while any hardness and want of elasticity in the design is compensated by the extreme richness and elaboration of the details. The Organ was designed by Canon Amigó, of Tortosa, and erected in the year 1563. It is of great size, and rises to the vaulting of the cathedral. The front consists of seventeen compartments of pipes, each with a carved shade. The base is decorated with niches, figures, and much costly detail. Rows of trumpets project forth from the lower frieze, as is usual in Spanish instruments; while in front of the gallery is the Choir Organ, with a semicircular pediment. The case is entirely of oak, without gilding, and is dark with age. Two enormous shutters or doors stretch out on either side, with majestic effect. They are well painted on canvas with representations of the Adoration of the Magi and the Resurrection."

By substituting Greek architectural detail for the free Renaissance enrichments, and forming the pipe-shades of refined Greek scrollwork, the Tarragona case could be turned into a beautiful Classic design. It would, if placed in a favorable position, gain much by having its principal divisions advanced.

There is an organ-case very freely treated in St. George's Hall, at Liverpool, which, although it cannot be called highly artistic or beautiful, harmonizes fairly well with the fine Roman architecture of the great hall. It was designed by the talented architect who finished the Hall; and presents no details inconsistent with the materials of which it is constructed.

Organ pipes have fixed structural forms which admit of no important modifications to suit the whims of the case designer; they must be accepted in all their conventionality; and encased or disposed in as artistic a manner as ingenuity and taste can devise. One thing connected with their form and disposition may be mentioned here; namely, the advisability, in cases of Greek design, of having their feet all of one height in each group or flat. This treatment obtains throughout the Tarragona case. In a case designed to harmonize with a building in Roman architecture, the heights of the pipe-feet may vary, throwing the mouths of the pipes into arched or concave lines.

In designing organ-cases for Romanesque buildings, the architect or artist must studiously avoid the introduction of structural forms directly copied from stone architecture. The massive character of such forms in stone renders a travesty of them in light woodwork, supporting or inclosing metal or wood pipes, simply absurd. Again the designer should ask himself: Given such organ-pipes and planks of oak, what would a Romanesque architect or organ builder have done with them? That he would in his admiration for solidity of construction

FIG. XXIV.

have used too much wood is highly probable, at all events he would have put the case together in rather a massive form. Notwithstanding this, he would have put it together in a perfectly legitimate manner, as a piece of woodwork having a definite purpose. Not an arch, buttress, pillar, or any other constructive feature peculiar to stonework would have appeared in it; save, perhaps, in some refined ornamental character, and in an unmistakable wood rendering. He would have moulded certain members in his usual bold style, and enriched others with quaint carving; and he would have put together all the structural members of the case with undisguised tenons, simply wedged or pinned. If the Romanesque architect or organ builder would have done all this, then the modern designer should follow in his steps: and if he is gifted with a fair amount of reasoning and inventive powers there is no cause why he should not succeed in producing an organ-case suitable for any Romanesque building. Plain, polished tin pipes are unquestionably the most appropriate for a case of so bold and severe a style; but, when richness of effect is desired, gilded pipes, decorated with simple Romanesque patterns in black or brown, may be freely used. The salient members and the mouldings of the case may also be enriched with gold and dark colors. The case should be of oak or some rich hardwood.

Gothic cases admit of a great variety of treatments: and fortunately enough of mediæval woodwork has been preserved to the present day to inspire the designer. In this, as in all other purely architectural styles, no attempt should be made, in designing an organ-case, to produce a work resembling a piece of stone architecture; and, accordingly, the fewer pointed arches, crocketed gablets or canopies, pinnacles, buttresses, pillars, and suchlike structural features, are introduced the better. None of these are necessary to the production of a perfect Gothic case, although certain of them, artistically treated, may be pressed into service by the designer who will not lose sight of the fact that he has to meet the conditions imposed by wood construction. If he will care less for what is commonly considered the distinctive features of Gothic architecture, and more for the spirit which pervades Gothic art in general, he will produce more artistic and satisfactory results in organ-case designing.

Unfortunately few organ-cases of the Gothic periods exist. Those which have been preserved are, of course, of late date, and highly suggestive. There existed in Strasbourg Cathedral an important instrument of the thirteenth century, but unfortunately nothing remains of it. For the earliest cases at present in existence we have to go to Spain. There are two Organs in Zaragoza, constructed during the first quarter of the fifteenth century. The one in the Cathedral was erected in the year 1413; and that in the Church of San Pablo was built about seven years later. Both these instruments have pure Gothic cases of exceptional interest; but as there is a great similarity in their general treatment, we content ourselves by reproducing only one of Mr. Hill's drawings—that of the Organ in the Cathedral, Fig. XXV. The design presents three quadrangular towers, surmounted by bold cornices and concave roofs, ornamented with crockets and finials, and separated by small curtains surmounted by bold crestings. The flat treatment of the front, with its five compartments on one vertical plane, is characteristic of a certain class of Gothic organ-cases. It was probably adopted to allow shutters or folding doors to be conveniently applied. The manner in which such folding doors are fitted to a three-towered flat case is shown in Fig. XIV., which represents the Organ in the Church of St. George, at Nördlingen, with its painted doors closed.

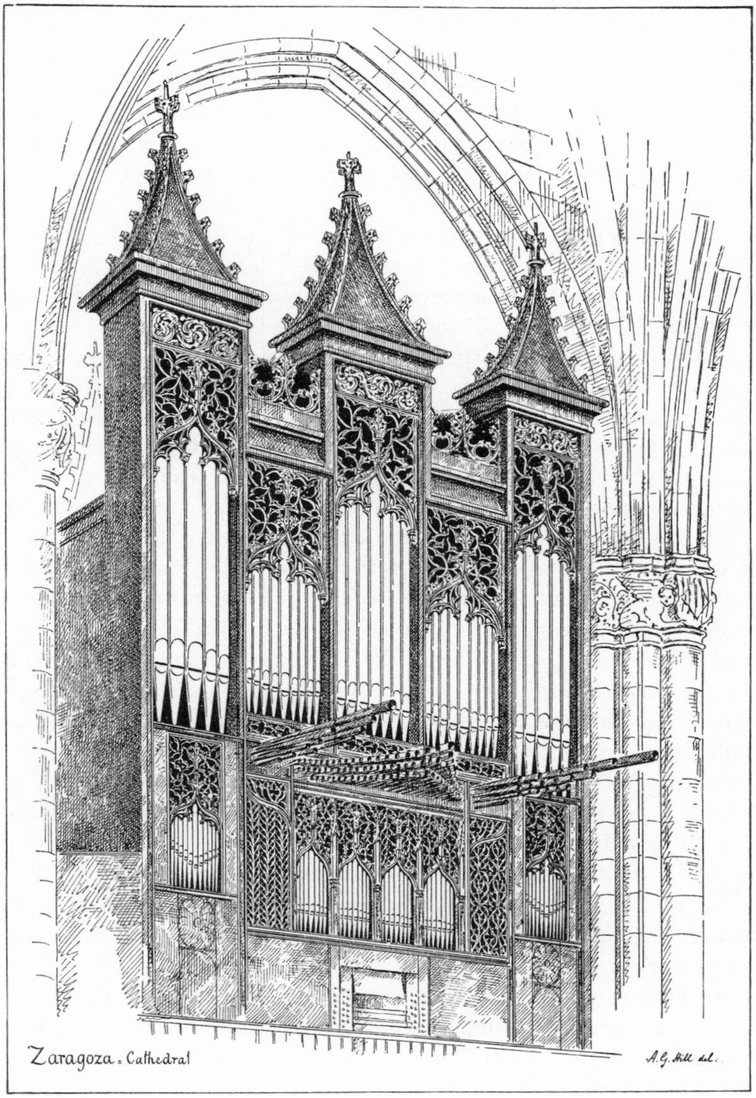

Fig. XXV.

The manner in which the five large compartments are enriched with arched, carved, cusped, and pierced pipe-shades is beautiful and full of true Gothic feeling. The lower compartments, which are in perfect keeping with the upper ones, are charming in design, imparting a wonderful variety and richness to the entire composition. The case of the Organ in San Pablo has also three quadrangular towers, of the same height, surmounted with cornices, elaborately carved crestings, and pierced roofs enriched with crockets and finials. These are separated by curtains, corniced and crested to correspond with the towers. The flanking towers contain single compartments of large pipes, while the central tower has two compartments in its height. The curtains have each two compartments filled with small pipes. The pipe-shades are similar to those shown in Fig. XXV. The lower part of the case is quite plain. Both these remarkable cases furnish valuable suggestions for modern Gothic case-work.

In our historical notes we give a drawing of the Organ-case in the Cathedral of Perpignan (Pyrénées-Orientales), Fig. XVII. The most remarkable feature in this immense case is the flat treatment which obtains throughout the entire front. This is to allow the whole to be covered by the great folding doors which are hinged to the outer edges of the case. These are covered with paintings of the Adoration of the Magi, the Baptism of Our Lord, and the four Evangelists. The height of the central portion of the case is about forty-five feet; and the pipes which are inclosed in the lateral compartments belong to the MONTRE, 32 FT. The clever graduation of the compartments of pipes, from the sides inward and upward, deserves special study; but the objectionable arrangement of inverted pipes, in the central compartment, indicates a greater love for novelty than for beauty and propriety on the part of the designer. Such a disposition should certainly never be adopted in modern work. This central compartment would have been quite satisfactory had it been filled with a single rank of pipes, shaded with pierced tracery, to correspond with the other compartments. The tracery throughout the case, though not very pure in style—the case dating from the closing years of the fifteenth century—is disposed in an artistic and satisfactory manner, and is thoroughly characteristic of the material in which it is executed. Speaking of this case, M. Viollet-le-Duc remarks: "Le buffet de la cathédrale de Perpignan est bien exécuté, en beau bois de chêne, et sa construction, comme on peut le voir, établie sur un seul plan, est fort simple; elle ne se compose que de montants et de traverses avec panneaux à jour. Presque tous les tuyaux de montre sont utilisés. L'organiste, placé derrière la balustrade, au centre, touchait les claviers disposés dans le renfoncement inférieur; la soufflerie est établie par derrière dans un réduit."

For Late Decorated or Perpendicular Gothic organ-cases, the Perpignan design furnishes a suggestive model. One charming modern-case designed on somewhat similar lines, but of small dimensions, exists in the Church of St. John the Baptist, Tuebrook, near Liverpool. It consists of a number of well-arranged flat compartments, formed by slender standards and moulded horizontal members, the whole being surmounted by a characteristic cornice. The compartments have pipe-shades of Perpendicular tracery, and are filled with burnished metal pipes, some of which are ornamented with embossed patterns after ancient examples. The oak of which the case is constructed is stained almost black, and partly decorated with gold and colors. The case is cleverly connected with the stall-work of the chancel, producing a most satisfactory composition. The case was designed by Mr. Bodley, the celebrated English ecclesiastical architect.

Of all the styles of Gothic architecture, the English Perpendicular lends itself most readily to the exigencies or requirements of the organ-case, being equally adapted for a flat or a broken-up treatment: and very good results, both from practical and artistic points of view, may be obtained with a moderate expenditure of material and labor. The Late Decorated woodwork which has been preserved to our time is full of beautiful details which the accomplished designer can press into his service; its beautiful flowing tracery and foliated ornament being perfectly suitable for pipe-shades, panel-work, and other decorative features.

In the accompanying illustration, Fig. XXVI., is given a sketch of the interesting Gothic case preserved in the Church of Hombleux (Picardie), constructed about the year 1500. This case is cast in a different mould from that of the preceding; and it represents a treatment which seems to have been held in high favor by the designers of the period. The Gothic cases in the Cathedral of Strasbourg, and in the Marienkirche, at Dortmund, are of a similar overhanging treatment. It was also adopted by the designers of the Renaissance in their earlier and retained in several of their later cases. The treatment obtains, in an exaggerated form, in the Organ of the Annenkirche, at Augsburg, and in the nave Organ of the Cathedral of Freiburg in Breisgau. In a more timid form, it appears in the Organs in the Church of Notre-Dame, at Argentan, the Church of Aire sur la Lys, the Cathedral of Bruges, the Church of Gonesse, and in Exeter Cathedral.

The Hombleux case, as it at present exists, has undergone some "restoration" at the hands of Renaissance workmen, which accounts for the incongruity obtaining in the carved and pierced pipe-shades of the several compartments. Those of the central and lateral compartments belong to the Gothic period; while those of the intermediate compartments, containing the coats of arms, are Renaissance. The ornamentation of the paneling in the lower portion of the case is also of the Renaissance period. Taken altogether, this case is an admirable model for a moderately sized Organ, providing the bellows are located away from the instrument. Large and dignified Gothic cases can be designed by an extension of this treatment, as is shown in the fine and modern case of the Organ in the Church of St. Bartholomew, at Armley, Yorkshire, England, an illustration of which is given in Plate III.

The design of the Hombleux case is of the highest suggestive value; its simple disposition of parts commending it for imitation, while its purely ornamental features admit of almost countless artistic treatments. In conjunction with this case, the designer should study the somewhat earlier case of the Organ in the Marienkirche, at Dortmund, an illustration of which is given in the preceding Chapter, Fig. XV. In this beautiful case there are three projecting semicircular features, each supported by a *cul-de-lampe*, and filled with large pipes; the two flats between them having small pipes arranged in two stages. The carving of the pipe-shades, crestings, panels, etc., is extremely rich and effective. Criticising this design, we may remark that the central feature is too wide for the rest of the composition, and that the lateral semicircular features are too low. The design would have been greatly improved had these been carried above the cresting of the adjoining flats or curtains. A treatment like this, carefully carried out in pure Late Decorated or Perpendicular Gothic would have a magnificent effect; and

FIG. XXVI.

such a case, executed in dark stained oak, would admit of a beautiful scheme of decoration in gold and colors. The pipes could be of plain, burnished tin, or of plain metal, gilded, and decorated with Gothic diaper patterns executed in dark brown or black. When it is necessary to have as much room as possible in the lower portion of the case, the lateral overhanging parts need not be carried out very far.

FIG. XXVII.

In the Cathedral of Strasbourg stands to-day one of the finest Gothic organ-cases in existence. It was constructed in the year 1497. Through Mr. Hill's kind permission, we are able to give an illustration of this remarkable instrument, Fig. XXVII. The treatment throughout the Gothic portion is extremely good and suggestive. It was this Organ that the late Sir George Gilbert Scott took as a model when he designed the beautiful case which is projected from the triforium of the choir of Ely Cathedral. Speaking of the Strasbourg instrument, Mr. Hill correctly remarks: "On the north side of the nave, projecting out from the triforium, is one of the most beautiful Gothic Organs that remain to us. The organist's gallery is a Gothic *cul-de-lampe*, in front of which is the Choir Organ or Positif. The ribs of the gallery are beautifully cusped, and the cresting or brattishing of the Organ above is very excellent and characteristic. The shades of the pipes are most elaborately carved. . . . The beautifully carved wings which project from the sides of the main case are Renaissance additions, made, most probably, to replace the painted doors which originally formed part of the design." The late German Gothic details are highly characteristic, and are replete with the wandering vagaries of the style. In imitating such a design, details of a more refined character should be adopted. For severe work the Perpendicular style should be followed; while for florid treatments the English Decorated or the French Flamboyant styles may be adopted. All lend themselves to legitimate woodwork. From the bottom of the *cul-de-lampe* to the top of the cresting of the main division, the Strasbourg Organ is about fifty feet in height. From this some idea of the imposing character of the composition can be formed. It is certainly a grand piece of work.

Another remarkable Gothic organ-case—the most complete and elaborate one in existence—is to be found in the Church at Jutfaas, in Holland. This originally belonged to the Nieuwerzÿds-Kapel, at Amsterdam, whence it was removed in 1871, and reërected at Jutfaas. The accompanying illustration, Fig. XXVIII., is reproduced from Mr. Hill's copy of a drawing by Mr. P. J. H. Cuypers, of Amsterdam. The style of the case is the florid and impure one that obtained in Northern Europe in the opening years of the sixteenth century, when Gothic architecture had reached its last stage of decay. The plan of the case is unique, being based on rather more than a semicircle—a form very badly suited for the internal economy of an Organ, and one not likely to be followed in modern work. The whole is supported on a richly moulded and traceried *cul-de-lampe*, which occupies a spandril between two arches, as indicated, and has a total height of about thirty-five feet. The lower part of the case, immediately above the *cul-de-lampe*, and in which is arranged all the displayed pipe-work, is formed of three semicircular and two V-shaped towers, placed alternately, and divided by four segments of the main body, as indicated in the small plan given in the illustration. These segments have pipes arranged in two stages, while the towers contain large pipes only. The towers are carried above the pipes in tall and richly detailed canopy-work of several stages; and the intermediate segmental compartments are finished with foliated pipe-shades, curved pinnacles, and pedestals supporting figures of angels holding shields. The main standards at the junctions of the towers with the main body of the case terminate upward in tall and slender, crocketed pinnacles. From the center of all rises a lofty and very elaborately treated polygonal lantern, terminating in an open, crocketed spire of unusual design. The whole composition is

Fig. XXVIII.

extravagant; and although we do not recommend it for imitation, the designer of to-day can obtain valuable hints from a careful study of its architectural treatment.

In Fig. XXIX. is given a sketch of the immense Organ in the Marienkirche, at Lübeck. The case of this instrument affords a noteworthy example of the flat

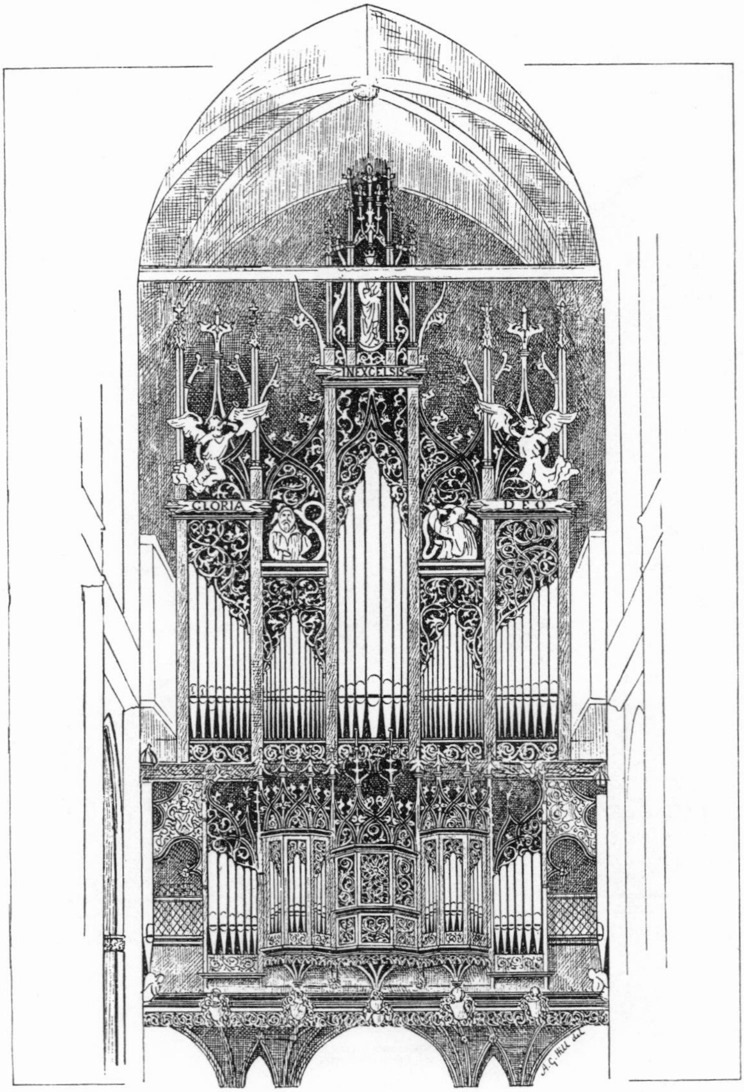

Lübeck Marienkirche.

FIG. XXIX.

treatment characteristic of Gothic design in connection with the Organ. Describing this important work, Mr. Hill says: "It is placed in a gallery at the west end, some forty feet from the ground, and the case itself is nearly eighty feet high and is forty feet wide. The church is 125 feet to the apex of the vaulting. This case was erected in the year 1504, though the Choir Organ is later, the date 1561 being carved upon it. The case consists essentially of five flats of pipes, of which three are carried up to form towers, the spaces between them at the top being filled in with elaborate tracery and carving. The way in which the crocketed pinnacles are twisted about should be noticed—it is characteristic of late German work. Upon the cornice mouldings of the three towers scrolls have lately been placed, bearing the inscription 'GLORIA IN EXCELSIS DEO.' Above the center tower is a figure of the Blessed Virgin Mary with the Infant, and over the two lower flats are figures of prophets with texts inscribed on scrolls. These three figures appear to be of the same date as the Organ, but the angels with expanded wings, at the sides, are of Renaissance workmanship. The design of the Choir Organ is very elaborate, and here we have a good example of the twisted pinnacles. Like most old Organs, this has but little depth, being only 7 feet from back to front. The sound-boards are disposed in tiers." Cases designed on these general lines, and in a pure and refined Gothic style, would be, comparatively speaking, inexpensive, and at the same time extremely effective. The introduction of figures imparts a very artistic appearance to a case, provided that they are not made on too large a scale, as in many old examples.

Numerous organ-cases of a refined and appropriate character were designed by English architects during the Gothic Revival, notably those for instruments of moderate dimensions. The larger cases, such as those in Chester Cathedral and the Church of St. Mary, Nottingham, are of a very elaborate description, but can hardly be pronounced entirely satisfactory. In these more important works there is a restlessness of treatment and a straining after effect which somewhat impairs their dignity. Simplicity and breadth of treatment in large cases, which have of necessity to be viewed from a considerable distance, are more effective and satisfactory than the most lavish display of broken-up features and carved enrichments. One may tolerate, or even approve of, the absence of repose, and the presence of an excess of elaboration, in a Renaissance design, but hardly in a pure Gothic one. Of the more artistically treated large organ-cases in English churches, that in the Church of St. Bartholomew, at Armley, illustrated in Plate III., may be considered the most satisfactory. It is extremely effective in work, and enshrines one of Edmund Schulze's choicest instruments. The Organ stands on an arcaded and vaulted stone gallery in the north transept of the church, the arch of which it almost fills. The case is of oak throughout, boldly traceried and carved. Its general design and the disposition of its several parts are appropriate and harmonious, many of the details furnished by ancient organ-cases and mediæval woodwork of late date having been skilfully made use of. Light bands of ornamental wrought-iron are introduced to support the displayed pipes. Two figures of angels holding musical instruments surmount the canopies at the angles of the projecting portion of the case. These angle features, containing three large pipes each, are supported, as it were, by large figures of angels carrying stringed instruments. Severe criticism might pronounce these figures out of place; certainly their omission would in no way injure the architectural propriety of the work. The three triplets of large pipes give great strength to the composition, and are well disposed. The overhanging wings are boldly and artistically designed; while the compartments, filled with comparatively small pipes, on each

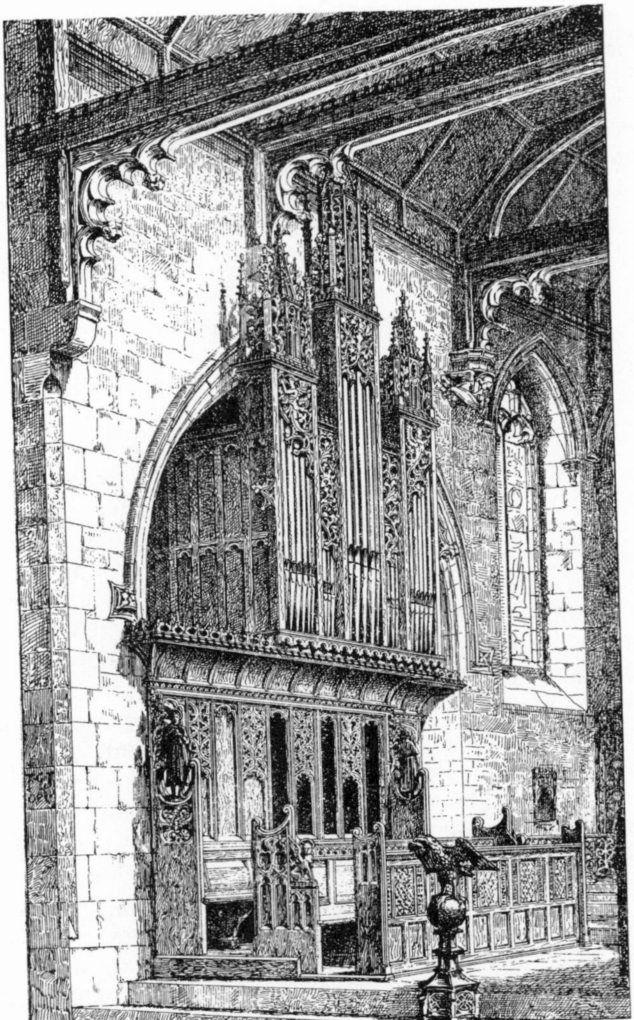

FIG. XXX.

side of the central feature, are beautifully and correctly treated. All the details are pure in style, and are executed in the true Gothic spirit. This case deserves to be carefully studied and used as a model. The organist's seat is in the central

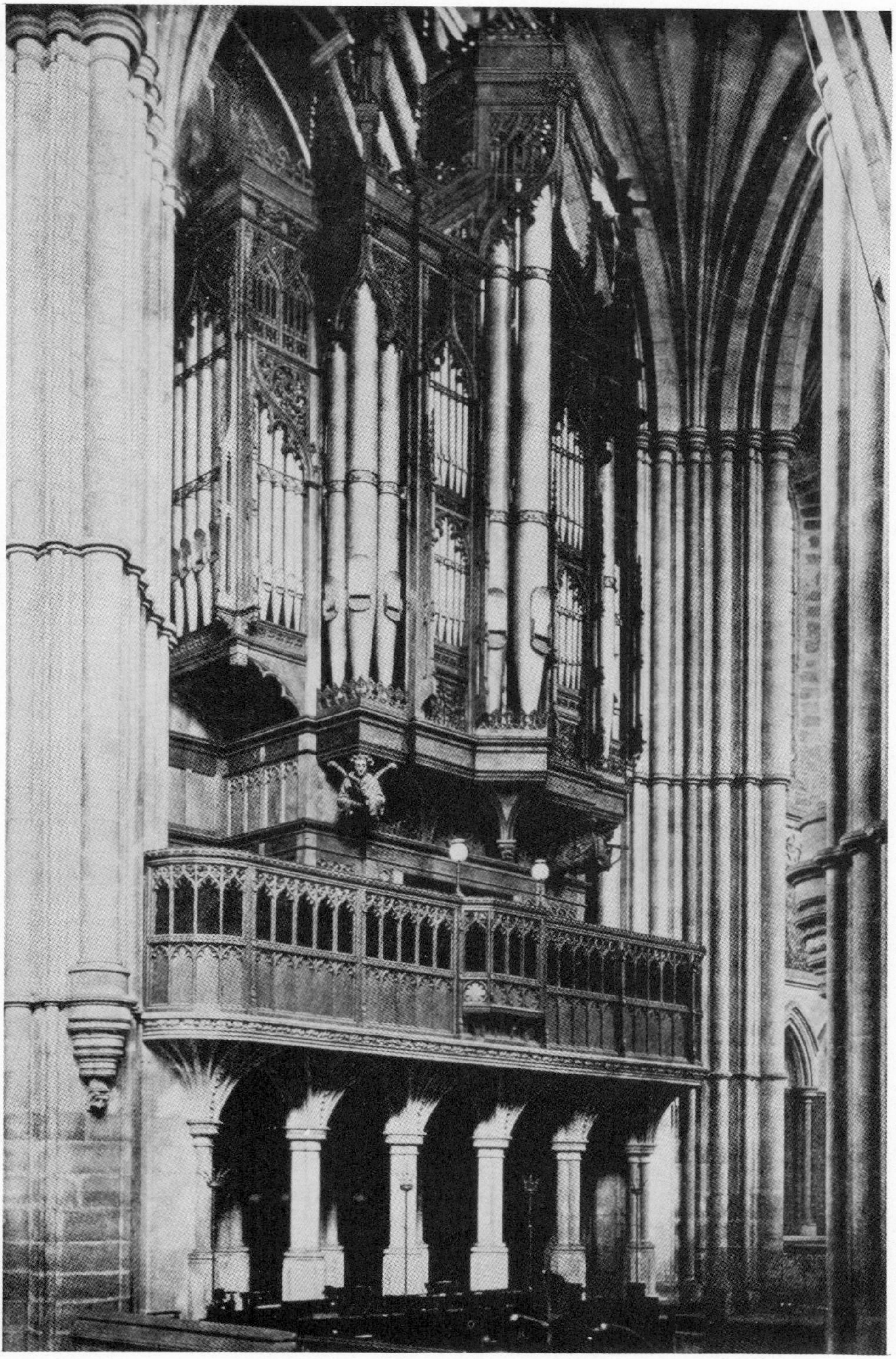

advanced portion of the elaborately traceried oak screen which fronts and surmounts the stone gallery, and gives so much value, in an architectural sense, to the entire composition.

Without a series of elaborate illustrations it would be profitless to describe the representative Gothic organ-cases which have been designed by the leading church architects in England. Some of the smaller cases are in all respects satisfactory and show a careful study of old models. One example may be given to show what has been accomplished in the shape of a small Chancel Organ. In Fig. XXX. is given a drawing of the Organ in Northington Church, Hants, designed by Mr. T. G. Jackson. It is obvious that, although this case is carried out in pure English Gothic, such cases as those of the Organs in the Cathedral of Zaragoza (Fig. XXV.), and the Marienkirche, at Lübeck (Fig. XXIX.), have been studied by the architect. In general effect the Northington case is extremely good; and the treatment throughout is perfectly in accord with the material used in its construction. We may point out, by way of a hint to those who may be disposed to copy this pretty case, that the carved pipe-shades in the flats between the towers are carried too far down, dwarfing the pipes which stand below. The absence of an artistic connection between the Organ and the screen is to be regretted. The existing treatment conveys the idea that the Organ was an afterthought, and, according to the general practice of architects in organ matters, it very probably was so. The organist sits behind the open portion of the screen. This is a very objectionable position, as it renders it extremely difficult for him to realize the effect of the Organ and hear the voices of the choir.

We cannot close our brief remarks on modern Gothic organ-cases without directing attention to the remarkable conception by the late William Burges, the distinguished English architect, which is illustrated in the succeeding Chapter on the Decoration of the Organ. This case is designed in a style of early Gothic of which Mr. Burges was a past master. The idea which he had in his mind—he invariably had some leading idea controlling or pervading each artistic work he essayed—was evidently that of a Castle of Sound and Music. The strong resemblance in the leading features to the castellated architecture of the Middle Ages, and the remarkable system of pictorial decoration applied throughout, certainly support our opinion respecting the artist's motive. The entire case was designed for the reception of a complete polychromatic embellishment, which, had it been carried out under Mr. Burges' careful supervision, would unquestionably have made the work the most expressive and artistic of its class ever designed. As a full description of the pictorial decoration is given in the succeeding Chapter, it is unnecessary to touch upon it here. The upper part of the case seems unnecessarily close and obstructive to the egress of sound; but as the whole is merely a screen the sound would not be interfered with to any appreciable extent. The small Choir Organ, in front, with its elaborately sculptured and painted support, is a beautiful conception. It is greatly to be regretted that this design was never carried out.

Organ-cases of Renaissance character present very few difficulties to the accomplished designer. Invention has free scope in works of this class, only requiring to be curbed by good taste and the sense of architectural fitness and artistic propriety. A great variety of materials may be used in combination, and decorative painting may be applied with good effect.

The front of a Renaissance organ-case may be divided, vertically and horizontally, to any desired extent, admitting the introduction of all the effective arrangements of pipes, large and small.

We are strongly of opinion that the designer in search of inspiration would do well to study the most refined and artistic architectural remains of the Renaissance period, and also its ecclesiastical and domestic furniture, rather than rest content with copying such Renaissance organ-cases as have been preserved. Indeed, such cases, while many of them contain very valuable suggestions, are, on account of their generally debased character, unsuited for wholesale imitation. The designer should especially avoid copying such gimcrack and piled-up tabernacle-work, and the still more meritricious adjuncts, as are to be found in the organ-cases in the Cathedrals of Chartres, Le Mans, and Amiens, and the Churches of Caudebec, Notre-Dame, at Argentan, and Saint-Bertrand de Comminges. The designer should also avoid the introduction of such monstrously disproportioned figures as those which surmount and seem to crush the organ-cases in the Cathedral of Bruges and the Church of Notre-Dame, Saint-Omer. In addition to such pronounced and unnecessary features, the accomplished designer would throw aside, as worthless and unworthy of imitation, the elaborate systems of built ornament which crowd such cases as those in the Cathedral of Würzburg and the Church of Aire sur la Lys.*

After these remarks, it may reasonably be asked how we advise the architect to proceed in preparing a Renaissance design. We unhesitatingly recommend him to observe the greatest possible simplicity in the leading forms and disposition of the several divisions of the case; striving after a dignified architectural treatment, perfectly consistent with the requirements of the Organ, as a musical instrument, and with the materials to be used in its construction. A careful study of the best examples of Renaissance woodwork will prove of immense assistance to the designer; and he will do well to bear in mind that, although there may be considerable freedom indulged in in the treatment of Renaissance work—for the Renaissance styles are lawless,—he should display quite as much artistic repose, taste, and refinement in his design for a Renaissance case as he would be expected to show in a design for a severe Classic or a correct Gothic one.

Let the designer, who desires to discriminate between a refined and a debased Renaissance treatment, compare the organ-case in the Cathedral of Tarragona, represented in Fig. XXIV., with such cases as those in the Cathredral of Bruges and the Church of Aire sur la Lys, illustrated by Mr. Hill. There can be no question as to the great artistic beauty of the Tarragona case. It deserves to be carefully studied; and along with it should be studied the case in the Church of St. John, Bois le Duc, represented in Fig. XXIII. We may remark that while in the Tarragona case there is nothing one would desire to see omitted, in the Bois

* Drawings of all the cases named in this paragraph will be found in Mr. Hill's valuable Work.

le Duc case there are several features which could be omitted or very greatly improved, notably the crowning feature above the main cornice of the central division and the altogether meaningless and unnecessary wing features. The former is open to a great improvement to accord with the rest of the design, while the wings should be entirely removed. The introduction of the inverted pipes in the four smaller compartments of the central division is certainly to be condemned. On the other hand, there is an admirable regard for architectural propriety observed throughout the composition; and all the statues are to the proper scale. Taken altogether, it would be difficult to imagine anything grander in its style than this remarkable work. In the drawing, Fig. XXIII., the side divisions are shown, for the sake of clearness, as if they extended straight from the sides of the central group; but in the actual work they are splayed backward, giving great prominence to the central composition, the wings returning to the straight direction. In the beautifully designed Choir Organ, in front of the gallery, the retiring side divisions are correctly delineated. We have much pleasure in giving Mr. Hill's remarks on this case. He says: "The instrument stands in a western gallery, and is of such vast proportions that the topmost portion of the woodwork rises to a height of 100 ft. above the pavement. The extreme internal height of the church is 120 ft. The width of the Organ is 40 ft., and its depth from back to front is about 10 ft. It would be difficult to conceive a more stately or magnificent design than is presented by this organ-case. The V-shaped towers are admirably contrived, and a splendid effect is obtained by splaying backwards the great side compartments of pipes. All the cornices and pilasters are richly carved, while carving is also lavishly used in the pipe-shades and great base-corbels of the case. The composition of the upper portion of the structure is extremely fine. The center pipes of some of the compartments are elaborately chased and punched out, while the greater number are of burnished tin. The large pipes in the side flats belong to the Great Organ PRINCIPAL, which extends as far as the 32 ft. F, a rather remarkable compass. The gallery which supports the Organ is of the same date as the case [1602], and is a beautiful specimen of Renaissance work. . . The effect of the huge Organ, with its bright pipes richly contrasting with the dark and sumptuously carved case, is really very magnificent."

As another example of North German Renaissance, the Organ in the Marienkirche, at Stralsund, illustrated in Fig. XXII., deserves to be studied by the designer of to-day. Few old cases present a more varied and finer arrangement of displayed pipe-work. The treatment of the richly carved pipe-shades leaves nothing to be desired in this direction. Of the objectionable features of this noteworthy case we have already spoken. The magnificent Organ in the Ægidienkirche, at Lübeck, an illustration and a brief description of which are given in our First Chapter, also merits the careful study of the modern designer. In this case, in addition to the pipe-shade proper, each compartment has a richly carved lower or inverted shade, behind which the feet of the displayed pipes rest on the speaking-block. This treatment imparts an extreme richness to the case, and is one worthy of imitation. The general architectural disposition, with its grouping of segmental and V-shaped towers, is very effective; while the manner in which the

Choir Organ is connected to the sides of the large lateral towers of the main instrument is singularly happy. In this case, as in several others of the Renaissance

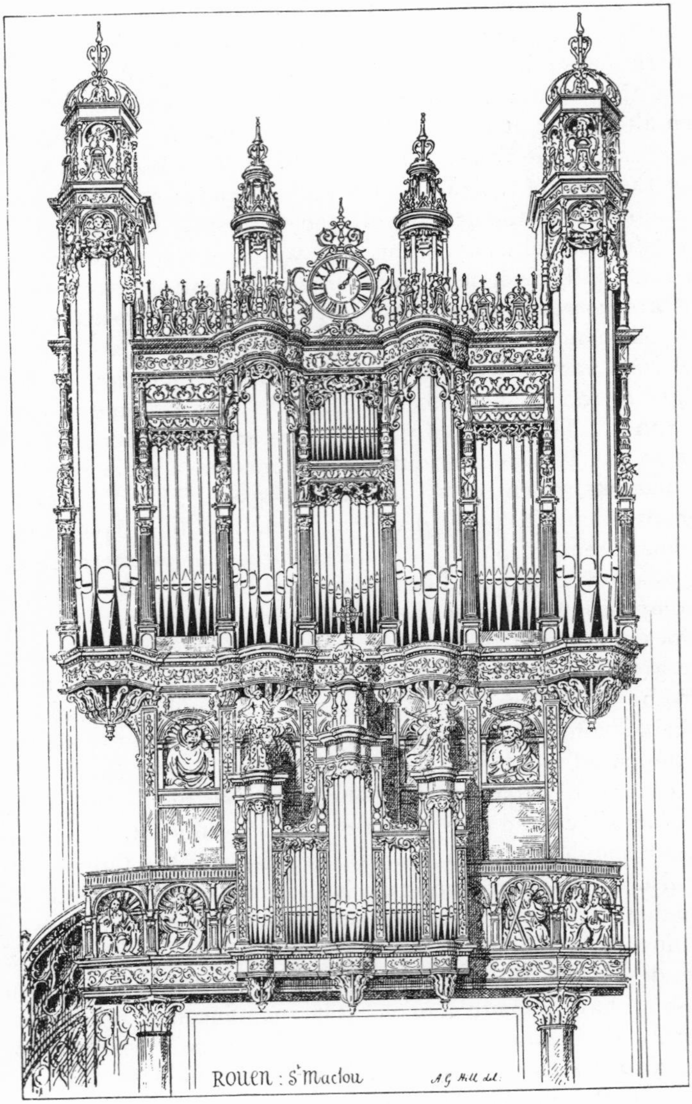

FIG. XXXI.

period, we find the objectionable wing features. Here they seriously injure the composition, being altogether too clumsy and out of scale with the other details of the case. The lanterns, or pagoda-like erections, which surmount the towers, are entirely out of sympathy with the work below; so much so that we cannot believe them to have been the work of the architect who designed the rest of the case. How easy it would have been to make these features artistic in themselves and in perfect keeping with the general architectural treatment.

The finest example of a French Renaissance organ-case is that in the Church of Saint-Maclou, at Rouen, Fig. XXXI. No work of its class and period deserves more careful study than this beautiful case—beautiful both in design and execution. Critical as one may be, it seems impossible to find fault with any portion of this remarkable work of Renaissance art. Mr. Hill furnishes the following interesting particulars: "The case is magnificently executed in a wood resembling chestnut and is of a light color. It stands in the western gallery. The work is chiefly by the hand of Nicholas Castel, and dates from the years 1518–21, while fifteen years later Martin Guibert, and his assistants, Mancel, Gillaume Dubost, and Robert Carolus, executed further work at a cost of 180 livres, being aided by the advice of Antoine Jousselme, organ builder, who received 140 livres. . . . Nicholas Quesnel, image maker, executed the figures of angels on the case. The whole work was originally decorated in gold and color, from a design furnished by Gougeon [Jean], and executed by Jacques de Seéz, painter, at a cost of 300 livres. This has, unfortunately, been removed of late years, and the woodwork entirely cleaned, and left in its natural tone. This is greatly to be regretted, as the decoration was, no doubt, of high excellence." We heartily join Mr. Hill in this expression of regret; for, while we examined the actual case in its present condition, we realized how much it must have gained by its artistic decoration under the direction of so accomplished a master as Jean Gougeon. The general architectural disposition, and the relative proportions of the several features of the case, are admirable. The arrangement of the displayed pipes in the towers and flat compartments is perfectly satisfactory. The Choir Organ, while of very pleasing design, does not correspond in all respects with the main Organ; we should pronounce it a later work by a different designer.

Of the Renaissance organ-cases designed by modern French architects, the most important is that of the Grand Organ in the Church of Saint-Eustache, at Paris. This was designed by M. Baltard, and was erected in 1854. The general treatment is strictly architectural, and is, accordingly, undesirably heavy and solid in appearance. The displayed pipes in the main case are all of large dimensions. In each of the lateral towers there are three independent groups of three great pipes, while the central tower contains five large pipes. In each of the curved curtains between the towers are eight pipes of lesser dimensions, making a total of thirty-nine displayed pipes. The towers are finished, upward, in an extremely heavy manner, having elaborately ornamented entablatures surmounted by architectural compositions in which large pedestals, niches, statues, festoons, vases, and other details appear. The Choir Organ, in front, is designed on similar lines and cannot be pronounced a satisfactory work.

The most ambitious and, at the same time, the most artistic modern design for a Renaissance organ-case, is that prepared by M. A. Simil for M. Cavaillé-

Coll's great project for a Monumental Organ in Saint Peter's at Rome. We give, in Plate IV., an illustration of this notable design, reproduced from a photograph presented to us by the late M. A. Cavaillé-Coll. The illustration is so clear in all the details that a description of the design is unnecessary.

In Fig. XVIII. in our historical notes, and Fig. XXIV. in the present Chapter, are given sketches of representative Spanish Renaissance organ-cases. The former, in the Cathedral of Barcelona, is highly suggestive; and one can see that, by removing the objectionable grotesque features which surmount the cornices of the several divisions, and finishing the principal divisions with pediments and ornamental terminals or figures of angels, a truly beautiful composition could be arrived at. The general disposition of the compartments and the arrangement of the displayed pipe-work are singularly happy. It will be observed that the large pipes in the lateral compartments are of their correct speaking lengths, and are, accordingly, all of different heights. The pipe-shades are cleverly treated to meet this irregularity. The same consistent treatment—consistent with the nature of organ pipes—is observed in all the larger compartments of the beautiful case in Tarragona Cathedral, Fig. XXIV. The lower portion of the Barcelona case, the small Choir Organ, and the front of the gallery, are all beautifully designed. Studying this work, one can imagine several very artistic and comparatively inexpensive renderings. For instance, such a case, constructed of plain wood, enameled warm white, and decorated with delicate Renaissance arabesques stenciled in black, would have a charming effect, resembling ivory inlaid with ebony. In such a case the displayed pipes should be of tin, burnished, and in prominent situations tastefully embossed, as in the upper central compartment of the Barcelona case. Other painted treatments will suggest themselves to the architect skilled in decorative art.

A general description of the case of the Organ in Tarragona Cathedral has already been given, and it is only necessary to add a few remarks here. To the modern designer of organ-cases in the Classic or Renaissance styles, this case is a mine of valuable suggestions. It is a work of wonderful dignity and repose, created by the architectural propriety which pervades its entire composition. A large case of this class, executed in dark oak, relieved with gold and colors, and having burnished tin pipes, or gilded pipes tastefully decorated with arabesques in brown, would have a magnificent effect at the west end of a Classical or Renaissance church.

In Mr. Hill's valuable book, to which we are so largely indebted, there is a drawing of the elaborate Renaissance case of the Organ in the Cathedral of Tortosa. This case is of much later date than that in Tarragona Cathedral, and is, accordingly, less pure in style and refined in detail. The ornamentation is extremely rich. The displayed pipes are of their proper speaking lengths, and several of the pipes in the four smaller compartments are embossed. The Choir Organ is of pleasing design and is, along with the gallery front and base of the main case, most elaborately carved. The entire work deserves to be carefully studied by the modern designer.

Organ-cases of Italian Renaissance present several distinguishing features

PLATE IV

characteristic of the architecture of the period. An interesting example is furnished by the Organ in the Church of Santa Maria della Scala, at Siena, a drawing of which is given in Fig. XXXII. The leading characteristic of the Italian

Fig. XXXII.

Renaissance cases is a square architectural treatment, in which bold angle pilasters, carrying a richly decorated horizontal entablature, and inclosing the displayed pipe-work, are the principal features. This treatment is shown in the Santa Maria Organ, and also in that in the Palazzo Pubblico, in the same city, an illustration of which is given in our historical notes, Fig. XIX. Speaking of the case in the

Church of Santa Maria, Mr. Hill remarks: "The organ-case under consideration was erected, most probably, about the year 1510, and is a very elaborate and fine piece of work. It is placed in a gallery or tribune at some height from the ground, the gallery being likewise much ornamented. It will be seen that the pipes in the organ-case are kept clear of the canopies or arcades, while they are cut to their natural speaking length without regard to exactitude of rake. All the details of this case are extremely well designed and executed, and the entire front is illuminated in blue and gold, red being very sparingly used. The frieze of the entablature and the panels of the columns are richly carved, the raised portions being gilded and the ground colored blue. In the two side circles are figures representing the Annunciation." The design of the filling-in, between the angle pilasters, is of a very curious character, but highly effective in the actual work. The entablature is surmounted by a composition of a very artistic and pleasing description, on the highest part of which stands a figure of the Blessed Virgin and Child. In the case in the Palazzo Pubblico, the filling-in, between the angle pilasters, is of a much more severe character, the cusped arches which spring from the square standards showing a lingering of the earlier Gothic feeling. The entablature is surmounted by a Classic pediment. This design (Fig. XIX.) is extremely dignified and highly suggestive. The irregular treatment of the pipes, characteristic of both Spanish and Italian Organs, is here very marked and is certainly not without its charm. In the four smaller compartments this irregularity is extremely pleasing, and is much to be preferred to a symmetrical arrangement. One can easily imagine what a magnificent case could be produced on the lines of this design, supposing it to be designed by an artist, executed by a master hand, and richly illuminated with gold and harmonious colors, like so much of the gorgeous Italian furniture and woodwork of the fifteenth and sixteenth centuries.

We may conclude our brief remarks on Italian organ-cases by directing attention to the grand Organ in the Church of Santa Maria di Carignano, Genoa, a reduced copy of Mr. Hill's clever drawing of which we give in the accompanying illustration, Fig. XXXIII. This remarkably beautiful case, although both designed and executed in Italy, cannot be pronounced a specimen of Italian Renaissance art. Beyond the irregular treatment of the displayed pipes, there is very little indicative of Italian taste. The manner in which the flanking towers are designed, the center portion is relieved by semicircular and V-shaped projecting features, the pipe-work is arranged, and the pipe-shades are treated, leaves nothing to be desired. As it stands, elevated in a western gallery, and with its painted shutters outspread, this Organ has a magnificent effect. Mr. Hill informs us that "the case is the work of Georges Heigenmann in its main features, the carvings being executed by Guilio Lippi, G. B. Hola, and Santino Guintino. The paintings on the shutters and the gilded decoration were carried out by Paolo Brozzi and Domenico Piola, the brother of the celebrated Pellegro." The work was executed about the year 1660.

There are very few English organ-cases of the Renaissance period that have escaped the ruthless hands of the "restorer," and this is much to be regretted. One of the earliest existing organ-cases is that of the smaller instrument in

Tewkesbury Abbey. This Organ was built by Harris for Magdalene College, Oxford, in the year 1637, and one hundred years later it was removed to Tewkes-

FIG. XXXIII.

bury Abbey. Of all the old examples in England we commend the case of this Organ to the attention of the architect and designer of to-day. The principal details of the case are Elizabethan in character; and these go far to show what an admirable style the Elizabethan is for the ornamental woodwork of an organ-

Fig. XXXIV.

case. Almost numberless fine works of the period, both in architecture and furniture, exist in the mansions of England. As drawings of these can be found in several art books, designers need not lack inspiration and suggestions. In Fig. XXXIV. is given a reduced reproduction of Mr. Hill's sketch of the Tewkesbury case. The general treatment of the woodwork and the arrangement of the displayed pipes are admirable. The Elizabethan character of the lower entablature

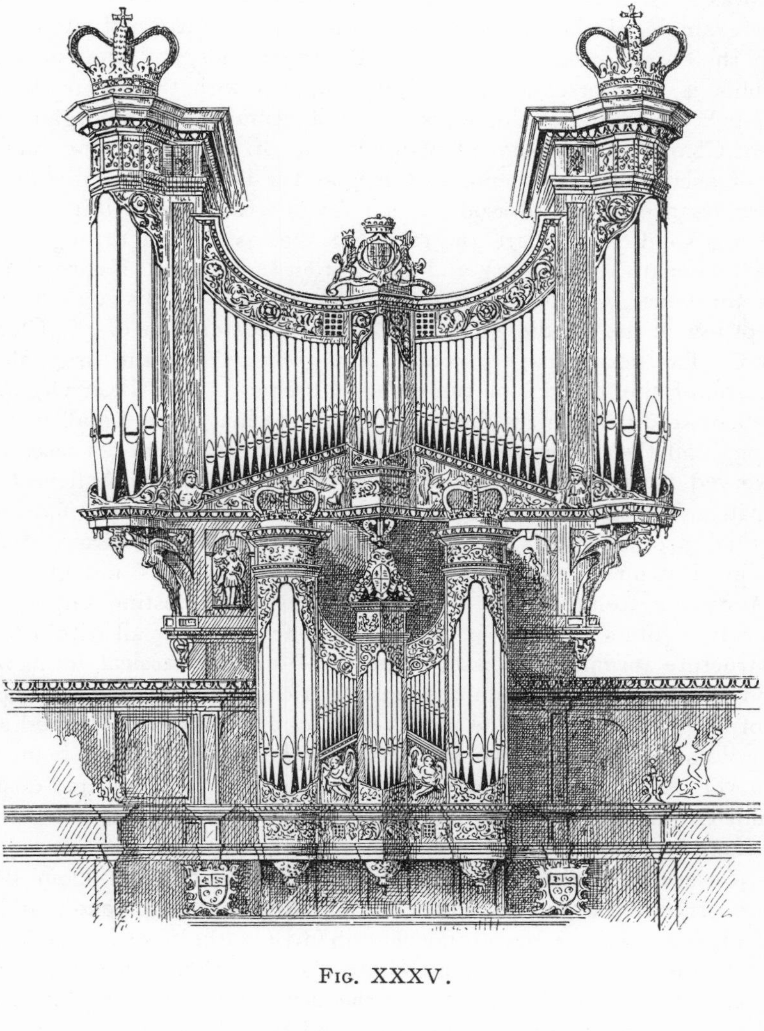

FIG. XXXV.

and its pendant arches is unmistakable; while a strong feeling in the same direction obtains throughout the upper portions of the case. The introduction of the several embossed pipes in the small V-shaped towers and the flats imparts great richness to the front.

Organ-cases of all classes, from the simplest to the most elaborate, can readily be designed in pure Elizabethan, for it presents much of the flexibility and spirit of Gothic work.

Another extremely interesting English Renaissance organ-case is furnished by the instrument in the magnificent Chapel of King's College, Cambridge. A sketch of this case, reproduced from Mr. Hill's work, is given in Fig. XXXV. This case was constructed in the early years of the seventeenth century, and is an admirable example of the taste of the period. The introduction of the large crowns on the entablatures of the towers, the royal arms, and the Tudor rose and the portcullis, is, of course, special and in sympathy with the architectural details of the Chapel. Speaking of this work, Mr. Hill remarks: "The organ-case in the magnificent Chapel of the above College is one of the oldest and most perfect examples of such work that remain in England. The instrument stands upon a superb Renaissance screen of wood which divides the Chapel into two portions. This screen is solid (save where the main entrance is pierced through the center, immediately beneath the Organ), and dates from the time of Henry VIII. It is, doubtless, the finest Renaissance work of its class left in this country. . . . The case is kept low in the middle, so as to allow of a better view of the Chapel from end to end. The design is very good, but a good deal of the original effect is lost by reason of the absence of the embossed pipes. The Choir Organ front is most excellent, and harmonizes thoroughly with the magnificent stall-work below."

Although all the important mediæval and Renaissance organ-cases that have been preserved have displayed pipes, we have good reason to believe that many smaller instruments were constructed in the cases of which no pipes were displayed. One instance of this treatment exists in the old Cathedral of Salamanca, Spain. This instrument is illustrated in "The Organ-cases and Organs of the Middle Ages and Renaissance." Speaking of this interesting Organ, Mr. Hill remarks: "It exhibits no pipes in front, but conceals them all within the square wooden structure forming the case. This is of strictly classical form, with pediments and angle pilasters, while the base is richly ornamented with arabesque patterns of excellent design. The panels or sides are elaborately carved and decorated in gold and color, the two subjects shown in the drawing being a Radix Jesse, and the Assumption, executed with much power and spirited design. . . . This quaint Organ dates from about the year 1540, and is in many respects a valuable example of old work." Doubtless numerous other works of a similar class are preserved in old Spanish churches. At the time of Dom Bedos, the idea of constructing organ-cases of a highly ornamental character and without displayed pipes must have been somewhat in favor; otherwise he would not have inserted in his important work the elaborate Plate, entitled "Idée d'un grand Buffet d'Orgues sans Tuyaux Apparents," at the same time recording his disapproval of the idea. The conception of the case alluded to is so novel that we give, in Fig. XXXVI., a reproduction of the Plate on a small scale. Notwithstanding the bizarre character of the design, it is not without value to the modern artist.*

* Dom Bedos remarks: "Ce Buffet consiste en un grand corps de menuiserie, décoré d'un nombre de figures & d'ornements, relatifs & analogues à l'Instrument. Il sera commode pour la construction intérieure de

Having considered the general design of the organ-case, we may now direct attention to the several features or portions of the instrument which enter into the composition of the external design of the Organ.

Fig. XXXVI.

At this point the swell-box may be mentioned as a portion of the Organ suitable for, and deserving of, artistic treatment whenever it is exposed. In the

l'Orgue ; comme il est tout à jour, le son se fera bien entendre. L'avant-corps, qui est au milieu sur le devant, est fait pour cacher l'Organiste, ou bien, pour y placer le positif, si on ne veut pas le mettre dans le grand Buffet. En ce cas, on lui donnera une profondeur convenable. Le tout peut être posé sans aucun inconvénient sur une tribune de quelque espèce qu'elle soit, pourvu, comme nous l'avons recommandé ailleurs, qu'elle soit ferme & inébranlable."

generality of instances the swell-box is either put out of sight, or shown without any attempt to beautify it; but as there is a considerable advantage gained so far as acoustic effect is concerned by elevating the swell-box, and also making it as high in itself as circumstances permit, there is no reason why its exterior should not be treated in an ornamental fashion and turned into an important feature in the general design. Of course a swell-box can only be so treated when the Organ occupies a position where there is ample height, and when it can be brought forward so as to be seen in combination with the case. In Chamber Organs of moderate dimensions and proper construction, the swell-box may become a most important central feature, and should, accordingly, be effectively designed and decorated, rendering anything in the shape of a screen unnecessary. The only portions of the swell-box that present any difficulty in the way of artistic treatment are the louvres or moving shutters; but as in all properly constructed instruments these will be placed vertically, the difficulty may be overcome, either by some relief ornamentation on their faces or by painted decoration; or, in some special works, by the union of both. In Gothic work, the faces of the louvres may be covered with light traceried paneling, such as is met with in the Late Decorated and Perpendicular styles; and this paneling may be artistically relieved by painting and gilding. Each louvre must be treated so as to be complete in itself, and to produce in combination with all the others a pleasing whole. The angles and tops of swell-boxes admit of a great variety of treatments. The angles may be simply moulded, or have corner standards surmounted by capitals carrying figures of angels, or may terminate in crocketed pinnacles. The top of the swell-box may have a rich cornice, carrying a battlemented, traceried, or foliated cresting; or it may assume the form of a quaint Gothic roof, appropriately painted.

The greatest display of ingenuity and taste is possible in designing the cases of Chamber Organs, although very little has been achieved in this direction. The old-fashioned style of case, closed entirely at the sides and almost completely in front, has the advantage of protecting the interior from much of the dust periodically disturbed by the housemaid's brush; but as an Organ, if at all worthy of its name, is a rather bulky affair, it follows that a closed case must appear a very cumbersome and inartistic piece of furniture. To overcome this objectionable appearance, the case or the exterior of the instrument should be broken up into well-marked features or divisions, and relieved by variously arranged groups of pipes. The sides of the Organ may appropriately be relieved by the wooden Bourdon or Open Diapason pipes of the Pedal Organ, carefully finished, and varnished or decorated. The front corners of the instrument may have towers of bright metal pipes, such as those which form the lowest octave of the chief manual Open Diapason; and the space, in front, between the towers, may be richly treated in several ways. Up to the level of the front wind-chest the case will usually be of ornamental woodwork, paneled and carved, or, what is much more to be desired, painted with subjects and designs relating to music. The upper part of the front may be designed in compartments, with or without projecting features; or treated in a broad and dignified manner, with single or double ranks of large metal or wood pipes, in advance of a richly decorated and ornamented swell-box. The metal pipes should be of burnished tin or the finest spotted metal, while the wooden pipes should be richly decorated with gold and colors.*

A Chamber Organ may be more closely cased up than any other class of Organ, simply because its sounds have neither to travel so far nor to so prominently assert themselves; indeed, as a rule, the stops in a Chamber instrument are all the better for having their voices refined. Great care must be taken, however, in designing the case, not to render the tone of the stops unequal by inclosing one part more than another. The mechanical portions of the instrument cannot be too much inclosed, provided arrangements are made for easy access to them for regulation and repairs; for the more completely the mechanism is protected from dust and currents of damp air the better it will be for all delicate parts of the action.

In the designing of all classes of organ-cases, save that class which disguises the nature of the instrument inclosed, the proper treatment of the displayed pipework is of the greatest importance. Speaking pipes only should be employed, except in cases where some decided disadvantage attends their uniform adoption. Dumb pipes may be introduced when a difficulty arises in the proper conveyance of wind; or when an odd pipe or two may be necessary to fill up a given space, or to render a group symmetrical. Both metal and wood speaking pipes may be introduced in the same design, either in separate compartments, or associated together in double ranks.

The ways of arranging and grouping external pipes are very numerous, and admit of almost countless changes, in which the heights of their bodies, the relative proportions of their feet, the lines created by their mouths, and their dispositions on plan, are the chief factors.

Large metal pipes, such as those belonging to the DOUBLE OPEN DIAPASON, 32 FT., the OPEN DIAPASON, 16 FT., VIOLONE, 16 FT., or DULCIANA, 16 FT., of the Pedal Organ; and the DOUBLE OPEN DIAPASON, 16 FT., of the Great Organ, may be appropriately and effectively grouped in salient features, or arranged in projecting clusters, commonly, in organ nomenclature, called towers. These usually comprise three, five, or seven pipes; the largest occupying the central and most

*In the Chamber Organ designed and constructed by the author of this treatise, the front swell-box (there are two in the instrument) is most elaborately treated. It comes forward to within about nine inches of the front line of the case below, and has only a single rank of stopped wood pipes in advance of it. These pipes fall downward in a curve to the center so as to allow the upper part of the swell-box to be seen. The box is enriched at each end with arched paneling, fully decorated; and is surmounted by a deep moulded cornice and battlemented cresting, also richly decorated. The louvres, horizontally placed, in front, are painted with a conventionalized rose-tree spreading over a gold trellis, the horizontal bars of which fall at the lower edges of the louvres. The wooden pipes, in advance of this, fifteen in number, are entirely gilded on their exposed surfaces and decorated with a quaint, 15th-century, diaper executed in black and brown: their caps are moulded and accentuated with quiet coloring. As the pipes are stopped and their stopper-handles are ornamental and shown, it is obvious that all the fifteen are of different lengths. This irregularity has been studied, and imparts a pleasing feeling of freedom to the front. The pipes have been so carefully scaled and regulated that their heights graduate in a symmetrical manner, and exactly the same amount of each stopper-handle appears. The diaper pattern is correctly graduated, so that all the pipes are alike as regards the number of repeats in length and width. The effect produced by these gold and black pipes against the rose-trellis background of the swell-box is extremely rich and refined.

prominent position in each group. These groups may assume a triangular, square, semicircular, or polygonal disposition, which will, as all the pipes are

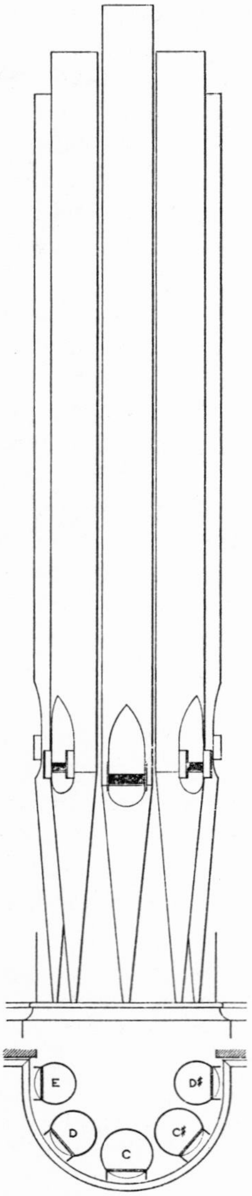

Fig. XXXIX.

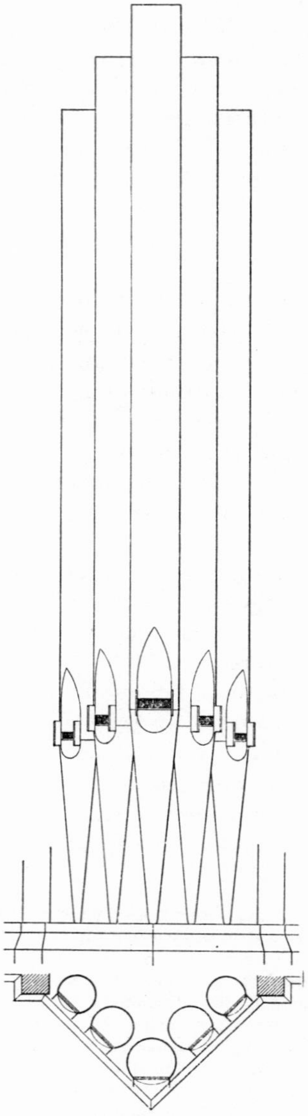

Fig. XXXVII.

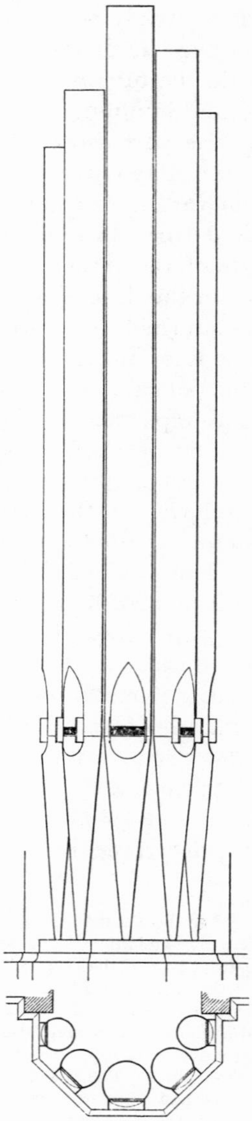

Fig. XLI.

cylindrical, be chiefly indicated by the forms of the supports on which they are planted, and the shades, cornices, or other features which surmount them. In the accompanying Fig. XXXVII. is represented a triangular tower of five pipes, suitable for all styles of cases. The feet are graduated in proportion to the heights of the bodies; and the tops are cut symmetrically, as if they are to be left free. The triangular tower may have only three pipes; a good example of which is to be seen in the central feature of the Armley Organ, Plate III. There also is to be seen the arrangement of three pipes as a corner feature. In these triplets the mouths are kept at one level, while in our Diagram they are on three different levels, with the highest in the center. Another example of a triangular tower is to be seen in the Hombleux case, Fig. XXVI.

Square towers may be used for certain positions, but are the least pleasing of all the forms in use. They cannot well be formed, like the triangular towers, of pipes only, requiring, for a satisfactory treatment, standards at their angles, as indicated in the Plan, Fig. XXXVIII. Square towers are suitable for Gothic

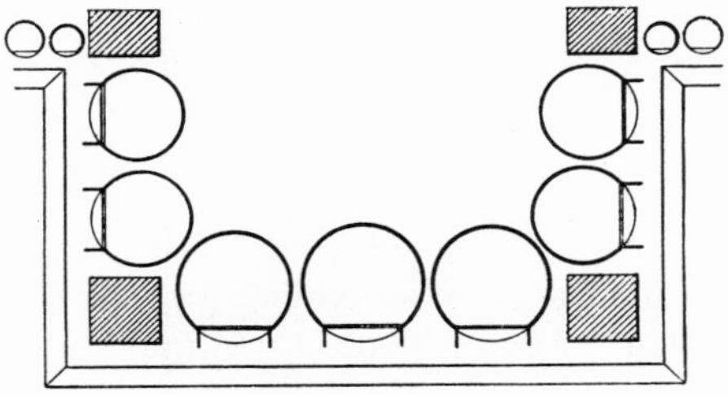

Fig. XXXVIII.

organ-cases, and admit of very effective treatments in their upper portions. They can also be introduced in Classic and Renaissance designs.

Towers formed of pipes disposed in a circular fashion are very commonly met with in old cases, and are generally pleasing in effect. When pipes so arranged occupy an arc less than a semicircle, the group cannot correctly be called a tower, but may be designated a breasted or convex compartment; such groups can be formed of a considerable number of small pipes, as will be shown. A semicircular tower is represented in Fig. XXXIX., composed of five large pipes. This is the smallest number of pipes a tower of this form should contain, for triplets naturally belong to triangular towers, as has been shown above. In our Diagram the mouths of the pipes are disposed in a manner directly contrary to that shown in Fig. XXXVII.: this is done to illustrate different methods. It will be understood that there are no rules relating to the arrangements of mouths or heights of pipe-feet, such details being almost entirely matters of taste. The semicircular tower is well adapted for an important central feature of a Classic, Romanesque, or Renaissance design; but is not suitable in a Gothic one, although it is not without precedent in that style. It appears in a pronounced form in the Organ in the Marienkirche, at Dortmund, where it is formed of nine pipes. In this interesting case, two lesser towers of similar form, containing seven pipes each, occupy lateral positions. Semicircular towers, alternating with triangular ones, are to be found in the fine late Gothic case in the Organ in the Church at Jutfaas. In old Rennaissance organ-cases semicircular towers or features are very common. Towers of seven pipes, occupying two-thirds or three-quarters of a circle on plan, are well adapted for salient features at the angles of a case, as indicated in the Plan, Fig. XL.

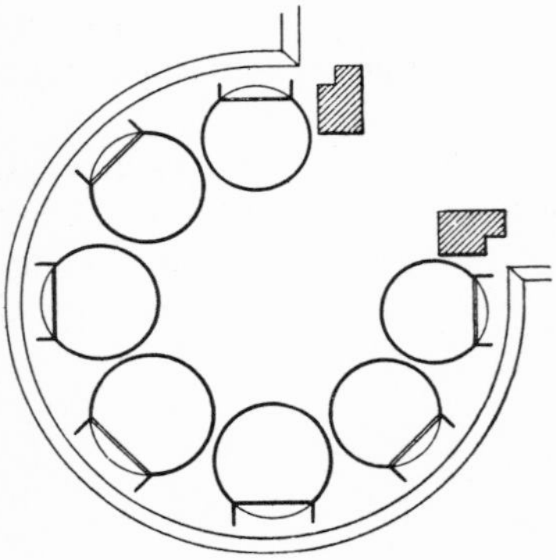

FIG. XL.

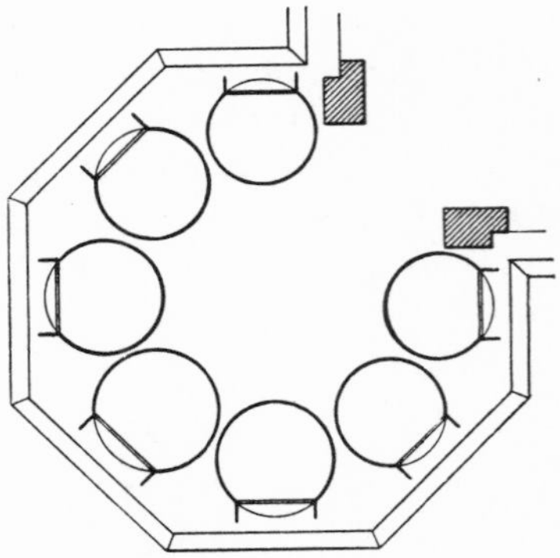

FIG. XLII.

Fig. XLI. is a Diagram of a semi-octagonal tower of five pipes, the only number suitable for such a plan. It will be observed that there is practically no difference in the positions of the pipes in the semicircular and semi-octagonal towers; their respective forms being defined only by the pedestals or supports on which they stand, and by the forms of any ornamental bands or crestings of woodwork which may enter into the design of the organ-case. Semi-octagonal towers can be introduced in designs in any style of architecture. The bodies of the pipes are here shown of unequal lengths, approximating their true speaking lengths, a treatment which has a fine appearance when the tops of the pipes are shown, without shades or other woodwork. For angular positions, towers presenting seven sides of an octagon and seven pipes are very suitable. A Plan of such an angle tower is given in Fig. XLII. Smaller angle towers, of five pipes, can be constructed with five sides of a hexagon, as indicated in Fig. XLIII.: and large towers of nine sides and nine pipes may be introduced in important cases. When the latter are adopted, they should be composed of tall pipes of small scale, and surmounted by ornamental woodwork. In the generality of properly treated and artistically designed organ-cases, all the towers and tower-like features are finished with perforated pipe-shades, entablatures, crestings, or canopy-work of wood; and all the pipes are carried up so as to finish behind the woodwork, irrespective of their speaking lengths. A tower-like feature, or what may be termed a quasi-tower, occupies the central position in Loosemore's case in Exeter Cathedral. This is formed of five large pipes, the center one of which is projected in front of the others, as shown in the plan, Fig. XLIV. This causes an angular projection both in the *cul-de-lampe* which carries the pipes and the entablature which crowns the group.

The dimensions of towers will, of necessity, be dictated by the size of the Organ, and the more important stops it contains that can be utilized. In instruments of the first magnitude, such as those in the Royal Albert Hall, London, and St. George's Hall, Liverpool, the chief towers are formed of pipes from the 32 feet open stops. The Albert Hall Organ has the finest towers ever introduced in an English instrument. They are formed of the lower pipes of the DOUBLE OPEN

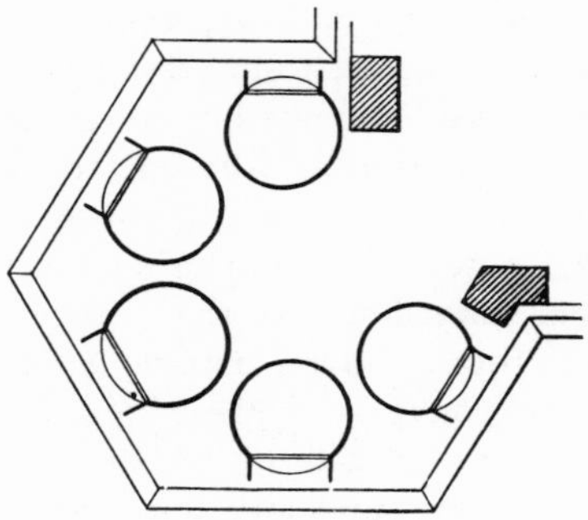

FIG. XLIII.

DIAPASON and the CONTRA VIOLONE, of the Pedal Organ: they are nearly pure tin, and the largest pipe of each tower measures about forty feet in height. In instruments of lesser size, which may have a single 32 ft. open metal stop of medium scale, two triplet towers may be formed of the GGGG pipe and the five following pipes above, the pipes in each group being of corresponding heights. In Church Organs, effective towers may be formed from the six or ten larger pipes of the 16 ft. metal stop, preferably the DOUBLE OPEN DIAPASON of the Great

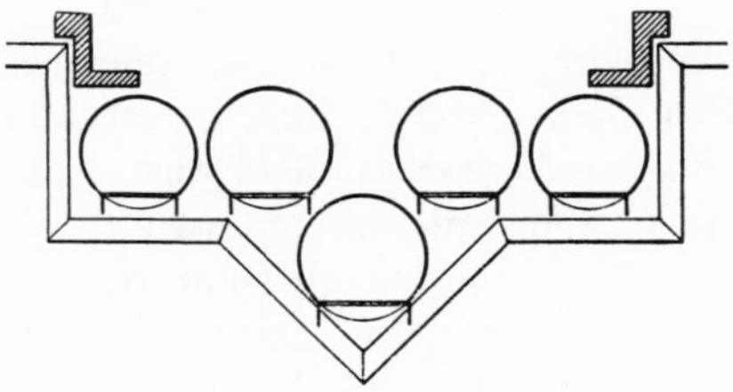

FIG. XLIV.

Organ. Secondary towers, or *tourelles*, in large Organs, should be formed from 16 ft. open metal stops; and in Church Organs, from 8 ft. stops, such as the OPEN DIAPASON, SALICIONAL, or DULCIANA. The towers of Chamber Organs of moderate size should be formed with the larger pipes of the uninclosed OPEN DIAPASON, 8 FT., of the manual department; the CC and CC♯ pipes of which, with properly proportioned feet, and bodies slightly in excess of their speaking lengths, will be about eleven feet in height.

In arranging speaking pipes in towers of any of the shapes above described, care must be taken to so place them as to secure an optical uniformity or balance. This renders it necessary to place the pipes on one side of a central pipe wider apart than those on the other, as clearly indicated in all the plans we have given. When dumb pipes are used, they can be made of similar sizes so as to render perfect uniformity possible; but in all cases such pipes should be sparingly used. Dumb pipes add expense without giving an adequate return; and it would be better, in all instances, to tolerate a little irregularity, especially as it springs from the nature of the instrument, than to resort to anything false.

Perhaps enough has been said respecting the arrangement of large pipes in towers, so we may now direct attention to different arrangements of smaller pipes in curtains, wings, and other divisions of an organ-case. The curtain is any space which extends between two towers or projecting features; while wings are the flanking portions of a design, subordinate to the central mass, and so treated as to terminate the composition, laterally, in an artistic manner. Curtains are usually flat, but may be concave or convex; while wings may assume bold sweeping curves or any form on plan that the taste of the designer may suggest, controlled only by the necessities of the instrument and the space at his disposal. Curtains may be composed of bold arrangements of medium sized pipes, preferably of small scale, spreading entirely across from tower to tower; they may be cut up into two, three, or more divisions by vertical standards; or divided both vertically and horizontally into several compartments, filled with numerous small pipes. The last method frequently obtains in rich cases, and when well arranged has, from an artistic point of view, much to recommend it: it is, however, attended with considerable expense on account of the elaborate nature of its woodwork, and the unavoidable demand for numerous dumb pipes to fill all the compartments remote from the wind-chests. As an illustration of the extent to which this vertical and horizontal subdivision has been carried in old work, we may mention the Organ in the Church of St. Nicholas, at Stralsund. The curtain work, between the heavy lateral towers, which is on plan a succession of concave and convex features, is divided into no fewer than thirty-three compartments, filled with pipes large and small, and very cleverly disposed. Great taste and skill can be displayed in the designing of large curtains; and considerable variety can be imparted to their compartments, not only by the various heights and scales of the pipes introduced, but also by the lengths of their feet, and the marked lines, horizontal, inclined, and curved, formed by their mouths. The curtains may be straight, curved, or wavy, in plan; or may be compounded of all these forms.

In designs for Gothic cases, the curtains should be flat, and their compartments so proportioned as to present an artistic display of traceried pipe-shades and an effective arrangement of displayed pipes. In the accompanying Diagram, Fig. XLV., is given Plans of the three arrangements of pipes suitable for flat compartments; and above them three ways in which their mouths can be appropriately ranged. In the Renaissance case of the Organ in Chartres Cathedral we find a flat compartment with an unusual arrangement of pipes. The Plan of this is given in Fig. XLVI. The large pipe forming a projection in the center of the compartment gives an opportunity for the introduction of some relieving feature in the design.

Breasted compartments are frequently met with in old organ-cases, and are

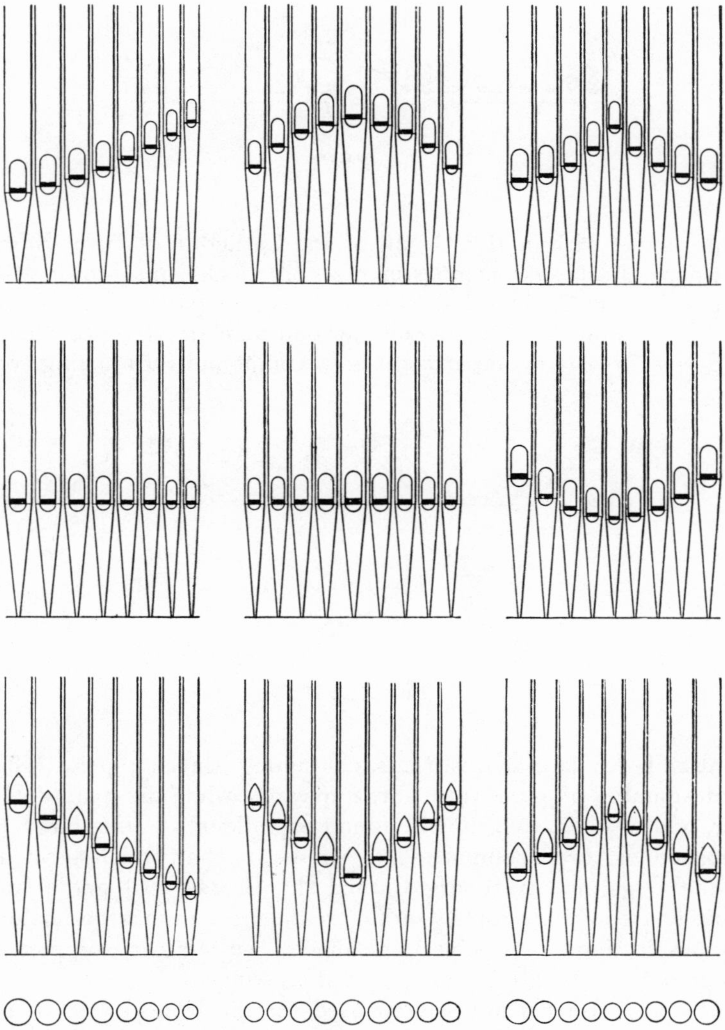

FIG. XLV.

valuable features in the hands of the skilled designer. They assume several forms, as indicated in the accompanying Plans, Fig. XLVII. A is a canted, or obtuse-angled, breasted compartment, of nine pipes, but it may be formed of any odd number of pipes; and it may have any degree of projection desired, so long as it does not assume the form of the triangular tower. A compartment of the form illustrated is to be seen in the Organ of the Church of Wesel, on the Rhine. B is a three-sided breasted compartment, of eleven pipes, but can be made of any odd number of pipes above seven with a satisfactory effect. An exception to this

FIG. XLVI.

desirable rule is met with in the Organ of the Cathedral of Saint-Brieuc (Côtes-du-Nord), where the lateral compartments—practically quasi-towers—have only four pipes, as shown at C. D is a convex breasted compartment of the usual form, composed of eleven pipes. Here again any odd number of pipes above five can be used. E is a breasted compartment of a compound form, being composed of

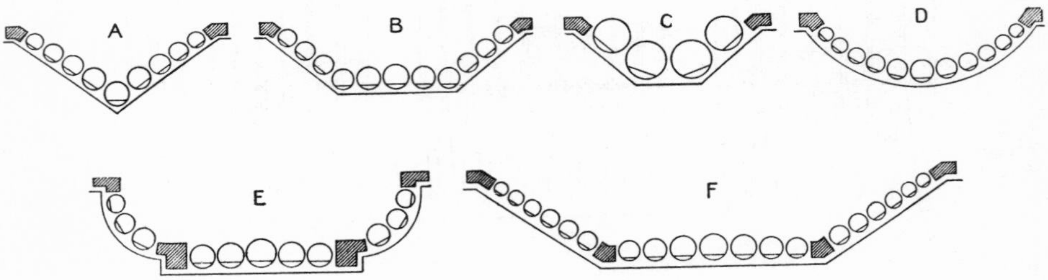

FIG. XLVII.

a central flat and two lateral quadrants, containing eleven pipes. The flat may have any odd number of pipes from three upwards, while the quadrants may have any number, odd or even, that may be found expedient. F is a large three-sided breast composed of three compartments, similar to that which forms the central feature of the Organ in Strasbourg Cathedral. Breasts with angle standards, as in this example, are suitable for a Gothic treatment, and may be made very beautiful, with pipes in single or double tiers, shaded with tracery or pierced foliage, and surmounted by rich cornices and pierced crestings.

Concave compartments are seldom used for the fronts of cases, being, comparatively speaking, ineffective. When the compartments are small and their concavity is considerable, the pipes have a huddled appearance, with their mouths approaching each other in a manner not pleasing to the eye. When the concavity is very slight the same objections do not obtain. Concave compartments are useful in connecting prominent divisions of a front with others that are recessed. A good example of this treatment is to be seen in the Organ of the Church of

St. Nicholas, Stralsund, where concave compartments, filled with small pipes, connect the central convex division of the case with the lateral projecting divisions. A somewhat similar disposition occurs in the Organ of the Cathedral of Würzburg. Plans of four concave compartments are given in Fig. XLVIII., showing different

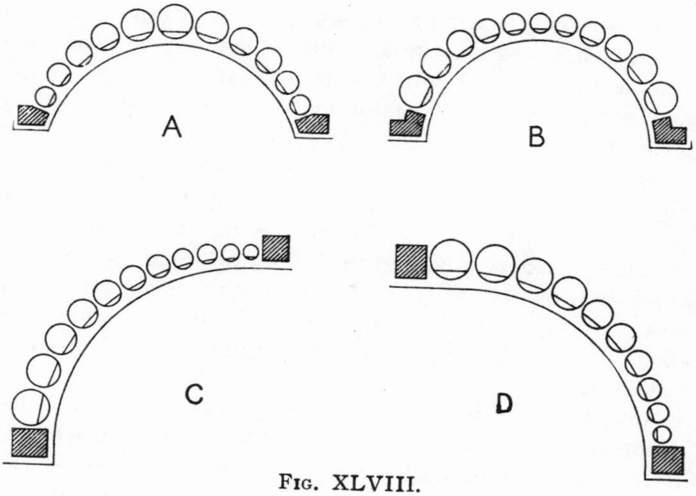

Fig. XLVIII.

arrangements of pipes. A and B are compartments, of the nature of niches, for introduction in fronts of cases, between features of equal projection; C and D are compartments for connecting features of different projection. Large concave

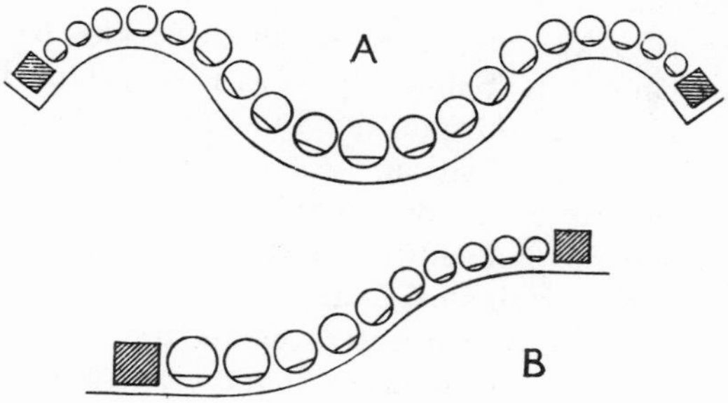

Fig. XLIX.

sweeps, of the nature of the latter two Plans, are suitable for wings of cases; or for connecting recessed wings or lateral towers with a main advanced division. Concave compartments are not to be recommended for cases in the Gothic styles.

Only two other forms of pipe arrangements or compartments need be alluded to here, those shown on plan in Fig. XLIX. A is the wavy compartment suitable for some central position; and B is the ogee compartment, only suitable for lateral positions, being similar in this respect to C and D, Fig. XLVIII.

When greater variety is desired in the exposed pipe-work of an organ-case than that which can be secured by the use of cylindrical metal pipes, or those which are alone introduced in the cases of the Mediæval and old Renaissance Organs, the designer may use pipes of some other forms, such as the graceful pipes of the SPITZFLÖTE and GEMSHORN stops, which taper from their mouths to a smaller circumference at top, and the BELL GAMBA, the pipes of which have tapered bodies surmounted by graceful bells. Such pipes must, however, be introduced sparingly and with great judgment, and preferably in flats of small dimensions. On acoustical grounds they are better than cylindrical pipes, because they do not obstruct the passage of sound to the same extent. Tastefully decorated wood pipes of small scales may be used in flat compartments with satisfactory effect; but they must be confined to leading or some special divisions of the case. In lateral divisions or wings, set back from the main body of the case, the tall and small-scaled pipes of the Pedal Organ VIOLONE, of wood, may be introduced with advantage, as they will throw the bright metal pipe-work of the main case into greater relief.

There is one other system of pipe arrangement that must be mentioned, although it is one not likely to be used in English or American Organs; we allude to the peculiarly Spanish method of placing reed pipes of the TRUMPET class horizontally, and projecting from the front of the Organ, at the level of the main wind-chests, or immediately below the feet of the lower series of the vertical, displayed pipes. An example of this treatment obtains in the Organ of Tarragona Cathedral, as shown in Fig. XXIV. Other noteworthy examples are furnished by the grand Organs in the Cathedrals of Toledo, Cordova, Burgos, Barcelona (Fig. XVIII.), Seville, and Zaragoza (Fig. XXV.). Reed stops disposed in this fashion are distinguished by the French organ builders by the term *en chamade*. There is a TROMPETTE HARMONIQUE en chamade in the Récit Expressif of the Grand Organ in the Church of Saint-Sulpice, at Paris. One English example was furnished by the York Minster Organ, the TUBA being there displayed projecting from the case in a horizontal position. As we strongly condemn the inartistic practice of placing powerful reed stops in an uninclosed and expressionless condition, we naturally cannot recommend the designer to follow the Spanish treatment.

In the center flats or curtains of Chamber or small Church Organs, in which the case-work is of the skeleton character, metal and wood pipes may be effectively arranged in two ranks, placed closely together. In Fig. L. the front rank is composed of OPEN DIAPASON pipes, preferably of burnished tin; while the back rank is of quadrangular wood pipes, such as those of the CLARABELLA or MELODIA; or they may be of LIEBLICHGEDECKT pipes, having their stopper-handles shown. These wood pipes should be decorated in a quiet and refined manner so as to form a background to the bright tin pipes. The metal pipes may be also decorated, either in a richer scale of color, or with a black or brown diaper on a gold ground. In Fig. LI. is shown an arrangement directly the reverse of the preceding. Here the front rank is of STOPPED DIAPASON, LIEBLICHGEDECKT, or small-scaled BOURDON pipes; while the back rank is formed of open cylindrical pipes, such as those of the SALICIONAL or DULCIANA. When tastefully decorated wood pipes are thus used, in advance of polished tin or plain gilded pipes, a curtain is produced which has a most artistic appearance; and especially so when the whole is placed immediately in front of a richly decorated and ornamental swell-box. It will be observed, on referring to Fig. LI., that the pipes are not arranged in a perfectly symmetrical manner, that is, in pairs of equal length on each side of the

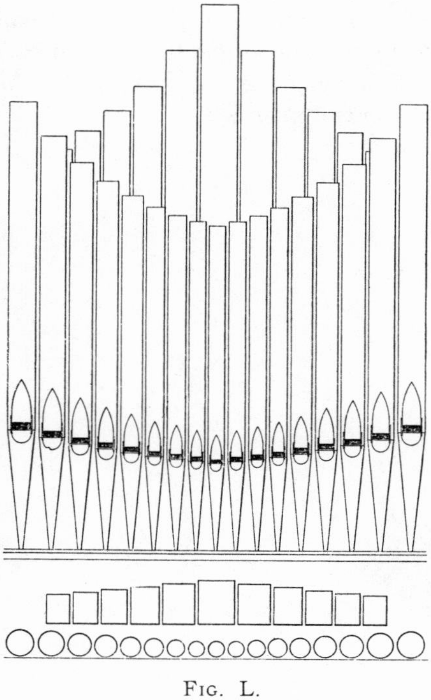

FIG. L.

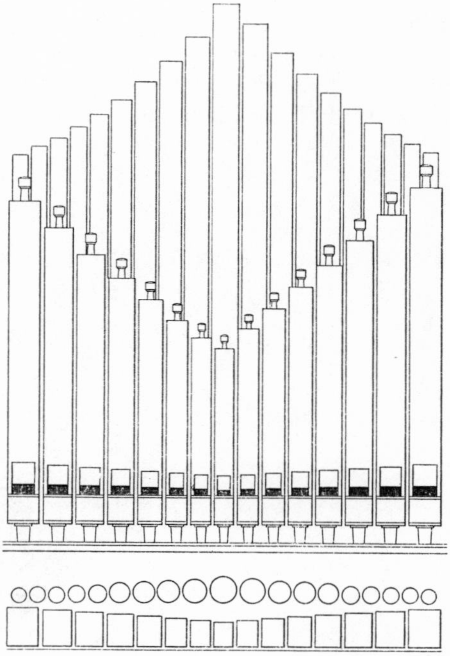

FIG. LI.

central odd pipe. Such an arrangement, following the Spanish and Italian custom, is less stiff and formal than that shown in Fig. L.; and must commend itself to anyone who knows anything about the nature of organ pipes; just as the irregular arrangement commended itself to the old Spanish and Italian artists.

In organ-cases in which the woodwork is carried upward and finishes in some ornamental fashion above the tops of the displayed pipes, it is usual for the pipes to terminate behind pierced tracery or carved scroll-work or foliage. Under these circumstances, the forms assumed by the free edges of the ornamental woodwork or pipe-shades impart distinctive characters to the several groups or ranks of pipes; and, accordingly, it is not a matter of great importance at what heights the pipes terminate behind the woodwork. In some designs, such as those of old

Spanish cases, the groups of pipes terminate immediately under the carved pipe-shades; and as it is necessary that each pipe be, at least, its proper speaking length, it is usual for the ornamental woodwork to be designed to meet as closely as possible the varying heights of the different groups. In all these matters the designer will do well to seek inspiration from ancient examples, bearing in mind that in the designs for such woodwork he has an immense field for the exercise of his individual ingenuity and taste.

We have extended the subject of the present Chapter somewhat beyond the limits prescribed by the general scheme of our treatise; yet we feel that not a line too much has been written. The subject is one deserving of much more study and general attention than it has received in recent times. It is to be regretted that it has been neglected in all the practical treatises on organ-building hitherto published; and this fact increases the debt all lovers of the Organ owe to Mr. Arthur G. Hill for his monumental work on ancient organ-cases.

CHAPTER IV.

DECORATION OF THE ORGAN.

AS a practical continuation to what is said in the preceding Chapter, the following hints on the Decoration of the Organ will not be without interest to the architect and decorative artist. This subject, like all others connected with the art of organ-building, admits of a lengthy dissertation; but such is not possible within the limits of the present treatise. In this Chapter, as in the preceding, a few hints only are given in the hopes that they may prove suggestive to those who have to design and decorate the cases for Church, Concert-room, and Chamber Organs.

Of late years there has been an opinion growing in certain artistic quarters that Organs should present no colored or gilded decoration whatever; that they should depend, for their beauty of appearance, on well-designed and carefully-executed woodwork devoid of painting of any description, and displayed pipe-work of burnished tin. This may be designated the legitimate treatment, while it is at the same time the most exacting and expensive, especially when the Organ is of large dimensions and calls for an elaborate design. One may at once admit that when an organ-case is artistically designed, carefully constructed of choice oak or some richly-colored hardwood, and mounted with tastefully grouped pipes of highly burnished tin, there is little left to be desired. But we do not hesitate to assert that even such a case would be greatly enhanced in artistic value and beauty of appearance by the addition of such decorations, in gold and colors, as would accentuate its leading lines and features and add force to its entire design. We have ample support for such an opinion in the works of the Middle Ages and Renaissance. We are free to admit that all the gilding and colored decoration possible will fail to redeem a badly-proportioned and coarsely designed organ-case; indeed, where deformities exist it is certain that the addition of color and gilding will make them more apparent to the eye. Generally speaking, decorative painting is resorted to with the view of hiding inferior materials and workmanship; and, under such circumstances, it usually attends cheap building, and is

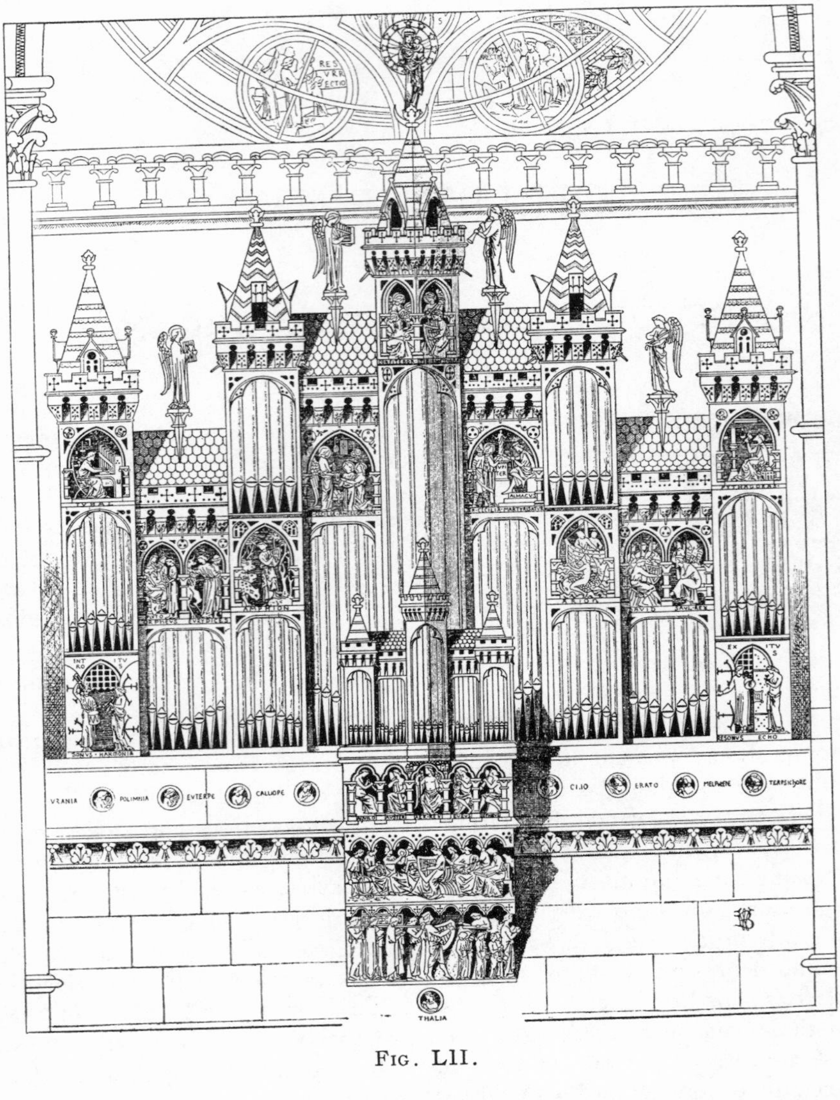

FIG. LII.

almost invariably inartistic in conception, coarse in execution, and crude and gaudy in coloring.

It is by no means easy to design an organ-case which shall be an artistic and thoroughly consistent work—consistent with the nature and demands of the

Organ as a musical instrument;—but it is a far more difficult problem to decorate it so that the result shall be at once rich and refined, and through which neither perfect workmanship nor choice materials shall be hidden.

In the first place, as regards the woodwork of the case, when oak is used alone or in combination with other contrasting woods, there is seldom any decorative painting added, unless elaborately-decorated surroundings demand it. Gilding, when judiciously and sparingly applied, so as to emphasize the leading forms and salient features of the design, has a very satisfactory effect. When the organ-case is to be entirely covered with decorative painting, a less expensive or more easily-worked wood than oak is commonly used. But in work carried out in the true mediæval spirit, and when the decorative painting is to be of the highest order, assuming the form of beautiful and appropriate figure subjects, it becomes obvious that only the finest quality of wood and workmanship should be associated with it. Under such circumstances, oak is adopted on account of its close association with mediæval work, and because of its strength and durability; and as the decorative painting is more valuable than the wood upon which it is executed, it is accordingly carried partially or entirely over it, as the aim of the artist may dictate.

The application of appropriate figure subjects to an organ-case may be well exemplified by the unique design prepared by the late William Burges, of London, for the Organ of the Cathedral of Lille, given in the accompanying illustration, Fig. LII.* The entire woodwork of this instrument was designed with the

* Reproduced from the engraving given in the "Annales Archéologiques," Vol. XVI., where the following interesting description is also given:

"Tous ces personnages représentent la musique, dont l'histoire est partagée en différentes zones, ou plutôt en différentes époques qui vont se dérouler successivement. Pour le moment, car nous allons y revenir, nous négligerons les deux rangées de sujets qui s'étagent sous le positif, et nous aborderons de suite la zone qui s'étend sous la largeur entière de l'orgue, au-dessus de la frise.

"M. Burges aime à remonter à la source des choses. Au jubé, où est figuré le sacrifice, il a dessiné les éléments, l'eau, la terre, le feu et l'air, qui servent de matière au sacrificateur; car, sur l'autel juif on brûle avec le feu, on arrose avec l'eau, on saupoudre avec le sel la victime, qui se résout en cendres et qui s'évapore en fumée dans l'atmosphère. Ici, sans air et sans vent, car le vent n'est que l'air agité, il n'y aurait pas de musique, et l'orgue n'existerait pas. L'air est donc le principe vital, l'âme de cette grande machine pneumatique. En conséquence, au centre de la première zone, nous voyons l'Air personnifié; couronné comme un roi, il porte un long sceptre qui va devenir le bâton de commandement de ce grand chef d'orchestre. Il est ailé, car les ailes sont à l'air ce que les nageoires sont à l'eau, les organes de la locomotion. Il est escorté des quatre vents cardinaux, l'Aquilon, l'Auster, l'Eurus et le Zéphir, qui sifflent et mugissent, mais, sous la discipline de leur maître, avec ordre et mesure. L'Aquilon et l'Auster, vents du nord et de l'est, soufflent dans une trompette orageuse; l'Eurus, vent du midi, fait retentir sa note sur un tambour, et le Zéphir, vent du soir, soupire sur un chalumeau. C'est de la musique, mais de la musique élémentaire; du bruit fort ou faible, plutôt que de la mélodie. . . .

"De ce réservoir, où le bruit roule à flots confus, comme le chaos avant la création, le son se détache; puis il monte à la seconde zone, qui est la seconde époque de la musique. A gauche de cette zone, est l'entrée ('Introitus'), à droite la sortie ('Exitus') du son qui vient de naître dans les profondeurs orageuses de l'orgue. A l'entrée s'ouvre une porte qui donne accès dans l'édifice sonore, et sur les jambages de laquelle se tient debout le Son. Cette personnification nous offre un homme de haute et forte stature qui frappe sur un tambour, pour en tirer l'élément musical; à gauche est debout ce même élément, le son, mais redoublé simultanément et produisant l'harmonie. L'Harmonie est une jeune fille pleine d'élégance, qui joue d'une double flûte, et c'est du mariage de ce son double que naît la partie la plus importante de la musique. Le son et l'harmonie parcourent l'instrument tout entier, comme le sang circule dans les veines et les artères; puis il en sort à l'extrémité opposée, par la porte où sont debout la Résonnance et l'Écho. La Résonnance est un homme qui tient une clochette, car c'est surtout dans la cloche qu'on entend nettement la répercussion du son; l'Écho, une jeune fille

view of giving the most favorable opportunity for a display of high-class decorative painting. It will be observed, on reference to the illustration, that the designer has wisely left all the pipe-work plain, intending it to be all of burnished tin.

It is greatly to be desired that more attention be paid to the external design of Organs; and that, in designing organ-cases, either for Church or Concert-room instruments, some provision be made for their decoration by appropriate and expressive figure subjects. The nature of the Organ does not favor the use of large surfaces for the display of figure subjects, unless we reintroduce the large folding shutters so common in late mediæval times. Mr. Burges' design shows all that can be done, without such shutters, to receive subject painting. Here the maximum amount of flat surface has been provided; indeed, from an acoustic point of view, it is probable that for Organs in anything like confined situations too much is closed up with solid woodwork. It is obvious that in providing sufficient fields for figure decoration, there is no necessity to go further, as Mr. Burges has done, and add heavy roofs and such like architectural features, which are certainly not necessary to a good mediæval treatment.

While on the subject of figure decoration, mention may be made of carved figures, which, when properly treated, form pleasing adjuncts to organ-cases. In all instances these must be judiciously introduced; and modeled in a style of marked simplicity and severity. Nothing approaching the rococo and sprawling monstrosities to be seen in many of the Organs on the Continent of Europe must

languissante, respire la fleur qui l'a fait mourir. Avec la Résonnance, le son va mourir, car c'est le reflet du rayon sonore; avec l'Écho, il meurt, car après l'echo c'est le silence. La Résonnance s'apprête à fermer un des battants de la porte par où sort le son; mais l'autre battant, contre lequel l'Écho s'appuie, est déjà complétement fermé.

"Telle est la seconde époque de la musique: à la première, naissance du bruit dans l'air; à la seconde, croissance du bruit en son, en harmonie, en résonnance et en écho; à la troisième, développement de la musique dans les instruments qui vont lui servir d'organes. Jubal, 'père de ceux qui chantent avec la cithare et l'orgue, touche de ce petit orgue, tel qu'on l'avait au moyen âge et qu'il vient de fabriquer avec l'équerre, le ciseau et le marteau suspendus au mur de son atelier. Il est à gauche, au sommet de la tourelle au bas de laquelle le Son et l'Harmonie s'apprêtent à entrer. A droite, Pythagore, l'inventeur du monochorde, sur le dessin de Reims, fait retentir avec un marteau les plateaux sonores d'une balance, pour peser, en quelque sorte, et pour mesurer le son.

"L'homme est en possession de la musique, mélodie et harmonie, mesurée et rhythmée; à la quatrième époque, nous allons le voir s'en servir pour dompter et charmer la nature. C'est avec elle qu'Orphée, descendu aux enfers, suspendit les souffrances de ce royaume du feu; avec elle qu'Amphion rendit sensibles les blocs de pierre, qui s'animèrent et vinrent se poser en assises pour former la ville de Thèbes; avec elle qu'Arion charma les flots, ou les vagues marines, et fut porté vivant par un dauphin sur le cap Ténare; avec elle, enfin, que David calma la frénésie de Saül.

"Ici, la musique dompte l'eau par Arion, la terre par Amphion et le feu par Orphée; mais elle a oublié le quatrième élément, l'air. En outre, dans cette zone, il s'agit des temps mythologiques ou antéhistoriques, et il n'aurait pas fallu y accoler David et Saül, que l'histoire réclame. Je sais bien que M. Burges a voulu montrer la toute-puissance de la musique, non pas sur les éléments, mais sur les monstres: sur les monstres des enfers, sur les monstres de la terre, sur les monstres marins et sur la folie humaine qui change un homme en bête et qui fit de Saül un animal féroce. Mais, sous la tyrannie de cette idée, M. Burges a dû représenter Amphion adoucissant les bêtes, tandis que le prince thébain a tout simplement animé des pierres. Enfin, Il a dû, ce qui me contrarie et me trouble dans ma symétrie, que j'estime si haut, mêler l'histoire sainte à la mythologie. Je propose donc à mon ingénieux ami de faire remonter plus haut, dans la section historique, David et Saül, et de compléter la toute-puissance de la musique sur les éléments en montrant Apollon, le dieu du jour, le commensal du ciel, l'habitant de l'air olympien, jouant de la lyre et donnant le ton, pour ainsi dire, au divin Orphée. Ainsi nous aurons charmé par la musique les quatre éléments et leurs habitants: le ciel ou l'air par Apollon; l'enfer ou le feu par Orphée, la pierre ou la terre par Amphion; la mer et les monstres marins par Arion.

be contemplated under any circumstances. In Church Organs, figures of angels playing musical instruments may occupy elevated positions on the tops of angle posts or canopies, or in niches or arcades designed to receive them; or with outspread wings, and carrying musical instruments or inscribed scrolls, at advanced angles or other salient points. While these and other appropriate figures may be executed in the same wood as the case and left plain, they will be much enhanced in value, for decorative purposes, if painted after the fashion of middle age sculpture. The treatment of the case generally will to a large extent dictate the method of decorating the figure work. For important positions in the case, other figures, such as King David with his attribute the harp, St. Cecilia bearing a Regal or Portative, St. Genesius with the violin, and St. Dunstan with his harp, are appropriate enrichments.

For the decorations of the cases of Concert-room and Chamber Organs, allegorical figures, representations of mythological personages connected with music, and statues of the great masters of organ music, may appropriately be introduced.

The general woodwork of the case, even when of elaborate design and workmanship, admits of several decorative treatments in colors and gold. It may be left in its natural soft brown color (to darken by age), and simply relieved, in its mouldings, tracery, and carvings, with gold; it may be stained throughout deep brown or black, rubbed to a waxy polish, and enriched both with colors and gold, as in the case of the beautiful Organ in the Church of St. John the Baptist, Tue

"Nous procédons ici comme dans la création, par la voie ascendante, et nous montons du brut à l'organisé, du fabuleux à l'historique. L'histoire est prise au peuple juif et au peuple chrétien. Les juifs ont leur roi-prophète, qui chantait sur la harpe et même dansait les psaumes qu'il avait composés. Je regrette que M. Burges ait oublié le cantique d'actions de grâce après le passage de la mer Rouge. En effet, la sœur de Moïse et d'Aaron, un tambour à la main et suivie des juives qui formaient des chœurs, aurait fourni le sujet d'une belle scène. Puis les murs a Jéricho, qui tombent aux sons formidables des sept trompettes et aux cris de toute l'armée des Hébreux, apportaient le sujet d'un autre tableau très-approprié surtout à nos orgues modèrnes, qui savent si bien mugir et trop bien ébranler les murs de nos églises. Ensuite serait venu David entouré de ses musiciens, et enfin, pour compléter cette gamme variée de joies et de douleurs, les captifs suspendant aux saules mélancoliques de l'Euphrate leurs instruments de musique pour pleurer à leur aise au souvenir de Sion et de la Judée.

"A ces quatre scènes de la musique juive auraient pu répondre quatre sujets de la musique chrétienne: le cantique divin, qui fut dit après la Cène, immédiatement avant le départ pour le jardin des Oliviers; saint Cécile entourée de tous les instruments de cette musique chrétienne dont elle est la gracieuse personnification; saint Grégoire le Grand constituant le plain-chant sur ses tons authentiques et plagaux; saint Thomas d'Aquin composant l'office du saint Sacrement, qui date du XIIIe siècle, et qui, peut-être à cause de cette époque, est le plus sonore et le plus magnifique des offices de l'Église. De ces quatre sujets, un seul malheureusement, celui de sainte Cécile, a été représenté par M. Burges. Un ange descend dans la chambre de sainte Cécile, toute remplie d'instruments de musique, et remet à la jeune vierge et à saint Valérien, son fiancé, les deux couronnes de lis et de roses immortelles qu'il avait apportées du paradis. Il est vrai que la légende de sainte Cécile se continue et qu'on voit la sainte condamnée à mort par Almacus, le gouverneur de Rome, qui siége au pied de la statue de Jupiter. Mais ce sujet prend une place précieuse qui ne lui appartient pas sur ce bel orgue, et que nous aurions donnée de préférence soit à saint Grégoire, soit à saint Thomas d'Aquin.

"Enfin, dans la dernière zone, nous quittons ce monde, nous quittons la terre et l'histoire humaine pour nous élever plus haut. Sur tous les points culminants de cet orgue, la musique se fait dans le ciel, par les anges, qui chantent. 'Confitebor tibi in cithara et organo,' et qui jouent d'instruments à cordes, à vent ou de percussion."

The remainder of the description of this Organ is with reference to its form and architectural treatment. The foregoing description of its decorative painting cannot but be of interest to all readers who pay any attention to artistic matters connected with the Organ; and of much suggestive value to those who may have to design important organ-cases, and desire to beautify them with expressive painting.

Brook, Liverpool, the design of the talented architect G. F. Bodley; or it may be most elaborately illuminated with colors and gold, as in the Cathedral of Manchester. Several fine and elaborate cases of undecorated oak are to be found in English cathedrals and churches, as in the Cathedral of Chester, and the Church of St. Bartholomew, Armley.

It is of course impossible to give rules of universal application for the decorative painting of Organs; but there is one piece of advice that may be given here, worthy of being remembered by decorators—Never overdo the work, but rather confine the decoration to that which is necessary to accentuate and harmonize all the features of the design; err on the side of simplicity rather than on that of over-elaboration; and employ only colors of refined and subdued tones, using gilding chiefly with the view of defining the leading structural and ornamental forms of the case. Gold is, however, not necessary, and unless used with great taste and judgment is better omitted; but this latter remark applies with equal force to all decorative painting.

The amount and style of decoration on the cases of Concert-room Organs will largely, if not entirely, be dictated by the decoration of the rooms in which they stand. The decorative painting should not be a very difficult matter if the cases have been designed in strict harmony with the architecture which surrounds them.

Great liberty is given in the decorative painting of Chamber Organs; and as it is comparatively small in extent, and will be closely viewed, it should be of the most beautiful and accurately executed character. Figure subjects painted in quiet colors upon gold grounds are desirable decorations. The framework and ornamental features may be of some rich wood, or stained black and relieved with gilding. The pipes may in all cases be delicately painted or of burnished tin, as individual taste may direct. A pleasing effect of soft color may be obtained by the use of woods of different tints, ranging from the soft white of holly to the black of ebony. Gilding may be again introduced to add richness to the design.

Decorative painting so far as Organs are concerned is, as a general rule, confined to the displayed pipe-work, true or sham, being used on pipes formed of zinc or common pipe-metal. Pipes formed of fine materials—tin or rich spotted metal—are rarely decorated. To decorate an organ pipe in a refined and thoroughly artistic manner requires careful study and no little ingenuity and skill; for it must always be remembered that the decoration must not appear to disturb the true form or construction of the pipe, on the contrary, it ought to accentuate its form. No words are sufficiently strong to condemn the meaningless and tasteless class of decorative painting almost universally met with in modern Organs, in which the coarseness of the patterns used is only surpassed by the vulgarity of the coloring.

Circular metal pipes are more difficult to decorate in an effective manner than quadrangular wooden ones; yet the latter are comparatively seldom, and in our opinion far too seldom, used for decorative purposes. In metal pipes, the foot and mouth present some difficulties in their treatment, and seem to demand a style of design which is out of sympathy with that most suitable for the cylindrical body. Diaper-work, band-work, and powderings, which are, generally speaking, suitable patterns for the body of a pipe, do not lend themselves to the conical surface of the foot or the conventional form of the mouth. This difficulty is overcome by having the foot and lower part of the body, up to a short distance above the upper lip of the mouth, either of plain gold or some quiet color, having a horizontal band of a simple pattern carried round its upper edge, so as to clearly mark the two divisions of the pipe. The cylindrical body, above this band, may be enriched in a great variety of ways, all of which group themselves under the three general classes of decoration above alluded to; namely, diaper-work, band-work, and powderings. Diaper-work includes all designs or patterns of a connected character, which repeat at regular intervals, and may be carried over any extent of surface. The most beautiful patterns of this class are those suggested by the rich velvets, cloths of gold, and silk brocades, of the fourteenth, fifteenth, and sixteenth centuries. Band-work includes those patterns which are composed of plain or ornamental bands or ribbons, disposed horizontally, vertically, diagonally, or in zigzag or chevronwise, or in any of these ways combined. The mural paintings and the illuminated manuscripts of the Middle Ages furnish good models for this class of decoration. Powdering is that class of ornamentation which, as its name implies, consists of detached devices, powdered or disposed at regular intervals over a plain ground. For Church Organs, powderings of symbols, emblems, and monograms are highly suitable; while for other Organs, any devices are available that taste may suggest.

In the decoration of pipes, any of the above classes may be used alone on all surfaces suitable for their reception; but the introduction of horizontal bands along with either diapering or powdering has a good effect. In these compound treatments, colors must be introduced with caution so as not to produce disturbed and bizarre effects. Diaper patterns will, of necessity, be executed on plain grounds, either of color or gold. Black or dark brown diaper-work, of some evenly distributed and flowing design, executed on a mat gold ground has a singularly rich and refined effect. If a quieter and somewhat antique effect is desired—resembling that of old gilded leather decoration—the brightness of the gold ground should be toned down by the application of a tawny or light brown lacquer or varnish. A great amount of artistic taste and skill may be displayed in such high class pipe decoration.

Band-work and powderings may be applied to either gold or colored grounds, or to the bright surface of tin or spotted metal. A very pleasing effect is produced by gilding the lower portion of a spotted metal pipe, banding it at the top edge of the gold (as previously directed), and then powdering the upper surface of the body with a conventional floral or symbolical device, executed in bright colors and gold outlined with black. We have decorated towers of large pipes in this manner with most satisfactory results. To preserve the decorations and gilding, and also to prevent the surface of the spotted metal becoming tarnished and dull, we varnished the whole with a single coat of fine French oil varnish. After twenty years of exposure, and repeated washings with clean cold water, we found the surface of the pipes as perfect as the day they were finished. For this class of decoration, we prefer pipes made of a metal having a large and boldly-marked spot to the finer confluent variety which almost resembles pure tin in appearance.

It is somewhat surprising that the desirable practice of protecting the surface of bright metal pipes with a colorless varnish or lacquer does not commonly obtain. As even the best burnished tin soon becomes dull and dirty in the atmosphere of towns, and spotted metal turns a dead grey in a few months time, it is to be regretted that the slight expense of protecting them is not incurred. Varnished pipes do not change; and all they may require is to be sponged over with cold water and wiped dry with a wash-leather, once in two or three years.

Pipes entirely painted should not be varnished, unless some special effect is aimed at; for, as a rule, they should be as free from gloss as possible. The case is different with polished metal pipes, only partly gilded or decorated with color; the varnish in this instance brightens the metallic surfaces, subdues the gilding and imparts to the colors the appearance of enamel.

Quadrangular wood pipes are not so difficult to decorate as cylindrical metal ones. This is owing to their having uniform flat surfaces with defined edges, and, under usual conditions, presenting only the front surface for ornamentation. Beside this, they have neither the awkwardly-shaped mouths nor the long conical feet of the metal pipes; indeed, such feet as they have are rarely shown in such a way as to require anything beyond plain painting. The mouths of wood pipes, which consist (except when inverted) of a plain sloped part within quadrangular lines, are best treated in a perfectly plain manner, either gilded, or colored some appropriate tint, contrasting with the rest of the painting. The caps, below the mouths, may be decorated in various ways. They should, to start with, be formed with a view to their ultimate decoration, having some simple mouldings worked upon them, horizontally, for the reception of lines of color. It is hardly necessary to say that in flats, formed of quadrangular pipes, the decoration should be such as to produce a satisfactory general effect; that is, all the pipes should be treated alike in design and coloring. Sometimes pipes have been painted in two designs, alternating; but, except in small groups, say of three or five, this treatment is rarely successful. Whatever description of pattern is selected for the pipes, it must be graduated in all its measurements and details to suit the different sizes of the same. There will, accordingly, require to be as many drawings, stencils, etc., as there are pipes to be decorated. We have tested this system of decoration with an eminently successful result. A flat of fifteen small-scaled BOURDON pipes was decorated with a graduated diaper and band design, executed in black and brown upon gold grounds; brighter tints appearing only on the mouldings of the caps and the stopper handles. The diaper pattern began and ended in precisely the same manner on every pipe, being accurately drawn to suit the different lengths and widths in all cases.

Powderings and banded patterns are more easily graduated to fit the different sizes of pipes than diaper designs; but they do not produce effects of so pleasing a character. Bands, whether applied to cylindrical metal or quadrangular wood pipes, should never be placed spirally or diagonally, like the bands on a barber's pole; for, so disposed, they produce an unpleasant and restless effect, destructive of all dignity and artistic propriety. On metal pipes, they should be placed only horizontally or in chevron fashion; and on wood pipes, they should be chiefly used in the horizontal position; but in certain designs, for large pipes, vertical bands, close to the angles of the pipes, have a satisfactory appearance. The golden rule in organ-pipe decoration is: Use no designs which tend to destroy the true forms of the pipes, and select those which are simple in their forms and combinations. Avoid all loud and vulgar coloring, and a great variety of colors.

Wood pipes occupying subordinate positions in the design of an organ-front or screen, and when constructed (on their exposed sides) of some good and agreeably-tinted wood, or of clean white pine carefully stained and varnished, require, comparatively speaking, little aid from painted decoration. Ornamental bands above the mouth and a short distance below the top are sometimes all such pipes require on their bodies. A simple geometrical, or free ascending, pattern may be carried between the bands and up to the top of the pipes when a richer treatment is desired. On such pipes very low-toned colors should alone be used, such as sage green, slate blue, brick red, chocolate, greenish or tawny yellow, black, and white. As has been already said, the mouths of wood pipes should be either gilded or painted some plain color in harmony with the rest of the decoration; on no account should their slopes be patterned. A narrow border of contrasting color, margin-lined, should be carried round the sloping mouths to separate the same from the general surface of the pipes. The caps may have a design of some geometrical character stenciled on them.

In a general treatise, like the present, it is quite impossible to discuss a complex subject, such as the artistic decoration of the Organ, in any degree of completeness; and no detailed description of decorative systems would be understood without an elaborate series of colored designs, which is quite beyond the limits of this Work. Enough has been said, perhaps, to induce those really interested in organ-building and its artistic development to pay more attention to the proper decoration of the different classes of instruments. At present the art is in a most neglected state; and we fear it will remain so until the Organ is once more looked upon as worthy of the highest consideration by architects and decorative artists of eminence and skill.

CHAPTER V.

THE CHURCH ORGAN.

PRIOR to about the middle of the last century the art of the organ builder was almost exclusively concentrated on the construction of instruments for church use: and at the present day, although Church Organs cannot be said to embrace the largest and most complete instruments fabricated in modern times, they certainly continue to form the most numerous, the most useful, and, accordingly, the most important class. Concert-room and Chamber Organs, however perfect and beautiful they may become, will always remain, comparatively speaking, few in number; and in point of general utility will always occupy a subordinate place to those instruments which are constructed for public worship. Such being the case, it is obviously desirable that the most earnest study and the greatest skill and care should be expended on the tonal appointment and general construction of Church Organs.

That the Church Organ, even in its most advanced form, as found to-day in all the organ-building countries of the world, is what it should be, or is all that can be desired for modern requirements, is open to very grave question. Organ builders generally, and we may say the whole organ-playing world, seem satisfied with it and disposed to leave it no better, so far as its tonal aspect is concerned, than what it was when they first made its acquaintance. We are, however, far from satisfied with the past and present methods of Church Organ appointment, just as we object on scientific and artistic grounds to the systems,—if any systems can be said to obtain,—followed in the construction and tonal appointment of Concert-room and Chamber Organs. In the present Chapter we offer a few hints and directions with the view of improving the stiff and colorless method of building which appears to be generally followed in the construction and tonal appointment of Church Organs.

For particulars respecting the rise and progress of Church Organ building prior to the eighteenth century, we must refer the reader to our First Chapter: but, at the risk of some repetition, we desire to introduce our present important subject with a few particulars respecting the state of the Church Organ in England in the eighteenth century.

In the year 1710, Renatus Harris erected an Organ in Salisbury Cathedral; and this instrument is described, by Francis Dewing, on an engraving of its "East Front," as follows: "This instrument, consisting of four sets of keys, and fifty stops, stands over the choir door, and is above 40 foot high and 20 foot broad; the arch under which it stands, being lofty, but narrow, and would admit no larger extention in breadth; and yet it was judged necessary to carry the finishing very high, to render this figure more lively and proportionable to the structure of the church (which is, from the pavement to the vaulting thereof, 80 foot high). The organ blower, as well as the bellows which are very large, have room in the body of ye case, in which are all ye movements, keys, roller-boards, and eleven stops of Echos, and yet the sight of the work is conceal'd from him, as he is from the people in the Church or Gallery. This organ is a new contrivance, and on it may be more varietys express'd, than by all ye organs in England, were their several excellencies united. The figures designed for the finishings of the choir organ are not as yet set up, neither are ye finishings of ye great organ fore shortned in this print according to perspective, because all parts of the Instruments should answer the Scale."

This was evidently the most advanced type of Organ, as well as the largest constructed up to that date in England. It had fifty speaking stops, distributed in four manual divisions, one being an Echo of eleven stops; while Smith's celebrated Organ in the Temple Church had only twenty-three stops in the three manual divisions; and his Organ in St. Paul's Cathedral had thirty-two stops (originally schemed for thirty-five), in, apparently, only two manual divisions. As space was very restricted in St. Paul's, and a powerful instrument was imperative for so large a building, it is easily understood why an Echo Organ was dispensed with.

Both in England and on the Continent at that time the mechanism or action of the Organ was of the simplest and heaviest description; and no mechanical appliances were yet introduced to aid the organist in the manipulation of the stops.

It will be seen on reference to our historical notes that long before the date of the Salisbury Organ, the German organ builders had made very important advances in their art. They seem, however, to have always paid most attention to the means of producing vast volumes of sound, neglecting the almost equally important means of controlling them. In the earlier years of the seventeenth century Germany possessed larger Organs than any other country. It appears certain that in some instances they contained pipes of 32 feet speaking length. Seidel, speaking of about the middle of this century, tells us that there were in Germany several large Organs, having four manuals and a compass of above four octaves: and under the date of 1686, he informs us that A. Schnitker built the Organ in St. Nicholas, Hamburg, with sixty-seven speaking stops, four manual divisions, and a

Pedal Organ; the latter containing, among other important stops, a Counter Diapason, 32 ft., of metal, placed in front, and a Trombone, 32 ft. This noteworthy instrument is said to have contained nine stops of 16 ft. pitch. Such, then, appears to have been the state of the Church Organ, in its highest development, in Germany, when Father Smith was busy in London laying the foundation of the modern school of organ-building in England.

It is a somewhat remarkable fact that although both Smith and Harris must have been well acquainted with the Pedal Organ, which was acknowledged all over Germany as an important, if not an indispensable, department of the Organ at the time Smith left that country to settle in England, they never put a pedal department or even a pedal clavier in their instruments. That the Pedal Organ was firmly established in Germany at this period is amply proved by the great prominence Bach gave to it in his matchless Preludes, Toccatas, and Fugues. Forkel, in his "Life of Bach," commenting on the importance of this department, says: "The Pedal is an essential part of the Organ: by it alone it is exalted above all other instruments; for its magnificence, grandeur, and majesty depend upon it. Without the Pedal, this great instrument is no longer great: it approaches those little Organs called in Germany *Positivs*, which are of no value in the eyes of competent judges." Although Bach did compose pieces for two manuals only, yet all his greater works for the Organ were written for the instrument with an independent pedal department.

Speaking on this subject, Dr. Hopkins remarks: "It is not a little remarkable that Smith and Harris,—the former of whom studied his art in Germany, and the latter in France,—should never have made a Pedal Organ, or even pedals, in England. What the cause of this striking omission could have been, cannot now be positively ascertained; but we know that nearly every other real improvement in the Organ met with the greatest opposition,—as the introduction of Doubles, the establishment of equal temperament, the restoration of the CC compass, &c.,—and probably the idea of introducing pedals met with no better reception. Be this as it may, pedals were not introduced into England till nearly the end of the last century. According to an autograph letter, written by the late Charles Wesley, the Savoy Organ by Snetzler [probably about 1785], was the first that had a pedal-board, without, however, any pipes, and which formed part of Snetzler's original work. Another account states the Organ in St. Matthew's Church, Friday Street, to have been the first to have pedals; and, further, that they were of the two-octave CCC in compass, with a complete set of Stopped Diapason pipes of 16-feet tone attached; and were made in 1790, under the direction of the late Rev. Mr. Latrobe. A third account is, that the first pedals made in England were those applied to the Organ in Westminster Abbey, by Avery; that they were a *ninth* in compass, GG to gamut A, with an octave of unison open pedal-pipes attached; that they were such a novelty and curiosity that people used to go from far and near to hear and see them; and that Dr. Benjamin Cooke, who died in 1793, composed his fine Service in G for the opening of the instrument after receiving those additions." Whichever of the above pieces of information may be correct, one cannot help wondering what the English musicians and organ builders could have been thinking about, for quite a whole century, to allow such a primitive state of affairs to exist. At the time of Avery's *important* addition to the Organ in Westminster Abbey, Bach had, for nearly half a century, been at rest in his unmarked grave in St. John's churchyard, at Leipzig; and all his great compositions for the Organ, with their pedal obbligatoes, had been given to the musical world.

All the essays in the direction of an independent Pedal Organ made at the end of the eighteenth century in England were very timid and decidedly tentative; indeed, it was not until several decades of the nineteenth century had passed that the Pedal Organ, as an all-important part of the Church Organ, was fully recognized and its desirable compass decided. But after all, English musicians and organ builders continued very half-hearted in the matter; and we regret to say that at the present day, so far as the average Church Organ is concerned, the pedal department is most grievously overlooked, and that to the serious sacrifice of the grandeur, dignity, and musical value of the instrument. The generality of those interested in organ-building forget, if they have ever heard, Forkel's truthful statement that "the Pedal is an essential part of the Organ;" and that "its magnificence, grandeur, and majesty depend upon it,"—depend upon the provision of an *adequate Pedal Organ.*

A few more words may be said respecting the Church Organ, as represented by the large instrument erected by Harris in Salisbury Cathedral. It is stated to have had four manual claviers, and, accordingly, four distinct divisions. It is beyond question that it had no pedal department; and that it had no Swell Organ is equally certain. It contained, however, the division which may be looked upon as the precursor of the Swell; namely, the Echo Organ. This consisted of several half-stops, usually duplicating the treble octaves of some of the stops in the other divisions, inclosed in a box of wood without any special provision for the egress of sound, so as to render their tones very subdued and distant, and, when played immediately after the corresponding loud and exposed stops, imitative of a natural echo. This miserable division of the Organ seems to have pleased the musical taste of the period immediately preceding the construction of this instrument. It will be seen, on reference to our Chapter on The Swell in the Organ, that in the year 1712, the true Swell Organ was invented and introduced by Abraham Jordan and Son, of London. The construction of the swell-box was subsequently improved by Samuel Green, of London, who appears to have been the introducer of the so-called "Venetian swell" in the Organ.

At this time the English were in advance of the rest of the world in the art of organ-building, insomuch that they had invented the Swell Organ, but there their superiority ceased. Whoever it was who first added a pedal department to an English Organ, it is quite certain that it was an accomplished fact in Green's lifetime; but how paltry and altogether insignificant were the essays in comparison with what had already been done on the Continent. It is right to bear in mind that at the distance of only about 220 miles, as the crow flies, from London, Müller had erected his magnificent Organ in the Cathedral of Haarlem, with its fine series of sixty speaking stops, including a pedal department of fifteen stops, containing two stops of 32 ft., and three stops of 16 ft. pitch; and, furthermore, that this instrument—well-known and celebrated—had been in existence for the third of a century, when the pedal clavier, with its single stop of about an octave in compass, was first added to an English Organ. It should be remembered by the student that long before the Pedal Organ was introduced in England the great Silbermann had labored and died, leaving a legacy of silver-toned masterpieces to attest his genius and skill: and that Johann Gottfried Hildebrand had constructed his Organ in the Church of St. Michael, at Hamburg, with its noble list of seventy stops, including a pedal department of sixteen stops. This Pedal Organ contained three stops of 32 ft., six stops of 16 ft., and five reed stops.

We now enter upon what may be correctly considered the modern epoch in the art of organ-building; and one which in England, France, and America has witnessed great improvements, and a general advance in almost all matters connected with the Organ. We omit the other European countries from our enumeration here; for, except in certain details, chiefly mechanical, derived probably from English or French inventions, the systems of construction and tonal appointment followed in Germany, Holland, Switzerland, Italy, and Spain may be said to have differed little from what they were at the close of the eighteenth century.

England had need to make progress, and the need, unfortunately, still obtains; for, as has been shown, organ-building was in anything but a creditable state there at the end of the eighteenth century; and it is, so far as the average Church Organ is concerned, not in the highest desirable state of advancement at the present time. We cannot shut our eyes to the fact that the average Church Organs in England, and also in the United States, have, in their tonal appointments, been little in advance of the average Church Organs of Germany and Holland of the eighteenth century; and at the present time they are decidedly inferior to them in the tonal appointment of the pedal department. The necessity for a truly adequate Pedal Organ seems never to have been fully recognized in England and the United States; and Church Organs have lost much in both dignity and utility accordingly. After the introduction of the pedal department in English instruments it remained for many years in a miserably inefficient state; indeed, it was not until Robson built the Organ for the Church of St. Michael, Chester Square, London, that even the proper compass for the pedal clavier was decided. Speaking of this Organ Dr. Hopkins remarks: "This instrument, built by T. J. Robson, in 1847, is designed upon the German principle, with special reference to the requirements of an Organ intended for the accompaniment and support of congregational singing. It consists of three manual Organs, viz., Swell, Great, and Choir, together with an independent Pedal Organ. The manuals are of the orthodox range, from CC, ascending from thence to g^3 in altissimo, 56 notes. The pedal board, with the Pedal Organ running *throughout*, extends from CCC to Tenor F, 30 notes, being the *first* Pedal Organ erected in London of this complete compass."

We do not desire it to be understood by the above remarks on the Pedal Organ compass that England was behind Continental nations in adopting the proper one, of 30 notes; for, on the contrary, England led the way in this important matter. In Germany,—that land of Pedal Organ renown,—very few instruments have pedal claviers of this compass. They commonly terminate at C, or, in more advanced examples, at D, 27 notes; indeed, the latter upward limit was fixed by German authorities, in 1877, as the correct one. Walcker's large Organ, of eighty speaking stops, in the Cathedral of St. Stephen, at Vienna, built in 1886, has its Pedal Organ compass from CCC to D, 27 notes; and the same builder's Organ, of one hundred and two speaking stops, in the Cathedral of Ulm, has its double pedal claviers of the same compass. Many examples of shorter compass could be given.

When we turn our attention to the stop appointment of the pedal department of the Church Organ, we must acknowledge the inferiority of the English and American systems to that adopted in Germany and other Continental countries. Let the reader glance over any number of Specifications of our ordinary Church Organs, containing from fifteen manual speaking stops upward, and then compare the relative appointments of their pedal departments with the appointments met with in corresponding examples of Continental organ-building. For the sake of ready reference, we here give a list of Churches, and the numbers of the manual and pedal stops their Organs contain or did contain:—

	No. of Manual Stops.		No. of Pedal Stops.
Lutheran Church, Vienna, . . .	15	—	8
Lutheran Church, Warsaw, . . .	18	—	9
St. Emmeran, Regensburg, . . .	18	—	8
Catholic Church, Trebniz, . . .	22	—	11
Cathedral of Verden,. . . .	25	—	9
St. Stephen, Vienna, ...	28	—	13
St. Maria, Cologne, ...	30	—	10
Cathedral of Antwerp, ...	34	—	10
SS. Peter and Paul, Goerlitz, . . .	36	—	19
St. Maria, Wismar, ...	40	—	16
Cathedral of Breslau, ...	42	—	18
Parish Church, Mühlhausen, . . .	42	—	18
Cathedral of Haarlem, ...	45	—	15
St. Paul, Frankfort, ...	52	—	22
Monastery Church, Weingarten, . .	53	—	17
Cathedral of Merseburg, . . .	61	—	20
Cathedral of Ulm, ...	71	—	31

Striking an average, roughly, of the above numbers, we find that the Pedal Organs contain closely upon five-twelfths of the number of stops contained in the manual departments. This is an average which could not be approached even in the most favorable list of English or American Church Organs.

It was not until about the middle of the nineteenth century that the great importance of the Swell Organ was fully recognized, and its compass extended to accord with the other manual divisions. Now it is invariably made of the full compass of the manual department; and under no circumstances should that practice be departed from, unless, indeed, it is to extend its compass, upward, beyond what is usually considered sufficient for the Great and Choir divisions of the Church Organ.

These few words are sufficient by way of an introduction to our subject. They bring us to the state of the art of organ-building as it obtained about the middle of the last century, beyond which it cannot be said to have progressed, in any decided manner, toward a more scientific, artistic, and logical system of tonal structure; toward a more convenient system of departmental appointment; and toward the production of a more flexible and expressive type of instrument. We do not deny that in the hands of certain leading builders improvements in voicing, and in the production of a higher standard of tone in certain classes of stops, have been reached: but these very facts cause deep regret that such improvements have not been utilized in the direction which tends to the greatest advantage of both performers and listeners.

Organ builders work in grooves of their own or, what is more common, their predecessors' creating; and it is, accordingly, a matter of great difficulty, even with sound logical reasoning, to induce them to study new methods, or to depart, to a slight extent, from the ways of doing things which they have so long been accustomed to. Many probably gave their allegiance to the traditional methods of their art when they did little more than make tapped-wires or sweep their masters' workshops; and it seems that such early impressions have ever since prevented their escaping from the traditional grooves. During an interesting conversation with one of the most progressive organ builders of the nineteenth century, we were led to ask: "How is it that you organ builders leave anything to be taught you by outsiders?" He replied: "We all work, day after day and year after year, in the grooves handed down to us by past generations of builders, and we thoughtlessly and conceitedly follow those grooves until we can see nothing good outside them." This admission was made, in 1886, by an organ builder who, of all men known to us, had displayed the least disposition and necessity to blindly follow in the footprints of others. It can only be this tendency to go on year after year in the well-beaten paths that accounts for the little progress and individuality displayed, during the last half century, by organ builders of reputation and unquestionable talent in the general appointment of their Church Organs. Now, this adherence to traditional ideas cannot but produce a certain degree of narrow-mindedness, and foster a conviction that there is nothing more to be learnt or done in the art of organ-building. And it is probable that, in numerous cases, organ builders nurse their own conceit to such an extent as to look upon any attempt to convince them of errors of judgment as a gross impertinence. When an artist, in any branch of art, is satisfied that he has learnt everything, and that he has reached the highest point of excellence, he has begun his downward course. A true artist is always dissatisfied with his best endeavors, and is ever striving to achieve something above and beyond them. In the foregoing remarks allusion is made only to the higher order of organ builders—to men who are above mere money-making ideas and trade trickery, and who are working, in all good faith, up to their lights.

We feel rather reluctant to speak of the lower class of builders who look upon Organs as merely so much merchandise, connected with which profit is the one important consideration; and who will build an Organ on any lines whatever so long as they make a satisfactory sum of money out of "the job." These men flourish on the credulity and ignorance of the public, or that section of it more or less interested in musical matters, but who know nothing about the science and art of organ construction. They secure contracts by alluring Specifications, presenting impressive lists of stops (generally insufficient and badly chosen) to catch the eye of inexperienced Organ Committees, or please the taste of special organists. Among the majority of persons, who profess to be musical yet know very little about the nature and construction of the Organ, there is a pretty general impression that an instrument with numerous stops, whatever their size may be, must be a better and more effective Organ than one with a lesser number. This is altogether an erroneous and an unfortunate belief, and one that has done incalculable mischief, and, we regret to say, continues to play into the hands of not over-scrupulous tradesmen, to the detriment of genuine art. It can hardly be wondered at that builders, not over-burdened with commissions, take advantage of this common impression, especially while the undesirable practice of competitive tendering is encouraged; while the organ builders are permitted to submit their own skeleton Specifications, committing them to very little beyond a number of stops bearing impressive names; and while inexperienced persons adjudicate and award.

The very general ignorance and apathy of the musical public have been important factors in the retardation of the art of organ-building; and no substantial progress will be made, we feel certain, until those for whom Organs are built know how their instruments ought to be constructed and appointed, and take full and reliable measures to secure a satisfactory result. We trust the following few words may be taken as a warning.

The usual course of proceeding when a new Organ is required for a place of worship, is to appoint a small committee from the leading members of the congregation (with or without an organist's coöperation), with powers to invite specifications and estimates from organ builders whose names may be known or mentioned to the members, and ultimately to decide either from some direct interest brought to bear upon it, or from a superficial examination of the skeleton specifications, who shall be entrusted with the construction of the Organ. Now, this proceeding might be fairly satisfactory, and might lead to desirable results, if the members of the Church Organ Committee were experts, or even reasonably conversant with the art of organ-building, and had some knowledge of the scientific principles on which the tonal structure of the Organ should be developed; but, in the great majority of cases, not one of the well-meaning gentlemen knows how the sounds of an Organ are produced; and probably not one could tell a TRUMPET from a FLUTE pipe. This is, generally speaking, not an exaggerated statement of matters. With a Committee so constituted at the head of affairs, the *tradesman* has an overwhelming advantage over the *artist;* for while the latter, in all honesty of purpose, may submit an artistically conceived Specification, comprising a moderate number of weighty and properly balanced stops, calculated to produce the dignified and richly-colored tones so desirable in an instrument for church use, demanding at the same time a price in just accord with the character of his work;

the *tradesman* builder sends in a Specification which presents a much longer list of stops than the other one, and a quotation of cost considerably under that of his competitor. The Committee sits in grave deliberation on the rival Specifications, and with a natural leaning, in its complete ignorance of the real question at issue, toward the longest list of stops and the lowest tender, ultimately decides in favor of the more imperfect and, in the long run, the dearest instrument. The members, worthy men, have doubtless acted up to their lights, just as they would in the open market over a consignment of bacon, a shipment of grain, or a keg of nails; and, as they shake hands at parting, mutually congratulate each other on having achieved a clever stroke of business for their church. Alas for art! What would such wiseacres say if it was proved to them beyond question that the Organ they rejected, because it would contain fewer stops and cost more money, would be a much finer and more useful instrument, and far cheaper in the end than the one so cunningly decided on?

There is another matter which should be touched upon for the good of all parties interested in the building and procural of Church Organs; but which we speak of with considerable reluctance, notwithstanding the fact that it has done much in the past to debase the art of organ-building. We allude to the pernicious and dishonest system of *sub rosa* commissions, or what may with equal propriety be called "black-mail"—a system which unfortunately has obtained far too long in connection with organ-building; but which we are glad to say is now repudiated by the leading builders, whose reputation renders it unnecessary for them to secure orders by other than legitimate and strictly honorable means. No person who is likely to impose or receive a *sub rosa* commission from an organ builder should be intrusted with the scheming and superintendence of an Organ; and no organ builder who is known to recognize such a commission should be intrusted with its construction. Let Church Organ Committees and purchasers of Organs bear in mind that such a commission, paid without their knowledge or consent, does not come out of the organ builder's pocket: it is either added to the contract price, or is subtracted from the value of the instrument by the use of inferior materials, the introduction of money-saving expedients, and the employment of cheap labor. It must also be borne in mind that the person who receives a secret commission from an organ builder can exercise neither the right nor the power to dictate to that builder how, or with what class of materials, the Organ is to be constructed. Without going deeper into this distasteful matter, we may content ourselves with pointing out a remedy, and one that will be accompanied by a marked improvement in the art of organ-building. Let there be organ architects, just as there are architects who are devoted to the study and practice of civil architecture; men properly qualified to undertake such duties as the giving of sound and reliable advice respecting the proper position and provision for the Organ in a church or other building, regarding its dimensions and tonal character, and with reference to its general treatment and design. Such men should be generally conversant with architecture and the science of acoustics, have both a musical taste and training, and be experts in the theory and practice of organ construction. Let such men be honorable and above suspicion; and let them be both able and willing to fulfil their duties to their clients in the matter of organ-building, just as architects of reputation are in the larger matter of church-building. When such experts are forthcoming, and are intrusted, in a business-like manner, with the scheming, designing, and superintendence of the construction of Organs, a new era will commence in the art of Church Organ building.

Both in Germany and France the construction of a Church Organ is a matter of great importance, and is usually attended to by a properly appointed Commission of musicians and experts. In the procural of the Grand Organ for the Cathedral of Notre-Dame, at Paris, the Commission appointed was of a most distinguished and remarkable character.*

A Church Organ to be thoroughly useful and appropriate, both from an artistic and a practical point of view, must be schemed and constructed to suit the place in which it is to be erected and the work it has to do. This is a golden rule which can never be violated with impunity. A Church Organ must, therefore, be more or less powerful in tone in exact proportion to the internal dimensions and the acoustical properties of the building in which it stands; power being, in this case,

* The following is an extract from the *procès-verbaux* of this Commission :—

"Pour compléter la magnifique restauration de l'église métropolitaine Notre-Dame de Paris, le Gouvernement avait commandé à la maison Cavaillé-Coll un orgue à proportions monumentales. En raison de l'importance exceptionnelle de cet instrument, S. Exc. le garde des sceaux, ministre de la justice et des cultes, par une décision en date du 17 février 1868, a nommé une commission spéciale pour en vérifier et recevoir les travaux.

Les membres de cette commission sont:

MESSIEURS

DUMAS, sénateur, président de la Commission;
AUBER, membre de l'Institut, directeur du Conservatoire;
AMBROISE THOMAS, membre de l'Institut;
ROSSINI, membre de l'Institut;
Baron SÉGUIER, membre de l'Académie des sciences;
Général FAVÉ, aide de camp de l'Empereur, commandant l'École polytechnique;
Mgr. SURAT, archidiacre de Notre-Dame;
DE PLACE, archiprêtre de Notre-Dame;
FÉLIX CLÉMENT, membre de la Commission des arts et édifices religieux;
L'abbé LEGRAND, curé de Saint-Germain l'Auxerrois, membre de la Commission des arts et édifices religieux;
BENOIST, professeur d'orgue au Conservatoire, membre de la Commission des arts et édifices religieux;
LISSAJOUS, professeur de physique au lycée Saint-Louis;
LEFÈVRE, directeur de l'École de musique religieuse;
HAMILLE, directeur de l'administration des cultes, président de la Commission des arts et édifices religieux;
DE LA MOTTE, chef de la 2e division à l'administration des cultes, membre de la Commission des arts et édifices religieux ;
VIOLLET-LE-DUC, architecte de la cathédrale;
L'abbé LAMAZOU, auteur d'écrits scientifiques sur l'orgue, secrétaire de la Commission.

"Dans sa première réunion générale du 20 février 1868, la Commission, sur la proposition de M. Dumas, président, s'est adjoint les trois étrangers de distinction désignés par M. le ministre des cultes pour prendre part à la réception des travaux de l'orgue:

MESSIEURS

Le chanoine DEVROYE, président du Congrès international de musique sacrée à Liége;
Le chevalier VAN ELEWICK, secrétaire du Congrès international de musique sacrée à Louvain;
LEMMENS, professeur d'orgue aux Conservatoires de musique de Londres et de Bruxelles.

"Sur la proposition de M. le président et de M. le directeur de l'administration des cultes, la sous-Commission, chargée de faire une étude spéciale des travaux et de préparer le rapport, a été ainsi composée: MM. le baron SÉGUIER, président; LISSAJOUS, FÉLIX CLÉMENT, DE LA MOTTE, chanoine DEVROYE; l'abbé LAMAZOU, rapporteur. Dans la dernière séance générale du mercredi 4 mars, M. l'abbé LAMAZOU a donné lecture du rapport sur la vérification et la réception des travaux."

understood to be volume and pervading character rather than loudness, in its simple state, which is of necessity accompanied by unmusical harshness and noise. A harshly-voiced and noisy Organ is an unmitigated abomination to the refined and musical ear. The leading characteristic of a Church Organ should be grandeur, combined with the greatest possible refinement of tone; so that it may be perfectly adapted for the appropriate accompaniment of choral and congregational singing, and the performance of voluntaries and other incidental music of a solemn and dignified character. It must never be forgotten that such an Organ is essentially, and before and above all, an accompanimental instrument; its capabilities for the display of florid skill in secular music on the part of the organist being an altogether secondary consideration, if it is a consideration at all. How often, however, do we find, on testing the tonal appointments of Church Organs, or carefully analyzing their lists of stops, that true dignity, grandeur, and usefulness have been sacrificed for the insertion of several ear-tickling and imitative stops for which many organists have so inordinate a predilection. An organist's Specification can generally be detected by the appearance of such fancy stops and the absence of that strictly accompanimental character which ought to distinguish the Church Organ. In the case of small, or even medium-sized, instruments this is fatal; but in large Organs there is generally ample material for both accompanimental and solo playing, although all may be deficient in flexibility and powers of expression. An English writer* of evident knowledge and experience has made the following apposite remarks on this subject:—

"In the first place, the Organ should be of a size and power proportionate to the building and the congregation it will contain. We see in some churches, Organs erected out of all proportion to the requirements of the service; as an instance, let that of St. Mary at Hill, London, be adduced—a very fine instrument is to be found there; but it is far too large and noisy for the comparatively small church. This instrument, although possessing great merit, is not a Church Organ in its true sense. The same fault applies to the recently-erected Organ at St. Andrew's, Well-street, London; the instrument is far too large and noisy for the size of the church, placed, as it is, near the congregation. One more example, by way of contrast: take St. Alphage, London Wall; here is a small church, and an Organ designed for the church—a Church Organ *par excellence*. It is unnecessary to go farther into detail upon this point: a Church Organ is an Organ designed to accompany the voices, and to be at the same time capable of rendering with effect the voluntaries before and after service. When the musical demands of an ordinary Sunday service are considered, and the large proportion of accompaniment to voice-singing in which it consists, it is certain that noise is not the attribute best suited to the Church Organ, but rather the more mellow tones of the foundation-stops—the DIAPASONS, and those registers which best accompany the voice. Now, the stops of this class are much more costly than the chorus and mutation stops, and a properly-constructed Organ of this type, with, say, twenty musical and well-balanced registers, would cost as much as an Organ of forty stops upon the quantity principle of endless small pipes. This may be explained more clearly by stating that the last twelve notes of the 8 ft. register on the keyboard cost about as much as the remaining forty-eight pipes; and hence, in the cumbrous 'churchwarden's Organ,' it will be noticed how often the foundation-stops are cut off at tenor C, 4 ft., and grooved into a common bass, or left altogether incomplete, without any bass at all; while a number of ranks of

*In the *Musical Standard* of June 23, 1877.

small pipes are introduced without any proper counterbalance of the foundation tone, either upon the Pedal Organ or keyboards. We now see why one specification of an Organ costing the same money may apparently represent a much more extensive instrument. Again, a Church Organ requires that in its design the tone of the Pedal Organ should be commensurate with the rest of the Organ; the Pedal Organ ought to carry down the last octave of the keyboard an octave lower without any very apparent break in the tone. Comparatively few of our present church instruments have any Pedal Organ at all. A single 16 ft. open wooden stop of a deep booming sound has to do duty alike for the full Chorus Organ and the soft Choir Organ-vocal accompaniment. It is very rare to find a properly balanced Pedal Organ, even upon the most recently constructed Church Organs. The fact is, the cost of a proper Pedal Organ nearly equals that of the Organ it has to balance upon the keyboard. Our present Church Organs are, as a rule, ill-constructed instruments; and, more or less, are erected in a commercial spirit, and form a transaction like the placing of the bricks, stones, and mortar of the building. No one takes any special interest, partly from a want of the necessary knowledge, and partly because 'it is no one's business.' What is wanted is a portion of that pure artistic spirit which animated the 'Father Schmidts' and other builders and organists of former days: men whose aim was too high for mere money-getting, and who gloried in the progress of the sublimest of all the constructive arts."

The strictures of this writer are perfectly just, and although they were written twenty-six years ago they are equally applicable to the Church Organs of to-day. With his remarks anent the general deficiency of Pedal Organs we cordially agree; and they are worthy of the serious consideration of the student of the art of organ-building.

It is perhaps unnecessary to point out that in approaching the subject of the proper tonal appointment of the Church Organ, one enters on the consideration of a problem widely different in its special bearings to those presented by the appointment of Concert-room and Chamber Organs. Between the true Church Organ and either of the instruments just named there are very few points in common beyond those which relate to general excellence of manufacture and refinement and purity of tone. Just as the three instruments are destined for different spheres of usefulness in the realms of music, so must they, when properly schemed and appointed, be widely different in their tonal resources, departmental treatment, and musical coloring. Excellence of workmanship, perfection of voicing, and the highest flexibility and powers of expression, are alike required in every class of Organ.

A Church Organ should be schemed throughout on the simplest and most thorough principles: there should be no ambition on the part of its designer to make a display in the form of a great number of speaking stops; but, on the contrary, a determination to have, in every possible way, a work of art—developed on the soundest lines, and true and perfect in materials and workmanship. The tonal structure of the instrument, be it small or large, should be characterized by gravity, dignity, and softness:—gravity, secured by an adequate and properly-balanced pedal department; dignity, by volume of foundation-tone in all the divisions of the instrument; and softness, by skilful voicing with a copious wind stream at a moderate pressure. Dignity combined with softness cannot be secured by small-scaled foundation unisons, numerous incomplete stops, and many ranks of high-pitched pipes, blown by high-pressure wind until they scream a coarse apology for their serious shortcomings. Gravity combined with softness of tone cannot be secured by one master-of-all-work pedal stop—a "booming" OPEN DIAPASON, 16 FT., or a large-scaled, tubby-toned BOURDON, in which the prime tone and the second upper partial (the Twelfth) seem to be perpetually struggling for the mastery.

A properly appointed Church Organ, containing nothing but complete stops of proper scales and an adequate pedal department, constructed of the best materials and by a conscientious builder, must of necessity be a somewhat costly affair; but it will fully represent the money expended, and prove a lasting satisfaction to all concerned in its fabrication and use. Such an Organ, under proper care, should last for centuries.

Just a few words of advice to those who may be interested in the procural of a Church Organ, and we shall pass on to the consideration of matters of detail. When an Organ is required, and the funds immediately available are limited (as is almost invariably the case), there are two straightforward and sensible modes of procedure, with reference to its construction, open to the purchaser. First, if the church is small, do not aim at having an instrument out of all reasonable proportion to it; but be satisfied to accept the judgment of your organ architect, who has no interest in misleading you, and procure an Organ which will be amply sufficient to sustain, in refined and dignified accompaniment, the choir and congregation in all portions of the musical service. Follow this course firmly, and intrust the work to a builder of proved taste, skill, and probity. Remain persistently deaf to the expostulations of your enthusiastic organist, and the allurements of the *tradesman*, who, with a lengthy and fascinating list of small and short stops and specious promises, offers tempting and *apparently* substantial advantages.

Secondly, if the church is large, and the funds immediately forthcoming are obviously insufficient for the purchase of an Organ of the necessary size and tonal character, built as a Church Organ ought to be built, do not aim at having a complete instrument all at once,—cheap, badly constructed, and a continual source of trouble and disappointment. The best course to adopt is as follows: Call in a reliable expert; furnish him with full particulars regarding the music of your services; allow him to carefully inspect the church and test its acoustical peculiarities (every church differs in these); and instruct him to prepare a Specification for a true Church Organ, embodying all legitimate requirements and meeting all conditions, and of just sufficient volume and variety of tone for the church and the extreme demands of the most elaborate musical service ever likely to be held therein. Then state the present limit of your funds, and consult him as to the most desirable way of expending them on the projected instrument.

Let the scheme, so far as the bellows and their adjuncts, the wind-chests, the entire action and mechanical accessories, and the case, are concerned, be carried out in its entirety; and let preparation be made for all the tonal forces contemplated. The balance of the funds, after paying for the above, should be devoted to the procural of the foundation-stops and those most necessary for the simple accompaniment of the musical services. The remaining stops can be added subsequently and by degrees as money is obtained. Private generosity is ever at work in church matters, and an unfinished Organ is a favorable field for its operations. When it is known that the Organ has, so far, been constructed on the most perfect known lines, and that provision has been made for the reception of further speaking stops, the list of which can be inspected, one may calculate on the completion of the instrument at no very distant date. It will be a great and lasting satisfaction to all parties concerned to know that nothing has been done in a cheap and careless manner, and that all the work has been constructed of the proper materials, under experienced supervision. The voice of the Organ will speak for itself. The beginning has been wisely and well essayed; and the ending, albeit somewhat delayed, cannot but be entirely satisfactory.

Of course, when funds are ample all the difficulties hinted at above have practically no existence: but, in the name of art and common sense, let the money be expended in procuring an Organ of the highest possible quality, constructed of the finest and most durable materials and with the best of workmanship, and containing the requisite number of properly-balanced and beautifully-voiced stops, suited for the highest class of ecclesiastical music; rather than a large and unwieldy instrument of inferior workmanship and materials, which will eventually prove a huge disappointment to every one connected with its procural and use, and which will entail a continual expenditure to keep it in working order. *The better an Organ is built the cheaper it will be in the end.* This is a fact to be added to the great advantages, in the musical direction, secured by the scientific and artistic treatment of the tonal forces.

GENERAL SCHEME OF THE ORGAN.

In the remarks which immediately follow it is to be understood that a single Organ only is contemplated as necessary for a church; and that it has to be constructed to meet all demands likely to be made upon it in the legitimate musical services. Later on we shall consider the question of two Organs in the same church, and their respective natures and uses.

DIVISIONS AND CLAVIERS.—The true Church Organ should not have less than three, whilst it need never have more than four independent divisions, including the Pedal Organ. When of three divisions, the two manual claviers will command respectively the Great and Swell Organs; and when of four divisions, the three manual claviers will command the Great, Choir, and Swell Organs. The compass of these claviers should never be less than 58 notes; namely, from CC to a^3. The common compass has been from CC to g^3, but that is not to be recommended for new Organs. A greater compass than that recommended is unnecessary for accompanimental music and the desirable class of voluntary and incidental playing, but there is no objection, especially in instruments containing a moderate number of stops, to carrying the compass up to c^4 = five octaves. This compass does not add much to the cost, and it is valuable in octave coupling. In an Organ of two manual claviers, the Great one should occupy the lower and the Swell the higher position. This is the accepted arrangement at the present time. When there are three claviers, the lowest should command the Great, the middle the Choir, and the highest the Swell Organ. We strongly recommend this arrangement in connection with the system of tonal appointment we advocate; and it was invariably specified by the greatest player of last century, the late W. T. Best, of Liverpool. It is not the old-fashioned one, and will, accordingly, be objected to by groove-loving organ builders and organists for some time to come. It is the proper and logical arrangement, notwithstanding contrary opinion.

We feel, that in advocating only three manual divisions, we shall be blamed by the whole world of ambitious organists, who are naturally proud of their executive abilities and desire Organs of the first magnitude,—of the Concert-room type or, at least, with all its resources,—whereon they can display, not their self-restrained and musicianly powers in the dignified and refined style of playing suited to ecclesiastical music, but the full extent of their powers as performers in *all classes* of music,—sacred and profane. It is quite certain if such organists cannot properly render, on a well-appointed three-manualed Organ, *all* the music that can be called for within the walls of a church, they will fail to do so on an instrument of four or five manuals. We cannot avoid, and do not seek to avoid, the condemnation of such performers. We adhere to the artistic and common-sense view of the matter, simply defining the true Church Organ as an instrument *sui generis;* unhesitatingly affirming that it is not a Concert Organ, and that it should not be impaired by any attempts to make it like one, with the inevitable result of rendering it insufficient for its chief, and, indeed, its only proper office. In an instrument of moderate size, schemed on the many-claviered, Concert-room type, a serious loss of grandeur and dignified volume of tone will be sacrificed to secure solo or "fancy" stops of indifferent mixing and building-up powers. A small Organ under such conditions becomes an "ear-tickler," rather than a solemn and noble-voiced instrument, fit for the appropriate accompaniment of the sacred songs of the Church. Of course, the simple multiplication of keyboards does not affect the sounds of the pipe-work; it merely cuts the instrument up into small, and often ineffective, divisions, and gives the performer facilities for making frequent and rapid changes of tonality,—changes by no means indispensable or generally desirable in the accompaniment of church music.

In English Church Organs of the first magnitude, designed for the accompaniment of the full cathedral service, four manual divisions are deemed sufficient; while the great majority of the finest Organs have only three manuals. In France, however, Church Organs of the largest size, built in recent times, have five manual divisions; for instance, the Grand Organs of the Cathedral of Notre-Dame and the Church of Saint-Sulpice, at Paris. Such instruments invariably occupy the west-end position, and are seldom, if ever, used for simple accompaniment. Another small and strictly accompanimental Organ is provided and placed in the choir in each instance. In the Church of the Madeleine, at Paris, the Grand Organ is elevated over the central entrance, while the Choir Organ (L'Orgue d'Accompagnement), an instrument dignified and refined in tone, is placed at the opposite end of the church, behind the high altar. The celebrated Organ in the

Cathedral of Haarlem has only three manuals. In Germany, while several Church Organs, which have been built or altered in recent times, have four manual claviers, the generality of the large Organs have only three. In the United States there are no lines of demarkation recognized between a Church and a Concert-room Organ; and, indeed, the fashionable and altarless American auditorium strongly resembles a concert-room, and much of the music performed therein lacks the true ecclesiastical character.

Every Church Organ, whatever may be its size and the number of its manual divisions, must have an independent pedal department with a clavier of not less than 30 keys, that is, with a compass of from CCC to F, inclusive.

THE ACTION.—The selection of the class of action most suitable for a Church Organ will depend greatly on the relative positions of the sound-producing portions of the instrument and the claviers; and also on the construction of the wind-chests. Cost may likewise be a factor in the question, although it should not be a controlling one. In the Church Organ, as in all the varieties of the instrument, the choice has to be made from the four following kinds of clavier action; namely, the simple tracker action, the pneumatic tracker or pneumatic lever action, the tubular-pneumatic action, and the electro-pneumatic action. It is not, however, imperative that any one should be carried throughout the entire instrument; on the contrary, it may be advisable, if not necessary, to use two or even three kinds of action in an Organ peculiarly disposed or divided. For instance, it was a very common practice, a few years ago, to apply the pneumatic lever to one clavier (usually the Great Organ) and the principal couplers, while the other claviers,—manual and pedal,—had the common tracker action. The pneumatic lever action, so commonly used in England and France a few years ago, has almost altogether gone out of use in the former country, the simpler tubular-pneumatic action having supplanted it. Again, both tracker and tubular-pneumatic actions may be found convenient in certain forms of the Organ, or one may be used for the manual and the other for the pedal claviers. Again, one or more divisions of the Organ may be electro-pneumatic, while the rest are tubular-pneumatic. Alluding to the electro-pneumatic actions, we may here repeat the golden rule given in our Chapter on The Concert-room Organ: Never depend upon electricity in organ-building when anything more reliable can be used. As the approved forms of all these actions are touched upon in the Chapters devoted to action-work, it is unnecessary to do more than mention their names here. Leaving the question of cost out of consideration, we may briefly allude to the selection of such actions as are necessary or advisable when the claviers are differently located with respect to the sounding portions of the Organ.

In the case of a small, or even moderately-sized Organ, and when the claviers are attached, and the organist sits directly in front and facing the instrument, there is seldom any real necessity for anything beyond the best form of tracker action; and when this class of action is made in the most careful manner, of the best materials, and adjusted in such a way as to produce a light and even touch, there is not much left to be desired. The only real disadvantage attending a perfect tracker action is the increased strain the couplers throw on certain claviers. In these Organs it is desirable, for more than one reason, to apply the tubular-pneumatic action to the Pedal Organ. Here it will be almost as cheap as the ordinary tracker action; and it will certainly be less noisy and less liable to go out of order by rough pedaling. It must be mentioned that in localities where the Organ is subjected to great atmospheric changes, and in which much moisture prevails at certain periods of the year and drought at others, tracker actions should not be used.

In an instrument which has a reversed and detached console, placed at a moderate distance from the sounding portion, the tubular-pneumatic action should be used throughout every division. The combined tracker and pneumatic lever action has frequently been applied to such instruments, notably in France; but the more recent tubular-pneumatic system is preferable in every way.

When the Organ is divided, that is, with a section on each side of the chancel or choir, and the console is attached to one section, or is placed, in a detached form, somewhere between the sections, the tubular-pneumatic will prove perfectly satisfactory, if properly constructed, and the distance from the console to either section is not very great. When, however, the console is placed far from the Organ, the electro-pneumatic action becomes imperative. In all cases where two Organs, such as a chancel Organ and a distant west-end Organ, are erected in the same church, and are arranged to be played from one console in the chancel or its neighborhood, the electro-pneumatic action becomes a necessity.

The foregoing remarks have been made without reference to any special conditions affecting the preservation or reparation of the Organ. It goes without saying, that as the mechanism becomes more delicate and complicated it also becomes more liable to injury, and to derangements, temporary or otherwise; and that such derangements are more difficult to repair the more complicated the action is, also goes without saying. Repairs are always difficult in the tubular- and electro-pneumatic actions, and require the hand of the experienced builder who is conversant with their special construction. As a rule, all properly constructed and well arranged tracker actions are less liable to go out of order than any other kind, and they are easy of access; and any derangements therein are both readily seen and repaired by the organist or any person having a rudimentary knowledge of organ-work. The case is widely different, as we have above pointed out, when derangements occur in the pneumatic levers, the delicate mechanism of the tubular-pneumatic system, or in the still more delicate and complicated mechanism of the electro-pneumatic action.

We desire to point out to all persons likely to be interested in the procural of a Church Organ, that the questions affecting its preservation and reparation cannot be overlooked with impunity. When the instrument is located in the neighborhood of the builder's factory, or when arrangements can be made with him or some other skilled organ builder to visit it and repair it on all necessary occasions, the selection of the class of clavier action may be decided on the considerations first stated: but when the Organ is placed in a country church and far away from skilled help, we unhesitatingly advise the adoption of the simplest, surest, and most accessible action that ingenuity can devise,—an action easy to understand and easy to repair when injured. It must be remembered that the most perfect action ever invented is only perfect when it is in perfect order. We have, even after a long and careful study of all the systems used, no prejudice against the simple tracker action, which, when skilfully made, only fails where it should not be used. In a moderately-sized Organ, of compact form, we prefer the direct tracker action for the manual divisions to all others; and when attached to a modern wind-chest, on the exhaust system, it leaves very little to be desired.

COUPLERS.—The number of couplers necessary, or advisable, to be introduced in the Church Organ varies according to circumstances. In instruments of small size, say of two manuals and under twenty-five manual speaking stops, all the ordinary couplers should be inserted, for through their agency the power and variety of the tonal combinations are greatly increased. In large instruments, the coupling system, even in its simplest desirable form, will present a goodly list of mechanical agents.

There are three different classes of couplers which act on the manual claviers. First, those which connect one clavier with another in three ways,—in the unison, the octave, and the sub-octave. Secondly, those which act upon a single clavier, uniting its notes in octaves or sub-octaves. Thirdly, those which connect the lower thirty notes of each manual clavier to the keys of the pedal clavier. The proper selection of the purely manual couplers is a matter of judgment and taste; but at the same time the selection should be made with strict reference to the stop appointment of the different divisions of the instrument.

It is desirable that an ordinary Church Organ, with two manual claviers, should have all the following couplers, especially if the stops which the claviers command do not exceed twenty-five in number:

I. Swell to Great, Unison coupler.
II. Swell to Great, Octave coupler.
III. Swell to Great, Sub-octave coupler.
IV. Great to Pedal.
V. Swell to Pedal.

In larger instruments, which may have a stop or stops of 16 ft. pitch in one or both of the manual divisions, the Swell to Great, Sub-octave coupler, may be omitted without any disadvantage. Some organists prefer the Octave coupler to affect the Great clavier only or the Swell clavier only; but we are convinced that in Organs of the class we advocate, the Swell to Great, Octave coupler, will be found to be more generally useful. It is true the Octave coupler on the Swell clavier only can also be commanded by the Great clavier when the Swell to Great, Unison coupler is drawn; but this involves the unison on the Swell in addition to the octave sounds, an effect not always desirable. This coupler question, so far as the true Church Organ is concerned, is not, however, one of paramount importance. A carefully schemed and well-balanced instrument will meet all legitimate demands made upon its musical resources even when it has only the Unison manual coupler and the two manual to pedal couplers.

In Church Organs with three manual claviers the following manual and pedal couplers are to be recommended :

I. Swell to Great, Unison coupler.
II. Swell to Great, Octave coupler.
III. Swell to Choir, Unison coupler.
IV. Choir to Great, Unison coupler.
V. Choir to Great, Sub-octave coupler.
VI. Great to Pedal.
VII. Choir to Pedal.
VIII. Swell to Pedal.

As in the preceding case, when there is a stop of 16 ft. pitch in the Great or Swell divisions, the Sub-octave coupler may be omitted; and, when the Choir Organ is an expressive division, a Choir to Great, Octave coupler, is a valuable addition. The resources of the Great clavier are materially increased by the Octave couplers, especially as they affect stops which are capable of being artistically adjusted to accord, in strength of tone, with the unison stops on the unexpressive clavier. At this point the reader should glance at the remarks on the couplers in the Chapter on the Manual Claviers. All the couplers which add to the tonal resources of any division of the Organ are practically stops belonging to that division; and, accordingly, their draw-knobs, stop-keys, or touches, should be placed in the group controlling the speaking stops of the division. The three Pedal Organ couplers (Nos. VI., VII., and VIII.) should be similarly treated, and, in addition, should be commanded by double-acting, or on-and-off, foot-levers, conveniently located side by side.

THE DRAW-STOP AND COMBINATION ACTIONS.—In all Church Organs above those of the smallest size and simplest construction, the draw-stop action should be pneumatic throughout. A proper pneumatic action—lever or tubular—leaves the draw-stop knobs or other mechanical appliances very little to do, removing all strain from them, and favoring the introduction of a perfect combination action, fixed or adjustable. When ventil, sliderless wind-chests are used, the draw-stop action may be either tubular-pneumatic or tracker; and in either form there is no necessity for it to be heavier than an ordinary key action. The same remark applies to the electro-pneumatic draw-stop action. While it is desirable that when draw-stop knobs are used they should be made to draw a short distance only, it is also desirable that they should offer just so much resistance to the hand as will make the feeling of drawing them comfortable. As the different forms of draw-stop actions are touched upon in subsequent Chapters it is unnecessary to dwell upon them here.

The draw-stop knobs, belonging to the speaking stops, should be conveniently and compactly arranged in distinctly marked groups, as close to the right and left cheeks of the manual claviers as possible, so as to be within easy reach of the performer while properly seated at the instrument. In all cases of direct action, and when no insuperable difficulties obtain, the draw-stop jambs should be placed at an angle, so that the knobs can be drawn toward the performer, and be within the control of either hand, on both sides, whilst the other hand is engaged on the keys. This arrangement may entail some additional mechanism; but the cost of the same is well represented in the greater convenience secured to the organist. Some organ builders, who have shown themselves both painstaking and artistic in all such matters, prefer to arrange the draw-stop knobs in stepped tiers, practically continuing the clavier disposition some distance, laterally, from the clavier cheeks. This is a clear and compact arrangement, and one that is very convenient when the claviers are in a detached console. M. Cavaillé-Coll, of Paris, carried this treatment to its extreme development in the reversed consoles of his large Church Organs. In these consoles the stepped, draw-stop jambs assume the form of quadrants, the several tiers or steps being carried directly from the cheeks of the claviers. This arrangement allows a large number of knobs to be placed within easy reach of the organist seated at the keys, without the necessity of locating any of them higher than the level of the hands while playing the uppermost clavier.

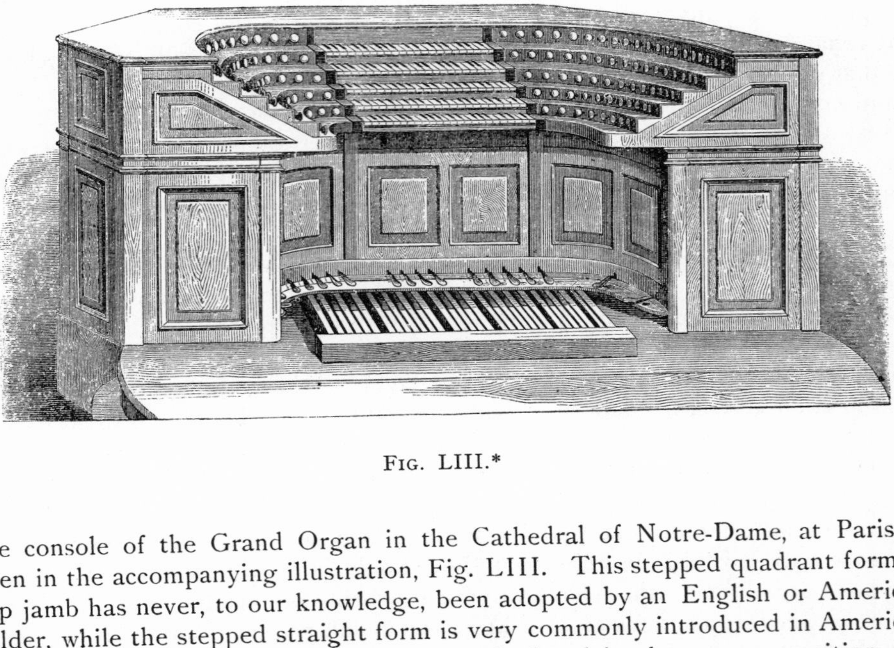

FIG. LIII.*

The console of the Grand Organ in the Cathedral of Notre-Dame, at Paris, is given in the accompanying illustration, Fig. LIII. This stepped quadrant form of stop jamb has never, to our knowledge, been adopted by an English or American builder, while the stepped straight form is very commonly introduced in American Organs. When the console is detached and placed in the reverse position, the low, stepped stop jambs are to be recommended: and whilst there is no necessity in Organs of moderate dimensions to adopt the quadrant form, it is certainly advisable to construct the jambs so that they leave the clavier cheeks at a convenient angle, and so place the draw-stop knobs within easy reach of the performer's hands. Neither a tubular-pneumatic nor electro-pneumatic action will be complicated by this arrangement. Very neat and convenient, plain draw-stop jambs

* At the time this page was printed we had met with no example of this form of console in an American Organ. The form now obtains in certain important instruments.—G. A. A.

were invented and patented in 1898* by Mr. Ernest M. Skinner, of Boston, Mass. These jambs are movable, being hinged to the ends of the console, close to the cheeks of the manual claviers. When the console is shut up, the jambs are parallel to the clavier cheeks: but when the console is opened, the jambs are moved into the necessary and convenient angular position. Apart from the convenience thus secured, the arrangement allows the console to be reduced in length and to be made singularly compact and portable. This form of console is commonly adopted by the Hutchings-Votey Organ Company, of Boston, for its electro-pneumatic Organs.

Whatever the position of the draw-stop knobs may be, we strongly advise their being very carefully and distinctly grouped, so that those belonging to each division of the Organ may be readily distinguishable. In the stepped form of stop jambs, the knobs commanding the stops of each division should be placed directly in line with the clavier of the division. The use of knobs of differently colored ivory or wood, faced with white ivory for the inscriptions, is greatly to be recommended. To one thoroughly acquainted with an Organ this matter of marked distinction is of small importance, for he can lay his fingers on the proper knobs without a glance at them; but to a stranger a ready means of distinguishing the several divisional groups is of the greatest service. One thing is certain, if the Organ is schemed so as to give the greatest possible facilities to the strange performer, it will be equally convenient to the organist who is fully conversant with it; but the reverse will not hold good. Matters such as these cost little beyond thought, ingenuity, and care.

In tubular-pneumatic and electro-pneumatic Organs, such appliances as stop-keys, or rocking or lever tablets, are likely to entirely supersede the ordinary and somewhat clumsy draw-stop knobs; but time will be required for so radical a departure from the old method. In certain quarters to-day the use of draw-knobs has been abandoned in electro-pneumatic work.

In addition to a satisfactory draw-stop action, commanded by draw-knobs, stop-keys, or rocking tablets, every Church Organ should have a sufficient and well arranged combination action, and this should in all possible cases be made adjustable. In instruments which have the old style of pallet and slider wind-chests, and the ordinary slider-drawing, rod and lever, stop action, the combination action will have to be commanded by foot-levers; but in Organs constructed on the tubular-pneumatic or electro-pneumatic systems, the combination action should be commanded by push-buttons, 'pistons,' or some similar appliances, conveniently placed under each manual clavier and within easy reach of the thumbs of the player. In addition to these, small foot-levers, situated conveniently above the toe-board of the pedal clavier, should be provided for drawing combinations simultaneously in all the divisions of the instrument. The number of thumb-pistons will, of course, be dictated by the size of the Organ and its tonal appointment; but no manual division should have less than three, producing, in the case of a fixed action, a *forte*, *mezzo forte*, and *piano* combination respectively. No Organ

*United States Letters Patent No. 11,669, dated June 14, 1898.

should have fewer than three combination levers, producing three of the most generally useful combinations in all the manual divisions, with suitable pedal combinations; and these should not clash with the combinations drawn by the thumb-pistons. When the Organ is large and is furnished with an adequate pedal department, it is desirable to arrange that certain of the thumb-pistons of each manual division will draw suitable stops or combinations in the Pedal Organ. This arrangement would go far to prevent the use of unsuitable basses, and would greatly help the performer in making rapid and well-balanced changes in tonality.

The importance of imparting greater flexibility to the Pedal Organ and bringing its grave voices more thoroughly and more immediately under artistic control cannot be over-estimated. At this point we cannot do better than quote some passages from the writings of the pioneer in this important branch of artistic organ construction. Mr. Thomas Casson, in his *brochure* on "The Modern Organ" (published in 1883), says:—

"Assuming that the German CC theory be adopted, it is unjust not to carry it out fully. The essential principle of that theory is, that the Pedal Organ shall be provided with basses for the chief manual stops. This is done by the Germans to the extent of providing the stops; but owing to their pedantic method of playing (their stops being generally 'set' beforehand) this mere fulfilment of the letter of their theory is practically useless in other countries, where ever-varying tones are demanded during performance: owing, nevertheless, to universal lack of system, no method of control has ever been applied to the pedal stops. Thus the Pedal Organ is either monotonous and inappropriate from lack of stops, or out of control from lack of system—the stops forming a forest of unwieldy handles, demanding perpetual manipulation at the very times when the hands and feet can be least spared.

"If, however, the spirit of the German theory be fully adopted, it will be perceived that not only should the pedal basses represent their manual counterparts individually, but that they should be grouped to form separate Pedal Organs to represent their manual counterparts collectively. This is made clear in some modern German instances, where this theory has been carried out to some extent with the awkward expedient of two Pedal Organs with separate pedal claviers.*

"It is impossible to have more than one convenient pedal clavier. Two must be cramped and clumsy; and since three or more are quite impracticable, the theory cannot be completely carried out in this fashion. Separate parts, as between two Pedal Organs, are however neither written nor required. All that is necessary is that a separate Pedal Organ be provided for each manual, with means for instantly attaching it to the one pedal clavier, to the simultaneous exclusion of the Pedal Organs not required; together with means for working the manual-to-pedal couplers simultaneously and appropriately.

"By this means we give to the pedal stops all the accessibility and variety hitherto peculiar to the manual stops; and if the combination action be arranged to act upon each manual organ simultaneously with its Pedal Organ and coupler, it is obvious that either by the combination action or draw-stop arrangement, the attachment of any Pedal Organ to the pedal clavier may be made in all cases to provide instantaneously the *exact* pedal bass required. It is not intended that, in playing, the bass combination shall necessarily be the exact counterpart of that of the manual. On the contrary, the separate Pedal Organs enable the organist to use contrasting or solo pedal combinations in exactly the same way as

* "Messrs. Walcker & Co. inform me (27th February, 1883), that they now group their pedal stops into separate Pedal Organs, attachable by pedals to one clavier; the action simultaneously throwing off the Pedal Organs not required. This is on the same theory as mine, and confirms it. Their action does not, however, work the pedal couplers, and would be of comparatively little use in English Organs."

he uses those of the manuals, of course far more readily than is possible by any present method. *The pedal clavier becomes in fact a great hand, which may be applied at will to any of the Pedal Organs.*

"It is not denied that *at the will of the performer* the Pedal Organ should be capable of producing tones of special character or weight; but it is maintained that the organist alone should have the option of either making it do so, or of producing an unobtrusive and strictly appropriate *bass*. The present English method does not provide a reasonably good bass, either by way of match or contrast, to any manual combination whatever—except so far as the contrast may exist between music on the one hand and noise on the other; and it especially ignores the necessity for basses for the Swell and Choir. [The same remarks hold good to-day with regard to the prevailing American method of Pedal Organ appointment and disposition.] If organists were, as they invariably should be, placed where they could hear their instruments, the noisy, monotonous, inappropriate 'Pedal Organ' would not long survive.

"Even were the invariable relatively obstreperous individuality of the pedal bass correct in theory, however, we are still without any *system* of control. It is worthless, from an artistic point of view, to have contrivances for 'reducing the Pedal Organ to a soft 16 ft. tone,' bringing on and off the 'Great to Pedal' coupler, &c. There must, in the Organ of the future, be means for instantaneously reducing or augmenting the Pedal Organ to exactly the bass required, whether the stop be a Stopped Bass, 16 ft., VIOLONCELLO, 8 FT., BASSOON, 16 FT., CLARIONET, 4 FT., or what not; while, as to the couplers, the 'Swell to Pedal' and 'Choir to Pedal' are of quite as much importance as the 'Great to Pedal'—not of course as a mere question of silencing so much noise, but as a question of producing certain musical sounds: yet no provision is made for the control of these useful adjuncts. I do not say that a method of control, other than that of the separate Pedal Organs, may may not be devised hereafter; but up to the present time it has not been produced. If the separate Pedal Organ system be adopted, even for pipes of enlarged scale, they must be grouped; and if so, they must be grouped in the order that long experience has shown to be necessary in the manual departments, viz.:—

Full and ponderous.	Expressive.
Light accompanimental.	Orchestral.

"This brings us to where we were before—giving us again pedal basses for the Great, Choir, Swell, and Solo *Organs*.

"Another objection to the German theory that the Pedal Organ should consist of *basses* for the manual stops is, that if it were correct, the object could be better attained by abolishing the Pedal Organ altogether, elongating the manual Organs to CCC, and providing couplers in 16 and 8 foot pitch for each manual [acting on each manual]. This was, I think, a plan advocated by the late Mr. Turle, and other eminent English musicians. It is infinitely to their credit; for there can be no doubt that if *thoroughly carried out*, it would have been immeasurably superior to the CC Organ, as generally constructed. Unfortunately it was but a plan, however: it was never completely carried out—probably on account of its great cost, for it would have necessitated carrying *all* the stops through to the CCC key, in order to avoid breaks at CC, such as are still perpetrated at tenor C by even eminent English builders. Still more unfortunately, it would have been prohibitory of contrasting obbligato or solo passages for the pedals; for these could not have been obtained without altering the combinations of other manuals to obtain them—an altogether impracticable idea. The six couplers, too, would have been out of control. The College of Organists, by its suggestions of elaborate contrivances for the control of only one pedal coupler, more than proves this. The chief objection, however, is, that contrasting obbligato and solo passages would be unattainable. The suggestion of the College of Organists as to pedal stops for melodic use is by far the most artistic and valuable of any in its scheme:

but I know of no quarter, save this, in which it has received the slightest attention. The fact is, that pedal solo stops are of no more use without separate Pedal Organs, in which to group them and make them available, than solo stops for the manual would be without separate manual Organs.

"By way of contrast, let the musician figure to himself an Organ in which an appropriate and sufficient, but unobtrusive bass is provided by touching a pneumatic stud, the bass of the Swell rising and falling with its manual power, the Choir endowed with sweet soft basses, Pedal contrasting obbligato and solo effects at once accessible, immediate antiphonal response of Pedal, as well as of manual, obtain in divided Organs, all worry with the Pedal Organ and pedal couplers absolutely abolished. He can then judge for himself as to the merits of the system."

In every Church Organ of any importance the combination action should be adjustable; for surely the day is past for the old-fashioned and inartistic fixed combination actions, which admit of no alteration in the combinations drawn by them unless the organ builder is called in to change the mechanism. The late Mr. Hilborne L. Roosevelt, of New York, was the first builder to demonstrate in a practical manner the great advantage of an adjustable combination action. The importance of such an action to the artistic organist and musician is clearly pointed out in the following remarks, printed in 1883, on the "Roosevelt Patent Adjustable Combination Action":—

"By this novel contrivance the player is enabled to place *any* combination of stops he may require, under immediate control, altering such combination as frequently as may be desired, instead of being compelled to use invariably an arbitrary and unalterable selection placed at his disposal by a builder who solely relies on the usual Combination Pedals. The mechanism is controlled either by a series of Pistons placed under each manual, or by ordinary Pedals; but inasmuch as the effect is not identical in each case, it will, perhaps, be advisable to describe them separately.

"When Pistons are employed—and they are in many respects preferable—a series of them affecting the stops in each department of the instrument is placed under the corresponding manuals. Rows of small vertical levers will also be found, agreeing in number with the Pistons, and displayed on the right and left of the keyboards above the draw-stops. These levers represent the registers, and are labeled accordingly, and the pressure of the lower end of any one of them will cause the stop it represents to be 'drawn on' when the Piston is used which controls the row in which the lever in question is situated, so that any desired combination may be readily 'set' on each of these appliances. The Pedal stops are connected with the Great Organ Pistons, in addition to which, Pedals are inserted whose action governs them exclusively. The Couplers also are controlled by this mechanism, those belonging to each manual being acted upon by its Pistons. It is likewise worthy of remark that the use of this mechanism renders the partial drawing of the stops an impossibility, and as the registers are *visibly* operated, the tonal condition of the Organ can always be ascertained by a casual glance, which is a matter of the utmost importance to an organist when dealing with an unfamiliar instrument, and even under other circumstances is highly desirable.

"In order to make the matter clearer we will quote an instance by means of which its practical comprehension will be ensured. Take the case of a three-manual Organ containing 50 speaking stops thus distributed: Great—13, Swell—17, Choir—12, Pedal—8, and Couplers—7, those allotted to Great and Choir being placed on the right of the player, the remainder, belonging to the Swell and Pedal, on his left, the Couplers occupying a position immediately above the Swell keyboard.

"Presuming that Swell and Great have 5 Pistons each, and the Choir, 3, also that there are three adjustable Combination Pedals controlling only Pedal Organ; 8 rows of adjustable levers will be found on each side. Five of those on the right will each represent in duplicate the 13 stops of the Great Organ, the 8 belonging to the Pedal, and the 4 Great Organ Couplers (a total of 25 in each row), and are governed by the 5 pistons respectively that will be found beneath that manual. In rendering Great Organ Piston No. 1 available for producing required changes of tone, it is only requisite to push in the lower ends of levers on the highest row bearing the names of desired stops, in order to cause them to be 'drawn on' when the Piston is pressed, those levers remaining in a reversed position, causing *their* corresponding stops to be 'drawn off' at the same time. The operation can be repeated in the case of No. 2 by a similar use of the levers in the second row, and so on.

"The 3 lower rows control the Choir Organ stops as well as its Couplers; while the upper 5 on the opposite side affect the registers of Swell Organ and its Couplers in a precisely similar manner when their pistons are used; the lower 3 rows governing the Pedal Organ stops independently by means of the 3 Adjustable Pedals referred to. If Pedals are substituted for the Pistons, the rows of levers do not represent separate departments as in the former case, but each of them contains a lever for every stop in the instrument. Thus any combination, however comprehensive, may be prepared on any Pedal, a distinctive brass number placed above each of them indicating the particular set of levers affected, which is also distinguished by a corresponding number. Every complete row of levers (extending to the right and left of the player) represents the entire contents of the Organ, and therefore the resources of each Pedal are practically unlimited."

The adjustable combination action as above described, controlled by thumb-pistons, was applied to the Organ of the First Congregational Church, Great Barrington, Mass.; and, controlled by a series of foot-levers, to the Organ of the Cathedral of the Incarnation, Garden City, L. I., in the year 1883. As the adjustable combination action forms the subject of a separate Chapter, it is unnecessary to enlarge on it here.

EXPRESSION LEVERS.—In a Church Organ of two manual divisions there will be, or ought to be, one division inclosed in a swell-box; and, as will be seen later, it may be considered desirable to introduce two swell-boxes. In Organs of three manual divisions there ought to be two expressive divisions inclosed in independent swell-boxes; and it may be considered advisable to have a certain portion of the tonal forces of the remaining division also inclosed in one of the swell-boxes. In each case the swell-boxes must have expression levers (commonly called swell-pedals) which should be of the French or balanced form. The position of the single lever should be immediately above the EE and FF keys of the pedal clavier. When two expression levers are required they should be placed side by side, and with not more than half an inch of space between their inner edges. This space should be directly over the space between the two pedal keys just named. This position places the levers slightly to the right of the true center, and, accordingly, convenient for the right foot of the performer. The left lever is easily reached with the left foot, when the Pedal Organ is silent, and when both levers are required to be operated in contrary motion at the same time. The reason why the levers should be placed side by side is to enable the right foot to control both together in similar motion, or one after the other in contrary motion.

When only one expression lever is required, as in the great majority of Church Organs as at present constructed, the returning form may be adopted if preferred. It certainly should not be of the old-fashioned, hitch-down, pattern, but should be provided with an automatic appliance, fixing it, at any point of its upward or downward motion, on the removal of the foot. When two or more expression levers are necessary, as they certainly will be in all properly appointed Organs having three manual divisions, it is imperative that they be of the balanced form, that is, if the swells are to be properly controlled and artistically used.

TREMOLANT.—When judiciously and artistically used, the TREMOLANT imparts a pleasing effect to the voices of certain stops; but a too liberal and a tasteless employment of its *tremolo* is essentially vulgar and distressing to the educated ear. As its artistic use is far more uncommon than the reverse, many persons with refined musical sense have advocated the omission of the TREMOLANT from the Church Organ; but we do not consider their argument to be a good one. An Organ should be designed for the *artist* and not for the *bungler;* for it may be said, that under the hands of the latter not only the TREMOLANT but every stop and appliance in the instrument runs a great risk of being abused in some fashion.

No rule save a very general one can be given for the introduction or application of the TREMOLANT in the Church Organ; for, in the absence of a list of its speaking stops, it is impossible to say where the *tremolo* is required, or, indeed, if it is necessary at all. The general rule alluded to confines its application to manual stops inclosed in a swell-box; and when the division has more than one pressure of wind, to the portion in which the stops of a solo character are congregated. There is only one speaking stop in the Organ whose characteristic voice depends on the effect of the TREMOLANT: we allude to the VOX HUMANA. The introduction of this stop involves the application of the TREMOLANT.

Should there be more than one TREMOLANT in a Church Organ? This question can only be answered after an inspection of the scheme of the instrument. If there are two expressive divisions, and both contain soft and solo voices which are suitable for the *tremolo* effect, then each division may have a TREMOLANT affecting those stops.

WIND PRESSURE.—Before proceeding with our brief remarks on the speaking stops most suitable and desirable for the Church Organ, it is, perhaps, expedient that the question of wind pressure—a question of no slight importance in the present epoch of organ-building—should be considered.

It must be admitted, we venture to think, by all true lovers of the Organ, that there has been of late years, especially in England, a decided tendency to over-blow the Organ, and to produce as much sound as wind can provoke from its pipe-work, without proper regard to the quality of tone, by a system of heavy-pressure blowing, and, of necessity, strained voicing. That all Organs built on this system have lost immensely in the elements of refinement and beauty cannot be questioned by any one endowed with musical taste, and possessed of some knowledge of the acoustics and musical properties of organ pipes. It is simply painful to listen to the generality of the Organs which have been placed in Churches during recent years; and one almost yearns, notwithstanding the knowledge of certain advances in the art of pipe making and voicing, for a return to the old style of tone as produced by early masters. Let any one compare, for instance, an unspoiled Silbermann, Father Smith, Harris, or Snetzler, OPEN DIAPASON with one of our modern over-blown, screaming affairs of the same name, and judge for himself.

The practice of using heavy pressures of wind is the necessary offspring of cheap and crowded organ-building, provoked by confined and badly-designed organ-chambers and other equally serious blunders of the church architects of to-day. Organ builders, for motives best known to themselves, strive to get as much sound as wind can produce from pipes of insufficient scales, sacrificing their proper musical tones for the sake of power and noise. Pipes of small scales weigh less, and, accordingly, cost less, than those of large or adequate scales; and the temptation to use the former and to cover their inherent weakness by means which cost nothing is too great to be resisted by builders who desire large profits, or who undertake work at low competition prices. There can be no question that the tones yielded by full-scaled and substantial metal pipes, blown by a copious supply of wind at a moderate pressure, are vastly superior to those produced from small-scaled pipes, blown with wind at a high pressure. For the true accompanimental Church Organ there can be no comparison between the two classes of tone; for that yielded by the full-scaled pipes is characterized by richness, volume, refinement, and great traveling power,—just the qualities required for dignified choral accompaniment,—whilst the harsh, thin, and forced tone of the over-blown small-scaled pipes utterly fails to satisfy the ear and meet the conditions of a sympathetic, refined, and artistic accompaniment.

In addition to the reasons above given, we must seek a little farther for the cause which induces some of the most renowned organ builders to adopt high pressures of wind even with large scales. We are confining our remarks to the large family of labial stops which may be said to form the vertebræ of the Organ; and are not alluding to certain classes of imitative stops (comparatively few in number) which gain much of their characteristic intonations from the use of high-pressure wind. Such builders seem to us to have labored so long in the face of architectural and acoustical disadvantages, which, in the natural order of things, compelled them to resort to extreme measures in the voicing of their stops, that their ears have become deadened to soft sounds, and have lost much of that delicate and sensitive perception which lies at the bottom of all pure musical sense. This is perhaps the most correct, as it is the most kindly way, of accounting for the production of that strictly modern tone, in the DIAPASONS and stops of a kindred nature, which is positively offensive to a properly educated and sensitive ear.

As might reasonably be expected, there is some diversity of opinion among those who favor the adoption of low pressures with reference to the most suitable pressure for the manual divisions of the Church Organ; that is to say, when only a single pressure is used throughout them. In large instruments, and, indeed, in those of any pretensions to completeness, it is necessary to have two or more different pressures of wind. An extreme and noteworthy example of the use of several pressures is furnished by the fine Organ in the Parish Church of Leeds, Yorkshire, which has no fewer than five, as in the subjoined list:

Pedal Organ, . . .	Wind pressure	3¾	inches.
Great Organ, generally, . .	"	3¾	"
Great Organ, TUBA only, . .	"	7	"
Swell Organ, . . .	"	3	"
Choir Organ, . . .	"	2½	"
Echo Organ, . . .	"	1½	"

While it may be considered advisable, as a rule, to adopt a safe medium pressure, say 3½ inches, for Organs of small size in which only one pressure is introduced, we are strongly in favor of a more frequent use of a slightly lower pressure for small Church Organs. When full-scaled pipes are skilfully voiced on a *copious supply* of wind of 2¾ inches the richest and roundest qualities of tone are obtained, and that without any objectionable hissing or windiness—the qualities of tone which best support and blend with the human voice in the dignified and solemn music of the Church. A pressure of 3 inches may also be safely used.

There is a very remarkable OPEN DIAPASON, 8 FT., in the Leeds Parish Church Organ, made by the great Schulze, probably the finest of its class in England. It is of full-scale, the CC pipe measuring 6·25 inches in diameter, and is very copiously winded at 3¾ inches pressure. The tone of this stop is majestic and full beyond description; indeed, it is a Great Organ in itself. Stops of this class are, however, hardly suitable for Church Organs of the usual size, or in buildings of moderate dimensions, although there can be no question as regards their impressiveness and supporting powers. What is really required in the average-sized Church Organ, in any building less than a cathedral in its proportions, so far as the chief OPEN DIAPASON is concerned, is a stop of similar scale and wind supply, but voiced on wind of lower pressure.

In instruments of medium size, with three manual divisions and pedal department, three pressures of wind should be used. For these we advise 3½ inches for the Pedal and Swell Organs; 3 inches for the Great Organ; and 2½ inches for the Choir Organ. Large scales should be used for the Great Organ, medium scales for the Pedal and Swell Organs, and small scales for the Choir Organ. A rich and impressive grandeur should characterize the general tone of the Great, brilliancy that of the Swell, and quiet sweetness and repose that of the Choir. These are facts sometimes disputed and almost invariably ignored by builders of Church Organs. It is now extremely difficult to get moderate or what may be called low pressures properly tested by our organ builders, for the high pressure craze is strong among them: and one experiences a hopeless feeling when one has a 3½ inch wind advocated for such an instrument as a Chamber Organ on the sole ground that such a pressure is necessary for the *tubular-pneumatic action* employed. There must be an impression lurking in such men's minds that the Organ, as a *musical instrument*, exists in its mechanical, not in its sound-producing, portion. For our part, we would willingly sacrifice everything in the shape of pneumatic appliances to secure that grand and refined volume of tone which places the Organ on the throne, and gains for it the title of the "King of Instruments."

SPEAKING STOPS.—The selection of the speaking stops for all classes of Organs is a matter of the greatest importance; and one which in all cases should be governed by the purposes for which the instruments are destined, and the demands which, in the proper order of things, are to be made on their musical resources. It is either from an entire misconception of the matter, or an equally serious neglect of the problem it involves, that so many modern Church Organs have been spoiled or rendered insufficient instruments. There is another cause for many failures. When the organist of a church is allowed to specify the contents of a new Organ, he is very apt to make it a personal matter, and either purposely or intuitively adapt the Specification to his own fancy and style of playing; forgetting that other organists are to come after him who are certain to disapprove of his arrangements. All this makes the advent of the independent organ expert highly desirable—the designer who will work on broad principles, born of science and art, and indulge in no personal whims and caprices.

Modern ingenuity has added numerous stops, chiefly of an imitative character, to the list of stops which was at the disposal of the organ builders of the eighteenth century and the beginning of the nineteenth; and, accordingly, the designer of Organs in the present day is subjected to considerable temptation when engaged in making a selection for any instrument. Unless he has a comprehensive knowledge of the nature and tonal qualities of all the organ stops at his disposal, and a practical acquaintance with their behavior on different pressures of wind; and unless he steadily holds in view the nature and uses of the instrument he is scheming, he is almost certain to make serious mistakes; sacrificing that which should be the governing feature in the tonal scheme, for what may be mere ear-tickling effects. There is little doubt that the ambition of organists to have the Church Organs, schemed by them, adapted for solo or recital purposes, has done much to incapacitate instruments of small, or even moderate, dimensions for their true and legitimate office—the dignified and appropriate accompaniment of sacred song. When Organs are large, there is scope for the insertion of tonal materials for all classes of music: and so long as the Organ proper, in its true church aspect as an accompanimental instrument, is amply appointed, there need be no exception taken to the addition of stops suitable for solo playing or for the production of varied orchestral effects.

The most important stops, and, indeed, those upon which the whole tonal structure of the Organ is based and built up, are commonly classed under the general appellation of *Foundation-work*. The name is appropriate, and fully expresses the important office fulfilled by the stops in question. In the manual department of the Organ such stops are formed of open metal pipes of cylindrical form, yielding tones, peculiar to organ pipes, of great purity and volume. Their tones are, generally considered, of a simple nature, that is deficient in harmonic or upper partial tones. First in order of importance among the stops forming the foundation of the Organ are those known in English speaking countries as OPEN DIAPASONS;* and subordinate are those derived from, and strictly attendant on, the DIAPASONS, yielding sounds which represent or corroborate the upper partial tones of the prime or unison tones. There can be no question that upon the scaling and voicing of the fundamental DIAPASONS, and upon the relative scaling and strengths of tone of all the derived, harmonic-corroborating stops, the Church Organ stands or falls as a worthy instrument. First of all, therefore, it is imperative that they should receive the greatest consideration in all matters connected with their manufacture and voicing. In all cases tin or the richest spotted metal should be used in the fabrication of their pipes; and it is essential that the metal should be of sufficient substance or thickness to render the pipes perfectly firm in their speech with the most copious windage they can be subjected to. It is impossible to obtain the full, round tone required in a true OPEN DIAPASON from pipes of bad metal, or from those of insufficient thickness in any metal. Zinc pipes have of late years come into common use, chiefly on account of their cheapness; and if their durability could be assured probably no serious objection could be advanced against them, especially when of large size and of good substance. Zinc pipes should invariably be fitted with spotted metal mouths and all parts that require manipulation in the process of voicing and regulating. No zinc should, under any circumstances, be used for labial pipes under four feet speaking length; and we may add that in good work it should never be employed for smaller pipes than those of eight feet speaking length.

As the matter of scaling is gone into with sufficient fulness in subsequent Chapters, it is unnecessary for us to pass more than the most general remarks on it here. As has been already hinted, there is a tendency among organ builders, and especially among those who work at low prices, to reduce the scales of metal stops, notably the heavy and expensive ones of the DIAPASON family, endeavoring to make up for their shortcomings in scale by increased wind pressures. When high class materials, such as tin and the richest spotted metal or 'confluent metal,' are used, the temptation to economize is greater: and when one bears in mind that the difference of half an inch in the diameter, or scale, of the CC pipe of the OPEN DIAPASON means a strip of metal about 9 feet long (including the foot) by 1½ inches in width, and so on, in proportion, in every succeeding pipe of the stop, one can hardly be surprised if the temptation frequently proves too strong to be resisted. The cure for such a state of affairs is simple. Let every one who designs an Organ know what the proper scales should be and see that he gets them. Scales are, however, not everything; for thickness of metal, properly proportioned to the scales used, is quite as important a matter for the production of a full and firm tone, to say nothing of durability. Hard and springy metal such as tin and zinc may, as a rule, be used somewhat thinner than spotted metal or any of the inferior alloys of tin and lead.

*It will be seen on reference to the Chapter on a Systematic Organ Stop Nomenclature, that we do not approve of the present heterogeneous naming of stops followed by English and American organ builders; and that we venture to suggest a more systematic method for future adoption. We have, however, deemed it expedient to use the present and commonly understood style of nomenclature throughout all the other Chapters of this treatise, so as to prevent misunderstanding or confusion in the minds of our readers.

We have already alluded to the scale of the chief manual OPEN DIAPASON in the Organ of the Parish Church of Leeds, as being that desirable for the same stop in all good Church Organs. This scale, which gives 6·25 inches as the inside diameter of the CC pipe, is the largest that need be contemplated under all ordinary circumstances. The smallest scale which should ever be used for the chief DIAPASON of a Church Organ gives the CC pipe an internal diameter of 5.5 inches.

When two or more OPEN DIAPASONS are planted in the same Organ, it is imperative that their scales be as widely different as practicable, and that their voicing be markedly dissimilar; if they are on winds of different pressures the result will be all the better. Not only does the treatment secure a desirable diversity of tone and different degrees of power, but it prevents a loss of volume in their combined tone through what may be called acoustical sympathy, the operation of which is not well understood. In very large Organs, or in instruments which have to fill large and spacious churches, it is desirable to add to the metal OPEN DIAPASONS an OPEN DIAPASON, 8 FT., of wood. The fine open wood pipes inserted by Schulze in his grand Organ in the Church of St. Bartholomew, at Armley, near Leeds, clearly show what can be achieved in this direction. English builders are, as a rule, adverse to the introduction of wood stops, of any class, in the manual departments of their Organs, and this is to be regretted. It is quite certain that Organs of all classes lose greatly in breadth and fulness of tone, to say nothing of variety, by the practice of depending almost entirely on metal stops.* On this important subject we speak more fully later on.

To retain or secure the requisite domination of the unison sounds of the foundation-work, it is necessary to select scales for the *derived* stops considerably smaller than those of the unisons. The general practice of introducing large-scaled and loudly-voiced octave and mutation stops is most injurious to the musical character of the Organ. Why this is so is fully explained in our Chapter on The Tonal Structure of the Organ. Of these harmonic-corroborating stops the most important are those which represent the first, second, and third upper partial tones; namely, the OCTAVE, or so-called PRINCIPAL, the TWELFTH, and the FIFTEENTH or SUPER-OCTAVE—stops respectively of 4 ft., 2⅔ ft., and 2 ft. pitch. In small or even medium sized instruments it is seldom advisable, in any single division, to go beyond these three harmonic-corroborating stops, in the form of independent and complete ranks: but in all instruments in which anything approaching completeness of tonal structure is aimed at it is imperative that further ranks of pipes, associated in the form of MIXTURES, be inserted, to add brilliancy and richness to the organ-tone by corroborating the higher upper partials. Without the full complement (from the practical, and not the theoretical, point of view) of

*On the occasion of our visit to Mr. Willis' factory for the purpose of viewing the Concert Organ for the Royal Albert Hall, while in process of construction, we remember the distinguished builder drawing our attention to the omission of wood stops from all the manual divisions, with, if we remember rightly, a single exception in the shape of a covered stop of 16 ft. pitch. On asking the builder how he was going to get the wood tone so desirable in an Organ, he replied: "I can get wood tone out of metal pipes, and *better*." We then remarked it is *true wood tone*, and not the "*better*," resulting from the use of metal pipes, that is required in the Organ. We say so still.

harmonic-corroborating stops, simple and compound, the Organ cannot be considered complete; and it will certainly not possess that complex character of tone which is one of the chief elements of its beauty and impressiveness. We freely admit, however, that, in the generality of existing examples, the Church Organ would be more agreeable to the ear without the MIXTURES which it may contain; but that fact is a reflection on the knowledge and musical sense of the builder, not upon the valuable and characteristic family of stops known as MIXTURES. A properly proportioned series of harmonic-corroborating stops cannot but add materially to the beauty of the Organ in which it is placed; while, on the other hand, a badly proportioned series is fatal to the musical character of the instrument.

The greatest care and judgment must be exercised in all matters relating to the introduction of the compound stops, as all stops of the MIXTURE class may be generally termed; and, strange to say, little or nothing beyond negative teaching is to be derived from a study of the works of the old organ builders. It is beyond all reasonable question that the early English and Continental builders and their immediate successors erred in making their MIXTURES far too assertive, by introducing inordinate scales and loud voicing, and by an unwise multiplication of them in their Organs. For instance, Father Smith inserted in his Temple Church Organ, which contained in all only twenty-three speaking stops, no fewer than five MIXTURES. These comprised 713 pipes out of the total number of 1,715 pipes in the instrument. Again, in the Great division of the Organ built by Renatus Harris for the Church of St. Sepulchre, Snow Hill, London, three MIXTURES were included in the list of fifteen stops.* Loudly-voiced MIXTURES, introduced in such numbers, go entirely beyond their province in the tonal structure of the Organ, and entirely upset the acoustical conditions which guarantee the introduction of such peculiar stops in proper form and proportion.

Erring on the other extreme, organ builders of to-day are introducing too few, or are altogether omitting, MIXTURES. Such a practice may have originated in the observation of the objectionable clang produced by the over-use of such stops; but probably the chief factor in the matter is the desire for cheap building. A MIXTURE of four or five ranks, with, respectively, 232 and 290 pipes, is both a costly and a troublesome stop; yet it is represented in an instrument by a single draw-knob, and in a Specification by a single number. When an Organ is competed for, and its contents are left to the tender mercies of the competing builders, there is a very strong temptation to omit stops calling for so much skilled labor in their construction, and so much space and additional labor on the wind-chests. Their argument, when challenged on the omission, is that such compound stops are neither necessary nor desirable in a Church Organ. They are correct in one respect. The MIXTURES *they* would be likely to introduce would, judging from the past, be both unnecessary and undesirable. Accordingly, inartistic, if not unreliable, builders are allowed to have their own way in a scientific and artistic matter in which, so far as their personal interests are concerned, they should have no controlling voice. For all practical information on the nature, office, and com-

*For further information on this subject, see the Chapter on The Compound Stops of the Organ.

position, of the compound stops, the reader must refer to the Chapter devoted to them.

Next in importance to the foundation unisons and their harmonic-corroborating companions, come the so-called DOUBLES, or manual sub-octave stops of 16 ft. pitch. While it is necessary to be careful in the introduction of such grave voices, there can be no question as regards their great value in the Church Organ. Considering the instrument in its most important function,—that of accompaniment to a number of voices singing in harmony,—it will be observed that the unisons, combined with the octave and the higher harmonic-corroborating stops, sustain the Treble voices in a perfectly satisfactory manner; but that the Tenors and especially the Basses are not supported and enriched to the same degree. To meet this requirement a soft stop of 16 ft. pitch is required. Hence the importance of having at least one stop of the class in the manual department of every Church Organ of any pretension to completeness. In addition to the importance of having a sub-octave stop for ordinary accompanimental music, such a stop is of great value in imparting fulness and dignity beyond what is attainable by any multiplication of unison stops. Dr. Hopkins, speaking on this subject, remarks:—

"If a chord be played in the treble part of the Great Organ of an instrument in a large building, and not having any stops lower in pitch than the unison, there will be perceived a certain *smallness* of effect, which makes it evident that, although the treble may possess sufficient brightness and intensity, perhaps even amounting to shrillness, yet it lacks the amount of fulness and volume necessary to produce an ample and dignified tone. This arises from the fact of even the unison pipes in the treble being comparatively acute in their sound; and, therefore, in the very nature of things, unpossessed of stately impressiveness. It thus becomes obvious that the harmonic-corroborating series of stops alone do not present *all* the resources necessary to form a satisfactory Organ. Something that is essential appears to be wanting; and a fresh element is felt to be necessary to supply that absent property. The property wanting is *gravity;* which possesses a character peculiar to itself, and for the absence of which no amount of *intensity* in the other sounds will compensate. Of the traveling and filling-up character of grave sounds we have already spoken; and of the fact itself, a sufficient illustration is given in the circumstance of a chant sung by twenty tenor and bass voices, in unison, pervading a building more completely than if sung by thrice the number of trebles. Again, the deep tone of a pedal DIAPASON will travel through a building more entirely than a double chord of six or seven notes played on the manual DIAPASONS from middle c^1 upwards. Its sound will certainly not be nearly so well defined; but it will be of a more pervading character. The want felt, and above specified, however, is not a *substitute* for the harmonic sounds, but a new element, which, *added* to them, shall render the general tone larger and more ample.* It is worth mentioning, that this want was so much felt, nearly three centuries and a half ago, abroad, that means were, even at that period, taken to supply the deficiency. It was about the year 1508, that a covered stop, of 16 ft. size of tone was invented in Holland; and

*For the correct and scientific explanation of this effect, see our Chapter on The Tonal Structure of the Organ.

which, to some extent, imparted the necessary, deep, resonant, *humming* effect to the other stops, and was hence expressly called *Bourdon;* a name that means a hum or drone; and which stop has never ceased to be highly valued abroad to this day."

From the above remarks, the reader can hardly fail to realize the importance of one or more stops of 16 ft. pitch on the manuals; and it now remains for consideration what description of stop should be introduced in Organs of different sizes; and at what point, with reference to the contents of any manual division, so grave a voice becomes advisable if not imperative. The latter question may conveniently be taken first. So soon as sufficient unison, octave, and higher harmonic-corroborating tones are provided to accompany, in a fairly effective manner, the voices of the choir and congregation, then, and then only, should a stop of 16 ft. tone be contemplated; and it should be added in preference to any further multiplication of unison stops, or the introduction of stops of an orchestral or fancy character. When the manual divisions are furnished with the proper tonal forces to support, equally, all the voices in full harmony, then may imitative and fancy stops be inserted, with the view of further enriching the general tone, and securing the means of imparting variety of coloring and strength of tone to the lighter accompanimental and incidental music of the services. Speaking by way of general guidance, we recommend that every Church Organ be provided with a stop of 16 ft. tone in the manual department, even when that department comprises only a dozen stops in all. Turning to Roosevelt's published series of Specifications, we find this recommendation supported. In his Church Organ, "Style Thirteen," the single manual department comprises only nine speaking stops, one of which is a BOURDON, 16 FT., throughout. Every Church Organ from this size upwards to say twenty speaking stops, should certainly have one manual stop of this pitch: and Organs containing a greater number, distributed in two manual divisions, should have one stop of 16 ft. pitch in each division. The Great Organ should have an open metal stop, and this may be a DOUBLE OPEN DIAPASON, DOUBLE DULCIANA, or CONTRA-GAMBA. The present very general practice of having only one stop of 16 ft. pitch, even in Organs of considerable pretensions, and that usually a covered wood stop placed in the Swell Organ, must be condemned; and more particularly because it usually happens that such indifferently appointed instruments have inadequate pedal departments.

With reference to the description of the DOUBLES most suitable for Church Organs of different sizes, and for insertion in their separate manual divisions, the following suggestions may be worthy of consideration. In instruments of the smallest serviceable size, and when the church is of small dimensions, a LIEBLICHGEDECKT, 16 FT., which neither occupies much space nor costs a large sum, will be sufficient to support the bass voices and impart dignity and gravity to the full manual tone. When the Organ is a two-manualed one, of from twelve to twenty stops, exclusive of those in the pedal department, with the full complement of couplers, the sub-octave stop should be placed in the expressive division. In somewhat larger instruments a BOURDON of medium scale should be placed in the Swell Organ; while, in all possible cases, a small-scaled and softly-voiced open metal stop of 16 ft. should be inserted in the Great Organ. This should be a DOUBLE DULCIANA. In still larger instruments, a large-scaled DOUBLE DULCIANA or a CONTRA-GAMBA should be placed in the Great; and when this division assumes important dimensions, a medium-scaled DOUBLE OPEN DIAPASON becomes necessary, voiced to a full round tone. In Church Organs of the first magnitude, with three or four manual divisions, a labial stop of 16 ft. pitch should be inserted in each division, selected in each case to suit, in quality and strength of tone, the unison voices. In addition to these labial stops, one or two reed stops of 16 ft. tone should appear in the most suitable expressive divisions.

It is scarcely necessary to point out that the Swell to Great, Sub-octave coupler, gives the organist ready means of adding several varieties and strengths of 16 ft. tone to any combinations in the Great Organ, down to Tenor C: and, further, that the same coupler furnishes the Great manual with a soft 32 ft. tone, down to the same note, when the LIEBLICHGEDECKT or BOURDON in the Swell Organ is drawn. The utility of this coupler is thus made evident. Few Church Organs have a stop of 32 ft. pitch in any manual division. Two noteworthy instances may be mentioned:—the Organ in the Parish Church of Leeds has in its Great division a SUB-BOURDON, 32 FT., of wood and metal, down to Tenor C; and the Organ in the Parish Church of Doncaster has a stop of the same name, pitch and compass, in its Great division. Both these stops were made by the renowned Schulze, of Paulinzelle, who evidently believed in the value and beauty of grave tones in the manual department. We cannot, however, advocate the direct introduction of the 32 ft. tone, as furnished by an independent stop, in anything save Pedal Organs of important size. Should so grave a sound ever be required on the Great Organ clavier, it can be obtained, in sufficient volume for any legitimate musical effect, by the use of the Sub-octave coupler, as above mentioned.

On the subject of other labial stops which are desirable in the Church Organ little need be said here; nevertheless it must not be passed over altogether. Up to the present point we have, with the exception of the covered sub-octave stop suitable for the manual department, and the SUB-BOURDON as introduced by Schulze, spoken of open stops, or those important ranks of pipes which form the backbone of the Organ proper; now attention may be directed to another class of stops, secondary only in importance to the open foundation-work. We allude to the stopped or covered ranks known by the names, STOPPED DIAPASON, LIEBLICHGEDECKT, ROHRFLÖTE, DOPPELFLÖTE, etc. All these stops, when of proper scales and artistically voiced, produce tones of good mixing and filling-up qualities; imparting to the tones of the open metal stops great roundness and increased solidity and sonorousness. This is due to the entire dissimilarity of their voices; and, accordingly, to the total absence of that acoustical sympathy which seems to reduce power by absorption. Of the stops just named, the DOPPELFLÖTE, 8 FT., is by far the most desirable and effective for the Great Organ, where a full volume of pervading tone is essential. It is much to be regretted that this beautiful stop is practically unknown in England. We are unaware of a DOPPELFLÖTE having been inserted in any Organ in that country prior to the year 1884, when we placed one in the expressive Great division of our own Chamber Organ. English organ builders, in their conservatism, do not seem disposed to undertake the manufacture of the wood DOPPELFLÖTE. The notion, in which the wish is father to the thought, that the voluminous and characteristic tones of stops of this class can be produced from ordinary, large-scaled metal pipes, has, as we have already hinted, done, and will continue to do, much to retard the proper use of wood pipes, and to circumscribe the range of tonal effects in the Organ generally. We unhesitatingly affirm that the peculiarly rich and sonorous filling-up qualities of the true DOPPELFLÖTE cannot be obtained from a single-mouthed metal stop; or even from a double-mouthed one, a sample pipe of which is before us as we write.

Next to the true organ-tone, as represented by the foundation-work, is that known as flute-tone; such tone as is yielded by the covered stops just enumerated, and by numerous other stops of both wood and metal, open and covered. Flute-tone, when of a refined quality, is extremely valuable for the accompaniment of the voice; and also for imparting that desirable variety in tonal coloring which may be resorted to in church music without any sacrifice of its general dignity. As a general rule, flute-tone should be kept strictly subordinate to the true organ-tone, for it is a quality the ear soon tires of; but in instruments of large size, such as those suitable for cathedrals or spacious churches, it will be expedient to insert two or more FLUTES of 8 ft. and 4 ft. pitch, having powerful and penetrating voices. We here allude to the HARMONIC FLUTES, the imitative ORCHESTRAL FLUTES, and such a stop as that introduced by Roosevelt in certain Church Organs, under the name of PHILOMELA. The last-named stop is formed of open wood pipes with two mouths; and when blown with wind of moderately high pressure has a voice of singular fulness and grandeur, both alone and in combination.

Stops producing sounds which imitate, more or less closely, the rich compound tones characteristic of the family of orchestral bowed instruments, although of less value in the Church Organ than those previously mentioned, may with great advantage be introduced in the chief expressive division. In instruments of moderate dimensions it is desirable to insert in the Swell Organ a VIOLONCELLO, 8 FT., of strictly imitative character. Such a stop, when skilfully used and played with appropriate expression, forms a beautiful accompaniment to a Tenor or Bass solo, while it furnishes most brilliant passages in combination with the higher voices. All the stops of the VIOL or so-called GAMBA class, on account of the specially rich harmonic structure of their sounds, enter into combination with all the other stops of the Organ but do not lose their individuality by absorption; accordingly, they produce bright and telling effects, and materially enrich the tonal resources of the instrument.

It is hardly necessary, in speaking of the Church Organ, to particularly allude to those stops which are justly classed as "fancy stops." Such may be allowed, or even considered desirable, in large, many-manualed instruments; but their value is questionable in the ordinary Church Organ, where, it is more than probable, their presence is secured at the sacrifice of stops of infinitely greater utility and importance. The craze which obtains among young and inexperienced organists, and a large section of the organ-loving public, for ear-tickling stops is about as absurd as it is pernicious to true art in organ-building. The golden rule here is:—Let fancy stops be added to an otherwise perfect Organ, but never be depended upon to perfect an insufficient or faulty instrument.

When a Church Organ has been properly appointed with respect to its foundation-work and labial stops generally, it requires but little aid from reed-work. Its presence is, however, very desirable, for it imparts what may be called a golden sheen to the already richly colored embroidery of sounds. Dr. Hopkins has tersely described the offices of the great families of organ stops in the following words: "Open stops of the Diapason kind, alone, would produce rather a cutting tone; an Organ entirely of Covered Stops would sound weak and muffled; while one composed entirely of Reeds would be too strong and penetrating. The four great classes of organ stops—Open, Covered, Flute, and Reed—are, in fact, to a great extent dependent on each other for the production of the most satisfactory result. The Covered Stops impart a quiet solidity to the Open Stops; the Open Stops bestow roundness and firmness on the Covered Stops; the Flute Stops give variety and increased character to the soft combinations; while the Reed Stops impart to the full organ stateliness and splendor, and in return receive fulness and brightness from the Open series of Stops." These remarks are true in the main; yet they must be read in the light of the instruments the writer was acquainted with, many years ago, when he penned them. The "cutting tone" of the open stops was doubtless due to the inordinate scales and voicing of the harmonic-corroborating stops so prevalent at the time. The "weak and muffled" effect of the covered stops was due to the few and comparatively tame varieties commonly met with in the English Organs. They seldom extended beyond the STOPPED DIAPASON and BOURDON, and their voices were very commonly both weak and muffled. The DOPPELFLÖTE, LIEBLICHGEDECKT, and ROHRFLÖTE, were practically unknown quantities, yet they are the highest types of covered stops.

In the ordinary Church Organ, the most important of all the manual reed stops is the TRUMPET, 8 FT.; and when properly scaled and voiced by a master hand it adds a highly desirable "stateliness and splendor" to all combinations into which it enters. It is also, when under the control of a swell, well adapted for solo passages of a pronounced character. In every Church Organ of any importance the TRUMPET ought to appear in one of the expressive divisions, or in the Swell Organ when there is only one expressive division. It is undesirable to place so potent a voice in an uninclosed position; but when it is so placed, it is advisable to modify and refine its tone. This is specially pointed out in our subsequent remarks on the Great Organ. The Octave of this stop, called the CLARION, 4 FT., is a useful adjunct when the instrument reaches sufficient importance to require a very pronounced octave tone. The CLARION, as an attendant on, and the diminutive of, the TRUMPET, should follow it in tone and disposition. It should be of smaller scale and have a softer voice than the unison reed.

Next to the TRUMPET, in general usefulness comes the OBOE or HAUTBOY, 8 FT., a pleasant soft-toned reed. In small Organs placed in churches in which even a softly-voiced TRUMPET would prove too prominent, the OBOE is the most appropriate reed stop. Under these circumstances, the normal class of OBOE should be selected in preference to the thin-voiced, imitative stop known as the ORCHESTRAL OBOE, which is insufficient for, and out of sympathy with, the true Church Organ. The OBOE should invariably be placed in an expressive division.

In order of interest and utility, now comes the highly characteristic reed stop, the CLARINET, 8 FT. This is a reed of imitative and pleasing quality, which imparts an agreeable variety to the softer combinations, and a peculiar richness of coloring to all in which it may enter. This stop is generally placed to great disadvantage in modern Church Organs, and even in those which have been constructed by eminent builders from Specifications by equally eminent organists. Precedent has been followed in an unreasoning manner; for, although of all organ stops it may be said to be *the one* which literally calls aloud for powers of expression, it is almost invariably relegated to a manual division which, in English Church Organs at least, is never inclosed in a swell-box. Reference to the Specifications of Church Organs appended to this treatise will hardly show the extent to which this unwise and inartistic practice has been carried in both old and recently built instruments; but if the interested reader will glance at the numerous Specifications given by Dr. Hopkins, in the Appendix to his Work,* he will find of one hundred Organs there specified that only three have stops of the CLARINET species placed in the Swell division; whilst no fewer than ninety examples have the CLARINET (either so called, or under such names as CREMONA, CORNO DI BASSETTO, or KRUMMHORN) placed in the Choir Organ, and, accordingly, without means of expression. Of the remaining seven examples, six have the stop in the Great, and one has it in the Solo division, all in an unexpressive condition. It is gratifying, for the sake of art, to observe in this as in other matters connected with the Organ, that American organ builders have displayed more intelligence. The greatest builder who has lived in the United States entirely abandoned the old practice of placing the CLARINET in an uninclosed position. In forty-four schemes for Organs of different sizes, given by the late Mr. Roosevelt, in his handsome *brochure* on the Organ, not one case obtains in which the CLARINET is specified to be outside a swell-box. When placed in the Choir Organ, that division is entirely expressive; and when included in the Great Organ, the CLARINET, along with certain other stops, is inclosed in a special swell-box. This is exactly as it should be.

Of the other unison reed stops suitable for Church Organs of average size, such as the HORN, CORNOPEAN, and BASSOON, little need be said in this place beyond pointing out that they should in all cases be placed in expressive divisions. The VOX HUMANA, of which so many vile examples exist in modern Church Organs, occupying the place of really important and badly-wanted stops, may safely be considered both useless and undesirable. It must be classed among the ear-ticklers already spoken of. It is, even when in its best form, of very limited use in solo music; while in legitimate accompanimental music it is of no use whatever, unless it is to show what a miserable travesty it is of the *human voice*.

* "The Organ, Its History and Construction." London, 1870.

When space will permit, and even in Church Organs of medium size, it may be found desirable to insert a reed stop of 16 ft. pitch in one of the manual divisions: this stop may be a small-scaled DOUBLE TRUMPET, 16 FT., a DOUBLE BASSOON, or a CONTRA-OBOE, 16 FT. It is hardly necessary to remark, after what has been said respecting other reed stops, that the selected one of 16 ft. must be placed in some expressive division, preferably the Swell Organ.

Except in instruments of the first magnitude, placed in cathedrals or very large churches, the introduction of reed stops voiced on high pressures is very undesirable. The dignity and grandeur of their voices cannot be disputed, and when skilfully used their effect is impressive; but they should invariably be looked upon as adjuncts to an otherwise complete Organ, rather than as integral parts of a necessarily circumscribed tonal structure. Such powerful voices really belong to the Concert-room Organ, in which they represent certain orchestral brass instruments.

These brief notes on the Speaking Stops may be appropriately closed with a few words on the more desirable stops belonging to the pedal department of the Church Organ. In the proper appointment of this most important department two difficulties very commonly present themselves; namely, circumscribed space for the accommodation of pipes of the necessary number and large dimensions; and insufficient funds for the purchase of the somewhat costly stops. An adequate Pedal Organ is, of necessity, a costly and cumbersome affair; but if a perfect, or even a thoroughly useful, instrument is aimed at, an adequate Pedal Organ must be provided. It is out of all reason to expect one or two stops of 16 ft. pitch to furnish a proper and satisfactory bass for all, or indeed any considerable portion of, the manual department; yet the number of modern Church Organs which have one or perhaps two such stops forming their only pedal resources is legion.

The unison pitch of the Pedal Organ is 16 feet; and the most useful labial stops of this pitch are the OPEN DIAPASONS, metal and wood, the VIOLONE or DOUBLE BASS VIOL, DULCIANA, BOURDON, and LIEBLICHGEDECKT. In all possible cases an OPEN DIAPASON, 16 FT., should be introduced, providing the foundation tone of the department and the true bass for the manual DIAPASONS. In old Organs this stop (of wood) has been inserted of inordinate scales; but under a more sensible modern treatment most effective stops have been made of comparatively small scales. For all ordinary Church instruments, the CCC pipe of the wood OPEN DIAPASON may range in scale between 10 inches by 12 inches and 8 inches by 10 inches, inside measurement. In large Organs a metal OPEN DIAPASON, 16 FT., of medium scale, may with advantage be added. The VIOLONE or DOUBLE BASS VIOL may be either of metal or wood, formed of open pipes of small scale, and voiced to imitate the tones of the orchestral Double Bass. This stop, when of a soft and refined quality, is invaluable in both accompanimental and solo music. The DULCIANA, 16 FT., is a very softly voiced metal stop, smaller in scale than the metal VIOLONE, yielding a pure organ-tone. As this invaluable stop is all that can be desired for the bass of the softest accompaniments, it should in every possible instance be inserted in the Pedal Organ. The BOURDON, 16 FT. TONE, a much abused and much over-used stop,—the delight of the cheap organ builder,—is unquestionably a valuable stop in its correct place in the tonal structure of a complete Pedal Organ; but it should never, under ordinary circumstances, be depended upon for the principal unison tone of the department, even in the smallest Church instrument. The LIEBLICHGEDECKT, 16 FT. TONE, a small-scaled, covered wood stop, is extremely valuable; and when carefully voiced on a copious wind of medium pressure is suitable for insertion in the smallest Church Organs, when a stop of 16 feet speaking length can neither be afforded nor accommodated. It is preferable to the BOURDON on account of the purity and clear intonation of its voice.

Every Pedal Organ, however small it may be, should have an OCTAVE, 8 FT., of some description. In the case of instruments for which either space or funds are limited this OCTAVE may be borrowed from the unison stop, by means of an Octave coupler and the inexpensive addition of an upper octave of pipes. But in all possible cases an independent stop of 8 ft. speaking length should be inserted, either in the form of a BASS FLUTE, of open wood, or a VIOLONCELLO, of metal or wood. In the case of a borrowed OCTAVE it is, of course, impossible to have it softer in tone than the unison from which it is derived; and both scientifically and artistically considered this is an objection which deserves attention. When the OCTAVE is an independent stop, it should be voiced considerably softer in tone than the principal stop of 16 ft. pitch in the department.

In instruments of medium size, a QUINT, 10⅔ FT., may be inserted. When drawn in combination with an open stop of 16 ft., it produces, though somewhat faintly, an impression on the ear of the sub-octave or 32 ft. tone. The reason of the acoustical phenomenon is fully explained in the Chapter on The Tonal Structure of the Organ. In more important Organs a CONTRA-BOURDON, 32 FT. TONE, should be inserted and the QUINT omitted. It is, of course, desirable to introduce an open stop of this pitch, the DOUBLE OPEN DIAPASON, 32 FT., but as this stop is expensive and demands considerable room and height for its accommodation, it is only to be contemplated for Organs of the first magnitude or exceptional character. It may be added that it is not really necessary to insert a stop of 32 ft. pitch in the Pedal Organ unless the Double, or 16 ft. tone, is amply represented in the manual department.

In addition to the unison and octave stops above alluded to, every complete Pedal Organ should contain several harmonic-corroborating stops, including a GRAND MIXTURE, without breaks. All Pedal Organs, in which anything approaching completeness is aimed at, should have, at least, one reed stop of unison pitch. This may be either a BASS TROMBONE, 16 FT., or a DOUBLE BASSOON, 16 FT.; and in large and properly appointed Pedal Organs an octave reed should be added to both the above, preferably in the form of a TRUMPET, 8 FT. A 32 ft. reed is not necessary in the ordinary Church Organ.

GREAT ORGAN.

It is a prevailing and, indeed, at the present time an almost universal impression—an impression which, in the minds of almost all organists and organ builders, admits of no reasonable doubt—that the Great Organ is both the most important and the most generally useful division of the Church Organ; and that it should contain the loudest and most assertive stops in the instrument, or, in short, that it should be able to produce as much sound as all the other divisions put together. This idea has been derived from a study of the old German system of organ-building which obtained before any attempt was made to impart powers of expression to the instrument, or to give any part of it the means of producing a *crescendo* and *diminuendo* without a perpetual manipulation of the draw-stop knobs.

We unhesitatingly affirm, on all grounds of art and taste, that the Great Organ, as an *absolute* and *unexpressive* division, should neither be looked upon as the most important and useful nor be made the loudest and most assertive part of the instrument. Now let us see if the opinion just expressed can be supported on any reasonable argument, or if it is based on any sensible foundation.

The Organ cannot be compared with any other musical instrument ever invented: as an instrument under the control of a single performer it stands alone. The only musical machine before which it assumes a secondary place is the complete Orchestra; and it is with this complicated and animated piece of mechanism alone that any comparison can be instituted. Now, for the sake of argument and illustration, let us suppose the Orchestra to be divided into two or more sections, fairly complete in themselves; and that the destiny of one section is to produce sounds of a uniform strength or intensity at all times, without the possibility of any variation—*crescendo* or *diminuendo:* and that the other section or sections are permitted to exercise their full powers of musical expression. Which of the said sections would the musician decide should be the loudest and best appointed? That which he is always compelled to listen to and use at its full and unvarying power, or those sections which are capable of every gradation of tone and effect of light and shade? The answer is obvious. Would he not unhesitatingly say: Let the *unexpressive* section be composed of those instruments which produce the purest, roundest, and quietest tones; to the uniform and expressionless flow of which the ear may listen with as little fatigue as possible, if not with absolute enjoyment: and let the *expressive* sections embrace all those loud, pungent, and assertive instruments, as well as the greatest number and variety of instruments, which must be played with expression to be tolerated by the musical ear or to satisfy the musical sense?

Turning, now, to the Organ, what does this lesson of the divided Orchestra teach us? Surely that we do wrong to follow the old-world system, and make the *unexpressive* division, called the Great Organ, the largest, loudest, and most assertive portion of the instrument. The old German builders were logical and perfectly correct in their treatment of the several divisions of their Organs, because all the divisions were alike unexpressive, and had their difference marked almost solely by strengths of tone. The Great Organ (Hauptwerk) in their instruments was, as the name implies, the largest and loudest manual division. The Organ, as we now know it, calls for a different treatment; and while the term Great Organ may be retained—a practice we do not approve—it should not carry the meaning it did in olden times before the swell-box was invented or adopted.

Putting aside the argument based on the illustration or lesson we have ventured to draw from the divided Orchestra, there is another consideration which supports our proposition—one which has a more direct bearing on the question at issue. When it is borne in mind that the so-called Great, like all the other divisions of the Church Organ, has for its chief office the accompaniment of the human voice, it must be obvious that, in its *unexpressive* state, the tonal structure of the entire division should be characterized by a full volume of quiet, refined tone—reposeful and dignified—rather than by those bellowing and screaming qualities which characterize the Great divisions of almost all Church Organs, ancient and modern. It must not for a moment be understood that we advocate the impoverishment of the Great Organ, for such is very far from our intention. We seek, rather, to eliminate from it the elements of coarseness and noise; and, in the other direction, to increase its dignity and usefulness by adapting it, in a true musical sense, to the place it occupies in the instrument and the office it has to fulfil; and by imparting to it that rich refinement of tone and volume of subdued intensity which almost do away with the necessity for light and shade. In our opinion the Great division of the Church Organ should be a normal Organ, producing sounds and combinations of sounds strictly born of, and peculiar to, the Organ, and unproducible by any other instrument or combination of instruments.

The question now arises: How is such a Great Organ to be schemed, and how should it be appointed with respect to the other, and especially the expressive, divisions of the instrument? We have already expressed an opinion with reference to the important matter of wind pressure, accordingly it is not necessary to say more here than recommend, for the Great Organ, the general adoption of moderate pressures; copious windage, ample scales, and a refined style of voicing, for the pipe-work following as a matter of course. All these virtues are necessary for the production of that amiable quality of tone on which the utility and true beauty of the Great Organ depends.

The tonal scheme of the Great Organ deserves most thoughtful consideration. First of all the proper quality and quantity of unison tone has to be provided by OPEN DIAPASONS and certain other labial stops of 8 ft. pitch. In small instruments, one OPEN DIAPASON, of full scale, will be sufficient, supported by two or three other unisons of good mixing quality and varied strength of voice: but in Great Organs having any pretensions toward completeness, two metal OPEN DIAPASONS will be necessary to provide the true foundation tone of the division. These must be of different scales, as has been previously directed, for use both separately and together. The first OPEN DIAPASON should be of large scale, voiced to yield a tone characterized by great volume and roundness—a tone forming, as one might say, a cushion of sound upon which all other sounds of the division will rest in perfect repose. The second DIAPASON should be much smaller in scale, and voiced to yield a lighter and brighter tone than the preceding. This marked diversity of tone is valuable on two grounds. First, it greatly enhances the mixing properties of the two stops, and prevents any robbing of power in their combination; and, secondly, it renders them, conjointly and severally, valuable for accompaniment and as foundations for many effective combinations. As a rule, in modern Organs, when OPEN DIAPASONS are duplicated in any division, they are made far too near each other in scale, character, and strength of tone; and, accordingly, their independent utility is minimized, and an unsatisfactory result is attained by their combination. As has been previously remarked, in large Organs where more foundation tone is desired, an OPEN DIAPASON of wood, constructed on the Schulze model, should be added in preference to a third DIAPASON of metal.

The next unison stop in order of importance is either an open wood stop of the CLARABELLA or MELODIA class; or when there is an OPEN DIAPASON of wood, as above recommended, a covered stop of round and filling-up quality. The best form of the latter is the DOPPELFLÖTE, 8 FT. This stop is peculiarly valuable in the Great Organ, being of full intonation, and mixing perfectly with the OPEN DIAPASONS and all other open metal stops, and imparting a peculiar body to the reed stops. The DOPPELFLÖTE is, as we have already remarked, unlikely to make its appearance in English Organs; so the organ-lovers of that country will have to be content with the STOPPED DIAPASON, 8 FT., or the LIEBLICHGEDECKT, 8 FT. When properly voiced, these stops are very desirable and useful; but on account of the characteristic softness of their voices, when at their best, they are more suitable for other divisions of the Organ.

Difference of opinion has a fair field concerning the other unison stop or stops to be introduced in the Great division, because now circumstances alter cases, and individual taste may exercise itself within reasonable bounds. The size of the church, the situation of the Organ, and the number and tonal character of its divisions, have each and all to be taken into consideration. Again, the question as to how much, if any, of the Great Organ is to be rendered flexible and expressive, by inclosure in a swell-box, must be considered in the selection of additional stops of unison pitch. It may, however, be said that when there is no second, small-scaled, OPEN DIAPASON in the division, a SALICIONAL, KERAULOPHON, a full-scaled DULCIANA, or a DOLCAN, may be inserted with advantage. A unison stop of the VIOL species will be a desirable and valuable addition, giving a diversified tone-coloring to combinations for accompanimental purposes, and a crispness to the general unison tone of the division. If this stop—a GAMBA, 8 FT.—is uninclosed it should be voiced to yield a rich and full string-tone rather than a pungent and rasping one. The latter quality of tone is more appropriate for a VIOL which is inclosed in a swell-box.

Of the stops of 4 ft. pitch, the OCTAVE, in relation to the fundamental OPEN DIAPASON, is the most important in the Great Organ. With reference to the scale of this stop nothing special need be said here; but a few words, even at the risk of our being blamed for repetition, may be said on its relative strength of voice and its office in the tonal structure of the division. On referring to the Chapter on The Tonal Structure of the Organ, it will be seen that the first upper partial tone of a prime tone is its octave, produced by twice the number of vibrations of the prime, and, accordingly, in the Organ, by a pipe half the speaking length (theoretically) of that yielding the prime tone. This teaches us that the true office of the relative OCTAVE, 4 FT., in the tonal scheme of the Great Organ is to corroborate the first, and most important, upper partial tones of the sounds produced by the foundation unisons; and that organ builders err when they introduce OCTAVES of too large scales and of too loud and assertive tones. When scientifically proportioned, the OCTAVE materially enriches, brightens, and ennobles the tones of the unison stops, without in any way disturbing their pitch; but when of too powerful a voice it imparts a hard and screaming character to the compound tone, and goes far to disturb the tonal balance of the Organ. There are points in every tonal structure beyond which the harmonic-corroborating sounds must not go in power and assertiveness; and he is the true artist who knows those points and never oversteps them in his work. *The laws which govern and apportion musical sounds cannot be neglected or broken with impunity.*

When the size of the Great Organ renders a second labial stop of 4 ft. pitch necessary, it should be introduced in the form of an open FLUTE of full and clear voice. This will prove valuable both in combination and alone in solo effects. More than two labial stops of this pitch are never really necessary save in Great Organs of very large size; and when a third is introduced it should be a string-toned stop, serving as the OCTAVE to the unison GAMBA.

We now come to the consideration of the mutation, super-octave, and compound stops necessary for the completion of the 8 feet harmonic series. The only mutation stops introduced in English Organs, in a complete form, are the OCTAVE QUINT or TWELFTH and the TIERCE or SEVENTEENTH. In Organs of ordinary size, the latter stop is quite unnecessary notwithstanding that it was apparently a favorite with the old builders. The TWELFTH, furnishing the second upper partial tone, when kept unobtrusive, materially enriches the foundation tone of the division, although it may be omitted in small instruments. The TWELFTH requires the SUPER-OCTAVE or FIFTEENTH, which furnishes the third upper partial tone. The SUPER-OCTAVE should always find a place in the Great Organ; but in what form it should be introduced may be considered a matter of taste. In all cases it is essential that its tone be kept subordinate to that of the OCTAVE and nearly equal to that of the TWELFTH.

We consider one or more compound stops or MIXTURES to be absolutely necessary in every properly appointed Great Organ; and every endeavor should be made to provide at least one good stop of the class. It has been previously remarked that the old builders and their followers were prone to the excessive use of compound stops, and invariably voiced them too loudly. Modern builders have thoughtlessly brought these invaluable stops into disrepute by following and even exaggerating the old practice. This practice is decidedly injurious, if not absolutely destructive, to that round and grand volume of tone which we maintain should characterize the Church Organ generally, and its Great division in particular. When a MIXTURE is of a powerful and piercing character, it is, of necessity, available only on rare occasions or in full combinations. This is an undesirable narrowing of its utility, which no artistic builder should be guilty of and no musician tolerate. A softly-toned and scientifically-voiced MIXTURE, such as properly corroborates the higher upper partials of the foundation unisons, without imparting any disturbing elements to their tones, will be suitable with soft as well as loud combinations. When the Great is partly expressive, the MIXTURE inserted in the swell-box—it should always be placed in the expressive section—may be of rather stronger intonation than when altogether uninclosed; but even then it must not be too loud for the full Great.

No stop of 16 ft. pitch should be introduced in the Great Organ unless the full complement of 8 ft. tone is provided and the tonal structure is otherwise complete. When introduced, the 16 ft. tone should be sufficient to enrich the general tone of the division without having any obvious power of drawing the unison tone downward. The true pitch of the division must on no account be interfered with either by grave or acute voices. As we have, in the remarks on the speaking stops suitable for the Church Organ, said all that is necessary on those of 16 ft. pitch, the subject need not be enlarged upon here.

Little need be said with reference to reed stops for the Great Organ. When the division is only sufficiently large to call for one stop of the class, preference should be given to the TRUMPET, 8 FT.; and in larger instruments the CLARION, 4 FT., should be added. When these reeds are inserted in an uninclosed state, their tones should be characterized by fulness and smoothness rather than by a brassy and piercing intonation—a common fault in indifferent specimens of the stops. Like the harmonic-corroborating stops, these reeds are greatly enhanced, both in general usefulness and effectiveness, when they are inclosed and rendered flexible and expressive. When inclosed, their tones may be of a brighter and more orchestral character. No stops of an essentially solo or orchestral character should be inserted in the Great, or, indeed, in any manual division of the Organ, unless provision is made to impart powers of expression to them. This may be accepted as a fundamental principle in artistic organ-building, ignored at present, simply because organ builders are, with rare exceptions, no artists, and artistic organ-building is practically unknown in the general trade.

Having introduced the question of expression in connection with the Great Organ, it will not be out of place to discuss it here, and before passing on to the consideration of the Swell Organ. Up to the present time no steps, so far as our knowledge extends, have been taken by English, French, or German builders, of the present organ-building epoch, to apply the swell-box, and consequently powers of expression, to the Great division of the Church Organ. It was left to the greatest of American organ builders to establish the new treatment of the Great Organ which we have advocated for a period of nearly forty years. By way of illustrating what the late Mr. Hilborne L. Roosevelt achieved in this important direction, we here give the scheme of the Great division of the large Organ erected in Trinity Methodist Episcopal Church, Denver, Colorado.

GREAT ORGAN.

UNEXPRESSIVE SECTION.

1. DOUBLE OPEN DIAPASON, 16 feet.
2. DOUBLE MELODIA, . . 16 "
3. OPEN DIAPASON, . . . 8 feet.
4. OPEN DIAPASON, . . . 8 "

EXPRESSIVE SECTION—IN CHOIR SWELL-BOX.

5.	GEMSHORN, ...	8 feet.	12.	OCTAVE QUINT, . . .	2⅔ feet.
6.	VIOLA DA GAMBA, . .	8 "	13.	SUPER-OCTAVE, . . .	2 "
7.	PRINCIPALFLÖTE, . . .	8 "	14.	MIXTURE, . .	IV. and V. ranks.
8.	DOPPELFLÖTE, . . .	8 "	15.	SCHARF, . .	III. and IV. "
9.	OCTAVE, ...	4 "	16.	OPHICLEIDE, ...	16 feet.
10.	GAMBETTE, ...	4 "	17.	TRUMPET, ...	8 "
11.	FLÛTE HARMONIQUE, . .	4 "	18.	CLARION, ...	4 "

It will be seen that only four stops out of the total number of eighteen contained in this division are planted in an uninclosed position; namely, the two OPEN DIAPASONS and the labial DOUBLES; all the remaining stops being planted in the swell-box in which the entire Choir Organ, of twelve stops, is inclosed. We may just remark, before commenting on the arrangement of this Great Organ, that of the entire number of fifty-five manual stops in this noteworthy instrument, only the four above-named stops of the Great Organ are planted outside the swell-boxes, of which there are three in the instrument. Under these conditions, we are strongly of opinion that a larger selection of the Great stops could with advantage have been left exposed. Without implying a full approval of the general tonal scheme of the Great, as above given, we think that stops from Nos. 1 to 9, inclusive, should have formed the unexpressive section. By such an arrangement a much greater variety of tonal effects would have been secured, by the combination of the several unisons with the harmonic series in varied degrees of strength. Very beautiful effects are obtained by the tones of the harmonic-corroborating stops being thrown, in *crescendo* and *diminuendo*, upon the stationary and full tones of the unison and double stops. This is not possible when the unisons of the same division are also expressive or inclosed in the same swell-box as the harmonic series.

On the subject of the swell-box and its extended introduction, and also of its use and abuse, we speak at length in subsequent Chapters; but there is no objection to our remarking, at this point, that it must not be supposed that the use of the swell in connection with the Great Organ is limited to the ordinary see-saw style of operation so much affected by unmusicianly performers. For although many charming musical effects and *nuances* can be produced by using the swell as the means of expression in the ordinary way, perhaps its most important office, in this division of the Organ, is to render it possible to graduate the strength of the voices of all the inclosed stops to balance with whatever strength of unison tone may be yielded by the uninclosed pipe-work. For instance, with the swell-box closed, it is practicable to throw the entire harmonic-corroborating series upon a single unison, of any strength, in the unexpressive section; and then, at will, to adjust this chorus to any increased combination.

It is usually the practice to place the Great Organ in a front and commanding position, the Swell and other divisions, when there are more than two manual divisions, being located in some positions in the rear. There is, of course, no serious objection to such a relative location if the entire instrument occupies a favorable place in the church, free from obstructions to the emission of its sounds: but it is unfortunately a fact that nine out of every ten Church Organs are crammed into badly constructed chambers, or jammed into corners or recesses totally inadequate and unsuitable. When the Organ has to be placed in a chamber, or anything of the nature of a chamber, care must be taken to give the most important expressive division a favorable position so that its accompanimental office may be satisfactorily fulfilled. The traveling and uniformly delivered sounds of an unexpressive Great Organ allow it to be placed, with but little sacrifice of its utility, in a position which would seriously impair the effect of the Swell Organ. In some cases it may be found advisable to divide the Great Organ into two or more parts, placing them in commanding positions, but so as to present no impediments to the free emission of the sounds of the expressive divisions. It is impossible, however, to do more in this important matter than point out the advisability of exercising great care and judgment in the disposition of the Great and other divisions. No rules of general application can be given, for every Organ must be disposed in accordance with the provision made for its accommodation.

SWELL ORGAN.

From the preceding remarks it will be observed that we lay more stress upon the value and use of the swell-box, and the proper appointment and location of the expressive division or divisions of the Church Organ, than any other writer on the subject has thought it advisable to do. Of necessity, the Swell Organ will always be the most important expressive division of the Church Organ, and of the highest value in true accompanimental music; accordingly, every matter connected with it deserves most careful consideration.

The Swell certainly has, ever since its inception in the year 1712, undergone a gradual but very decided development; but it would be rash to say that it has reached, in the present year of grace 1903, its highest point of excellence. So far as regards the form and construction of the swell-box, we are strongly of opinion that perfection has not yet been attained.

In an instrument specially designed for the accompaniment of the voice, it must be obvious that its most important and resourceful division should be rendered capable of every possible gradation of tone, and endowed with the highest possible powers of expression. As a rule, the Swell Organ is not accorded its true dignity and value by European builders in any class of instrument manufactured by them; traditions of an earlier time hang over them still. This is especially the case with the German organ builders, who in all matters of construction and appointment are singularly conservative. In both Germany and England the swell is very commonly neglected and its value underrated. Even when the Swell Organ is fairly well appointed and under favorable conditions would prove efficient, it is too often relegated to a locality in the depths of a chamber or some other objectionable place which proves fatal to its effectiveness. Serious complaints are leveled against the swell-box, because the stops placed within it are believed to suffer a species of annihilation. There may be reason in such complaints in numerous cases, for, unquestionably, swell-boxes are too frequently very sorry affairs,—true exponents of cheap organ-building,—constructed without proper regard to acoustical laws, and with equal indifference respecting the office they have to fulfil. Greater knowledge and care are required in all matters connected with the planning and construction of the swell-box, and also in matters affecting the disposition and planting of the speaking stops within it. In a properly proportioned and scientifically constructed Swell Organ we expect a perfectly pure and distinct tone both when its shutters are closed and open; with a well-marked and effective gradation from a clear *piano* to a brilliant *forte*. The mile-away sound annihilation, which too many organ builders seem to think is the acme of perfection in a Swell Organ, is neither requisite nor desirable.

As the Swell Organ is a manual division essentially and entirely flexible and expressive, it is apparent that the considerations which obtained with so much force in relation to the Great Organ have no direct bearing on its tonal structure. It will be remembered that in our illustration of the divided orchestra we expressed the very natural belief that a musician would decide that the *unexpressive* section should be composed of those instruments which produce the purest, roundest, and quietest tones; and that the *expressive* section should embrace all those loud, pungent, and assertive instruments, which must be played under proper control and with expression to be tolerated by the musical ear, or to appeal to the musical sense. From these remarks it will be gathered that we hold the view that the expressive division or divisions should contain louder and more assertive stops, and also a greater number and variety of stops, than any unexpressive division. Such is our firm conviction. While the Great Organ, in its dignity and refinement, is of great value and importance in the general scheme of the Church Organ; there can be little doubt that when the Swell division is fully appointed, and inclosed in a properly constructed swell-box, it is *the* division that will be resorted to for the highest and most expressive class of accompanimental music. If vocal music is required to be expressive in every sense of the word, surely the accompaniment, and such an accompaniment as the Organ furnishes, in particular, should be as flexible and expressive as possible.

In advocating the introduction of louder-voiced and more assertive stops in the Swell than those recommended for the Great Organ, it must not be imagined that we mean coarse, screaming stops, such as one only too often hears in Church Organs. The stops we advocate are those of rich and marked intonation; having sufficient power, individuality, and distinctness of voice to be effective under the extreme conditions in which they are used. Probably in no branch of the art of organ-building can the true artist show himself more clearly than in the tonal appointment and structural treatment of the Swell Organ.

To secure the character and brilliancy of tone desirable in an expressive division, stops of medium scales, specially voiced, and having marked individuality of tone should alone be used. They should be planted on ample wind-chests, in as open an order as practicable, with the fullest amount of speaking room, and the larger pipes must be kept away (several inches or a foot if possible) from the back and sides of the swell-box, so as to allow the sound to reach the entire internal surface of the same. These are all essential conditions toward the production of a satisfactory and efficient Swell Organ.

Generally speaking, a higher wind pressure than that advocated for the unexpressive Great may with advantage be adopted for the Swell Organ. In large instruments two or more pressures will, in all probability, be apportioned to so important a division. This, however, largely depends upon the natures of the stops embraced in its tonal scheme.

In scheming the tonal appointment of the Swell division, care must be taken to secure a due proportion of true organ-tone and character by the introduction of one or more unison stops of the DIAPASON class, and as complete a series of harmonic-corroborating stops as space and funds will allow. It may be pointed out that it is even of more importance here than in the Great Organ that a full harmonic structure should be present; for that ringing brilliancy so desirable in the Swell Organ, which enriches but does not overbalance the fundamental tones, can only be secured by its presence. To this foundation should be added, according to the size of the Organ and the legitimate calls to be made on its tonal resources, so many stops, of unison and octave pitch, of an imitative and solo character as can be accommodated, and one or two stops of 16 ft. pitch. It must be understood that the resources of this important division cannot be too great.

In speaking of imitative and solo stops, we here allude to those which impart a refined and distinctive coloring to all the combinations into which they enter, and which can also be used alone or with varied soft accompaniments—stops which, in short, throw an orchestral reflection on the solid background of pure organ-tone, varying and enriching it without impairing its dignity. For notes on the imitative or orchestral stops reference may be made to the following Chapter on The Concert-room Organ.

Purely fancy stops, including the VOX HUMANA and the so-called VOIX CÉLESTE, may be left to individual taste; and when introduced they should be placed in either the Swell Organ or an expressive Choir Organ. Such stops are, however, far from being necessary or desirable in an accompanimental instrument; they certainly should never be inserted in small Organs, where their presence is at the expense of much more valuable voices.

Having given, by way of an example in a certain direction, the scheme of the Great division of the Roosevelt Organ in Trinity Church, Denver, we may now give the scheme of the Swell Organ of the same instrument, and a few remarks thereon :—

SWELL ORGAN.

INCLOSED IN A SPECIAL SWELL-BOX.

1.	BOURDON,	16 feet.	6.	VOX CŒLESTIS,	8 feet.
2.	OPEN DIAPASON,	8 "	7.	CLARABELLA,	8 "
3.	SALICIONAL,	8 "	8.	STOPPED DIAPASON,	8 "
4.	SPITZFLÖTE,	8 "	9.	QUINTADENA,	8 "
5.	ÆOLINE,	8 "	10.	OCTAVE,	4 "

11.	SALICET, ...	4 feet.	16.	CORNOPEAN, ...	8 feet.
12.	HOHLFLÖTE, ...	4 "	17.	OBOE, ...	8 "
13.	FLAGEOLET, ...	2 "	18.	VOX HUMANA, ...	8 "
14.	CORNET, . III., IV., and V. ranks.		19.	CLARION, ...	4 "
15.	CONTRAFAGOTTO, . . .	16 feet.	I.	TREMOLANT.	

This is unquestionably an imposing scheme, with its two stops of 16 ft. pitch and eleven of 8 ft. pitch; but, as a representative one, we think it falls short of what a Swell Organ ought to be. In the first place, its harmonic structure is not sufficiently complete for so great a weight of unison tone. Following the OCTAVE, there certainly ought to be a two-rank stop formed of a TWELFTH and FIFTEENTH, and instead of the CORNET, as specified, such a division should have a MIXTURE of VI. or VII. ranks throughout. To make room for these compound stops, the QUINTADENA and CORNET may be removed. Although the SALICIONAL is a fine and desirable stop, we are of opinion that, in a division having so strong a body of reed-tone, a stop of fuller and richer voice should take its place, such as the GEIGENPRINCIPAL or VIOLIN DIAPASON, which, on account of its distinctive quality of voice, would combine admirably with the full and pure-voiced fundamental OPEN DIAPASON; and at the same time aid in building up the foundation tone of the division. In addition to what has already been provided of organ-tone, a soft stop of a similar tonality should be inserted. This should be a true DULCIANA, 8 FT., having a pure, liquid voice without a trace of string-tone or reediness. None of the stops above mentioned should be slotted. We mention this because the pernicious practice of cutting slots in such stops, for the convenience of tuning, is much too frequently indulged in, to the almost total destruction of the grand and solemn tones of stops of the OPEN DIAPASON class. The DULCIANA may take the place of the ÆOLINE,—a stop better suited for the Choir Organ than for the Swell division.

The Roosevelt scheme is entirely without imitative or assertive string-tone, and in this respect is decidedly faulty. In an expressive accompanimental division of the Church Organ, string-tone is only secondary in value, importance, and beauty to the pure, foundation organ-tone; and this fact should not be overlooked in scheming the tonal appointment of the Swell Organ. A VIOLONCELLO, 8 FT., of broad, imitative quality, should take the place of the ear-tickling and practically useless VOX CŒLESTIS: and a VIOLETTA, 4 FT., should be substituted for the SALICET, 4 FT. A large-scaled BOURDON, 16 FT., of a dull 'humming tone' should not be introduced in the Swell Organ, for its voice can never be desirable. Purity and brightness should characterize all expressive divisions of the Church Organ. Instead of such a stop, a medium-scaled LIEBLICHGEDECKT, 16 FT., voiced to yield the ground tone in an almost pure condition, should be inserted. The presence of the first harmonic upper partial tone of a covered stop of 16 ft. pitch is undesirable in a properly balanced 8 ft. tonal structure.

Flute-tone is not sufficiently pronounced in the Roosevelt scheme; accordingly, we suggest the substitution of a CONCERT FLUTE, 8 FT., HARMONIC FLUTE, 4 FT., and HARMONIC PICCOLO, 2 FT., for the SPITZFLÖTE, HOHLFLÖTE, and FLAGEOLET.

The five reed stops of the scheme do not seem altogether satisfactory or well balanced. We suggest the following: Double Trumpet, 16 ft., Fagotto, 8 ft., Oboe, 8 ft., Trumpet, 8 ft., and Clarion, 4 ft. The Trumpet and Clarion should be voiced to yield brilliant and ringing tones of great traveling power, distinct from the round tones of the Great Organ stops of the same names.

We now give, for the sake of ready reference and comparison, the scheme as developed in the foregoing criticism. The more desirable stops in the original Specification have been retained.

SWELL ORGAN.

MODIFIED SPECIFICATION.

	ORGAN-TONE.	
1.	Open Diapason, . . .	8 feet.
2.	Geigenprincipal, . .	8 "
3.	Dulciana, ...	8 "
4.	Octave, ...	4 "
5.	Twelfth and Fifteenth,	2⅔ & 2 "
6.	Mixture, ...	VII. ranks.
	OPEN FLUTE-TONE.	
7.	Concert Flute, ...	8 feet.
8.	Clarabella, ...	8 "
9.	Harmonic Flute, . .	4 "
10.	Harmonic Piccolo, . .	2 "
	COVERED FLUTE-TONE.	
11.	Lieblichgedeckt, . .	16 feet.
12.	Lieblichgedeckt, . .	8 "
	STRING-TONE.	
13.	Violoncello, ...	8 "
14.	Violetta, ...	4 "
	REED-TONE.	
15.	Double Trumpet, . .	16 "
16.	Fagotto, ...	8 "
17.	Oboe, ...	8 "
18.	Trumpet, ...	8 "
19.	Clarion, ...	4 "

I. Tremolant.

This Specification is arranged in a completely new form—a form which we recommend for general adoption, because it enables an analysis of a tonal scheme to be made at a glance, showing its strength or weakness in an unmistakable manner. Were all Organ specifications tabulated in this form, we venture to think fewer mistakes in stop appointments would be perpetrated; and it would not be so easy for unscrupulous builders to mislead their clients, providing their clients have some musical knowledge. It must be remarked, however, that it is not sufficient for a tonal scheme to look well on paper, it must be carried out in a correct and truly artistic manner. Every stop must be scaled and voiced with relation to every other stop in the division; and each division must be appointed as a part of the grand whole—the complete and perfect Organ. Accordingly, it is possible to make a most unsatisfactory Organ from a perfectly satisfactory Specification. No Specification can do more than direct the artist, or furnish him with proper materials for his skilful manipulation; it cannot create or provide the artist. These are simple truths that should never be forgotten by purchasers of Organs.

A Church Organ with a Swell division of nineteen speaking stops, as above specified, would probably have a Choir division also; so it is but just to remark that our modified tonal scheme has grown out of the criticism of that in the

Roosevelt instrument, and has not been constructed with reference to either a special Great or Choir Organ. Such being the case, our scheme must be accepted as suggestive only.

CHOIR ORGAN.

Taking it for granted that both the Great and Swell Organs are based on, and furnished with, adequate harmonic structures, and are provided with the full complement of pure organ-tone, it may be presumed that this third, and least important, manual division may be schemed on freer lines: and when there are only three manual divisions (there need seldom be more in the ordinary Church Organ) the third division may conveniently partake partly of the nature of a softly-toned accompanimental Organ and partly of an effective Solo Organ. This dual capacity or character at once ushers in the question: Should the so-called Choir Organ be *expressive* or not? Reference to precedent in the works of European organ builders gives us an almost unqualified reply in the negative; but, on the other hand, a positive, and by no means timid, reply is furnished by the works of America's most renowned builder. We remember on the occasion of our delivering a lecture, on 'The Swell in the Organ,' before the members of the Royal College of Organists, that some of the good old-fashioned organists present condemned the proposition to inclose the Choir Organ in a swell-box; but their condemnation was born of prejudice, and was unsupported by any logical reasoning. It is such a spirit as this that has materially stayed the development of the art of organ-building. The Dr. Fell style of argument, if argument it can be called, should be firmly discouraged in the matters of organ construction. A thing is either right or wrong; and in either case is open to logical reasoning and proof by positive experience.

If it is decided that the Choir Organ is to be unexpressive throughout, let all stops imitative of orchestral instruments and those of a purely solo character, to which expressive power is as the breath of life, be omitted; and let the tonal forces of the division be composed of very soft organ-toned stops, delicately voiced flute- and string-toned stops of an unimitative class, and octave and harmonic-corroborating stops of the most delicate intonation that the skill of the organ builder can achieve. But even with all this carried out in the most artistic manner the utility of the unexpressive Choir, as an accompanimental division, is most undesirably circumscribed.

No organ builder who has ever lived realized this truth as the late Mr. Hilborne L. Roosevelt did; and his conviction of the importance of rendering the Choir Organ entirely expressive was conveyed to us in unmistakable terms. Speaking of the Choir division of the large Organ he erected, in 1883, in the First Congregational Church, at Great Barrington, Mass., he says in his Description: "The Choir Organ is inclosed in a box of its own, a device which greatly enhances its value, and is productive of many charming effects of expression, in general only obtainable by the use of the Swell Organ. . . . It will be readily seen that, with such an unprecedented proportion of the whole instrument placed within swell-boxes, viz., thirty-eight out of fifty-five (exclusive of the Echo), a *crescendo* or *diminuendo* of startling intensity becomes feasible to an extent impossible under other circumstances, besides which a beautiful and novel effect is produced by gradually closing one swell while opening the other."* The Specification of this Roosevelt Organ is given in the concluding portion of this treatise.

We can easily understand, and to a large extent sympathize with, the love which obtains in some quarters for the sweet, soft, singing, old-fashioned, uninclosed Choir Organ; and doubtless the tone of the Choir Organ as made by the old English masters formed a charming accompaniment to the fresh and joyful voices of the singing boys. But great changes have come over the construction of Church Organs, and the demands made upon their musical resources by skilful and musicianly performers: and something more than the sweetly-voiced but somewhat colorless, old-world Choir Organ has become an artistic necessity in these advanced times; and it is only prejudice mixed with a dash of ignorance in such matters that can close one's eyes to this fact.

We strongly favor the idea of doing away with the old-fashioned and traditional Choir appointment, by infusing its tonal structure with more distinctive coloring,—coloring not to be found in either the Great or Swell divisions. Seeing that the true Church Organ, as a dignified and resourceful accompanimental instrument, is provided in the latter two divisions, there need be no hesitation in introducing certain new qualities of tone in the third manual division; never, however, ignoring the legitimate use and purpose of the instrument. In the first place, as it is likely that in neither the Great nor Swell Organs can accommodation be found for those very soft stops whose voices are as beautiful as they are useful in accompanimental music of the most delicate character, we suggest that one moiety of the Choir division be devoted to their reception; while the other moiety be furnished with certain stops having a pronounced orchestral character of tone.

The softly-voiced stops may be selected from the following list:—VOX ANGELICA, 8 FT.; ÆOLINE, 8 FT.; ECHO DULCIANA, 8 FT.; DOLCE, 8 FT.; VIOLA D'AMORE, 8 FT.; VIOLA DA GAMBA, 8 FT.; SPITZFLÖTE, 8 FT.; LIEBLICHFLÖTE, 8 FT.; OCTAVE DULCIANA, 4 FT.; GAMBETTE, 4 FT.; FLAUTO D'AMORE, 4 FT.; FLAUTO DOLCE, 4 FT.; GEMSHORN, 4 FT.; CELESTINA, 4 FT.; OBOE FLUTE, 4 FT.; SUABE FLUTE, 4 FT.; NASON, 4 FT.; LIEBLICHFLÖTE, 4 FT.; SUPER-OCTAVE DULCIANA, 2 FT.; GEMSHORN FIFTEENTH, 2 FT.; PICCOLO D'AMORE, 2 FT.; and FLAGEOLET, 2 FT. All these stops should be on low pressure wind, not exceeding 2½ inches.

A Choir Organ can scarcely be considered complete without certain harmonic-corroborating ranks; accordingly, we would suggest a five-rank CORNET, contain-

*This was written in the year 1883; but about the year 1870 the Author of the present treatise had anticipated the "novel effect," commented on by Mr. Roosevelt, by placing different sections of the Great division of his own Chamber Organ in two distinct and independent swell-boxes, and the Choir division also in a swell-box. The entire instrument could be designated a Swell Organ. So far as we know this Chamber Organ remains unique in the respect that its Great division has two distinct and independent *expressive* sections and one *unexpressive* section, all commanded by the Great Organ clavier. By this arrangement the combined and crossing effects of *three swells* are obtained while the hands are performing on *two* claviers and the right foot is operating *two* expression-levers in a varied manner.

ing a third-sounding rank, formed of small-scaled DULCIANA or VOX ANGELICA pipes. The effect of such a chorus, in combination with the other tones of the division, would be beautiful in the extreme. The stop may be composed thus:—

DULCIANA CORNET—V. RANKS.

CC	to	BB,	. . . . .	19—22—24—26—29.
C	to	B,	. . . . .	12—15—17—19—22.
c^1	to	b^1,	. . . . .	8—12—17—19—22.
c^2	to	c^4,	. . . . .	1— 8—10—12—15.

The orchestral-toned stops from which a selection may be made are here given:—CONCERT VIOLIN, 8 FT.; ORCHESTRAL FLUTE, 8 FT.; ORCHESTRAL OBOE, 8 FT.; ORCHESTRAL CLARINET, 8 FT.; ORCHESTRAL BASSOON, 8 FT.; COR ANGLAIS, 8 FT. (Free reed); MUSETTE, 8 FT. (Free reed); OCTAVE FLUTE, 4 FT.; OCTAVE OBOE, 4 FT.; and ORCHESTRAL PICCOLO, 2 FT. All these stops should be on wind of 3 inches.

Should a stop of 16 ft. pitch be desired, a LIEBLICHBOURDON may be inserted in the swell-box; or a small-scaled VIOLONE, 16 FT., or DOUBLE DULCIANA, 16 FT., may be planted outside, when the swell-box cannot be contrived to hold the bottom octave. It would, perhaps, be better to inclose all save the bottom octave in the swell-box, because expression is less important in the grave tones of a softly-voiced stop. It must be understood, however, that we do not countenance the dividing of stops save in exceptional cases such as that just mentioned.

A word may be said, in conclusion, with reference to the swell-box for the Choir Organ. The first question which presents itself is: Should it have a separate swell-box, independently controlled? Mr. Roosevelt, in his important Church Organs, commonly placed the entire Choir division in the same swell-box with the inclosed stops of the Great Organ. There is no serious objection to this treatment from a musical point of view, whilst there would be very serious objections to the association of the Swell and Choir stops in one box. Of course a very large swell-box becomes necessary when it has to contain both the expressive section of the Great and the entire Choir division; and, accordingly, special provision has to be made for its proper reception and placing. When the Choir stops are placed in the Great Organ swell-box, only two expression-levers will be required in the three-manualed Organ. This is a convenience, but one of no great moment.

When all conditions are favorable, it is desirable to inclose the Choir in an independent swell-box, and have three expression levers. In instruments which have a fourth manual division,—a Solo Organ,—the inclosure of the Choir in the Great swell-box becomes almost a necessity, the third swell-box and its expression lever being required for the Solo division. It is just a question, when the Organ comprises an expressive Solo division, if the Choir requires to be made expressive. Should it be decided to follow ancient precedent in this matter, the tonal appointment of the division must be schemed to suit the conditions. All orchestral-toned stops will naturally find their place in the Solo Organ; and the Choir will assume the form of a very softly-voiced, normal organ-toned, and unimitative division. It will require, and should have, no reed stops of any kind. Reeds should, in the sacred name of Music, have both flexibility and powers of expression given them.

SOLO ORGAN.

Notwithstanding what has been said with reference to the undesirable or unnecessary addition of a fourth manual clavier to the ordinary Church Organ, our remarks would doubtless be considered incomplete without some direct allusion to the fourth division, commonly called the Solo Organ. This division is never really a necessity in the Church Organ; and certainly need never be contemplated for instruments under the first magnitude; and then only for Organs which are certain to be used for very elaborate musical services, recitals, etc. For all usual demands, the expressive Choir Organ, as already described, will prove sufficient in its dual nature of Choir and Solo.

Whatever may be decided as regards the inclosure of the Choir Organ, it is, on musical grounds, imperative that so assertive a division as the properly appointed Solo Organ be inclosed in a separate swell-box. An *unexpressive* Solo Organ must always be a musical anomaly, to use no stronger term; yet how commonly this important fact has been ignored by organ builders. In England the practice of inclosing the Solo division is so rare that it is difficult to find more than two or three examples. One is furnished by the new Organ in Worcester Cathedral, and another by the older Organ in the Cathedral of Winchester. The designer of the latter instrument, while he recognized the importance of giving powers of expression to the Solo stops, made the great mistake of inclosing them in the Swell Organ box. Under some conditions this error may not be very evident; but there can be no question that the utility and musical resources of both the divisions are interfered with by this common inclosure. Even in Church Organs of the largest size, the Solo division need never comprise many stops; from four to eight stops of well marked tonal character being ample. The swell-box will, accordingly, not be of such dimensions as to render its accommodation a matter of difficulty. Care must be taken, however, to so locate the swell-box that the sounds of the inclosed stops may meet with little or no obstruction; and the box should be provided with the greatest possible amount of shutter-work. For particulars on this subject see the Chapter on the Construction of the Swell-box.

It has been the general practice in what is supposed to be the advanced School of Church Organ construction to insert in the Solo division, unexpressive or otherwise, stops of very powerful intonation, voiced on wind of high pressures. This practice may be accepted as suitable in the tonal appointment of the Concert-room Organ, but we gravely question its wisdom in connection with an accompanimental instrument like the legitimate Church Organ. The height of absurdity is reached, both on practical and artistic grounds, when we find a builder, professing to be artistic, contemplating the insertion of a TUBA MIRABILIS, 8 FT., in a Church Organ, voiced on wind of one hundred inches pressure. Such a stop should be labeled TUBA MISERABILIS. Our idea of the true office of the Solo division in the Church Organ is not to make a deafening noise, but to yield sounds of great purity, richness, and dignity, like those produced by orchestral instruments in the hands of artists. Extreme wind pressures are not required for this purpose; and no true artist, with sound musical knowledge and taste, would resort to them. Such pressures, and such pressures only, should be used as are necessary to produce the characteristic orchestral qualities of the Solo stops, without straining or imparting harshness to them.

The Solo Organ should be true to its name; and when it is introduced, it should be the storehouse of special solo effects, placing at the disposal of the musician glowing and varied tonal colors, to be used by him, in accompanimental music, with judgment and due reserve.

PEDAL ORGAN.

It is quite safe to say that of all the divisions of the Church Organ, as it is constructed in English speaking countries, the Pedal Organ is the most deficient and radically imperfect. The short-comings of this important department are attributable to several causes; such as, want of a proper and lively conception of its true office; shortness of funds or unwise parsimony; deficiency of space for the reception of an adequate instrument, through blundering on the part of the architect; and ignorance of the art of organ-building, associated with the blind following of bad methods. The neglect of the Pedal Organ has always been a reproach to every one connected with the construction of English Church Organs; and it is obvious that the legitimate office and use of the Pedal Organ have either been greatly misunderstood or wilfully ignored by organ builders and designers; and that it has been systematically sacrificed or denuded of its tonal resources for the sake of the manual department. Nothing could be more short-sighted than such a mode of procedure.

As has already been pointed out, the true office of the Pedal Organ is to provide a suitable bass for all the important stops and combinations of stops of the manual divisions. To fulfil this office in a satisfactory and artistic manner, it is necessary that the pedal department should be furnished with appropriate and well-chosen stops, numbering about the fifth part of the entire list of speaking stops contained in the instrument. As will be seen by the list given in the earlier part of the present Chapter, numerous Continental Organs have their pedal departments greatly in excess of the proportion just given. Several of the Organs enumerated in the list have pedal departments containing about one-third of the total number of speaking stops: this proportion, however, may be considered excessive under all ordinary conditions. Although it may not be necessary to follow any abnormal and extravagant development of the Pedal Organ, it is not too much to say that we need never hope to have satisfactory or thoroughly efficient Church Organs until we follow, more closely than has ever yet been done, the lines laid down by the great German masters in this direction.

We are, of course, aware, that the large pipes necessary for the unison and double stops of the Pedal Organ are both cumbersome and costly; and that shortness of funds on the one hand, and the mistakes of church architects on the other, have generally militated against a more liberal introduction of them. But, in the name of art and common sense, it is surely more advisable to scheme an Organ with *all* its divisions properly balanced and suited to each other, however modest and circumscribed they may have to be, than to have the manual divisions unduly enlarged at the expense, if not to the ruin, of the Pedal Organ; and, accordingly, to the serious crippling of the entire instrument in every class of music.

Where is there an English or American Church Organ schemed on such lines as those followed in the stop appointment of the moderately-sized instruments in the Lutheran Churches of Warsaw and Vienna? The former has eighteen manual stops and nine pedal stops; while the latter has fifteen manual and eight pedal stops. Eight or nine pedal stops are considered by English builders, from the highest to the lowest, to be ample for Church Organs of from forty to fifty speaking stops. There are a few exceptions which prove the rule. By far the greater number of Church Organs in England have miserable pedal departments. Four stops are considered a liberal allowance; while in instances too numerous to be counted, one or two stops have to serve as the pedal department in instruments containing many manual stops. We have elsewhere commented on the absurdity of depending on one master-of-all-work, loud 'booming, OPEN DIAPASON,' or, what is infinitely worse, a 'tubby BOURDON,' to supply a proper bass to fifteen or twenty manual stops, so need not enlarge on the subject here. But we may remark that it is truly lamentable to note the shifts organists are continually put to in performing on instruments with totally inadequate pedal departments; and the expedients they resort to, in methods of pedaling, to make some loud stop serve as the bass to some soft manual combination, just, as a moment previously, it served as the bass to the full organ, are worthy of all praise.

In scheming a Pedal Organ on proper lines, the condition that it must provide appropriate basses for all the manual divisions, and, indeed, for all the more important manual stops and combinations, must be held steadily in view. In addition to this, it should in all possible cases have a fairly complete harmonic structure; and any of its stops which specially call for powers of expression may with advantage be inclosed in one or other of the manual swell-boxes. We feel confident that before long, and when artistic organ-building becomes generally understood, the advisability of imparting flexibility and powers of expression to the more assertive stops of the Pedal Organ will be freely recognized. On this important question, the reader may consult what is said, in the following Chapter, on the pedal department of the Concert-room Organ.

The matter which first claims attention in the tonal appointment of the Pedal Organ, is the provision of several different strengths and qualities of 16 ft. tone,—the unison pitch of the department,—and in no case should there be fewer than three distinct strengths and qualities in an instrument of any pretensions toward completeness or utility. The total absence of anything in the nature of a softly-voiced unison stop in this department has rendered the great majority of Church Organs in England and America very unsatisfactory instruments. A softly-toned bass is a *necessity* in every Organ used for accompanimental music, or, indeed, music of any refined character; and we urge our readers never to overlook this really important fact when engaged in designing or purchasing Organs. For an instrument of small dimensions, having only two stops in the pedal department, we recommend an OPEN DIAPASON, 16 FT., of wood, 10″×12″ scale, and a DULCIANA or softly-voiced VIOLONE, 16 FT., of metal. With two such stops, three serviceable strengths of tone are available. At a small additional expense, an Octave action or coupler and the extra top octave of pipes may be provided in connection with the DULCIANA or VIOLONE, giving a valuable soft-toned OCTAVE, or VIOLONCELLO, 8 FT., as the case may be. Apart from the value of this OCTAVE, when used alone, it materially adds to the resources of the department both as regards variety and strength of tone. There is no reason why the Octave attachment should not be applied to the OPEN DIAPASON also, providing what may be called a BASS FLUTE, 8 FT. We strongly approve of any legitimate expedient whereby a small Pedal Organ may be improved; and we recommend the addition of the extra octave of small and inexpensive pipes and the Octave coupler in all cases in which either cramped space or shortness of funds renders a small Pedal Organ imperative. In proof of the utility of such additions in a department of two stops or ranks of pipes, such as has just been mentioned, we may state that while without the Octave attachments the tonal effects are limited to *three*, with the Octave attachments the possible effects are increased to *fifteen;* several, if not all, of which will be found useful. The same number of tonal effects are, of course, obtained by four independent stops; while with four stops and two Octave attachments no fewer than *sixty-three* tonal changes are possible.

It is unnecessary to again give a list of the stops best suited for the pedal department of the Church Organ, seeing that the matter has already been touched upon in our general remarks on the Speaking Stops: but we must again, and in conclusion, impress upon all who are interested in the construction of Church Organs the absolute necessity of providing properly proportioned pedal departments, with as complete harmonic structures as circumstances will permit. Let the idea which has too long obtained that the Pedal Organ is an inferior department, or one secondary in importance to the Great, Swell, and Choir Organs, be set aside forever; and let it be recognized, once for all, that the Pedal Organ is quite as important in relation to the other divisions of the instrument, as the bass part of any musical composition is in relation to the upper parts thereof.

GRAND AND CHANCEL ORGANS.

A very few words will suffice on the subject of double Organs, that is, two Organs placed in one church. When two independent Organs are introduced, one commonly occupies an elevated, west-end, position, or what, for the sake of distinction, may be designated the west-end position, while the other is located in the neighborhood of the chancel or sanctuary. The former instrument, called the Grand Organ, is usually of important dimensions, and is used for incidental and, in some cases, for responsive music of a solemn and dignified character: and in the most notable examples it partakes, in its tonal character and resources, of the nature of the Concert-room Organ. Such Organs are to be found in the French cathedrals and large parish churches. The Organs in the Cathedral of Notre-Dame, the Madeleine, and the Churches of Saint-Sulpice and Saint-Eustache, at Paris, are among the best works of the class. The Organ which occupies the choir position is usually of moderate size, and is strictly of an accompanimental character, furnished with a carefully selected series of refined and softly-toned stops, chiefly of pure organ-tone, admirably adapted for the dignified and impressive accompaniment to the voices of the choir, and also as a support to the orchestral instruments frequently associated with it in fuller accompaniments. The Grand Organ supplies all the tonal qualities not strictly necessary for an effective accompaniment, while it is admirably fitted for the rendition of solo and incidental music. In the French churches the Choir or Sanctuary Organ, properly so called, is used for the accompaniment to plain-song; and its tones are full and rich, without any tendency to coarseness or a screaming character. The Orgue d'Accompagnement of the Madeleine is a representative example.

The practice of introducing a Grand Organ and a Choir Organ, or what is practically a divided Organ, is rapidly gaining favor in the United States in cases where the architectural conditions are suitable. The divided Organ in the Church of St. Bartholomew, New York, is a recent and noteworthy example. This instrument is in two main divisions. That designated the "Gallery Division" is located on an elevated gallery at the end of the nave, one hundred and thirty feet from the chancel, and contains a Great Organ of eighteen stops, a Swell Organ of twelve stops, a Solo Organ of six stops, and a Pedal Organ of twelve stops. The "Chancel Division" is subdivided, containing, in the south portion, a Great Organ of twelve stops, a Choir Organ of eleven stops, and a Pedal Organ of ten stops; and, on the north side, a Swell Organ of seventeen stops. The action is electro-pneumatic: and all is played from a compact, portable console. The Specification of this large Organ is given in the concluding part of this treatise.

CHAPTER VI.

THE CONCERT-ROOM ORGAN.

DOUBTFUL as the true position of the English school of organ-building may be as regards the Church Organ, there can be no question, we venture to think, that, with all its obvious short-comings, it occupies the highest position with reference to the Concert-room Organ. It is not too much to say that the latter instrument is the outcome of national genius and musical enterprise and taste. The first Concert-room Organ, at all worthy of the name, was designed and constructed in England; and in no other country is the importance and value of this class of Organ so generally recognized. There is hardly a town of any importance in Great Britain that has not a Concert-room Organ either in its Town Hall or Concert Hall. Several towns can boast of two such instruments. Notwithstanding these facts, it can not be wondered at that, at the outset, the construction and tonal appointment of the Concert-room Organ did not differ materially from those of the ordinary Church Organ, save in the simple matter of size and in some mechanical details; and, indeed, at the present time little in the direction of a radical departure from the time-honored systems has made its appearance in the Concert-room instrument. This is greatly to be regretted; for it is obvious, as we shall endeavor to prove, that there still remains much to be done before the Concert-room instrument can be accepted as reasonably perfect. It may be freely admitted that it is not in the nature of the Organ, as a musical instrument, to be *perfect;* but it is surely in its nature to be much more complete in its musical structure and resources, and more flexible and expressive, than it has ever yet been made. There is every evidence that, in the near future, a certain distinguished organ builder in the United States will take the lead in the artistic construction and tonal appointment of the Concert-room Organ.

With the history of the Concert-room Organ, one name will ever be honorably linked; we allude to the greatest English organ builder who has ever lived—Henry Willis, of London. The masterpiece of this artist, so far as true musical qualities are concerned, is his earliest great work, the Grand Organ in St. George's Hall, Liverpool;* and not only did he never surpass this achievement, in respect to general tonal character and richness of musical resources, but no other builder in the world has yet approached it (1903). With such a beginning, one cannot help wondering and regretting that not one of Mr. Willis' subsequent great Concert-room Organs display any evidence of progress, either in the disposition of the tonal forces, or in the direction of increased flexibility and powers of expression. He proved his skill to be so great in matters relating to organ construction, that no one would dream of questioning that he had capacity to cope with any problem in his art that might present itself to his mind: and, accordingly, we cannot but believe that the conditions which are held by some persons at the present time, and those which we individually hold, as essential to a satisfactory musical instrument of so complex and assertive a nature, were either never contemplated by him, or were put aside, after probably a hasty consideration, as departures of too radical a nature to agree with old-established methods.

By way of an introduction to the remarks and suggestions we purpose making on the appointment of the Concert-room Organ, we may pass under hasty review some of the representative instruments which have been constructed by leading builders. The reader will, accordingly, be able to arrive at a tolerably clear idea of the present condition of the Concert-room Organ.

The largest Concert-room instrument in Great Britain is that in the Royal Albert Hall, South Kensington, London. This immense Organ was constructed by Henry Willis; but although it is an instrument of great resources, and was constructed long after the Organ in St. George's Hall, Liverpool, was brought to its most satisfactory state, it shows no advance toward a better type of instrument. So far as its tonal effects are concerned, it is decidedly inferior; but much of its short-comings in this direction must be attributed to the vast hall in which it is located, which is, as is well known, most imperfect acoustically; and also to the expedients adopted in the voicing of the pipe-work to render the instrument effective in the great space. St. George's Hall cannot be said to be a satisfactory room from an acoustical point of view, although it must be allowed that it is highly favorable for certain classes of modern organ music, especially that of a slow, *cantabile* character. A fugue on the Organ in St. George's Hall, if at all quickly rendered, is just as unsatisfactory to the critical ear as a slow melodic subject, skilfully accompanied, is charming. What both these large Organs are seriously deficient in are flexibility and powers of expression:—lamentable short-comings in so important and many-purposed an instrument as the Concert-room Organ. As we have treated this subject of flexibility and expression at some length in our Chapter on The Swell in the Organ, we shall say no more than is absolutely necessary on it here.

*This instrument was built in 1855 by the late Henry Willis from a scheme prepared by Dr. S. S. Wesley. In 1867 it was altered to equal temperament and greatly improved by the builder under the direction of the late W. T. Best, Corporation Organist. In this stage it was at its highest point of excellence in its tonal powers. In 1898 it was again altered, being then reduced from the GGG to the usual CC manual compass downward, and otherwise modified: the result being, in our opinion, a loss of some of its former grandeur. See Specification in the concluding part of this treatise.

The disposition of the speaking stops in both these immense Organs is by no means all that could be desired. Fine as their several divisions are, there is a decided absence of logical and artistic classification, grouping, and local coloring, which materially cripples their tonal resources. Our meaning will be made clear in our subsequent observations, and by the scheme we suggest for the tonal appointment of a Concert-room instrument of the first magnitude.

In the Liverpool Organ, pure organ-tone is fully provided for, there being in the Pedal Organ two DOUBLE OPEN DIAPASONS, 32 FT., two OPEN DIAPASONS, 16 FT., two PRINCIPALS, 8 FT., and harmonic-corroborating stops comprising ten ranks of pipes; and in the manual divisions there are three DOUBLE OPEN DIAPASONS, 16 FT., eight OPEN DIAPASONS, 8 FT., four PRINCIPALS, 4 FT., and what may be considered a full complement of mutation and compound harmonic-corroborating stops. Reed-tone is amply represented by a superb series of thirty-four beautifully-voiced reed stops. What the Organ is notably deficient in is imitative and pungent string-tone. In the Great Organ there are two weak string-toned stops, a VIOLONCELLO, 8 FT., and a VIOLA, 4 FT.; in the Choir Organ there are also two, a VIOLA DA GAMBA, 8 FT., and an octave GAMBA, 4 FT. In the Pedal Organ there is no stop of this class, unless the SALICIONAL can be considered one, which we question. But what was most remarkable in the original scheme of this large Organ (100 speaking stops), was the total absence of string-tone in both its Swell and Solo divisions. Accordingly, there was not a single string-toned stop in the instrument having powers of expression. So seriously was this deficiency felt, that, during the recent renovation and alteration of the Organ, a VIOLA DA GAMBA, 8 FT., and an OCTAVE VIOLA, 4 FT., were substituted for other stops in the Swell Organ; and a VIOLA DA GAMBA, 8 FT., was substituted for the DOUBLE DIAPASON in the Solo Organ, the latter stop having to "be removed to provide room for the new swell-box." The Solo Organ is now partly expressive.

In the Albert Hall Organ, which contains one hundred and eleven speaking stops, we meet with a tonal scheme of greater variety, in certain directions, than that above commented on; but as regards the general principle observed in the grouping and disposition of the stops throughout the several divisions there is, as we have previously remarked, no decided advance on the earlier instrument. Pure organ-tone is not so fully represented in the manual divisions as it is in the Liverpool Organ. Reed-tone here, as in all Mr. Willis' great instruments, is represented to the fullest desirable extent; for we find thirty-eight reed stops;—one of 32 ft., eleven of 16 ft., twenty of 8 ft., and six of 4 ft. Considering the immense size of this Organ, we have again to mark the deficiency in the direction of string-tone of a pronounced and imitative character. Certainly more has been done here than in the Liverpool Organ, but far more might have been done with advantage. In the Pedal Organ there are three stops whose names indicate string-tone; namely, a CONTRA-VIOLONE, 32 FT. (certainly non-imitative), a VIOLONE, 16 FT., and a VIOLONCELLO, 8 FT. In the Great Organ there are four, a CONTRA-GAMBA, 16 FT., VIOLONE, 16 FT., VIOLA DA GAMBA, 8 FT., and VIOLA, 4 FT. In the Swell Organ there are two, a VIOLA DA GAMBA, 8 FT., and VIOLA, 4 FT. In the Choir Organ there is one, a VIOLA DA GAMBA, 8 FT.; and in the Solo Organ there is a VIOLA D'AMORE, 8 FT. In our opinion the above-named stops are insufficient for a Concert-room Organ of one hundred and eleven speaking stops, more especially as they are so distributed as to render anything like effective massing impracticable during a performance. Again, only two out of the entire number are rendered expressive. We look in vain, in the general scheme of this colossal instrument, for any economy or definite system of tonal appointment or grouping of tone-color.

We must not leave the works of this celebrated builder without some reference to the scheme of the large Concert Organ erected by him in the Alexandra Palace, Muswell Hill, near London. This instrument has eighty-seven speaking stops. Its true organ-tone is furnished by two DOUBLE OPEN DIAPASONS, 32 FT., two open stops, of 16 ft., of the Diapason class, and two OCTAVES, 8 FT., in the Pedal Organ; by one DOUBLE OPEN DIAPASON, 16 FT., three OPEN DIAPASONS, 8 FT., and one PRINCIPAL, 4 FT., in the Great Organ; and by one DOUBLE OPEN DIAPASON, 16 FT., two OPEN DIAPASONS, 8 FT., and one PRINCIPAL, 4 FT., in the Swell Organ. All these foundation stops are supported by mutation and compound harmonic-corroborating stops. Reed-tone is amply furnished by four stops in the Pedal Organ; five in the Great Organ; seven in the Swell Organ; three in the Choir Organ; and seven in the Solo Organ. String-tone of an imitative character is here, as in Mr. Willis' other instruments, poorly represented. In the Solo Organ are the only two string-toned stops which are claimed by the builder to be imitative; namely, the VIOLONCELLO, 8 FT., and VIOLA, 4 FT. In the Great Organ there is a VIOLA DA GAMBA, 8 FT.; in the Choir Organ there are a CONTRA-GAMBA, 16 FT., a VIOLA DA GAMBA, 8 FT., and a VIOLA, 4 FT.; and in the Pedal Organ there is a VIOLONE, 16 FT. It is strange that in the Swell Organ—the only expressive division of the instrument—there is not a single string-toned stop of any description. We hold it as a canon of artistic organ-building, that all imitative stops must have powers of expression; and that those that imitate or represent, in the Organ, the Violin, Viola, Violoncello, and Double Bass of the orchestra, should, above and before all others, be given all the powers of expression possible in the Organ. While in the stop appointment of this instrument we can trace some recognition of the value of tonal grouping, yet it displays little in the way of a departure from old and time-honored lines, and nothing calling for special comment.

There is a large Concert Organ in the concert-room of the Town Hall of Leeds, Yorkshire, originally built by Messrs. Gray and Davison, of London, in the year 1859; and practically reconstructed by Messrs. Abbott and Smith of Leeds, in the year 1896. This Organ contains ninety-one speaking stops and a CARILLON; but beyond its size it presents no noteworthy feature as it at present stands. For a Concert-room Organ of the first magnitude it is, in its tonal disposition and resources, singularly commonplace. Its deficiency in imitative string-tone is lamentable, and we are surprised that this deficiency was not realized at the time of its reconstruction. There are only three manual stops professing to be imitative in this class,—a VIOLA, 8 FT., in the Great Organ, a VIOLIN and VIOLONCELLO (one stop) in the Swell Organ, and a VIOLA DA GAMBA in the Choir Organ. The total absence of string-tone in the Solo Organ is, even in the present indifferent state of stop appointment, unpardonable. With such a state of affairs, the satisfactory rendition of a great orchestral work is an utter impossibility; and surely in an Organ of ninety-one stops and six divisions this difficulty should not obtain. To be just, we may remark that in the appointment of the so-called Choir Organ we can trace an impression in the builders' minds that there is something to be gained by grouping a family of stops. The impression is evidently a fleeting one. The Pedal Organ of sixteen stops is insufficient in so large an instrument; and it does not contain a single soft-toned unison, unless the VIOLONE can be called one, which can hardly be granted.

The Concert Organ built by Messrs. T. C. Lewis and Company, under the direction of the late W. T. Best and Henry Smart, in the concert-room of the Public Halls, Glasgow, shows a slight awakening to the importance of expression and flexibility in instruments of the class; while the tonal scheme, and the disposition and grouping of the several classes of stops, show no departure from old grooves.

We may now direct attention to the largest and most ambitious Concert-room Organ ever constructed by an English organ builder; namely, the Organ in the Centennial Hall, at Sydney, New South Wales. In the general tonal structure of this immense Organ of one hundred and twenty-six speaking stops, and in the disposition of the tonal forces in the different divisions, there is no indication of an advance or any departure from old ways of doing things. As might be expected from its builders,—Messrs. Hill and Son, of London,—true organ-tone has been amply provided in all the chief divisions of the instrument. In the Pedal Organ there are two DOUBLE OPEN DIAPASONS, 32 FT., two OPEN DIAPASONS, 16 FT., and two OCTAVES, 8 FT.; in the Great Organ there are one DOUBLE OPEN DIAPASON, 16 FT., four OPEN DIAPASONS, 8 FT., and two PRINCIPALS, 4 FT.; in the Swell Organ there are one DOUBLE OPEN DIAPASON, 16 FT., one OPEN DIAPASON, 8 FT., one DULCIANA, 8 FT., and one OCTAVE, 4 FT.; in the Choir Organ there are one CONTRA-DULCIANA, 16 FT., one OPEN DIAPASON, 8 FT., one DULCIANA, 8 FT., and one OCTAVE, 4 FT.; and in the Solo Organ there are two OPEN DIAPASONS, 8 FT., and one OCTAVE, 4 FT. This almost overwhelming mass of foundation-tone is fairly supported by twenty mutation and compound harmonic-corroborating stops, comprising forty-eight ranks of pipes. Reed-tone is represented by thirty-three stops. Again, in this Organ, we find a serious deficiency of imitative and effective string-tone, which positively cripples the orchestral qualities of its several divisions. Of the one hundred and twenty-six stops this instrument contains, there are only eleven that can claim to yield a string-like quality of tone, and not one of these can claim to be considered imitative, to an effective extent, of any of the orchestral strings. In the Pedal Organ there are a GAMBA, 16 FT., a VIOLONE, 16 FT., and a VIOLONCELLO, 8 FT.; in the Great Organ there are a VIOLA, 8 FT., and a GAMBA, 8 FT.; in the Swell Organ there is a VIOLA DA GAMBA, 8 FT.; in the Choir Organ there are a GAMBA, 8 FT., and a VIOLINO, 4 FT.; in the Solo Organ there is a VIOLA, 8 FT.; and in the Echo Organ there are a VIOLE D'AMOUR, 8 FT.; and a VIOLE D'AMOUR, 4 FT. It will be observed that while the above list is somewhat striking, it is impossible to obtain a massing of string-tone for the adequate rendering of orchestral music; accordingly some of the grandest musical effects will never be heard from this very large but commonplace Organ. As the Specification of, and notes on, this Organ are given in the concluding part of this treatise, no further remarks on its tonal structure and shortcomings need be made here.

The most satisfactory scheme for a Grand Concert-room Organ ever prepared by an organ builder, was that submitted by the late Mr. Roosevelt, of New York, for the Organ for the Centennial Hall, Sydney, N. S. W., and very unwisely rejected by the Sydney authorities in their ignorance of the subject of practical and artistic organ construction. Among the important Specifications appended to this treatise, two are given relating to this large Organ. No. 1, the Specification of the instrument as built by Messrs. W. Hill and Son, of London; and No. 2, the Specification as submitted, in competition, by the late Mr. Hilborne L. Roosevelt. We have annotated these Specifications so as to assist the student of organ-building in comparing them; and, accordingly, may refer him to our notes for particulars that we have no space for here.

We may remark that had Mr. Roosevelt's scheme been carried out, as he would have carried it out, it would have resulted in the most remarkable and beautiful Organ ever built. Its almost limitless powers of expression, in conjunction with its rich tonal resources, would have produced, under the control of an experienced organist, musical effects absolutely impossible on any Grand Organ in existence at the present time.

It will be seen, however, on reference to the Specification, that the apportionment and disposition of the speaking stops in this scheme do not accord with our ideas on the subject; and we hold that a much smaller instrument, constructed under our system, would be more effective in everything save absolute power of sound at the full; and it must be remembered that the full effect of a large Concert Organ is rarely if ever resorted to in legitimate music. There is no necessity for Organs with one hundred and thirty speaking stops; indeed, it is questionable if a Concert Organ, of the first magnitude, need ever exceed eighty speaking stops. We certainly give, in this Chapter, a scheme for an Organ with considerably more stops than eighty; but this is done with the view of practically covering the subject of tonal structure and coloring so far as the Concert-room Organ is concerned. It is left to the taste and judgment of those interested in Concert Organ construction, to reduce the size of the instrument as schemed by us, keeping in view a just proportion of all parts, and paying careful attention to balance of tone and the retention of the expressive and flexible qualities of the instrument. We may remark that the reed stops admit of being considerably reduced in number; but with regard to the string-toned stops as small a reduction as possible should be ventured upon. This remark induces us to mention the deficiency in Mr. Roosevelt's scheme in the matter of string-tone. In this immense scheme, of one hundred and thirty speaking stops, there are only ten stops of anything approaching a string-tone in the several divisions, distributed thus:—In the Pedal Organ, a VIOLONE, 16 FT., a GAMBA, 16 FT., and a VIOLONCELLO, 8 FT.; in the Great Organ, a VIOLA DA GAMBA, 8 FT., and a GAMBETTE, 4 FT.; in the Swell

Organ, a Bell Gamba, 8 ft.; in the Choir Organ, a Viola d'Amore, 8 ft.; and in the Solo Organ, a Contra-Gamba, 16 ft. Judged on old lines, this number may be considered ample; but it must be observed that the stops are so distributed in the several divisions as to be available only singly or in very small groups. Such an arrangement we pronounce, and shall attempt to prove later on, to be insufficient for the demands on the Concert Organ, and for much of the music now rendered thereon. To produce something approaching the massive and complex effect of the string department of the orchestra, it will be necessary to mass a number of imitative string-toned stops together; and that with due regard to correct harmonic structure so that the compound tones of the stringed instruments may be produced as closely as possible by the pipes. Much may be done in this direction that has never yet been essayed.

We may now turn from the Sydney Organ scheme, which unfortunately exists only on paper, to the brief consideration of the most important Concert-room Organ built by Mr. Roosevelt—the Organ in the Auditorium, at Chicago. Although this instrument does not contain so many speaking stops as the Organ in the Centennial Hall, at Sydney, it is greatly superior to it tonally; and is unquestionably the most perfect Organ in all matters of flexibility, powers of expression, and mechanism, ever constructed. Like all the large instruments above considered, this Organ displays, in its tonal structure and in the disposition and grouping of its stops in the different divisions, no advance or noteworthy features. The Organ comprises one hundred and seven speaking stops, and two mechanical bell stops, formed respectively of steel bars and bell-metal tubes. The stop apportionment is as follows: The Pedal Organ contains nineteen stops, all of which are, unfortunately, unexpressive; the Great Organ contains twenty stops, thirteen of which are rendered expressive and flexible by being inclosed in a swell-box; the Swell Organ comprises twenty-three stops, all of which are, of course, inclosed in a special swell-box; the Choir Organ has sixteen speaking stops and a Carillon, of 24 steel bars, all inclosed in a special swell-box; the Solo Organ contains fourteen speaking stops and Chimes, of 25 tubular bells, all inclosed in a separate swell-box; the Echo Organ has eleven stops, inclosed in a special swell-box; and the Stage Organ consists of four uninclosed stops. It will be observed that of the one hundred and seven speaking stops no fewer than seventy-seven are rendered flexible and expressive by being inclosed in five independent swell-boxes, controlled by three balanced-levers.

Had the tonal structure and grouping been more logical and systematic, this important instrument would have marked a new era in the art of organ-building. This Organ affords another instance of the neglect of the imitative string-toned family of stops. In the Pedal Organ there are a Violone, 16 ft., and a Violoncello, 8 ft.; in the Great Organ there are a Contra-Gamba, 16 ft., a Viola da Gamba, 8 ft., and a Viola d'Amore, 8 ft.; and in the Solo Organ there are a Violoncello, 8 ft., and a Viola, 4 ft. It is noteworthy that there is no string-toned stop in the Swell, Choir, Echo, or Stage Organs. The seven string-toned stops, none of which are strongly imitative, are insufficient for so large an Organ; and it is difficult to imagine how the organist will produce many of the more striking and characteristic effects in renditions of important orchestral scores. It is quite certain the problem cannot be worked out on paper. It is greatly to be regretted that this Organ occupies a confined position, quite unsuitable and unworthy; but the blunders of architects in this direction are notorious.

We now come to the consideration of the works of the renowned French organ builder, the late M. A. Cavaillé-Coll, of Paris. Of the Concert-room Organs constructed by this artist, that in the Palais du Trocadéro, at Paris, and the expressive instrument in the Albert Hall, at Sheffield, are the most worthy of attention. It is right to remark that the former Organ was designed, up to a certain point at least, for the Church of Notre-Dame, Auteuil, being subsequently enlarged by the addition of a Solo Organ and certain other features to better adapt it for concert purposes. The Organ comprises sixty-six speaking stops, distributed in five divisions. The apportionment and grouping of the stops present, as might be expected, no noteworthy features, being carried out on the lines one is familiar with in the larger Church Organs of this builder. It is right to mention, however, that much credit is due him for the noble Pedal Organ. It is of unusual proportions, comprising sixteen stops out of the total of sixty-six, or, practically, one stop for every three in the manual divisions. This fine Pedal Organ contains two stops of 32 ft., six of 16 ft., six of 8 ft., and two of 4 ft.; and of these two are string-toned and seven are reeds. As in all French Organs, the string-toned family of stops is here inadequately represented. In the Great Organ there is only a VIOLONCELLO, 8 FT.; and in the Solo Organ a VIOLONCELLO, 8 FT. These stops furnish all the string-tone in the manual department of fifty stops.

As regards powers of expression, this Organ takes a good position among European Concert-room instruments; for we find that both the Récit and Positif divisions are inclosed in separate swell-boxes, controlled by balanced-levers. It is somewhat remarkable that so artistic a builder as M. Cavaillé-Coll, in adding the Solo division, did not place it under control. The tonal structure of this division is in no way noteworthy; but its utility and beauty would have been increased tenfold had it been given powers of expression. It was a strange want of taste which permitted the placing of the only CLARINET in the Organ in this unexpressive division. There is, however, a stop of this class, called a CROMORNE, in the Positif.

As we touch at some length on the Organ in the Albert Hall, Sheffield, in our Chapter on the Swell in the Organ, it is unnecessary to allude to its expressive powers here. Of its tonal structure little need be said; for, beyond an unusual proportion of 16 ft. tone in the manual divisions (a questionable gain), the stop appointment and distribution present no novelties. The tonal character of this Organ, taken as a whole and in its full effects, is, we venture to observe, not altogether satisfactory to ears accustomed to the roundness and dignified tones of such an Organ as that in St. George's Hall, Liverpool, and other works of England's greatest builder. Beyond matters of expression and excellence of workmanship, we have no desire to see this Organ taken as a model for future Concert-room instruments.

A glance at the Concert Organ schemes of the most renowned German organ builders, Messrs. E. F. Walcker and Company, of Ludwigsburg, Würtemberg, shows nothing but an adherence to old world grooves; in fact they do not differ in any essential points from the schemes of their important Church Organs. Glancing at the Specification of the Organ in the Crystallpalast, at Leipzig, which shows sixty speaking stops distributed, in the old-fashioned manner, over three manual divisions and a Pedal Organ, we fail to detect a single feature which marks this instrument as designed for the rendition of all classes of concert-room music. Its scheme is decidedly commonplace; and in powers of expression it is singularly deficient, the Swell Organ containing only ten stops, of which the following is the list:—

SCHWELLWERK.

1.	Lieblichgedeckt,	16 feet.	6.	Flöte,	8 feet.
2.	Lieblichgedeckt,	8 "	7.	Fugara,	4 "
3.	Geigenprincipal,	8 "	8.	Flöte,	4 "
4.	Aeoline,	8 "	9.	Trompete,	8 "
5.	Voix Céleste,	8 "	10.	Clarinette,	8 "

The Concert-room Organ in the Gewandhaus at Leipzig, the work of the same builders, is designed on the same commonplace lines as the preceding. It contains fifty-four speaking stops, only nine of which are rendered expressive by being inclosed in a swell-box. The only expressive division is called the Echowerk, probably because it contains softly-voiced stops only. This is well, for it certainly does not rise to the dignity of a Swell Organ.

"The Great Concert Organ" of the Liederkranz, Stuttgart, erected in 1895 by Carl G. Weigle, of Stuttgart, is another marked instance of commonplace stop appointment: and on a careful examination of the general disposition of the tonal forces one is at a loss to see in what direction this so-called "Great Concert Organ" differs from a good old-fashioned Church Organ, unless it be in the matter of the high pressure stops patented by the builder. In the grouping of the voices, in the several divisions of the instrument, there is absolutely no attempt to place at the disposal of the *virtuoso* the ready means of producing complicated orchestral effects or of massing special tone-colors. The instrument is very deficient in orchestral or imitative string-tone; and what string-tone there is is so distributed as to be of comparatively little value unless it is brought together by coupling all the manual divisions. The necessity of coupling for such a purpose is to be condemned, for it immediately cripples the entire instrument for the production of other orchestral effects at the same time. Such a state of affairs should never obtain in a properly appointed Concert Organ. German builders do not appear to realize the self-evident fact that a Concert-room Organ has to be constructed on lines widely different from those on which a true, accompanimental, Church Organ should be schemed.

Before going into details connected with the appointment of the Concert-room Organ, it is, perhaps, desirable to briefly define the nature and requirements of such an instrument when in its true and complete form. It is quite certain that no other class of Organ is called upon to meet so many and such varied demands upon its resources as that designed for the Concert-room. A Chamber Organ, which, when of considerable size, may be considered most akin to the Concert-room Organ, has, at most, to meet very reasonable calls in solo and accompanimental or concerted music: while the Church Organ, in its legitimate office, has only to accompany the voices of the choir and congregation, and to lend itself to the rendition of a limited range of dignified solo music. On the other hand, the Concert-room Organ has a threefold office to fulfil, and that to the fullest extent possible in an Organ. It must be capable of taking part, in conjunction with a full orchestra, in the accompaniment of Oratorios and other important choral works. It should be equally capable of accompanying such works, furnishing an able substitute for the grand orchestra, in the rendition of their full instrumental scores, when an orchestra is not provided. It must furnish the musician (we do not mean the average organist, whose demands are limited) with proper tone-colors, properly grouped, and properly placed under his control, for the effective interpretation of the artistic conceptions of his own and other minds, and for the effective rendition of the most complex compositions written either for the Organ or orchestra. In short, the Concert-room Organ should be a perfect Organ and a full orchestra combined.

It must be obvious that to fulfil all these purposes, and to meet the most exacting demands of the accomplished musician and improvisatore, the Concert-room Organ must ever be an extremely complicated instrument; yet both its tonal and mechanical structures should be founded and appointed upon a system so perfect, that simplicity will appear to characterize all matters connected with its control. We may assist the reader by explaining briefly what is meant by the above remarks. First, all the speaking stops in the different divisions of the instrument should be grouped on a definite and easily recognized system; and when this is done, their number, however great, ceases to present the slightest element of confusion. Secondly, the means provided for the manipulation of the complete series of stops, singly or in any desired combination, should be so perfect and so easily mastered, that the memory of the performer is not severely taxed, and but a slight acquaintance with the instrument is necessary. Thirdly, each division of the Organ should be wholly or partly expressive and flexible; and the mechanical means for controlling the several swells should be as simple as they are complete. Fourthly, the claviers should be so located with respect to the sound-creating departments of the instrument, that the performer may hear perfectly the effects he is producing. Every musician will admit that these conditions are simple, reasonable, and necessary; yet there is not an Organ of any class in existence which comprises them all, or even any two of them in perfection. Not a single English Concert-room Organ presents any one of them properly developed. Do not these simple facts show how much has yet to be done before a reasonably perfect Organ makes its appearance?

The positions of the Concert-room Organ and its claviers have been considered in the Chapter on the Position of the Organ, so need not be touched upon here.

GENERAL SCHEME OF THE ORGAN.

DIVISIONS AND CLAVIERS.—No Concert-room Organ should have fewer than five independent divisions, commanded by one pedal and four manual claviers. Instruments of the first magnitude should have a pedal and five manual claviers. When circumstances are unfavorable to the introduction of a fifth manual clavier, or when, as may frequently and properly be the case, the fifth clavier is omitted for the sake of simplicity, convenience, and comfort, two minor divisions can be commanded by one of the four claviers, in the manner explained further on.

We feel somewhat reluctant to interfere with the old-established nomenclature of the divisions and their claviers; but we can hardly see how it can be retained for the Concert-room Organ under the new method of stop disposition, and the multiplication of expressive divisions, which we have to propose. In the first place, in an instrument containing three or four expressive divisions, the term Swell Organ has no definite significance when applied to either of them. It is open, accordingly, to serious question whether the name should be retained. The term Great Organ certainly has much to recommend it; while the terms Choir Organ and Solo Organ have no serious objections to be advanced against them. The term Echo Organ should be swept away entirely from the general nomenclature of the Organ. It is a meaningless and undignified appellation in connection with any part of a Concert Organ; for it smacks of trickery, and of fanciful, ear-tickling effects unworthy of so noble an instrument. If the effect of an echo is at any time required it can be readily obtained, and that in any quality of tone, from one or other of the expressive divisions. Such an effect is very rarely necessary in dignified organ music, and should certainly not give its name to an entire division of the Organ.

Probably the simplest solution of the entire question regarding the distinction of the manual divisions, is to abandon the common terms Great Organ, Swell Organ, Choir Organ, etc.; and use the sufficiently distinctive names First Organ, Second Organ, Third Organ, etc.; or, in the most musical of languages, *Organo Primo*, *Organo Secondo*, *Organo Terzo*, etc.

With respect to the compass of the manual and pedal departments of the Concert-room Organ a very few words will suffice. All the Concert Organs in existence, known to us, have the note CC, 8 ft. tone, as their manual compass downward. Up to the year 1898 the grandest Concert Organ ever built had its manual compass from GGG to $a^3 = 63$ notes; but at the present time, as already stated, this instrument has its manual compass from CC to $c^4 = 61$ notes. We allude to the Organ in St. George's Hall, Liverpool. In the compass upward, the practice has not been uniform, the notes g^3, a^3, and c^4 having been adopted by different builders in different instruments. All authorities agree to-day that c^4 is the proper note for the manual claviers of the Concert-room Organ. The correct compass of all the manual claviers is, accordingly, CC to c^4. The Concert Organs in St. George's Hall, Liverpool; the Royal Albert Hall, London; the Public Halls, Glasgow; the Albert Hall, Sheffield; the Centennial Hall, Sydney; the

Town Hall, Melbourne; the Auditorium, Chicago; and the Music Hall, Cincinnati, have all this approved compass. The German organists and organ builders do not seem to have realized the importance of this compass; for we find that the instruments in the Gewandhaus, the Crystallpalast, and the Conservatorium, at Leipzig, which were constructed by Messrs. Walcker, have the compass of CC to $a^3 = 58$ notes: while the much lauded "Great Concert Organ" of the Liederkranz, at Stuttgart, has the old-fashioned compass of CC to $g^3 = 56$ notes. So much for progressive organ-building in Germany.

The proper compass of the Pedal Organ in the Concert-room instrument is that adopted by Mr. Willis in the Organs of St. George's Hall, Liverpool, and the Royal Albert Hall, London; namely, from CCC to G = 32 notes. There are other instances of this useful compass in English Organs, which was introduced as early as the year 1850, by Jackson, of Liverpool, in his Organ in the Collegiate Institution of that city. The two additional notes, above the usual compass, are very useful, especially when melodic passages are performed on the pedals, or when they are played in octaves. In scheming a Concert-room Organ every possible call upon its resources should be considered and anticipated; and it may be accepted as a fact that every addition to the capabilities of the instrument, although it may be in advance of immediate requirements, will tend to improve organ playing, and will inspire writers for the Organ to greater achievements.

COUPLERS.—Next in importance to the claviers themselves are the mechanical accessories introduced for the purpose of connecting them together so that two or more can be commanded by the hands or feet from a single clavier. While in all Organs couplers are of considerable use, in the Concert-room Organ they are of the first importance; and as complete a system as circumstances will permit should in all cases be introduced. Adopting the nomenclature already suggested for the several divisions of the advanced Concert Organ, we give complete systems of couplers for instruments having a pedal and four and five manual claviers. The nature and use of several of the couplers will be readily realized on reference to the tonal appointments of the different divisions given farther on.

ORGAN WITH A PEDAL AND FOUR MANUAL CLAVIERS.

FIRST ORGAN SYSTEM—FIRST CLAVIER.

I.	Second Organ to First Organ, ...	Unison coupler.
II.	Expressive Subdivision of Second Organ to First Organ,	Octave coupler.
III.	First Subdivision of Third Organ to First Organ, . .	Unison coupler.
IV.	Second Subdivision of Third Organ to First Organ, .	Unison coupler.
V.	Second Subdivision of Third Organ to First Organ, .	Octave coupler.
VI.	Fourth Organ to First Organ, ...	Unison coupler.
VII.	Fourth Organ to First Organ, ...	Octave coupler.
VIII.	Fourth Organ to First Organ, ...	Sub-octave coupler.

SECOND ORGAN SYSTEM—SECOND CLAVIER.

I.	First Subdivision of Third Organ to Second Organ, .	Unison coupler.
II.	Second Subdivision of Third Organ to Second Organ, .	Unison coupler.

III.	Expressive Subdivision of First Organ to Second Organ,	Unison coupler.
IV.	Fourth Organ to Second Organ, ...	Unison coupler.
V.	Second Organ on itself, ...	Octave coupler.

THIRD ORGAN SYSTEM—THIRD CLAVIER.

I.	Expressive Subdivision of First Organ to Third Organ,	Unison coupler.
II.	Expressive Subdivision of Second Organ to Third Organ,	Unison coupler.
III.	Expressive Subdivision of Second Organ to Third Organ,	Octave coupler.
IV.	Fourth Organ to Third Organ, ...	Unison coupler.
V.	Fourth Organ to Third Organ, ...	Octave coupler.
VI.	Fourth Organ to Third Organ, ...	Sub-octave coupler.

FOURTH ORGAN SYSTEM—FOURTH CLAVIER.

I.	Unexpressive Subdivision of First Organ to Fourth Organ,	Unison coupler.
II.	Expressive Subdivision of First Organ to Fourth Organ,	Unison coupler.
III.	Expressive Subdivision of Second Organ to Fourth Organ,	Sub-octave coupler.
IV.	First Subdivision of Third Organ to Fourth Organ, .	Unison coupler.
V.	Second Subdivision of Third Organ to Fourth Organ, .	Unison coupler.
VI.	Second Subdivision of Third Organ to Fourth Organ, .	Octave coupler.

PEDAL ORGAN SYSTEM—PEDAL CLAVIER.

I. Unexpressive Subdivision of First Organ to Pedal Organ.
II. Expressive Subdivision of First Organ to Pedal Organ.
III. Second Organ to Pedal Organ.
IV. First Subdivision of Third Organ to Pedal Organ.
V. Second Subdivision of Third Organ to Pedal Organ.
VI. Fourth Organ to Pedal Organ.
VII. Pedal Organ, Octave Coupler on itself in Expressive Division only.

When the Organ has a pedal and five manual claviers, the following couplers require to be added to those given in the preceding list :—

FIRST ORGAN SYSTEM—FIRST CLAVIER.

IX.	Fifth Organ to First Organ, ...	Unison coupler.

SECOND ORGAN SYSTEM—SECOND CLAVIER.

VI.	Fifth Organ to Second Organ, ...	Unison coupler.

THIRD ORGAN SYSTEM—THIRD CLAVIER.

VII.	Fifth Organ to Third Organ, ...	Unison coupler.

FOURTH ORGAN SYSTEM—FOURTH CLAVIER.

VII.	Fifth Organ to Fourth Organ, ...	Unison coupler.

FIFTH ORGAN SYSTEM—FIFTH CLAVIER.

I.	First Organ to Fifth Organ, ...	Unison coupler.
II.	Second Organ to Fifth Organ, ...	Unison coupler.
III.	Second Organ to Fifth Organ, ...	Octave coupler.
IV.	First Subdivision of Third Organ to Fifth Organ, . .	Unison coupler.
V.	Second Subdivision of Third Organ to Fifth Organ, .	Unison coupler.
VI.	Fourth Organ to Fifth Organ, ...	Unison coupler.

PEDAL ORGAN SYSTEM—PEDAL CLAVIER.

VIII. Fifth Organ to Pedal Organ.
IX. Fifth Organ to Pedal Organ, in the Octave.

All the couplers given in the above lists must be looked upon as strictly belonging to the tonal forces of the Organ, and should be considered along with the speaking stops of their respective divisions. The draw-knobs, stop-keys, or touches which control the couplers should, accordingly, be located in a convenient position immediately adjoining the draw-stops of the divisions to which they strictly belong. To make this grouping of the couplers quite clear to the reader we have divided them into distinct systems. The lists doubtless seem rather formidable, and several unusual couplers appear therein; but the value and utility of the full complement in a properly appointed Concert-room Organ will be realized by the organist of the advanced modern school when he studies the new and logical scheme which we formulate for the apportionment of the tonal forces in the several divisions of the instrument—the Concert-room Organ of the Future.

The couplers which connect divisions which are commanded by lower claviers to those commanded by higher claviers are extremely valuable; for while they couple in the manner set forth they leave the lower divisions free and self-contained when their own claviers are manipulated. In every case the coupling is solely in the direction expressed: for instance, in the Third Organ system, the Unison coupler which connects the expressive subdivision of the First Organ to the Third Organ does not in any manner couple the Third Organ to the First Organ. This backward coupling, so to speak, is necessarily carried to the full extent in the Fifth Organ system.

It must at this point be understood that we do not advocate the multiplication of couplers for the sake of loud and overwhelming effects of sound, or, in other words, noise; but primarily for the production of subtle orchestral effects and *nuances,* in which compound swells play no unimportant parts. The variety of tonal combinations—practically limitless—is one thing; but the surprising effects imparted to the combinations of tones by the skilful and musicianly management of two or more independent swells are, in our estimation, of much greater importance in an instrument schemed on the lines laid down in the present Chapter. The highest use to which the independent swells can be put depends largely upon the number and nature of the couplers. In the matter of couplers, it may be remarked that their use has in many quarters fostered a doubtful taste for loud effects—the same vitiated taste that is gratified by the uncontrollable roar of *uninclosed* TUBAS on 30 inch wind. This fact disposes one to believe that there are few things in connection with a large Organ more generally abused in their use than the couplers, at least in the hands of the average player who seems to think that organ music amounts to little unless it is deafening. Now, once for all, be it understood that the multiplication of speaking stops and couplers is not for the production of ear-splitting crashes; but, on the contrary, for the obtainment of those refinements of light and shade,—musical *chiaroscuro,*—and the rich tonal colorings which are to the musician what the 'well-set palette' is to the painter.

DOUBLE-TOUCH.—Secondary only in importance to the complete equipment of manual couplers, if secondary at all, is the proper installation of the Double-touch in the Concert-room Organ. The remarkable effects which the Double-touch gives the skilful musician the power of producing, with ease and certainty, are as difficult to realize as they are to describe; indeed, they are so varied and complex as to defy description. The Double-touch has only recently made its advent in certain English electro-pneumatic Organs; while at the present time (1903) it is absolutely unknown in the United States. That the advantages which attend its introduction in the Concert-room Organ only require to be understood to secure its universal adoption for all important instruments is, in our opinion, a certainty. The ease with which it can be introduced in electro-pneumatic Organs is, of necessity, much in its favor.

The Double-touch consists in giving to a manual clavier a twofold fall or action. When the keys are lightly depressed they reach a level at which they are apparently arrested; but on a greater pressure being used by the fingers, the keys sink to another level, where, of course, they are finally arrested. On the initial depression of the keys the first electrical contacts belonging to them are made; while on the further depression the second electrical contacts are added. Now, if the musician will suppose that either one complete manual division or a subdivision is commanded by the first motion of the keys, and another division or subdivision is commanded by the second motion of the keys, he can readily imagine the wonderful tonal colorings that are possible and easy of production, and the startling *sforzando* and complex orchestral effects that can be obtained, instantaneously, at the will of the performer, and that without removing his fingers from the keys.

Objections to the adoption of the Double-touch will, in all probability, be advanced by groove-loving organ builders and worthy organists of the old school, on the grounds that so delicate a mechanism will be costly and liable to derangement, and that it will lead to endless blunders on the part of unskilful performers. That it will cost more to construct a console with the Double-touch we freely admit; but when such an instrument as a Concert-room Organ is contemplated, the small additional cost is undeserving of consideration. It rests altogether with the skill and careful workmanship of the builder whether the necessary additional mechanism will go out of order or not. Such an Organ as calls for the addition of the Double-touch is not, in the proper order of things, intended for the blundering performer; he will find himself out of his depth on a Concert-room Organ of any description. It must be borne in mind that while the double motion of the keys obtains at all times, the second depression is operative only when the Double-touch is 'drawn on.' Under these circumstances the Organ is, when so desired, an instrument of the ordinary class, so far, at least, as the clavier actions are concerned. The Double-touch is for the *virtuoso* and the profound musician, who know when, where, and how to use it. The Double-touch can, of course, be applied to any or every clavier in a Concert-room Organ; but it will be found of most value when it is applied to those claviers which have their voices apportioned in two subdivisions. This arrangement will be shown in the Specification given in the present Chapter.

DRAW-STOP AND COMBINATION SYSTEMS.—We do not treat of purely mechanical matters in the present Chapter; our aim being simply to point out what is requisite and desirable for the proper appointment and equipment of the Concert-room Organ, not to touch on details of construction.

In an instrument of so great a number of speaking stops and couplers as the Concert-room Organ, the position and arrangement of the draw-stop knobs, stop-keys, or lever-touches, are matters deserving careful consideration on the part of the organist as well as on that of the organ builder; for on their systematic arrangement and convenient position will, to a very large extent, depend the easy and proper control of all the tonal forces of the instrument.

In all the important Concert-room Organs hitherto constructed the ordinary draw-stop knobs are used, placed in groups in splayed stop-jambs or stepped horizontal tiers. The chief objection to both these methods of disposition in large instruments, especially where there is no adjustable combination action, is the difficulty, sometimes amounting to an impossibility, experienced in placing all the draw-stop knobs within the easy reach of the performer while properly seated at the claviers. In Organs such as Mr. Roosevelt built, fitted with his "automatic adjustable combination action," the position of the draw-stop knobs was not a matter of paramount importance, such as it must always be in instruments which have no adjustable combination appliances. In the case of a Roosevelt Organ, such as that in the Auditorium, at Chicago, it is unnecessary for the organist to touch a single draw-stop knob during the performance of any composition of an ordinary character. When draw-stop knobs are used, care must be taken to render those belonging to each division of the instrument as distinct as possible; those controlling the couplers in each group being clearly marked. This is especially necessary in the Concert-room Organ, which will, in the ordinary course of events, be performed on by numerous organists who may have had only a very short acquaintance with the instrument. The methods of distinguishing the several groups will continue to be matters of taste or convenience; for it is hopeless to look for the adoption of any uniform treatment in this or any other similar detail of organ construction. Each group of draw-stop knobs may be of a differently-colored wood or ivory, with name-plates in white; or each group may be of the ordinary white ivory, placed on a differently-colored ground, distinctly defined by lines, and labeled with the name of the division to which it belongs. In addition to such distinctive methods it is desirable to separate the groups by placing them as far apart as practicable. In short, everything ingenuity can suggest should be done to aid the organist in individualizing the different groups. The draw-knobs controlling the couplers should be placed immediately under or adjoining those controlling the speaking stops of the divisions to which they belong. The practice of placing all the couplers together, in a row above the claviers, or in some other separate situation, is to be strongly condemned.*

With respect to the positions of the stop-keys, rocking stop-touches, or other mechanical devices for stop control, introduced in electro-pneumatic actions, no

*For further particulars respecting the positions of the draw-stop knobs, see the remarks, under the heading "The Draw-stop and Combination Actions," in the preceding Chapter on The Church Organ.

hard and fast rules can well be given, beyond the one which insists on the positions being in every way convenient for the performer. Probably in large Organs, having four or five manual claviers, the most convenient positions for stop-keys would be in stepped jambs extending obliquely from the cheeks of the claviers. When rocking stop-touches are used, they can be conveniently disposed on splayed or concave jambs, the latter having a radius adapted to the natural movement of the arms from the shoulders, when the body occupies the correct, central position on the organ-seat.

In a large Concert-room Organ, the most important adjunct in connection with the draw-stop system is the mechanism whereby the performer is able, with perfect ease and certainty, to control the entire series of speaking stops and couplers, and that without having to remove his hands any distance from the keys while playing. We do not hesitate to affirm that it is absolutely necessary for the properly appointed Concert-room Organ to be furnished with a complete adjustable combination action; by means of which the performer can prepare all the combinations of speaking stops and couplers, on every clavier, manual and pedal, that he will require during the rendition of any piece of music; and that in such a clear and orderly manner that very little exercise of memory will be called for.

It is to be regretted that the leading European organ builders have paid so little attention to adjustable combination actions. Since the introduction, in England, of the pneumatic action with fixed combinations, controlled by thumb-pistons and foot-levers, no general advance has been made. We find no fault with the pistons and levers *per se;* but we do object to their restricted operations. It is out of all reason, in this advanced age of mechanical art, that the performer on an immense Concert Organ, containing a hundred or more speaking stops and numerous couplers, should be compelled, during the rendition of an elaborate and exacting musical work, to choose between two evils; namely, to rest content with such fixed combinations of stops as the organ builder has thought proper to provide, or to undertake the manipulation of the stops in detail. In fact, it is not too much to surmise that throughout a long recital of varied music, or during the accompaniment of an important choral work, the organist may fail to find one of the fixed combinations exactly suitable; and will, accordingly, if he is an artist and acquainted with the orchestration of the work, have to manipulate the stops independently of any mechanical assistance. To the organist who knows nothing better than the old-fashioned fixed combination system, and who has never experienced the convenience of an adjustable combination action, the present ordinary appointment of Organs may appear satisfactory: but under no possible conditions can it be satisfactory or even tolerable in a Concert-room Organ. Yet all the large Concert Organs constructed by Willis and Hill have fixed combination systems. What is wanted, and what the complete Concert Organ must have, is a combination action controlled by thumb-pistons or combination-keys, located under or immediately adjoining the manual claviers, and a series of foot-levers, with an unlimited means of adjustment so far as the stops to be drawn are concerned. The organist should be able, before commencing a piece, to arrange on the pistons and levers all the combinations and changes of speaking stops and couplers he will require during its performance: he should be able at a glance to see the record of all the combinations he has placed on the pistons and levers, and so be saved an undesirable effort of memory. It is desirable, if possible, that the combinations, as they are drawn by the pistons or levers, be made evident to the eye by the movement of the draw-stop knobs, stop-keys, or touches.

The adjustable combination action should be so easily and quickly manipulated that the organist will find no difficulty in arranging his several combinations, and preparing an entirely new series for all the divisions of the instrument, in the usual interval between any two pieces of music. As a rule, however, during a recital or the accompaniment of a lengthy choral work, the operations alluded to will rarely extend beyond some slight modifications of the series of combinations arranged before commencing the performance.

There can be no question as to the great importance and value of such an adjustable combination action, yet this does not appear to be realized by the great European organ builders. How is this to be accounted for? Are European builders deficient in ingenuity and mechanical skill? Or are they too indifferent regarding matters relating to their art to trouble themselves with problems which the playing world around them has not imperatively demanded the solution of? It seems little short of absurd that the largest Concert Organ ever constructed, with its one hundred and twenty-six speaking stops and thirteen couplers, should only have thirty-three fixed combinations on the thumb-pistons of its five manual divisions. These are supposed to answer equally well for all musical compositions that may be performed year after year, or until the organ builder is called in to alter them. It is, however, satisfactory to know that the importance of automatic adjustable combination actions is now being recognized by certain builders.

The introduction and practical application of adjustable combination actions appear to be due to the ingenuity and skill of Canadian and American builders. In the year 1880, MM. Casavant Frères, of St. Hyacinthe, Province of Quebec, introduced a simple and tentative form of adjustable combination action in the Organ constructed by them for the Church of Notre-Dame de Lourdes, at Montreal. In 1883, Mr. Hilborne L. Roosevelt was using a very complete adjustable combination action;* and in 1889 his successor, Mr. Frank Roosevelt, was using another form of adjustable combination action invented and patented by M. Salluste Duval, of Montreal, Canada. At these dates not a single attempt had been made by European builders to introduce an action of a similar character. We do not wonder at this so far as German and French builders are concerned. The former remained satisfied with their humdrum, but time-honored, mechanical appliances; while the latter remained content with the insufficient tonal changes rendered possible by their "ventil system."

There is now no excuse for constructing important Concert-room Organs with any kind of fixed combination actions: and as organ builders, with a few notable exceptions, are most reluctant to move beyond their well-worn and comfortable grooves, it behooves the purchasers of Concert-room Organs and those

* The builder's description of this action is given in the preceding Chapter on The Church Organ, under the heading "The Draw-stop and Combination Actions."

interested in their playing, to insist on having a perfect automatic adjustable combination system inserted, and to resist all compromise that may be suggested by builders or other conservative parties.

EXPRESSION-LEVERS.—No Concert-room Organ should have less than three expressive manual divisions commanded by two balanced expression-levers; while properly appointed instruments of the first magnitude should have four or five expressive manual divisions commanded by three or four expression-levers. The difficulty which appears to obtain in finding space for, and in controlling, more than three expression-levers, especially when they are all of the French or balanced form, militates greatly against the introduction of a fourth. When two expression-levers are required they should be placed side by side, and located so that the small space between them (about half an inch) is directly over the space between the EE and FF keys of the pedal clavier. When a third lever is added it should be placed on the left of the pair in the position above directed. When a fourth lever is added it should occupy a position on the right of the group. Arranged thus, the right foot of the performer can easily command all the levers singly, or in pairs. When passages are played with compound expression, *sans pédales*,—namely, with two swells at the same time, but independently of each other,—the left foot can be placed on the first or second and the right foot on the second or third; or the left foot can actuate both the first and second simultaneously, while the right foot confines itself to the third lever; or the left foot can confine itself to the first lever, while the right foot actuates the second and third at the same time. When the tonal scheme of the properly appointed Concert Organ is properly understood, the astonishing musical effects that can be produced by a skilful and artistic use of the expression-levers will be readily realized. In the Concert Organ in the Auditorium, at Chicago, constructed by the late Mr. Frank Roosevelt from the noteworthy Specification prepared by Mr. Walter F. Crosby, the three expression-levers are grouped together, and placed in a central position with respect to the manual claviers over. The lever on the left controls the expressive division of the Great and the Choir Organ; the middle lever controls the Swell Organ; and the lever on the right the Solo and Echo Organs. There are five separate swell-boxes in this important instrument. In our scheme for the Concert-room Organ there is an expressive subdivision of the Pedal Organ. While this should be controlled by a special lever, arrangements should be made to enable the performer to connect this subdivision to any of the expression-levers belonging to the several manual divisions. The importance and value of such an arrangement is self-evident. On this branch of our subject we speak fully in the Chapters on The Swell in the Organ, and The Construction of the Swell-box.

In addition to the balanced expression-levers, the Concert-room Organ should have two levers, placed side by side on the right of the balanced levers; one of which, on being put down by the foot, opens all the swell-boxes simultaneously; while the other, on being depressed, closes all the swell-boxes in the like manner. These levers are to be found in the Auditorium Organ.

CRESCENDO- AND DIMINUENDO-LEVERS.—The foot-levers which actuate the mechanism which draws all the stops in the Organ in the order of their strength of tone, and which silences them in reverse order, are very important accessories, notwithstanding the fact that such tonal effects as they produce are rarely resorted to in legitimate playing. These levers are to be found in the Auditorium Organ, placed on the right of those which open and close all the swell-boxes.

Another foot-lever, called the Sforzando-lever, is also valuable. Through its agency a sudden and transitory increase of tone is produced. The *sforzando* so produced is extremely effective when artistically managed.

TREMOLANTS.—The number of these mechanical accessories necessary in the Concert-room Organ is dictated by the number of expressive divisions in the manual department; for it is never desirable to attach a tremolant to an unexpressive division. No tremolant should be attached to the expressive subdivision of the Great Organ, or what we call the First Organ in our Concert Organ scheme; but there need be no hesitation in furnishing one to each of the other expressive divisions. It is desirable to apply the tremolant to such stops in the divisions as are suitable for the *tremolo*, and to those only. As a rule it is undesirable to affect any of the foundation, mutation, and harmonic-corroborating stops; or those stops which yield pure organ-tone, and belong to the fundamental tonal structure of the instrument. There are several advantages attending this partial application of the tremolant. In the first place it circumscribes the possibility of its illegitimate and tasteless use; and in the second place, it favors the production of numerous full effects of a complex character, such as those produced by the combination of wavy tones of an assertive nature with rich volumes of steady organ-tone.

Much of the utility and beauty of the tremolant depends upon the character and speed of the *tremolo* it generates. Generally speaking, tremolants are both too powerful and too rapid. The result is unpleasant in the extreme; and the refined quality of the stops they affect is changed into a hooting or sobbing intonation. The action of a tremolant should be only sufficient to impart a gentle wave-like ripple or undulation to the natural speech of the pipes, and that sufficiently slow to allow the ear to recognize their true musical tones.

As the tremolant is an appliance which should always be sparingly used, and is, except in the case of the VOX HUMANA, the imitative quality of which greatly depends upon the *tremolo* effect, chiefly required in short passages during the performance of a piece, convenient arrangements should be made whereby the organist can control its entry and exit instantaneously and easily. In addition to the ordinary draw-stop arrangements, each tremolant should have a double-acting thumb-button or stop-key, placed in a convenient position under the clavier of the division it affects. These things may appear trifles; but they will be found, along with other small matters, to go far toward reducing the labor and worry of the performer, especially in so complicated an instrument as a large Concert-room Organ. Here is a golden rule: Let the organ builder, in scheming an Organ, do everything possible to save the organist unnecessary labor in playing it. If builders would only realize the importance of this rule, it would be greatly to their advantage; for the skill of a builder is commonly judged by the musical results easily obtained on his instruments. Organists, as a rule, do not deeply study the construction of the Organ; and, in their ignorance of what can and should be done, are content to accept just such conveniences and helps the organ builder is good enough to give them. Organists do not systematically think out all an instrument's short-comings, and, in the builder's interest, set themselves, with ungrudging labor and ingenuity, to hide them, or, with consummate skill, to make up for them by extraordinary exertions of hands and feet.

THE KEY ACTION.—As has been pointed out, in the Chapter on the Position of the Organ, when a Concert-room Organ is properly treated and placed, the console or key-case is located at a considerable distance from the sound-producing portions of the instrument. This arrangement certainly points to the electro-pneumatic action as the only suitable one to be adopted. But when the console is only reversed and placed immediately in front of the instrument, as in Cavaillé-Coll's Organ in the Albert Hall, Sheffield; or when the claviers directly join, or are practically buried in, the body of the instrument, as in the Organs in St. George's Hall, Liverpool, and the Royal Albert Hall, London, either a tubular-pneumatic or tracker and pneumatic lever action can be used. The latter action is used in the Sheffield Organ, but is not to be recommended for new instruments. When circumstances favor its adoption, the tubular-pneumatic action is to be preferred; but it is evident that for important Concert Organs having distant or movable consoles the electro-pneumatic action is imperative.

SPEAKING STOPS.—In approaching the all-important subject of the speaking stops for the Concert-room Organ,—a subject which can only be glanced at in a general Chapter like the present,—the question of wind-pressures, upon which so much of the beauty and tonal effect of the instrument depends, comes naturally to the front. The subject of wind-pressures is a general one; yet the question, so far as the Concert-room Organ is concerned, may well be decided on its own merits and from a special point of view. In the Concert Organ sufficiently high pressures should be used, and those only, to produce the richest and most musical tones from the various stops. In so comprehensive an instrument there should be just so many different pressures employed as are necessary to meet the peculiar demands of all the different classes of speaking stops in its tonal appointment. We do not approve of extreme or even what may be called ordinary high pressures for the larger part of the pipe-work of any Organ; and we gravely question if the greatest demands music makes, even to the strained and vitiated ear, compel us to blow organ pipes until they yield sounds approaching the bellowing of fog-horns or the screaming of steam-whistles. Let it not be understood, however, that we condemn, or even undervalue, such commanding stops as the TUBAS and other heavy pressure reeds, or the STENTORPHONE, and other dominating labial stops bearing high-sounding names. All we ask of the organ builder, who is not an artist in his calling, is to draw a line in the wind-pressures for such stops just a little under that which separates a musical tone from a musical noise, if such a paradoxical term is admissible. Let high pressures be confined to such characteristic and assertive stops as are only employed for extraordinary effects in organ music; and then let us have reasonable, moderate, and even low pressures for all those stops which, after all is said and done, are, and will ever continue to be, the true glory of the Organ.

The importance of having the greatest possible variety and the most marked individuality of tone in the numerous families of stops in the Concert Organ cannot be overrated; but such variety and individuality are best arrived at by differences of form, scale, and voicing, and not by piling weights on the long-suffering reservoirs. Every true musician will agree with us in this.

We may conclude these brief remarks on the organ-wind, by pointing out that higher pressures may be consistently adopted for the Concert instrument than for either the Church or Chamber Organ; and that the inclosure of the greater part of the pipe-work in swell-boxes renders it advisable to use the highest safe pressures that the stops will take, without an impairment of their purity and refinement of intonation. Each division of the Concert Organ will require at least two different pressures of wind, while some may require so many as four. The number of pressures and their respective measurements will not only depend upon the stop appointment of the instrument, but largely on the artistic sense of the organ builder, leaving the question of cost out of consideration.

In an earlier part of the present Chapter we endeavored to define, in a few words, the nature and offices of the properly appointed Concert-room Organ; and the conclusion to be arrived at from that definition is that such an Organ may be considered a perfect Organ and a full orchestra combined. Allowing such an idea to be correct, it is quite obvious that the speaking stops which compose the tonal forces of the instrument must group themselves under two classes; one embracing the organ-toned or unimitative stops, and the other the orchestral or imitative stops. In the former group are all those foundation, mutation, and harmonic-corroborating stops which build up the complex tonal structure of the Organ proper;* and which give it its unique grandeur, richness, and rolling volume of sound. No love for display in orchestral coloring or simple beauty in solo effects should divert attention from the all-essential foundation-work and its attendant family of organ-toned stops. Unless the Organ proper is fully appointed, the instrument, however rich it may be in imitative tones, will be hopelessly insufficient.

The different groups or families of stops must be so apportioned in the several divisions of the Organ that, while they mutually enrich and support each other, the two classes of tonality may be kept distinct. To secure this desirable end, a special classification of stops must obtain in each manual division, with just such an encroachment on each other's terrritory as will impart the requisite flexibility and variety to the divisions, and give the performer the maximum of facili-

* See our Chapter on The Tonal Structure of the Organ.

ties for varied combinations and rapid changes of tonal coloring. This all important matter may be left for the present, for it will come prominently forward when we treat of the tonal appointment of the different divisions of the Organ.

In the scaling and voicing of all the pure organ-toned stops, great care must be taken to secure that full volume of refined and characteristic tone which places the Organ beyond imitation by any kind or number of orchestral instruments: and, outside the great family of stops which completes the complex harmonic structure of the instrument, both in the manual and pedal departments, as great a variety of quality and strength of tone should be aimed at as can possibly be obtained, without positively encroaching on imitative qualities. No two stops in the Organ should be exactly alike in tone or strength of voice.

As regards the purely imitative stops little need be said here. They form a fertile field for the genius and manipulative skill of the pipe maker and voicer. In certain directions most satisfactory results have been attained by individual artists in this branch, but much still remains to be done. A much closer imitation of the tones of the orchestral brass instruments is to be desired, notably those of the Horn, the Euphonium, and the Saxophones. The best imitation of the characteristic tones of the Saxophones known to us is that produced by a labial stop invented by Mr. W. E. Haskell, of Philadelphia, Pa. We are strongly of the opinion that if ever the tones of the orchestral Horn are successfully imitated in the Organ, they will be produced from metal, labial pipes, and certainly not by reeds of the ordinary construction. We should be pleased to see organ builders generally set seriously to the interesting task of producing satisfactory imitations or organ equivalents of the string quartet of the orchestra. Certain organ builders have shown what is practicable in this important direction. Prominent among these was the late Edmund Schulze, of Paulinzelle, and the late William Thynne, of London. Nothing has as yet, to our knowledge, been accomplished in the shape of wood, string-toned stops surpassing those made by the former; while the metal VIOLINS and VIOLONCELLOES made by the latter remain as eloquent records of his remarkable skill. We have specimens of Mr. Thynne's work in our possession; and we were for several years intimately acquainted with him, taking a lively interest in his artistic methods of scaling and voicing; we, accordingly, can speak with some authority on the subject of his artistic achievements. Mr. Thynne has had an able successor in the person of Mr. John W. Whiteley, of London, who has invented and made some remarkably fine imitative string-toned stops. These stops are described elsewhere. We have carefully examined and studied all the best works of Edmund Schulze in his English Organs, and can bear testimony to the general excellence of his imitative string-toned stops. What has been done can surely be done again; so we do not despair of finding string-toned stops of great beauty of tone, massed in the manner we advocate, in the Concert-room Organ of the future.

We have already pointed out, in the brief survey of what has been done in the tonal appointment of the Concert-room Organ by leading builders of modern times, that the string-toned forces of the instrument have been very unwisely, and we venture to think very seriously, neglected; yet this class of tone is the backbone of the Organ in its orchestral character. It is remarkable that German, French, and American organ builders have systematically overlooked the great importance and value of these imitative and singularly rich voices.

Remarks on the different families of speaking stops will be found in the following divisional articles, and also in future Chapters.

FIRST ORGAN.

LOWEST CLAVIER—PARTLY EXPRESSIVE.

In speaking of divisions and claviers, we have alluded to the difficulty there obtains in adhering to the old and well-known nomenclature of the several divisions of the manual department in the class of Concert-room Organ now proposed. We remarked that while we are reluctant to interfere with the old-established nomenclature, we can hardly see how it can be retained for the divisions of an instrument in the appointment of which so much that is old-fashioned is swept away, and in which the essential conditions which gave rise, with some sort of reason, to that nomenclature, no longer obtain. We have pointed out that the term Swell Organ, so appropriate in the case of an instrument with only one expressive division, can have no definite significance in relation to an instrument which has every one of its divisions wholly or partly inclosed in swell-boxes. No division is specially a Swell Organ, when the entire instrument may, under certain conditions, be correctly designated one grand Swell Organ. Two other terms should also drop out of use; namely, Choir Organ and Echo Organ. The former is essentially meaningless in connection with the true Concert Organ, whilst the latter is simply absurd and has no *raison d'être* in relation to the modern Organ in its legitimate and dignified treatment. There may not be the same objection to the retention of the terms Great Organ and Solo Organ; but even these are not altogether applicable to any division of the advanced Concert Organ.

Such being the case, we have decided to employ the simple, appropriate, and easily understood terms: First Organ (lowest clavier); Second Organ (second clavier); Third Organ (third clavier); Fourth Organ (fourth clavier); and Fifth Organ (fifth clavier). The term Pedal Organ, being perfectly applicable to the department commanded by the feet of the performer, is retained. All manual divisions, as above enumerated, may be classed under the name of Manual Organ.

The First Organ must be treated as the true foundation of all the manual divisions; forming, in conjunction with a portion of the pedal department, the Organ proper. Its tonal structure should be as complete and correctly proportioned as science can direct and skill accomplish. First of all, the full amount of true organ-tone of the manual unison, or 8 ft., pitch must be provided, with double, or 16 ft., tone added in due subordination: then both the eight and sixteen feet harmonic series must be introduced; the latter being subordinate in every respect to the former. While it is desirable, in this division of the Organ, to have a due amount of 16 ft. tone and its harmonic upper partials, it must be borne in mind that the true manual pitch is that of 8 ft., and that nothing is gained by lowering the pitch an octave, and so assimilating it with the Pedal Organ unison pitch. Whatever stops of 16 ft. pitch are introduced in the First Organ, they must be both in strength and penetrating quality of tone strictly subordinate to the corresponding unison stops; and still more must those stops which strictly belong to the 16 ft. harmonic series, and corroborate certain upper partial tones of the 16 ft. tone, be subordinated to all stops near them in pitch which belong to the 8 ft. harmonic series. It may be mentioned that the only stops, or ranks of pipes in the compound stops, which will have to be considered, belonging to the 16 ft. series, are the QUINT, 5⅓ FT., and the TIERCE, 3⅕ FT. These stand in relation to the 16 ft. tone as the TWELFTH and SEVENTEENTH. The other intervals of this harmonic series are represented by stops of 8 ft., 4 ft., 2⅔ ft., and 2 ft., but as all these intervals likewise belong to the more important 8 ft. harmonic series, the respective stops are provided and proportioned with regard to the foundation unisons of the division, and not to the double or 16 ft. stop or stops. These are rules that must be observed if a well-established unison pitch and a perfect balance of tone is to be secured. There is one question which may present itself to the reader's mind at this point. What character and strength of tone should the organ-toned stop of 16 ft. pitch have with regard to the OPEN DIAPASONS? From both a scientific and artistic standpoint, there can be little doubt that the quality of tone should be similar, but considerably softer or lighter, so as to secure due subordination to the foundation unison when sounding in combination. If a second stop of 16 ft. be desired, it may with advantage take the form of a soft string-toned, open metal stop. Such would be found most valuable in full combinations, relieving the dull effect which too often attends the use of pure organ-toned, manual double stops.

Notwithstanding the practice which has been followed by certain German organ builders of adding a stop of 32 ft. pitch to the chief manual division of their large Church Organs, we unhesitatingly question the wisdom and utility of its introduction in any size or description of Organ; and we fail to discover a single reason, scientific or æsthetic, for the presence of so grave a voice in a division whose true unison pitch is two octaves higher. It certainly need not be contemplated in the scheme for a Concert-room Organ, even should it be of the very largest size. We are pleased to note that in none of the important Concert Organs we have spoken of has such an abnormally grave stop been introduced in any manual division. Should it, however, be thought desirable to introduce so grave a voice, we suggest the addition of a QUINT, 10⅔ FT., which, when drawn with the DOUBLE DIAPASON, 16 FT., will produce the differential tone of 32 ft. pitch—the so-called 'resultant' or 'acoustic tone.' This differential tone will prove quite as much as the manual division can stand from a musical point of view. It will be heard by the sensitive ear, and that is all.

In all the manual divisions the fundamental 8 ft. tone must assert itself with overwhelming predominance, but in no division more so than in the one under immediate consideration. The fundamental tone of the First Organ should be furnished by at least two OPEN DIAPASONS of metal, one of large scale and powerful intonation, with a voice full, round, and commanding; the other of contrasting quality, smaller in scale, and with a voice of rich and somewhat penetrating character. This decided contrast, apart from variety, is of great value in preventing sympathy between the stops, and a consequent loss of power and volume in their combined voices. In Organs of the first magnitude, a third OPEN DIAPASON, 8 FT., should be added, formed of wood pipes, as made and voiced by Schulze.* This, again, with the view of materially increasing the variety and volume of unison tone, and avoiding any tendency toward sympathy. The next unison stop should be a covered stop of great body and filling-up quality. No better stop than the DOPPELFLÖTE can be adopted, for its tone is characterized, when it is voiced by a master-hand, by great volume, dignity, and sonorousness: as a mixing stop it is singularly valuable. With the four unisons already mentioned, the true foundation-tone of the First Organ is secured; but, leaving reeds and other inclosed unisons out of consideration for the moment, at least one other open metal stop of 8 ft. ought to be added, uninclosed; and this, to secure variety and contrast, should be a GAMBA, of a broad, normal string-tone, sufficiently pungent to assert itself through the whole pure organ-tone of the division.

We now enter on the important subject of the harmonic structure based on the foundation unison or diapason-tone. There can be no doubt that the First Organ—the true Organ—should be characterized by as great a completeness as possible in its tonal structure; and all the facts that the science of acoustics has revealed must be carefully utilized in its development. In the unison harmonic series, the first element, after the fundamental tone, is the OCTAVE, which furnishes the first and most important upper partial tone. The stops which represent this tone are of 4 ft. pitch, and should be, to some extent, under control, so that the tone may be graduated in intensity to suit the strengths of the different fundamental unisons. All the stops which corroborate the higher upper partial tones should be under control for a similar end. These facts have, however, never been practically recognized by any European builder, if we judge by existing English and Continental Organs. An OCTAVE, 4 FT., formed of open metal pipes of about the same scale and strength of tone as the smaller OPEN DIAPASON, may with advantage be planted, along with the double and unison OPEN DIAPASONS, on an uninclosed wind-chest; but all the other stops of 4 ft. pitch and the two stops already named as belonging to the 16 ft. harmonic series, should unquestionably be inclosed and rendered flexible.

Let it be understood at this point that we advocate, in relation to the division of the Concert Organ now under consideration, the planting of the stops of 16 ft., the OPEN DIAPASONS, 8 FT., the other stops of 8 ft. pitch, as already mentioned, and at least one open metal OCTAVE, 4 ft., on an uninclosed wind-chest; and that every other stop introduced in the division be planted on a wind-chest inclosed in a swell-box. By this treatment the First Organ becomes partly flexible and expressive, and has all its higher harmonic-corroborating stops and its reed stops under proper control. The unexpressive subdivision may be considerably added to in instruments of very large size.

* Magnificent pipes of this class are to be found in the Organ, by Schulze, in the Church of St. Bartholomew, Armley, England.

The stops required to complete the 8 ft. harmonic series are as follows: 1. A small-scaled metal OCTAVE, 4 FT., having a bright voice of medium strength. 2. A TWELFTH, 2⅔ FT., representing the second upper partial tone: this should be slightly softer than No. 1. 3. A SUPER-OCTAVE, 2 FT., representing the third upper partial tone: to be somewhat softer than No. 2. 4. A TIERCE or SEVENTEENTH, 1⅗ ft., representing the fourth upper partial tone: this may be considerably softer than No. 2. 5. A LARIGOT or NINETEENTH, 1⅓ ft., representing the fifth upper partial tone: this should be slightly softer than the preceding. 6. A SEPTIÈME, 1⅐ ft., representing the sixth upper partial tone: this stop need only be introduced in Organs of large size; and when introduced it must be of small scale and of comparatively soft intonation. 7. A TWENTY-SECOND, 1 ft., representing the seventh upper partial tone: voiced softer than No. 5. Of course these remarks on the relative strengths of tone must be accepted as of general application only. Every Organ should be carefully schemed and artistically balanced in its tonal structure; and this cannot be accomplished on paper, but only in actual work, under the cultivated ear and the artistic sense of the musician.

It may be objected by the organ builder that it is inexpedient to introduce stops of so high a pitch as the NINETEENTH, SEPTIÈME, and TWENTY-SECOND, especially in an instrument which has a manual compass to c^4, on account of the difficulty of carrying up such small ranks to the top note. But this need be no barrier to their introduction, for they may be discontinued where their pipes become undesirably small, or break into the octave below at any convenient note in the top octave. The stops should be discontinued or broken on different notes. They may be associated together as a MIXTURE, but much will be gained by having them under independent control.

Notwithstanding the unusual completeness of the above scheme, the general harmonic structure of the First Organ will not be satisfactory without the addition of one or more compound harmonic-corroborating stops, which will carry the harmonic series of upper partial tones still higher throughout the lower octaves of the manual compass and considerably enrich the upper octaves. Such MIXTURES, when carefully schemed, and scientifically proportioned in strength of tone with regard to the other harmonic-corroborating stops, are of the greatest value, imparting a mysterious richness of tonal coloring, and a fascinating complexity of structure to the pure organ-tone, which no other class of stops can furnish.

Having devoted an entire chapter to the Compound Stops of the Organ, it is undesirable to do more here than convey a clear idea of what would be suitable for such a division of the Concert Organ as we have now under consideration. The two following compositions for full-toned MIXTURES may be accepted as representative :—

FULL MIXTURE—VI. and V. RANKS.

CC	to	B,	. . . .	15—19—22—24—26—29.
c^1	to	b^1,	. . . .	8—12—15—17—19—22.
c^2	to	b^2,	. . . . .	8—12—17—19—22.
c^3	to	c^4,	. . . . . .	1— 8—10—12—15.

FULL MIXTURE—V. RANKS.

CC to e^1,	. . . . . .	15—19—22—26—29.
f^1 to b^2,	. . . . . .	8—12—15—19—22.
c^3 to c^4,	. . . . . .	1— 5— 8—12—15.

The first MIXTURE comprises a third-sounding rank throughout, placed in the most favorable position for such an interval. From CC to $b^1 = 36$ notes, there are, in addition to the third-sounding rank, three octave- and two fifth-sounding ranks; and in the treble, from c^2 to b^2, there are, in addition to the continued third-sounding rank, two octave- and two fifth-sounding ranks; and from c^3 to c^4 there are one unison-, two octave-, one third-, and one fifth-sounding ranks. This last break theoretically belongs to the 16 ft. harmonic series, and on this account imparts fulness to the acute portion of the manual compass. The second MIXTURE has no third-sounding rank; octave- and fifth-sounding ranks alternating throughout. In both compositions, the highest rank of each break is octave-sounding, for that interval is unquestionably the best, tonally considered, in such a position. It is not, however, imperative that such an arrangement should obtain. In the scaling and voicing of these MIXTURES, and, indeed, every compound stop in the Organ, the builder must accept the teaching of the natural phenomena of sound as produced by the human voice and the more perfect orchestral instruments. Just as we find that in a rich, compound musical sound the upper partial tones decrease in strength as they ascend in pitch until they become inaudible, so must all the ranks of pipes inserted in the Organ with the view of corroborating the upper partial tones of the fundamental unisons be similarly graduated in strength of intonation. Probably no teaching of acoustical science has been more grievously misunderstood or more pertinaciously ignored by organ builders than this. The early mediæval Organ was simply a large MIXTURE; but the higher-pitched ranks it comprised were not introduced for the purpose of corroborating upper partial tones. The series of pipes on each note formed a musical chord, and all the pipes were practically equal in strength of tone. When the Organ was developed from this early model, and large stops of an independent character were introduced, the MIXTURE was not abandoned: on the contrary, it was retained and occupied a very prominent position in the tonal appointment. Later it was discovered that stops of the MIXTURE class produced certain remarkable acoustic effects: but the early organ builders seriously blundered in their treatment of these assertive stops, probably through imperfect knowledge, or a natural clinging to tradition or precedent. Their successors followed much on the same unscientific lines, for they had no observer like Helmholtz to teach them the true office of the compound stops and their scientific relationship to the prime tones of the Organ. So matters went on in the time-honored grooves century after century. The inartistic character, to use no stronger term, of all the old harmonic-corroborating stops, in their uncontrollable condition, has gradually induced some organ builders, of observation and refinement, to restrict to an undesirable extent the introduction of MIXTURES and certain harmonic-corroborating ranks in their later Organs. We will not say that the pocket has had nothing to do with this modern spirit of restriction. Compound stops, if properly made, voiced, and regulated, are comparatively expensive and very troublesome; and few indeed are the organ builders of to-day who are sufficiently artistic, or sufficiently well paid, to forget such facts. We may add that there are very few organ builders who have studied acoustics and the phenomena of sound sufficiently to realize the importance of the harmonic-corroborating stops, or to treat them in a thoroughly scientific manner. In this, as in too many other tonal matters, the rule of thumb prevails in the organ-building world to-day. There are hopeful signs, however, of an improvement in scientific and artistic treatment. Let us hope, with our present knowledge of the phenomena of sound and the complex structure of the several varieties of musical tones, that nothing will be omitted from the tonal structure of the Concert-room Organ that is conducive to the production of pure organ-tone and imitative orchestral-tone. Prominent among the forces which aid in building up complex musical sounds in the Organ, and which enter as potent factors in *timbre* creation, stand the compound harmonic-corroborating stops.

One word more with reference to the harmonic-corroborating stops. It is understood that they are to be inclosed in a swell-box,—say swell-box No. 1,—and so placed under control as to be capable of having any desirable degree of softness given to them. Now comes the obvious question: What should their strength of tone be when heard at their full power, with the swell-box open? This is very easily answered. Let all the stops of the division which yield the fundamental unison organ-tone, and which are outside the swell-box, be drawn; then let all the stops which represent the 8 feet harmonic series be so voiced and regulated as to complete the desirable unison *compound tone* in the manner consistent with scientific teaching, and according to a true and refined musical sense. Let there be no scream, or crash like breaking glass, as the notes are put down by the fingers: on the contrary, let the whole complex structure combine in one grand volume of rich and refined sound, of which the sensitive ear feels assured it could never tire. When such a result is attained, the Organ in its proper form is safe; and the modifying operation of the swell may enter on its mission—to throw upon the several combinations of unison tone various garments of subtile and mysterious beauty, changing in musical texture and color at the will of the performer.

Such an Organ—call it a Great Organ if you will—is no longer the loud intractable thing one meets with in all instruments built on old lines, but a flexible and responsive division, bending itself to the will and requirements of the musician in a way unknown and scarcely foreshadowed in the present prevailing system of organ construction and appointment.

The First Organ, having its foundation-work and its harmonic structure complete, calls for only a few other stops for the purpose of imparting variety and richness to its many combinations. Another labial stop of 8 ft. pitch should be inserted; and this may assume the form of a large-scaled covered, or half-covered, metal stop of broad and filling tone, similar to the BOURDON, 8 FT., in the Great division of the Concert Organ in the Town Hall, at Manchester, constructed by Cavaillé-Coll; or it may be a large-scaled covered wood stop of full and sonorous intonation. Another stop of 4 ft. pitch should be added, preferably in the form of a HARMONIC FLUTE of large scale. Three reed stops are desirable in this division, while two are essential. The three stops comprise a DOUBLE TRUMPET, 16 FT., a TRUMPET, 8 FT., and a CLARION, 4 FT. All these should be of a bold and broad tone, imparting great dignity to the full combination when the swell is open, and great richness to the foundation-tone when modified in power by the action of the swell. In an Organ of medium size the DOUBLE TRUMPET may be omitted.

The following is the Specification of the complete division, based upon the particulars above given. It is, however, merely suggestive; while for a Concert-room Organ of the first magnitude it is essentially complete:—

FIRST ORGAN—LOWEST CLAVIER.

PARTLY EXPRESSIVE—COMPASS CC to $c^4 = 61$ NOTES.

UNEXPRESSIVE SUBDIVISION.

1.	DOUBLE OPEN DIAPASON,	Metal. 16	ft.	6.	OPEN DIAPASON, .	Wood. 8	ft.
2.	CONTRA-GAMBA, . . .	Metal. 16	"	7.	GAMBA, ...	Metal. 8	"
3.	SUB-QUINT, ...	Wood. $10\frac{2}{3}$	"	8.	DOPPELFLÖTE, . .	Wood. 8	"
4.	OPEN DIAPASON, MAJOR,	Metal. 8	"	9.	CLARABELLA, . .	Wood. 8	"
5.	OPEN DIAPASON, MINOR,	Metal. 8	"	10.	OCTAVE, MAJOR, .	Metal. 4	"

EXPRESSIVE SUBDIVISION.

Inclosed in Swell-box No. 1.

11.	BOURDON, ...	Metal. 8	ft.	19.	SEVENTEENTH, .	Metal. $1\frac{3}{5}$	ft.
12.	GROSSFLÖTE, ...	Wood. 8	"	20.	NINETEENTH, . .	Metal. $1\frac{1}{3}$	"
13.	QUINT, ...	Metal. $5\frac{1}{3}$	"	21.	SEPTIEME, . . .	Metal. $1\frac{1}{7}$	"
14.	OCTAVE, MINOR, . . .	Metal. 4	"	22.	TWENTY-SECOND, .	Metal. 1	"
15.	HARMONIC FLUTE, . .	Metal. 4	"	23.	MIXTURE, . .	VI. and V. ranks	
16.	TIERCE, ...	Metal. $3\frac{1}{5}$	"	24.	DOUBLE TRUMPET,	Metal. 16	ft.
17.	TWELFTH, ...	Metal. $2\frac{2}{3}$	"	25.	TRUMPET, . . .	Metal. 8	"
18.	SUPER-OCTAVE, . . .	Metal. 2	"	26.	CLARION, . . .	Metal. 4	"

The Expressive subdivision to be brought on and put off the First Clavier by thumb-pistons or touches; and to be also commanded by the Double-touch of the clavier.

Stops Nos. 11, 12, 15, 24, 25, and 26 to be on wind of 6 inches; and all the other stops to be on wind of 4 inches.

SECOND ORGAN.

SECOND CLAVIER—PARTLY EXPRESSIVE.

We now come to the consideration of the second division of the Concert-room Organ—one which, while it is of hardly less importance than the first division, must present in its tonal appointment a marked contrast. Indeed, it is one of the leading principles in the system of organ construction we are now advocating that each division shall have clearly and boldly marked tonal characteristics of its own. The present worn-out system of stop disposition, which to a very large extent makes each manual division (with, perhaps, the exception of the Solo Organ, when such a division is provided) little better than a duplicate of the others, is radically wrong; and results in a great loss of variety, and, accordingly, in a serious sacrifice of the beauty, scope, and utility of the instrument.

The importance and value of having a different range of distinctive tonal coloring in each of the divisions of the Concert Organ (and indeed in every description of Organ) must be freely acknowledged by the *musician*,—not only on account of the immense facilities it gives him in painting his most complex and expressive tonal pictures, and in keeping all his different effects distinct, but also in leading him to the realization of musical compositions hitherto practically impossible of interpretation through the medium of the Organ. The Organ constituted as we propose becomes an instrument for the *virtuoso;* and, with its limitless range of tonal combination and powers of expression, is only second to that great musical machine—the Grand Orchestra.

This question is just worth serious consideration: Are Organs to be constructed for the pleasure and profit of the organ builder, or for *art* and the *musician?* Let each reader answer this question as his sense dictates. We can imagine only one rational reply.

In the first place, let it be understood that the Second Organ is to be, in its chief part, expressive; and, accordingly, will have the larger number of its stops inclosed in the swell-box No. 1, which contains the expressive subdivision of the First Organ. There can be no question that an independent swell-box for the Second Organ would be an advantage so far as tonal effects and *nuances* are concerned; but, on the other hand, the difficulty of readily commanding and comfortably operating a number of expression-levers must be freely acknowledged.

Now with reference to the tonal or stop appointment of this Organ. As the First Organ must be characterized by all that makes the true Organ the unapproachable instrument it is—grandeur, majesty, and sublimity of tone—so must the Second Organ, in valuable contrast, be characterized by subdued dignity, refinement, and liquid brightness of tone. There should be no sympathy, in the acoustical sense of the term, between the voices of the respective Organs, while there must be the closest bond of union between them in all that relates to musical expression and tonal light and shade.

Although in the Second Organ, as in all the manual divisions, there must be a decided predominance of unison tone, the sub-octave should not be neglected. Here, for more than one reason, it should be furnished in the unexpressive subdivision by the DOUBLE DULCIANA, 16 FT., and in the expressive subdivision by the LIEBLICHGEDECKT, 16 FT., preferably of wood throughout. As one of the distinctive features of the Second Organ should be the presence of the LIEBLICHGEDECKT family of stops in its complete form, the several members, in addition to the above-named double stop, may be given here; namely, the LIEBLICHGEDECKT, 8 FT., wood and metal or all wood if preferred; LIEBLICHGEDECKT OCTAVE, 4 FT., metal; LIEBLICHGEDECKT QUINT, 2⅔ FT., metal, of small scale, and soft intonation; and the LIEBLICHGEDECKT SUPER-OCTAVE, 2 FT., metal, also of soft intonation. The upper octave of this last-named stop will require to be of open pipes. That of the QUINT may be similarly treated. It is perhaps unnecessary to point out to the musician the charming effects and combinations which can be produced by this family of sweetly-voiced stops alone; yet only in a very few instances are more than two members of the family found together in one division of an Organ, and, accordingly, the beauty and peculiar character of such combinations are not commonly realized by organists. In no Organ known to us is the complete family inserted even in a distributed fashion.

The more important labial stops for the Second Organ are the GEIGENPRINCIPAL, 8 FT., of medium scale, voiced to yield a bright tone of considerable volume and good mixing quality; the SALICIONAL, 8 FT., of rich silvery tone; and the KERAULOPHON, 8 FT., voiced to yield a round, horn-like tone. As the Second Organ will be largely used for accompaniment, still softer-voiced unisons are necessary. These may be a DULCIANA, 8 FT., of pure organ-tone; a VIOLA DA GAMBA of imitative tone; and a VOX ANGELICA, 8 FT., of the softest intonation possible in organ pipes. These three stops will form charming combinations with the LIEBLICHGEDECKT family.

As there is a stop of 4 ft. pitch provided in the LIEBLICHGEDECKT series, it will only be necessary, or essential, to add another stop of the same pitch. This may be a FLAUTO TRAVERSO, 4 FT. Should it, however, be deemed desirable to insert an octave stop in the unexpressive subdivision, a SALICET, or OCTAVE SALICIONAL, 4 FT., would be suitable. The three stops of octave pitch will be ample both for the amount of unison tone in the division and for the production of the necessary variety of tone in combination.

One additional SUPER-OCTAVE should be included in the scheme; and as that in the LIEBLICHGEDECKT series is a covered stop, the second may appropriately be a FLAGEOLET, 2 FT., formed of open metal pipes, with a clear voice slightly softer than the higher octaves of the FLAUTO TRAVERSO.

As every division of an Organ, in which the majority of the unison stops produce sounds naturally deficient in upper partials, should have those harmonic elements which are requisite for the production of rich musical *timbres* and satisfactory compound tones, it is necessary, in the division now under consideration, to further extend its tonal structure by the addition of a compound stop, corroborating several of the higher upper partials of the fundamental unison tone. In the OCTAVES, QUINT, and SUPER-OCTAVES, the three most important upper partials are adequately represented; but these are not sufficient, in combination with the unisons, to produce the desirable richness of compound tone; and, accordingly, a softly-voiced MIXTURE such as the following becomes necessary:—

DULCIANA CORNET—VI. RANKS.

CC to BB, . . .	15—19—22—24—26—29.
C to f^1, . . .	8—12—15—17—19—22.
f♯ to f^2, . . .	1— 8—12—17—19—22.
$f♯^2$ to c^4, . . .	1— 5— 8—10—12—15.

This MIXTURE should be made of DULCIANA pipes, carefully voiced and artistically regulated so as to give the octaves and fifths a slight predominance over the third-sounding rank. Such a compound stop is of the highest value in an accompanimental division of the Organ; and may be used in hundreds of combinations in which a louder and less complete MIXTURE would be tonally objectionable.

Having provided in the Second Organ what may be considered the essential labial stops, we have now to decide what should be inserted in the form of reed stops. In this matter two questions claim our consideration: First, seeing that the division is in its nature well adapted for accompaniment, ought the reed stops to be similarly adapted, and be of a quiet and refined mixing character, rather reinforcing and enriching the general tone of the division than introducing decidedly independent elements into it? Secondly, seeing that the labial stops of the division are, amongst themselves, deficient in prominent solo voices, should not this deficiency be made up by the reed stops? If it was of the first importance that the stops of each individual division of the Organ should display extremes of tonal contrast among themselves, rather than that such extremes of contrast should obtain between the stops in the separate divisions, then the second question would certainly have to be answered in the affirmative. But, on the contrary, as it is most important that each division of the Organ should have a distinct tonal character, as well as a definite chief office in the general scheme of the instrument, it is evident that the affirmative reply should be given to the first question. By a careful and judicious selection of the reed stops it will be possible to meet all demands made on the Second Organ. It is desirable that the reeds should be of a light, mixing, and reinforcing character, while they should also lend themselves to certain solo effects, distinct from those possible in the other divisions of the instrument.

The first reed should, in our opinion, be a softly-toned stop of 16 ft. pitch, of a quality resembling, as closely as practicable, the family of orchestral Saxophones. A stop of this character was made for us by the late Mr. Hilborne L. Roosevelt. It is a free reed with slender conical tubes. As a stop of 16 ft. pitch it should be labeled CONTRA-SAXOPHONE. The desirability of introducing such a quality of tone into the Concert-room Organ may be realized from the following remarks on the orchestral Saxophones, by Berlioz:

"These new voices given to the orchestra possess most rare and precious qualities. Soft and penetrating in the higher part, full and rich in the lower part, their medium has something profoundly expressive. It is, in short, a quality of tone *sui generis*, presenting vague analogies with the sounds of the Violoncello, of the Clarinet, and Corno Inglese, and invested with a brazen tinge which imparts quite a peculiar accent."

A stop with a tone resembling that described by Berlioz would be of the greatest value for both combinational and solo effects, while it would hold itself perfectly distinct from all the other reed stops of the same pitch in the Organ.

The next reed stop suggested for the Second Organ is the CORNO INGLESE, 8 FT. tone. This should also be a free reed, as usually made by certain European builders. It would be a most valuable unison voice, and an admirable octave to the Contra-Saxophone, while it would aid materially in keeping the distinctive character of the division. Berlioz, speaking of the Corno Inglese, says: "It is a melancholy, dreamy, and rather noble voice." The quality of the instrument is somewhat similar to that of the Oboe; but it is of a more sombre and grave character. It is usual in certain quarters, as it was with Mr. Roosevelt in particular, to put the Corno Inglese on wind of a somewhat high pressure. This practice is, we venture to think, a mistake; for with a high pressure it is impossible to secure that "melancholy, dreamy, and rather noble voice" which Berlioz justly considers to be the characteristic beauty of the orchestral instrument.

When the Organ is large, other unison reed stops may with advantage be added to this division. The most valuable, in our opinion, bearing in view the general character of the Second Organ and its stop appointment, would be the Musette or Schalmei, a small-scaled stop of 8 ft. tone, which would form charming combinations with the several Lieblichgedeckts and other soft stops of the division, as well as prove extremely useful for characteristic passages in music of the *Pastorale* style. Should a bolder-voiced stop be desired, either a small-scaled Clarinet, or Oboe and Bassoon, 8 ft., may be inserted. As both these stops are made by German and French reed voicers with free reeds, they should be here used in that form, completing the free reed family in this division of the Organ. Should they be preferred in their usual form,—as striking reeds,—care should be taken to voice them in a distinctive manner, so that they may contrast with the full-toned and imitative stops of the same names in the other divisions of the instrument. There is a decided prejudice among English organ builders against the introduction of free reed stops of all classes, almost amounting to contempt, but not a contempt born of familiarity, rather one proceeding from want of knowledge and from indifference. The amount of indifference in relation to artistic matters connected with organ appointment evinced by English and American organ builders of the average class, is as great as it is regrettable. Free reeds are out of the every-day course, and demand both extreme care and the expenditure of considerable time in their construction; accordingly our organ builders profess to condemn them as insufficient, and systematically set their faces against the insertion of such stops in Specifications. Two or three examples exist in English Organs: there is a Cor Anglais in the Concert Organ of the Town Hall, Leeds, and in the Organ of Westminster Abbey. The latter was made by Messrs. Abbey, of Versailles, for Messrs. Hill and Son. Both these stops are free reeds.

There is a class of stops which, in small Concert-room Organs, might be adopted instead of the stops above mentioned. We allude to the German Physharmonica, as met with in the Lucerne and Freiburg Organs, inserted by Herr Haas. In both these instruments the Physharmonica appears of 8 ft. pitch, and as free reeds inclosed in small special swell-boxes. In the former Organ the reeds have no resonators; but in the Freiburg Organ we found resonators attached to them, to the increase and great improvement of their tones. The Physharmonica lends itself to many pleasing accompanimental effects; notably in combination with some soft-toned labial stop, as an accompaniment to solos of a flute character. Of course, it is impossible for stops of the Physharmonica class to rival either in volume or dignity of tone such legitimate organ stops as the CONTRA-SAXOPHONE, CORNO INGLESE, and MUSETTE.

A reed stop of 4 ft. pitch, preferably of the OBOE class, might with advantage be added to this division; but, except in very large Organs, and when cost and space are of no consideration, such a stop may be dispensed with. In our representative scheme we have provided ample 4 ft. tone for all ordinary purposes: for very full combinations, when both the First and Second Organs are coupled, as one grand Swell Organ, supported by the unexpressive OPEN DIAPASONS, etc., the CLARION will amply meet all requirements.

A TREMOLANT should be attached to the expressive subdivision of the Second Organ, affecting only the most suitable stops.

A few words may be added on the subject of the swell-box which is shared by the expressive subdivisions of both the First and Second Organs. The position of the instrument and the space at the disposal of the organ builder will, of necessity, affect both the construction and proportions of the swell-box, so no hard and fast directions can be given on these matters: but we may point out the desirability of having this swell-box fitted with the largest possible amount of shutter-work, so that when it is open the minimum of obstruction may be presented to the free emission of sound. When circumstances permit, the front and both ends of the box should be shuttered; the shutters or louvres being pivoted vertically, and made to open in the manner best calculated to throw the sound directly into the concert-room. The following is the Specification of the Second Organ:—

SECOND ORGAN—SECOND CLAVIER.

PARTLY EXPRESSIVE—COMPASS CC to c^4 = 61 NOTES.

UNEXPRESSIVE SUBDIVISION.

1.	DOUBLE DULCIANA, .	Metal. 16 ft.	3.	VIOLA DA GAMBA, .	Metal. 8 ft.
2.	SALICIONAL, . . .	Metal. 8 "	4.	DULCIANA, ...	Metal. 8 "

EXPRESSIVE SUBDIVISION.

Inclosed in Swell-box No. 1.

5.	LIEBLICHGEDECKT, . .	Wood. 16 ft.	12.	LIEBLICHGEDECKT, .	Metal. 2⅔ ft.
6.	GEIGENPRINCIPAL, . .	Metal. 8 "	13.	LIEBLICHGEDECKT, .	Metal. 2 "
7.	KERAULOPHON, . . .	Metal. 8 "	14.	FLAGEOLET.	Metal. 2 "
8.	VOX ANGELICA, . .	Metal. 8 "	15.	DULCIANA CORNET, .	" VI. ranks
9.	LIEBLICHGEDECKT,	Wood and Metal. 8 "	16.	CONTRA-SAXOPHONE, .	Metal. 16 ft.
10.	LIEBLICHGEDECKT, .	Metal. 4 "	17.	CORNO INGLESE, . . .	Metal. 8 "
11.	FLAUTO TRAVERSO, .	Metal. 4 "	18.	MUSETTE, ...	Metal. 8 "
			I.	TREMOLANT.	

This Expressive Subdivision to be brought on and put off the Second Clavier by thumb-pistons or touches; and to be also commanded by the Double-touch of the clavier.

Stops Nos. 7, 8, 11, 14, 16, 17, and 18 to be on wind of 3½ inches; and all the other stops to be on wind of 3 inches. The TREMOLANT to affect the stops on wind of 3½ inches.

THIRD ORGAN.

THIRD CLAVIER—ENTIRELY EXPRESSIVE.

The division of the Concert-room Organ we have now to consider is, according to our method of appointment, the most extensive, and, viewed from the orchestral standpoint, the most important, in the instrument. We here propose a system of appointment which has never been suggested by any organ builder, or been outlined in any published treatise on organ-building; but which we feel certain will, sooner or later, be adopted in all properly constituted Concert Organs. Such matters, however, move slowly, whatever their merits or advantages may be, simply because organ builders are a most conservative class of men, very reluctant to trouble themselves with new ideas; and, on the other hand, their clients and the organ-playing world in general are curiously indifferent on all matters connected with the science and art of organ construction. A very different state of affairs will in all probability obtain when, in the case of the erection of an important Organ, the services of an Organ Architect will be deemed as essential as are the services of the architect who directs the erection of the concert-room in which the Organ is to stand. The Organ Architect must have a thorough knowledge of all the branches of organ-building,—scientific, artistic, and practical,—and after he has prepared the scheme and plans of the instrument he must have the superintendence of its construction, as in ordinary architectural practice. Until this business-like method of procedure is adopted all unskilled purchasers of Organs will practically be at the mercy of organ builders. The architect's commission must be paid by the client; for under no circumstances must any money pass from the organ builder into the architect's hands in the form of commission, *sub rosa*, or otherwise.

As our Third Organ practically occupies the place of the ordinary Swell Organ, in the instruments at present constructed on old lines, it is almost unnecessary to state that it is to be *entirely expressive*, and that to the extreme limit possible in the Grand Organ. In our scheme, so far developed, there is one large swell-box inclosing sixteen stops of the First Organ and fourteen stops of the Second Organ; affording the performer, with and without the uninclosed subdivisions, immense resources in tonal coloring, degrees of power, and expressive effects. Pure organ-tone, or that broad and dignified quality of tone which belongs to the Organ proper, being adequately provided in the First and Second Organs, we may now turn our attention to other classes of tonal coloring.

For the Third Organ the orchestra becomes the field of study and inspiration. We propose dividing this Third Organ into two sections, practically independent of each other; yet, as they are to be played from the same clavier, they will unite in producing an inexhaustible series of charming and effective combinations of an orchestral character. Each of these sections or subdivisions is to have an entirely distinct tonal appointment and coloring; and so that the maximum powers of flexibility and expression may be secured, as well as the most varied *nuances*, we propose inclosing each section in an independent swell-box, which, for clearness of description and easy reference, may be designated swell-box No. 2, and swell-box No. 3.

Although it is a matter of little moment which of the sections of the Third Organ is first considered, it may be convenient to take that which occupies swell-box No. 2. This section comprises the stops which represent the stringed instruments of the grand orchestra.

We may here remark, in addition to what has already been said in the short review of certain representative Concert-room instruments, that all the Concert Organs hitherto constructed are, in proportion to their size, lamentably deficient in imitative string-toned stops; and that this deficiency is all the more apparent through the few stops of the class, which are inserted, being dispersed in different divisions and so rendered incapable of being massed or concentrated for special and desirable effects. Now, the massing of the imitative string-toned stops, under proper conditions, in an instrument such as the Concert-room Organ, is about as important, from a musical point of view, as the massing of the stringed instruments in the orchestra. We were the first to formulate this idea with reference to the Organ,* and we feel convinced it will, with some more of our advanced ideas, receive recognition in the near future.

Glancing at the string section of the orchestra, we find four classes of instruments used, all members of the Violin family; namely, Violins, Violas, Violoncelloes, and Double Basses. To these the Harp is occasionally added; but, as it does not produce tones similar to those of the bowed instruments, it need not be considered here. In the orchestra, the number of instruments of the Violin family is usually and correctly more than twice that of all the other instruments put together. Berlioz gives in his scheme for a full orchestra of 119 performers, 41 Violins, 18 Violas, 15 Violoncelloes, and 10 Double Basses—in all 84 bowed instruments. For a smaller orchestra of 80 performers there should be provided, say, 30 Violins, 12 Violas, 10 Violoncelloes, and 7 Double Basses. From these figures it must be apparent how important the body of strings is in the tonal structure of the orchestra; and surely they must teach us that in a Concert Organ, which will be constantly used for the rendition of music originally composed for the orchestra, the complete family of imitative string-toned stops should be inserted, and that in such a manner as to be immediately available for massive passages and the richest effects of compound string-tone.

It must be borne in mind that of all the instruments invented by man, the bowed instruments are the richest in harmonic upper partial tones; and that organ pipes generally are essentially weak in such upper partial tones. Certainly the small-scaled pipes used for the imitative string-tone stops, as voiced by a Schulze, a Thynne, or a Whiteley, are richer in harmonic upper partial tones than any other description of labial pipes; but after all is done that can be done, their voices are naturally deficient in comparison with the wonderful compound tones produced by the bowed instruments. Such being the case, it is useless to attempt to represent the complex sounds, produced by the stringed instruments of the

* In the series of "Notes on the Concert-room Organ," published in *The English Mechanic*, in 1887–8.

orchestra, in the Organ by the simple association of three, four, or five unison and double string-toned stops, which are all that can be found in the largest Organs constructed up to the present time. No: if the problem is to be solved, and an adequate and truly characteristic imitative string-toned section is to be secured, all must be done on strictly scientific lines, tempered by an artistic feeling and a consummate musical sense.

The section of the Third Organ which is inclosed in swell-box No. 2 can, however, only embrace what may be considered the main, unison portion of the imitative string-toned forces; for the chief sub-octave portion, which furnishes the equivalent of the Double Bass tone of the orchestra, must be placed in the Pedal Organ. This is necessary, not only on account of the space such large stops require for their proper accommodation, and the consequent difficulty of providing room for them in swell-boxes of reasonable dimensions, but so that the bass may be kept independent from the tenor and treble parts in elaborate passages for the strings, and in other orchestral movements. Independence is so necessary in all the parts, that provision must be made for freedom and separate expression in the upper parts by placing two or three imitative string-toned stops, of 8 ft. pitch, preferably of a marked solo and very assertive character, in another division.

The foregoing remarks have been deemed necessary for the proper understanding of the matter under consideration. We may now proceed to the stop appointment of the first section of the Third Organ. Every stop in this section should either be of the VIOL family, or of a quality of tone conducive to the production of the rich, compound, imitative quality of string-tone aimed at. In the first place, a sufficient volume of unison or ground tone must be provided by four or five stops of 8 ft. pitch, made to different scales and voiced to different strengths. To these should be added a covered stop, preferably a QUINTATEN,* of 8 ft. pitch, for the purpose of imparting to the pungent and somewhat thin tones of the VIOLS the full and sonorous qualities of the orchestral instruments. The tonal appointment may be as follows: Let two VIOLS, of a full and bold tone, be inserted, tuned in perfect unison, and be considered in the scheme of the section as two VIOLONCELLOES, 8 FT.; then let two unisons of bright and pungent quality be added, and considered as two VIOLINS, 8 FT. To these should be added a VIOLA, 8 FT., of softer tone, tuned a beat or two sharp, but only sufficiently so to impart to the general volume of unison string-tone the *nervous* character of a number of bowed instruments played in unison. We do not here mean anything approaching the objectionable out-of-tunism which characterizes the mis-called VOIX CÉLESTES of so many organ builders. And to complete the foundation-tone of the section, let the QUINTATEN, 8 FT., of soft intonation, be inserted. These six stops, if artistically made, may be accepted as representing, in the Organ, the fundamental or prime tones of several Violins, Violas, and Violoncelloes; but the resultant tones are still deficient in respect to that rich and complex tonal coloring which is the glory of the sounds produced by those orchestral instruments.

*The stop here signified is commonly labeled QUINTATON or QUINTATÖN, but both modes of spelling are incorrect. The correct name is QUINTATEN, the abbreviated rendering of *Quintam tenentes*.— See Helmholtz's work "On the Sensations of Tone," London, 1875; pages 50 and 142.

As we have remarked, the stops of the VIOL family are richer in natural upper partial tones than any other class of labial stops; and to the prominence of these over-tones is due the *timbre* which so closely imitates the sounds of the bowed instruments: but still it is quite impossible to produce a satisfactory imitation of the compound sounds of a mass of orchestral stringed instruments by the simple multiplication of unison stops. Scientific investigation has told us wherein lie the peculiar richness and distinctive character of the tones of the Violin family; and we must accept the teaching if we desire to produce truly artistic results. Accordingly, in addition to the ground-work of unison tone, already provided, a series of harmonic-corroborating stops must be inserted, just as in the First Organ; but here infinitely more care and skill must be exercised in the just gradation of strength and assertiveness in all the ranks. In the first place, two OCTAVES should be inserted, of different strengths of tone, so as to be available, singly, in combinations of different degrees of fulness; but, with both drawn, the octave tone should not be too assertive for the full strength of the unison. A TWELFTH, FIFTEENTH, and SEVENTEENTH should be added to corroborate the second, third, and fourth upper partials. These are the most important of the harmonic series, and all their pipes should belong to the VIOL class, and be voiced in a similar manner to those forming the unison VIOLS. The series need not be carried farther in independent stops, but should be completed with a VIOL MIXTURE of VII., VI., and V. ranks, the composition of which may be as follows:—

VIOL MIXTURE—VII., VI., and V. RANKS.

CC to F♯, . .	15	19	22	26	29	33	36
G to e^1, . .	8	12	15	19	22	26	29
f^1 to d^2, . .	1	8	12	15	19	12	26
d♯^{2} to b^2, . .	1	5	8	12	15	19	22
c^3 to f^3, . .		1	5	8	12	15	19
f♯^{3} to c^4, . .			1	5	8	12	15

This MIXTURE must be composed of small-scaled VIOL or GAMBA pipes, voiced to yield a soft string-tone of a singing character; and it must be regulated so that each rank is softer than the larger rank preceding it. It must be entirely devoid of anything approaching a screaming character, and it must be perfectly balanced within itself. Its use, in conjunction with the graver harmonic-corroborating stops, is to impart to the general volume of string-tone the fulness and richness of structure which can alone satisfy the musical ear, and produce a proper imitative quality.

The tonal structure of this section of the Third Organ is practically complete, so far as the unison tone and its harmonic series are concerned. It will be observed, however, that in the higher octaves of the treble the unison pitch has been interfered with by the introduction of the QUINT, strictly belonging to the 16 ft. harmonic series. This will prove perfectly satisfactory; indeed, it will impart singular richness to these octaves. The question now arises as to how far it is desirable to introduce the 16 ft. tone throughout the compass of the section. That its presence would be valuable for many musical effects there can be no doubt; and there need be no hesitation in adding a soft-toned covered stop of 16 ft. pitch, preferably of the true QUINTATEN character, in which the ground tone is but little stronger than its first harmonic over-tone.* This would be unobtrusive in its voice, while it would add considerable dignity to the full volume of the section. As a proper proportion of viol-tone of 16 ft. pitch is provided in the Pedal Organ, and one open DOUBLE BASS, 16 FT., is inserted in the second section of the Third Organ, now under consideration, it is unnecessary to increase the dimensions of swell-box No. 2 for the reception of a stop of 16 ft. speaking length.

The following is the Specification of the contents of the first expressive section of the Third Organ, as above detailed :—

THIRD ORGAN—THIRD CLAVIER.

ENTIRELY EXPRESSIVE—COMPASS CC to c^4 = 61 NOTES.

FIRST EXPRESSIVE SECTION.

Inclosed in Swell-box No. 2.

1.	QUINTATEN,	Wood & Metal.	16 ft.	8.	OCTAVE VIOL,	Metal.	4 ft.
2.	VIOLONCELLO,	Metal.	8 "	9.	OCTAVE VIOL,	Metal.	4 "
3.	VIOLONCELLO,	Metal.	8 "	10.	QUINT VIOL,	Metal.	$2\frac{2}{3}$ "
4.	VIOLIN,	Metal.	8 "	11.	SUPER-OCTAVE VIOL,	Metal.	2 "
5.	VIOLIN,	Metal.	8 "	12.	TIERCE VIOL,	Metal.	$1\frac{3}{5}$ "
6.	VIOLA (Tuned sharp)	Metal.	8 "	13.	VIOL MIXTURE, VII., VI., & V. ranks		
7.	QUINTATEN,	Metal.	8 "	II.	TREMOLANT.		

This First Expressive Section to be brought on and put off the Third Clavier by thumb-pistons or touches. To be commanded by the Double-touch of the clavier.

Stops Nos. 2, 3, 4, 5, 6, and 8 to be on wind of 5 inches; and all the other stops to be on wind of 3½ inches.

The TREMOLANT to affect all the above stops on wind of 5 inches.

In the scaling, voicing, and regulating of the several stops in the above string-toned section, a problem of no mean difficulty is presented for solution; and the true artist can display his knowledge, skill, and taste, to an extent rarely possible in the ordinary tonal appointment of Concert-room Organs.

In strict accordance with the principles which guide the development of our tonal scheme, we have now to find an entirely new stop appointment for the second section of the Third Organ—an appointment which will furnish several very important and distinctive orchestral voices. If we turn our attention to the grand orchestra we find the voices ready for our purpose; namely, those which are grouped under the denomination 'wood-wind,' and which are yielded by the Flutes, Oboes, Clarinets, and Bassoons. The grouping of the stops, which are the organ equivalents of these important orchestral instruments, in the Third Organ, side by side, so to speak, with the string-toned stops, is a singularly happy

* A covered or stopped pipe of 16 ft. tone cannot be made to yield the octave, which is strictly the first upper partial tone of the 16 ft. series. The first harmonic of such a pipe is, accordingly, the Twelfth or Octave Quint.

arrangement, as every musician will admit who takes the trouble to study our appointment. The orchestral effects and *nuances* possible in this Third Organ alone, with its two independent expressive sections, its perfect system of control, and its double-touch, cannot easily be realized by the mind. They certainly cannot be produced on any Organ hitherto constructed.

At this point it is proper to insert the Specification of the contents of the second expressive section of the Third Organ :—

THIRD ORGAN—THIRD CLAVIER.

SECOND EXPRESSIVE SECTION.

Inclosed in Swell-box No. 3.

14.	Contra-Basso, . .	Wood. 16 ft.	24.	Contra-Oboe, . . .	Metal. 16 ft.
15.	Principale, . . .	Metal. 8 "	25.	Contrafagotto, . .	Wood. 16 "
16.	Grobgedeckt, . . .	Wood. 8 "	26.	Fagotto, ...	Wood. 8 "
17.	Doppelrohrgedeckt,	Wood. 8 "	27.	Corno di Bassetto, .	Metal. 8 "
18.	Orchestral Flute, .	Wood. 8 "	28.	Orchestral Oboe, .	Metal. 8 "
19.	Harmonic Flute, .	Metal. 8 "	29.	Orchestral Clarinet,	Metal. 8 "
20.	Octave, ...	Metal. 4 "	30.	Horn, ...	Metal. 8 "
21.	Harmonic Flute, .	Metal. 4 "	31.	Vox Humana, . III. ranks.	8 "
22.	Harmonic Piccolo, .	Metal. 2 "	32.	Octave Oboe, . .	Metal. 4 "
23.	Grand Cornet, . .	V. ranks.	III.	Tremolant.	

This Second Expressive Section to be brought on and put off the Third Clavier by thumb-pistons or touches. It is commanded by the first or single-touch only.

Stops Nos. 18, 19, 21, 22, 25, 26, 27, 28, and 29 to be on wind of 5 inches; and all the other stops to be on wind of 4 inches.

The Tremolant to affect all the above stops on wind of 5 inches.

The advantages, from a musical point of view, of the unique tonal scheme above set forth for the Third Organ must be obvious to the musician who is skilled in orchestration, and who will give our scheme careful consideration. Beyond an examination of the two lists of stops, he must bear in mind that both sections are independent of each other; that both are independently flexible and expressive; and that both can be brought on the Third Clavier, separately or together, and silenced at the performer's will by a slight pressure on a pneumatic or electric piston or touch. It would require many pages of details to give even a faint idea of the practically limitless resources of this single manual division, in which are grouped the organ equivalents of the string and wood-wind forces of the orchestra; so these resources must be left to the imagination of the reader.

It is only necessary to pass a few remarks on the stops introduced in our scheme for the second expressive section, so that our intention may be clearly understood. The Contra-Basso, 16 ft., is inserted here for more than one reason. In the first place, being an open wood stop, with its largest pipe about sixteen feet in length, it can only be accommodated in a swell-box of large dimensions. In the second place, it is a stop which will often be required on the clavier in combination with the string-toned section, so as to impart Double Bass tone to the same: and in the third place, the stop is a most valuable element in the tonal structure of its own section, to which it imparts great richness and dignity. In addition to this, the CONTRA-BASSO will be valuable for bass solo passages, and for accompaniment, in which its imitative character will be heightened by combination with the harmonic voices of the first section, subdued by the closed swell.

In the section now under consideration are grouped a most effective series of flute-toned stops, including the ORCHESTRAL FLUTE, 8 FT., and the family of the HARMONIC FLUTES, 8 FT., 4 FT., and 2 FT. These four stops will amply supply imitative flute-tone. The GROBGEDECKT, 8 FT., and DOPPELROHRGEDECKT, 8 FT., are effective filling-up stops which will be extremely useful in combination with the orchestral reed stops. Pure organ-tone, for combination purposes, has not been neglected, as the presence of the PRINCIPALE, 8 FT., and the OCTAVE, 4 FT., proves. The GRAND CORNET has a very important office to fill in this section; and its ranks are carried throughout the compass without a break. The composition of the stop to be as follows: The first rank to be a QUINT, 5⅓ FT., formed of metal, ROHRFLÖTE pipes of medium scale and quiet intonation. The second rank to be an OCTAVE, 4 FT., formed of small-scaled, open, cylindrical pipes, yielding an organ-tone of a bright silvery character. The third rank to be a TIERCE, 3⅕ FT., formed of GEMSHORN pipes of small scale, very softly voiced. The fourth rank to be a TWELFTH, 2⅔ FT., formed of small-scaled, DOLCE pipes, voiced softer than the OCTAVE. The fifth rank to be a SUPER-OCTAVE, 2 FT., formed of small-scaled, cylindrical pipes, voiced softer than the TWELFTH.

The fine group of reed stops inserted in this section,—CONTRAFAGOTTO, 16 FT., FAGOTTO, 8 FT., CORNO DI BASSETTO, 8 FT., CLARINET, 8 FT., and OBOE, 8 FT.,—along with the FLUTES above mentioned, complete the organ equivalents of the wood-wind forces of the orchestra. As all the powerful brass-toned reed stops are inserted in another division, the six imitative stops above named should in no way be strained in their intonation. The series of reed stops is further enriched by the addition of a soft-toned double, unison, and octave, in the form of a CONTRA-OBOE, 16 FT., a HORN, 8 FT., and an OCTAVE OBOE, 4 FT. One reed stop remains to be mentioned and, perhaps, apologized for. All investigations and experiments have satisfied us that it is impossible to produce a satisfactory imitation of the human voice, in its cultivated musical character, from organ pipes: but as no Concert-room Organ would at the present day be considered complete without the so-called VOX HUMANA, the least one can do is to try and make it inoffensive to the ear. We feel assured, after a careful study of the VOX HUMANA, as made in Germany, France, and England, that the stop can only be made moderately imitative and tolerably agreeable in a compound form; that is to say, by adding to the reed stop, in its most perfect construction and intonation, one or two ranks of labial pipes. As it is practically impossible to find in the same division of the Organ, stops exactly suitable to be drawn with the VOX HUMANA, the adoption of the special compound treatment becomes in every way desirable; the necessary expense being put out of the question. Allowing that the VOX HUMANA is made in the most approved form and properly voiced, the labial stops most suitable to be associated with it are a softly-voiced, covered metal QUINTATEN, 8 FT., and a small-scaled DULCET, 4 FT. These two ranks require to be very carefully and artistically graduated in tone, so as to combine perfectly with the reed, forming a rich, full sound somewhat resembling that of the human voice.

FOURTH ORGAN.

FOURTH CLAVIER—ENTIRELY EXPRESSIVE.

The Fourth Organ, commanded by the Fourth Clavier, now claims consideration. We shall first consider it in the tonal appointment suitable for a Concert-room Organ having only *four* manual divisions and claviers. This division occupies practically the same position in our general scheme as the Solo Organ occupies in all the Concert-room Organs hitherto constructed. In our scheme, however, the Fourth Organ is much more than an ordinary Solo division, for it enters as the representative of an important section of the grand orchestra; namely, that which embraces all the brass wind instruments. This, at least, is its most pronounced characteristic; but in addition it contains several effective stops of imitative voices, suitable for solo passages; thereby relieving the other manual divisions from the necessity of making rapid and frequent changes of tonality, calculated to seriously interfere with their utility in the rendition of orchestral compositions.

In the previously described divisions of the Concert-room Organ the highest wind pressure is 6 inches, whilst in the division now under consideration that is the minimum pressure, the maximum being 20 inches. The latter pressure, however, can only be fixed theoretically: in practical work it will be dictated, to a very large extent, by the size and acoustical properties of the room or hall in which the instrument is to be erected. Higher pressures have been used by the lovers of noise rather than of music; or by those who have simply aimed at outdoing others, or at doing what others have wisely left undone.

The orchestral brass wind instruments which have to be tonally imitated as nearly as skill can accomplish by means of reed pipes are the Trumpet, the Trombones, the Horn, the Ophicleide, the Bass Tuba, the Sax Tuba, and the Cornopean. A few words may be passed on each imitative stop. The ORCHESTRAL TRUMPET, 8 FT., should have a bright, clear, ringing tone of medium strength, as closely resembling that of the orchestral instrument as art can attain. This stop will, accordingly, be quite distinct in quality from the broad-toned TRUMPET in the expressive subdivision of the First Organ. The ORCHESTRAL TRUMPET is a most valuable solo stop, while it enters admirably into combinations of varied tonality. Two TROMBONES should certainly be introduced: one termed BASS TROMBONE, 16 FT., and the other TROMBONE, 8 FT. These being on heavier wind than the ORCHESTRAL TRUMPET will have more powerful intonations, their voices standing about midway between the medium and high-pressure reed tones. The TROMBONES should be brilliant and have a brazen clang, in imitation of the *forte* tones of the orchestral instruments. As this brassy character almost entirely disappears when the swell-box is closed, the effect of the Trombones when softly played is fairly well imitated; and the effect is improved by the addition of a full-toned labial stop. The TROMBONES, when properly voiced, are of the greatest value in the Concert Organ, for they supply tones of a powerful and assertive nature for numerous passages in which the quieter reeds would be insufficient, and the heavy-pressure reeds overwhelming and offensive. Here, as in every other division of the Organ, the value of tonal contrast cannot be overrated. No successful imitation of the "noble and melancholy" voice of the orchestral Horn (notably that without pistons) has as yet been achieved by the organ builder; and it is a grave question if it will ever be closely imitated by an organ reed stop. The closest resemblance to the true tones of the Horn we have ever heard were produced by a labial stop of the KERAULOPHON species, of large scale, and constructed of thick plain metal in the composition of which lead largely predominated. It is probable, as in the case of the VOX HUMANA, that the best result will be obtained by forming the HORN as a compound stop, associating with a smooth-toned reed a unison labial stop of the KERAULOPHON class. The latter to be of large scale and formed with a somewhat narrow mouth. The HORN in the present division should be much fuller in tone than the stop of the same name in the second expressive section of the Third Organ, thereby securing the desirable distinction between the two voices. The OPHICLEIDE should be a large-scaled stop of full and smooth intonation, with as little brassiness as possible, in this respect contrasting with that of the TROMBONE, 8 FT. The OPHICLEIDE, 8 FT., as contemplated in our scheme, would be chiefly used as a filling-up voice. The OPHICLEIDE, 8 FT., in the Solo division of the Organ in St. George's Hall, Liverpool, is on wind of 22 inches ; and, in its loud and uncontrollable condition, its tones are ably described by Berlioz, in his remarks on the Ophicleide of the orchestra, as "rude" and "wild." "There is nothing," says this able writer on instrumentation, "more coarse,—I might almost say, more monstrous,—or less fit to harmonize with the rest of the orchestra, than those passages, more or less rapid, written in the form of *solos* for the Ophicleide medium in some modern operas. It is as if a bull, escaped from its stall, had come to play off its vagaries in the middle of a drawing-room." The latter sentence exactly describes the voice of the unexpressive OPHICLEIDE in the Solo division of the Liverpool Organ; and, indeed, the voices of all similar high-pressure reeds when left without powers of flexibility and expression. Bad as the orchestral Ophicleide may be at its best, what would it be if it had to be played at full blast and without a trace of expression? The CORNOPEAN, 8 FT., should be of a clear intonation with no brassiness, resembling the most refined and unforced tones of the instrument from which it takes its name. Its strength of voice should be nearly that of the ORCHESTRAL TRUMPET; from which stop it must, however, be kept perfectly distinct by its widely different *timbre*.

With respect to the pressures of wind for the above-described reed stops, we are of opinion that, under ordinary conditions, 6-inch wind should be furnished for the HORN; 7-inch wind for the ORCHESTRAL TRUMPET, OPHICLEIDE, and CORNOPEAN; and 10-inch wind for the TROMBONES.

We have included in the tonal appointment of the Fourth Organ four important reed stops, to be voiced on wind of from 15 inches to 20 inches; the exact pressure to be decided by the size and acoustical properties of the concert-room. Higher pressures have been adopted by the leading English organ builders, for stops of the class we now allude to, but it is very questionable if anything in the nature of legitimate musical effect is gained by them. First in order of dignity and importance comes the BASS TUBA, 16 FT., with a voice rolling and majestic, but as free as possible from brassy clang, which, if present to any pronounced degree, would impart to the tone too great assertiveness in respect to the unison tone of the division. Here, as in all the other manual divisions of the Organ, the unison (8 ft.) pitch must reign supreme. The TUBA, 8 FT., should have a voice similar in quality to that of the preceding double stop, but of greater fulness and assertiveness. For very prominent solo passages, as well as for the grandest combinations, another and much more powerful unison reed is inserted in the form of the HARMONIC TROMBA, 8 FT. This must be the loudest and most assertive voice in the entire Organ, capable of dominating the otherwise full power of the instrument. The fourth high-pressure reed must be of octave pitch. It is introduced in the form of the HARMONIC CLARION, 4 FT., with a voice full and bright, second in strength of intonation only to that of the HARMONIC TROMBA, to which it stands as the true OCTAVE. This completes the series of 'brass-wind' stops, but by no means completes the tonal appointment of the Fourth Organ, which has still to be considerably enriched in other directions.

It must be borne in mind that the six following labial stops are to be voiced on the second pressure of the division; namely, 7 inches.

For the purpose of imparting volume and richness to the unison voices of this division at times when either the BASS TROMBONE or BASS TUBA would prove too powerful, it is necessary to introduce a labial stop of 16 ft. pitch, having a tone of full, round, and sonorous quality. The GROSSDOPPELGEDECKT, 16 FT., meets all the requirements. This important stop is formed of large-scaled, deep, wood pipes, having double mouths and leather-covered upper lips. It requires to be very copiously winded. It may be found sufficient to carry the double mouths down to tenor C, the bass octave being carried down in large-scaled, single-mouthed pipes. No further stops of 16 ft. pitch are necessary. The chief unison labial stop introduced in this division is the STENTORPHONE, 8 FT., of large-scaled, open, cylindrical pipes, made of very thick plain metal, and yielding a very powerful and majestic tone admirably suited for the support of, and combination with, the assertive reeds of the division. Fine examples of the STENTORPHONE have been made by Roosevelt; but it has never, to our knowledge, been introduced in any English or Continental Concert-room Organ. Next in importance is the DOPPELGEDECKT, 8 FT., a large-scaled, covered, wood stop, having, as its name implies, double mouths. Its tone must be of a full and round fluty character, valuable in combination with the reeds, and especially so in combination with the ORCHESTRAL CLARINET, 8 FT., should it be a reed alone.

We add two flute-toned stops, the HARMONIC FLUTE, 4 FT., and HARMONIC PICCOLO, 2 FT., of imitative quality and clear intonation. These are necessary, both for the harmonic structure of the division, corroborating two important upper partial tones of the unison, and for prominent Flute and Piccolo solo passages. The harmonic structure is further extended and enriched by the addition of the following GRAND CORNET of VI. and V. ranks:—

GRAND CORNET—VI. and V. RANKS.

CC to g^2,	. . . . .	8—10—12—15—19—22.
$g\sharp^2$ to c^4,	. . . .	1— 8—10—12—15.

This CORNET should be formed of medium-scaled OPEN DIAPASON pipes, voiced to yield a full and solid tone, in keeping with the powerful character of the division. While the first rank (octave and unison) should be about the ordinary strength of an OPEN DIAPASON, all the higher ranks must follow the same rule of gradation of tone as is observed in all properly treated compound harmonic-corroborating stops.

Four important and very desirable stops still remain to be considered. First in order is the CONCERT VIOLONCELLO, 8 FT., of a purely imitative and penetrating quality of tone, and with a more powerful intonation than any of the string-toned stops in the other manual divisions of the Organ. The CONCERT VIOLONCELLO is extremely valuable for solo and melodic passages, accompanied by contrasting combinations in either the Second or Third Organ. Next is the CONCERT VIOLIN, 8 FT., a companion to the preceding stop, and having, like it, a purely imitative voice for solo passages. In combination with the CONCERT VIOLONCELLO it would be extremely fine and commanding. The CONCERT VIOLIN should not be quite so strong in tone as the VIOLONCELLO, so as to prevent sympathy and to provide variety. To these stops is added a VIOLETTA, 4 FT., calculated to impart great brilliancy to the unison voices of the VIOLONCELLO and VIOLIN, by corroborating to the desirable extent the first upper partial tone. It is well known by scientific investigators that in the richest quality of orchestral string-tone, as produced by the bowed instruments, the first upper partial tone is not only next in importance to the prime tone but is only slightly inferior to it in intensity; hence the value of the VIOLETTA.

The last stop which, for several reasons, we consider desirable in the Fourth Organ is the ORCHESTRAL CLARINET, 8 FT. This valuable stop should be made of two ranks of pipes of unison pitch; one being the usual cylindrical, metal reed stop, and the other a medium-scaled, wood or metal, covered stop, yielding a somewhat hollow quality of tone in which the second upper partial or twelfth is prominent. The orchestral Clarinet has a cylindrical tube, the proper tones of which correspond to the third, fifth, seventh, and other uneven partial tones of the prime. Such being the case, the importance of associating with the CLARINET a stop of the QUINTATEN class is self-evident. Apart from the harmonic-corroborating property, the labial rank imparts to the reed tone the hollow, wood-like tone peculiar to the orchestral Clarinet, especially in the chalameau part of its compass.*

* In our own Chamber Organ we invariably drew the FLAUTO PRIMO (a DOPPELFLÖTE, 8 FT.) with the CLARINETTO when the full orchestral quality was required for solo passages.

This double-ranked stop should, along with the three string-toned stops above described, be voiced on wind of 6 inches—the lowest pressure of this division.

The Specification of the complete Fourth Organ is as follows:—

FOURTH ORGAN—FOURTH CLAVIER.

ENTIRELY EXPRESSIVE—COMPASS CC to c^4=61 NOTES.

Inclosed in Swell-box No. 4

1.	Grossdoppelgedeckt,	Wood.	16 ft.	6.	Grand Cornet,	VI. and V. ranks.	
2.	Stentorphone,	Metal.	8 "	7.	Ophicleide,	Metal.	8 ft.
3.	Doppelgedeckt,	Wood.	8 "	8.	Cornopean,	Metal.	8 "
4.	Harmonic Flute,	Metal.	4 "	9.	Orchestral Trumpet,	Metal.	8 "
5.	Harmonic Piccolo,	Metal.	2 "				

The above nine stops to be on wind of 7 inches.

10.	Concert Violoncello,	Metal.	8 ft.	13.	Orchestral Horn,	Metal.	8 ft.
11.	Concert Violin,	Metal.	8 "	14.	Orchestral Trumpet,	Metal.	8 "
12.	Violetta,	Metal.	4 "	15.	Orchestral Clarinet.	II. ranks.	8 "

IV. Tremolant.

The above six stops to be on wind of 6 inches.

16.	Bass Trombone,	Metal.	16 ft.	17.	Trombone,	Metal.	8 ft.

The above two stops to be on wind of 10 inches.

18.	Bass Tuba,	Metal.	16 ft.	20.	Harmonic Tromba,	Metal.	8 ft.
19.	Tuba,	Metal.	8 "	21.	Harmonic Clarion,	Metal.	4 "

The above four stops to be on wind of from 15 inches to 20 inches according to the requirements.

Before passing our concluding remarks on the tonal appointments of the several manual divisions of the Concert-room Organ, we may properly consider the modified appointment for the Fourth Organ and the scheme for the Fifth Organ in an instrument comprising five independent manual divisions commanded by five claviers. The following is the Specification of the Fourth Organ which is now essentially of a solo character:—

FOURTH ORGAN—FOURTH CLAVIER.

ENTIRELY EXPRESSIVE—COMPASS CC to c^4=61 NOTES.

Inclosed in Swell-box No. 4.

1.	Lieblichgedeckt,	Wood.	16 ft.	4.	Viola da Gamba,	Metal.	8 ft.
2.	Flûte à Pavillon,	Metal.	8 "	5.	Viola d'Amore,	Metal.	8 "
3.	Hohlflöte,	Wood.	8 "	6.	Cymbal,	III. ranks.	

The above six stops to be on wind of 4 inches.

7.	Concert Violoncello,	Metal.	8 ft.	12.	Concert Piccolo,	Metal.	2 ft.
8.	Concert Violin,	Metal.	8 "	13.	Euphonium,	Metal.	16 "
9.	Concert Flute,	Wood.	8 "	14.	Orchestral Oboe,	Metal.	8 "
10.	Saxophone (Labial)	Wood.	8 "	15.	Orchestral Clarinet,	II. ranks.	8 "
11.	Violetta,	Metal.	4 "	16.	Glockenspiel (Tubes or Steel Bars).		

IV. Tremolant.

The above nine stops to be on wind of 6 inches.

The Double-touch of this Fourth Clavier is to command the Fifth Organ when required.

The Fifth Organ, the tonal appointment of which is given in the following Specification, may be correctly designated the 'brass-wind' division of the Organ.

FIFTH ORGAN—FIFTH CLAVIER.

ENTIRELY EXPRESSIVE—COMPASS CC to c^4=61 NOTES.

Inclosed in Swell-box No. 4.

1.	Grossdoppelgedeckt,	Wood.	16 ft.	3.	Grand Cornet,	VI. and V. ranks.	
2.	Stentorphone,	Metal.	8 "	4.	Ophicleide,	Metal.	8 ft.

The above four stops to be on wind of 7 inches.

5.	Bass Trombone,	Metal.	16 ft.	6.	Trombone,	Metal.	8 ft.

The above two stops to be on wind of 10 inches.

7.	Bass Tuba,	Metal.	16 ft.	9.	Harmonic Tromba,	Metal.	8 ft.
8.	Tuba,	Metal.	8 "	10.	Harmonic Clarion,	Metal.	4 "

The above four stops to be on wind of 20 inches.

In all the foregoing remarks on, and the schemes for, the different manual divisions of the Concert-room Organ, it must be understood that what has been aimed at is simply the laying down of general principles of stop disposition and divisional appointment, and not the furnishing of directions which are to be followed to the letter; indeed, in such a complex matter as the scheming of a large Concert-room Organ, any other course would be out of all reason. It must be obvious that when so many conditions obtain in connection with the matter, such as the space available for the reception of the Organ, the funds provided for its construction, and the chief purposes for which the instrument is destined, hard and fast rules are impracticable. With the system, or rather the want of system, which has obtained in the organ-building world up to the present time we have no sympathy; and we certainly fail to recognize any decided skill or knowledge in the multiplication of divisions which display little or no marked individuality, no distinct grouping of tone-colors, and no decided contrast in tonal effects. In the large Organs which have been built, at home and abroad, there is certainly a great waste of material through the aimless repetition of stops in certain divisions, the absence of distinctive voicing, and the want of grouping or concentration of the leading families of stops. Such Organs produce the minimum effect with the maximum of effort on the part of the performer. Concentrated, contrasted, and distinctive tonal colorings, such as one hears in the grand orchestra, and which one certainly ought to hear in such a colossal instrument as the modern Concert-room Organ, are impossible under ordinary management, and are without doubt extremely difficult to produce on that instrument, as at present constructed, under any management whatever. This state of affairs ought no longer to be tolerated by musicians: and if in such important matters organ builders will neither lead nor be led, they should be driven.

The reader who has not given the subject under discussion serious thought and careful study will probably fail to see the full force of the remarks just made. To him the largest Concert-room Organs in existence will doubtless appear to be all that the art of the organ builder can be made to achieve. Such, however, we venture to affirm is far from being the case. The advance that is so desirable in the art of Concert Organ construction must not be looked for in the direction of still larger instruments than are at present in existence; for we are satisfied that the mere multiplication of speaking stops and mechanical appliances, on old-time lines, will do nothing toward making the Organ the perfectly satisfactory musical instrument it ought to be. More science, more musical taste and knowledge, and, certainly, more common sense, must be brought to bear on the art of organ-building, before any substantial modification in departmental disposition and appointment of the tonal forces, improvement in general tonal structure, and the desirable simplification of all details affecting the correct control of the many and varied voices of the Organ, can reasonably be looked for.

It will be readily granted, perhaps, that of all the art inventions made by man not one can be said to surpass the Concert Organ in complexity of structure, or in the wonderful nature of its effects; and, of all musical instruments yet constructed, it occupies the most exalted position, imperfect as it still is in many essential matters. Such an instrument is the result, not of any one man's genius, but of centuries of gradual and extremely slow development—a work built up, piece by piece, on certain traditional rules, which have been added to age after age, but which do not appear to have at any time been seriously questioned or radically altered under the steadily increasing light of musical and acoustical science, and the ever-growing demands of art, refinement, and taste. It is the blind following of such traditional rules, the perpetual running in old grooves, the unquestioning belief in precedent, that have kept the art of organ-building what it is at the present time—behind the requirements of the age.

In the largest Concert-room Organ in the world to-day no great and fundamental improvements, no marked strides in advance of what had previously been accomplished, and no departures from established methods, are apparent. Both the tonal structure and general stop apportionment are essentially on traditional lines; and, accordingly, are imperfect and insufficient for coming, and, indeed, for present, demands. It would not be difficult to scheme an instrument of much smaller size which would, at one step, place the gigantic Organ alluded to in the list of old-fashioned instruments; and in the present Chapter we have hurriedly sketched how this can be done. There is, doubtless, an impressiveness about the very idea of an Organ with one hundred and ten or one hundred and twenty speaking stops; but we unhesitatingly affirm that no Organ yet constructed with such an immense array of stops could be made to produce, under the most skilful manipulation possible on the part of the performer, anything approaching to the range of tonal effects, decided contrasts of sound, concentrated musical colorings, and such easy and rapid changes and groupings, as would be simple matters of course in a very much smaller instrument built upon the model shadowed forth in this Chapter. We lay no stress on mere power or volume of sound; for without absolute flexibility with reference to divided, contrasted, concentrated, and combined tonal effects, such volume of sound is practically a disadvantage. A noisy orchestra is not of necessity either a fine or a useful one; and such an orchestra, with all its instruments jumbled together, without system, classification, and concentration, would be about as difficult to command as the ordinary Concert-room Organ of to-day. Of course, the reader will say, especially if he is an organ builder, What on earth have we to do with the orchestra and the arrangement of its instruments? We have this much to do with the orchestra—it is the only model which, if intelligently studied, can directly help us to solve the difficulties which beset the stop appointment and tonal structure of the true Concert Organ.

PEDAL ORGAN.

PEDAL CLAVIER—PARTLY EXPRESSIVE.

In approaching the subject of the stop appointment and other matters connected with the pedal department of the Concert-room Organ, it may be well to briefly define the position it occupies in the general scheme of the instrument; and to consider its proper office in relation to the several manual divisions and subdivisions previously described.

In the Concert-room Organ, as in the other classes of Organs, the first and most important office of the pedal department is to furnish suitable basses for all the more important stops and combinations of stops in the manual divisions. This involves the introduction of several stops similar in form and tone to the leading manual stops, but an octave lower in pitch. In the Church Organ, as will be seen on referring to the Chapter on that instrument, the office of the Pedal Organ need not extend beyond this direct relationship to the manual divisions; but in the Concert-room Organ it should also be a thoroughly self-contained department, suitable for the production of a large range of solo effects, and adapted for the completion of the instrument in its orchestral aspect. Such being the case, it is obvious that the Pedal Organ must be full in its compass, comprehensive in its tonal range, and capable of a considerable degree of expression,—the highest degree possible in so colossal a department.

In scheming the Pedal Organ, it is necessary to refer to the stop appointment of all the manual divisions, and to continue to the fullest extent practicable the principles there observed. It must be pointed out that the two important functions of the Pedal Organ in the Concert-room instrument—namely, the furnishing of a proper bass to the leading manual stops and combinations, either distinct from, or in conjunction with, such manual work; and the furnishing of sufficient materials for special solo and accompanimental effects, suitable for melodic and thematic passages—render it necessary for the tonal forces of the department to be grouped into two subdivisions, one of which remains, in accordance with old usage, uninclosed, while the other is, in accordance with our system, inclosed in a swell-chamber and rendered *expressive*.

Respecting the unexpressive subdivision, nothing beyond general hints for its stop appointment need be given: but a few remarks regarding the application of expressive powers to the Pedal Organ cannot be out of place at this point. In the Chapter on the Church Organ, we remark that certain of the Pedal Organ stops should, even in a Church instrument, be made *expressive* by being inclosed in one of the swell-boxes; and, of course, this method may also be followed in the Concert-room Organ, and most certainly should be followed when an independent swell-chamber is impracticable in the pedal department. When space and funds are very limited, it may not be possible to provide a completely independent expressive division, or to so enlarge the swell-boxes of the manual department as to accommodate any of the appropriate pedal stops: in such a case, and in such a case only, should manual stops be *borrowed* to fill up the deficiency in the Pedal Organ. One of the most notable examples of such borrowing, that has come under our notice, is presented by the pedal department of the Concert Organ in the Town Hall, Manchester, constructed by Cavaillé-Coll. In this instance the very poor accommodation provided by the architect no doubt compelled the organ builder to resort to his system of wholesale borrowing.

Whilst we are on the subject of borrowing, it may be remarked that even when the Pedal Organ is practically complete in itself, a certain amount of borrowing is not only admissible, but desirable. In this age of tubular-pneumatic and electro-pneumatic actions, there is no difficulty in attaching appropriate stops belonging to the manual divisions to the pedal clavier, so that they may be played therefrom without at the same time sounding on the manual claviers. This must at once strike the mind of the musician as a most desirable, as it is a most legitimate, reinforcement of the Pedal Organ; and one that the ordinary system of manual-to-pedal clavier coupling does in no adequate manner furnish. In many instances, during the rendition, for example, of a complex orchestral movement, it may be found desirable to have special combinations of stops on the manuals, while only certain of the stops which enter into those combinations are desirable on the pedal clavier. Again, it is possible to render a solo passage, on one of the manual stops, on the pedal clavier, while the accompaniment is being played, by both hands, on the manual clavier of the division which contains the solo stop: and, again, it may be desirable to have on the pedal clavier a combination of stops borrowed from the manual divisions, and so secure charming effects of *compound expression*, while none of the borrowed stops need sound in any of the manual combinations. The variety of treatment is almost limitless, so these hints may suffice for the present. All manual stops borrowed in this manner may be called, in contradistinction to the Pedal Organ stops proper, Pedal Organ *auxiliary stops*.

We are certainly not in favor of the *partial* borrowing of stops from manual divisions to complete Pedal Organ ranks; for the practice, under ordinary conditions, leads to such made-up stops being unequal in tone, through their upper portions being inclosed in swell-boxes while their lower pipes are left uninclosed. When this class of borrowing is resorted to in an Organ, it is usual to provide the lower octave of pipes in the pedal department, and to borrow the eighteen or twenty pipes necessary to complete the compass. Now, if for any good reason this method is to be followed, let it be confined to stops which are altogether uninclosed, unless arrangements are made to have the octave specially belonging to the pedal department inclosed in the same swell-box with the borrowed pipes. When the borrowing takes place from an uninclosed manual stop, no special disposition of the lower octave of pedal pipes is necessary; for it may be planted on a wind-chest at any convenient distance from the manual wind-chest. Of course it is desirable that both portions of the stop should be as near each other as possible.

As the unison or foundation tone of the Pedal Organ is of 16 ft. pitch, the stops of that pitch are of necessity the most important in the department; and they must, accordingly, be more numerous than those of any other pitch. We have pointed out in the earlier part of the present Chapter that the First Organ must be looked upon as the true foundation of the manual divisions—as forming, in conjunction with a portion of the Pedal Organ, the Grand Organ or the Organ proper. It is, therefore, advisable to treat of the portion of the pedal department alluded to before touching on that which is more or less of an orchestral character.

If the reader will refer to the Specification of the First Organ he will readily see what the Pedal Organ will require to enable it to furnish, without resort to coupling, true basses to the foundation-work therein provided. Taking the stops of unison or 8 ft. pitch first, it is obvious that an OPEN DIAPASON, 16 FT., of metal and of large scale, is required to furnish the bass to the OPEN DIAPASON, 8 FT. (No. 4); that another OPEN DIAPASON, 16 FT., of metal and of smaller scale, is desirable to supply the correct bass to the OPEN DIAPASON, 8 FT. (No. 5); and an OPEN DIAPASON, 16 FT., of wood and of medium scale, is required to furnish the proper quality of bass to the OPEN DIAPASON, 8 FT., of wood (No. 6). The GAMBA, 8 FT. (No. 7), should find its characteristic bass in a GAMBA, 16 FT., in the Pedal Organ; and the DOPPELFLÖTE, 8 FT. (No. 8), should be carried down by a DOPPELGEDECKT, 16 FT., or a medium-scaled BOURDON, 16 FT. These are all the Pedal Organ labial stops, of unison pitch, that may be said to be strictly complementary to the foundation-work of the First Organ: accordingly the five stops of 16 ft. pitch, above named, form the foundation of the Pedal Organ.

The harmonic structure of the Pedal Organ must be filled up so far as is desirable by the insertion of a QUINT, 10⅔ FT.; OCTAVE, 8 FT.; TWELFTH, 5⅓ FT.; SUPER-OCTAVE, 4 FT.; GREAT CORNET, VI. Ranks; and COMPENSATIONSMIXTUR, V. Ranks. The two compound harmonic-corroborating stops just named, being different from those commonly used in Pedal Organs, may be described. The GREAT CORNET should be formed of small-scaled OPEN DIAPASON pipes, voiced to yield a smooth, bright, silvery tone of properly graduated strength; for here, as in the several compound harmonic-corroborating stops in the manual divisions of the Organ, the acoustical laws connected with upper partial tones must be very carefully observed and respected. The GREAT CORNET should be composed, without breaks, as follows:—

GREAT CORNET—VI. RANKS.

CC to G, ... 8—12—15—17—19—22.

This CORNET will impart great fulness and richness to the harmonic structure of the pedal department, and add clearness of articulation to the grave foundation-tone. Being under perfect control, its usefulness cannot be overestimated. It can be drawn with any single unison stop, or any combination of stops, in the department.

The COMPENSATIONSMIXTUR, V. Ranks, is unquestionably a valuable compound stop, imparting distinctness of tonality and speech to the graver notes of the pedal compass. It should be formed of GEMSHORN pipes, of rather large scale, and voiced to yield a bright tone, carefully graduated until the top notes of the several ranks can only just be heard. The reader will find full particulars of the composition and construction of this uncommon stop in the Chapters on The Compound Stops of the Organ, and Names and General Particulars of Organ Stops.

It is, of course, imperative in an Organ which has so considerable a number of stops of 16 ft. pitch in its manual divisions that the pedal department should contain appropriate basses for them, in the form of stops of 32 ft. pitch. Of labial stops it will only be necessary to insert two; namely, a DOUBLE OPEN DIAPASON, 32 FT., of metal, and a DOUBLE OPEN DIAPASON, 32 FT., of wood. A third stop of this grave pitch, in the form of a SUB-BOURDON, 32 FT., is very desirable, seeing that there are several covered stops of 16 ft. pitch in the manual divisions. The fulness and richness of the Pedal Organ can be somewhat increased by the introduction of the SUB-QUINT, 21⅓ FT. The general idea obtains that by its combination with stops of 32 ft. pitch, notes belonging to a 64 ft. scale are created. This is a misconception, simply because notes of so grave a pitch are far below the limit of audible sounds. In this case the *differential* tones are of no value, so we must look to the *summational* tones, and the harmonics created by its combination with the stops of different pitch, for the special tonal effects produced by the SUB-QUINT, 21⅓ FT. This subject is a somewhat complex one and need not be enlarged upon here. The reader will find the subject fully treated in the Chapter on the Tonal Structure of the Organ.

Of the other necessary unison labial stops, required to furnish suitable basses for important families of stops in the manual divisions, nothing need be said. It is only requisite to give their names in the Specification. The same holds good with respect to the desirable reed stops. Such being the case, and for the purpose of rendering our further remarks more intelligible, the Specification of the entire Pedal Organ may now be given:

PEDAL ORGAN—PEDAL CLAVIER.

PARTLY EXPRESSIVE—COMPASS CCC to G=32 NOTES.

UNEXPRESSIVE SUBDIVISION.

1.	Double Open Diapason,	Metal.	32 ft.
2.	Double Open Diapason,	Wood.	32 "
3.	Sub-Bourdon, . .	Wood.	32 "
4.	Sub-Quint, . . .	Wood.	$21\frac{1}{3}$"
5.	Open Diapason, Major,	Metal.	16 "
6.	Open Diapason, Minor,	Metal.	16 "
7.	Open Diapason, . .	Wood.	16 "
8.	Gamba, ...	Metal.	16 "
9.	Violone, ...	Metal.	16 ft.
10.	Dulciana, . . .	Metal.	16 "
11.	Doppelgedeckt, . .	Wood.	16 "
12.	Octave, . . .	Metal.	8 "
13.	Bassflöte, . . .	Wood.	8 "
14.	Compensationsmixtur, .	V. ranks.	
15.	Contra-Bombardon, .	Wood.	32 "
16.	Bombardon, . . .	Metal.	16 "

All the above stops to be on wind of 4½ inches.

EXPRESSIVE SUBDIVISION.

Inclosed in a Swell-chamber.

17.	Double Bass Viol, .	Wood.	16 ft.
18.	Lieblichgedeckt, .	Wood.	16 "
19.	Quint, ...	Wood.	$10\frac{2}{3}$"
20.	Violoncello, . .	Metal.	8 "
21.	Hohlflöte, . . .	Wood.	8 "
22.	Twelfth, . . .	Metal.	$5\frac{1}{3}$"
23.	Super-octave, . .	Metal.	4 "
24.	Hohlflöte, . . .	Wood.	4 "
25.	Great Cornet, . .	VI. ranks.	
26.	Bass Trombone, . .	Metal.	16 ft.
27.	Contrafagotto, . .	Wood.	16 "
28.	Euphonium (Free reed),	Metal.	16 "
29.	Double Trumpet, . .	Metal.	16 "
30.	Trumpet, . . .	Metal.	8 "
31.	Clarion, . . .	Metal.	4 "
32.	Octave Clarion, . .	Metal.	2 "

Stops Nos. 17 to 28 inclusive to be on wind of 6 inches. Stops Nos. 29, 30, 31, and 32 to be on wind of 10 inches.

AUXILIARY DIVISION.

BORROWED FROM EXPRESSIVE MANUAL DIVISIONS.

FROM SECOND ORGAN.

5.	Lieblichgedeckt, ...	16 ft.
16.	Contra-Saxophone, . . .	16 ft.

FROM THIRD ORGAN.

1.	Quintaten, ...	16 ft.
14.	Contra-Basso, ...	16 "
24.	Contra-Oboe, ...	16 ft.

FROM FOURTH ORGAN.

1.	Grossdoppelgedeckt, . .	16 ft.
16.	Bass Trombone, . . .	16 "
18.	Bass Tuba, ...	16 ft.

It is unnecessary to enlarge on the advantages of this auxiliary division. The great additional tonal resources presented by the eight effective stops of 16 ft. pitch, distributed in three of the manual swell-boxes and controlled by their expression-levers, must be obvious to every experienced organist.

It will be observed that the *unexpressive* subdivision is practically a complete Pedal Organ, comprising four stops of 32 ft. pitch; one of 21⅓ ft. pitch; eight of 16 ft. pitch; two of 8 ft. pitch; and a compound harmonic-corroborating stop. The *expressive* subdivision furnishes the necessary extension of the harmonic structure, and several impressive voices valuable both in combination and for solo effects. In short, the Pedal Organ is provided with all that is required to enable it to meet every call made upon it by the manual divisions.

The series of harmonic-corroborating stops is here inclosed and rendered flexible for precisely the same reason as has already been advanced for the inclosure of the same class of stops in the First Organ. The two fifth-sounding stops, Nos. 19 and 22, the SUPER-OCTAVE, 4 FT., and the GREAT CORNET, VI. Ranks, voiced with assertiveness sufficient to complete the tonal structure of the entire unexpressive subdivision, and also of the full Pedal Organ, are, under the control of the swell-chamber, capable of being used in the same effective manner with any one of the stops of unison pitch in the unexpressive subdivision. The great value of the expressive subdivision is the power it gives the performer, not only to produce an effective *crescendo* and *diminuendo* on all the sixteen inclosed stops, and through them on the entire Pedal Organ, but to set all or any portion of its tonal forces to any degree of strength that may be desirable for the pedal passages to be rendered, and to increase or diminish that strength at his pleasure. Most effective solo or melodic passages are so made easy without the necessity of coupling any manual division to the pedal clavier. By our arrangement the Pedal Organ becomes as flexible and self-contained as the First Organ. In this respect, as well as in its complete tonal structure, our Pedal Organ scheme may claim to be the most perfect ever formulated up to the present time.

It is not necessary to enlarge on the speaking stops of the Pedal Organ; so we may pass on to the consideration of the mechanical appliances required for the proper control of the shutters of the swell-chamber which incloses the expressive subdivision. In the first place, a special lever, preferably of the balanced form, must be provided, and placed either on the right of, and adjoining, the levers of the manual divisions, or on the extreme right, over the highest key of the pedal clavier. When in the latter position, it may be of the hitch-down form, as already described. This lever must be permanently connected with the special mechanism for operating the shutters of the swell-chamber; and is to be used for setting the division to any required degree of strength; and also, when necessary, for producing a *crescendo* and *diminuendo* in simple solo or melodic passages. In the second place, a draw-stop, piston, or foot-lever system should be provided, whereby the special mechanism of the pedal swell-chamber shutters may be instantaneously connected to any one of the expression-levers belonging to the manual divisions of the instrument. By this latter arrangement, it is obvious that the expressive subdivision of the Pedal can be made to move, in perfect accord, with any of the manual expressive divisions. Crossing or compound effects can readily be produced by connecting the Pedal swell to a lever immediately adjoining the expression-lever belonging to the manual division in use. In this case, the foot of the performer has merely to slip from one lever to another in producing compound effects; or to be placed so as to actuate both levers simultaneously when a uniform effect is desired.

It must be quite evident to the musician that a Pedal Organ constructed on the scheme outlined above would be, to all intents and purposes, independent of coupling as commonly resorted to. We cannot but look upon the necessity of coupling the manual divisions to the Pedal Organ as a decided weakness in the scheme of a large Organ; but, at the same time, we have no desire to see the manual-to-pedal couplers omitted in any scheme. The Pedal Organ should be so appointed, and its tonal structure should be so complete, that it need in no essential way depend on aid from the manual divisions. The adoption of the suggested series of Pedal Organ auxiliary stops would do still more to reduce the utility of the couplers. The more perfect the tonal appointment of the Organ becomes, the less will the manual-to-pedal couplers be resorted to by the musician in his desire to obtain richness and clearness of tonal effect. It will chiefly be for the massing of the different families of stops in a bass part, or for the production of immense volumes of sound in pedal passages, that the couplers will be resorted to.

In our foregoing schemes for the several divisions of the Concert-room Organ we have purposely avoided introducing any of the new-fangled names which have been given to certain modifications or developments in stop construction and voicing. The stops to which such names have been given have to be subjected to long and severe tests, under varied conditions, before they can take a recognized and permanent place in the tonal appointment of properly schemed instruments. When they have proved their value as refined and noble voices, there will be no difficulty in finding their proper places in the tonal appointment of the Concert-room Organ.

Much more might have been said on the important and interesting subjects of the past treatments, and the future and desirable developments, of the Concert-room Organ: but enough has probably been said in this Chapter to show the short-comings of existing Organs; and to point the way to a more artistic, logical, and resourceful tonal structure and appointment. Whether our suggested methods be right or wrong, the imperative necessity for a more scientific and artistic treatment of the sound-producing portion of the Organ cannot be questioned by thoughtful musicians and those competent to judge.

CHAPTER VII.

THE CHAMBER ORGAN.

HAVING treated of the two leading classes of Organs, we now come to the consideration of the Chamber Organ and matters connected with its proper appointment. In treating of the Chamber Organ we have to recognize and accept conditions widely different from those which control, or should control, the construction and tonal appointment of both Church and Concert-room Organs, as set forth in the two preceding Chapters. Nothwithstanding this, the Chamber Organ, in its most desirable form, may be accepted as belonging to the family of concert-room instruments, being, in its highest development, a diminutive of the Concert-room Organ.

In no work on the art of organ-building published up to the present time has the Chamber Organ received the amount of consideration which is strictly its due; indeed, in what has long been pronounced the most important treatise on the subject hitherto published, from the pen of an English writer, the existence of such a thing as a properly-appointed Chamber Organ is completely ignored, not even a single Specification of a Chamber Organ appearing in its two hundred and sixty-six pages of Specifications. This can, however, be accounted for by the simple fact that at the time the work first appeared the Organ in its chamber form was not recognized by musicians, and was almost unknown to the musical amateur. It is not too much to say that in the year 1855, when "The Organ," by Hopkins and Rimbault, was published, there was not a single Chamber Organ, worthy of consideration, in any house in England, or, in fact, we may say, in the world. We may go still farther and remark that up to the present day, notwithstanding the number of instruments of large and small dimensions which have been erected in private houses in England, France, and America, there is evidence that organ builders, as a body, have not given the construction and tonal appointment of the

Chamber Organ the study and care they deserve. We are glad, however, to observe signs of awakening interest on the part of a few progressive builders, notably in America. It is scarely to be hoped, however, that the somewhat troublesome matter of the Chamber Organ will be taken up in an enthusiastic spirit by the general body of professional organ builders; for, as has already been said, organ builders are the least likely of all art-workmen to lay down or create a new line of operation for themselves, and depart of their own free will from their traditional practice. To the large majority of organ builders a Chamber Organ, commonly so called, is simply a *small Organ*, built on ordinary lines, out of the manufacture of which but little profit can be made, and that little attended with considerable trouble and worry. By many others it seems to be regarded as a toy, unworthy of earnest study and artistic development. Need we say that in holding either of these views organ builders are standing most stupidly in their own light? The Chamber Organ, as a special instrument, adapted to special requirements, cannot longer be ignored or neglected; and it is the office of the present Chapter to make all matters connected with its scheming and tonal appointment clear to the inquiring student.

Musicians, and organists in particular, are apt to side with the organ builders n their prejudiced and trade-tied views; and this unfortunate sympathy will do, as it certainly has done, much to retard the proper development of the Chamber Organ. As a rule, organists are accustomed to perform on large and powerful instruments; and it naturally follows that their ears become so familiar with the volume and grandeur of the full manual combinations and the majestic roll of the pedal department of their Organs, that they feel dissatisfied and out of place when seated at the keys of a comparatively small and delicately-voiced instrument, such as one might reasonably expect to find in a private music-room or drawing-room. But, given that the Chamber Organ has been properly appointed and artistically-voiced, this feeling, on the part of an organist, is about as reasonable as would be the objection, on the part of a musician, to a string quartet on the sole ground that it failed to produce the volume and grandeur of sound that emanates from the full orchestra. Each is right and adapted to its place, and the results obtained are equally worthy and artistic. Again, generally speaking, organists are not a scientific and deep-thinking class of men, at least so far as matters connected with the construction and tonal structure of the instrument on which they perform are concerned; and they are, accordingly, too prone to form their opinions, as regards the capabilities of the Chamber Organ, from the commonplace specimens builders have been content to place before them. Such being the case, organists may be said to have right on their side when they emphatically condemn the usual types of so-called Chamber Organs. These instruments are, when of moderate dimensions, sadly circumscribed and expressionless affairs, with little more than loudness of tone to make up for lack of variety of effect and flexibility: and, when large, are either simply deafening with their noise, or muffled to the utmost limit with the view of producing what has been described as the "*true chamber-tone*." So truly are their tones *chamber ones*, that they have some difficulty in escaping from the chambers into which the pipe-work is crammed.

If any decided progress is to be made in the art of Chamber Organ construction, the initiative must come from outside the organ-building trade, and the somewhat inexperienced and prejudiced section of the organ-playing world. The music-loving and enthusiastic amateur, free from prejudice and traditional influences, can alone be depended upon to inaugurate and foster the correct and artistic school of Chamber Organ appointment. From him the demand must come; and he must be able to clearly define how and in what manner his directions are to be carried out. When the demand steadily sets in, there can be little doubt that intelligent organ builders will realize that it is to their interest to prepare themselves to meet it with study, patience, and skill. To start with, it is absolutely necessary that the client should be conversant with organ-building details generally, and perfectly satisfied in his own mind regarding the lines upon which the Chamber Organ,—if it is to be an instrument deserving the name,—must be constructed and appointed. Secondly, he must be prepared to clearly lay down those lines for the builder's guidance; and be ready to combat the old-fashioned views and trade objections which will, in nine cases out of ten, be advanced against his innovations, or what will of a certainty be considered "new-fangled ideas." The average builder will raise objections because he will immediately see difficulties ahead, and probably nothing but what will seem to him to be tedious and troublesome ways of overcoming them: he will see that a very high standard of workmanship, and extreme care in scaling, voicing, and regulating the pipe-work, will be imperatively demanded. Under such circumstances, the Organ will be an unknown quantity. New methods of working involve uncertainties in time and outlay, and if the builder contracts for the Organ his profits are doubtful, if not quite inadequate to recompense him for the personal labor and study entailed by the exceptional nature of the work. A small Organ, built in the every-day style, buried in a chamber or smothered by a close case to ameliorate the harshness or irregularities of its tone, presents no difficulties and involves no unknown expenditure; accordingly the organ builder will naturally advocate something of the kind, throwing, with many assumptions of past experience, cold water on the amateur's scheme, and endeavoring to direct his client's footsteps into safe pastures, or, at least, into pastures with which he (the builder) is well acquainted.

Investigations go to prove that from the earliest period of what may be designated modern organ-building, the Organ, as a home instrument, has been better known in England than in any other country. This is probably attributable to the peculiar love for domestic life which has always characterized the English people, as well as their natural love for music.

On the subject of the primitive Regal and Positive it is unnecessary to speak here. The student will find particulars of these small instruments in the first Chapter of this treatise. The earliest Chamber Organs, properly so called, were tentative affairs, consisting of only a few manual stops of the ordinary character, commanded by a single keyboard, and devoid of any power of expression beyond that obtained by the skilful manipulation of the keys. The stops introduced were almost invariably an OPEN DIAPASON, STOPPED DIAPASON, PRINCIPAL, TWELFTH, and FIFTEENTH. The contents of Mace's Chamber Organ, of which particular mention is made in our Chapter on The Swell in the Organ, are given in the following quotation from the description of the instrument which appeared in the year 1676. "There are in this Table [Organ] Six Stops, the first is an Open Diapason; the second, a Principal; the third, a Fifteenth; the fourth, a Twelfth; the fifth, a Two-and-Twentieth; and the sixth a Regal. There is likewise (for a pleasure and light content) a Hooboy Stop, which comes in at any time with the foot; which stop (together with the Regal) makes the Voice Humane. The bellows is laid next the ground, and is made very large, and driven by the foot of the player, or by a cord at the far end." This instrument was, for more reasons than one, a remarkable work in its time.

Dom Bedos, in his great work, gives some space to the description and illustration of small, unexpressive, instruments, under the heading: "Des Orgues convenables dans des Salles ou dans des Chambres." His examples represent the most advanced conceptions of the Chamber Organ at the date of his work (A. D. 1766–1778) in France. He opens the subject thus:—

> "On peut faire, pour des salles de concert ou pour tout autre appartement, des Orgues de bien des manieres, selon la grandeur de la piece qui doit le contenir, selon l'usage auquel on le destine, & selon la dépense que l'on veut y faire. Si l'Orgue est pour une bien grande salle, & qu'on le destine à servir dans un grand concert, il convient de le composer de façon à produire l'effet qu'on doit en attendre. Nous allons en décrire de plusieurs especes, depuis le plus considérable, pour un semblable usage, jusqu'au plus petit, dans autant de Sections, afin qu'on ait lieu de choisir le devis convenable à l'objet qu'on se propose & à la dépense qu'on veut faire."

This reads in a promising manner; but we find nothing following it that places the Chamber Organ, as an instrument constructed on special lines, in a different category from Church and Concert-room instruments. To Dom Bedos, as to the organ builders of his time, the Chamber Organ was simply a small Organ, the pipes and mechanical portions of which were crowded into a closed case; the whole being made to appear a handsome piece of furniture. From Dom Bedos we, accordingly, receive no help toward the development of the Chamber Organ as an instrument designed on special lines for a special purpose.

We may pass over the Chamber Organ as it appeared in England during the eighteenth and first half of the nineteenth century; for it remained, what it was at its inception, a small and ineffective instrument all through that period. Later efforts, however, were certainly promising, for they possessed two manual claviers,—the upper, in the more advanced types, commanding a small expressive division, or Swell Organ, of short compass; and the lower commanding such stops as have been already mentioned. In some isolated examples the enterprising spirit of their builders carried them so far as to add an octave or so of pedal keys, by means of which the bass notes of the manual clavier were drawn down by the feet of the performer; but to which no independent pedal pipes responded. The Chamber Organ remained for a long time in this pseudo-efficient state; and both the builders and owners of the time appear to have been satisfied that the highest point of excellence had been reached in its direction; so satisfied, indeed, that it is a matter for congratulation that any advance was subsequently deemed necessary. Who the enterprising and ambitious innovator was who first added separate pipes to the pedal keys of a Chamber Organ history deponeth not; nor does it record the place or year in which this noteworthy step out of the beaten track was taken. Once taken, however, there was no going back; and, accordingly, what may be considered the normal type of Chamber Organ became an established fact. This effort on the part of the organ builder comprised a Great division of five or six stops; a Swell division of four or five stops, and usually of short compass; and a pedal clavier of thirteen or twenty-five notes, commanding only a single covered stop of 16 ft. pitch. Of the stops selected little need be said beyond the fact that they were identical with those introduced in the smaller Church Organs of the same period; in the most favorable instances voiced with some reference to the places in which they were to be heard. We have not gone into the matter of dates, for this is not a historical Chapter; but that the last-mentioned type of Chamber Organ brings us very close upon the present epoch may be gathered from the following description of the "Grand Orgue de Salon," constructed by the most distinguished French builder for the Exposition Universelle, Paris, 1878, and which was catalogued thus:—

"Un Grand Orgue de Salon à double expression (nouveau système), à deux claviers et un pédalier en console, dont la composition suit :

CLAVIER DU GRAND ORGUE.

d'Ut à Sol, 56 notes.

1.	Bourdon,	de 16 pieds.	4.	Prestant,	de 4 pieds.
2.	Principal,	8 "	5.	Doublette,	2 "
3.	Bourdon,	8 "	6.	Trompette,	8 "

CLAVIER DU RÉCIT.

d'Ut à Sol, 56 notes.

7.	Flûte Harmonique,	de 8 pieds.	10.	Voix Célestes,	de 8 pieds.
8.	Viole de Gambe,	8 "	11.	Basson-Hautbois,	8 "
9.	Flûte Octaviante,	4 "	12.	Voix Humaine,	8 "

CLAVIER DE PÉDALES.

d'Ut à Fa, 30 notes.

13.	Soubasse,	de 16 pieds.	14.	Basse Ouverte,	de 8 pieds.

PÉDALES DE COMBINAISON.

1. Effets d'orage.
2. Tirasse du Grand Orgue.
3. Tirasse du Récit.
4. Expression du Grand Orgue.
5. Expression du Récit.
6. Copula des claviers.
7. Tremolo.
8. Prolongement harmonique."

Again, in 1882, M. Aristide Cavaillé-Coll sent another "Grand Orgue de Salon" to the Exposition des Arts Décoratifs. This Organ was in all respects similar to the above, giving an unquestionable proof that he was at that time convinced he could suggest or construct nothing better in the shape of a Chamber Organ. On subjecting both these instruments to a very careful examination, and hearing them repeatedly performed upon, we were forced to the conclusion that they were simply small Organs of the church type, slightly modified in tone but still infinitely better suited for a small church than for a private music-room. They were built on wrong lines, as Chamber Organs, save in one direction. They were instruments of "*double expression*,"—that is, both the manual divisions were rendered expressive by their stops being inclosed in swell-boxes. Beyond this, it is difficult to realize what had been accomplished toward rendering the instruments examples of a "*nouveau système*."

This treatment was doubtless new in France in 1878; but its novelty could not be extended to England, simply because, eleven years before, we had constructed a Chamber Organ of *triple expression*—the first Organ ever constructed with such extended powers of flexibility and expression. When the distinguished musician M. Saint-Saëns performed on our Organ, he pronounced it unique, and remarked that he wished he had such an instrument at his disposal in Paris.

If the list of stops in M. Cavaillé-Coll's Organ be examined, it will be seen that very few satisfactory combinations or pleasing tonal effects are possible; and that an instrument so appointed must, even under the most artistic manipulation, be deficient in flexibility and variety. Take the Great division (Grand Orgue) for instance; the BOURDON, 16 FT., must be recognized as of little use in so small a division, being only effective in the full combination; and with the five remaining stops very few combinations presenting marked varieties of tonal coloring are possible. It is true, that with six stops fifty-seven different combinations are possible; but of these only a very small number could be resorted to in an Organ appointed as above specified. This important matter evidently did not present itself with full force to the builder's mind: he had the traditions of his art ever before him, and was content to work in accordance with them.

According to the ordinary English nomenclature, the stops placed in the Great division are BOURDON, 16 FT., OPEN DIAPASON, 8 FT., STOPPED DIAPASON, 8 FT., PRINCIPAL, 4 FT., FIFTEENTH, 2 FT., and TRUMPET, 8 FT. Of these only three could well be used singly, and only one could be properly designated a solo stop,—the TRUMPET,—and that, on account of its powerful voice, would be of very limited use in refined chamber music. Almost any other unison reed would have been more satisfactory here.

The appointment of the Swell division (Récit) is equally open to objection. Two stops must be set aside, not only as practically useless in combinations, but as available on occasions very few and far between: we allude to the VOIX CÉLESTES and VOIX HUMAINE. All that remain for general use are the FLÛTE HARMONIQUE, VIOLE DE GAMBE, FLÛTE OCTAVIANTE, and BASSON-HAUTBOIS. These are capable of producing very few satisfactory combinations: and if they are considered to be solo stops, how are they to be properly accompanied on the Great division? On that clavier the BOURDON, 8 FT., is the only stop on which a suitable accompaniment could be rendered.

The paucity of Couplers materially cripples the tonal resources of the instrument; for, instead of its manuals being furnished with Unison, Octave, and Sub-octave couplers, and the pedal clavier with couplers acting on the manual claviers, only a single coupler is introduced; namely, the manual Unison coupler.

While we admit that this "Grand Orgue de Salon" is an essay worthy enough in intention, we may, at the same time, express the opinion that it is an essay, almost from first to last, in its tonal appointment, in a wrong direction. We criticise with some reserve the work of one of the greatest and most artistic organ builders of modern times; but we must add, in duty to our subject, that we consider M. Cavaillé-Coll's "Grand Orgue de Salon," viewed as a Chamber instrument, a grand mistake. With Organs of this class,—inefficient, uninteresting, and expensive,—it will, or ought to be, a long time before French musicians favor their introduction into the private music-room.

Having given particulars of the representative Chamber Organ, as schemed by one of the most distinguished organ builders of the nineteenth century, we may now direct attention to a scheme for an instrument of the same class, by one of the greatest organists of the same epoch—the late Mr. W. T. Best, of Liverpool. We give the following Specification verbatim, from the autograph in our possession:—

"SPECIFICATION of a CHAMBER ORGAN : 2 Keyboards; CC to a^3=58 notes. Pedal-board CCC to F=30 notes.

GREAT ORGAN.

(LOWEST KEYBOARD.)

Inclosed in a swell: the 'pedal' of which must be in the center of the pedal-board, above the middle 'E and F' keys; and balanced so as to remain open at any point desired.

1. LIEBLICH BOURDON—closed wood from Gamut G upwards; the remaining pipes derived from the pedal BOURDON, . . 16 ft.
2. OPEN DIAPASON—metal, ... 8 ft.
3. LIEBLICH GEDACKT,—12 lowest pipes in stopped wood; the rest in stopped metal, ... 8 ft.
4. VIOLE DE GAMBE—metal. From Gamut G; lowest 7 pipes from OPEN DIAPASON, ... 8 ft.
5. VOIX CÉLESTES—metal. Of VIOLE DE GAMBE pipes; one pipe smaller; tuned sharp. Tenor C to treble c^3=3 octaves. The stop-handle to draw with it the VIOLE DE GAMBE, ... 8 ft.
6. GEMSHORN—metal, ... 4 ft.
7. PICCOLO—metal, ... 2 ft.
8. CARILLON—metal. A repeated MIXTURE of III. ranks :—

CC	to	BB, . .	15—19—22.
C	to	B, . .	12—17—22.
c^1	to	b^1, . .	12—15—17.
c^2	to	b^2, . .	8—12—15.
c^3	to	top, . .	1—5—10.

9. TRUMPET—metal, ... 8 ft.

SOLO ORGAN.

(*UPPER KEYBOARD.*)

10. Echo Dulciana—metal, ... 8 ft.
11. Flauto Dolce—Lowest 12 pipes in closed wood; the rest in open wood. Of soft tone, ... 8 ft.
12. Flûte Harmonique—metal. The lower 24 pipes not harmonic. From middle c^1 to the top in harmonic pipes, *i. e.*, of double length, ... 4 ft.
13. Cor Anglais—metal. Three octaves only; from tenor C to treble c^3. Of imitative tone, ... 8 ft.
14. Clarinet—metal. Of similar compass to Cor Anglais, . . 8 ft.

Both these stops [Nos. 13 and 14] in a swell to render the tone expressive.

PEDAL ORGAN.

15. Sub-Bass—closed wood. Pipes of substantial thickness, and firm tone, so as not to sound the 'Twelfth' above, as is commonly the case, ... 16 ft.

This stop must have forty-two pipes on the sound-board; *i. e.*, 12 more than the pedal-board compass; from which is derived:—

15a. Flute-Bass, ... 8 ft.

COUPLERS.

I. Great to Pedals.
II. Solo to Pedals.
III. Solo to Great.
IV. Great—Octave on its own keyboard.
V. Solo—Sub-octave on its own keyboard.

"It is recommended that the keyboards be placed at the side of the room, so as to avoid the usual awkward position in front.

"To avoid the cumbrous and noisy action of 'Composition Pedals,' which thrust the stops continually backward and forward, and in so small an Organ are not necessary, a sin-single Wind Ventil is recommended for the stops in the Great Organ; which, when fixed down, takes away the wind from the stops numbered 6, 7, 8, and 9; and *vice versa*, when again raised, allows them to sound, the stop-handles being in each case drawn, and not moved.

"The Swell Pedal to the Solo stops named to be placed at the side [right] of the other Swell Pedal (acting on the entire Great Organ), and to be of similar construction.

"The Couplers are not to be brought into operation by stop-handles, but by small Pedals above the pedal-board, all of which fasten down to the right or left."

This is unquestionably a much better scheme of tonal appointment than that adopted by Cavaillé-Coll, and would be productive of numerous satisfactory combinations and accompanimental and solo effects; it marks a decided advance in English ideas, so far as the inclosure of the Great Organ is concerned; but we had inaugurated a still more radical departure nearly ten years before the date of this Specification, having introduced in our own Chamber Organ a divided Great Organ, inclosed in two independent swell-boxes—a thing never before attempted in any Organ. In the Solo Organ, Mr. Best wisely specified the Cor Anglais and Clarinet to be inclosed in a special swell-box, "to render the tone expressive;" but it is difficult to understand on what grounds he left the other three stops exposed and unexpressive. The Flûte Harmonique would have been most valuable, in an expressive state, for solo purposes. The Pedal Organ is very deficient, having only a Bourdon and a derived stop of 8 ft. tone; but this is a fault shared with thousands of more important instruments in England, and a treatment apparently sacred in the minds of English organ builders.

The intelligent and growing taste for the Organ, combined with the national love of home-life and elevating social enjoyments, are leading toward a widespread introduction of the instrument, in one form or other, into the private dwellings of the wealthier classes. Even at the present time there are many Chamber Organs to be found in the houses of musicians and amateurs, and their number is on the increase. The majority of these are, however, too closely allied to the original type of Chamber Organ to claim any notice here. The consideration of others, after the Cavaillé-Coll "Grand Orgue de Salon" class, but without the advantage of "double expression," causes feelings of disappointment and regret—regret that so much money should have been expended in a wrong direction. Others, again, the works of intelligent builders, show a decided advance in the comprehension of the problem to be solved. In a few cases, one can see that the true conditions under which a Chamber Organ should be constructed have been tentatively realized; but in nearly all such cases unsatisfactory courses have been taken to approach the desired result. In no instance known to us has an English organ builder, or, indeed, an organ builder of any other country, fully and boldly grasped the problem and worked it out to its legitimate solution. Accustomed to look upon the large Church or Concert-room Organ as the acme of their art, as the one end and aim of their artistic labors, the leading builders have disdained to bend their minds to the humbler, but no less difficult, task of producing the true Chamber Organ.

When commissioned to build a Chamber Organ, the popular organ-building mind at once conceives an instrument formed on the model of a small Church Organ, the usual harsh tones of which shall be subdued by some boxing-up process, or by the common practice of huddling the whole affair into a closed case, a confined recess, or an adjoining room. With reference to the tonal appointment, if the client has not provided a Specification, the builder produces some stereotyped list of stops, to be cut down by the remorseless scissors of dollars or pounds sterling. It does not appear to have occurred to those interested in Chamber Organ construction that the church type of instrument is the last one that should be taken as a starting point; and that, if they desire to produce artistic instruments which shall prove thoroughly suitable and interesting for chamber use, they must approach the model furnished by a properly appointed Concert-room Organ. A Chamber Organ built after the former model may be made to yield a few effective combinations of tone, and full effects of some dignity in what is commonly understood as *organ-tone*, but it will certainly be deficient in solo, orchestral, and accompanimental effects. Such being the case, the instrument would be unsatisfactory for the best and most interesting class of chamber music; and of very circumscribed use in concerted music with the piano and stringed instruments. On the other hand, if it is schemed on the lines of the Concert-room Organ (as set forth in the preceding Chapter), replete with decided and well-selected contrasts of tone, and capable of producing numerous rich musical effects and refined *nuances*, it becomes a perpetual source of interest and intellectual enjoyment to every one brought within its influence.

The true Chamber Organ should be on the Concert Organ model; it must, in fact, be the home orchestra—the center of the musical forces of the household. Whatever instruments may otherwise be available,—the Piano-forte, Violin, Violoncello, Flute, etc.,—all should take their positions here in relation to the dominating instrument—the Organ. With one or two, or with all four combined, the true Chamber Organ leads to artistic results of never-ending variety, beauty, and interest. In this matter we speak with an exceptional experience of above a quarter of a century.

Although we have pointed to the Concert-room Organ as the fountain of inspiration in scheming the Chamber Organ, we do not desire it to be understood that any absolute copying is to be contemplated; for between an instrument of from sixty to one hundred and odd speaking stops, including pedal stops of 32 ft., and an instrument of from fifteen to thirty stops, such a thing as direct reproduction is impracticable. On the contrary, it must, once for all, be understood and recognized that the true Chamber Organ is an instrument distinct and peculiar,—a work constructed on special lines, for a special purpose, perfect within its necessarily circumscribed limits, and aiming at nothing beyond its legitimate powers. Viewed in this light, the Chamber Organ assumes a dignity not hitherto accorded it, and becomes a study of great interest to the artist.

We have alluded to the almost universal failure, considered from a purely musical point of view, of the usual types of Chamber Organs, which have been produced by eminent organ builders and others at home and abroad, and in connection with which no reasonable outlay has been withheld; now it may not be uninteresting to note the more direct causes of this failure.

First, it will be found that nothing special or distinctive is presented by their contents; their stops being precisely those one would expect to find in ordinary Church Organs of the same dimensions. Secondly, it will be observed that little if any attempt has been made to adapt the stops, by special scaling, voicing, and regulating, to the conditions under which they are to be used and heard. Thirdly, that the instruments, as a general rule, are sadly deficient in powers of expression. Fourthly, that to obtain the requisite softness of tone the instruments have been crowded into chambers closed on all sides but one; or so inclosed with casework that muffled sounds, entirely devoid of character and brilliancy, are alone producible.

The best effect possible under such adverse conditions closely resembles that of a loud-toned Church Organ as heard from outside the closed doors of the church. Such an effect may be pleasing so far as it goes; but unfortunately it does not go far. It would be out of all reason to expect a musician to accept it as the *ne plus ultra* of chamber-organ tone; for it is obtained at the sacrifice of all free power of expression, brilliancy of tonal coloring, and grandeur. It is, in short, produced by a misdirected attempt to reconcile imperfectly-voiced and badly-chosen stops to the conditions which are necessarily imposed on a chamber instrument. If such a tonal effect could be followed, at will, by a grand *crescendo*, there would, perhaps, be less to say against it; but the very means which have beēn resorted to, to secure the subdued effect, render anything approaching an effective *crescendo* impossible. In fact, in instances of important and expensive Chamber Organs which have come under our own observation, this muffled, through-door, Church Organ effect was all they were capable of producing when at their full powers. Chamber Organs of the last type alluded to are certainly eloquent in negative teaching; but it is undesirable to occupy valuable space in enlarging on their too obvious short-comings.

We now come to the consideration of the practical branch of the present subject,—to the consideration of all those matters on which the true beauty, distinctive character, and flexibility of the Chamber Organ depend. We allude to the general scheme and scope of the instrument; the scaling, voicing, and disposition of the speaking stops, and their selection for the production of effective combinations of tone, for suitable accompaniments, and for solo passages; and the means of properly controlling and imparting flexibility and powers of expression to all the divisions of the instrument.

It must be obvious that in so complicated an instrument as a complete Chamber Organ, in which so much has to be provided in a limited space, the greatest ingenuity and care must be expended on its general scheme. The comparatively small number of speaking stops which can be properly accommodated in such an instrument renders their selection, scaling, and voicing matters of the very highest importance. Next to the proper treatment of the tonal forces, and hardly less in importance, come the mechanical appliances required to impart flexibility of voice and powers of expression to all, or nearly all, the speaking stops in the instrument.

The construction of a Chamber Organ which shall be worthy of the name, and which shall be to the private music-room or drawing-room what the grand Concert Organ is to the public concert-room, is a problem quite worthy of both the professional builder's and the musician's earnest attention. That the problem can be solved we have, at least to our own mind, satisfactorily proved; and that its solution is not attended with extreme difficulty, or with more than reasonable expense, can be safely asserted. For a successful issue, it is necessary that the individual who makes the essay should approach the matter without any prejudice or preconceived ideas, founded on previous teachings, or derived from the ordinary existing examples of so-called Chamber Organs.

GENERAL SCHEME OF THE ORGAN.

The general scheming and planning of Chamber Organs depend on so many circumstances, and are influenced by so many different considerations, that it is only possible to give here instructions and suggestions of common application. Although the positions which the Organs are to occupy, the dimensions of the apartments in which they are to be erected and heard, the range of the uses to which they are to be put, and the numbers of their divisions and speaking stops, should in all cases modify their schemes and direct their planning, yet the general principles we are about to lay down should direct everything and be alike observed in every instrument.

DIVISIONS AND CLAVIERS.—A great number of Chamber Organs have been made with only a single clavier, and, accordingly, with only one department. This one-ply type has already been mentioned, and may here be dismissed with a few condemnatory words. It is an instrument so hopelessly imperfect that it is a matter for wonder that it should have continued in use to the present time. Its introduction in the early epoch of modern organ-building may be understood; but its retention is not easily accounted for. We presume that it is the grandeur of tone characteristic of organ pipes which has alone recommended it; for from no other point of view is a one-manualed Chamber Organ, devoid of a pedal department, equal to a piano or a good harmonium. In powers of expression, and for the purpose of interpreting musical thought, it is far inferior to either of these instruments. The grandeur of tone just alluded to is certainly one of the chief glories of the Organ; but there are other equally important matters which must be held steadily in view in scheming an Organ. We desire to impress our readers with the necessity of imparting to the Chamber Organ the fullest possible powers of expression; and to assure them that every expedient that can be devised to increase the tonal flexibility of the instrument will be of the highest value from a musical point of view.

The first important question which arises under the present heading is—How many manual claviers should a properly appointed Chamber Organ possess? The answer is: In the largest and most fully developed instrument three; and in all other lesser instruments two. The three claviers should be designated either First, Second, and Third; or Great, Choir, and Solo respectively: and the two claviers should, in like manner, be called either First and Second; or Great and Solo respectively. The First or Great Organ clavier should invariably occupy the lowest position. It will be observed that in neither instance is the term Swell Organ adopted; the reason for this departure from the almost universal nomenclature will become evident later on.

Save in the large-sized Chamber Organs,—say of thirty speaking stops,—the adoption of three or two manual claviers may be left to individual judgment and taste; for, within ordinary limits, they do not imply the necessity for different contents so far as the speaking stops are concerned. Thus, fifteen or twenty stops may, with equal propriety, in accordance with our system, be distributed in two or three divisions and their subdivisions. In matters of mechanical and controlling appliances, the three-manualed Organ will, of necessity, be a more complicated and costly affair than the two-manualed instrument. In the Chamber Organ, as in the other classes of Organs, the introduction of three manual claviers gives the performer many facilities for the production of varied combinations and rapid changes of tone; and the value of these is almost as great in chamber as in concert-room music. It is, accordingly, quite proper to recommend the adoption of three manuals in all instruments of above twenty speaking stops.

The next important question is that relating to the compass of the manual claviers. The remarks already made anent the compass of the claviers of the Concert-room Organ also apply here. The compass of the Chamber Organ should invariably be from CC to c^4=61 notes. This compass will be found necessary in much chamber music, and especially in concerted music; and it gives facilities for the production of many brilliant effects by octave coupling.

Every Chamber Organ must have an independent pedal department commanded by a proper pedal clavier, the compass of which should be from CCC to G=32 notes. Of the proper form and proportions for this clavier, as well as those of the before-mentioned manual claviers, nothing need be said here, for all particulars respecting these important portions of the Organ are given in the Chapters devoted to them.

COUPLERS.—From the consideration of the manual and pedal claviers, in separate form, we naturally come to those mechanical appliances which are introduced for the purpose of connecting them together. In this matter it might seem sufficient to refer the reader to what has been said in preceding Chapters; but we think it a tiresome method, and withal a lazy one, to be continually referring to what may be found elsewhere. A little trouble, and perhaps some repetition, on our part will spare the patience of the reader, and probably prevent uncertainty as to our meaning.

In an instrument with rather limited resources, so far as the number of speaking stops is concerned, it is highly desirable to introduce as many couplers as are practicable; for through their agency numerous useful combinations and tonal effects are rendered available, which without such mechanical aids could not be obtained. For Chamber Organs with a pedal and two manual claviers, all the following couplers are to be recommended:

I. Solo to Great, Unison coupler.
II. Solo to Great, Sub-octave coupler.
III. Solo to Great, Octave coupler.
IV. Great to Pedal.
V. Solo to Pedal.

It is impossible to overrate the utility of the full complement of couplers in an instrument of two manuals and, say, fifteen or twenty speaking stops. Allowing that all the stops have been carefully selected with reference both to individuality of tone and mixing qualities, the three manual couplers add immensely to the variety of tonal effects as well as to the general power of the instrument.

Let us note, as an illustration of our meaning, what can be done with *two manual speaking stops* and the *three manual couplers*. Supposing that a TRUMPET, 8 FT., is drawn on the Great manual and a FLUTE, 8 FT., on the Solo manual, we find that, placing our fingers on the Great keys, no fewer than *seven combinations* or different tonal effects are producible by the simple manipulation of the *three couplers*, thus:—

I.—Drawing the Unison coupler gives the combination of TRUMPET, 8 FT., and FLUTE, 8 FT., throughout the entire compass=CC to c^4.

II.—Drawing the Octave coupler gives the combination of TRUMPET, 8 FT., and FLUTE, 4 FT., from CC to c^3

III.—Drawing the Sub-octave coupler gives the combination of FLUTE, 16 FT., and TRUMPET, 8 FT., from tenor C to c^4.

IV.—Drawing the Unison and Octave couplers gives the combinations of TRUMPET, 8 FT., FLUTE, 8 FT., and FLUTE, 4 FT., from CC to c^3; and TRUMPET, 8 FT., and FLUTE, 8 FT., from $c\sharp^3$ to c^4.

V.—Drawing the Sub-octave and Unison couplers gives the combinations of FLUTE, 16 FT., TRUMPET, 8 FT., and FLUTE, 8 FT., from tenor C to c^4; and TRUMPET, 8 FT., and FLUTE, 8 FT., from CC to BB.

VI.—Drawing the Sub-octave and Octave couplers gives the combinations of FLUTE, 16 FT., TRUMPET, 8 FT., and FLUTE, 4 FT., from tenor C to c^3; TRUMPET, 8 FT., and FLUTE 4 FT., from CC to BB; and FLUTE, 16 FT., and TRUMPET, 8 FT., from $c\sharp^3$ to c^4.

VII.—Drawing the Sub-octave, Unison, and Octave couplers gives the combinations of FLUTE, 16 FT., TRUMPET, 8 FT., FLUTE, 8 FT., and FLUTE, 4 FT., from tenor C to c^3; TRUMPET, 8 FT., FLUTE, 8 FT., and FLUTE, 4 FT., from CC to BB; and FLUTE, 16 FT., TRUMPET, 8 FT., and FLUTE, 8 FT., from $c\sharp^3$ to c^4.

With the above illustrations of what are possible in the case of *two stops only*, it is unnecessary to enlarge on the utility of the three manual couplers, or to direct attention to the practically countless tonal effects they are the means of producing in an Organ of only twenty speaking stops.

In important instruments having three manual claviers, the following couplers should certainly be introduced:

I. Choir to Great, Unison coupler.
II. Choir to Great, Sub-octave coupler.
III. Choir to Great, Octave coupler.
IV. Solo to Great, Unison coupler.
V. Solo to Choir, Unison coupler.
VI. Great to Pedal.
VII. Choir to Pedal.
VIII. Solo to Pedal.

There is another manual coupler of some value; but, for the Chamber Organ, we lay no stress on its introduction: we allude to the Octave coupler acting on the same clavier. Such a coupler may be applied to any clavier, but preferably to that of the Solo Organ.

It may be pointed out that in Organs which have a stop of 16 ft. pitch in either the Great or Choir divisions the Sub-octave coupler may be omitted. Its chief use is to introduce the 16 ft. tone on the Great clavier in small Organs which comprise nothing larger than 8 ft. stops in their manual divisions: notwithstanding this, we advocate the introduction of the Choir to Great, Sub-octave coupler, even when either division so coupled contains a stop of 16 ft. pitch.

DRAW-STOP KNOBS, ETC.—The proper arrangement of the draw-stop knobs commanding the speaking stops and couplers is a matter of no little importance; for on it depends the easy control of the tonal forces of the Organ. Every knob should be within the reach of the performer's hands without compelling him to move his body out of the correct central position.

In small Chamber Organs containing about ten speaking stops, the draw-stop knobs may conveniently be placed in a row above the upper clavier; but in larger instruments the knobs controlling both the speaking stops and couplers should be compactly disposed, in two groups, as close as practicable to the right and left cheeks of the claviers. As Chamber Organs are certain to be performed on by many persons who have had little or no previous knowledge of their peculiar arrangements and resources, and frequently at a moment's notice, it is very desirable that every assistance be provided by a distinct grouping of the draw-stop knobs belonging to each division; and also, when possible, by some distinctive treatment of the knobs themselves, whereby the eye can quickly recognize the divisions to which they belong. A decided difference of color is clearly the best way of doing this; and woods of different tints and stained ivory lend their aid in a perfectly satisfactory manner. In all cases the knobs must have face disks of white ivory, with clearly engraved inscriptions, uniformly black. It may be argued that the colored system has not the clean and elegant appearance of that in which knobs of white ivory alone are used: this may be so, but we place utility and convenience in such an important matter before mere beauty of appearance. We have frequently observed the inconvenience, in a Chamber Organ, of the uniform character of the draw-stop knobs, especially when strangers sat at the keys. However, this matter may be left to individual taste and judgment: but the proper grouping of the knobs in convenient positions, and the distinct labeling of each group, should never be neglected even in so humble an instrument as a small Chamber Organ.

It is unnecessary to speak here of those modern appliances which, in electro-pneumatic and tubular-pneumatic actions, are sometimes introduced in place of the ordinary draw-stop knobs. They will be found described elsewhere.

COMBINATION LEVERS AND PISTONS.—It is an open question as to what extent combination appliances should be introduced, or to what extent they are really necessary, in the average-sized Chamber Organ: but it may be taken for granted that each manual division should have, at least, two foot combination levers or two combination pistons; and that three additional foot-levers should be provided, two acting on all the speaking stops of the instrument, and the third bringing on and releasing, by double-action, the more important couplers. It would be found very convenient to have a separate foot-lever for each of the Pedal Organ couplers. In instruments of large size a more elaborate combination system is necessary, somewhat resembling that required in the Concert-room

Organ. Such being the case, we may refer the reader to the particulars, on Combination Systems, given in the preceding Chapter.

In Organs in which neither tubular-pneumatic nor electro-pneumatic actions are used, the combination system must be controlled by foot-levers only: but when either of the above actions obtain, the combination system may be controlled by thumb-pistons, combination-keys, or small rocking touches. Foot-levers may conveniently be retained for the full combinations and the important couplers.

EXPRESSION-LEVERS.—For a Chamber Organ the best and, indeed, the only suitable form of the expression-lever is the balanced. In even the smallest instrument, constructed on the system here advocated, two expression-levers are required for the manual divisions; while in the larger forms of the instrument three are necessary. The levers should be placed side by side, the lever on the left occupying the central position, above the pedal clavier. In this situation they can be commanded by either foot, or, as is frequently desirable, for the production of effects of compound expression, by both feet at the same instant.

As space is very valuable, in every direction, in a Chamber Organ, and everything approaching clumsiness is to be avoided, the expression-levers should be made only large enough to receive comfortably the sole of an average-sized shoe. Their inner edges should not be more than half an inch apart, so that the foot of the performer may be rapidly passed from one lever to the other, or may comfortably operate two levers at the same time.

In instruments which have an expressive Pedal Organ, it may be considered desirable, in addition to the mechanical arrangements which connect the shutters of its swell-chamber with the expression-levers of the manual divisions, to have an independent expression-lever placed above the right end of the pedal clavier, treated in the manner suggested for the Concert-room Organ.

TREMOLANT.—Every Chamber Organ of any pretensions should have a tremolant, affecting the division or divisions which contain the solo stops of most importance, or those which are best suited for the *tremolo* effect. In treating of the General Scheme of the Organ, it is only necessary so far as the tremolant is concerned to point out its importance, and to allude to the arrangements required for its proper command. In the first place, it should be brought on by the ordinary draw-stop action; its knob, key, or touch, being located, in the most convenient position, in the group belonging to the division of the instrument which it affects. In the second place, the tremolant should also be commanded by a foot-lever, which should hang, vertically, close to the outside edge of the expression-lever of its division, so that a slight lateral movement of the foot, while operating the expression-lever, will bring the tremolant into action; and the removal of the pressure will immediately stop it. The convenience of this arrangement must be obvious to the musician, rendering, as it does, a *tremolo* on a few notes, or even on a single note, possible at will, and that during a *crescendo* or a *diminuendo.*

Matters such as those alluded to in the foregoing brief remarks may appear of little importance in themselves, or when considered singly; but in the aggregate they are of the highest value in an instrument whose powers of flexibility and expression must be developed to the utmost limit if it is to become a worthy interpreter of refined musical thought. A Chamber Organ, worthy of the name, admits of no crudities either in its tonal forces or its mechanical appliances; it must, from first to last, be an instrument for the *virtuoso*, replete with refinement of voice, and susceptible of the most delicate effects of light and shade, subtile *nuances*, and marked tonal expression. It must be borne in mind that a Chamber Organ of only ten speaking stops, furnished with the most complete means of expression, will be a more perfect *musical instrument* and a more lasting source of pleasure than one of twice the number of stops not under satisfactory control.

SPEAKING STOPS.—In the Chamber Organ, as in the Organs considered in the preceding Chapters, the first matter claiming attention in connection with the speaking stops or sound-producing section of the instrument is the pressures of the wind advisable to be used. The importance of the wind-pressures cannot be overrated, for upon them depend the entire scaling and voicing of the pipe-work, and, accordingly, the volume, refinement, and prevailing quality of the tone of the instrument.

It is imperative that all the stops of the Chamber Organ be of a delicate and refined intonation, with, at the same time, sufficient volume, brilliancy, and distinctive character to render them effective both in combination and in solo effects. Voices of this satisfactory class, having slightly different musical values, may be secured by two different methods of procedure: First, by adopting very small scales and a moderately high pressure of wind; and, Secondly, by using medium, or even fairly large, scales and a low pressure of wind. The latter method is preferable for all Organs of importance, in which only one pressure of wind is used, simply because the tones produced are characterized by greater volume and grandeur than those yielded by pipes of small scales on wind of higher pressure. In Chamber Organs of considerable size it is desirable, if not necessary, to employ different pressures of wind, and a corresponding variety in the scales of the stops.

We have no hesitation in saying that, as a rule, wind of too high a pressure is adopted for Chamber Organs. Here, in particular, organ builders show their unwise advocacy of heavy wind. The average pressure hitherto used for important Chamber Organs is 3¼ inches: but we hold that this is too high for the general pipe-work, because of its tendency to make an Organ coarse, and too assertive for association with the Piano-forte and other instruments suitable for a private room. The introduction of tubular-pneumatic actions in the Chamber Organ has doubtless contributed to the retention of high pressures; but the use of pneumatic actions is certainly no argument for the adoption of an undesirable pressure in the sound-producing section. In all Organs in which pneumatic actions are desirable or necessary two or more pressures of wind should be provided.

It is highly desirable, at the present time, that some definite conclusion should be arrived at anent the most desirable wind-pressures for the speaking stops. We are firmly of opinion that the maximum pressure for the manual divisions, except, perhaps, in the case of a special Solo Organ, should not exceed 2½ inches; while certain softly-voiced stops in the Choir Organ may require the minimum pressure of 1½ inches. The adoption of a higher pressure than the maximum above given for the general pipe-work is not to be recommended, even when small scales are used, because it would impart a harsh and screaming intonation, very undesirable in a Chamber Organ. Experience has taught us that a pressure of 2⅜ inches is perfectly suitable for all the stops necessary in an ordinary Chamber Organ, and for both manual and pedal stops which are of medium scales, and are required to yield tones combining fulness with sufficient brilliancy for chamber music. With this pressure, sufficient wind can be supplied to all pipes to produce, with skilful voicing, the smooth and velvety tones which are so pleasant to the ear, without a trace of hissing or disagreeable windiness. It must be borne in mind that a Chamber Organ should be *all tone*—that is, the tone should be entirely free from the disturbing sound of rushing wind and every other objectionable quality which interferes with its purity.

A Chamber Organ, when properly located, is heard under most exacting conditions—conditions widely differing from those which obtain in the case of either a Church or a Concert-room instrument. A Chamber Organ has not the advantage of distance or great space to exercise a refining or other ameliorating influence on its tonality: it is listened to and judged by critical ears within twenty, and in many instances within ten, feet of its pipes. This is surely a sufficient reason for our insisting on extraordinary care being taken to secure absolute purity and refinement of tone in every pipe in the instrument. We have proved that this can be done by skill and care; and what has been done can be done again.

Unquestionably one of the most important matters connected with the speaking stops is their scaling; and for a Chamber Organ it demands more than ordinary consideration. On the question of scales not a little difference of opinion obtains among experts; accordingly, it is difficult, and perhaps undesirable, to lay down hard and fast rules on the subject. It is certainly undesirable to bind the accomplished organ builder to follow any definite course in a matter with which the artistic sense and a knowledge of the special requirements of each case have so much to do.

The commonly accepted idea of deriving the scales of the subordinate, organ-toned, stops from the scale of the chief foundation stop—Open Diapason, 8 ft.—should not be carried out in the tonal structure of the true Chamber Organ. It no doubt appeared the correct thing to the old-fashioned, conservative, builders of past times, whose notions of a Chamber Organ did not extend much beyond a one-manualed instrument, comprising only an Open Diapason, Stopped Diapason, Principal, Twelfth, and Fifteenth; but in an instrument which may reasonably be expected to accord more closely with modern musical taste and the deductions of advanced acoustical science, in which the old-world ideas find no support, it is unnecessary, as it is undesirable, to blindly follow traditional lines simply because they seem time-honored.

With an ample supply of wind of 2½ inches, scales sufficiently large to yield tones of great fulness and purity may always be adopted for the more important labial stops. For the Great Organ Open Diapason, 8 ft., a scale of from 5 inches to 5·5 inches will be found perfectly satisfactory; while, on the same wind, the scale of the Pedal Organ Open Diapason, 16 ft., of wood, may be 8 inches by 10 inches. On a similar wind pressure, reed stops of moderately large scales can be introduced with perfect safety; and they can be voiced to yield full and rich tones, devoid of the disagreeable buzz and brassiness only too common in such stops voiced on wind of the higher pressures usually adopted. The scales most desirable for the flute-toned and string-toned stops depend greatly on the qualities and strengths of the tones aimed at, and the special treatments of their voicers. We are in favor of medium scales for the former and small scales for the string-toned stops; indeed, small scales are absolutely necessary for the production of *imitative* string-tone. It is proper to point out that of all classes of organ stops, those producing imitative string-tones are the only ones which can be said to suffer loss of character from a low-pressure wind (we are confining our remarks to stops suitable for the Chamber Organ); accordingly, when possible, a slightly heavier wind, say of 3 inches, should be furnished for stops of this class, and certain others of a pronounced orchestral character. The very delicate string-toned stops, such as the Viola da Gamba, Viola d'Amore, and the labial Æoline, produce their most desirable tones on a wind of moderately low pressure.

There is one drawback attending the use of such scales as we have advocated for the more important stops in the Chamber Organ; namely, the space requisite for their proper accommodation. It is likely, therefore, that in many cases, where space is very limited, smaller scales will be adopted, accompanied by a slight increase in the wind pressure. The general tonal character of the instrument will suffer by this latter treatment; at least, the desirable volume of pure velvety tone will be replaced by a certain thinness and extreme brightness which is liable to fatigue the sensitive ear.

It will be gathered from the preceding remarks that we are not in favor of the general adoption of small scales for the stops of a properly-appointed Chamber Organ. Indeed, the contrary is the case. For the more important unison stops, or those which form the backbone of the Organ, so to speak, we advocate what, for such an instrument, may be considered large scales; depending upon skilful voicing, moderate wind-pressure, and absolutely perfect regulation, to produce the dignified, round, even, and absolutely pure tones required. These remarks specially apply to the foundation unison stops; for when one comes to consider the octave, super-octave, mutation, and compound stops, which build up, scientifically, the tonal structure of the Organ, one must recognize the necessity of rejecting old-time methods in favor of those dictated by the natural laws of musical sounds; and, by proper scaling and voicing, avoid any tendency toward that screaming character of tone which would limit the usefulness of such highly pitched stops to a very undesirable extent.

Considerable judgment must be exercised in the selection and treatment of the octave stops (4 ft.); because, in a Chamber Organ, whose tonal resources are necessarily circumscribed, they must not only fulfil their proper function in the tonal scheme of the instrument but be available for solo effects. It should never be overlooked in scheming a Chamber Organ that every one of its stops should be equally useful, and practically independent of each other; while they should be so balanced in relation to each other as to render it impossible to draw a useless or a disagreeable combination. As matters relating to the tonal structure of the Organ are gone into, with some degree of fulness, in the Chapter devoted to that subject, it is unnecessary to enlarge on it here: it is sufficient to say that in the introduction, in the Chamber Organ, of all stops which corroborate the harmonic upper partial tones of the foundation unison, the principles laid down in that Chapter should be carefully observed.

In Chamber Organs of moderate size, hitherto constructed, little or no science has been brought to bear on their tonal appointment; and much of their poverty of tone may be attributed to this fact. The multiplication of unison and what may be called fancy stops can never make up for a serious short-coming in the true tonal structure of the Organ proper. Let the tonal structure be adequately provided, and then any number of solo and fancy stops may be added with a reasonable certainty of improving the instrument.

Every properly appointed Chamber Organ must have a foundation unison of dominating voice in the chief manual division,—the First or Great Organ,—and this will of course be an Open Diapason, 8 ft. Too much care cannot be expended on the construction and voicing of this all-important stop, for upon it depends much of the grandeur of the complete instrument. When wind of 2½ inches is used, the scale of the CC pipe should be 5·24 inches; and the scale may be increased to 5·46 inches when a pressure of 2¼ or 2⅜ inches is adopted. In its voicing, a full volume of round organ-tone should be secured, in preference to the bright and somewhat thin quality, approaching a string-tone, which characterizes many of the so-called Open Diapasons of the present time. In all cases every trace of windiness must be eradicated by a just apportionment of wind to each pipe, and a perfect regulation of the tone throughout the compass. Any marked imperfections in the tone of the Open Diapason will be fatal to the beauty of the division in which it is placed, if not to that of the entire instrument. *It is impossible to build up a worthy structure upon a bad foundation.*

Next in importance, in the tonal structure of the Organ, is the stop which corroborates the first upper partial of the foundation unison; namely, the Octave, 4 ft., or so-called Principal. In all instruments designed to produce a satisfactory tonal effect, an Octave specially related to the Open Diapason should be introduced; but its adjustment to the foundation unison need not circumscribe its usefulness either in combination or as a solo stop. As it has to be voiced many degrees softer, and of a lighter and more silvery tone, than the Open Diapason, it forms a brightening element in many combinations of the softer unison stops. The Octave should be of a scale considerably smaller than that of the pipes of the same speaking length in the Open Diapason. By way of a guide, we may remark that when the 4 ft. pipe of the Open Diapason measures 3·21 inches in diameter, the 4 ft. pipe of the relative Octave need not exceed 2·62 inches in diameter, while, under certain conditions, it may be of a still smaller scale with advantage.

The next important component part of the tonal structure is the stop, called the TWELFTH, $2\frac{2}{3}$ FT., which corroborates the second upper partial tone of the foundation unison. It is just a question, however, how far this mutation stop is necessary in the Chamber Organ. In an instrument of small dimensions its presence may be dispensed with; and, indeed, unless it is scientifically treated as regards strength and character of voice, it may not prove, in any instrument, a desirable element in the tonal scheme. It may be added, however, that, as it corroborates one of the more important upper partials, and as the true compound organ-tone cannot be produced without it, it should find a place in the tonal appointment of every complete Chamber Organ, scientifically adjusted in strength of intonation. As the TWELFTH should invariably be covered by a SUPER-OCTAVE or FIFTEENTH, 2 FT., which corroborates the third upper partial, it may be convenient to associate the two stops in the form of a MIXTURE. The pipes forming this MIXTURE should only be slightly larger than the usual DULCIANA scale, and be voiced to yield a quiet and singing tone.

The introduction of an independent SUPER-OCTAVE, in the form of a solo stop, is rendered more easy by the insertion of the above MIXTURE; for it is no longer necessary to consider it in the light of a harmonic-corroborating stop, fashioned under exacting natural laws. Accordingly, it may with great propriety be introduced in the form of an ORCHESTRAL PICCOLO, or, softer in tone, in that of a FLAGEOLET, 2 FT.

We now come to a rather important question—that relating to the high-pitched compound stops for the Chamber Organ. Opinions differ as to the advisability of introducing compound stops of any description in such an instrument; but we venture, in advocating their systematic introduction, to think that those, outside the practical organ-building world, who are adverse to them, judge, not on scientific grounds, but from the miserable screaming specimens with which they are acquainted in ordinary Church Organs, without pausing to think that what is right theoretically may also be made, by judgment and skill, right practically.

We are quite satisfied that it is desirable, if not imperative, that every Chamber Organ, worthy of the name, should contain at least one compound harmonic-corroborating stop; for, as we have elsewhere said, it is impossible to obtain the true compound organ-tone without the presence of its high harmonic sounds. It must be obvious to every musician, who has given any attention to tonal combinations, that as loud and penetrating MIXTURES are of questionable value in large Church and Concert-room Organs, they must of necessity be out of place in a Chamber Organ of any dimensions. When they approach a screaming intonation they can only be tolerated in full combinations, in which the foundation unisons and the entire harmonic series of stops are present. This is a most undesirable narrowing of their value and utility, and such a treatment should be avoided. In a properly-balanced Chamber Organ the MIXTURE exercises an important influence on its tonal capabilities; the range of that influence of course depending entirely upon its composition and tonal character. It should be of the softest and most musical intonation, secured by pipes of very small scale, voiced on the smallest supply of wind compatible with perfect speech. To test the proper quality of a Chamber Organ MIXTURE, let it be drawn with the DULCIANA,

8 FT., or some other equally delicate unison stop; if it is what it ought to be, it will form not only a satisfactory but a really beautiful combination. This severe test has been suggested by our own experience. In our own Chamber Organ the DULCIANA, 8 FT., and the CORNET, of five ranks (in different swell-boxes), formed one of the most beautiful combinations that could be desired.

The MIXTURE, whatever the number of its ranks or the nature of its component intervals may be, must be formed of pipes of extremely small scale, voiced and regulated in such a manner as to give the mutation ranks less prominence in tone than those representing such intervals as the 8ve, 15th, 22nd, and 29th. The composition of compound stops suitable for the Chamber Organ deserves careful consideration; and is, of course, largely influenced, if not absolutely dictated, by the general tonal scheme of the instrument.

Three representative examples of compositions, perfectly adapted for the MIXTURES of Chamber Organs of different sizes, are here given. All their breaks are on the same notes; but in the event of any two of these MIXTURES being introduced in the same Organ, it will be desirable to alter in one of them the notes on which the breaks occur. No two compound stops in one instrument should break on the same notes.

CARILLON—III. RANKS.

CC	to	BB,	15—19—22.
C	to	B,	12—17—22.
c^1	to	b^1,	12—15—17.
c^2	to	c^4,	8—12—15.

This stop should be formed of small-scaled tapered pipes, of the GEMSHORN class, voiced to yield a bright and delicate tone. It has, when properly made, a bell-like quality that is very charming in combination with the voices of the softer unisons, and especially with those of the flute-toned stops.

DULCIANA CORNET—V. RANKS.

CC	to	BB	19—22—24—26—29.
C	to	B,	12—15—17—19—22.
c^1	to	b^1,	8—12—17—19—22.
c^2	to	c^4,	1— 8—10—12—15.

Formed of small-scaled DULCIANA pipes, and voiced to yield a singing character of tone, this CORNET is in every way suitable for the Chamber Organ. It must be regulated to the utmost nicety; care being taken to keep the third-sounding rank—the 24th, 17th, and 10th—more subdued than the others. Much of the beauty of this stop is due to its highest rank being of octaves, which correctly cover the lower mutation intervals and give a completeness to its tonal character. The DULCIANA CORNET is a model softly-toned compound stop, most effective in combinations of all kinds. In every respect it is superior to the CARILLON; but a stop comprising 305 pipes of so small a scale, all carefully voiced and regulated, is, of necessity, a rather troublesome and costly affair. On this account it will not be commonly introduced in Chamber Organs: it is, however, as we know from direct experience, well worth all the trouble and money it costs. Its harmonic-corroborating powers impart great richness to the full Organ, without producing any shrillness, or a trace of that screaming character which invariably accompanies the use of loud-voiced and large-scaled MIXTURES; while it invests soft combinations with almost indescribable charms.

HARMONIA ÆTHERIA—V. RANKS.

CC	to	BB,	15—19—22—26—29.
C	to	B,	12—15—19—22—26.
c^1	to	b^1,	8—12—15—19—22.
c^2	to	c^4,	1—5—8—12—15.

Properly made, this is the most delicately-toned compound stop in the Organ. Its pipes should be of the VOX ANGELICA or of the ÆOLINE class, according to the character of tone desired. When made of the former class of pipes, its voice will be of almost pure organ-tone; while, made of the latter class, its tone will be slightly stringy. The delicate quality of the stop is favored by its having only octaves and fifths in its composition; and by the full character of its upper break of two octaves, in which one member of the 16 ft. harmonic series appears. The HARMONIA ÆTHERIA is most suitable for the Choir division of the Chamber Organ, voiced on wind of about 1½ inches pressure.

The flute-toned stops, of which there is a considerable variety at the disposal of the modern builder, are of the greatest value in the Chamber Organ, especially when the instrument is designed for concerted playing with the piano and stringed instruments. Every Chamber Organ of any importance should have at least two stops of this class, including, in all cases, a FLAUTO TRAVERSO, or ORCHESTRAL FLUTE, preferably of 8 ft. pitch. The second unison flute-toned stop may with great advantage be a DOPPELFLÖTE, 8 FT., the tone of which, carefully voiced on 2½ inch wind, is singularly rich and full, with perfect mixing qualities. Probably there is no stop in the Organ more valuable for combination with the reed stops: with the CLARINET it produces an imitation of the orchestral instrument of a truly striking character. After those just named, the most desirable FLUTES are those which group themselves into the family of LIEBLICHGEDECKTS. These are covered stops of 16 ft., 8 ft., 4 ft., and 2 ft., pitch, with tones of a quiet and refined quality. Probably the most beautiful octave flute-toned stop for the Choir division of the Chamber Organ is the FLAUTO D'AMORE, 4 FT., a half-covered stop of an extremely delicate intonation, most valuable for soft accompaniments, in combination with the DULCIANA, 8 FT., VIOLA D'AMORE, 8 FT., ÆOLINE, 8 FT., VOX ANGELICA, 8 FT., or other softly-voiced stops.

Of the fuller-toned FLUTES, formed of open wood pipes, suitable for the Chamber Organ, the most generally useful are the CLARABELLA, 8 FT., the HARMONICA, 8 FT., and the ZARTFLÖTE, 4 FT. To these may be added the MELODIA, 8 FT., yielding a full and rich flute-tone, and being perfectly suited for the Great division. Descriptions of all the above named FLUTES will be found in the Chapter on the Names and General Particulars of Organ Stops.

VIOLS, or imitative string-toned stops, come next in order of importance; and it is desirable to introduce at least one characteristic member of this family in every Chamber Organ, however small it may be; while in instruments approaching a complete form there should be one or more placed in every division. In the Pedal Organ, the stop will appear as a VIOLONE, 16 FT., CONTRA-BASSO, 16 FT., or VIOLONCELLO, 8 FT. As floor space is always a matter of consideration in a Chamber Organ scheme, it may be desirable to derive the VIOLONCELLO from the CONTRA-BASSO by means of an octave action; the latter stop having an extra top octave of pipes added to complete the compass of the VIOLONCELLO. In the manual divisions, the string-toned stops will chiefly be of 8 ft. pitch; and will appear under the names of VIOLIN, VIOLA, and VIOLONCELLO, according to their tonal character. These must be voiced to be as strongly imitative of the respective orchestral instruments as skill can accomplish; for, although they are valuable in combinations, their great value lies in their solo voices.

The secondary class of string-toned stops should be imitative of the more ancient and delicately-toned bowed instruments, such as the Viola da Gamba and Viola d'Amore; and the stops may, reasonably, bear their names.

The string-toned stops above alluded to will frequently be used in rendering passages originally written for the Violin or Violoncello, and for producing, in combination, certain characteristic orchestral effects. It is not too much to say that no Chamber Organ can approach completeness, or become an interesting and effective instrument, unless it contains two or more stops of the VIOL family. In an instrument of the largest chamber type, a VIOLETTA OR OCTAVE VIOL, 4 FT., may be introduced with advantage; but it must be of very soft intonation. It is extremely valuable in combination with the unison VIOLS, materially enriching their compound tones.

How far it may be advisable, in the large Chamber Organ, to have a subdivision entirely devoted to string-toned stops, after the manner so strongly advocated in connection with the Concert-room Organ, is a question which may well be left to individual taste and other controlling circumstances. When money is no object and space is ample, we should strongly advise the adoption of this subdivision. It should be commanded by the second clavier, being instantaneously brought on or silenced by a pneumatic ventil operated by thumb-pistons.

Having briefly touched upon the more important labial stops, we may now consider, in an equally brief manner, the reed stops which are best adapted for chamber music, and which should, accordingly, find a place in the Chamber Organ. Of those suitable for the manual divisions, the TRUMPET, 8 FT., OBOE, 8 FT., and CLARINET, 8 FT., are unquestionably the most generally useful. Being of unison pitch, they impart great richness and dignity to the fuller combinations; while as solo voices they are of the first rank. An octave reed stop is not of any great value in a Chamber Organ; but should one be desired, it should be an OCTAVE OBOE, 4 FT., of the softest intonation consistent with its true character.

The TRUMPET should be of a medium scale, and voiced to yield a clear ringing quality of tone, free from the harsh, brassy tone which so many voicers appear to delight in. The moderate wind pressure we have advocated will go far to secure the agreeable quality necessary for the refined character of the true Chamber Organ. As the tubes of the TRUMPET can be mitred in any direction, generally with advantage to the tone, there is no difficulty, even in swell-boxes of moderate height, in carrying the stop throughout the entire compass of the division. On no account should so important a stop be inserted in an incomplete form; for the absence of the bass octave very seriously impairs the general utility of the whole, disturbs the balance of the division in which it is planted, and denudes the stop of the chief part of its grandeur. The TRUMPET is the most important reed for the First or Great Organ.

The OBOE should find an honored place in every Chamber Organ, small or large, being invaluable in combinations of medium strength, and beautiful in solo passages. Perhaps no reed stop in the Chamber Organ is more valuable than the OBOE; and, as its slender tubes admit of mitring, it should invariably be introduced of full compass. The stop is voiced in two ways; one producing a soft, round, normal reed-tone of pleasing quality, mixing well with all the other classes of tone in the Organ; and the other yielding a thin, delicate sound, closely resembling (in the best examples) the tone of the orchestral instrument. The selection of either of these qualities may be left to individual taste and judgment in the generality of cases; but it may be pointed out that when a generally useful reed is aimed at, or when, in a very small Organ, one reed only is to be inserted, the former, or normal reed-tone, is to be preferred. When, on the other hand, a highly characteristic solo voice is desired, the imitative stop, or ORCHESTRAL OBOE as it is usually called, is certainly the one to be selected. The ORCHESTRAL OBOE produces many charming effects in music of light and pastoral character, and imparts a peculiar orchestral coloring to numerous soft combinations. In an instrument furnished with a TRUMPET, as above described, the ORCHESTRAL OBOE is decidedly the best to be adopted. As the Oboe of the orchestra does not go below B♭, the greater part of the two lower octaves of the organ stop has no relation to the instrument proper: but as the orchestral Bassoon or Fagotto furnishes the true bass to the Oboe, the lower portion of the organ stop—from CC to A—should be voiced to imitate the Fagotto. Under this arrangement the complete stop should be labeled OBOE AND FAGOTTO, 8 FT. We may just remark that it would be found convenient to divide this stop at A—B♭, and let the divisions be drawn separately. The advantage of such a method will be obvious to every musician.

As an imitative stop, with a decided coloring, the CLARINET may justly be considered the most satisfactory of all the reeds introduced in the Organ. Such being the case it should, in all possible instances, find a place in the Chamber Organ: and as its pipes occupy less space than those of any other reed stop (save, perhaps, some forms of the VOX HUMANA)—the CC pipe, producing the 8 ft. tone, being only about 4 feet 10 inches in total length by about 1·65 inches in diameter—the stop can conveniently be carried throughout the manual compass, even in swell-boxes of very moderate dimensions. When skilfully voiced and regulated, the CLARINET is a most charming solo stop; and it is also very pleasing in combination with all classes of labial stops. The stop must be provided with means for its perfect regulation, for this is an important matter in so delicately-toned an instrument as the true Chamber Organ. On the perfect smoothness and equality of tone, from the lowest to the highest note, depend much of the peculiar beauty and pleasing character of the CLARINET.

The manual reed stop which may be considered next in importance (for the Chamber Organ) is, perhaps, that known as the VOX HUMANA, 8 FT. It must be granted that the insertion of this stop in such an exacting instrument as the Chamber Organ is a matter deserving more than ordinary consideration. If good in tone, and perfectly adapted to its position, there can be no question as to its interest and value: but if it is so made and voiced as to yield the usual harsh and nasal sounds, and to require distance to lend enchantment to its tones, then it is an abomination in a private room, beyond the power of polite language to describe. The expedient of giving artificial distance to the VOX HUMANA, by inclosing it in a separate box placed within the main swell-box, has only been to a small degree successful. By such means the tones of the stop are literally smothered; and it becomes a question if the cure (if it can be so termed) is not worse than the disease. We utterly condemn everything that muffles, or in any manner interferes with, the free delivery of its tones. If the VOX HUMANA is to be inserted in a Chamber Organ, it must be made and voiced, by the hands of an artist, specially for the position it is to occupy. All the delicacy and character required must be inherent in the stop itself; and, while distance cannot but impart additional charms to its voice, it must be independent of its ameliorating effect. That such a rare stop can be made, and, indeed, has been made, we have absolute proof.* It is well known that the imitative quality of the VOX HUMANA is almost altogether dependent on the *tremolo* effect imparted to it by the Tremolant; but it is not commonly realized that, when properly voiced, it is, without the *tremolo*, a very valuable reed in combination with various labial stops. Such, however, is the case; and it is evident that a VOX HUMANA which is perfectly satisfactory in its dual capacity must form an important addition to the Chamber Organ.

It is much to be regretted that English and American organ builders and reed voicers have not given the construction of *free reed* stops their earnest attention; for had they done so, the list of reed stops, suitable for the Chamber Organ, would at the present time be considerably larger than it is. The perfectly smooth tone of the free reed would go far to favor its liberal introduction in Organs

* Writing, in the year 1889, of the author's Chamber Organ, and specially alluding to its VOX HUMANA, Mr. Clarence Eddy, the well-known Concert Organist, says: "To the eye it is 'a thing of beauty,' while to the ear it is a constant surprise in the variety of its tonal coloring and peculiarly charming effects. In voicing, your Organ is the most unique of all the Chamber Organs with which I am acquainted. Each stop is individual in character, and yet it assimilates in combination with every other stop in the Organ in a manner rarely heard. It would be a pleasure, if time would permit, to dwell upon the beauty of each department, but mention must be made of the extraordinary five-rank MIXTURE, which is quite after my own heart in its delicacy of voicing. The reeds are exceptionally fine; and it would be difficult to find so satisfactory a VOX HUMANA, while its accessory, the Tremolo, is absolutely perfect. I do not remember ever to have heard one so quiet and at the same time so efficient.

"The degree of expressive power contained in your beautiful Organ is remarkable; and let us hope that this feature at least will receive just recognition, and prove a source of emulation to organ builders."

designed for small rooms, in which it would greatly enrich the tones of the labial stops, without imparting the brassy clang which commonly attends the liberal use of the striking reed stops, and which always requires the saving grace of distance to refine and smoothen it to the ear. There are certain orchestral instruments which could be more or less successfully imitated by free reed stops, which at present receive practically no attention from reed voicers; we allude to the Horn, Cor Anglais, and the Saxophones. Stops successfully imitating these beautiful instruments would, indeed, be valuable additions to Organs of every class. The builders of Germany and France are not so backward as English and American builders are in the use of free reed stops; for, in addition to the PHYSHARMONICA, as found in the Lucerne and Fribourg Organs, they make the CLARINET, OBOE, COR ANGLAIS, and EUPHONE, as free reeds.

These brief remarks anent the stops suitable for the manual divisions of the Chamber Organ may be concluded with a few words respecting certain valuable stops which may be considered to be outside the different classes already touched upon. First, in order of importance, is the DULCIANA, 8 FT., and no Chamber Organ can be considered complete, or even to approach completeness, unless it contains this refined and beautiful stop. For the most delicate solo effects, and for the lightest class of accompaniment, it is invaluable. Considerable diversity of opinion obtains respecting the strength and coloring of the tone of the DULCIANA, as made for ordinary instruments; but we venture to think there can be no question that the DULCIANA in the Chamber Organ should be a perfect echo to the OPEN DIAPASON, yielding an extremely delicate, singing, and pure organ-tone of perfect mixing character. This quality will be found to be generally useful.

The still softer stop commonly called the VOX ANGELICA, 8 FT., is the most delicate of all the organ voices, and is admirably adapted for the small Chamber Organ. It should not, however, take the place of the DULCIANA, unless it is voiced much louder than its normal tone. When introduced along with the DULCIANA, the VOX ANGELICA should have a contrasting tone, approaching the ÆOLINE in character.

How far it is desirable to follow the favorite practice of introducing the stop known as the VOIX CÉLESTES in the Chamber Organ is open to question—at its best it is a matter of taste. That the peculiar compound tremulous sound, produced by the two 8 feet ranks out of tune with each other, is a great favorite with countless organists there can be no doubt; but, as they favor so many things in organ appointment that are unquestionably imperfect, their approval of the common, so-called, VOIX CÉLESTES counts for little. This question is discussed elsewhere, so need not be pursued here.

In considering the important question of the stops necessary and desirable for the Pedal Organ, the chief difficulty which presents itself is the space they demand for their proper accommodation. It is this difficulty of finding adequate floor space and height which has, in the generality of instances, and even in apartments of considerable dimensions, prevented the introduction of open stops of 16 ft. speaking length, and has caused the too general adoption of covered stops of 16 ft. tone. It is quite evident that in rooms of the average size, which cannot be altogether sacrificed to the Organ, it is impossible to locate the lower octave of an open stop of 16 ft., unless some special arrangement has been made for its reception. If the pipes forming the stop are of wood, and in nearly all cases they are certain to be so, all that are above ten feet in length may be mitred; and the four or five larger pipes may be laid horizontally, in any convenient place, behind the Organ. If a recess or shallow chamber can be formed from the room, or, what is better, planned along with the music-room in the first instance, all difficulty in connection with the appointment of an adequate Pedal Organ disappears. To further economize space, the CCC, DDD, and EEE pipes of the wood OPEN DIAPASON can be made, by an arrangement of pneumatic valves, elsewhere described, to yield also the CCC♯, DDD♯, and FFF notes; thereby saving three pipes of large size. By this expedient considerable economy of both space and money is arrived at.

There can be no question as to the immense value of an open 16 ft. stop in a Chamber Organ, notwithstanding the rarity of its introduction except in instruments of the first magnitude; for its pure, quiet, and dignified tone imparts a grandeur otherwise unattainable in a small instrument; while it supplies a perfect groundwork of sound on which all varieties of manual combinations may rest, enriched, but otherwise undisturbed. The best scale for the CCC pipe, 16 ft., is 8 inches in width by 10 inches in depth. Except when voiced on higher pressures than that previously recommended, stops of smaller scales will, in their lower octave, be rather weak and slow of speech. The OPEN DIAPASON, 16 FT., should be voiced to yield a pure prime tone of unobtrusive character, which will support and not outweigh the rest of the tonal forces of the instrument. At the same time it must be sufficiently clear and self-assertive to render independent passages distinctly.

The stop almost invariably introduced in small Chamber Organs is of the BOURDON or LIEBLICHGEDECKT species, of 16 ft. tone. The longest pipe being about 9 feet, of smaller scale than that above mentioned, the introduction of the stop presents no difficulties. The chief peculiarity in the speech of the BOURDON is its tendency to combine the second upper partial with the ground or prime tone. This peculiarity is sometimes affected in the voicing of the stop, and, as a distinguishing appellation, it is then called a QUINTATEN, 16 FT. When there is no open stop of 16 feet, it is desirable that the BOURDON or LIEBLICHGEDECKT should be of medium scale, and voiced to yield the prime tone as free from the twelfth as possible. But when there is also an OPEN DIAPASON, 16 FT., in the Pedal Organ, the covered stop of the same pitch may, with advantage to the general effect of the division, be of the QUINTATEN class. When crisply voiced it forms an effective stop, somewhat resembling the orchestral Contra-Basso in tone, materially enriching the resources of the Organ.

In all instances where space permits it is advisable to introduce an independent open stop of 8 ft. speaking length. This should be a VIOLONCELLO, as closely imitative of the tones of the orchestral instrument as the voicer's art can accomplish. This will always prove a valuable voice, both in ordinary bass and in melodic passages. Should a second octave stop be contemplated, it ought to be an open wood FLUTE, 8 FT., of soft intonation. When space is the only consideration which militates against the introduction of this independent FLUTE, the equivalent may be obtained by adding an octave of pipes to the OPEN DIAPASON, 16 FT., and inserting a pedal Octave coupler. The octave stop thus obtained will be more powerful than is required for the perfect balance of tone in combination, but in full effects the defect will not be very evident. The stop will be valuable for melodic and solo passages on the pedals.

When the Organ is large, and is placed to full advantage in a properly constructed music-room, a metal DULCIANA, 16 FT., should certainly be added to the pedal department. The value of a very delicate and refined bass for soft accompaniments cannot be overestimated. Nine-tenths of all the Chamber Organs in existence are seriously impaired by the want of a soft pedal stop. The lowest octave of the DULCIANA will form admirable towers in the design of the organ-front.

A reed stop of 16 ft. pitch is a most desirable addition to the Pedal Organ; but its introduction, in a perfectly satisfactory form, is attended with certain difficulties. If a striking reed of the ordinary construction is contemplated, it will be found almost impossible to get it sufficiently smooth and refined in tone. The vibrations of the larger tongues are generally accompanied by a rough and disagreeable noise, impossible to be sufficiently subdued to be pleasant in a small or ordinary apartment. If it is a free reed, it unfortunately demands considerable space for its accommodation. Perhaps it may be desirable to explain what is to be understood by the last remark. Although the metal tubes of a free reed stop of 16 ft. tone are not larger in diameter, and are considerably shorter, than the corresponding tubes of a striking reed of similar pitch, the boots are altogether different affairs, being immense in comparison to the ordinary boots of the striking reed pipes. For instance, the wooden boot of the CCC pipe of the CONTRA-SAXOPHONE, 16 FT. (as placed in our own Chamber Organ), measures 4½ inches wide by 5 inches deep, and no less than 4 feet 3 inches high. The metal tube, of the usual inverted conical shape, is about 10 feet in length. The tubes can be mitred in any convenient fashion, and usually with advantage to the tone. The tones of free reed stops are of remarkable smoothness and purity, and while the graver ones have a characteristic reedy quality, they are entirely free from the buzz more or less pronounced in every striking reed.

Such a stop as the free reed BASS or CONTRA-SAXOPHONE, 16 FT., is of great value in the pedal department, both in combination with the other stops and for solo or melodic passages. It forms a satisfactory bass for the manual reed stops of soft intonation. Should this free reed stop be difficult to obtain, a labial stop constructed on the Haskell model may be substituted.

Having thus briefly touched, in a general way, on the question of the speaking stops most suitable for the properly-appointed Chamber Organ, without, however, alluding to certain fancy and ear-tickling stops which will be found described in their proper place in our pages, we have now to consider the apportionment of such stops in the different divisions and subdivisions of the instrument, and the means to be adopted to secure for them adequate powers of flexibility and expression.

THE FIRST OR GREAT ORGAN.

LOWER CLAVIER—PARTLY EXPRESSIVE.

The division of the Chamber Organ which, for our present purpose, we prefer to designate the First Organ, is, under our proposed treatment, the most extensive, complete, and important one of the instrument. In this division should be congregated the chief organ-toned stops,—namely, the Open Diapason, 8 ft., Octave, 4 ft., Super-octave, 2 ft., Mixture, etc.,—two or three of the full-toned reed stops, and a proportion of the chief labial stops suitable for solo passages and accompaniment. The full tone of this division should be characterized by depth and richness of harmonic structure, while its leading combinations should afford considerable variety of tonal coloring. Every care should be taken, in the selection of the stops, in the relation of their scales, and in their voicing, to render it difficult, if not impossible, to draw an unsatisfactory combination. When the Organ is of moderate size, or when the total number of the manual speaking stops is about fifteen or sixteen, it is advisable to place about two-thirds of the number in the First Organ; the remaining stops being apportioned to the Second Organ, commanded by the upper clavier. When the instrument is of larger dimensions, and comprises three manual divisions, the First Organ may conveniently contain about three-fifths or two-thirds of the manual stops.

Now comes the all-important question how to impart perfect flexibility of tone and the maximum power of expression to the First Organ; for without a system of complete control, in both these directions, the Chamber Organ, as a musical instrument, is a "delusion and a snare." Let there be no misunderstanding in this very important matter. The only stop which it is desirable to place beyond the control of the expression-levers, and outside the swell-boxes, is the Open Diapason. The pipes of this important stop may with advantage be displayed on the exterior of the Organ, forming the chief towers in small instruments, and subordinate features in large ones. Such salient positions secure for the stop perfect freedom of speech and predominance of tone, placing it at once in the prominent position it is entitled to hold in the general tonal scheme.

The other stops of the First Organ should be about equally divided, and inclosed in *two* independent swell-boxes. Let the student of organ-building pay special attention to this disposition of the tonal forces; for, so far as can be ascertained, the Author of the present treatise is the first who has suggested the desirability, and practically proved the advantage, of dividing any *one division* of an Organ into *two distinct expressive sections*, while both can be played together or separately on *one clavier*.* This arrangement forms one of the most important steps, in our opinion, toward rendering the Organ a thoroughly flexible and expressive instrument, and one better suited than any ordinary tonal apportionment for the satisfactory interpretation of the inspirations of the great composers, and the

* The partition of the First Organ into three subdivisions—two *expressive* and one *unexpressive*—was first carried into effect, about the year 1872, by the Author in his own Chamber Organ, and with highly satisfactory results musically.

musical thoughts of the *improvvisatore*. For the production, with perfect ease and certainty, of complex orchestral effects, subtile *nuances*, and a greatly increased range of *crescendo* and *diminuendo*, no method, so far as is known to us, can equal the one here suggested.

We must now give some further details respecting this arrangement, so that it may be thoroughly understood and its peculiar advantages realized by the student. Let it be supposed that the First Organ comprises thirteen stops, to be apportioned as above directed; six of these will be placed in what may be designated, for convenient recognition, the *back swell-box;* and six in what may be called the *front swell-box*. The OPEN DIAPASON, 8 FT., will be placed outside the latter, while it derives its wind from the inclosed wind-chest, or from a special wind-chest commanded by the same mechanism. Six stops are thus apportioned to each of the expressive subdivisions of the First Organ. The independent valves of both wind-chests must be connected by one action with the single clavier of the First Organ. This arrangement would, however, be of little value, at least in one of its important offices, unless means were provided for instantaneously connecting or disconnecting, at the will of the performer, either of the subdivisions to or from the clavier. This is conveniently secured by simple pneumatic ventils which control the wind supplied separately to each subdivision. The ventils are commanded by thumb-pistons or touches, placed immediately under the First Organ clavier. Should the action be electro-pneumatic, the connecting and disconnecting of the two expressive divisions can be readily accomplished close to the clavier. The clavier can with great advantage be furnished with the Double-touch, enabling the performer to combine the subdivisions at any instant, in any manner, and on any notes, according to his desire, while rendering a composition.

The selection of the stops to be inclosed in the separate swell-boxes is a matter deserving careful study; for much depends on their proper apportionment. This apportionment may, on first thoughts, appear a very simple matter; the most obvious arrangement seeming to point to the grouping of all the stops strictly belonging to the harmonic structure of the Organ, as based on the OPEN DIAPASON, in the front swell-box; and the solo and accompanimental stops in the back swell-box. Such a mode of procedure, however rational it may seem, would result in much disappointment, and a serious narrowing of the more important offices of the twin swells. In fact, the diametrically opposite course should be followed. If the chief foundation stop—the OPEN DIAPASON, 8 FT.—is connected, as suggested, with the wind-chest of the front swell, the OCTAVE, 4 FT., the mutation stops, and the MIXTURE should be located in the back swell; while the SUPER-OCTAVE, 2 FT., which in the best type of Chamber Organ will in all probability be a PICCOLO or a stop of a solo character, should be placed in the front swell. The accompanimental and solo stops should be divided between the two swells, care being taken to secure as marked a contrast of tone as possible in the two subdivisions. Thus, if a solo FLUTE be placed in one, let an equally characteristic solo stop, such as the CLARINET, be opposed to it in the other. Again, as the chief labial stop—the OPEN DIAPASON—is connected with the subdivision in the front swell, let the most powerful reed—the TRUMPET—be placed in the back swell.

Again, let an imitative string-toned stop be contrasted with a flute-toned covered stop, and so on.

Before going farther, it may be advisable to put the reader in possession of one or two facts connected with the operation of the twin swells. In the first place, it may be pointed out that while the back swell contains about half of the stops apportioned to the First Organ, the front swell should be made large enough to contain all the stops apportioned to the Second Organ as well as the remaining subdivision of the First Organ. By this arrangement, the back swell will contain about one-third, while the front swell will contain about two-thirds, of the entire list of manual stops. In the second place, each swell will have an independent expression-lever, of the balanced form, located side by side, in the position previously recommended. So placed, they can be operated one after the other, or both together, with *one foot;* or in different directions at the same moment, with *both feet*, when the Pedal Organ is silent. This absolute control over both the expression-levers is essential to the full utility of the twin swells.

It may be questioned why the Second Organ should not have an independent swell-box and an accompanying expression-lever. On first thoughts it might appear advisable, seeing that the First Organ stops are placed in two swell-boxes, for the Second Organ stops to be inclosed in a third and distinct one: but the additional space required for such an arrangement, the increased number of mechanical parts, and the difficulty (in reality very slight) of operating effectively the *three* expression-levers, can hardly be said, in the case of a two-manualed Organ of the size already contemplated, to be repaid by the third independent swell. But we have no wish to undervalue the effect of this third expressive division; and may remark that when a third expression-lever for compulsory use is objected to, a simple mechanical appliance can be introduced whereby the action of the Second Organ swell may, at will, be connected with one of the levers belonging to the subdivisions of the First Organ. This arrangement will enable the right foot of the player to open or close the three swell-boxes simultaneously, by simply placing it so as to press equally on both of the levers of the First Organ. Thus united, the manual divisions may be said to form one grand Swell Organ.

When there are three distinct manual divisions, commanded by three claviers, three independent swell-boxes become necessary in the true Chamber Organ. Leaving the Second and Third Organs for future consideration, let us, for the present, hastily glance at some effects rendered possible through the agency of the twin swells of the First Organ.

First, suppose all the First Organ stops are drawn, and the wind is admitted to both the subdivisions; with both swells closed, the effect will be that of an OPEN DIAPASON, at its full value, with a richly-toned but subdued background, to which the closed swells impart the effect of restrained power. Now, the slightest touch of the foot on either of the expression-levers greatly enriches the tonal combination to the ear, by bringing one-half of the background of compound tone, if we may continue to use the term, nearer and more prominent. Leaving the lever thus first touched where it has been moved, the foot may be shifted to the lever of the other subdivision, and sufficient pressure applied to open its swell rather more than in the preceding case, and bring the tones of the inclosed stops still more prominently forward. Many and marked differences of tonal effect are produced by the alternate operation of the two expression-levers. The above-described mode of proceeding may be carried on step by step, or by almost imperceptible gradations, until the full Organ peals forth at its maximum strength.

Secondly, suppose the OPEN DIAPASON, 8 FT., FLUTE, 4 FT., and PICCOLO, 2 FT., to be drawn in the front subdivision; and the TRUMPET, 8 FT., OCTAVE, 4 FT., and MIXTURE, to be drawn in the back subdivision; and the wind to be admitted to the front subdivision only, to begin with. With a closed swell, the effect will be that of a full-toned OPEN DIAPASON in combination with a very soft OCTAVE and SUPER-OCTAVE. Let the tone be brightened, by a partial opening of the front swell, until a satisfactory balance is obtained between the unison and the octaves; and then, at a favorable moment, let the pneumatic piston be touched and the wind admitted to the back subdivision. Instantly the ear is arrested by the addition to the tone of a mysterious and subdued chorus effect, filling up and enriching the original combination. The chorus effect is rendered more striking if the tremolant belonging to the back swell is drawn. Following this, at the proper time, let the tremolant be silenced, and the swell be slightly opened. The result is now a rich organ-tone in which the harmonic structure is practically complete, colored by a prominent reed- and flute-tone. If both expression-levers are now operated simultaneously a most effective *crescendo* is obtained, thrown upon the stationary and commanding voice of the unexpressive OPEN DIAPASON. The wind of the front subdivision may be cut off at any desired moment, leaving the TRUMPET, OCTAVE, and MIXTURE (a perfect combination) at the disposal of the organist.

Thirdly, suppose the CLARINET and a string-toned stop are drawn in one subdivision, and a flute-toned combination (say the FLAUTO TRAVERSO and PICCOLO) in the other, and the wind is admitted to both. Now, while the performer is engaged in rendering a florid composition of an orchestral character, he can, with right foot alone, bring countless *nuances* and varied colorings to enrich and add charms of expression to his performance;—now subduing the penetrating flute-tones and swelling the rich unison of the reed- and string-tones; and now producing a complete *crescendo* or *diminuendo* on all the stops drawn. And, in any passages where the Pedal Organ is silent, he can, by placing both feet on the twin expression-levers, produce, by crossing the different qualities of tone, so to speak, charming and varied orchestral effects replete with light and shade.

We cannot help feeling how inadequate the above sketchy remarks are in conveying even a faint idea of the countless complex and refined musical effects which are practicable and easily produced on a single clavier, when the stops it commands are divided and inclosed in separate swell-boxes, in the manner described. If the reader is a musician, in the true sense of the word, he will have no difficulty in realizing what such a treatment is capable of in the sphere of expression; and how by its aid musical ideas may be rendered with a degree of refinement and expression absolutely unobtainable on Organs built on ordinary lines.*

* As the suggestions made in this Chapter, respecting the tonal appointment of the Chamber Organ, may appear strange, and, perhaps, of doubtful value, to the average reader, we here give a short extract from a letter

THE SECOND OR SOLO ORGAN.

UPPER CLAVIER—ENTIRELY EXPRESSIVE.

This division is, as before noted, of less size than the First Organ, and, accordingly, subordinate thereto. It has been suggested that only about one-third of the manual speaking stops should be apportioned to it; and that its stops should differ, both in quality and strength of tone, from the stops of the First division. The Second Organ has a dual office; it should serve both as a solo and an accompanimental division, containing a few stops of an imitative or orchestral character, and a few stops of a very delicate intonation suitable for combination with the solo stops in the same division, and for accompaniment to the stops of a solo character in the First Organ. In an instrument of fifteen or sixteen manual speaking stops, the Second Organ may conveniently contain six,—five stops of unison and one of octave pitch,—three being solo and three accompanimental. Of the solo stops, the first should be a reed, preferably an ORCHESTRAL OBOE AND FAGOTTO, 8 FT., or, when an OBOE is placed in the First Organ, an ORCHESTRAL CLARINET, 8 FT. The second solo stop should be a VIOLIN AND VIOLONCELLO, 8 FT., of the most pronounced imitative quality. The third solo stop should be an ORCHESTRAL FLUTE, 8 FT. The three stops, accordingly, represent reed-tone, string-tone, and flute-tone, in their most favorable development in the Organ. The three softly-voiced accompanimental stops may be a DULCIANA, 8 FT., an ÆOLINE or VIOLA D'AMORE, 8 FT., and a FLAUTO D'AMORE, 4 FT. These will supply several charming combinations for accompaniments to any solo voices in the First Organ; while they will combine perfectly with the solo stops in their own division. The effect of the full Second Organ will be very fine if the six stops are carefully voiced and regulated so as to blend their tones perfectly. The above list of six stops for the Second Organ is merely suggestive: it may be modified to any desirable extent to produce the necessary contrasts of tone to the voices of the First Organ. It is impossible here to give more than an outline of general principles of stop apportionment.

In the remarks on the First Organ, we alluded to the desirability of inclosing the stops of the Second Organ in the front swell-box, along with the stops forming one subdivision of the First Organ; questioning the necessity of occupying valuable space and increasing the number of mechanical appliances by the introduction of a third and independent swell-box. Judging from long practical observation, we are inclined to maintain that no disadvantage worth consideration attends the proposed two-swell arrangement. It is only on extremely rare occasions that the independent Second Organ swell appears to be called for; and, even on such occasions, the exercise of a little ingenuity and skill on the part of the performer overcomes all ordinary difficulties which may present themselves. When

written to the Author, in the year 1888, by Daniel J. Wood, Esq., Mus. Doc., Organist of Exeter Cathedral. After alluding, in terms of admiration, to the Chamber Organ constructed by the Author of the present treatise, in which the tonal appointment above described was for the first time carried out, Dr. Wood says: "*It opened to my imagination quite a vista of new and previously impossible effects in organ playing.*"

the Second Organ is used alone, of course no inconvenience is experienced in its management. When used as an accompaniment to certain solo voices in the First Organ, the worst that can happen is that the accompaniment will have precisely the same kind and degree of expression imparted to it—so far, at least, as the influence of the swell is concerned—as may be deemed appropriate for the solo. This, however, only obtains when both the solo and accompanimental stops are in the same swell-box; for when the solo stop is in the back swell of the First Organ, and the accompanimental stops are in the Second Organ (inclosed in the front swell) or *vice versa*, the performer can keep the expressive effects of both the solo and accompaniment perfectly distinct.

In a two-manualed Chamber Organ of larger size than that above contemplated, say from twenty-five to thirty speaking stops, we would recommend a further development of the swell appointment. For this three independent swell-boxes would be necessary. The swell No. 1 would contain, say, two-fifths of the First Organ stops; swell No. 2 would contain about two-fifths of the First Organ and one-half of the Second Organ stops; and swell No. 3 would contain the remainder of the Second Organ stops. By this unique arrangement about one-fifth of the First Organ stops would be left uninclosed; while all the rest of the instrument would have compound expression, thus:—

FIRST ORGAN—	Unexpressive subdivision.
"	First expressive subdivision, in swell No. 1.
"	Second expressive subdivision, in swell No. 2.
SECOND ORGAN—	First expressive subdivision, in swell No. 2.
"	Second expressive subdivision, in swell No. 3.

With such an arrangement, combined with a carefully selected and well-contrasted apportionment of stops in the five subdivisions of the manual department, an instrument of practically limitless powers of compound expression and astonishing tonal flexibility would be produced. Three expression-levers would be necessary: and each subdivision should be furnished with an electro-pneumatic control, or a wind ventil commanded by thumb-pistons, and also by a double-acting foot-lever when such can be conveniently applied.

Returning to our original and more modest scheme, and referring to the list of manual couplers given, it will be found that we recommend three for the purpose of connecting the Second to the First Organ clavier; namely, the Unison, Sub-octave, and Octave couplers. With this complete system of coupling, the Second Organ becomes a very important factor in the tonal structure of the instrument. When the Unison coupler is drawn, the entire number of the inclosed stops forms one grand Swell Organ, the hands being confined to the First Organ clavier, and both the expression-levers being operated together. If the levers are operated separately, the organist has at his disposal a great range of *crescendo* and *diminuendo* effects. By drawing the Octave coupler any desirable degree of additional brightness can be imparted to the First Organ, through the introduction of sounds of octave and super-octave pitch; and this without in any way interfering with the true pitch of the Second Organ as commanded by its own clavier. If stops of 8 ft. and 4 ft. are drawn in the Second Organ, and the claviers are connected by the Sub-octave coupler, an additional dignity and gravity is imparted to the tones of the First Organ by the entry of sounds of 16 ft. pitch, down to tenor C, and of 8 ft. down to the same note.

Numerous pages could be written, in addition to the few remarks contained in this Chapter, on the almost countless combinations and tonal effects to be obtained by the joint manipulation of the stops and couplers; but the remarks made must suffice for the present purpose. Any reader who may feel curious to realize what can be done with a divided First Organ of eleven stops and a Second Organ of six stops, in conjunction with the three couplers, should take up his pen and work out the sum of the possible combinations. We can promise him a feeling of surprise when he has arrived at the end of his task; and he will then be prepared to agree with the statement that a Chamber Organ of, say, sixteen or seventeen manual stops, built on the lines here suggested, is by no means a paltry or insufficient instrument; and that it will require a very industrious and ingenious organist to get to the end of its resources. It may be interesting to give the numbers of the combinations possible with different numbers of stops, without the use of the couplers:—

Number of Stops.	Number of Combinations.
5	31
6	63
10	1,023
15	32,767
17	131,071
20	1,048,575
30	1,073,741,823

By the use of the Sub-octave and Octave couplers, the above numbers of combinations would be immensely increased.

THE THIRD OR SOLO ORGAN.

THIRD CLAVIER—ENTIRELY EXPRESSIVE.

The present Chapter would obviously be incomplete without some notice being taken of the Chamber Organ with three claviers and independent manual divisions. The adoption of three claviers opens up a much larger choice of treatments and stop apportionments than is practicable when only two claviers are used; but the general principles which we have endeavored to outline, in relation to the two-manualed instrument, should be held in view while scheming a Chamber Organ with three manual divisions; namely, First or Great Organ, Second or Choir Organ, and Third or Solo Organ.

The adoption of three claviers necessitates the introduction of three independent swell-boxes,—that is, if the Organ is to be constructed on the lines already laid down,—but the selection of the speaking stops for the respective divisions of the instrument, and their disposition in the different swell-boxes, must, beyond the provision of the fundamental tonal structure of the instrument in the First Organ, be largely matters for individual judgment and taste. The chief use to which the Organ is to be put will properly influence the selection and disposition of the stops to a considerable extent; therefore, in scheming the instrument, a careful survey should be taken of the offices it will be called upon to fill in solo and concerted chamber music.

The question now arises, whether the stops of the First Organ should, in the case of the three-manualed instrument, be divided in the manner proposed for the two-manualed one; or whether they should be confined to one swell-box, of course excepting the OPEN DIAPASON, 8 FT., and any other stop or stops which taste may decide to leave uninclosed. Knowing the immense value, from a musical point of view, which attends the divided First or Great Organ, we unhesitatingly recommend that the First and Second Organs should be treated in the three-manualed instrument precisely as they are treated in the previously described instrument with two claviers. Such being the case, the third clavier commands an entirely independent expressive division—the Third or Solo Organ.

In a Chamber Organ of about twenty manual stops, the Solo Organ should contain four or five special stops, imitative of orchestral instruments. A selection may, accordingly, be made from the following list:—ORCHESTRAL FLUTE, 8 FT.; FLAUTO TRAVERSO, 4 FT.; ORCHESTRAL PICCOLO, 2 FT.; VIOLIN AND VIOLONCELLO, 8 FT.; ORCHESTRAL OBOE AND FAGOTTO, 8 FT.; ORCHESTRAL CLARINET, 8 FT.; COR ANGLAIS, 8 FT. (free reed); and ORCHESTRAL TRUMPET, 8 FT. The insertion in this division of the last-named stop does not necessitate the omission of a TRUMPET in the Great Organ; but care must be taken to secure a decided difference in their respective voices. The Solo TRUMPET should be more powerful in tone and brilliant in character than the First Organ stop: it should be to the Chamber Organ what the TUBA is to the Concert-room instrument. Should a very assertive stop be desired, suitable for a large music-room, the Solo TRUMPET may be made of large scale, with open reeds, and be voiced on wind slightly higher in pressure than that already recommended for the Chamber Organ generally. On no account should the pressure exceed 3½ inches, while in all but exceptional cases 3 inches will be ample.

The insertion of the ORCHESTRAL OBOE in the Solo Organ does not prevent the introduction of an OBOE of normal unimitative tone in another division: and, in like manner, the insertion of the ORCHESTRAL CLARINET would not prevent the introduction of a stop of the same family, such as a softly-voiced CORNO DI BASSETTO, 8 FT., in the Second or Choir Organ.

It might seem that when a VOX HUMANA is included in the list of selected stops it should find a place in the Solo Organ; but there is good reason to place it away from the stops of an orchestral character. In such an instrument as we are endeavoring to outline, the best place for the VOX HUMANA is the second expressive subdivision of the First Organ. Here it will be in the position to be accompanied by the soft combinations of the Second Organ, and by the orchestral stops of the Third or Solo Organ, all being in different swell-boxes.

In the three-manualed instrument, the Second or Choir Organ should contain stops of the softest intonation, selection being made from such stops as the following:—SALICIONAL, 8 FT.; DULCIANA, 8 FT.; VOX ANGELICA, 8 FT.; VIOLA DA GAMBA, 8 FT.; VIOLA D'AMORE, 8 FT.; ÆOLINE, 8 FT.; ECHO OBOE, 8 FT.; LIEBLICHGEDECKT, 8 FT.; FLAUTO DOLCE, 8 FT.; FLAUTO D'AMORE, 4 FT.; CŒLESTINA, 4 FT.; FLAGEOLET, 2 FT.; GEMSHORN, 2 FT.; HARMONIA ÆTHERIA, V. RANKS; CORNO DI BASSETTO, 8 FT.; MUSETTE, 8 FT.; OBOE, 8 FT.; and OCTAVE OBOE, 4 FT. All these stops will yield beautiful and varied qualities of tone when voiced on wind of 1½ inches to 2 inches. The pressure for the Second Organ should not exceed the latter figure.

In the three-manualed instrument, now under consideration, the Second Organ would be chiefly used for accompaniment; but it would also furnish the soft combinations and subdued effects which are so charming in the rendition of the more refined classes of chamber music. With a Second Organ of so delicate a character, the First or Great Organ may be made to yield tones of a rich and majestic nature, through a reasonably complete harmonic structure and stops of full intonation which are appropriate in both its subdivisions.

With the three independent swell-boxes the same number of expression-levers will be necessary. These should be placed, in the position already recommended, in the following order from left to right—First Organ, Second Organ, Third Organ. This arrangement will be found to be the most convenient. First, because, by placing the foot on both the first and second levers, a *crescendo* and *diminuendo* can be produced on the full First Organ, or on the First and Second Organs combined; to be followed up and most effectively prolonged by a *crescendo* on the Third or Solo Organ. Secondly, because it favors the production of compound expression in the different divisions, and the crossing effects of the First Organ subdivisions, already commented upon. Thirdly, because it is most favorable to the production of striking effects of light and shade and refined expression in both solo and accompaniment.

PEDAL ORGAN.

PEDAL CLAVIER—PARTLY EXPRESSIVE.

There can be no question that one of the chief difficulties, if not the chief difficulty, in connection with the stop appointment of the Chamber Organ, is the furnishing of an adequate pedal department. As has already been said, there is generally a difficulty in finding sufficient floor-space and height, in the usual type of domestic apartments, for the accommodation of the most important and desirable class of Pedal Organ stops; namely, open stops of 16 ft. pitch; yet without, at least, one stop of this size, the bass of the instrument will lack its principal element of grandeur. Every endeavor should be made to include such a stop in the tonal scheme. In organ music, pure and simple, its deep and impressive tones are invaluable; while in *ensemble* playing—that is, when the Organ is used along with the Piano-forte, Violin, Violoncello, and other orchestral instruments—the effect of such a stop as the OPEN DIAPASON, 16 FT., is magnificent and singularly impressive. Such a grave stop is, however, attended, in the generality of private rooms, by one disagreeable effect. It has a decided tendency to set up sympathetic vibrations in doors, windows, and certain pieces of furniture, including the organ-case. Such vibrations should be listened for, traced, and cured; for they invariably proceed from some imperfection of workmanship or looseness in the objects affected, which a little ingenuity can put right. As we have gone into the principal matters connected with this stop, in our remarks on the speaking stops suitable for the Chamber Organ, it is only necessary to add the following hints here.

While the larger pipes of the OPEN DIAPASON, 16 FT., may have to be stowed away within a chamber, or behind the displayed portion of the Organ, the pipes of lesser size, say from AAA upward, may be ranged in view, and utilized as an effective feature in the general design of the instrument. Of course, for this purpose, the pipes should be carefully finished, and the smaller ones made considerably longer than their true speaking lengths, and cut out behind. They may all be tastefully decorated* or simply varnished. Whatever the disposition may be, it must be borne in mind that it is almost imperative and altogether desirable that every pipe should be placed either directly upon, or very close to, its wind-chest.

The advantage of having a softly-voiced open metal stop of 16 ft. in the Chamber Organ cannot be overrated; but it is not likely that such a stop will be freely introduced except in large instruments placed in lofty rooms. The larger pipes may either be laid horizontally, or mitred, so as to reduce their height, when placed vertically. So treated, the stop can be accommodated in rooms of thirteen feet in height. In Chamber Organs of the largest desirable size, placed in specially constructed music-rooms of not less than twenty feet in height, a DULCIANA, 16 FT., or a delicately-voiced VIOLONE, 16 FT., should certainly be introduced in the Pedal Organ. The twelve or fourteen larger pipes may be used to form effective features in the external design; and this with much benefit to their tones.

Next in importance to the open stop or stops comes a covered stop of 16 ft. pitch. Such a stop is almost invariably found in the Pedal Organ of small instruments; and, unfortunately, too often found alone, doing duty as the bass for every variety of manual tone. As this stop, under the names of BOURDON, LIEBLICHGEDECKT, and QUINTATEN, has been mentioned with sufficient fulness in an earlier part of the present Chapter, no further remarks anent its tonal character need be made here: but with respect to its disposition in the Organ a few words will not be out of place. As the longest pipe, yielding the CCC note, does not necessarily exceed 8 feet 6 inches in total length, and, in the Chamber Organ, need never measure more than 7 inches in width and 8½ inches in depth, while it can be made considerably smaller, the stop can easily be planted so as to form effective features in the general design. We have tested the external disposition of the

*In the case of our own Chamber Organ, these pipes of the OPEN DIAPASON, 16 FT., of wood, were ranged close to the end wall of the music-room (a room 45 feet long by 20 feet wide, and 14 feet high), as wings to the ornamental portion of the instrument, which projected into the room in front of the chamber behind. The pipes were very carefully made and accurately finished at their mouths. They were gilded from their feet up to about one-third of their height and left plain: above this the pipes were painted black and covered with ornamental designs in gold. The lower pipes of the stop were placed in the large chamber behind.

pipes of the Bourdon, of the above scale, in the Chamber Organ already alluded to, and may briefly describe the method adopted. At the sides of the central and salient portion of the instrument, which comprised the front swell-box (containing one subdivision of the First Organ and the entire Second Organ stops), the Open Diapason, 8 ft., and the Bourdon, 16 ft. tone, the twelve lower pipes (CCC to BBB inclusive) of the latter stop were ranged upon stepped wind-chests—each pipe directly over its wind. In the front space, between the flanking towers of Open Diapason pipes (of varnished spotted-metal, decorated with figures of angels and flowers in colors and gold), and above the key-case and slightly in advance of the highly decorated swell-box, were ranged the fifteen pipes of the Bourdon, from CC to D, inclusive; the latter pipe occupying the central position. All the pipes, with the exception of the three higher ones, were in this manner used as integral parts of the design; with the advantage of having perfectly unobstructed speech toward the room, and admitting of the most delicate voicing and perfect regulation. Of course all the displayed pipes were carefully finished and richly decorated; those in front were gilded on all visible surfaces and enriched with a flowing diaper pattern executed in black and brown. An idea of what has been briefly described may be gathered from the accompanying Plate V., which is engraved from a photograph of the Organ.

The fact that the wood pipes of the Pedal Organ can so easily and appropriately be used in lieu of much cumbersome and costly case-work should never be lost sight of. Their external arrangement relieves the inside of the Organ of undesirable crowding, while the pipes benefit greatly from their exposed positions. The Bourdon, when so placed, can be voiced to yield the round 'velvety' tone which is so essential in the bass of a Chamber Organ; while its totally unshaded position allows it to be regulated to the utmost nicety, and its tones to be heard at their full value. Such a stop is too often packed away within closed cases, or crowded into recesses or confined chambers, so that its tones, as heard in the room, are little better than the buzzing of a score of humblebees; unless, indeed, the pipes are voiced undesirably loud. Perfect smoothness and regularity of tone are impossible under such conditions.

In the remarks already made anent the speaking stops suitable for the Chamber Organ enough has been said with reference to the octave, or 8 ft., stops and the reed stop for the pedal department. We may, however, impress all readers interested in Chamber Organ construction with the advisability, if not the absolute necessity, of providing the Pedal Organ with at least one stop suitable for solo or melodic passages. That the chief office of the Pedal is to supply a proper bass for all the manual divisions goes without saying; but this consideration should not cause it to be overlooked that the Pedal Organ is an independent department, having distinct functions as well as purely relative ones. Granted that there is to be one stop suitable for melodic passages; or, what is better, two stops—say a Violoncello, 8 ft., and a Contra-Saxophone or a softly-toned Contrafagotto, 16 ft.—the question arises whether it is or is not desirable to render them expressive, like the other solo voices in the Organ. Our opinion is decidedly in favor of inclosing them in some convenient species of swell-chamber,

PLATE V

so that they may be flexible as well as expressive. If the music-room has been planned for the reception of an Organ, by an architect who has any knowledge of its requirements, there will probably be no difficulty in grouping the stops on a special wind-chest and inclosing them in what will form an effective swell. For further particulars respecting the expressive Pedal Organ the reader may refer to the remarks on the subject in the preceding Chapter on the Concert-room Organ.

Whatever may be done in the direction just pointed out, let the great importance and value of the Pedal Organ be fully recognized in its tonal appointment. *No Organ is worthy of being called an Organ, however rich its manual resources may be, unless it has an adequate pedal department.*

Much more could be written on the engaging subject of the Chamber Organ; for it is one on which very little interest has been evinced by previous writers on the art of organ-building, probably because they failed to realize that the construction and tonal appointment of the instrument form a problem distinct from those connected with the larger types of Organs: but as the space at our disposal is not unlimited, we must conclude our remarks; trusting that enough has been said to point the way to a future development of the instrument, and to help its introduction, in a truly interesting and useful form, into the dwelling-houses of lovers of music. No other instrument is so well suited to be the focus of the musical exercises of the home circle.

CHAPTER VIII.

INTERNAL ARRANGEMENT OF THE ORGAN.

CONSIDERING the extremely complex structure of the Organ, the immense number of different parts which constitute its internal economy, and the necessity for means of ready access to every portion of the instrument for adjustment, repairs, regulating, tuning, etc., it becomes obvious that the greatest care, ingenuity, and skill should be expended on its Internal Design and Arrangement.

In small Organs the internal arrangement is usually a simple matter: but in the case of a large Church or Concert-room Organ the internal arrangement may amount to a problem, the solution of which, owing to some awkward conditions of locality or insufficient accommodation, is beset with great difficulties. When both floor-space and height are ample, the organ builder has a favorable opportunity to display taste as well as skill in the disposition of the several tonal divisions of the Organ, and in the arrangement of the numerous structural and mechanical portions. The tonal divisions of the instrument should be so disposed as to secure the most satisfactory results, musically; while all the mechanical parts should be so arranged as to be easily reached without interfering with, or displacing, any other work in the interior.

In the skilful and tasteful arrangement of the Organ no builder has surpassed Cavaillé-Coll, of Paris. We have formed this opinion after a careful examination of the interiors of several of his more important instruments. We may give one example of his system of arrangement which may be accepted as fairly representative; and with this view we select the Concert-room Organ erected by him in the Albert Hall, at Sheffield, England. Our brief description will be readily understood with the assistance of the accompanying Plan of the Organ, Fig. LIV. The instrument is erected on an elevated floor, level with the highest tier of the orchestra seats; and directly underneath this floor are placed the bellows, the several reservoirs, and the blowing mechanism; the wind-trunks ascending thence to the wind-chests in the Organ. On the floor level above alluded to is a low room (*rez-de-chaussée*) almost exclusively devoted to the pneumatic levers connected with the manual and pedal claviers, and the pneumatic draw-stop action for all the divisions of the instrument. The localities occupied by these mechanical appliances are indicated on the Plan by the small, dotted, and diagonally-crossed, oblong spaces, placed under or adjoining the divisions of the Organ to which they belong. During our inspection of this noteworthy instrument we were greatly impressed with the admirable arrangement of these important portions, and the perfect ease with which every adjustable part of the actions could be gotten at for

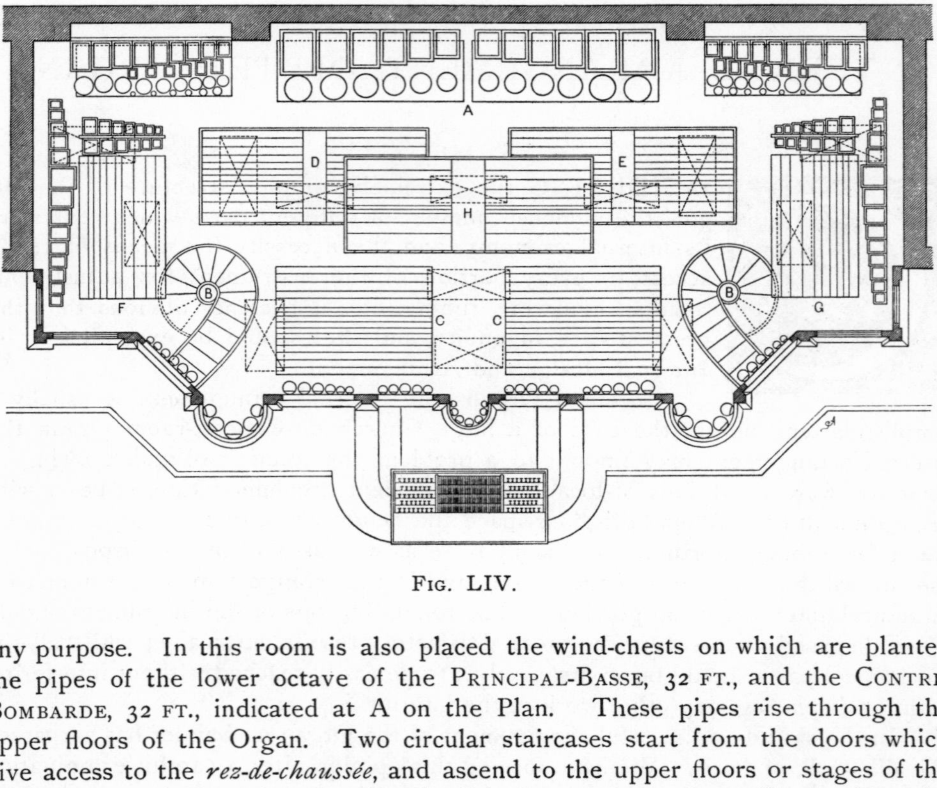

FIG. LIV.

any purpose. In this room is also placed the wind-chests on which are planted the pipes of the lower octave of the PRINCIPAL-BASSE, 32 FT., and the CONTRE-BOMBARDE, 32 FT., indicated at A on the Plan. These pipes rise through the upper floors of the Organ. Two circular staircases start from the doors which give access to the *rez-de-chaussée*, and ascend to the upper floors or stages of the instrument, as indicated at B. On the first floor or stage, immediately above the *rez-de-chaussée*, are placed, toward the front, the two large wind-chests of the Grand Orgue, C; and behind them the wind-chests and swell-boxes of the Récit Expressif, D, and the Positif Expressif, E; ample space being provided all round them for access, and for the free emission of sound. On this stage are also placed the remainder of the wind-chests of the Pédale, shown at F and G; all being most conveniently disposed and having free space on all sides. The arrangement of this stage is clearly shown on the Plan. On the second stage, which extends over the central portion of the instrument, are located the wind-chests and swell-box of the Solo. These are indicated at H, in the position they occupy in relation to the divisions in the stage below. It would be difficult to imagine a more convenient and effective arrangement for a large Organ, under the conditions imposed by the architect of the hall. The only exception that can be taken is to the position of the Solo division on a much higher level than the rest of the instrument, which, of necessity, subjects its pipe-work to the action of the warmer air in the upper part of the hall. No Organ known to us is more easy of access for inspection, tuning, and repairs.*

Before touching on the internal arrangement of Church Organs, we may mention the admirable treatment of the Organ in the Public Halls, at Glasgow, built by Messrs. T. C. Lewis & Company, of London. This instrument, taken altogether, presents as satisfactory an internal arrangement as is to be found in the works of English organ builders. The planning of the Organ is practically all that could be desired, and, considering the size of the instrument and the space at the disposal of the builders, is extremely skilful. The action from the claviers is direct, horizontal, and vertical. All the pneumatic levers are under their respective wind-chests, and perfectly accessible for adjustment and repairs. The passage-boards are wide and unyielding; indeed, firmness and stability pervade all parts of the Organ. The passage-boards and ladders are so arranged that there is no difficulty in reaching every portion of the instrument. The wind-chests are so large and so well disposed that all the pipes planted on them have ample room to speak, and all can be easily reached for regulating and tuning.

In the first or lower stage of the Organ, access is given to all parts by one longitudinal and four transverse passages. The central compartment is occupied by the manual actions; the pneumatic levers, the coupling mechanism, the tracker-work, etc., being so skilfully arranged that all centers, buttons, and the other adjustable parts, can be readily examined and manipulated. On each side of this action runs a passageway of convenient width. Between these passages and the other two lateral ones are compartments in which are placed the pneumatic draw-stop actions of the Great and Swell Organs; the pneumatic combination levers for the same; and two of the reservoirs containing the wind, of 3 inches pressure, for the bass sections of the Great Organ wind-chests. All these appli-

*The following description of the Organ in the Albert Hall, Sheffield, will be read with interest by the student of organ-building:

"L'instrument, dont le buffet a 12 mètres de largeur et 6 de profondeur, aura, une fois en place, 15 mètres de hauteur; il possède quatre claviers manuels de 61 notes, d'*ut* en *ut*, et un pédalier de 30 notes; il a 74 registres, dont 10 pour les mélanges, et de plus 21 pédales de combinaison. Sur ses 64 jeux complets, 2 sonnent le trente-deux pieds ouvert, 14 le seize pieds, 26 le huit pieds.

"Huit grands sommiers, disposés sur trois étages, portent les 4,082 tuyaux de l'orgue, auxquels six souffleurs au besoin peuvent fournir le vent. Pas un tuyau, pas une pièce mécanique à laquelle on ne puisse facilement, sans rien déranger, porter la main. Des passages larges et commodes permettent d'arriver sans gêne à toutes les parties de l'instrument. Deux escaliers tournants, aussi doux, aussi praticables que ceux de nos maisons, montent à l'intérieur de l'orgue pour en faire communiquer tous les étages. On pourra faire aux dames les honneurs de la mécanique intérieure de tout l'instrument, tandis qu'ailleurs on ne peut visiter un intérieur d'orgue sans faire une pénible et souvent dangereuse gymnastique."—Article by M. Albert Dupaigne, in *Le Monde* of May 7, 1873.

ances are conveniently arranged. The two lateral compartments are occupied chiefly by the four reservoirs, under two pressures, for the Pedal Organ.

Ascending to the second stage of the instrument, we find in the most favorable position the six wind-chests belonging to the Front and Back Great Organs, divided by passage-boards 22 inches wide. In front of these, toward the Hall and at a somewhat lower level, is placed the wind-chest of the Choir Organ, portion of which is inclosed in a small swell-box. In the rear of the Great wind-chests is located the Solo Organ inclosed in a swell-box. On both sides of the Great and Solo Organs, in the lateral spaces or wings of the instrument, are placed the wind-chests of the DOUBLE OPEN DIAPASON, 32 FT., and the other stops of the Pedal Organ. These wind-chests are so divided, and furnished with passage-boards of ample width, that every pipe planted on them can be easily gotten at for regulating and tuning. It would not be easy to plan a more convenient lay-out than that presented by the second stage of this Organ.

In the third stage is located the large Swell Organ, directly above the Solo swell-box and rear portion of the Back Great Organ. The wind-chests, four in number, are conveniently separated by longitudinal and transverse passage-boards; and as the bass pipes of all the stops are toward the ends of the swell-box, every facility is given for tuning. The swell-box is entered through a trap-door in the back passage-board; while a small door from the central passage-board opens to a platform in front of the swell-box. The longer pipes of the Pedal Organ rise, at each end of the swell-box, from their wind-chests on the second stage.

The arrangement and disposition of the tonal divisions of both the noteworthy Organs above spoken of are excellent and deserving of the attention of all interested in the proper planning of important instruments. Both the Organs are built on the pneumatic lever system; and, accordingly, considerable space is devoted to the accommodation of all the mechanical appliances connected therewith, and to the passage-ways necessary for proper access to all the adjustable parts. When tubular-pneumatic or electro-pneumatic actions are employed, much less space is required, for very little save the pneumatic tubes or electric wires intervenes between the console and the wind-chests. Careful provision must, however, be made for easy access to all the complicated mechanical parts of the key actions and the valves of the wind-chests. Whatever the mechanical or other action may be, it in no way affects the principles which direct the arrangement of the tonal divisions of the Organ: and in the case, for instance, of either the Sheffield or the Glasgow Organ, the adoption of an electro-pneumatic action would not of necessity alter any of the positions properly selected for the several manual and pedal divisions. The sound-producing and the sound-controlling portions of the Organ are as distinct in their principles of formation and treatment as are the violin and its bow. It is too often forgotten by organ builders and organ purchasers, that the Organ is, first of all, a musical instrument, and, secondly, an ingenious piece of mechanism. The inventive powers of the organ builders of today seem concentrated on the mechanical branch of their art, to the very serious neglect of the far more important musical or tonal branch. Organ builders are vying with each other in the production of tubular-pneumatic or electro-pneumatic actions and complicated mechanical appliances, to the almost total extinction of all worthy rivalry in the development and scientific appointment of the tonal forces of the Organ. Musical tones of greater variety, beauty, and flexibility, and less complexity in mere mechanism, are what are required in modern organ-building. Let it be realized that one good stop properly placed is better than two indifferent ones badly located; and that the former is more to be desired, with the simplest action, than the latter, with all manner of complicated mechanical appliances. Let this be clearly realized by the purchasers of Organs and there will soon be a new era in the practice of organ-building. The proper arrangement of the tonal divisions of the Organ, and the scientific and artistic appointment of the tonal forces in those divisions, are all-potent factors in the production of a perfect musical instrument: and when these important factors are present, the controlling mechanism need not be perplexingly complicated, as it is in too many of the unmusical Organs of to-day.

Turning now to the Church Organ, we find, unquestionably, the most perfect internal arrangements in the large French Organs, and notably in such instruments as the Grand Organs in the Churches of Saint-Sulpice and Saint-Eustache, at Paris. In the former, Cavaillé-Coll has displayed his consummate skill in the internal arrangement of a large Church Organ constructed on the pneumatic lever system. The Organ is constructed in five stages. The lowest stage, the floor of which is level with that of the gallery on which the instrument stands, contains the main series of pneumatic levers, directly connected with the lowest or first manual clavier, and operating on all couplers. Above are located the two series of pneumatic levers, acting, respectively, on the Grand Chœur (First Clavier) and the Grand Orgue (Second Clavier). On each side of these pneumatic machines are placed two large reservoirs, each formed of eight sets of ribs, and connected together by accordion wind-trunks. The upper reservoirs furnish wind of less pressure than that furnished by the lower reservoirs, and, accordingly, are always kept fully charged. At the extreme ends of this stage are placed the wind-chests of the Pédale CONTRE-BASSE, 16 FT., the pipes of the stop—fifteen at each end—being disposed horizontally so as not to encroach on the space of the second stage. Immediately above the upper reservoirs are placed the pneumatic draw-stop actions for the Grand Chœur and Grand Orgue. This first stage has passage-boards at about the middle of its height to give direct access to the several pneumatic actions, tracker-work, roller-boards, upper reservoirs, etc. The second stage of the Organ contains the wind-chests and pipe-work of the Grand Chœur and the Grand Orgue; and in lateral positions, adjoining the ends of the case, are here placed the main wind-chests and pipe-work of the Pédale; the PRINCIPAL-BASSE, 32 FT., of wood, rising thence to the highest stage of the instrument. The pneumatic actions for these pedal wind-chests are situated under them in the higher portion of the first stage. The third stage is devoted to the series of pneumatic levers and pneumatic draw-stop actions of the Bombarde (Third Clavier) and the Positif (Fourth Clavier). This stage occupies only a central position, allowing the larger pipes of the Grand Chœur, Grand Orgue, and Pédale to pass upward at each end of it. The fourth stage of the Organ contains the wind-chests and pipe-work of the Bombarde and Positif, placed one behind the other with a wide passage-board between them. The wind-chests of the Bombarde extend over the passage provided in the rear of the lower stages for easy access to all their various parts. The pipes of the PRINCIPAL-BASSE, 32 FT., and CONTRE-BOMBARDE, 32 FT., extend upward through this stage. The fifth stage contains, in its lower part, the pneumatic levers and pneumatic draw-stop action of the Récit Expressif (Fifth Clavier), and the wind-chest and pipes of the TROMPETTE HARMONIQUE, 8 FT., *en chamade.* Directly over the pneumatic levers are placed the wind-chests and pipe-work of the Récit Expressif inclosed in a large swell-box. We can speak from personal knowledge of the admirable arrangement of this Organ, for we had the privilege of examining it, some years ago, in company with its talented builder.

The internal arrangement of the Organ in the Church of Saint-Eustache presents nothing which differs so greatly from the general method followed in the Organ of Saint-Sulpice as to call for special description. It may be pointed out, however, that this instrument has a detached Positif, after the fashion of many old Organs, the performer sitting between it and the main body of the instrument—a most objectionable and uncomfortable arrangement be it said.

As an example of good internal arrangement in a divided Organ, we may direct attention to that of the instrument in the Church of Saint-Vincent de Paul, at Paris, constructed by Cavaillé-Coll. This Organ occupies an elevated gallery, and is divided into two sections so as to leave exposed the central rose window. The console is situated exactly in the center between the sections; the performer sitting with his face toward the one containing the Grand Orgue. The tracker-work from the pedal and three manual claviers is carried, to the sections, underneath the raised platform on which the console is mounted. Immediately at the ends of this platform, where it joins the case-work of the sections, are placed the series of pneumatic levers for the two principal manual divisions of the instrument. The pedal action is direct tracker, and extends, underneath the manual action, to both sections. In the section on the right hand, as one views the Organ from the church, are placed two large reservoirs, one above the other, furnishing winds of different pressures. Directly over these are located the bass and treble wind-chests of the Grand Orgue. In front of the treble wind-chest, but at a much lower level, is placed a small wind-chest from which the front exposed pipes derive their wind. Near the floor, and at right angles to the wind-chests of the Grand Orgue, is placed a wind-chest for one division of the Pédale. In the left-hand section we find double reservoirs, similar to those in the other section; and over them are located the wind-chests of the Positif and Récit Expressif, the latter being inclosed in a swell-box. Here there is another wind-chest for the exposed pipes, and a wind-chest for the remaining division of the Pédale. Special reservoirs are placed under the wind-chests of the Pédale, and open directly into their pallet-boxes through accordion wind-trunks. The feeders, receivers, and blowing mechanism are located in an adjoining room. The internal arrangement of this Organ is very convenient, for no part is crowded and every part can be easily reached for examination, repairs, and tuning. Each section of the instrument occupies a floor space of about 16 feet by 14 feet 6 inches.

The Organs erected in English cathedrals and churches present few noteworthy features in their internal arrangements, although, in numerous instances, they bear evidence of much ingenuity and skill on the part of their builders. In the great majority of cases the Organs occupy positions or chambers of so confined and inadequate a character that open and convenient internal arrangements are impracticable. The common practice of crowding large Organs into spaces quite inadequate for their accommodation has been a factor fatal to proper internal arrangement.

With the exception of the large Organs which occupy elevated positions at the end of the naves in Roman Catholic cathedrals and parish churches, and in a few Protestant Episcopal churches, the foregoing remarks are applicable to American Church Organs. Certain instruments erected by Roosevelt, of New York, in churches of other denominations, and which occupy commanding positions, are models of good internal arrangement. A noteworthy example obtains in the Organ in Trinity Methodist Episcopal Church, at Denver, Col.; which, notwithstanding the somewhat cumbersome nature of its several large swell-boxes, is most conveniently arranged, both for the free egress of sound from all its divisions and for easy access to all its parts.

There are two leading causes of the prevailing bad and indifferent internal arrangements of Church Organs. The first, and, perhaps, the most serious, springs from the want of proper knowledge on the part of the ordinary church architect, who, in his ignorance of its requirements, fails to provide suitable accommodation for the Organ. The second cause is the very common determination, on the part of the church authorities, to have an Organ out of all proportion to the accommodation provided for it, and frequently out of proportion to the legitimate requirements of the musical service of the church. Organ builders, for the most part, are tradesmen who find the practice of their art anything but highly remunerative; and are, accordingly, generally willing to cram a large instrument anyhow or anywhere, so long as they are well paid for doing so. In the present period of cheap and competitive organ-building it is natural that such a state of affairs should exist. From these fertile causes spring all manner of imperfect, or positively bad, internal arrangements, and correspondingly indifferent instruments.

As before pointed out, the perfection of internal arrangement practically obtains in such a disposition of the tonal and mechanical portions of the Organ that they can be readily and conveniently reached for inspection, tuning, adjustment, and repairs. This disposition amply provides, when the instrument is not confined in an unsuitable chamber, for the proper speech of the pipe-work, and the generally good acoustical effect of the Organ; except, of course, in a case where the several tonal divisions are in themselves badly appointed.

In the arrangement of the different tonal divisions—the Great, Choir, Swell, Solo, and Pedal—it is essential, for securing the best acoustical and musical effects, that their wind-chests be placed with as little of an obstructive nature in front of them as possible. When it is necessary to locate one division behind another, their wind-chests should be placed on different levels, the front ones being lower than those behind; so that the sounds of the pipe-work in the rear division may suffer the minimum of obstruction in their forward course. In the case of a large Organ, favorably placed in a lofty church, ample height is necessary for the best tonal results, allowing the manual divisions to be elevated in successive stages, as in the important French instruments previously alluded to.

It is invariably advantageous to arrange the Organ on a wide and shallow plan; and it is always objectionable to adopt a narrow and deep arrangement, and especially so when the instrument is closed in at the back and sides. In selecting the relative localities for the different tonal divisions, care must be taken to do each one full justice. Under no circumstances should one division be sacrificed for the sake of another, to the destruction of the artistic balance of the Organ. A softly-toned division must not be so buried behind a loudly-toned one that, when both are speaking, the tones of the former division are obscured or largely absorbed by the powerful sounds of the latter. A softly-toned division, such as the Choir Organ, is commonly used for delicate accompaniments; accordingly it is advisable to place it in an advanced position in front of, and somewhat lower than, the Great division, as in the Organ in the Public Halls, Glasgow; or detached from the main body of the instrument, as in Chester Cathedral, where the softer stops of the Choir Organ are placed in a small case located over the central entrance of the choir screen, some distance from the rest of the instrument which stands in the north transept. When the Choir division is inclosed in a special swell-box, it may be placed in front, as above advised, with its exterior ornamentally treated; or it may be located behind the Great Organ wind-chests, when they are divided by a central passage-board, and their treble pipes are planted toward the passage. If the Choir wind-chests are elevated two or three feet above those of the Great Organ, the tonal effect of the Choir will, in all probability, prove satisfactory. The Choir stops will, of course, have to be specially voiced to meet the conditions of their location. The adoption of divided wind-chests, planted tonally, for the Great Organ, as in the large instruments already mentioned, cannot be too strongly advocated. They not only favor the most open and convenient planting of the pipes, but they open up the central portion of the interior for the free passage of sound.

When it is decided to inclose a portion of the Great Organ stops in a swell-box,—a proceeding we strongly recommend for important instruments,—the arrangement of the interior of the Organ will have to be considered from a special stand-point. The swell-box must, of necessity, be located in the rear of the exposed wind-chests of the division, being simply divided from them by a narrow passage-board: and it will certainly be undesirable to place any other tonal division behind the swell-box, unless it happens that the space is so large and the Organ is so uninclosed that there is no liability of its sounds being locked in or seriously impaired. In certain Organs built by Roosevelt the inclosed stops of the Great division are placed in the swell-box which contains all the stops of the Choir Organ, as in the Organ in the First Church of Christ, Hartford, Conn. Under such a method of arrangement, the Choir Organ would properly be placed behind the uninclosed wind-chests of the Great Organ, and on a somewhat higher level. In the Roosevelt Organ in the First Congregational Church, at Great Barrington,

Mass., seven of the Great Organ stops are inclosed in the Swell Organ box. Under such an arrangement, the Swell Organ may be located behind the Great, allowing that there is a depth sufficient for its accommodation. The Swell division will be much more effective in such a location than the less assertive Choir Organ. When this arrangement obtains, the Choir Organ may occupy an elevated position, above the Swell division, or a low position in front of the Great wind-chests, as before recommended. When the space for the Organ is wide and shallow, the swell-boxes containing the Swell and Choir divisions may be placed, side by side, above the swell-box, or the rear portion, of the Great Organ: or the Solo Organ swell-box may occupy a central position above the Great, while the Choir and Swell divisions are placed, at an intermediate elevation, at the ends of the Great Organ. Other good arrangements are presented by the Organs in the Albert Hall, Sheffield, and the Public Halls, Glasgow, previously described; in both of which the several swell-boxes are properly placed. In whatever manner the tonal divisions of an Organ may be treated and arranged, it is imperative that ample and convenient means of access to every part of them be provided; and this should be done in a way so as not to create any obstruction to the free egress of sound, or to render the temporary removal of any pipes necessary. As the Organ is an instrument that requires frequent tuning and careful attention, such matters as those just mentioned are of the greatest importance. As the apportionment and arrangement of the stops in the different divisions of the Organ are considered, with the desirable degree of fulness, in other Chapters, it is unnecessary to go into the subjects here, where we deal with general rather than with special treatments.

In the internal arrangement of Organs of ordinary dimensions, the disposition of the large pipes of the pedal department is accompanied with more or less difficulty. The wind-chests of the 32 feet and 16 feet open wood stops occupy considerable floor-space; and, owing to the great length of many of the pipes planted thereon, much of this space is taken up throughout the entire height of the Organ. In the general run of Church Organs, built by English and American firms, the difficulty above alluded to rarely assumes serious proportions, simply because their pedal departments are, as a rule, little better than apologies. The average Pedal Organ rarely extends beyond three stops; and it frequently consists of one master-of-all-work stop in the shape of a loud Open Diapason, 16 ft., perhaps accompanied by an Octave Coupler to give the effect of a Bass Flute, 8 ft.* In too many cases the stops that are introduced are so buried in the depths of the instruments, behind large bellows and other obstructions, that their tones are denuded of all character beyond a muffled, rumbling sound. As the tones of all labial pipes are produced at their mouths only, it is necessary in the internal arrangement to place their mouths as high above the floor level as possible, and in spaces tolerably free from obstructions. It will be observed, from our descriptions, that in the Organ in the Albert Hall, Sheffield, all the wind-chests of the pedal department, save the two on which are planted the 32 ft. octaves of the Principal-

*For further remarks on the short-comings of English and American Pedal Organs, see Chapter on The Church Organ.

BASSE and the CONTRE-BOMBARDE, are placed on the same stage as are the wind-chests of the Grand Orgue; and that in the instrument in the Public Halls, Glasgow, all the Pedal Organ wind-chests are on a level with the wind-chests of the Great Organ. The arrangements are in both instances highly satisfactory. When pedal pipes have to be planted close to the floor on which the Organ stands, ample room should be given them for proper speech; and provision must be made for the free egress of their tones. These remarks do not apply to reed pipes, the sounds of which issue from the upper openings of their tubes. The wind-chests of reed stops must be so placed that the pipes planted thereon can be conveniently reached for tuning purposes.

The scales of the larger Pedal Organ stops exercise a great influence on their proper arrangement and accommodation. The inordinate scales so often adopted by organ builders in England have done much to retard the development of the Pedal Organ in that country. When it is known that in numerous instruments the CCC pipe of the OPEN DIAPASON, 16 FT., has an internal measurement of about 18 inches in width by 22 inches in depth, and that the wood forming such a pipe is probably not less than 1½ inches in thickness, some idea can be formed of the space required to accommodate the entire thirty pipes of such a stop. Correspondingly inordinate scales are often met with in the pipes of the DOUBLE OPEN DIAPASON, 32 FT. One instance may be given on the authority of Dr. Hopkins: he informs us that the CCCC pipe of the CONTRA OPEN DIAPASON, 32 FT., in the Organ erected by W. Hill, of London, in the Town Hall of Birmingham, "is 12 feet in circumference, and its interior measurement is 224 cubic feet." Calculating roughly, this pipe must have an internal measurement of 2 feet 6 inches in width by 3 feet in depth; and it must require nearly 9 square feet of floor space to stand upon. Stops of such immense and unnecessary scales are never found in Germany,—the birthplace and true home of the Pedal Organ,—and valuable lessons may be learnt from the works of its great builders in the matter now under consideration. For Pedal Organ PRINCIPALS, 16 FT., of wood, the great Silbermann was content with the scale of 9 inches in width by 11 inches in depth for the CCC pipe: and it is rare to find in the large Organs in Germany the CCC pipe of the MAJORBASS, 16 FT., measuring internally more than 10 inches in width by 12 inches in depth. The same small scales are to be observed in the open wood stops of 32 ft. speaking length. Edmund Schulze, of Paulinzelle, in his Organs in the Cathedral of Bremen, and the Church of St. Mary, Wismar, has introduced PRINCIPALBASS stops of 32 ft. which measure only 12 inches in width by about 14 inches in depth, internally, at their CCCC pipes. And Walcker, of Ludwigsburg, uses scales for similar stops which, at their CCCC pipes, measure from 11 inches to 16 inches in width.

It is somewhat difficult to account for the employment of such absurdly large pipes as one finds in many English Organs; unless it is on the ground that their builders, in introducing only one or two stops in their Pedal Organs, desired to make up for the deficiency in number by the size of the stops they did introduce. We can conceive no other reason for their adoption of inordinate scales.

With stops made to the small German scales, the proper arrangement of the

Pedal Organ becomes a comparatively easy matter. In the Organ in the Public Halls, at Glasgow, we find that the CCCC pipe of the DOUBLE OPEN DIAPASON, 32 FT., measures internally 19 inches in width by 22 inches in depth; while the CCC pipes of the OPEN DIAPASON, 16 FT., and the VIOLONE, 16 FT., measure, respectively, 12 inches by 14 inches, and 6 inches by 9 inches. The scales of the above DIAPASONS are as large as need ever be used; and much smaller ones will prove sufficient, with copious winding and proper voicing, for the largest Church Organs in which refinement of tone is desired in preference to mere volume.

When small scales are adopted, the proper appointment and arrangement of the Pedal Organ becomes, as we have already said, comparatively easy even in cases where space is very circumscribed. To help matters, the larger wood pipes may be disposed horizontally, one above the other, in the lower part of the Organ, care being taken to provide ample means of egress for the sound produced at their mouths. These pipes may be reduced in their horizontal length by being mitred toward their open ends. As further examples of what we may call sensible scales for Pedal Organ stops, we may mention the MAJORBASS, 16 FT., and the VIOLONE, 16 FT., in the noteworthy Organ, built by Edmund Schulze, in the Church of St. Peter, at Hindley, Lancashire. The CCC open pipe of the former stop measures 8⅜ inches in width by 11 inches in depth, internally; and the corresponding pipe of the latter stop measures, internally, only 5½ inches in width and depth. Notwithstanding the smallness of their scales, both these stops are remarkably full-toned and effective. The covered SUBBASS, 16 FT., in the same Organ, has its CCC pipe 5¾ inches in width by 8 inches in depth. This scale is generally largely exceeded in the BOURDONS introduced in the pedal departments of English Church Organs.

In arranging the pipes of the Pedal Organ stops, it is always desirable to avoid planting them semitonally. This is specially desirable in the case of large-scaled covered pipes, such as those of the SUB-BOURDON, 32 FT., and the BOURDON, 16 FT. The dividing of the Pedal Organ wind-chests, and the placing of them at different sides of the manual divisions, are practices commonly adopted by the great builders, and ones that should be followed in all possible cases. Large covered or stopped pipes planted close together semitonally, that is, in the order of the chromatic scale, have been found to be injuriously affected in their speech through some unexplained acoustical phenomenon; while small-scaled stopped pipes are not affected to any noticeable extent by semitonal planting.*

In Organs occupying confined or disadvantageous positions there will always be a difficulty in finding accommodation for an adequate or properly-appointed Pedal Organ; and as architects rarely provide sufficient room for instruments of reasonable size, this difficulty is likely to obtain in the majority of cases. The architect of the Town Hall of Manchester made a great mistake in not providing a suitable place for the Organ in the concert-room of that important building. When M. A. Cavaillé-Coll was called upon to construct the Organ, he was, as he personally informed us, much disappointed at finding so badly constructed a place

*Dr. Hopkins gives some interesting facts on this subject in "The Organ," p. 300. Edition of 1870.

for its reception. He found himself at a loss to insert a Pedal Organ such as he knew to be necessary; and so great was the difficulty that it could only be met by a wholesale system of borrowing—a system he naturally condemned. Notwithstanding the fact that we give the complete Specification of this instrument elsewhere, we may here give particulars of its Pedal Organ, as illustrative of the expedients organ-builders have to adopt when they are instructed to erect large Organs in places totally unsuited for their reception. The following list fully explains how Cavaillé-Coll contrived to provide a Pedal Organ of seven stops:—

1. CONTRE-BASSE, 16 FT.—Open wood throughout; with additional octave of pipes at top for the FLÛTE BASSE. (No. 3.)
2. SOUBASSE, 16 FT.—Stopped wood and metal. Borrowed entirely from the BOURDON of the Grand Orgue.
3. FLÛTE BASSE, 8 FT.—Borrowed from the CONTRE-BASSE (No. 1) with its extra octave of pipes.
4. VIOLONCELLE, 8 FT.—Borrowed entirely from the VIOLONCELLE of the Grand Orgue.
5. BOURDON DOUX, 8 FT.—Borrowed entirely from the BOURDON of the Grand Orgue.
6. BOMBARDE, 16 FT.—Metal throughout; with an additional octave of pipes at top for the TROMPETTE. (No. 7.)
7. TROMPETTE, 8 FT.—Borrowed from the BOMBARDE (No. 6) with its extra octave of pipes.

From this it will be seen that Cavaillé-Coll found room for only two independent Pedal Organ stops,—the CONTRE-BASSE and BOMBARDE,—and that he obtained the other five stops by borrowing; an expedient which should never be resorted to when room can be found for independent stops. It may be said, however, that an adequate Pedal Organ may be improved by borrowing one or two stops from some expressive division; for the great imperfection of the modern Pedal Organ lies in its absolutely unexpressive character and total want of flexibility.

The pedal department may in some cases be relieved by mounting one or more of its small-scaled wood stops as external ornamental features, as has been done, on our suggestion, in the wings of the Organ in Trinity Church, at Denver, Col. We have spoken on the desirability of employing wood pipes as decorative features in our Chapters on the External Design of the Organ and the Decoration of the Organ.

It is both a common and commendable practice to use the larger pipes of the open metal stops of the Pedal Organ for the main towers introduced in the external design of the Organ. Notable examples are numerous. They are to be found in the Organs in St. George's Hall, Liverpool, and the Royal Albert Hall, London. In the front of the Organ in the Cathedral of St. Bavon, at Haarlem, are mounted the larger pipes of the SUBPRINCIPAL, 32 FT., the CCCC pipe of which is about 40 feet in height and 15 inches in diameter. Germany furnishes many fine examples of this effective treatment of large metal pipes.

Although we have spoken chiefly of the wood stops of the Pedal Organ, because of the mistakes that have been made in adopting inordinate and undesirable scales for them, and the corresponding difficulty of finding room for them in Organs of moderate dimensions or in those occupying unfavorable positions, many of our remarks are applicable to the larger metal labial stops of the same department. English builders have frequently erred in employing undesirably large scales, gaining power, perhaps, but sacrificing quality. It is known to every organ expert that very large scaled metal pipes of the DIAPASON class or form do not yield the rich, bright, and singing tones of properly scaled OPEN DIAPASONS; but, on the contrary, produce rather powerful and heavy fluty tones. One of the grandest OPEN DIAPASONS, of 8 ft. pitch, we remember to have heard is the larger of the two in the Great division of the Organ in the Parish Church of Leeds, Yorkshire. This noble stop was made by Edmund Schulze to a scale largely favored by him, the CC pipe of which is only 6·25 inches in internal diameter. This scale carried down would give a diameter of about 10·5 inches for the CCC pipe, ample for any ordinary Pedal Organ OPEN DIAPASON, 16 FT., allowing the pipes are properly voiced and copiously winded, at a moderate pressure, as they are in the stop made by Schulze. Both German and French organ builders use reasonable scales for their 16 ft. open metal stops of the PRINCIPAL or DIAPASON family: their CCC pipes rarely exceed 10 inches in diameter, while in numerous instances they are little more than 9 inches. In English Organs the OPEN DIAPASON, 16 FT., in the pedal department, frequently exceeds 12 inches, and has been made 14 inches in diameter in some cases.

The saving of room in the Pedal Organ by the systematic adoption of the small scales commonly used by the great German masters is a matter of the utmost importance; for, under existing conditions, it can only be by such an adoption that one can hope to see the Pedal Organ improved in its tonal appointment, and brought into reasonable keeping with the manual divisions. With small-scaled stops there will always be less difficulty, than commonly obtains, in arranging a suitable Pedal Organ. In locating their wind-chests in spaces where larger ones could not be accommodated a substantial gain is secured, admitting of the insertion of one or more additional stops. Different degrees of tonal strength and variety of tonal character are as necessary in the speaking stops of the Pedal Organ as they are in those of the manual divisions; therefore it is desirable, in the cause of art, that every legitimate means be adopted to secure their presence in the tonal appointment of every Organ in which completeness is aimed at. In this opinion, we are convinced, all organists who are artists will support us.

We may conclude our brief remarks on the internal arrangement of the Organ with a few words respecting the locating of the bellows and reservoirs. It is desirable in all possible cases to locate the bellows—feeders and main receiver—outside the Organ, either in a chamber specially constructed underneath it, or in a room adjoining or at a reasonable distance from it. By so doing, the interior of the Organ is relieved of a very cumbersome structure; and all chance of unpleasant noises arising is prevented. It is only necessary, when the bellows are so removed, to provide means for the conveyance of air from the immediate vicinity of the Organ to the feeders, so that the pipe-work may be blown by wind of the same temperature and general condition as that which surrounds it.

Although it is not absolutely necessary, it is very desirable to place within the Organ the reservoirs which supply the wind of different pressures directly to the several wind-chests, as in the French Organs we have spoken of. Two reservoirs should always be provided in an Organ of any pretensions; one to supply the pedal department and the other the manual divisions. By this arrangement two pressures of wind can readily be obtained; and no class of pedal playing will interfere with the steadiness of the manual wind. This is a matter of no small importance. When the internal space is circumscribed, the reservoirs may be placed one above the other, as in the Organ in the Church of Saint-Sulpice, at Paris; the lower one supplying the pedal wind-chests, and the upper one furnishing wind of somewhat lower pressure to the manual wind-chests. When it is found impossible or very undesirable to place the reservoirs within the Organ, they can be located in the bellows chamber and connected to the Organ by proper wind-trunks.

Too much consideration cannot be given by the organ builder to the internal arrangement of the Organ, whatever its class may be; and the consummate artist is he who neglects no detail in the production of work of combined utility and beauty.

CHAPTER IX.

ACOUSTICAL MATTERS CONNECTED WITH ORGAN PIPES.

IT is not our intention to give anything approaching a dissertation on the Science of Acoustics, or to discuss the difficult questions which beset the theory of sound as at present taught; but we feel that a treatise such as the present, in which an attempt is made to give a fairly comprehensive view of all important matters connected with the science and art of organ construction, would obviously be imperfect without some allusion being made to the acoustical matters intimately connected with the sound-producing portion of the Organ—the pipe-work.

The sound of a labial organ pipe is generated at its mouth by the rapid vibratory action of the wind-stream which rushes from its wind-way, setting up shocks, pulses, or tremors throughout the internal column of air. This action we shall attempt to describe as we understand it. This much we know to be the case; but beyond this simple and evident fact we acknowledge we know very little. The varied opinions held by distinguished acousticians and others who seem to have given some attention to the subject, go to prove how unsatisfactory is our present knowledge of the behavior of the air in producing sound of different qualities in pipes of different form or construction. Considering the fertile field organ pipes furnish for interesting experiment and investigation, it surely is remarkable that so little of any true value has appeared in the standard works on acoustics and treatises on organ-building: and it is still more remarkable that what has been written by the several reputed authorities is strangely conflicting; so much so, that when their respective opinions and statements are compared the result is negative and practically valueless. In support of what we have ventured to assert, we shall quote what such scientific investigators as Helmholtz, Tyndall, and others of the same school, have advanced on the subject of the generation of sound by organ pipes. It must be admitted, after an exhaustive study of all the experiments made and the theories advanced by the acousticians who have written on the subject of organ pipes, that science has done very little to help the organ builder and pipe voicer, to whom, at the present time, simple traditional methods and practical experience are of infinitely more value than all that scientific research has placed at their disposal. Considering the great importance of the organ pipe as an acoustical instrument, it is just a little remarkable that acousticians should have said so little about it, should have said that little so badly, and have (obviously through scanty knowledge) made misleading statements anent it. This is specially the case in connection with reed pipes. Interesting as matters connected with reed pipes are, the student of organ acoustics will find those connected with labial pipes much more interesting. To this varied and important class of organ pipes we shall now direct the reader's attention.

Notwithstanding the fact that in other Chapters we treat at length on all the varied forms and modes of construction of labial pipes, it is advisable that we should give in this special Chapter a brief description of the two leading forms; namely, the *open pipe* and the *stopped pipe.* While the modes of construction of these pipes differ materially in certain directions, and the tones they produce differ in quality, it must be borne in mind that their sounds are generated in precisely the same manner and by the same means.

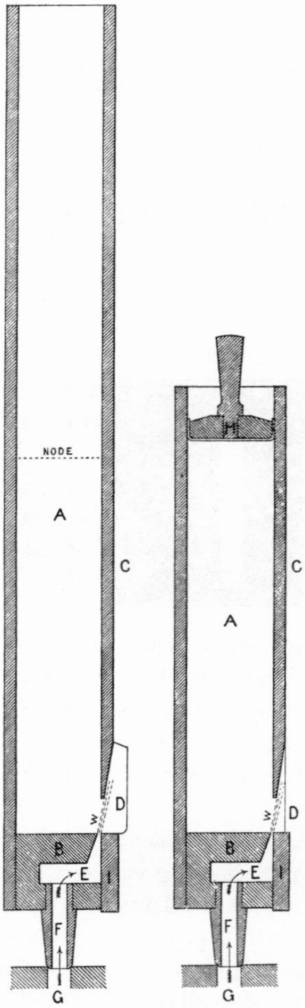

Fig. LV. Fig. LVI.

Fig. LV. is the Longitudinal Section of an open wood pipe, the body, A, of which is quadrangular in form, constructed of four boards glued together at their edges and to the block B. The face-board C is shorter than the others, and is thinned at its lower end so as to form the upper lip of the mouth of the pipe, D. The block B is cut to the section shown before it is glued to the back- and side-boards. The "throat" of the block, at E, is for the free passage of the compressed air which is sent from the wind-chest G through the channel bored in the pipe-foot F. The direction of the wind is indicated by small arrows. The front of the block B is covered by the cap I; and between the upper sharp edge of the block and the inner upper edge of the cap is a narrow slit, extending along the mouth of the pipe, forming the wind-way through which the compressed air rushes upward, in a thin sheet, across the mouth. The direction of this wind-sheet, immediately before the pipe speaks, is indicated by the dotted lines at W. On the sides of the mouth are projecting pieces of wood called ears, one of which is indicated at D. These are applied for the purpose of preventing the lateral spreading of the wind-sheet. In wooden pipes of moderate dimensions, the wood left at the sides in cutting the mouth forms the necessary ears, as at D in Fig. LVI. This, then, is the manner in which the open wood pipe, in what may be considered its normal form, is constructed.

Open metal pipes of ordinary form have cylindrical bodies; and in all essential features resemble wood pipes so far as the treatment of their mouths or sound-producing parts is concerned. A thick metal plate, cut to a sharp edge, takes the place of the block, and is called the "language" or "languid;" while a portion of the conical foot of the pipe is flattened so as to form the wind-way. The portion so flattened is designated the lower lip. The upper lip of the mouth is formed by cutting a portion from the cylindrical body and then flattening the pipe immediately above the mouth so as to bring it directly over the wind-way. We may just remark that in voicing labial pipes, both of wood and metal, the treatment of the upper lip is an important factor in tone production; but it is unnecessary for our present purpose to go into particulars respecting the art of voicing.

Returning to the open wood pipe, we have to briefly consider the manner in which it produces sound. The first fact to be observed, at this stage of our subject, is that when the pipe is made to speak its fundamental tone, the column of air contained within its tube or body, A, Fig. LV., divides itself into two unequal portions, separated by a stratum of air apparently at rest; both the divisions being in a state of tremor or molecular vibration. The dividing stratum of air, which is obviously the place of latent energy and opposing force, is commonly designated the node of the pipe; and its position (which is variable) is roughly indicated by the dotted line in the illustration, nearer to the mouth than to the open end of the pipe. It will be shown later on that when a pipe is made to speak its harmonic tones, two or more nodes are formed in its vibrating column.

In Fig. LVI. is given a Longitudinal Section of a quadrangular stopped or covered pipe, drawn to the same scale as the adjoining open pipe, so as to show, as nearly as practicable, the relative lengths of an open and stopped pipe yielding notes of the same pitch, that is, sounding in unison. It will be observed that the differences which obtain between the two pipes lie in their respective lengths, and in the addition to the shorter one of a stopper, H. This stopper is formed of wood covered with leather, so as to make it fit perfectly air-tight, and yet allow of its being raised or lowered, in the top of the pipe, in the process of tuning. The lower portion of the stopped pipe and the construction of its mouth and wind-way are essentially similar to those of the open pipe, as indicated in the illustrations. When such a stopped pipe speaks its fundamental tone, there is no node formed in any portion of its internal column of air, the entire column being set in motion or molecular vibration directly by the action of the wind-sheet sent from the wind-way across the mouth.

With reference to the respective internal lengths of open and stopped pipes of the same scale, yielding tones of exactly the same pitch, Tyndall states that "to make an open tube yield the same note as a closed one it must be twice the length of the latter. And since the length of a closed tube sounding its fundamental note is *one-fourth* of the length of its sonorous wave, the length of an open tube is *one-half* that of the wave it produces." Such a statement may be sufficiently accurate for the lecture-room, or for the pages of a popular text-book on acoustics, but it is certainly misleading when applied to open and stopped organ pipes. Everyone knows, who has more than a superficial knowledge of matters connected with the behavior of organ pipes, that if an open pipe is cut exactly in half, and the mouthed portion is stopped by a piece of wood being glued down over its open end, so as not to diminish, in any way, its internal length, the note yielded by it will not be of the same pitch as that originally yielded by the open pipe before it was cut. This is one practical proof that it is incorrect and misleading to state, in an unqualified manner, that "to make an open tube yield the same note as a closed one, it must be twice the length of the latter;" and it goes to prove—what we shall still more clearly prove farther on—that the lengths of the tubes of organ pipes bear little or no relation to the hypothetical lengths of equally hypothetical sound-waves. We are aware that the makers of the organ pipes commonly used by the professors and lecturers who teach the popular theory of sound, so scale and voice such pipes as to apparently prove what such sapient teachers desire to prove; and the professors and lecturers are careful not to bring forward other organ pipes the dimensions and tonal behavior of which would refute their teaching. That, of course, is not to be expected. In case we should be considered too severe in our condemnation of questionable teaching, we quote the following passage from the writings of the greatest authority on acoustical matters connected with organ pipes who has ever lived. Mr. Hermann Smith says:—

"Bearing in mind the working power of the air-reed, we are brought to consider the effects of the dimensions of the pipe and consequently of the form as well as the extent of the air-column whereon this power is impelled to act, and it is necessary to recur in passing to the question of length. Scientific writers affirm that the length of an organ pipe for a given note corresponds to the length of the wave in air with an absolute relation, thus expressed. Prof. Tyndall says: 'The length of a stopped pipe is one-fourth that of the sonorous wave which it produces, whilst the length of an open pipe is one-half that of the sonorous wave.' Prof. Balfour Stewart says, in his 'Elementary Lessons in Physics': 'In an organ pipe of this kind, the upper end closed, the primary note is that of which the wave length is twice the length of the pipe . . . the wave length of the sound produced by an open pipe is equal to the length of the pipe, so that it is only half of that produced by a shut pipe of the same length.' (One is curious to know why there is this difference of statement from two leading teachers of men; perplexing to the student in want of a leader.) Prof. Tyndall demonstrates his affirmation, showing that a stopped tube resounds to the note middle c^1 of 256 vibrations per second; the wave length in air of this note he states to be fifty-two inches; then in proof he measures the jar or tube, and says, 'by measurement with a two-foot rule I find it to be thirteen inches, precisely a fourth of the wave length.' [We treat this subject more fully farther on.] He then proceeds to affirm the same of organ pipes, and proves it by tuning-forks and by sounding the pipes to the same note, and believes he has justified his assertions. His hearers do him that justice, and go home believing also. The proof is, however, altogether illusive. No speaking organ pipe of that length ever gave the note of that pitch. Let us put the assertion to the test. My object lies beyond the rectification of a philosopher's misapprehension, and is meant to show not only that an organ pipe behaves itself in a manner different to that with which it is accredited, but also why it does so; to show how important a matter in the nature of its action is this neglected difference, and how wide its bearing on the whole system of musical instruments. Here at my hand is a stopped pipe sounding middle c^1. I measure it interiorly from languid to stopper; it is eleven inches in length, and has a diameter of one-and-a-half inches. Here is an open pipe, same pitch, same diameter, and its length is twenty-three inches. Observe, our stopped pipe is half an inch less in length than half that of the open pipe; yet again notice, it is longer than that pipe would be if severed at the true nodal distance from the languid. How can we read eleven as precisely thirteen, and twenty-three as twenty-six inches? Under the strange notion that it is no matter if there is a difference, this has been done, and the truth of facts lost sight of or disguised in the convenient phrase, 'approximately correct.' The phrase assumes that there is a standard claiming nature's allegiance. We want to know, not what is correct, but what is true. Further, remark that if you stop the same open pipe at the top, the note obtained will not be an octave deeper, it will be nearly a tone sharper than that; if you stop the pipe at the center, the note will not be the same as the open one, it will be considerably flatter; in neither case a good tone, since for its proper sounding in such condition the lip would require to be cut higher, mouth a little narrower, perhaps curved, and languid lowered. Every detail we come upon tells plainly of the working power of the reed [air-stream] affecting variably the results in pitch, and I think the reason for these distinctive sounding lengths will be discerned when we reach the consideration of the question of periods of vibration in pipes as tempered by rests. . . .

"A student well read in all that the best text-books in acoustics can teach, coming to the practical study of organ pipes and seeing in a grand Organ so multitudinous an array of pipes, the unison pipes of the several stops conspicuous for diversities of diameter as well as of length, would naturally expect that here, if anywhere, he would find confirmation of Reynault's law, 'The velocity of propagation of a wave of the same intensity in straight lines is *less according as the section of the tube is less.*' No! this small comfort is denied him; he is in a world of contrarieties; the law is abrogated; he will find the organ world *de facto* governed on principles the exact opposite, '*The velocity is greater as the section is less.*' Investigating further, he will find that, although in length the octaves of particular flue stops examined are each very closely upon half the length of the other, yet their diameters do not follow a similar rule, for instead of octave or double octave being in that ratio, he must from the pitch note count to the seventeenth pipe before he will arrive at a pipe half its diameter. For other seeming anomalies, let him proceed to the stops called BASSOON, TRUMPET, and TUBA, and he will find that here increase of diameter demands not less length, but greatly increased length, to accompany increase of scale. Books of latest authorities will tell him that in an organ pipe with a metallic reed 'the note produced depends upon the length of the pipe rather than upon the length of the reed. In fact, when the note is established the reed obeys the impulses it receives from the air in the tube. Its use is accordingly rather to economize air and to give certainty and percussion to the striking of the note.' Alas, it is inference by theory without test. Remove the whole of the eight or nine feet of the tube, leaving but the few inches of cup or socket, and you will have altered the pitch not more than a semitone.

"All organ pipes having metallic reeds act in conformity with Reynault's law, and the same holds good of wind instruments—trumpets, bassoons, and the like. All organ pipes possessing air-reeds, flutes also, and some whistles, not all, display an opposite law. The musical tones of all in both these systems are the result of 'suction by velocity,' and the distinction is that in the former the intermittence is produced by suction under a *propulsive current*, and in the latter by suction under an *abstracting current.* The fact announces the law and leads to its explanation."

The facts clearly stated in the above quotation go far to show with what caution one must accept the dogmatic and conflicting assertions of the popular teachers of acoustical science.

Before proceeding farther, it is perhaps desirable to consider the motions of the air within open and stopped pipes, as formulated by the authorities above alluded to. In the pages of "Sound" we find diagrams which are introduced for the purpose of conveying, in a graphic manner, an idea of the modes in which the vibrating columns of air within open and stopped tubes divide themselves when sounded by wind of different pressures. We give a series of these diagrams, retaining the *incorrect* positions of the nodes in them; but instead of the simple tube forms, we show them in the more expressive forms of sections of organ pipes.

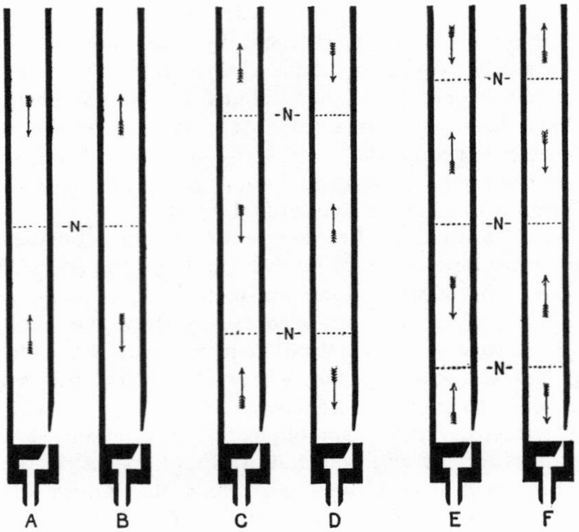

FIG. LVII.

The column of air within the body of an open pipe while yielding its fundamental tone is divided, according to the popular theory, into two equal parts separated by a node. This primal division is indicated by Diagrams A and B, Fig. LVII. The arrows show the supposed direction of the pulses in the process of condensation in the pipe A, and in that of rarefaction in the pipe B; similar motions obtaining on both sides of the node N. We are told by Tyndall that the length of an open pipe is "one-half the length of its sonorous wave," so that the length of each portion of the air-column, as indicated in diagrams A and B, must be, according to this authority, one-quarter the length of its sonorous wave. When the same pipe is made, by increased wind pressure or other means, to speak the first upper partial tone of its prime or fundamental tone, the column of air within it is divided into three parts, separated by two nodes, as indicated in Diagrams C and D. The nodes are at N, N. It will be observed that the central part of the column is equal in length to both the lower and upper parts added together. The arrows indicate the directions of the pulses in the condensations and rarefactions of the several parts. When the same pipe is made to speak its second upper partial tone, the column of air within it is divided into four parts, separated by three nodes, N, N, N, as indicated in the Diagrams E and F. Here it will be seen that the two larger parts, divided by the central node, are each equal to the two smaller extreme parts added together. The two equal parts, separated by the single node, in the Diagrams A and B, are termed by acousticians "semi-ventral segments." In the Diagrams C and D, the larger central part, between the two nodes, is termed a "ventral segment," and is said to be formed of two semi-ventral segments; and the smaller lower and upper parts are semi-ventral segments. In the Diagrams E and F, the larger parts between the nodes are ventral segments; and smaller lower and upper parts are semi-ventral segments. Therefore, it will

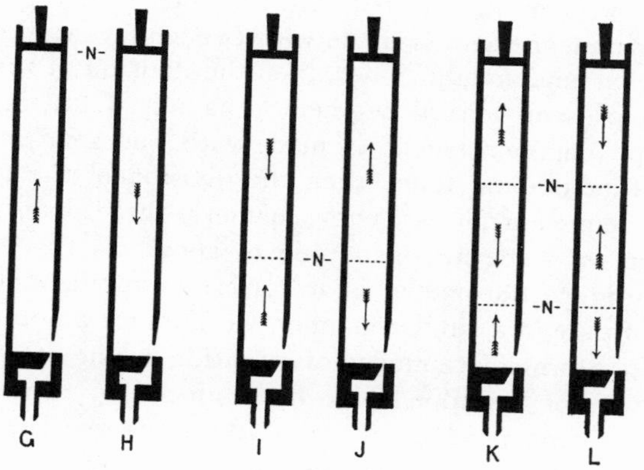

FIG. LVIII.

be seen that the mouth of a pipe is in all cases at the middle of a ventral segment; or, in other words, that the part of the column of air adjoining the mouth is a semi-ventral segment.

We will now consider the stated conditions of the air-column within a stopped pipe while it is yielding its fundamental and its first and second upper partial tones, employing another series of diagrams to elucidate the subject, Fig. LVIII. When a stopped pipe yields its fundamental tone no division takes place in the column of air within it, as indicated in the Diagrams G and H; for in this case the under side of the stopper occupies the place of the upper semi-ventral segment as it obtains in the open pipe, and, accordingly, serves as a node, at N. The sound pulse, we are told, "simply moves up and down from bottom to top, as denoted by the arrows." The complete column is, therefore, a semi-ventral segment, or one-quarter the length of the "sonorous wave" created by the pipe. We can now see how it is, according to Tyndall, that a stopped pipe measures one-half the length of an open pipe yielding a note of the same pitch as the stopped pipe. When the stopped pipe is made to speak its first upper partial tone, the column of air within it is divided into two parts separated by a node, as indicated in the twin Diagrams I and J; the under surface of the stopper continuing to be nodal. In this instance the lower part of the column is a semi-ventral segment, while the larger upper part is a complete ventral segment. It will be observed that the semi-ventral segment in Diagrams I and J is only one-third the length of that in Diagrams G and H. When the same stopped pipe is made to speak its second upper partial, the column of air is divided into three parts—a semi-ventral segment and two complete ventral segments—separated by two nodes and bounded by the nodal surface at the stopper, as indicated in Diagrams K and L. The semi-ventral segment in this case is one-fifth the length of that indicated in the diagrams G and H.

It is supposed that theoretically there is no limit to the division of the column of air in a tube or pipe, either open or stopped; but in practice its divisions are very limited, as all who are acquainted with the voicing of organ pipes are aware. In an open pipe commencement is made with two semi-ventral segments, the pipe yielding its prime or fundamental tone: then the division of the column proceeds in even numbers of semi-ventral segments; namely, four, six, eight, and so on. In a stopped pipe commencement is made with one semi-ventral segment, the pipe yielding its fundamental tone: then the division of the column proceeds in odd numbers of semi-ventral segments; namely, three, five, seven, and so on. Accordingly, when we voice an open pipe to speak its first harmonic or upper partial tone, we produce the octave of its prime or fundamental tone; but when we treat a stopped pipe in a similar manner, we produce a note a twelfth above its prime tone. "No intermediate modes of vibration are in either case possible. If the fundamental tone of a stopped pipe be produced by 100 vibrations a second, the first overtone will be produced by 300 vibrations, the second by 500, and so on. Such a pipe, for example, cannot execute 200 or 400 vibrations in a second. In like manner the open pipe, whose fundamental note is produced by 100 vibrations a second, cannot vibrate 150 times in a second, but passes, at a jump, to 200, 300, 400, and so on. In open pipes, as in stopped ones, the number of vibrations executed in the unit of time is inversely proportional to the length of the pipe. This follows from the fact," says Tyndall, "that the *time* of a vibration is determined by the *distance which the sonorous pulse has to travel to complete a vibration.*" This may be considered a good working hypothesis, but it cannot be said to be of universal application, as we shall endeavor to show.

As an introduction to the subject of resonance in organ pipes, Tyndall describes certain experiments with tuning-forks and resonant jars, the chief aim of which is the determination of the lengths of the columns of air which resound to certain definite tones. The experiments are simple and seemingly conclusive. They are certainly ingenious. The first experiment is as follows: A large tuning-fork is taken which vibrates 256 times in a second; and which we are told produces a sonorous wave 4 feet 4 inches long in air at the temperature of 60° F. It is detached from its resonant case, which, be it said, has an internal depth of only 11⅞ inches, so that when it is set in vibration its sound can hardly be heard by a distant ear. While in active vibration it is held over the open end of a cylindrical glass jar, 18 inches deep, formed with a flaring or trumpet-shaped mouth, which fails to resound to any marked extent to its note. While held in this position, water is poured, with as little noise as possible, into the jar. The water rises in the jar and the internal column of air shortens until a point is reached when the note produced by the fork bursts forth with considerable strength. This is the point of perfect resonance, or "maximum augmentation of the sound." The "next question is," says Tyndall, "what is the length of the column of air which resounds to this fork? By measurement with a two-foot rule it is found to be 13 inches. But the length of the wave emitted by the fork is 52 inches; hence *the length of the column of air which resounds to the fork is equal to one-fourth of the length of the sound-wave produced by the fork.* This rule is general, and might be illustrated by any other of the forks [with specially prepared jars, of course] instead of this one."

Further particulars respecting the above assertion are necessary before the action of the air in an organ pipe, according to the popular theory, can be clearly understood. In the accompanying illustration, Fig. LIX, is shown a Vertical Section of the glass jar, with the air column of 13 inches measured from the surface of the water, at D, to the mouth of the jar, at C. T is the tuning-fork held over the jar, as previously described, the dotted lines *a* and *b* indicating the swing of the lower prong while vibrating. The action is ingeniously described as follows: In the time required by the prong of the fork to move from *a* to *b*, the condensation it produces runs down to the surface of the water, is there reflected, and, as the distance to the water and back is 26 inches, the reflected wave reaches the lower prong of the fork at the moment when it is on the point of returning from *b* to *a*. The rarefaction of the sound-wave is produced by the retreat of the lower prong from *b* to *a*. The rarefaction also runs down to the surface of the water and back, overtaking the prong, nearest the jar, just as it reaches the limit of its swing, at *a*. From this we are expected to learn that the wave produced by the swing of the fork's prong must be twice 26 inches in length; and that the vibrations of the fork are perfectly synchronous with the vibrations of the aerial column within the jar, which is exactly one-quarter the length of the sound-wave produced by the fork. "In virtue of this synchronism," says Tyndall, "the motion accumulates in the jar, spreads abroad in the room, and produces this vast augmentation of the sound."

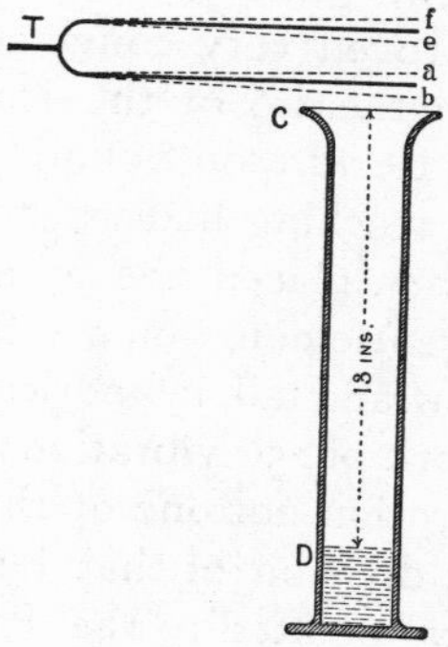

FIG. LIX.

This is all very ingenious and seemingly conclusive, but there are some slight difficulties which must be cleared away before such teaching can be accepted. In the first place, a very discreet silence is observed respecting the action of the second or upper prong of the fork used in the experiment, the swings of which are indicated, in a highly exaggerated manner, by the dotted lines *e* and *f*. It is, however, quite evident that while the under side of the lower prong, in moving from *a* to *b*, is generating the *condensation* spoken of, the under side of the upper prong, in moving, in the same instant of time, from *e* to *f*, is generating a *rarefaction;* and it is equally evident, according to the conditions of the experiment, that a condensed and a rarefied wave must pass simultaneously down and up the column of air in the resonant jar. How this physical impossibility is accomplished we are not told. At all events, a single thought will show the wisdom displayed by Tyndall in leaving out all mention of the upper prong; and in not directing attention to the simple fact that, according to his own teaching, if one side of a single prong generates a *condensation*, the other side must, at the same instant of time and in the self-same body of air, generate a *rarefaction*. Such being obviously the case, it follows, in accordance with the law of "interference of sound," that neither the fork nor the resonant jar could emit or generate sound. It is just worth while, with the view of aiding the inquiring mind anent this important subject, to quote an obviously logical statement made by Helmholtz. He says: "It is evident that at each point in a mass of air, at each instant of time, there can be only one single degree of condensation, and that the particles of air can be moving with only one single determinate kind of motion, having only one determinate amount of velocity, and passing in only one single determinate direction."

The glass jar experiment, which we have illustrated and described, doubtless proved very convincing to Professor Tyndall's audience which crowded the lecture-theatre of the Royal Institution of Great Britain, on the occasion of his Fifth Lecture on Sound: but what would the audience have thought of his dogmatic teaching had we stepped onto the platform with a basket of fifty glass jars, and then placed the collection in a row along the lecture table, saying: 'Ladies and gentlemen, you see these fifty glass jars, every one of which—wide and short, narrow and tall, cylindrical, globular, and conical—yields the maximum resonance to the fork of 256 vibrations per second; yet not one supports the Professor's theory, seeing that not one of them contains an air-column of 13 inches in length or any equal division of that length'? Again, what would the audience have thought, had we pointed to the Professor's tall bell-mouthed jar, with its necessary amount of water, and said: 'That jar has been ingeniously formed and proportioned so as to prove or support the theory which every one of my jars refutes. Alter its bell mouth in the slightest, and you will no longer have an air-column of 13 inches giving the maximum resonance to the fork of 256 vibrations in a second'? Facts are stubborn things!

We may now direct attention to the organ pipe, which may, for the moment, be looked upon, from the popular theory point of view, as a resonant vessel inverted. We are assured by Tyndall that the length of an open pipe is one-half the length of its sonorous wave: that an open organ pipe 26 inches long, filled with air, executes 256 vibrations in a second of time. Therefore, the length of its sonorous wave, measured from condensation to condensation, is twice 26 inches or 4 feet 4 inches. Multiplying this length by 256, we obtain 1,120 feet per second as the velocity of sound through air at the temperature of 60° F.

Now this statement respecting the organ pipe is just as accurate, and just as much supported by facts, as the preceding statement by Tyndall respecting the fork and resonant jar. The organ pipe, comprehensively considered in both its open and stopped labial forms and in its several reed forms, gives no support to the hypothetical sound-waves by indicating the equally hypothetical wave-lengths. Every organ expert knows that both open and stopped pipes, yielding the same note, vary in length according to their scales and the pressure of the wind used to give them voice; but our remarks on this important branch of our subject would be insufficient without some clear proof of their accuracy—an accuracy easily tested by any one skilled in pipe-making. At this point we may repeat the quotation previously given: "To make an open tube yield the same note as a closed one, it must be twice the length of the latter. And since the length of a closed tube sounding its fundamental note is one-fourth of the sonorous wave [as learnedly shown in the fork and glass jar experiment], the length of an open tube is one-half that of the sonorous wave it produces." It only remains for us to put this statement to a practical test, selecting the stopped pipe as the most convenient field for our investigation. In Fig. LX. are represented, accurately to scale, the fronts of three stopped wood pipes in our possession, formed with the view of testing the supposed relation of pipe lengths to the stated lengths of sound-waves. When accurately tuned, on the same wind-chest, and on the same pressure of wind, these pipes yield notes of precisely the same pitch; namely, that of the tuning-fork of 256 vibrations a second. Now, according to Tyndall's teaching and that of other authorities on the popular theory of sound, all these pipes *ought* to have an internal air-column of one-quarter the length of the sonorous wave said to be generated by a fork or other sounding body which vibrates 256 times in a second. Tyndall puts the wave-length down at 4 feet 4 inches, and the internal length of a stopped organ pipe at 13 inches, or one-quarter the wave-length. Turning to the three test pipes, A, B, and C, the student of acoustics will be surprised to find that, while they all produce notes of precisely the same pitch and vibrational number, not one of them contains a column of air of the required length of 13 inches. The dimensions of their respective air-columns are as follows: The longest pipe, A, measures 1 inch square internally; and the length of its air-column is 11¾ inches, measured from the upper surface of the block to the nodal surface of the stopper, as indicated. The middle pipe, B, measures 2 inches square internally; and the length of its air-column is 9¾ inches. The shortest pipe, C, meas-

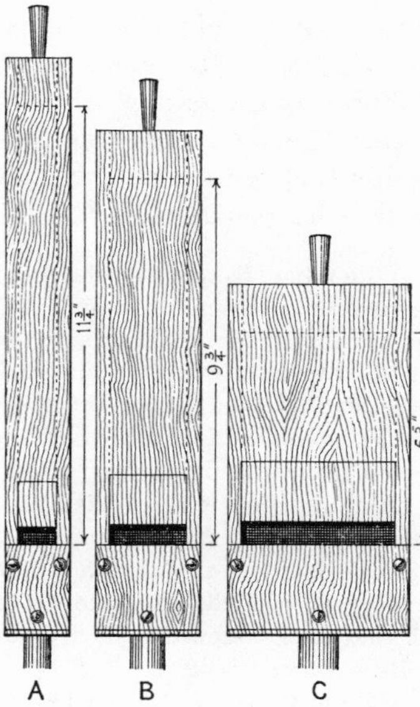

FIG. LX.

ures 4 inches square internally, and the length of its air-column is only 5⅝ inches. Not only do these pipes fail to show the hypothetical column of 13 inches; but not one of them contains a column of a length bearing any even numerical relation to that of 13 inches, or to the length (4 feet 4 inches) of the equally hypothetical sonorous wave.

Another fact connected with the behavior of these pipes may be pointed out; namely, that the lengths of their air-columns are not fixed, while the pitch of the notes they yield strictly accords with that of the fork of 256 vibrations. If the pipes are blown with wind of a lower pressure than that on which they were originally tuned, their stoppers will have to be driven down, and their air-columns shortened, to bring their notes in accord with the fork: and if, on the other hand, they are blown with a wind of a higher pressure, their stoppers will require to be raised, and their air-columns lengthened, to restore their notes to the correct pitch. These facts point conclusively to what Mr. Hermann Smith calls "the variability of the node," which obtains in open as well as in stopped pipes. What this distinguished observer and writer has said on this interesting subject is so valuable that we do not hesitate to give the following quotation from the article in which he discusses it.*

"The displacement of the node sometimes receives notice in works on sound, but with little further comment than an admission of some slight correction of Bernoulli's laws being necessary for bringing about actual conformity between scientific statement and natural fact. Even the evidence offered is in such general terms, that the attempted interpretation is of too doubtful a kind to attract the attention, and so the matter has escaped anything like thorough investigation. Beyond the knowledge of some displacement of the node from the theoretical position it was supposed to occupy, there is another fact to which I have called attention, and that is the variability of the position of the node according to conditions and influences. In my explanations of the acoustics of instruments, I have had to remark upon the nodal changes taking place under the impress of quality and pitch by the performer, according to his will and intent for musical ends, and have wished you to apprehend the truth that every outward change perceived by the ear is accompanied by an inward change equally real and positive.

"From the time of Savart it has been known that the nodal division of the open organ pipe does not take place at the exact half of the length, that the half nearest the embouchure is the shorter of these 'unequal halves'—a contradictory term apologized for yet sanctioned, I believe, by the late Prof. Donkin.

"The displacement of the node is perhaps the most significant fact that in the natural history of organ pipes presents itself to the attention of the investigator, be he student or teacher. Why it should have been passed by as though its meaning were not worth wrestling for is incomprehensible. Since Savart wrote no light has been thrown on this singular phenomenon, for the explanation which has been afforded (presently to be quoted) cannot be called in any degree satisfactory. In the illustrations of nodal division given in various scientific works there is a puzzling contrariety hardly to be accounted for except on the supposition that our engravers are as niggardly conservative in design as the buried Egyptians, or that the engravings themselves are the cherished heirlooms of our publishers. . . .

"Kœnig in his own illustrations represents the displacement of the node as it is indicated under experiment, for this one condition of truth to nature had been too often before him in his manometric flames to allow of his disregarding its faithful portraiture.

* *Musical Opinion*, February 1, 1884, page 210.

The difference he shows to exist as to position corresponds very closely with that we arrive at by other means, by calculation of scales, and by the practical teachings of experimental study of the relations and arrangements of organ pipes. Of the cause of the displacement Kœnig offers no elucidation.

"The following explanation is quoted from Prof. Airy's treatise on 'Sound and Atmospheric Vibrations.' In the section on open organ pipes, he says:—'It was found by Mr. Hopkins, of Cambridge, that the node next the open mouth of the pipe was somewhat less distant from it than that given by theory, or, which amounts to the same thing, that the place where the air has always density as the external air is not exactly at the pipe's mouth but somewhat exterior to it.'

"The extent of the disparity would be but very imperfectly comprehended under this vague delineation. Other authors have attempted explanation, in substance the same as the above, to account for the disparity; the summary of the whole is, that science brings forward no better plea than the surmise of a probable place, somewhat exterior to the mouth, which the air-wave of the *lower half* of the pipe has to attain before it can be properly said to be completed in length. Truly an illogical conclusion if this line of reasoning is carried out. In common fairness the *upper half* of the pipe may claim to be credited with a reasonable amount of wave-prolongation, seeing that at the higher orifice the internal column of air pulsates the atmosphere with far greater vigor than at the mouth, and consequently that for a similar attainment of density the due addition of wave-length would only serve to increase the disparity in relation to the *half below* the node. A displacement of some sort thus receives acknowledgment, although as yet the variability of the node is unsuspected.

"The actual extent of the disparity between the 'unequal halves' can be ascertained. It is subject to laws of relation of as definite a character as are found in other dynamical problems when the elements of calculation are delicately defined. An approximate estimate will be sufficient for the present purpose. For avoidance of the inconvenient 'unequal halves' it will be permitted me to coin two simple terms as more distinctly representative, and to speak of them as super-nodal and sub-nodal. If a standard OPEN DIAPASON pipe be made for some designed pitch, whatever that pitch may be it may safely be predicted that the pipe will stand considerably short of the full theoretical length; æsthetically judged for musical quality, it ought to be about one-eighth less, a difference much affecting the veracity of the scientific argument.

"Doubtless it would be somewhat a novelty for a scientific lecturer to tell his audience that one-eighth of the whole wave-length was lost by conversion into organ-pipe vibrations, yet, unless he innocently accepts the ironical reply of Galileo on the pump question, that 'perhaps nature is indifferent to a few feet,' he is strictly in this dilemma; if the pipe is a natural standard of wave-length, the velocity of sound in air computed on the basis of the pipe's length falls very far short indeed of the philosophical estimate, 1,125 feet per second; on this ruling the latter should be pronounced to be irreconcilably wrong, *or else* the frank admission made that there is no 'necessity of relation' [as there certainly is not] that the wave-length in an organ pipe, giving a defined pitch, and the wave-length in the free air [if such wave-lengths actually exist] corresponding to that note should be identical.

"Taking the several classes of pipes, from the DIAPASON to the VOX ANGELICA, ranging from the pipes of the most vigorous to those of the softest intonation, the amount of difference from full measure varies from one-eighth to one-twelfth *less* than that which theory demands. The loss is mainly due to the cause which enforces nodal displacement. Our immediate inquiry is: What is the extent of the displacement of the node, and what its variability? Divide the length of the already reduced pipe into seven equal parts, and the unequal halves will be in the ratio of 4 to 3. Four parts belonging to the super-nodal half, and three parts to the sub-nodal half, subject to a relative variability, according to the position of the pipe in the range of octaves, and subject to a fluctuating variability determined by force of wind, diameter of pipe, character of scale, relative size of mouth, mode of voicing, and other details, changing the proportion, perhaps, to 6:5, or even to 7:6. Whatever the extent of the variability, change in result rigidly follows change in details, with a calculable value. When, instead of the fundamental note, the pipe vibrates in harmonic nodal divisions, the lowest half-segment takes upon itself almost the whole difference, and not merely a proportional share in comparison with its segmental relation to the whole pipe. A remarkable fact, but one fully accounted for in the theory I have put forth, and which I have termed the aëro-plastic reed theory, for it is easy to me visibly to demonstrate that the harmonic-independent and the harmonic-concomitant are originated in the pipe by totally distinct natural processes."

The above able, but too brief, digest of a very important subject is deeply interesting, and points the way to a wide field for investigation and experimental demonstration. We regret that he has found it advisable to make direct allusion to the hypothetical air-waves and wave-lengths; for we believe that so long as such imaginary things block the way to unprejudiced investigation there will be indifferent progress made in the true understanding of the acoustical problems connected with organ pipes. Mr. Hermann Smith is, however, one with us in regretting the want of proper attention, on the part of professing acousticians and teachers of natural philosophy, to all matters connected with sound-production in organ pipes. This will be seen by the following remarks. He continues:—

"The nodal difference detected by Mr. W. Hopkins was much smaller in extent, but there is an important distinction not to be overlooked: his experiments (recorded in the *Transactions* of the Cambridge Philosophical Society, vol. 5) were not made with organ pipes, but with glass tubes supported in position over a glass plate, the plate being set in vibration by friction. He expressly rejected organ pipes by reason of their intractability and of the difficulty of obtaining results from them of the nature desired. In like manner we continually find experimentalists rejecting organ pipes as insubordinate pupils; they prefer dumb pipes [an eloquent fact] and the artificial speech of tuning-forks, and having obtained such negative evidence, make a clean transfer of their conclusions to all argumentative reasonings and expositions of the nature and functions of the original, living, speaking organ pipes. The Hon. A. Strutt, in his Paper on the Theory of Resonance, printed in *Phil. Trans.*, Nov., 1870, says: 'Independently of these difficulties, the theory of pipes or other resonators made to speak by a stream of air directed against a sharp edge is not sufficiently understood to make this method of investigation satisfactory. For this reason I have entirely abandoned this method of causing the resonators to speak in my experiments, and have relied on other indications to fix the pitch.'

"Prof. Airy is as evidently dissatisfied with the state of theory and experiment, using such phrases as these: 'the matter, however, demands more complete explanation;' 'that obscure subject, the production of musical vibrations in a pipe by a simple blast of air;' 'possibly when the mathematical calculus is farther advanced, this may be shown,' etc. Beyond the province of mathematical analysis his survey is keen, and with foresight of the results of possible experiments.

"At the present date our best authorities are in effect repeating the assertion of Biot that 'the particular properties of the vibrations of confined air in tubes are not yet sufficiently explained.' The disturbing influence of some unknown agency may be discerned in Dulong's experiments of filling organ pipes with various gases, and estimating the velocity of sound in these gases by the pitch produced. Similar experiments on this method are referred to by Herschel, and he, noticing how the results gave for hydrogen gas a velocity differing by one-fourth from that which theoretically had been calculated, could only account for it by supposing an impurity in the gas used for the experiments. There is little need to resort to the supposition of an impurity; it is quite sufficient to know that an agreement in length of organ pipe and aërial wave-length was assumed which does not exist, and that, moreover, the mechanical nature of the organ pipe, and its delicate apparatus so wonderfully balanced for the attainment of its ends, had escaped observation. . . .

"The confession of 'obscurity' amounts to a concession that the old theory has been found wanting, that it is inadequate to deal with facts. Whether in dealing with the larger questions here brought into discussion, or with the simpler class, the mere modifications of structure, it is equally incapable. If, for instance, a stopped pipe is pierced through the stopper and a short open pipe inserted, say a third or fourth the diameter and a third or fourth the length, what will be the effect of this on the pitch? The old theory would reply, the added length would cause a flattening of pitch, and then will come a proviso for safety's sake, that if the change converted it into an open organ pipe then the pitch would be raised in accordance with the open length. We go to Nature for her say in the matter, and find that the pitch is raised, not flattened, and that the extent is about a quarter of a tone, and that *further lengthening* of the smaller pipe takes back the pitch again just its quarter tone. If another stopped pipe is drilled at the back with a hole of a diameter a third or fourth of that of the pipe, but so that it shall be at a higher level than the lip or edge of the mouth, in effect shortening the air-column by admission of external air at a higher point, what will be the result? On the old theory we should expect the pitch to be higher in consequence. Appealing to the ear we know that, on the contrary, it is flattened. These results cease to be anomalies when viewed under the new theory, and indeed they would be predicted with confidence as the necessary outcome of the conditions.

"The proposition that in an organ pipe there is no constant wave-length for an ascertained pitch will no doubt be discountenanced as novel and revolutionary, but it is true and will have to be acknowledged. A further proposition that in an open organ pipe there are three different velocities speeding at different rates, concurring in every vibration, and essential to the synchronic time of its note, has a still more aggressive aspect defiant of law. Not so. It is because law—'known law,'—does not cover the facts, is unstable in its applications, and is deficient in prevision, that there is room for a new hypothesis which does not play fast and loose with nature; the utmost exactitude of length in an organ pipe is as indispensable in this as in the older theory, but the relation is one of proportion to a system, and the least and every variation will make imperative suitable or corresponding modifications in other portions of the structure. Only a whistle, yet with more to marvel at for delicacy of organization and beauty of adaptation 'than is dreamt of in philosophy.'"

We may now return to our subject where it was interrupted to quote Mr. Hermann Smith's instructive remarks. It must be obvious to any unprejudiced person conversant with the peculiarities of organ pipes, and who will recognize the teaching of the test described, that the tremulous motion or disturbance of the air within a pipe can neither resemble, nor have any connection with, what acousticians describe as sound-waves; for it becomes radically impossible, in the face of the facts we have given, for any calculations respecting the lengths of such sound-waves to be based on the dimensions—ever changing with alterations of scale, wind pressure, etc.—of the columns of air within organ pipes. That an intense molecular disturbance or tremor pervades the entire volume of air within a pipe, created by the action of the wind-stream at its mouth, is certain, but its *exact* nature has yet to be determined. There are other matters of interest which have not, up to the present time, been satisfactorily explained. Here is one: Seeing that the length of an open pipe has no more strict relation to the length of the sonorous wave it is said to generate than that of a stopped pipe, how does the air within an open pipe divide itself into two or more vibrating parts, separated by nodes, or planes of latent energy, whilst it is under the influence of the wind-stream at the mouth? Again, why—seeing that both the lower and upper parts of the air-column in an open pipe are in a state of tremor—is no sound produced anywhere but at the mouth of the pipe? Again, why is the tone produced at the mouth of the pipe instantly affected when a hand or other shading body is brought close to the open end, or when the shape of the open end of the pipe is altered? These questions do not seem to have been carefully considered by acousticians, for a complete silence is observed respecting them.

Our attention was, for the first time, forcibly directed to the fact that the vibrating air in the upper part of an open labial pipe did not produce sound, during our survey of the Organ in the Town Hall of Manchester. We were on the highest platform of the instrument, endeavoring to trace the system of borrowing in the Pedal Organ, when we experienced some difficulty in identifying a pipe that was speaking, the open end of which, along with several others, appeared above the level of the platform. The mouth of the pipe was thirteen or fourteen feet below, and speaking loudly; but by simply applying the ear to the open end of the pipe it seemed almost impossible to locate it. This astonished us very much, for at that time we did not question the teaching of the popular theory of sound. We soon, however, discovered the speaking pipe by thrusting an arm down it and observing the flattening of its note.

Scientific investigators have made several attempts to reconcile the lengths of the vibrating air-columns within pipes with the theoretical wave-lengths generated in unconfined air; but as yet no rule of universal application has been formulated. Max Allihn, in "Die Theorie und Praxis des Orgelbaues," fully discusses this subject, giving certain mathematical formulæ, and alluding to the investigations of Liscovius, Werthheim, and Wüllner, then sums the matter up by saying: "A comparison of the calculated and experimentally found quantities reveals such great and irregular differences that we cannot accept the formulæ." He remarks: "Werthheim experimented with small-scaled stopped pipes, which show a very different result from open pipes with regard to their deviation from theoretic lengths. Thus we are compelled to consider the question scientifically unsolved."

On January 23, 1860, M. A. Cavaillé-Coll addressed a "Note" to the Academy of Sciences, Paris, entitled, "De la Détermination des Dimensions des Tuyaux par rapport à leur Intonation." We give the substance of this communication, which cannot fail to be interesting to the student of organ-building:—

"Dans une série d'expériences faites en vue de déterminer exactement les sons harmoniques des tuyaux d'orgues, dans le but de créer des nouveaux jeux avec des séries de tuyaux donnant leurs harmoniques au lieu du son fondamental comme on l'avait fait jusqu'alors, j'ai reconnu: 1° que les longueurs des parties vibrantes de la colonne d'air à partir de l'extrémité ouverte des tuyaux se trouvaient toujours conformes à la théorie de D. Bernouilli, c'est-à-dire que ces parties étaient égales aux longueurs d'onde correspondantes au ton des tuyaux; 2° que le diamètre du tuyau n'avait aucune influence sur la longueur de ces subdivisions de la colonne d'air, mais que la partie contiguë à l'embouchure subissait, au contraire, un raccourcissement d'autant plus grand que le diamètre du tuyau était plus considérable.

"Cette dernière circonstance, observée par Bernouilli lui-même et par les physiciens qui ont étudié la question après lui, avait porté les théoriciens à faire abstraction de l'embouchure des tuyaux pour ne considérer que des tubes complètement ouverts aux deux bouts, ou bien entièrement fermés d'un seul côté. De cette manière on mettait à peu près la théorie d'accord avec l'expérience; mais ce genre de tubes sans embouchure ne pouvait recevoir aucune application dans la facture instrumentale.

"Toutefois, comme dans la pratique on ne peut pas se contenter des spéculations isolées de la théorie, il était nécessaire de considérer les tuyaux munis de leurs embouchures usuelles et de chercher à mettre la théorie d'accord avec les faits.

"Après quelques expériences sur des tuyaux de bois de différentes dimensions, je crus m'apercevoir que la véritable longueur du tuyau était égale à *la longueur de l'onde* (correspondante à son intonation) diminuée de *deux fois la profondeur intérieure du tuyau.* Les observations que j'ai eu occasion de faire depuis cette époque sont venues confirmer mes prévisions. Voici quelles furent mes premières expériences:

"Un tuyau de bois à base carrée donnant l'*ut* 2 (dit de 4 pieds), coupé en ton d'après le *la* normal de 880 vibrations [single vibrations] par seconde, ayant 0^{m} 08 de profondeur intérieure et pour longueur 1^{m} 13. Le ton de ce tuyau correspondant à 264 vibrations par seconde.

"Maintenant si nous supposons la vitesse du son à la température moyenne de 15 degrés de 340 mètres par seconde, l'onde sonore correspondante au tuyau précité sera de $\frac{340^{\text{m.}}}{264^{\text{vib.}}} = 1^{m}\ 288$, et si nous retranchons de la longueur de l'onde trouvée deux fois la profondeur du tuyau, c'est-à-dire $0^{m}\ 08 \times 2 = 0^{m}\ 160$, on aura, pour la longueur calculée du tuyau, 1^{m} 128, ce qui ne donne qu'une différence de 0^{m} 002 sur la longueur trouvée expérimentalement qui est de 1^{m} 130.

"L'*ut* grave de 32 pieds de la pédale de flûte de l'orgue de Saint-Denis avait été coupé à la longueur de 9^{m} 566; sa profondeur est de 0^{m} 48. Ce tuyau s'est trouvé trop long d'après le diapason de 880 vibrations par seconde, sur lequel cet orgue est accordé. Ce résultat est venu encore confirmer l'hypothèse ci-dessus.

L'onde sonore de ce tuyau étant de $\frac{340^{\text{m.}}}{33^{\text{vib.}}} = 10^{m}\ 30$	
en diminuant le double de la profondeur,	
c'est-à-dire $0^{m}\ 48 \times 2 = 0^{m}\ 96$, ci	0^{m} 96
il reste pour la longueur calculée du tuyau .	9^{m} 34

"Or, la différence de 0^{m} 226 en moins de la longueur calculée à la longueur d'abord fixée s'est trouvée justifiée par l'ouverture qu'on a dû pratiquer à l'extrémité du tuyau pour l'accorder en sa place.

"D'après ces premières observations, je fus naturellement conduit à vérifier cette loi sur des tuyaux de dimensions les plus opposées, et l'expérience ayant constamment confirmé mes prévisions, j'en ai conclu, ainsi que je l'avais tout d'abord remarqué, que la longueur des tuyaux en bois est égale à la longueur de l'onde sonore diminuée de deux fois la profondeur du même tuyau.

"Si nous désignons par V la vitesse du son, N le nombre de vibrations,* L la longueur du tuyau, P la profondeur intérieure, on aura, pour déterminer l'un de ces quatre éléments qui concourent à la détermination du ton,

$$(1)\quad L = \frac{V}{N} - 2P, \qquad (3)\quad P = \tfrac{1}{2}\left(\frac{V}{N} - L\right),$$

$$(2)\quad N = \frac{V}{L + 2P}, \qquad (4)\quad V = (L + 2P)\,N.$$

* The French acousticians count by single vibrations: that is, a swing in one direction is a vibration. English acousticians consider this only half a complete vibration.

"Soit, en langage ordinaire:

"(1) La longueur du tuyau est égale au quotient de la vitesse du son par le nombre de vibrations diminué de deux fois la profondeur.

"(2) Le nombre de vibrations est égal au quotient de la vitesse du son par la longueur du tuyau augmentée de deux fois la profondeur.

"(3) La profondeur est égale à la moitié du quotient de la vitesse du son par le nombre de vibrations diminué de la longueur du tuyau.

"(4) Enfin la vitesse du son est égale au produit de la longueur du tuyau augmenté de deux fois la profondeur par le nombre de vibrations.

"Dans une autre série d'expériences sur des tuyaux cylindriques en métal, nous avons été à même de reconnaître que la loi qui s'applique aux tuyaux prismatiques en bois à base carrée régit également les tuyaux cylindriques.

"Nous devons toutefois faire remarquer qu'il ne faut pas confondre la profondeur du tuyau avec son diamètre, comme on pourrait le supposer par analogie avec les tuyaux de bois à base rectangulaire. Dans ces derniers tuyaux, la profondeur est la même que la largeur du côté perpendiculaire à la ligne de l'embouchure, tandis que, dans les tuyaux cylindriques, la profondeur est nécessairement plus petite que le diamètre. L'aplatissement de la bouche, qui est habituellement du quart de la circonférence du tuyau, forme une corde soustendant un arc égal aux 3/4 de cette même circonférence. C'est ici la moyenne des perpendiculaires abaissées de cette corde sur l'arc opposé qui doit être prise pour la profondeur. Or, cette moyenne peut être représentée sans erreur sensible par les 5/6 du diamètre, et en remplaçant la valeur de P de notre formule par $D.\frac{5}{6}$, on aura

$$2P = D.\frac{5}{3};$$

d'où il suit que, pour les tuyaux cylindriques, notre formule sera

$$L = \frac{V}{N} - \left(D.\frac{5}{3}\right).$$

Soit enfin, en langage ordinaire: *La longueur des tuyaux cylindriques est égale au quotient de la vitesse du son par le nombre de vibrations moins les 5/3 du diamètre du tuyau.*

"Plusieurs tableaux d'observations rapportés dans ce Mémoire viennent à l'appui de cette nouvelle théorie, qui se trouve d'ailleurs confirmée par vingt années d'application à la construction des grandes orgues que j'ai exécutées depuis cette époque.

"La facilité des calculs de cette formule m'a permis de mettre entre les mains de mes plus simples ouvriers accordeurs des Tables et des règles où sont indiquées les vraies longueurs d'ondes sonores, et au moyen desquelles ils peuvent, par une simple opération d'arithmétique ou seulement de compas, déterminer directement et avec une exactitude rigoureuse la longueur normale des tuyaux pour le son fondamental, la position des nœuds de vibrations pour les sons harmoniques, le prolongement des tuyaux à ouvertures latérales, les proportions de ces mêmes ouvertures, à l'effet de régler exactement l'accord et l'homogénéité des sons."

While we hold in the highest respect the memory and opinions of the late M. Aristide Cavaillé-Coll—a kindly gentleman with whom we were for many years in most friendly relations, and in whose *atelier* we have spent many profitable hours—we are compelled to admit that our own investigations and experiments have not gone far to support his "*nouvelle théorie.*" In preference to stating our own experiences and views on the subject, we quote those kindly placed at our disposal by Mr. Hermann Smith. He remarks:—

"One organ builder, of scientific attainments, M. Cavaillé-Coll, has empirically determined a rule in regard to practical work which has suited his purpose with his own workmen, although it cannot lay claim to accuracy in the scientific sense. I know that on its first introduction for consideration we spent many hours in testing its truth on all varieties of pipe, and found that the rule would not work to any available extent in an English factory. That it should suit M. Cavaillé-Coll is reasonable enough, because, conditioned by a particular practice, a prescribed quality of tone, definite pressure of wind, and training of workmen accustomed to such routine as such a rule enforced, guidance of or by some set standard might prove useful,—as it were a sort of supernumerary master in the master's absence; but it is questionable if any other value attaches to it. In every factory there are set-out rods kept in permanence for every series of pipes, showing the lengths that have been determined upon by long usage. Still, the calculations are most interesting, and they serve to attract attention to the great discrepancies that exist between scientific theory and everyday practice in organ-building. From the calculated wave-length which it is assumed an open pipe should be for a specified pitch,—viz., one-half of the wave-length—deduct, in the case of square pipes or pipes of rectangular section, *twice the depth of the pipe*, and for round or cylindrical pipes an amount equal to *five-thirds of the diameter*. The latter proportion is thus less than the former, and evidently the need for the difference arises from the nearness of the acting wind-stream to the inclosing wall which surrounds the air-column, upon which its influence is to be effective and prompt. With such a guiding idea in estimating results, we can see why it should be so, and are not merely left to the conclusion that it is because it is.

"M. Cavaillé-Coll relies upon his method of calculating reduced lengths for the ascertainment of the nodal division in respect of pipes for the FLÛTE HARMONIQUE. Taking the exact length for the body of the pipe (less five-thirds diameter), he pierces the hole for the node at the exact distance, from the open end, of a quarter of wave-length ;* and the pipe then, providing the mouth is of proper height only, speaks the first harmonic tone instead of the fundamental. I cannot see, in the system adopted by M. Cavaillé-Coll, anything more than a rule-of-thumb procedure; for however much he may value it, in daily practice in the factory it must be subject to modifications from a variety of causes. To mention only one which is never remarked upon in scientific comments,—the wind admitted at the foot-hole; this is perhaps the most important, most governing influence that is brought to bear upon the behavior of the pipe. Diameter may be the same, width of mouth the same, bellows pressure the same; but, if the amount of wind admitted at the foot is increased, the whole aspect is changed, quality, pitch, power, are all in new relations, and these cannot be affected without affecting the length of pipe,—consequently the reduced length can never be adjudged to be any fixed amount of reduction by rule or ratio. In point of fact, additional amount of wind is equivalent to a change to higher pressure, and the size of the foot-hole is the foundation of the constitution of the pipe."

The facts above touched upon are deserving of most careful and thoughtful attention on the part of scientists who have regard for truth in matters connected with organ pipes, and who are prepared to conduct their investigations with open minds, untrammeled by the chains of untenable hypotheses and gratuitous assumptions. Up to the present time investigations in this interesting and instructive field of acoustical science, as presented in published text-books, have evidently been conducted in the most half-hearted and perfunctory manner; and have been cut off abruptly wherever they appeared to clash with preconceived theories or publicly-expressed personal opinions.

Having in the earlier part of the present Chapter, and in a necessarily brief

* This remark is apt to be misleading unless explained. The hole pierced in the pipe is not "*for the node*," but to *prevent the formation of a node* in its immediate neighborhood.

and somewhat sketchy manner, described the general construction of open and stopped labial pipes, and directed attention to certain matters connected with the behavior of their internal air-columns, we may now enter on the interesting question: How does an organ pipe of the labial class produce sound? We are compelled to admit that notwithstanding the study which apparently has been given to the question, it still remains beset with uncertainty. One might naturally expect to find it satisfactorily answered in the writings of the professors of acoustical science; for one surely has good reason to expect that such renowned investigators would never leave so important a question until it was answered beyond all reasonable doubt. The fact is, however, that it has never been squarely faced by any of the distinguished acousticians or physicists, unless Professor A. Privat Deschanel, in his "Natural Philosophy," may be said to have so faced it. This work has been translated by Professor Everett, and widely accepted as a learned and trustworthy text-book. Let us see what its author has to say on the question at issue. He says: "The air from the bellows arrives through the conical tube at the lower end [of the organ pipe], and, escaping through a narrow slit, grazes the edge of a wedge placed opposite [the edge of the upper lip of the mouth]. A rushing noise is thus produced, which contains, among its constituents, the note to which the column of air in the pipe is capable of responding; and as soon as this resonance occurs the pipe speaks." This plausible explanation or statement has, in all probability, been accepted as scientific gospel by nine hundred and ninety-nine out of every thousand of his readers, simply because it is dogmatically made and is supported by a distinguished name. Let us not forget the old saying:

> "The name is but the shadow, which we find
> Too often larger than the man behind."

Be this as it may; a more grievous mistake could not well be made by a scientific investigator. Professor Deschanel does not directly inform us what causes the "rushing noise," or what description of noise it is that contains the note to which the column of air within the pipe responds. This is disappointing, to say the least of it. Reading farther, however, gives us some insight into his views. In one place he says: "The period of vibration of the fundamental note of a stopped pipe is the time required for propagating a pulse through four times the length of the pipe. For let a condensation be suddenly produced at the lower end by *the action of the vibrating lip*. It will be propagated to the closed end, reflected back, thus traveling over twice the length of the pipe." And again: "The period of the *movements of the lip* is determined by the arrival of these alternate condensations and rarefactions; and the *lip*, in its turn, serves to divert a portion of the energy of the blast, and employ it in maintaining the energy of the vibrating column." From these quotations it will be seen that Professor Deschanel, when he wrote his treatise, held the erroneous belief that the *lip* of the pipe *vibrated* while sound was being produced. His "rushing noise" which contains so much music is, according to his theory, produced by the upper lip being set in vibration or movement by the wind escaping from the "narrow slit," or wind-way, and grazing the edge of the same. He accordingly believed in the necessity of the upper lip being *thin*. Professor Helmholtz, in describing an organ pipe, speaks of "the *mouth hole* where it is blown, terminating in a *sharp lip*." In speaking of tone-production in pipes he says: "Any air chamber can be made to give a musical tone, just like organ pipes, provided they have a sufficiently narrow opening, furnished with somewhat projecting *sharp edges*, by directing a thin flat stream of air across the opening and against its edges. These edges are the source of the musical tone. The directed stream of air breaking against the edges generates a peculiar hissing or rushing noise, which is all we hear when the pipe does not speak. . . . Such a noise may be considered a mixture of several inharmonic tones of nearly the same pitch. When the air chamber of the pipe is brought to bear upon these tones its resonance strengthens such as correspond with the proper tones of that chamber, and makes them predominate over the rest, which this predominance conceals. Hence in all such pipes [badly-voiced pipes] we always hear the tone accompanied more or less distinctly by a rush of wind, and this gives a peculiar character to its quality."

Following Helmholtz, Professor Tyndall remarks: "There are various ways of agitating the air at the ends of pipes and tubes so as to throw the air-columns within them into vibration. In organ pipes this is done by blowing a thin sheet of air *against a sharp edge*. . . . This thin air current breaks *against the sharp edge*, and there produces a fluttering noise, and the proper pulse of this flutter is converted by the resonance of the pipe above into a musical sound."

It is somewhat remarkable that the three distinguished scientists quoted should have believed in the necessity of the upper lip of a pipe being *thin* or *sharp* at its edge; for every one who knows anything about the construction and voicing of organ pipes, for the production of varied tone-colors, knows that neither a thin nor a sharp edge is essential, or of anything approaching universal adoption. Certain wooden pipes, producing pure and beautiful tones, have been made with upper lips three-quarters of an inch thick, and cut square; others with rounded lips half an inch thick; and others with cylindrical rods of considerable diameter attached to the edge of their upper lips. Metal pipes of the DIAPASON class have been greatly improved by having their upper lips leathered; so that, instead of coming in contact with a sharp edge, the wind-sheet finds a smooth surface to glide over while vibrating. Of course, both thin and sharp edges are used, but simply as a means for the creation of certain qualities of tone.

Professor Deschanel affirms, in unmistakable language, that the upper lip of an organ pipe *vibrates* under the action of the wind-sheet and the moving column of air within the pipe. Did this scientist ever give the organ pipe serious consideration? We should imagine not; for the ignorance displayed on the subject of the nature and office of the upper lip of the pipe mouth can only be accounted for on the hypothesis that he never studied the construction of labial pipes. The fact is, that neither the upper lip, be it thin or thick, nor any other portion of the mouth, vibrates, or is capable of being set in vibration, by the wind from the bellows. The upper lip, or so-called "wedge," may be damped by having a finger or a rod tightly pressed against it, so as to preclude the possibility of any rhythmical vibrations obtaining, without in any way impairing the speech of the pipe.

Or a solid steel wedge, quite incapable of being influenced in the slightest degree by the stream of compressed air, may be fixed in the mouth, instead of the ordinary wood or pipe-metal lip, and the pipe will speak a true note. Every organ expert knows that there is no vibration in the lip while the pipe is speaking; and he will assure one that if such a vibration should by any means occur it would render the tone of the pipe false, if it did not destroy it altogether.

While there is no difficulty in refuting the false teachings just discussed, there are real difficulties in arriving at an absolutely certain conclusion regarding the exact action of the wind-sheet or wind-stream in producing sound at the mouth of an organ pipe. While the motion of the wind-stream itself has been satisfactorily shown by a simple experiment, its exact action on the column of air within the pipe can only be guessed at; and it is highly probable that the mode of sound-production in a labial pipe will never be decided beyond doubt or question. It certainly never will be explained by such self-stultifying hypotheses as those formulated by the writers of text-books on the popular theory of acoustics.

Alluding to the behavior of labial pipes in the process of voicing and while speaking, Mr. Hermann Smith correctly remarks :—

"The art of voicing consists, in one particular, in so directing the stream of wind that it shall avoid striking the lip and shall glide past without concussion upon the edge, for the real vibration depends upon quite another causation. Professor Tyndall, following Helmholtz, puts forth a theory of a promiscuous assemblage of pulses, fluttering and clamoring at the lip of the pipe, one of which, out of a thousand or so, it selects, and that periodic pulse is installed as the reigning pitch of the pipe. This elegant fancy of a selective pitch is a fair-seeming explanation, and under the commanding name of this popular writer is generally accepted, for nothing better had been previously devised in the laboratory of the philosophers; yet the study of the organ pipe as it is, in every mood of its behavior, makes the theory quite untenable. In practice there is nothing adventitious,—the artist has some prescience of the powers that are to work his will. The pipe is a mechanism designed to a precise intent, which it fulfils: it speaks but as it must. There is no selective power, for the hand that fashions it ordains."

The same careful observer claims, and probably justly, to be the first to formulate what is unquestionably the most reasonable hypothesis of sound-production in the labial pipe,*—an hypothesis which accords perfectly with our own observa-

* While we freely admit Mr. Hermann Smith's claims, it is only just, in an unprejudiced review like the present, to lay before our readers the following quotation from Abbé Lamazou's "Étude sur l'Orgue Monumental de Saint-Sulpice": "Dans un mémoire présenté à l'Académie des sciences (Séance du 24 février 1849. *Études expérimentales sur les tuyaux d'orgues*, par M. A. Cavaillé-Coll.), l'artiste qui personnifie la facture d'orgue moderne a démontré, plus clairement qu'on ne l'avait fait avant lui, la véritable fonction du premier moteur du son dans l'embouchure des tuyaux à flûte, moteur qu'il assimilait à une anche libre aérienne. Il a fait remarquer l'analogie qui existe entre les vibrations transversales des lames vibrantes d'air et celles des lames vibrantes solides, analysées par Daniel Bernouilli, et qu'il suppose régies par la même loi. Il en tirait, par voie de conséquence, des données positives sur la hauteur à donner aux bouches des tuyaux en rapport avec leur intonation et la force élastique de l'air qui les anime. Mais comme ces observations scientifiques et d'autres non moins intéressantes ont été déjà communiquées depuis plusieurs années à l'Académie, nous n'en faisons pas même une mention sommaire."

While it is evident, from the above extract, that, so early as the year 1849, the great French organ builder had discovered the reed-like motion of the wind-stream at the mouth of the labial pipe, it seems that he did not carry his investigations very far, seeing that he compares its motion to that of a free-reed, governed by the same law of vibration. It was left to Mr. Hermann Smith to discover that the wind-reed at the mouth of the labial pipe was unique in its motions, and that it did not belong to the free-reed family.

tions and experiments. Such being the case it is only right to recognize the service he has done to true science; and we have the greatest pleasure in laying, with his kind permission, the results of his investigations before our readers.

Having already, in the present Chapter, briefly described and illustrated the forms and construction of ordinary wood pipes, we may now confine our remarks to the action that goes on at the mouths of such pipes while they are producing their musical tones; for it must be clearly understood that it is at their mouths, and at their mouths only, that their sounds are generated. If open pipes alone produced sound such a statement might be questioned, but as stopped pipes are equally good sound-producers it admits of no reasonable doubt. In essaying to explain the action of the wind at the mouth of a speaking pipe, as we believe it to be, we shall have to use, more or less closely, the words employed by the talented writer above quoted. We accordingly desire to acknowledge, without the repeated employment of quotation marks, the valuable assistance we derive from his writings on the subject now under consideration: at the same time we may say that in certain conclusions, of a minor nature, we are at issue with him.

At the outset, it must be understood that the compressed air (from the bellows) which issues from the wind-way, between the cap and block of the organ pipe, ascends across the mouth of the pipe in the form of a thin sheet. This wind-sheet or wind-stream takes a course, curving slightly in an outward direction, so as to escape striking the edge of the upper lip of the mouth.* This position of the wind-stream, taken at the first instant of its rush from the wind-way across the mouth, is roughly indicated in the accompanying illustration, Fig. LXI., which is a Vertical Section through the mouth and lower portion of an ordinary wood FLUTE pipe. M is the mouth of the pipe where the sound is generated, and W represents the wind-stream, issuing from the wind-way between the cap and block and passing across the mouth in an outward direction so as to escape the edge of the upper lip and glide along the outer sloping surface. When a pipe is properly voiced so as to speak promptly and firmly, this is the initial direction given to the wind-stream. If it is directed so as to pass a slight distance in front of the sloping surface, the pipe will be slow of speech; and if the wind-stream is directed still farther in the outward direction, the pipe will not speak at all. On the other hand, the pipe will produce no sound if the wind-stream is directed inward, or so

*Notwithstanding the length of time that this evident fact has been acknowledged by those intimately acquainted with organ matters, mistakes of a regrettable nature continue to be perpetrated in quarters where accuracy might naturally be looked for. For instance, in "A Handbook of the Organ," by J. Matthews (Second Edition, 1897), we find the remarkable statement that the air entering at the foot of the pipe, being checked by the block or languid, rushes out and is *cut by the upper lip, part of it passing out through the mouth of the pipe, and part ascending and passing out at the top.* Then in connection with the stopped pipe, we are assured that the *air passing up it is prevented from getting out at its upper end by the stopper, and, accordingly, has to descend in order to escape at the mouth.* (See pp. 27, 28.) Now, the fact is, that the conditions of the air-columns in both open and stopped pipes are precisely the same so far as the action of the wind at their mouths is concerned: and no wind from the wind-way passes out at the top of an open labial pipe any more than out of the top of a stopped one. The author of "A Handbook of the Organ" was evidently unaware that, so far as the passage of the exciting air is concerned, the open pipe is as effectually stopped as the one closed with the wooden stopper. In this respect an open pipe may be compared to two stopped pipes placed end to end with their stoppers between them. No pipe would speak if its wind-sheet was so directed as to be *cut by the upper lip* in the manner described by Mr. Matthews.

as to split against the edge—thin or thick—of the upper lip. These are facts well known to scientific voicers.

While the wind-stream remains in the initial position, indicated in Fig. LXI., no sound is created; but it is rapidly instituting a condition in the air-column within the pipe that will enable it to generate a musical note. It is impossible for a rapidly rushing stream of compressed air to be directed immediately across an opening in any tube or vessel, without its exerting a certain power of suction, and of drawing toward and into itself whatever is close to the opening and of a nature capable of being easily moved and carried away. This action of the wind-stream at the mouth of a large organ pipe is clearly proved by placing on the block or languid, within the mouth and immediately behind the wind-way, some filaments of cotton or down, and then admitting wind to the pipe: the filaments are shot out with considerable energy, showing the suction exerted by the wind-stream.

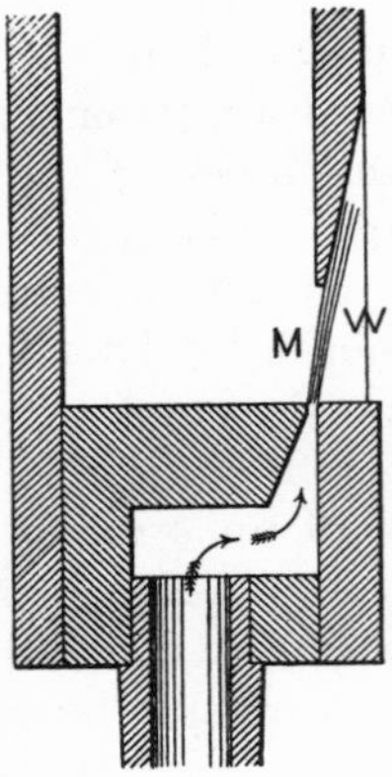

Fig. LXI.

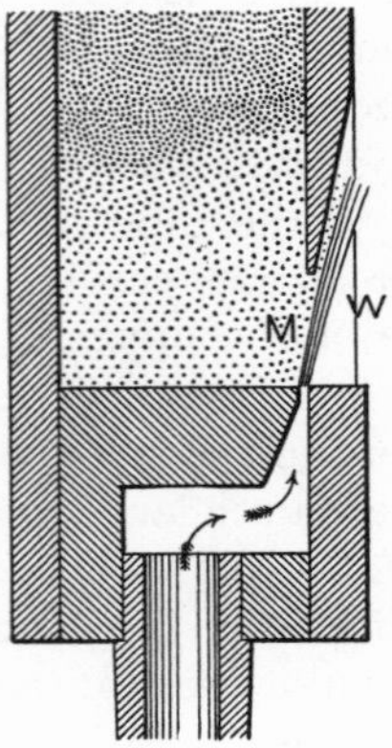

Fig. LXII.

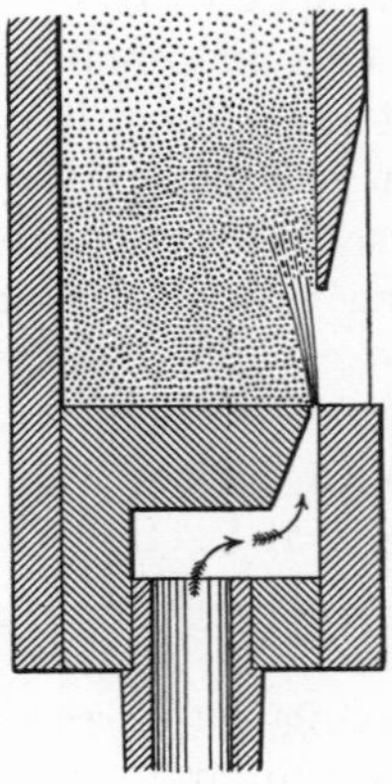
Fig. LXIII.

The first action of the rushing wind-stream is to abstract the air, within the pipe, which is in the immediate neighborhood of the mouth, forming, for the instant, a partial vacuum there. This state of the air within the pipe is diagrammatically shown in Fig. LXII., by the few and widely-spaced dots in the neighborhood of the mouth, M, in comparison with the closer and darker dotting higher in the pipe, which indicates the less disturbed portion of the air-column. As already said, the first effect of the suction exercised by the rushing wind-stream is the creation of a partial vacuum behind the stream; and this being increased by the continuity of the operating force becomes a more and more decided vacuum. To fill this partial vacuum the rest of the air-column in the pipe expands (to make our explanation clear let a stopped pipe be understood), and, in the natural order of things, sets in rapid motion every particle of air within the pipe. The active extraction of the internal air into the rushing wind-stream, and also between it and the outer surface of the upper lip of the pipe, causes the wind-stream to swell in volume and swing in an outward direction. This position of the wind-stream we have attempted to indicate in Fig. LXII. When the wind-stream has reached its outward limit, and has exerted all its power of suction, under the controlling conditions imposed by the nature and proportions of the pipe, a natural reaction sets in, caused by the rarefaction of the internal air, on the one hand, and the pressure of the external air, on the other; the latter pressing on the outer surface of the wind-stream in its attempt to fill up, or bring to an equilibrium, the exhausted air within the pipe. Mr. Hermann Smith correctly remarks: "Just as the only innate tendency of water is manifested in the effort of seeking to gain its level, so air is itself active only in one way, and, so to speak, displays its life in a perpetual endeavor to preserve its equilibrium whenever disturbed and from whatever cause. The pipe acts as a delayer of the time of regaining equilibrium, since it is only at the ends or outlets that the air-column is able to mix with the mass of air outside in any course going on, or that the outward air can gain access to the inside. Sound cannot proceed from an organ pipe unless its interior air is out of equilibrium, or disturbed from a state of rest."

At the second stage of its operation, above alluded to, the wind-stream swings inward, past the edge of the upper lip, first reinstating the equilibrium between the internal and external air, and then, inverting its initial operation, shocking the internal air-column by a sudden and forcible condensation, and creating at the same instant a partial vacuum in the external air immediately adjoining its outer surface. The direction of the wind-stream at this stage is diagramatically represented in Fig. LXIII., in which the supposed condensation is indicated by close and dark dotting. The instant this state of the internal air-column is reached an inevitable reaction takes place, and, relieved from active external pressure, and assisted by the condensed state of the internal column, which naturally seeks the state of equilibrium, the wind-stream swings outward, resuming its original position, with reference to the upper lip, and its active operation on the air within the pipe, now greatly assisted by its condensed condition. The slowness of speech in pipes under certain styles of voicing is probably due to the fact that the wind-stream is at the start unassisted by the air-columns within them, which are not then in a state of condensation.

It has taken many words and occupied several minutes to outline the operations of a single inward and outward swing of the wind-stream; but it must be realized that in the process of generating a musical tone these operations may have to be repeated many hundreds of times in a second, and that with unvarying precision and regularity. From the description given, it will be realized that the wind-stream at the mouth of an organ pipe is in reality a rapidly vibrating wind-tongue somewhat resembling the metallic tongue in the free-reed of the harmonium. Mr. Hermann Smith calls the air-stream an "aëro-plastic reed," or simply an "air-reed." He remarks: "The aëro-plastic reed forming with the pipe a *system* of transverse vibration associated with longitudinal vibration, and possibly another phase of vibration across the width of the reed enabling it to synchronize with the harmonic range of the pipe; the principle of action of the whole being termed, in my non-academic phraseology, suction by velocity; but if a more exact expression is found its explanation should imply, or better still, include the axiomatic phrase of Sir William Thomson, 'in a moving fluid the pressure is least where velocity is greatest.' To state the existence of an air-moulded free-reed is to give the key to its nature. . . . Velocity is power, and in every conjunction of reed and pipe the reed is dominant. Most distinctly it should be recognized that the air-reed does *work* and expends power in doing it."

Shortly after the first announcement of Mr. Hermann Smith's theory, an article by Herr Schneebeli, entitled "Zur Theorie der Orgelpfeifen," appeared in "*Poggendorff's Annalen*" (1874, vol. 153, pp. 301–305). Whether he derived his inspiration from Mr. Smith's articles which appeared in "*Nature*," or from independent investigation, we cannot venture to say; but his conclusions happily agree with those arrived at by Mr. Smith. As we have not had access to the original article, we must be content with quoting the remarks upon it by the late Alexander J. Ellis, in his Appendix to his able translation of Helmholtz's work, "Die Lehre von den Tonempfindungen." He says:—

"Herr Schneebeli had an experimental pipe constructed in the usual way; with glass back and a movable lip and slit or wind-way, through which was driven air impregnated with smoke, as is frequently done to make it visible. When he so placed the lip and slit that the stream of air passed *entirely outside* of the pipe, no sound occurred; but if he blew gently upon this sheet of air, at right angles, the pipe sounded, and the tone continued until he blew through the other end of the pipe; nevertheless under these circumstances it was very rare indeed to find that any smoke penetrated into the pipe. If the sheet of smoked air passed *entirely inside* of the pipe, there was also no sound; but then on blowing through the open end, so as to force some of it out, sound was produced, and it was stopped by blowing against the slit. This case was therefore the converse of the last. He concludes: 'That the stream of air which issues from the slit forms a species of air-reed (*Luft-Lamelle*, aërial lamina), and that this plays in the generation of vibrations in the mass of air, a part analogous to that of reeds in reed pipes.' He states that the vibrational nature of motion of the air between the slit and the lip can be shown by attaching a piece of silk-paper to the edge of the [lower] lip or slit, and pressing a point against it. . . . The source of tone, according to both Mr. Hermann Smith and Herr Schneebeli, is the formation of what the former calls an 'aëro-plastic reed,' and also simply an 'air-reed' and the latter a 'Luft-Lamelle,' which is produced outside of the pipe, and bends partly within it. For the formation of this reed both agree that it is essential for the exciting air to pass the lip, certainly not to enter the pipe. The existence of the reed is shown by Mr. Hermann Smith by interposing a thin lamina, a shaving, or crip tissue-paper, which is caught by the air and vibrates as a reed, and by Herr Schneebeli by the smoke mixed with air which enables the experimenter to see its motion directly, and also by a piece of silk-paper."

There can be no doubt, we venture to say, that some such action as above described takes place at the mouth of an organ pipe while it is speaking. Considerable force on the part of the wind-stream or air-reed is necessary to set instantaneously into a state of excitement or tremor the column of air in a large organ pipe; and one can hardly imagine any other motion or action of the wind-stream capable of imparting the necessary disturbance to the resonating and synchronizing air-column within the pipe. While the mode of sound-production at the mouth of the pipe is not easily realized, from analogy we may accept it as due to the intense vibration or molecular disturbance of the air immediately at the mouth, which vibration is influenced by both the form and dimensions of the internal air-column ; for, as we have already observed, no positive sound issues from the air-column itself. The exact nature of the synchronizing vibration or disturbance in the air-column cannot well be decided; but while it may have some relation to the velocity of sound conduction in air, its phenomena go to prove that it can have little to do with the hypothetical wave-lengths, as taught by Tyndall and other wave-theorists. That there is a close relationship between the rushing wind-stream at the mouth and the proportions of the responding and resonating column within the pipe, and that they exert a mutual influence, is self-evident ; but in exactly what manner this mutual influence is exerted, and what the conditions are that modify it in the way one observes in pipes of different forms, proportions of parts, scales, etc., have never been satisfactorily explained.*

As an appendix to what has already been said, we have much pleasure in giving the following quotation from Mr. Hermann Smith's admirable writings, kindly placed at our disposal by their author :—

"As regards music making, the pulses of the organ pipe are irrespective of space ranges, and issue from a fixed place, having a definite time-distance determined by the length of the pipe, the dimensions of the pipe, and the acting force in co-relation. A single pulse would die out instantly, and be of no effect; mechanically, it requires to be backed up by a succession of pulses, and this is accomplished by the agency of suction. I want you to follow me whilst I seek to make the process clear to you according to what I conceive to be the right interpretation of the way that nature works. . . .

"We can now consider my theory of the action of the working reed [stream-reed] upon the body of air encompassed by the pipe. The isolated reed, before any change takes place, has no innate tendency to swerve from uprightness; it can neither blow in nor out, nor can the atmosphere have influence, for it is equal on both sides; the air-column within the pipe is at rest, it has no self-stimulating power of vibration. What then disturbs this equilibrium? Some internal exciting cause is needed which shall produce, with determination of priority, condensation or rarefaction. Orthodoxy says that condensation comes first in order. According to my view it is rarefaction, for it is obvious that the reed, as it now stands, has no power to produce a condensation. It does not, as they [Helmholtz, Tyndall, and others] assume, strike against the sharp edge of the upper lip, it simply asserts its own strong upward-rushing force. The reed must bend before it will vibrate; but what is to make it bend? To cause this flexure, the only alternative is rarefaction, and in the stream-reed we possess a power exactly suited to exercise the required function. The act of rarefying occupies time, must take place within the pipe, yet is not spontaneous, but is only to be induced by some previous act. The provocation belongs to the reed. Consider its mode of action; in velocitous rush over the mouth, its dense stream making around itself a rarefied atmosphere, it causes the approach of the quiescent column, carries off all the particles of air

*We find the following pertinent remarks by Max Allihn in "Die Theorie und Praxis des Orgelbaues" (p. 84): "The whistle (Pfeife) is perhaps the most ancient and most used of all musical instruments. Everybody is familiar with its construction and knows how to cut it out of a piece of willow; nevertheless, the physical process which attends the sounding of it is far from having been understood with perfect clearness and certainty. We know the doings of the tone-wave (Tonwelle) in the body of the pipe, but the calculations arrived at by theory and those found by practice do not coincide, and, in the attempts made to explain the cause of this divergence, the stage of hypothesis has not yet been transcended. We know that the wind-stream (Anblasestrom) by striking against the upper lip gives the impetus for the wave (Welle) in the resonating body; but how this is done is a matter of speculation. It is known that the pitch and timbre of the tone are altered by the height of the mouth, the width of the wind-way, and the velocity of the wind-stream; but the conceptions held on the subject are only of a general nature, more or less definite."

lying in the nearest layers, and would go on abstracting indefinitely, if there were no counterbalancing causes coming into operation; but it brings down on itself the power that bends it. *Suction by velocity* has created a partial vacuum; the air-column passing outward with the impetus of expansion begins to bend the reed over, the excited air particles not only press forward to fill the places of the lost, but eagerly crowd out upon the top of the reed, irresistibly drawn into the zone of rarefaction around the mouth,—a region where velocity has insured least pressure; and, through this same 'law of least pressure,' there is, outwardly, a loss of support to the under surface of the reed near the tip, favoring there the curve of flexure, the pressure necessarily varying and diminishing from the root upward.

"As yet we have no vibration, for simultaneously with the exterior action the interior rarefaction is extending high upward, the air particles are rallying from further distances, awakened by the agitation of those in advance, throughout the whole length and breadth of the pipe, uneasy as bees in a hive; whilst these particles are swarming toward the mouth, they are drawing away from the main body of their supports, their own elastic energy is diminishing, they are more and more thinned in numbers, and the new levies come up to the front exhausted of their early vigor. Now is the supreme moment of the reed's advantage; now its watchful ally, the external air, pierces the weakest line just under the sharp edge of the lip, and with it dashing in as a wave of condensation with cumulative pressure drives back the outflowing wave, and the whole pulse of motion courses upward with impetuous vigor and precipitates itself expansively into the upper air; meanwhile the stream-reed, rising with renewed power to recover its upright position, which it had overpassed, commences again to further exhaust the lower region of weakened air particles which yet are able to make a bold front, to attack the reed again, and bend it outward; a second time the reed and the external air dash inward on the thinned ranks still holding the pipe; they advance far into the interior, but midway are met by a recruited army; the wave of rarefaction is returning as a wave of condensation;—then comes the shock of war, and vibration is established. The invading wave has been repulsed at the spot hereafter memorable as the *node*, and the conflict renewed and continued will chronicle no victory to either, unless other and foreign forces are brought in; for we have resources within command enabling us to sway the equipoise and give supremacy to the reed.

"'I do suppose,' as Dr. Hooke says in his quaint talk on 'springy bodies,' 'I do suppose the particles behave,' and that the action takes place, in the manner I have described; the analogy is not strained, nor have I used one phrase in association of ideas which I do not think fully justified by the physical relations of the process. Therefore, do not dismiss this as the sketch of a fancy battle. Watch for yourselves; place within the pipe at the back of the mouth some fine filaments of cotton, or fluff, or down; then with a wire or rod advance them from the interior to the inner edge of the wind-way, and you will see them shot with energy, not upward into the pipe, but outward, full in your face with an unmistakable trajectory. Do we not bring into activity the same force, 'suction by velocity,' when we blow through one little tube over another tube leading down to a well of perfume, and draw up thereby scent-laden globules caught in the belt of wind passing over the tube's orifice, dispersing fine odor sprays into the atmosphere? The work of the stream-reed is specifically to *abstract*. By reason of abstraction rarefaction ensues, condensation correlates therewith, and the product is vibration. The reed is the generator of power, and the node is the fulcrum of vibration, the place of reaction, with this peculiarity that it affords an elastic fulcrum sensitive to the encroaches of the column of air above it. In the stopped pipe, on the contrary, there is a stable unyielding fulcrum, and the results from this difference are very remarkable. . . . At present I can only allude to one result, which it seems desirable not to omit reference to at this stage of the exposition. It is an essential feature of my hypothesis that the initial movement or prelude to vibration in the pipe is distinct from successive movements both in its course and character; it extends throughout the pipe, is continuous but diminishing in degree, and is without a node, which is only fully established at the second course, and then because a contrary pulse motion has been set up, and we have rarefaction exhibiting itself as working in opposite directions. As corroborating my estimate of the mode of initiatory action, it may be important to notice that the interval between the first effort or gasp of the pipe, and the full possession of its powers, is distinctly perceived by the ear. All musicians acquainted with Organs are conscious of this, and it is matter of usual comment with them how that the stopped pipes are, on the contrary, remarkably quick of speech, instantaneous in articulation; they feel this without reasoning of the why or wherefore. As in stopped pipes there is no super-nodal air-column, no requirement for an effort, similar to that awakening motion to perfect vibration in open organ pipes, the verdict of the ear is in both cases consistent with and corroborative of the hypothesis.

"To recapitulate this mechanical process which I want you clearly to follow,—first, the stream-reed excites rarefaction in the pipe from the mouth upward, and is itself bent outward by the air it draws out, and it takes a curve in shape, because the pressure of the air on its outer face necessarily varies in degree of force, being strongest at the root, and weaker upon the middle and tip; consequently the yielding is expressed by a curve, just as it is in a blade of grass waving. As rarefaction proceeds it arrives, relatively to the coercive force then operating, at such a point of balance of effect that it begins to react, and actually to suck the reed back, which at the moment of rest it is able to do. So the reed strikes back, throws itself beyond its natural vertical line into the partial vacuum that it had created; then inevitably a portion of its substance is cast into the pipe; then from the impetus recovering itself—and a moment of rest is here also not to be avoided—it strikes back, cutting off from itself at the mouth's edge so much of its substance as during that brief interval between its entrance and exit has been issuing. It is an absolute severance of a mass of dense air, which forces itself upward, and leaves in its path of passage a still higher degree of rarefaction. Imagine this pith of air pursuing its course inside. But, before it has gone far, that recovery of the reed just stated will have begun, and, as soon as the stream regains its outward flow, it will have recommenced to rarefy, until once more its extreme outward curve has been attained.

"Imagine, then, this position of affairs:—the pith of air thinning the air more and more behind it, nears the outlet at the top of the pipe, and the stream-reed also thinning the air in the lower part of the pipe. Now, see the consequence:—these two rarefying powers pulling in opposite directions suddenly give way, and at the moment that (at the top of the pipe) the pulse of motion finds exit, the dense external air rushes in as an invading wave of condensation, so, at the self-same moment, the stream-reed, returning, enters, passes the mouth, throws in its wave of condensation, and the two waves meet in full shock, and are thrown back in recoil with equal vigor; and the spot where this takes place we call the node. It is said to be a place of no motion, a description which causes some misapprehension; it is rather the place of least translation of air, but will be best understood as being a very tight place. This course of action and reaction goes on in perpetual repetition whilst the pipe is sounding. The succession of shocks, rapid and periodic, constitutes musical sound,—literally and actually nothing but motion; and the time-distance between one shock and the next shock determines musical pitch."

While we willingly subscribe to the theory of action so cleverly set forth in the above quotation, we differ from Mr. Hermann Smith in "musical sound" being "literally and actually nothing but motion," as stated by him, in accordance with the dogmatic teaching of all the acousticians whose theories in connection with organ pipes he so eloquently and properly condemns; but as this is not an essential matter in this place we need not enter on the consideration of so complex a question. Mr. Smith gives us a graphic description of his first discovery of the stream-reed and its action at the mouth of a pipe; and as this cannot fail to be interesting to the student of organ-building, we have much pleasure in giving the following passage from his writings here:—

"I well remember the day when I first had the audacity to try and confirm by vision the action of the air-reed, which I had mentally conceived. I was like the astronomer, searching for an unknown planet, because it ought to be there. I thought that my ideal reed ought to be there, and a large metal pipe, a 16 ft. CCC, standing on the floor level, gave me one day my opportunity. . . . The moment when I was about to see the unrevealed was a moment of flush and fever. I was like the small boy in the temerity of firing his first cannon. Not a creature was there; all was silence. Nothing but this monster standing beside me, measuring a good yard round, with a wide mouth of about nine inches, and two inches in height. On the floor lay a broad shaving of pinewood; one that it is the pride of the workman to produce, of perfectly even texture, fine as a tissue, white and shining like silk, and this I shaped to my purpose. Stealthily I stepped round to the bellows, filled them with wind, wedged down the pedal key, and started the pipe into life; then I caught up the broad shaving, held it deftly to the mouth of the monster, and to my joy saw it absorbed by the stream as though it were lost, and in an instant starting upward the ideal reed of my imagination. Soon the stream failed at its source, and a great silence came, so that my own breath seemed panting to betray me to the first comer; then I sat down and pondered long. The all-possessing ardor of the enthusiast you perhaps may not know, but you can see what I saw, and verify my experience in calmer mood.

"There is a country custom, when the bees are about to swarm, to dredge them with flour as a means of identification; if the flour travels the bees will have journeyed with white jackets on. So I place a white jacket on my reed, and detect and display his movements. Take a piece of white tissue-paper—I should in my eagerness have used a Bank of England note if I had had one—and let it be nearly of the size and shape of the mouth of the pipe, with an additional margin to allow of gumming the edge to a card for convenience of holding it in the position wanted; then advance the card, holding it to the level of the *outer* edge of the wind-way; the tissue is, in fact, a paper reed, but flaccid and inanimate. As you advance it to the wind-way, no sooner is it caught in the current than it darts upright, and becomes incorporated with the wind-reed. . . .

"This same crisp little bit of paper will reveal to your eyes the treasured secret of the organ pipe, tell you how its wealth of varied tone is wrought, show you its fine arcs of flexure, how it bends less for its inward than for its outward stroke. Listen, and you shall hear the domestic wrangle of the reed and pipe; look, and you shall witness how in its high caprice it transmutes in a flash to harmonic speed, and leaps exultant to its octave. Truly, an Ariel imprisoned, held captive, endowed with form, and clothed with a white vesture, making it, in all its motion, visible as bees.

"Most marvelous is the energy of suction when the stream-reed—remember, it never ceases to be a stream—when in recoil it throws itself *inward* and bends over, for the rushing wind is there in full force,—actually there *under the curve* of the paper-reed. Notwithstanding the presence of the paper-reed, the tone of the pipe is not perceptibly affected, nor its speech injured in any degree, nor its power impaired."

At this point, the accompanying illustration, Fig. LXIV., will assist our readers in thoroughly understanding Mr. Smith's instructive description of the motions of the stream-reed. It is a Vertical Section through the mouth of a wood pipe, in which the dotted fan-like figure, which issues from the wind-way and curves outward and inward as it sweeps past the upper lip of the pipe, graphically portrays the swing of part of the stream-reed while the pipe is speaking. The swing is exaggerated for the sake of clearness. Mr. Smith continues:—

"That fan-like display is what you actually see before you; but, of course, the reed's *path* only is described by that form, since at one instant the paper is at the extreme outward line of the fan, and at another at the extreme inward edge; but you seem, through what is termed persistence of vision, to see it in all its places at once, so rapid is its real movement. Always the wind-stream is on the inner face of the paper-reed, and the paper by suction adheres to the wind,—the movement of the one is the movement of the other.

"The most interesting, and perhaps the most important, fact disclosed in my investigations of the physical action taking place at the mouth of the organ pipes, according to aëro-plastic reed theory, is this,—that the wind stream-reed has a law of its own, unique among the phenomena heretofore observed in musical vibrations. I have stated it in *Nature* [an English journal] in these terms: '*As its arcs of vibration are less, its spread is greater.*' All our knowledge of rods and strings, of plates and membranes, would lead us to expect the usual manifestation of the law of isochronism, that, in the air-reed considered as a *free-reed* or rod fixed at one end, and vibrating transversely, the law would be observed: 'Though the amplitude may vary, the times of vibration will be the same.' Yet here we meet with its absolute reversal,—viz., *the times vary with the amplitude.*

"The information does not rest on theory; every eye may verify it. A principle so strange, when first its action was observed, might well lead to disbelief in one's senses, although the mind had by its reasonings led up to the fact, and sought for it as the one thing needed to give consistency in theory, and make it a perfect whole. Familiar as the air-reed had been to me, the one secret had been hidden from my eyes; seeing, they saw not. Faith in the known mode of activity of the transversely vibrating reed had blinded me, and it was only after long reasonings forced upon me by presence of independent harmonics not belonging to a free-reed—whose first harmonic would be higher than an octave twelfth—that my faith was shaken. Then it was that, conceiving the new idea of the principle of action, I looked, hoping to find my reasoning confirmed; yet, let me confess it, the first sight of the reality startled me not a little with self-confusion. Here was an every-day fact, constantly before me it had been, beautiful in its simplicity, waiting to be acknowledged, and I so stupidly blind as not to see it. . . . Vary the experiment, repeat it again and again as I have done, and the fact will be confirmed beyond possibility of doubt, that, the length of reed remaining unaltered, if by extraneous influence the pitch of the note is lowered whilst the pipe is speaking, correspondingly with the changing sound, the path of the wind-reed will be lengthened; or, conversely, if the pitch be raised, simultaneously with the quickened velocity the wind-reed will be seen to shorten its stroke; no swelling of tone gaining power with gain of amplitude; not the counterpart in action of the metal reed, nor acting as a tuning-fork. The creature of air, it times itself to the element that sustains it. The aëro-rhythmic law provides the only way possible to the air-reed to work out the transmutations of energy essential to its functions. The constitution of air itself necessitates the conformity in mechanical relations. Certainly the stream-reed is not of the free-reed family."

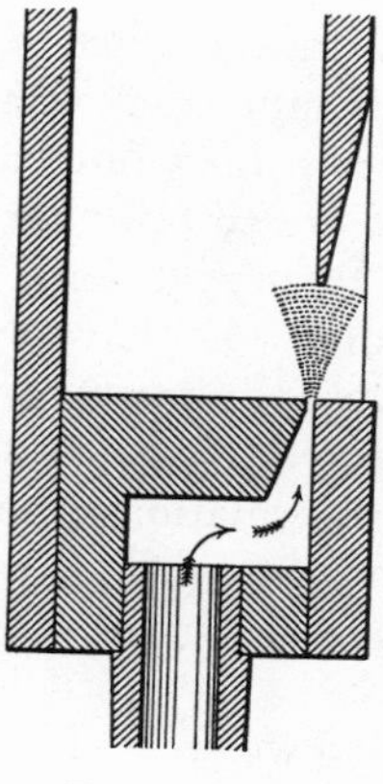

FIG. LXIV.

Experience and practice, aided by traditional methods, have taught the average organ builder and organ expert all they know about pipes and sound-production: acoustical science, in its popular aspect, teaching in direct opposition to known and self-evident facts, has given them absolutely no assistance. On the contrary, the modern acoustician has taken pipes from the hands of the organ builder, and, without careful study and investigation, has endeavored to extract some support to his pet theory from them. He has signally failed, as we have already pointed out. It is time some humility should be learned; and acknowledgment made that in matters of sound-generation and subsequent conduction very little is known beyond what natural phenomena seem to imply.

Respecting the absence of humility in matters of science, Wilkie Collins, in "Heart and Science," wisely says: "There are lectures and addresses by dozens which, if they prove nothing else, prove that what was scientific knowledge some years since is scientific ignorance now—and what is scientific knowledge now, may be scientific ignorance in some years more. There, in magazines and reviews, are the controversies and discussions, in which Mr. Always Right and Mr. Never Wrong exhibit the natural tendency of man to believe in himself in the most rampant stage of development that the world has yet seen. And there, last but not least, is all that the gentle wisdom of FARADAY saw and deplored, when he said: 'The first and last step in the education of the scientific judgment is—Humility.'"

With reference to the scarcity of painstaking, true investigators, William Black, the distinguished writer, says: "I can assure you that an accurate observer is a very rare bird indeed—far more rare among men of science than is supposed. There are so few who will take the trouble to look patiently; they must jump to their theory at once." How true this is with respect to modern professors of acoustics who have systematically ignored the truth enunciated by Froude, that "Philosophy goes no further than probabilities, and every assertion keeps doubt in reserve." We earnestly commend the above remarks to the attention of all who seek information in the dogmatic pages of Tyndall and Helmholtz, or in those of the more superficial writers on acoustics. We have endeavored to avoid any semblance of dogmatism on the subject of the present Chapter. To prove this to have been the spirit in which we have approached it, we may repeat a few of our opening words:—The sound of a labial organ pipe is generated at its mouth by the rapid vibratory action of the wind-stream which rushes from its wind-way, governed by the pulses or tremors set up in the internal column of air. This action we shall attempt to describe in due course. This much we know to be the case; but beyond this simple and evident fact we must acknowledge we know very little.

Great as are the difficulties in the way of our ascertaining, to a certainty, the manner in which the swinging air-stream or air-reed operates in producing the simple fundamental tone of a labial pipe; the question respecting its compound and evidently complex action in generating, at the same time, the prime tone and a series of attendant harmonics or upper partial tones, as in a pipe of the VIOL class, is infinitely more difficult to answer in any way approaching a satisfactory manner. The problem becomes apparently more and more perplexing the more fully we examine the several appliances and treatments that have been introduced and resorted to to obtain the compound tones, rich in harmonics, which imitate so closely the sounds of bowed instruments. It seems highly problematical if this question will ever be entirely freed from doubt. It would appear, however, on carefully examining the construction of the mouths, or at the mouths, of those organ pipes which yield sound rich in upper partial tones, that two causes are at work to produce the peculiar acoustical or tonal effects we hear; namely, a greater force or energy in the wind-stream, and a compound or special curve of vibration, probably formed by an outer current of free air, induced by the rush and consequent suction of the wind-stream and drawn against, and probably into, its outer surface. What we here mean will be shown more clearly in subsequent remarks. In the meantime we may profitably direct attention to Mr. Smith's opinion on the matter. He says:—

"In no work do we meet with any definite statement as to the causation of harmonic tones; yet it seems necessary for the full understanding of their nature and of the relation they bear to the instruments producing them that the mode of their origination should not be left unheeded. The conclusion derived from my own investigations is that the harmonics of musical instruments have their origin solely in the *surplus energy* of the generating force over and above that necessary to produce the fundamental tone; this superabundant vigor finds its outlet in accessory vibrations, and the harmonics are the escape-valves for securing to the fundamental tone freedom from fluctuations to which otherwise it would succumb. When the vibrating force is inadequate to waken the ground tone of an organ pipe it settles down into the harmonic nearest related to its power; the tone may be considered as surplus energy, since it is disproportionate to its work, and only becomes harmonic because it falls short of the fundamental after which it is striving. Except in this relation we should regard it as ground tone. When a pipe is overblown, the harmonics maintain themselves through the excess of energy to the complete exclusion of the fundamental, and they are sharp to the regulated pitch of the pipe. [And they are more fixed in pitch than the ground tone.] Harmonic tones when thus produced independently have considerably more intensity than the normal tones of pipes of corresponding pitch. [As in the case of the HARMONIC FLUTES.] In all the orchestral wind instruments it is the higher notes that require greatest wind-force for their production; the Clarionet alone differs as respects a certain range of its high notes, where the reverse is the case, the force being considerably less than for the lower range, but the structural conditions of the instrument sufficiently account for the peculiarity."

Before giving Mr. Smith's interesting dissertation on "The Building up of the Tone in the 'Gamba' Organ-pipe," which the author has kindly placed at our disposal, it is desirable that we briefly describe the representative forms and mouth treatments of the VIOLS, or string-toned pipes, which have been devised by masters in the art of voicing. These treatments are so varied that it seems almost a hopeless task to account, in any reasonable manner, for their apparently similar action on the wind-stream. As properly detailed drawings of the sounding parts of all the leading treatments of the string-toned pipes will be found in our Chapters on Metal Pipes: and Their Modes of Construction, and Wood Pipes: and Their Modes of Construction, it is only necessary to give here simple diagrams, sufficient for the purpose of the present dissertation. There are three leading treatments of mouth, apart from the dimensions of the opening of the mouth itself, which have been devised for, and found conducive to, the production of compound tones such as are characteristic of the stringed and bowed instruments of the orchestra. The first, and most effective of these treatments, consists of adding projecting ears to the lateral edges of the mouth, and placing between the ears a cylindrical or semi-cylindrical bar of metal or wood, which we prefer to designate the *harmonic-bridge.* This treatment is indicated in the diagram, Fig. LXV., which is a Vertical Section through the mouth of a metal pipe. The second treatment consists of omitting the lateral projecting ears (so important in the preceding treatment) and suspending in front of the mouth an inclined plate of thin metal, called the "*frein harmonique.*" * This treatment is indicated in the Section, Fig. LXVI. It is, like the harmonic-bridge, applied to both metal and wood pipes, as will be seen on examining the illustrations of string-toned pipes given in the Chapters on Metal and Wood Pipes already alluded to. The third and least effective treatment consists of forming in front of the mouth a quadrangular or a hopper-shaped box, open only at top. Large projecting ears form the ends of the box. This treatment is shown in the Section, Fig. LXVII. We

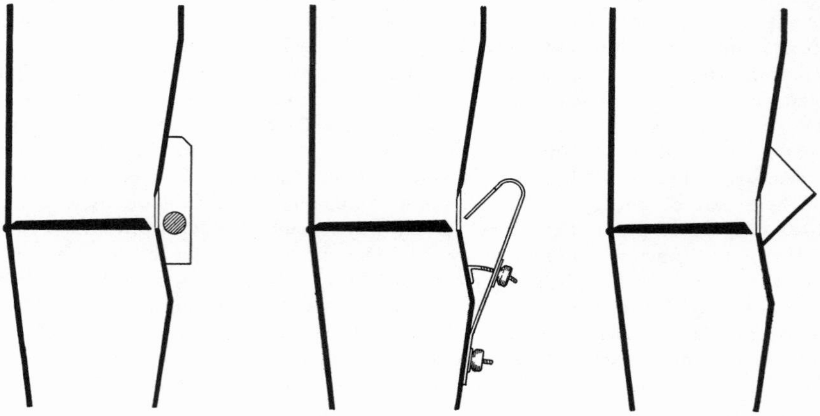

FIG. LXV. FIG. LXVI. FIG. LXVII.

may state that the distance below the lower lip of the mouth at which the bottom of the box is placed varies considerably in different examples of the treatment: and this fact renders it difficult to realize the action the air within the box exerts upon the wind-stream; while the different shapes and relative proportions of the box in different pipes only complicate matters. It will be observed that in the first and second treatments any external current of air, created by the rushing wind-stream, must come from below the mouth and pass upward between the wind-stream and the harmonic-bridge or the lower edge of the frein harmonique; but in the third treatment any current, created by the exhausting power of the wind-stream, must rush downward, over the outer edge of the box, and take a sudden turn when it reaches the bottom, to fill the partial vacuum created there by the suction of the wind-stream. We may now give Mr. Hermann Smith's able

* So named by its inventor, M. Gavioli, of Paris. The first stop with this frein harmonique introduced in an English Organ is the VIOLA D'AMORE, made by Zimmermann, of Paris, for our own Chamber Organ, sometime about the year 1878.

remarks which originally appeared in *Nature* (Feb. 25, 1875) under the heading "On the Building up of the Tone in the 'Gamba' Organ-pipe":—

"In considering the nature of this pipe, and in determining the relation of its air-reed and its air-column, one fact discovered in these investigations should always be borne in mind, that the pitch of the reed is dependent not on vibrating length, but on vibrating divergence—on the amplitude of the reed's motion. The pitch of the air-column is not necessarily the same as the pitch of the air-reed; they may be and often are at variance: and this pipe will afford a happy means of demonstration of the statement that the tone of every organ pipe is dual. As regards the reed, whatever the modifications of length by height of mouth, of thickness by varied wind-way, or of strength by amount of wind-pressure, the final result is bound by this law of divergence. In the typical air-reed, any deviation from the direct line of force taken by the stream of air is the beginning of vibration; its highest possible rate of vibration begins existence on its least divergence from the direct line; consequently, its highest pitch is its inceptive tone at this stage or condition of untamed energy. The bass has always been considered the basis and commencement of musical tone; every relation of tones has been examined on that ground, and it has undoubtedly been the source of many errors, one might almost say in the nature of superstitions, so tenacious has been its hold, so blinding its influence on the perceptions. Tone has its beginnings in the highest activity, and descends to the lowest and slowest; the development of its mechanical relations proceeds by definite degrees, and the issue depends on the affinity existing between the pipe and the reed, both possessing definite form, power, and character, and blending these by law. The vibration of the aëro-plastic reed is thus shown to be *isotonic*, not *isochronous*.

"It was my good fortune some time ago to have placed in my hands a specimen of a variety of 'GAMBA' devised by the famous organ builder, Schulze, of Paulinzelle. The 'GAMBAS' form a class of pipes variously constructed in scale, and they are so called from the quality of their tone imitating the old 'Viola da Gamba' and its modern representative the 'Violoncello.' The general characteristics of the class are—cylindrical pipe of comparatively slender scale, low-cut mouth, full-winded at foot, and slow in speaking; the slow speech is a necessity, and is caused by the wind being, as it is technically termed, 'much thrown out'; that is, the line of force of the current of wind is set more outward than ordinarily, for without such arrangement the fundamental or ground tone of the pipe would not secure its hold; some harmonic would usurp possession; for the air-reed, being short in consequence of low mouth, and strong from excess of wind, would keep to harmonics as the 'FLÛTE HARMONIQUE' does; the latter has a low languid (or interior level within the mouth), the 'GAMBA' has a higher languid in relation to the under lip, thus directing the stream at a more oblique angle to that level. The tone has decided introductory and transitive harmonics. Of their sequence, although but momentary, the ear conveys a clear impression to our consciousness. We call it a 'stringy quality,' and it is a very interesting inquiry how this peculiar pipe-tone is built up. The characteristic quality pertaining to all stringed instruments whose tone is elicited by the bow, does, we may well suppose, arise through a process bearing a close analogy to this.

"It is a disadvantage, this slow speech of the 'GAMBA,' often felt to be excessively slow.* Most skilful voicing is needful to give sufficient time for the appearance of the in-

*Commenting on this remark, we may say that Mr. Smith wrote it in 1875, before the art of the voicer had achieved marked success in the production of the more pungent and assertive string-toned stops, whose voices are as prompt as that of the Violin. It is true that the old German GAMBAS were very slow of speech; so much so as to require another stop—a helper—to be drawn with them to aid in covering the impediment in their speech. The renowned Schulze removed this impediment to such an extent as to render the attack in his beautiful string-toned pipes quick enough for every call save, perhaps, that of the most rapid playing and repetition. The VIOLINS and VIOLONCELLOES voiced by the late Mr. W. Thynne, of London, are as prompt and full in their intonation as the orchestral instruments after which they are named. Several distinguished voicers have, since his death, achieved equally satisfactory results in this direction.

troductory harmonics without too greatly delaying the fundamental, for it is a nice point to strike the mean between having the wind so much thrown out that the pipe will not speak any tone, and risking, by giving quicker speech, the sudden 'flying off to the octave,' with obstinate persistence not to descend.

"Take note of this. If you hold your hand or your finger near the mouth of any speaking organ pipe, there is forthwith a sensible flattening of its pitch, deepening with the nearer approach of the hand; in tuning Organs it is the ordinary custom to test pitch by this simple method, determining thereby whether the pipe will best bear flattening for its nearer approximation to a desired pitch or concord with others. Suppose yourself to be tuning a set of 'GAMBA' pipes: you would notice perchance that a restive pipe continually darting off to harmonics would be corrected and steadily held in check so long as your hand or finger was near or across its mouth.* We can thus well understand how it might occur to Schulze that the temporary expedient could be made permanent. This is what Schulze did: he fixed a small bar across the mouth. The device proved successful. In pipes thus treated the tendency of the [aëro-plastic] reed to settle at the octave is suppressed, speech is quickened, more wind may be given without danger, and the quality becomes in consequence more characteristic, more 'stringy.' Schulze has extended his method to large pedal pipes, producing a stop of remarkable beauty called the 'VIOLONE.'†

"Applying the air-reed theory to this Schulze's 'GAMBA,' we shall see how fruitful it is in illustration of the actual process of tone-making. Without diagrams and with but few technical terms it may be made clear and comprehensible. Let us take a specimen pipe. It is of slender, graceful proportions, what is called 'narrow scale,' length thirty-seven inches and a quarter, diameter one inch and five-eighths, mouth or *embouchure* in breadth one inch and a quarter, three-eighths of an inch high, and its pitch answers to the note E in the tenor octave. It has a very fine wind-way, large foot-hole, and is considerably overblown, for it will bear it. There is a bar in front of the mouth, fixed upon the little upright strips projecting at the sides about a quarter of an inch, which are termed ears; they are common to pipes [of a certain class] until the size is too small to require them. Builders say the ears are added to pipes to steady the tone. On the theory advanced in these papers, we find their purpose is to prevent any flank movement of the atmosphere during the vibration of our air-reed, for the angle formed by the vertical line of the mouth and the line of force of the outwardly inclined stream of air presents an opening of weakness, and these ears are as ridges or outworks thrown up to guard against any premature invasion by the external air which pierces through at the proper time only, just under the edge of the upper lip.

"We readily perceive that the 'GAMBA' pipe has three specialties: overblown wind, to give a stiffer reed; a low-cut mouth, as a provision for shortness of reed; and wind much thrown out, as a means compulsory for insuring a greater amplitude in the reed's motion,—the result of the combination being that the tone is rich in harmonics; harmonics precede the ground tone, and follow it, and coalesce into it, and linger behind as though the last to quit the pipe. There is nothing more beautiful in all the varied wealth of an Organ than a well-voiced 'GAMBA.' Every tone suggests a symphony, many-tinted, autumnal.‡ There is another remarkable feature peculiar to these—the artist can shade them with less depth of ground tone and more varied and delicate hues in the harmonics, which nevertheless come out more brightly in the contrast, and compensate the ear with a new variety, toned with

* Mr. Smith here alludes to the old German GAMBA which has no harmonic-bridge across its mouth.

† Descriptions and drawings of Schulze's string-toned pipes will be found in our Chapter on Wood Pipes: and Their Modes of Construction.

‡ These remarks are strictly true; yet, as will be seen in our criticisms of important Organs in the concluding part of the present treatise, no class of tone has been more neglected by organ builders. The extent to which we advocate the introduction of imitative string-tone will be realized on reading our Chapter on The Concert-room Organ.

less body yet with equal fulness, through the heightening of the harmonic color, and the more gradual blending of the whole.

"In the pipe we are examining we shall find that the wind is not so much thrown out as in the older class of the species, and herein lies the real meaning of the difference, for by the agency of the bar an equal amplitude is enforced in the air-reed, but one of new form: and see how gracefully it is drawn,—yes, happily we can see, for the new form bears an impress highly significant. A little bit of paper deftly applied will enable us to watch the process of nature. Take away the bar, and the pipe will not sound its ground tone—it is only able to produce its string of brilliant harmonics. Look at the air-reed: how minute a space it traverses whilst these high notes are thrilling in your ears. In substitute for the removed bar, now lay a small pencil across the mouth, and see how in coy consent the air-reed yields, comes out to you with a fine curve, and all the power of the pipe is affirmed coincidently with this visibly extended amplitude of the reed's motion. You can change it from one state to the other by this movable bar, and you have to notice that the reed is almost upright in stem, but bends over, arching at the tip,—notice also that the inward curve of the reed is less than the outward curve. The explanation of this influence will be quickly divined if you fully comprehend the way in which the reed builds itself up in a curve, leaning outward upon the external air: the air composing the reed issues from the wind-way in a dense stream; the particles are most compressed at the root, and gradually expand and become less energetic as they reach higher freedom—the velocity of the upward stream motion attracts the external air with force, strongly, to the root, bearing with lessened force on the less compressed portions higher up, and the gradation of force so manifested gives rise to the curve—the curve delineates the force, we may say the curve expresses the constant flow of the surrounding air to this diversified region of 'least pressure,' its impulses being in graduated power from root to tip. By the bar we interfere with the direction of this flow, concentrate it more on the lower portion of the stem, and shield the tip of the reed from its influence; the upper portion, having thus lost so much of its natural support, is bent by the outflowing nodal wave of the pipe in a more supple curve, and to an extent equal to the required amplitude for its pitch. The form differs now. The curve of the 'GAMBA' is not the same as the curve of the DIAPASON.

"The distinct agency of the air-reed and the nature of the air-column in relation therewith being evident, the inference follows that the note produced is dual, consists of two unisonous notes blended into one sound. Quite unexpectedly the chosen pipe furnished me with the talisman to prove its truth. When the reed and the pipe are suitably mated, the union is one of perfect harmony; but the reed rules always: it may be sharp to the pipe, but the pipe can never be sharp to the reed, for on the first intimation of such the reed is roused, and starts forth to a tone of higher velocity. How slight a matter may derange the union of the reed and pipe. If we tease the pipe with this pencil, peace is disturbed. Our beautiful little 'GAMBA' is very sensitive and high-spirited, and cannot help letting us hear a little of the inner life of the home when things go a trifle wrong. There is one particular place across the mouth for the fixture of the bar: if, resting the pencil at the upper points of the projecting ears, you leisurely bring it down, you will hear the changing harmonics; then, halting just a hair's breadth or so before the true position is arrived at, all tone will be lost, and there will suddenly break forth a wailing 'who-hoo, who-hoo;' that torture will continue until you relieve the suspense by moving the pencil another shade in descent, when the discord will resolve into the perfect tone, instantaneously, as two dew-drops when they touch melt into one. Precisely the same 'who-hoo' as we hear when tuning two separate DIAPASON pipes so nearly in tune that they are only a shade out of unison and just on the point of accord. The 'GAMBA' pipe and the reed were similarly at variance; the air-reed, not having quite yielded to the outward influence of the bar, was a trifle sharp to the pipe; the super-nodal wave was too short and unable to effect a synchronization with precision, and therefore the phenomenon of beats was manifested. We could have lengthened the super-nodal wave and flattened the note by adding a portion to the top of the pipe, when concord would have followed, as it did by lowering the bar, for in tuning it matters not which note of two is altered to bring about unison; we might alter either pitch of pipe or pitch of reed; but by the lowering of the bar we flatten the reed, and cause thereby the descent of the node (then an uneasy fulcrum) and the lengthening relatively of the super-nodal column. As a listener remarked, 'there was surely a fight going on inside,' we settled it by favoritism, taking sides with the little 'GAMBA,' and gaining the reed over in concession of its strength for the sake of concord. That is the explanation as it suggests itself to me, practically, exhibiting how a strong reed drives the node higher up in the pipe, and a weak reed favors the opposite; thus determining the variations in the lengths of pipes of unisonous pitch, so long an unsolved problem.

"Another point of some importance is also illustrated—that the earliest harmonics in the theoretical series may be out of tune with the fundamental. Here the introductory or transitive harmonics are, it is evident, all sharp to the ground tone, since the influence of the bar does not come into effect until its flattening power ushers in the fundamental; phenomena of this kind occur in other instruments mostly unacknowledged—it is admitted to be the case in the [old make of] Trumpet, which has No. 5 in the series flat, 7 still flatter, and 9 sharp. A DIAPASON pipe will, however, exhibit the same in the small pipes of the higher octave; they may be blown to imitate exactly the clash of the Trumpet.*

"As showing the essential nature of the curve of the reed under the influence of the bar, it is worth notice that in the earlier 'VIOLONE' stops thus treated a square-faced bar was fitted, but not with so good effect as when the rounded bar was adopted; and in the light of our explanation we see why it should be so, for the curve could not form itself truly.† The best form of bar is that given by a split pencil, the half-round, with the flat surface outward."

The above dissertation, from the pen of the investigator who has devoted more study and attention to acoustical matters connected with organ pipes than any other known man, deserves our most careful consideration: the only cause for regret is that it does not fully explain certain matters connected with the vibrating air-reed that seem to require further investigation and explanation. The writer tells us that when the harmonic-bridge or "bar" is removed from the mouth of a speaking GAMBA pipe, the pipe instantly refuses to "sound its ground tone—it is only able to produce its string of brilliant harmonics. Look at the air-reed:" he adds, "how minute a space it traverses whilst these high notes are thrilling in your ears." One recognizes this fact; but one is anxious to know in what peculiar and complex manner the air-reed is vibrating so as to produce, not a single, simple, high-pitched note, but the "string of brilliant harmonics" of several different pitches. The motion of the air-reed cannot be a simple swinging or pendular one,‡ such as we believe it to be in large-scaled, high-mouthed pipes, which, under

*This fact has induced organ builders to use such labial pipes for the top octave of the CLARION, 4 FT., instead of inconveniently small reed pipes.

†The most characteristic and beautiful VIOLONE, 16 FT., known to us is that in the pedal department of the Schulze Organ in the Church of St. Peter, Hindley, Lancashire. The harmonic-bridge of this stop has a square, sharp edge, of about one-third its length, placed in a central position underneath, while all the rest of its inner face is rounded. See the drawing of the mouth in our Chapter on Wood Pipes: and Their Modes of Construction. Cylindrical harmonic-bridges are now generally preferred to the half-round mentioned by Mr. Smith.

‡"G. S. Ohm was the first to declare that there is only one form of vibration which will give rise to no harmonic upper partial tones, and which will therefore consist solely of the prime tone. This is the form of

a moderate pressure of wind, yield ground tones with practically no over-tones. We think had Mr. Smith said that on the removal of the "bar" a new and higher prime tone—most probably the octave of the proper ground tone of the pipe—was instituted with its "string of brilliant harmonics," he would have correctly stated the position of affairs. It is extremely difficult to account for the compound action of the vibrating air-reed. The eye cannot possibly trace its peculiar motions, and the mind is baffled in its attempt to realize them. We know that some complex forces are at work in the air-reed, and there our knowledge ceases. The addition of the harmonic-bridge, or the *frein harmonique*, creating an auxiliary current in the free air, at once, and in some mysterious way, compels the air-reed to slacken the speed of its principal vibration so as to generate the ground tone belonging to the pipe, while its other compound vibrations continue creating the "string of brilliant harmonics." Such matters as these have very evidently perplexed the minds of dogmatic and know-all scientists; and their explanations, given with their usual voice of authority, are amusing. They could not afford to admit that they *do not know*. As Mr. Smith properly remarks: "The study of the organ pipe in every mood of its behavior will make untenable the elegant fancy of a promiscuous assemblage of pulses fluttering and clamoring at the lip of the pipe, one of which out of a thousand it selects. It is a fair-seeming explanation, and under the commanding name of Prof. Tyndall generally accepted, for nothing better had been devised in philosophy. Not too strictly interpreting an ideality of expression, there yet remains an implied theory which is not in any sense borne out by the teachings of experience. The artist has some prescience of the powers that are to work his will; in practice there is nothing adventitious; the pipe is a mechanism designed to a precise end which it fulfils; it speaks but as it must; there is no selective power, for the hand that fashions it ordains."

The concluding remark is strictly true, not only with respect to the pipes whose tones so closely resemble the rich compound tones of the bowed instruments, but with respect to those remarkable pipes, introduced by Mr. Haskell, whose voices so closely imitate those of the orchestral Oboe and Saxophone,—veritable triumphs of the voicer's art. These pipes are of wood, and so far as the general treatment of their mouths is concerned they do not appear to differ, in any essential particulars, from the wood pipes of the Schulze VIOLONE and VIOLA. A great difference must, however, obtain in the strength and initial direction of the wind-stream and in the manner it is influenced or affected by the cylindrical harmonic-bridge; otherwise, the peculiar voices of the Oboe and Saxophone, so widely different in their *timbres* from those of the Violin, Violoncello, and other bowed instruments, could not be produced. The whole matter involved is one of the deepest interest to the acoustician who really seeks after truth, and who cares to devote time and careful investigation to it, untrammeled by the dogmatic and misleading assertions of the writers of the popular text-books on sound. We give descriptions and drawings of the Haskell pipes in the Chapter on Wood Pipes: and Their Modes

vibration which we have described as peculiar to the pendulum and tuning-forks. We call these *pendular vibrations*, or, since they cannot be analyzed into a compound of different tones, *simple vibrations*."—Helmholtz' "Sensations of Tone," p. 34.

of Construction, which can be compared with those of the Schulze and Whiteley imitative string-toned pipes also given.

In all the preceding remarks we have confined ourselves to the labial pipes which have straight wind-ways and upper lips, and in which the wind-streams or "aëro-plastic reeds" are invariably straight in transverse section, in accordance with the wind-ways from which they issue. We may now direct attention to the fact that wind-streams having curved, semicircular, or circular transverse sections, and which issue from wind-ways of corresponding forms, are equally efficacious in the production of sound. The ordinary steam-whistle, which has a circular steam-way and upper lip, is a well-known illustration of this fact. In his desire to rival the tones produced by steam-whistles, and under the apparent conviction that powerful sounds, regardless of musical quality or refinement, are desirable in the Organ, W. T. F. Weigle, of Stuttgart, patented, in 1893, a form of organ pipe in which the mouth is semicircular in horizontal section, having semicircular wind-way and upper lip. We understand that this treatment has been further extended by the construction of a pipe on the steam-whistle model, in which the wind-way is circular, both the circular languid and the body of the pipe being supported by internal and external bridges or stay-bars. The increased power of the sounds produced by these pipes is entirely due to the increased superficial area and corresponding energy of their wind-streams. The motion of the semicircular or circular wind-stream differs somewhat from the simple swinging motion of the straight aëro-plastic reed; for while its form and dimensions remain the same where it issues from the wind-way, its upper portion expands and contracts in size as it alternately rarefies and condenses the column of air within the body of the pipe. Beyond the difference of motion just mentioned there appears to be no new element introduced in the acoustical problem we have ventured to discuss in the preceding pages.

A few remarks may now be made on the subject of sound-production in lingual or reed pipes. The construction of the lingual pipe is due to the fact, which has been known for thousands of years, that any contrivance which will admit a regular and frequently-recurring succession of puffs or jets of compressed air into a partially confined body or column of air at atmospheric pressure will create a sound more or less musical in character. All reed instruments, from the primitive pastoral pipe, with its split barley-straw, to the largest and most powerful lingual pipe ever constructed by the organ builder, have owed their powers of sound-generation to this simple acoustical phenomenon. As all matters connected with the construction of the several classes of lingual pipes are more or less fully treated in the Chapter on Reed Pipes: and Their Modes of Construction, it is only necessary to touch in the briefest manner on the subject here.

The mechanism commonly used in the lingual pipes of the grand Organ is extremely simple, while it calls for most careful workmanship and accurate adjustment. It consists, in its normal form, of a tube of brass or other suitable material, stopped at one end, and having an orifice or slit on one side where a perfectly flat surface has been produced by a file or some other means. The open end of this tube, called the reed or *échalote*, is connected with the lower and smaller end of another and much larger tube or resonator, formed of metal or wood, which assumes different forms and is open at its upper end for the emission of sound. Against the flat and perforated surface of the reed is placed, and firmly held at its upper end, a thin, flexible strip of metal, called the tongue or *languette.** This has been carefully filed to a perfectly smooth and even surface on both sides, so as to vibrate truly, and bed accurately against the face of the reed while vibrating. The tongue is slightly curved in its free portion, and, accordingly, bends away from the face of the reed while at rest. By means of a strong wire spring, shaped so as to press evenly and firmly against the outer surface of the tongue, and so fitted in the block that carries the reed and the resonator as to admit of its being raised or lowered in the process of tuning, the vibrating portion of the tongue is lengthened or shortened as required. The entire mechanism is inclosed in a chamber formed by what is called the boot. This brief description will be readily understood on examination of the accompanying illustration, Fig. LXVIII., which is a Vertical Section of the sound-producing apparatus of a striking reed organ pipe of normal form, or such as is commonly used for pipes of the TRUMPET class. The reed or *echalote* is shown at A, with its upper open end fixed in the perforation of the block B, and communicating, through it, with the lower end of the open resonant tube C, only a small portion of which is indicated. The vibrating tongue or *languette* D is secured firmly against the upper part of the reed by means of the wooden wedge F. The tongue is shown with a characteristic curvature and in its position while at rest. E is the tuning-wire with its cross end bearing firmly against the tongue and so limiting its vibrating length. The boot G incloses the whole, and forms a chamber which conveys the compressed air from the wind-chest to the reed through the hole H.

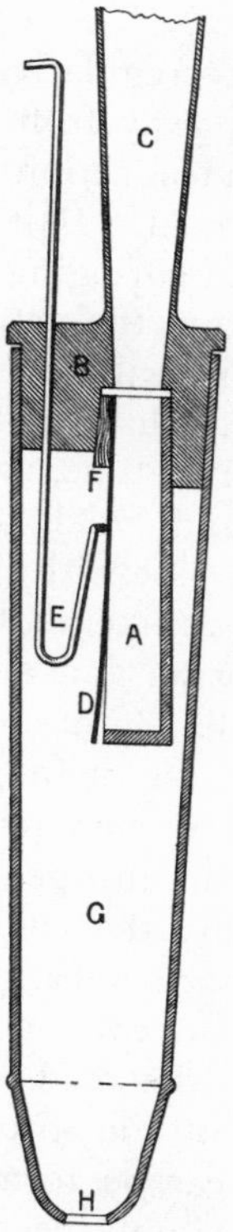

FIG. LXVIII.

The operation of the mechanism above described appears to be extremely simple, while the acoustical phenomena which attend it have never been satisfactorily explained. When the compressed air from the wind-chest is suddenly admitted into the boot, its first action is to inject a puff into the slit in the reed, beneath the curved tongue, causing a powerful suction there which draws the tongue toward the reed, or which allows the compressed air to exert its power on its outer surface and drive

*It will be observed, in organ nomenclature, that the term *reed* is used to designate the perforated tube against which the *tongue* vibrates. But in the nomenclature of the wood-wind instruments of the orchestra, the vibrating plates of cane are called *reeds* while they are, in strict terminology, *tongues*. This is especially the case in the Clarinets and Saxophones, which are constructed with single vibrating tongues in a fashion similar to that obtaining in the lingual pipes of the Organ. The chief difference lies in the fact that in the orchestral instruments the single tongues or reeds are straight and the surfaces against which they vibrate are curved.

it against the reed until it almost entirely closes the slit in the same. At this instant the spring power of the curved tongue, which is greater than the pressure exerted upon it by the compressed air, now unassisted by the initial action, asserts itself, and the tongue leaves the reed and swings back to a slight distance beyond its original position, allowing another puff of air to enter the reed, and itself to be caught on the rebound and again driven against the reed. It would seem that the compressed air in rushing into the reed generates a rarefaction on the inner side of the tongue, or reduces the pressure there in finding a means of egress through the reed. If such were not the case, the tongue could not be moved in the manner we know it is moved by the compressed air in the boot. The operations above outlined are repeated with great rapidity and absolute regularity, a sharp puff of air entering the reed each time the tongue swings away from its face. It must be borne in mind, so as to understand the mechanical action of the tongue, that it at no time absolutely closes the opening in the reed. If it bedded perfectly on the surface of the reed it would be incapable of springing away from that surface in the manner it does.

How the action of the tongue produces sound can only be guessed at, and probably will never be known with absolute certainty. We know the simple fact that the sharp puffs of compressed air, following each other many times in each second of time, enter the cavity of the reed and then and there generate a powerful sound, harsh, and anything but pleasing. This fact can be verified by sounding a reed pipe with its resonant tube removed. The action of the tongue and reed has been likened to that of the siren, which generates sound by emitting, in rapid succession and at regular intervals, puffs of compressed air into the atmosphere immediately in contact with its surface. There is certainly a close analogy here. The harsh sound produced within the reed is amplified, modified, and translated into a refined musical tone through the agency of a resonant column or body of air in an open tube, called the resonator, which opens at its contracted lower end into the cavity of the reed, as indicated in Fig. LXVIII. As in all the other acoustical problems connected with organ pipes, the manner in which this resonant column of air exerts so potent an influence over the sound generated within the reed can only be imagined. It must, however, be very different in its office of tone-production to the resonant column of air within a labial pipe. No node can be formed in a reed pipe analogous to that created in an open labial pipe, simply because there is an intermittent current of compressed air rushing through its resonator all the time the reed is speaking; while in the labial pipe no air whatever passes through its resonant column, as we have previously explained. Speaking on this subject, Max Allihn remarks:—

"Experience has long since taught that the vibrating tongue requires a resonating body: first, in order to give it prompt action; and secondly, to refine the tone of the reed and render it musically serviceable. It frequently occurs that the tongue, unaided, will not vibrate, while it will do so the moment a body or cone is added to the reed. . . . So soon as the body is added to the reed, the tone is altered and becomes rounder and fuller; the sharpness, the nasal quality, and the shrill admixture of tones vanish; and a sound of musical value springs into existence. This is most strikingly the case with the larger pipes of the TROMBONE, 16 FT. What is heard without the body is a crackling noise associated with high-pitched dissonant tones; but so soon as the body is put on the deep ground tone prevails. We suspect that here the air-wave going up and down in the body is the cause, *but cannot picture to ourselves the nature of the proceeding*, as the laws which have become known to us through the behavior of labial pipes do not hold good here. To the length of a labial pipe belongs a certain tone; but such is not the case here, as one can employ both long and short bodies. When the body of a labial pipe is reduced in scale, to obtain the proper pitch it must be increased in length. In a lingual pipe the reverse is the case."*

It seems quite evident that in investigating the acoustical phenomena connected with lingual pipes, one has to lay aside what one has gathered from the behavior of open and stopped labial pipes, and to start from an entirely new point. The only matter absolutely common to both lingual and labial pipes, so far as can be clearly seen, is that they are sounded by a stream of compressed air. It is true that there seems to be some parallel between the action of the wind-stream at the mouth of a labial pipe and that of the tongue of the so-called free reed within the opening of its frame; but there is practically little relationship between the free reed and the striking reed of the organ pipe. The tongue of the former swings freely, with a pendular motion, within its opening, while the tongue of the latter swings from and against the opening of the reed, uncovering and covering it alternately. Both the free and striking tongues separate the stream of compressed air into a regular succession of sharp puffs, creating aërial shocks which generate sound in the cavity or air chamber of the reed.

We remarked in the opening paragraph of our present notes on lingual pipes that the construction of such pipes is due to the fact, known for thousands of years, that any contrivance which will admit a regular and frequently recurring succession of puffs or jets of compressed air into a partially confined body or column of air, at the ordinary atmospheric pressure, will create a musical sound. About thirty years ago we had a noteworthy and unexpected illustration of this fact in our own Chamber Organ. The bass pipes of the PRINCIPALE GRANDE, 8 FT., forming the front towers, were supplied with wind from special small wind-chests, placed a short distance from them, and connected with the speaking-blocks by metal conveyances. The pallets of these wind-chests were in the form of small disc valves, suspended by long wires from the ends of backfalls. While engaged in adjusting the bedding of these valves to a nicety, with the pipes removed from their speaking-blocks, we were surprised to hear a rich and deep musical sound issuing from one of the conduits. We found it due to the rapid vibration —up and down—of one of the valves, under the influence of the compressed air in the valve-box and a slight spring in the long backfall. The valve was acting precisely in the same manner as the beating tongue of an ordinary lingual pipe, the conveyance or conduit serving as a resonator.

Availing himself of the long-known fact of which we have spoken, Mr. Robert Hope-Jones, M. I. E. E., took out a patent in the year 1894 for an apparatus for

* "Die Theorie und Praxis des Orgelbaues," p. 296.

producing musical tones; and in the following year he took out another patent, in which we find the following particulars:

> "This invention relates for the most part to improvements in modifications of the apparatus for producing musical tones described under the head of 'Diaphones' in the Specification of my application for Patent No. 22,414 dated November 20th, 1894.
>
> "Whereas in the Specification above referred to 'Diaphones,' in which a motor or its equivalent was directly connected with a valve, were more particularly described, now a portion of this invention relates to similar 'Diaphones' in which the motor or its equivalent is connected with its valve through the medium of a pneumatic relay,—that is to say, Diaphones in which the motor or diaphragm moves an intermediary valve which regulates the pressure exerted upon a second motor and thereby causes the movement of a valve which sets up or helps to set up or maintain sonorous vibrations in the pipe or resonator. In such Diaphone the wind which operates the first motor may be obtained from the same or from a different source from that which operates the second motor."

From the above particulars it will be gathered that the DIAPHONE consists of a pipe or resonator, open at top, and connected, at its lower end, with an apparatus so constructed as to admit into the air chamber communicating with the resonator a rapid and regular succession of puffs or jets of compressed air, generating sound therein precisely in the same manner as the beating tongue of the ordinary lingual pipe generates sound in the cavity of the reed. The DIAPHONE differs from the ordinary striking reed, however, in that when blown by different pressures of wind it alters its power and perhaps quality of tone without an attendant alteration of pitch; in this respect it closely resembles the free reed. It is well known that the slightest alteration of the wind-pressure causes a corresponding change in the pitch of the sound generated in the striking reed. In the DIAPHONE, while an increased pressure causes a more energetic action, and adds to the force of the puffs admitted into the cavity of the apparatus, the number of vibrations per second is not altered. Apparently any strength of tone may be obtained in the DIAPHONE. From an acoustical point of view it is extremely interesting and instructive. As a full description of the apparatus is given in the proper place it is unnecessary to say more on the DIAPHONE in this Chapter.

The free reed is rarely used by English and American organ builders, but the German and French builders have shown it considerable favor in the past, and continue to use it for certain stops of a soft and refined quality of tone. The German builders construct the characteristic stop called the PHYSHARMONICA with free reeds; and it is usually made with resonating chambers without the addition of tubes or pipe-bodies. The free reed consists of a thick, oblong plate of brass, perforated with a long and narrow opening, and a brass tongue which is closely and accurately adjusted to the opening so as to swing within it, without touching its sides. The tongue is securely screwed to one end of the plate, and close to its fixed end it is provided with a tuning clip, by means of which the vibrating portion of the tongue is lengthened or shortened to a small extent. When the free reed is associated with an open tube or resonator, after the fashion of the striking reed, it is usually screwed to the face of a wooden block, in which a chamber or resonant cavity is formed opening at its upper end into the resonator. This block is inserted into a large boot, for the free reed will only vibrate properly when surrounded with a considerable volume of condensed air. The office of the free tongue is like that of the beating tongue; namely, to admit a rapid and perfectly regular succession of sharp puffs or jets of compressed air into the column of air immediately behind it. The manner in which the puffs are admitted differs somewhat from that which obtains in the striking reed, and a different tonal quality is the natural result. It is impossible to procure the strength of tone from a free reed that is readily obtained from a striking reed. The free reed allows an increased pressure to be used without altering the pitch of its tone. This is due to the pendular and unarrested motion of the free tongue: under increased pressure, the amplitude of the swing of the tongue is increased, but the period of its vibration remains constant, as in the case of the swinging pendulum or the vibrating prong of the tuning-fork. In the case of the beating tongue of the ordinary organ reed, the slightest alteration of the wind pressure alters the pitch of the tone produced. In the remarks just made we have not considered the changes due to alterations of temperature. Further particulars respecting free reeds are given in the Chapter on Reed Pipes: and Their Modes of Construction.

It must be conceded that acoustical matters relating to sound-production and control in lingual pipes are at present in a very vague and undecided state. On this subject Max Allihn waxes eloquent. He says: "The subject of reed pipes is a question so intricate and obscure that it creates a sensation as of one trying to find a path through a forest with which one is unacquainted, and in which numberless stray paths lead away from the right road." Then, alluding to his own exertions, he modestly remarks: "If we undertake to offer our guidance to the reader in this realm, we do not presume to transform the rough ways into a smooth road; but with the consciousness of having taken pains in exploring the territory, and in the belief of having found some points from which right views and unprejudiced perspectives are possible." He then adds: "The organ builder has, at all times, had trouble with the reed stops. As experience accumulated, certain practical rules were evolved and certain conventional measurements adopted; but how different or conflicting are all such rules and measurements among themselves. TRUMPETS are constructed with short and long and narrow and wide bodies; with narrow and wide and hard and soft tongues; with and without boots; and requiring high and low wind-pressure. Each builder argues and claims his practice to be the right one, and no one finds it wholly satisfactory. . . . Also, in themselves, the processes in tone-formation show great irregularities. A body of a certain length is employed and then exchanged for others of greater lengths: the tone at first does not change at all, then it deepens in great skips, becomes muffled and sickly, begins to rattle, and then jumps back to the original pitch. Another time the tone drops lower and shortly afterwards jumps to a higher pitch. The TROMBONE, 16 FT., can in tuning be changed in pitch half an octave; the three-lined C can hardly be touched without its tone jumping, often into quite a foreign one, out of all relation to the proper scale. Then, again, the free tongue behaves differently from the beating tongue, which forms the tone more readily, but so far as the body of the pipe is concerned is more sensitive than the free tongue. Now, if the organ builder, in view of such incalculable mishaps, is reduced to groping experimentation, away from all methodical research, it is easily understood how he forms such a pessimistic opinion about reed-work as is expressed in the German saying 'Schnarrwerk—Narrwerk' (Reed-work—Fool-work).

"Under such circumstances, the practician justly turns to theory for enlightenment; but in this matter theory is just as helpless as practice. In the case of labial pipes it has been observed that the physical process of their sound-production has by no means been sufficiently grasped; the same is the case with reed pipes, with which very few expert scientists have concerned themselves."

The writings of Helmholtz, Tyndall, and their imitators, go to prove the correctness of Max Allihn's concluding remarks. In his work, "On the Sensations of Tone," Helmholtz devotes only about four pages to the subject of organ reed pipes; and during his remarks he makes the following misleading statement, so far as advanced organ-building is concerned: "Formerly, *striking vibrators* or *reeds* were employed, which on each oscillation struck against their frame. But as these produced a harsh quality of tone, they have gone out of use." All he says of any interest about organ reeds we give here:—

"We now proceed to investigate the *quality of tone* produced on reed pipes. The sound in these pipes is excited by intermittent pulses of air, which at each swing break through the opening that is closed by the tongue. A freely vibrating tongue has far too small a surface to communicate any appreciable quantity of resonant motion to the surrounding air; and it is as little able to excite the air inclosed in pipes. The sound seems to be really produced by pulses of air, as in the siren, where the metal plate that opens and closes the orifice does not vibrate at all. By the alternate opening and closing of a passage, a continuous influx of air is changed into a periodic motion, capable of affecting the air. Like any other periodic motion of the air, the one thus produced can also be resolved into a series of simple vibrations. We have already remarked that the number of terms in such a series will increase with the discontinuity of the motion to be thus resolved. Now the motion of the air which passes through a siren, or past a vibrating tongue, is discontinuous in a very high degree, since the individual pulses of the air must be generally separated by complete pauses during the closures of the opening. Free tongues without a resonance tube, in which all the individual simple tones of the vibration which they excite in the air are given off freely to the surrounding atmosphere, have consequently always a very sharp, cutting, jarring quality of tone, and we can really hear with either armed or unarmed ears a long series of strong and clear partial tones up to the 16th or 20th, and there are evidently still higher partials present, although it is difficult or impossible to distinguish them from each other, because they do not lie so much as a semitone apart. This whirring of dissonant partial tones makes the musical quality of free tongues very disagreeable. A tone thus produced always shows that it is really due to puffs of air. I have examined the vibrating tongue [free] of a reed pipe when in action with the vibrationmicroscope of Lissajous, in order to determine the vibrational form of the tongue, and I found that the tongue performed perfectly regular simple vibrations. Hence it would communicate to the air merely a simple tone and not a compound tone, if the sound were directly produced by its own vibrations.

"The intensity of the upper partial tones of a free tongue, unconnected with a resonance tube, and their relation to the prime, are greatly dependent on the nature of the tongue, its position with respect to its frame, the tightness with which it closes, &c. Striking tongues which produce the most discontinuous pulses of air also produce the most cutting quality of tone. The shorter the puff of air, the more sudden its action, the greater number of high upper partials should we expect, exactly as we find in the siren, according to Seebeck's investigations. Hard, unyielding material, such as that used for brass tongues, will produce pulses of air which are much more disconnected than those formed by soft and yielding substances.

"The tones of tongues are essentially changed by the addition of resonance tubes, because they reinforce and hence give prominence to those upper partial tones which correspond to the proper tones of these tubes, precisely as was the case for the rush of wind in the flute or flue pipes of Organs. In this case the resonance tubes must be considered as closed at the point where the tongue is inserted. A brass tongue such as is used in Organs, and tuned to *b♭*, was applied to one of my larger spherical resonators, also tuned to *b♭*, instead of its usual resonance tube. After considerably increasing the pressure of the wind in the bellows, the tongue spoke somewhat flatter than usual, but with an extraordinarily full, beautiful, soft tone, from which almost all upper partials were absent. Very little wind was used, but it was under high pressure. In this case the prime tone of the compound was in unison with the resonator, which gave a powerful resonance, and consequently the prime tone had also great power. None of the higher partial notes could be reinforced. The theory of the vibrations of air in the sphere further shows that the greatest pressure must occur in the sphere at the moment that the tongue opened. Hence the necessity of strong pressure in the bellows to overcome the increased pressure in the sphere, and yet not much wind really passed. If instead of a glass sphere, resonant tubes are employed, which admit of a greater number of proper tones, the resulting musical tones are more complex."

Attempts have been made by theorists, indifferently versed in stubborn practical facts, to devise some law of general application to the lengths of the resonators of reed pipes, with the view of reconciling the lengths of their internal, vibrating air-columns with the stated lengths of the acoustician's hypothetical sound-waves. These attempts have been as futile in the case of lingual as they have been proved to be in the case of labial pipes. The closest approximation to a practical law was propounded by Weber, in his essay on the theory of sound-production in lingual pipes.* He laid it down as the law in relation to reeds and resonant tubes, that three-fourths of the half of the wave length is the proper relation of the speaking length of tube of the compound, reed and pipe. It must be noted that in his investigations he employed reed pipes which differed materially from those used in the Organ. However closely this law may appear to apply to such a reed instrument as the Oboe of the orchestra, it apparently breaks down when applied to reed pipes of widely different forms and scales. On this subject, Mr. Hermann Smith remarks:—

"The true standard for all instruments of the propulsive class is to be regarded as modified in accordance with varying diameters; all larger diameters according to their degree of divergence demanding length to be increased, and also allowance to be made for greater or less amount of wind and for greater or less degree of pressure, for amount and degree are practically convertible in effect, the one often doing duty for the other. The organ TRUMPET is to be estimated on these lines, and not on those applicable to DIAPASONS and other pipes: hence its apparent relation to those in length is deceptive. It is the enlarged diameter that causes it to approach the open pipe length. The main impulse of the current passes into the cone of air in a central course; and thus in a wide pipe, as compared with its course in a narrow pipe, the current has exchanged the friction upon the sides for the lesser friction of air upon air. It is still restricted, but less so, as the cone expands,—

* Poggendorff's Annalen. Bd. XCII.

as of a swift river escaping the confinement of banks, flooding the full expanding delta with a distinct central stream, yet agitating its waters with gradually decreasing strength, and then becoming diffused in the surrounding ocean."

It is quite evident that both the dimensions and forms of the tubes or resonators have a strong modifying influence on the sounds produced by the associated reeds, imparting marked varieties of tonal-coloring and distinctive *timbres* to the resultant tones; but exactly in what manner, or by what peculiar modes of vibration of the air-columns in the resonators, the different tones are produced remain a mystery to the most painstaking investigators. In no form of reed pipe which has definite proportions can two tones of an equally good and perfect character be produced from differently formed or proportioned reeds. This fact seems to clearly point to some definite relationship existing between the vibrations natural to the tongue of the reed, under a special wind supply, and the vibrations proper to the air-column contained within the resonator. It may be safely accepted that the resonator exercises an all-important influence in establishing the *timbre* and correct intonation of the pipe. The best tonal result is obtained when the natural vibration of the tongue synchronizes in some distinctive or special manner with the period of vibration strictly belonging to the air-column in the resonator. As the various forms of resonators, used for the production of the several *timbres* or qualities of tone, are described and illustrated in our Chapter on Reed Pipes: and Their Modes of Construction, it is unnecessary to go into that branch of our subject here. We are certainly not prepared to treat it from a purely acoustical stand-point.

CHAPTER X.

THE TONAL STRUCTURE OF THE ORGAN.

MUCH of the unsatisfactory character of the majority of modern Organs may safely be attributed to imperfections or shortcomings in their Tonal Structure. This is the conclusion arrived at after careful study of a great number of representative instruments constructed by European and American builders; and the conviction is, accordingly, forced upon us that the true acoustical laws directly bearing on the tonal structure of the Organ are either generally misunderstood or insufficiently worked upon by organ builders. It is not too much to say that it is hopeless to expect an Organ to be entirely satisfactory unless the laws which govern the production of refined compound musical sounds are fully recognized and carefully followed in the development of its tonal structure. To direct the reader's attention to these laws, so far, at least, as they have a direct bearing on the stop appointment of the Organ, is the purpose of the present Chapter.

Our attention was first directed to the acoustical problem connected with organ-building about a third of a century ago by the great French organ builder, M. Cavaillé-Coll. This master of the subject entertained us in his studio, in Paris, with a long and interesting disquisition, illustrated by a very ingenious piece of apparatus, by means of which the several acoustical effects produced by organ pipes were made evident, in a striking manner, to the ear. Since then we have fully investigated the problem, satisfying our mind on the great importance of its proper recognition and its artistic solution in practical organ-building.

It is not universally known that all the stops, or ranks of pipes, higher in pitch than the prime or fundamental tones of the instrument, are introduced in the Organ in strict accordance with the natural laws of sound; and that the octave, and all the higher mutation tones are introduced, with the view of substantiating or corroborating similar tones naturally present, but in an undesirably weak condition, in the prime tones of the foundation unison stops, and of building up a complete harmonic structure, pregnant with tonal vitality and brilliancy. Such, however, is the case.

It is not proposed in this treatise to go into a lengthy scientific dissertation on the subject just introduced; but enough must be said to make its particular bearings clear to the reader.

It has long been known to certain physicists and special investigators that the ear, in attentively listening to the sounds produced by stringed and other musical instruments, realizes the presence of tones higher in pitch than those which are known as the fundamental or prime tones; and that it is owing to the perfect proportion and combination of these over-tones with the prime tones that the resultant compound sounds of the musical instruments are rich and beautiful to our sense of hearing. Theoretically the series of over-tones has a great, if not a limitless, upward range; but practically, it is bounded by the very circumscribed powers of the human ear. The over-tones forming this series are known as *harmonics*, *harmonic upper partial tones*, *upper partials*, or *over-tones* of the prime tone. The prime tone is designated, in addition to the simple term *prime*, the *fundamental tone*, the *ground tone*, and the *prime partial tone.* The prime tone is the lowest and most powerful and assertive of all the partial tones, and by it we judge the pitch of the whole compound tone. The term *compound tone* is used to designate the musical tone compounded of the predominant prime partial and all the upper partial tones it embraces. The upper partials bear a definite relationship to the prime tone; and this relationship is invariably the same in the compound tones produced by musical instruments. The complete series of upper partials is, however, not invariably present in such compound tones; their presence or absence, as well as their relative degrees of strength or assertiveness, determining the quality or *timbre* of the compound tones of which they are constituents. These are important facts in musical acoustics which should never be lost sight of by the artist in tone-production. Before proceeding farther it is desirable to lay before the reader particulars respecting the upper partial tones necessary to be recognized by the organ builder in the tonal structure of the Organ.

The *First Upper Partial Tone* is that generated by twice the number of vibrations required to produce the prime or fundamental tone. Thus, if the prime tone is CC, yielded by an open pipe of say 8 feet speaking length, which, for the sake of argument, may be accepted as having 64 vibrations per second, the first upper partial is C, the prime tone yielded by an open pipe of say 4 feet speaking length, having 128 vibrations per second. Accordingly, in the tonal structure of the Organ, in which the OPEN DIAPASON, 8 FT., represents the prime tone, the OCTAVE, 4 FT., represents the first upper partial tone.

The *Second Upper Partial Tone* is that generated by three times the number of vibrations required to produce the prime tone. Thus, if the prime tone is CC, of 64 vibrations, as above set forth, the second upper partial is G, the prime tone yielded by an open pipe of say 2⅔ feet speaking length, having 192 vibrations per second. This upper partial is represented in the tonal structure of the Organ by the TWELFTH or OCTAVE QUINT.

The *Third Upper Partial Tone* is that generated by four times the number of vibrations required to produce the prime tone. Accordingly, if the prime tone is CC, of 64 vibrations per second, the third upper partial is c^1, the prime tone yielded by an open pipe of say 2 feet speaking length, having 256 vibrations per second. In the tonal structure of the Organ this upper partial is represented by the FIFTEENTH or SUPER-OCTAVE.

The *Fourth Upper Partial Tone* is that generated by five times the number of vibrations required to produce the prime tone. Thus, if the prime tone is CC, of 64 vibrations per second, the fourth upper partial is e^1, yielded by an open pipe of say 1⅗ feet speaking length, having 320 vibrations per second. This upper partial is represented in the tonal structure of the Organ by the SEVENTEENTH or TIERCE.

The *Fifth Upper Partial Tone* is that generated by six times the number of vibrations required to produce the prime tone. Accordingly, if the prime tone is CC, of 64 vibrations, the fifth upper partial is g^1, yielded by an open pipe of say 1⅓ feet speaking length, having 384 vibrations per second. The fifth upper partial is represented in the tonal structure of the Organ by the NINETEENTH or LARIGOT.

The *Sixth Upper Partial Tone* is that generated by seven times the number of vibrations required to produce the prime tone. Thus, if the prime tone is CC, of 64 vibrations per second, the sixth upper partial tone, lying between $a\sharp^1$ and $b\flat^1$ of the physical scale, is yielded by an open pipe of say 1⅐ feet speaking length, having 448 vibrations per second. In the tonal structure of the Organ this upper partial is represented by the SEPTIÈME.

The *Seventh Upper Partial Tone* is that generated by eight times the number of vibrations required to produce the prime tone. Accordingly, if the prime tone is CC, of 64 vibrations, the seventh upper partial tone is c^2, yielded by an open pipe of say 1 foot speaking length, having 512 vibrations per second. This partial tone is represented in the tonal structure of the Organ by the TWENTY-SECOND or OCTAVE FIFTEENTH.

The *Eighth Upper Partial Tone*, generated by nine times the number of vibrations required to produce the prime tone, is not recognized practically in the tonal structure of the Organ.

The *Ninth Upper Partial Tone* is that generated by ten times the number of vibrations required to produce the prime tone. Thus, if the prime tone is CC, of 64 vibrations, the ninth upper partial tone is e^2, yielded by an open pipe of say ⅘ foot speaking length, having 640 vibrations per second. This upper partial is represented in the tonal structure of the Organ by the TWENTY-FOURTH or OCTAVE TIERCE.

The *Tenth Upper Partial Tone*, generated by eleven times the number of vibrations required to produce the prime tone, and lying between f^2 and $f\sharp^2$ of the physical scale, is not recognized in the tonal structure of the Organ.

The *Eleventh Upper Partial Tone* is that generated by twelve times the number of vibrations required to produce the prime tone. Accordingly, if the prime tone is CC, of 64 vibrations, the eleventh upper partial tone is g^2, yielded by an open pipe of say ⅔ foot speaking length, having 768 vibrations per second. In the tonal structure of the Organ this upper partial tone is represented by the TWENTY-SIXTH or OCTAVE LARIGOT.

The *Twelfth*, *Thirteenth*, and *Fourteenth Upper Partial Tones*, which lie close together from between a♭² and a² to b² of the physical scale, are never recognized in the tonal structure of the Organ.

The *Fifteenth Upper Partial Tone* is that generated by sixteen times the number of vibrations required to produce the prime tone. Thus, if the prime tone is CC, of 64 vibrations, the fifteenth upper partial tone is c³, yielded by an open pipe of say ½ foot speaking length, having 1024 vibrations per second. In the tonal structure of the Organ this upper partial tone is represented by the TWENTY-NINTH.

The *Nineteenth Upper Partial Tone* is that generated by twenty times the number of vibrations required to produce the prime tone. Accordingly, if the prime tone is CC, of 64 vibrations, the nineteenth upper partial tone is e³, yielded by an open pipe of say 4/10 foot speaking length, having 1280 vibrations per second. This high upper partial is represented in the tonal structure of the Organ by the THIRTY-FIRST.

The *Twenty-third Upper Partial Tone* is that generated by twenty-four times the number of vibrations required to produce the prime tone. Thus, if the prime tone is CC, of 64 vibrations, the nineteenth upper partial tone is g³, yielded by an open pipe of say ⅓ foot speaking length, having 1536 vibrations per second. This high upper partial is represented in the tonal structure of the Organ by the THIRTY-THIRD.

The *Thirty-first Upper Partial Tone* is that generated by thirty-two times the number of vibrations required to produce the prime tone. Accordingly, if the prime tone is CC, of 64 vibrations, the thirty-first upper partial tone is c⁴, yielded by an open pipe of say ¼ foot speaking length, having 2048 vibrations per second. This is the highest upper partial tone introduced in the tonal structure of the Organ, being represented by the THIRTY-SIXTH.

Now, although scientific investigation and the careful analysis of compound musical sounds assure us that all the harmonic over-tones above enumerated are present, and, indeed, still higher ones, in the tones produced by the vibrating strings of the orchestral bowed instruments, and in the sounds of certain other musical instruments and the human voice, so far as the Organ is concerned, only those harmonic upper partials or over-tones are favored which form strictly harmonious intervals. The introduction of the sixth upper partial tone—the SEPTIÈME—being the only one which, so far, has formed an exception to this generally recognized rule. The following Table, showing all the harmonious upper partial tones belonging to the 32 ft., the 16 ft., and the 8 ft. harmonic series which have been found available in the tonal structure of the Organ, will be found useful for ready reference. The column of vibrations is in accordance with the French physical scale, but is here given in double vibrations, instead of single vibrations as adopted by the French acousticians.

TABLE SHOWING THE NOTES AND VIBRATIONAL NUMBERS OF THE UPPER PARTIAL TONES AVAILABLE IN THE TONAL STRUCTURE OF THE ORGAN, IN THE 32 FT., 16 FT., AND 8 FT. HARMONIC SERIES.

NAMES OF NOTES	NUMBER OF VIBRATIONS	32 FEET HARMONIC SERIES	16 FEET HARMONIC SERIES	8 FEET HARMONIC SERIES	INTERVALS OF 8 FT. SERIES
CCCC [32 FT.]	16 *d. v.*	PRIME TONE.			
DDDD . .	18	—			
EEEE . .	20	—			
FFFF . .	21·33	—			
GGGG . .	24	—			
AAAA . .	26·66	—			
BBBB . .	30	—			
CCC [16 FT.]	32	1st Upper partial	PRIME TONE.		
DDD . . .	36	—	—		
EEE . . .	40	—	—		
FFF . . .	42·66	—	—		
GGG . . .	48	2nd Upper partial	—		
AAA . . .	53·33	—	—		
BBB . .	60	—	—		
CC [8 FT.]	64	3rd Upper partial	1st Upper partial	PRIME TONE.	1
DD . . .	72	—	—	—	2
EE . . .	80	4th Upper partial	—	—	3
FF . . .	85·33	—	—	—	4
GG . . .	96	5th Upper partial	2nd Upper partial	—	5
AA . . .	106·66	—	—	—	6
BB . . .	120	{ 6th SEPTIÈME 112 vibrations } —	—	—	7
C . [4 FT.]	128	7th Upper partial	3rd Upper partial	1st Upper partial	8
D	144	—	—	—	9
E	160	9th Upper partial	4th Upper partial	—	10

NAMES OF NOTES	NUMBER OF VIBRATIONS	32 FEET HARMONIC SERIES	16 FEET HARMONIC SERIES	8 FEET HARMONIC SERIES	INTERVALS OF 8 FT. SERIES
F	170·66	—	—	—	11
G	192	11th Upper partial	5th Upper partial	2nd Upper partial	12
A	213·33	—	— 6th SEPTIÈME 224 vibrations	—	13
B	240	—	—	—	14
c^1 . [2 FT.]	256	15th Upper partial	7th Upper partial	3rd Upper partial	15
d^1	288	—	—	—	16
e^1	320	19th Upper partial	9th Upper partial	4th Upper partial	17
f^1	341·33	—	—	—	18
g^1	384	23rd Upper partial	11th Upper partial	5th Upper partial	19
a^1	426·66	—	—	— 6th SEPTIÈME 448 vibrations	20
b^1	480	—	—	—	21
c^2 . [1 FT.]	512	31st Upper partial	15th Upper partial	7th Upper partial	22
d^2	576	—	—	—	23
e^2	640	—	19th Upper partial	9th Upper partial	24
f^2	682·66	—	—	—	25
g^2	768	—	23rd Upper partial	11th Upper partial	26
a^2	853·33	—	—	—	27
b^2	960	—	—	—	28
c^3 . [½ FT.]	1024	—	31st Upper partial	15th Upper partial	29
d^3	1152	—	—	—	30
e^3	1280	—	—	19th Upper partial	31
f^3	1365·33	—	—	—	32
g^3	1536	—	—	23rd Upper partial	33
a^3	1706·33	—	—	—	34
b^3	1920	—	—	—	35
c^4 . [¼ FT.]	2048	—	—	31st Upper partial	36

It is not possible to imitate or to reproduce artificially the wonderful natural structure of a rich compound musical tone, any more than it is possible to depict the wondrous glory of color in the western sky at sunset. Art has, in both directions, defined and very narrow limits. To produce artificially, in some way approaching completeness, the natural harmonic structure of a compound tone, such as that which accompanies the sweep of the bow on an open string of the Violoncello, we should have to graduate to a scientific nicety each and every upper partial artificially introduced. In proof of this, a very beautiful and instructive experiment can be performed with a harmonic series of tuning-forks, mounted on resonant cases in the usual way. The forks must, of course, be absolutely just, each one having its exact relative number of vibrations in a second of time, and be so placed as to exert an equal action on the ear. We arrange the forks, fourteen in all,—yielding the prime and the upper partial tones above enumerated,—in the natural order on a table. Now, with a well-resined bow we set the thirteen forks which represent the upper partial tones into vibration, commencing at the highest in tone and deliberately descending to the fork yielding the first upper partial tone. Allowing a few seconds to elapse, so that the harmonic series of tones may become sensibly subdued, then, with a vigorous sweep of the bow, we set the prime fork in vibration. The result is a little short of marvelous. All the upper partial tones, which previously struck the ear with an impression of an incomplete and restless tonality, are instantly absorbed in the predominating prime or fundamental tone, producing a rich volume of sound, to which one could listen for a long time without fatigue, and, indeed, with increasing satisfaction. The perfect success of this experiment depends on the proper gradation of strength in all the upper partial tones; for all the harmonic tones naturally produced by the vibrations of stretched strings and certain other sonorous bodies *decrease in strength as they rise in pitch*, and that in a very marked manner. It is with the view of approximating this natural gradation of tone that the forks are deliberately set sounding from the highest downward, and the prime fork last of all.*

Organ builders who desire to become tonal artists and scientific masters in their calling will do well to take the lesson taught by this instructive experiment very seriously to heart. At the present time the teaching of natural laws appears to be either misunderstood or totally disregarded so far as the tonal structure of the Organ is concerned. Organ builders are content to jog on, year after year, in traditional and well-worn grooves, formed at a time when many important musical instruments now used were in their infancy; and they more or less blindly follow methods, which have at least antiquity to recommend them, without investigating the causes of their original adoption, or questioning their scientific correctness or artistic value.

Organ builders are aware that the stop appointment of the Organ is based on some acoustical phenomena or principles, but exactly what they are and to what extent they have to be recognized in organ-building they seem, so far as our

*We first witnessed this beautiful experiment performed by Dr. Kœnig, of Paris, the celebrated acoustician and manufacturer of acoustical apparatus, while we were in Paris studying M. Cavaillé-Coll's system of organ-building.

experience extends, to have a very hazy notion. Such being the case, we may reasonably conclude that much of the unsatisfactory character of modern Organs as musical instruments—not as mechanical achievements—is attributable to this neglect of the teaching of acoustical phenomena.

As has already been remarked, practical application of the harmonic series of upper partial tones in the tonal structure of the Organ, however successful it may have been up to a certain point, has not favored the introduction of several members of that series. There are serious impediments to the successful introduction of such upper partial tones as the eighth, tenth, twelfth, thirteenth, and fourteenth. The chief difficulties lie in our imperfect method of tuning, the practical impossibility of keeping delicate pipes in perfect accord, and in making pipes of an intonation sufficiently soft. It must not be overlooked, in considering these and other difficulties, that each pipe, introduced with the view of corroborating or enforcing the upper partial tones of the pipe yielding the fundamental tone, produces its own series of upper partials, tending to create confusion out of what should be simplicity. In this direction it is but right to remark that tuning-forks do not run parallel with organ pipes. The vibration of tuning-forks is a simple pendular one, producing tones in which the lower and more important upper partials have no perceptible existence. The reverse is the case with a certain class of organ pipes, which resemble, to a limited extent, bowed strings in the production of compound tones. The following remarks by the late Professor Helmholtz may not be uninteresting here:—

"It is well known that the union of several simple tones into one compound tone, which is naturally effected in the tones produced by most musical instruments, is artificially imitated on the Organ by peculiar mechanical contrivances. The tones of organ pipes are comparatively poor in upper partials. When it is desirable to use a stop of incisive penetrating quality of tone and great power, the wide pipes (*Principal-register* and *Weitgedackt*) are not sufficient; their tone is too soft, too defective in upper partials; and the narrow pipes (*Geigen-register* and *Quintaten*) are also unsuitable, because, although more incisive, their tone is weak. For such occasions, then, as in accompanying congregational singing, recourse is had to the *compound stops*. In these stops every key is connected with a larger or smaller series of pipes, which it opens simultaneously, and which give the prime tone and a certain number of the first upper partials of the compound tone of the note in question. It is very usual to connect the upper Octave with the prime tone, and after that the Twelfth. The more complex compounds (*cornet*) give the first six partial tones, that is, in addition to the two Octaves of the prime tone and its Twelfth, the higher major Third and the Octave of the Twelfth. This is as much of the series of upper partials as belongs to the tones of a major chord. But to prevent these compound stops from being insupportably noisy, it is necessary to reinforce the deeper tones of each note by other rows of pipes, for in all natural tones which are suited for musical purposes the higher partials decrease in force as they rise in pitch. This has to be regarded in their imitation by compound stops. These compound stops were a monster in the path of the old musical theory, which was acquainted only with the prime tones of compounds; but the practice of organ builders and organists necessitated their retention, and when they are suitably arranged and properly applied, they form a very effective musical apparatus. The nature of the case at the same time fully justifies their use. The musician is bound to regard the tones of all musical instruments as compounded in the same way as the compound stops of organs.

"We have thus been led to an appreciation of upper partial tones, which, as it differs considerably from that previously entertained by musicians, and even physicists, must meet with considerable opposition. The upper partial tones were indeed known, but almost only in such compound tones as those of strings, where there was a favorable opportunity for observing them; but they appear in previous physical and musical works as an isolated accidental phenomenon of small intensity, a kind of curiosity, which was certainly occasionally adduced, in order to give some support to the opinion that nature had prefigured the construction of our major chord, but which on the whole remained almost entirely disregarded. In opposition to this we have to assert, and we shall prove the assertion, that upper partial tones are, with a few exceptions, a general constituent of all musical tones, and that a certain stock of upper partials is an essential condition for a good musical quality of tone. Finally, these upper partials have been erroneously considered as weak, because they are difficult to observe, while, in point of fact, for some of the best musical qualities of tone, the loudness of the first upper partials is not far inferior to that of the prime tone itself. There is no difficulty in verifying this last fact by experiments on the tones of strings. Strike the string of a piano or monochord, and immediately touch one of its nodes for an instant with the finger; the constituent partial tones having this node will remain with unaltered loudness, and the rest will disappear. We might just as well touch the node at the instant of striking, and thus obtain the corresponding constituent partial tones from the first, in place of the complete compound tone of the note. In both ways we can readily convince ourselves that the first upper partials, as the Octave and Twelfth, are by no means weak and difficult to hear, but have a very appreciable strength."

As the lengths of properly-scaled organ pipes, yielding the harmonic upper partial tones, may be accepted as bearing the same proportions to the length of the pipe yielding the prime tone, as the divisions of a vibrating string, yielding the same series of upper partials, do to the full length of the vibrating string, the following table giving all particulars may be useful for reference :—

DIVISIONS OF STRING YIELDING PARTIAL TONES.	NOTATION OF THE PARTIAL TONES.		THEORETICAL LENGTHS OF OPEN ORGAN PIPES.		NUMBER OF DOUBLE VIBRATIONS PER SECOND.
Full length		Prime tone.	8 feet	—	64
$\frac{1}{2}$ length		1st Upper partial.	4 "	—	128
$\frac{1}{3}$ "		2nd Upper partial.	$2\frac{2}{3}$ "	—	192
$\frac{1}{4}$ "		3rd Upper partial.	2 "	—	256
$\frac{1}{5}$ "		4th Upper partial.	$1\frac{3}{5}$ "	—	320
$\frac{1}{6}$ "		5th Upper partial.	$1\frac{1}{3}$ "	—	384

DIVISIONS OF STRING YIELDING PARTIAL TONES.	NOTATION OF THE PARTIAL TONES.	THEORETICAL LENGTHS OF OPEN ORGAN PIPES.		NUMBER OF DOUBLE VIBRATIONS PER SECOND.
$\frac{1}{7}$ length. Between	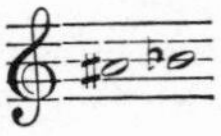 6th Upper partial.	$1\frac{1}{7}$ feet	—	448
$\frac{1}{8}$ "	 7th Upper partial.	1 "	—	512
$\frac{1}{10}$ "	 9th Upper partial.	$\frac{4}{5}$ "	—	640
$\frac{1}{12}$ "	 11th Upper partial.	$\frac{2}{3}$ "	—	768
$\frac{1}{16}$ "	 15th Upper partial.	$\frac{1}{2}$ "	—	1024

The careful investigation of the compound tones produced by the best of our modern musical instruments proves that the richest qualities of tone are those in which the first and second upper partials of the compound are powerful, the third and fourth of moderate strength, and all the higher partials comparatively weak and markedly diminishing in assertiveness as they rise in pitch.

Now, the pertinent question arises: What do these facts teach us, so far as the tonal structure of the Organ is concerned? Surely, that if we desire to secure a thoroughly satisfactory compound tone in what may be considered the Organ proper, we must carefully follow this natural order of things.

In the first place, the prime tone, represented in the tonal structure of the Organ by the normal OPEN DIAPASON, 8 FT., must be of sufficient volume and power to dominate and absorb within its own nature all the harmonic tones which are to be added to it. That is to say, however great a degree of brilliancy, or harmonic complexity and richness of coloring, may be imparted to it by the addition of numerous higher tones, its true prime pitch must not be disturbed. There must be no screaming quality, no flutter of acute tones as if they were endeavoring to drag the prime tone upward in pitch; on the contrary, the prime tone must be more firmly established and more satisfactory to the musical ear with the entire harmonic structure added than when heard without it. This most desirable result can only be attained by the accurate proportionment of all the upper partial tones to the prime.

The first upper partial tone, commonly furnished by the OCTAVE, or so-called PRINCIPAL, 4 FT., must be distinctly secondary in power to the prime tone, and of a sympathetic or mixing quality. Speaking in a general way, and in the full knowledge that circumstances alter cases, if we accept the strength of the prime tone to be equal to 100, we may accept the proportionate value of the first upper partial tone as 70. The effect produced by sounding a single note of the OPEN DIAPA-

SON and the OCTAVE, 4 FT., combined, must be distinctly different from that produced by the same note and its octave on the OPEN DIAPASON alone. This marked difference of tonal effect will not, under proper conditions, be due only to the different strengths of the tones of the two octaves; but to the fact that the independent OCTAVE correctly corroborates the first upper partial tone of the DIAPASON prime, and that it loses its individuality in that prime tone, enriching, without affecting, its pitch.

The second upper partial tone represented by the TWELFTH, 2⅔ FT., must be softer and lighter than the first upper partial; otherwise a disturbing and *timbre-creating* effect will be apparent. A perceptible difference will, however, be sufficient to secure tonal homogeneity and a rich musical coloring. Still accepting the value of the prime tone as 100, the second upper partial may have the proportionate value of 60. This and the first upper partial tone are the two most prominent harmonic over-tones commonly observed in the compound sounds produced by bowed strings and the small-scaled organ pipes of the VIOL family. Accordingly, such harmonics call for a more decided reinforcement or corroboration than any of those which are higher in pitch.

The third upper partial tone ranks next in importance; but should, in the tonal structure of the Organ, where it is represented by the SUPER-OCTAVE or FIFTEENTH, 2 FT., be considerably softer and less assertive in its tonality than the preceding upper partial. Its proportionate value may be accepted as 50, or just one-half the strength of the fundamental or prime tone. This and the two preceding upper partial tones may be correctly classified as harmonics of the first order.

The fourth upper partial tone, represented by the TIERCE or SEVENTEENTH, 1⅗ FT., must be decidedly weaker than the third upper partial; its proportionate value being about 40. When the TIERCE is inserted of too great a strength of tone it produces a somewhat harsh effect, giving to the harmonic a false or unnatural relation to the prime tone, rather than simply corroborating it and imparting a fulness to the compound tone. The TIERCE is by no means a common stop in modern Organs, having fallen into disrepute through the unscientific way in which it was almost universally inserted in the old instruments. But we unhesitatingly affirm that the tonal structure of the Organ lacks a very important constituent when the fourth upper partial remains uncorroborated.

The fifth upper partial tone, represented by the NINETEENTH or LARIGOT, 1⅓ FT., must be slightly softer than the fourth; its proportionate value in relation to the prime tone may be accepted as 35. This is also a somewhat uncommon stop in a complete and separate form, although, like all the following more acute harmonic-corroborating ranks, it frequently appears in the composition of MIXTURES or compound stops.

The sixth upper partial tone, which, in the complete tonal structure of the Organ, is furnished by the SEPTIÈME, 1⅐ FT., requires to be most skilfully proportioned in strength of intonation. This is essential from the fact that it is the first dissonant interval in the harmonic series—the so-called "sub-minor seventh." This stop has seldom been introduced by organ builders, doubtless on account of the difficulties which beset its scientific adjustment.

The most noteworthy instances of the introduction of the SEPTIÈME we know of are furnished by the Grand Organ in the Cathedral of Notre-Dame, at Paris, constructed by M. Cavaillé-Coll, in 1868. In this noble instrument the SEPTIÈME is introduced in the 32 feet, 16 feet, and 8 feet harmonic series, being respectively stops of 4 4/7 feet, 2 2/7 feet, and 1 1/7 feet speaking lengths. The same distinguished builder included the SEPTIÈME, also in the three harmonic series mentioned above, in his great project for the Grand Organ for the Basilica of Saint Peter, at Rome. The importance of this harmonic-corroborating stop may readily be acknowledged on the authority of France's most scientific and artistic organ builder.

The sixth upper partial is naturally weak; accordingly, the SEPTIÈME must be of very small scale and delicate intonation. As it corroborates an over-tone of comparatively small importance, it may be omitted except in Organs of the first magnitude in which completeness of tonal structure is aimed at. Its effect in the Notre-Dame Organ is highly satisfactory. The presence of this stop necessitates the introduction, in a complete form, of the stop which corroborates the next higher upper partial tone. The sixth must invariably be covered by the seventh upper partial tone.

The seventh upper partial tone, represented in the tonal structure of the Organ by the TWENTY-SECOND, 1 FT., the most acute stop ever introduced in a complete form,—that is, throughout the entire range of the manual clavier,—must be rather more assertive than the SEPTIÈME, being a perfect consonant of the prime tone. Its proportionate value may be accepted as being about 30. The TWENTY-SECOND, as a distinct and complete stop, appears in a few English, German, Dutch, and French Organs, but its general adoption seems to have met with little favor. Of course it appears in the Organ of Notre-Dame, where its presence is compulsory on account of the SEPTIÈME. In all instruments of any pretension to completeness the TWENTY-SECOND appears, in certain parts of the compass, as a rank in one or more of the MIXTURES.

It will be sufficient for our present purpose to speak of the higher upper partial tones as invariably represented, in a broken manner, in the tonal structure of the Organ by ranks of the compound stops or MIXTURES. The upper partials commonly corroborated by these ranks are the ninth, eleventh, and fifteenth, under the names, respectively, of TWENTY-FOURTH, TWENTY-SIXTH, and TWENTY-NINTH. In rare instances the still higher upper partial tones; namely, the nineteenth, twenty-third, and thirty-first, are corroborated by the ranks known respectively as the THIRTY-FIRST, the THIRTY-THIRD, and THIRTY-SIXTH. Owing to the small size of the pipes required for such high-pitched ranks, it is obvious that they can only be introduced in the bass octave of the manual compass. As a separate Chapter is specially devoted to the consideration of all important questions appertaining to the MIXTURES, it is unnecessary to enlarge here on the subject of the upper partial tones they are intended to corroborate, beyond stating, emphatically, that, in accordance with the natural phenomena of musical sounds, they must be softer than all the preceding upper partial tones, and be relatively softer as they rise in pitch.

From what has already been said in the present Chapter, the reader will have grasped much that is essential to be understood relative to the harmonic structure of the Organ; and the reasons for the introduction, throughout the compass of the instrument, of certain mutation ranks of pipes, which on first impressions might appear to be entirely out of place, and productive of discord rather than that solidity and grandeur of tone which places the Organ at the head of all musical instruments fabricated by man.

A writer on the Organ, speaking of the stops introduced for the purpose of corroborating the natural harmonics, says: "Now if we were to draw all these stops and produce all these sounds, for every note we used on the OPEN DIAPASON, the effect would be simply discord, and utterly unbearable. But it was never intended that artificial harmonics should be so used. Nature has suggested and produced these sounds as subordinate and attendant on their ground tones. And in using a simple DIAPASON stop, Nature has done enough for herself to satisfy our ears. But if, on the other hand, we deepen the tone by adding a 16 ft. and many other 8 ft. stops, 4 ft. tones are wanted to brighten these. And supposing that we have only a number of 8 ft. and 16 ft. stops in use, we have a heavy and almost dull droning. All the natural harmonics are subdued. The waves they are trying to produce are, as it were, conquered by the ground waves of the principal tones, they have no power of penetration and do not reach us, save in a blurred and confused sound, which adds heaviness to the general effect. But if we assist in adding these tones to our others, the effect is almost magical. Then the natural harmonics are reinforced, they find a strong wave sound of their own caliber, produced by the pipe of their own vibrating length, with which to blend; and they all come together to the fore, and are able to fill up Nature's proper intervals, and the result is that we have an effect that would be produced by one grand pipe or string of the loudness and caliber of the combined foundation stops. It would be, of course, impossible to get one pipe as loud as a full organ, and by the combination of many to produce such strength of tone the harmonics get mixed. But combine, also, these too, and the then result is beautiful in the extreme—in fact we have a natural sound with its proper attributes."*

We have quoted the above passage, not because we agree with all the opinions expressed, but because it is a representative resumé of the ideas held by a considerable number of persons who are understood to be lights in the organ-building world. Let us see how far its statements bear analysis.

The remark that if we draw all the harmonic-corroborating stops which strictly belong to the harmonic structure of the normal 8 ft. series, the prime tone of which is represented by the OPEN DIAPASON, the effect of such a thing as a full consonant chord of four notes "would be simply discord, and utterly unbearable," is evidently based on the acceptance of the crude and unscientific adjustment of the harmonic series of stops perpetrated by the inartistic and thoughtless organ builder. But if the stops representing all the upper partial tones have been scaled and voiced in accordance with the teaching of the natural

* "Organs and Organ Building."—C. A. Edwards, p. 150.

laws which affect the relation of harmonic tones to the parent prime, no such effect as discord will result from the sounding of any consonant group of notes. On the contrary, a very brilliant, full, and satisfying compound tone will be the outcome, marred only by the imperfection inherent in equal temperament. We shall speak of the effects produced by the addition of other unison stops later on.

The statement that "in using a simple DIAPASON stop, Nature has done enough for herself to satisfy our ears," is only partially correct. Stops of this species, even in their best form, are naturally deficient in upper partial tones, yielding very few that are appreciable by the unaided ear, and, accordingly, have a decided tendency to become heavy and dull in tone when used alone in harmony, especially in the bass and tenor octaves. The use of two or more unison stops of the same class in combination only increases the evil, and proves the inherent short-comings of the genus. The trained musical ear can never be altogether satisfied with the tone of a simple OPEN DIAPASON: the almost total absence of that quality which makes the compound tones of bowed instruments so rich and gratifying is realized by the ear with a feeling of dissatisfaction. The purer and grander the OPEN DIAPASON is, viewed from the position it should occupy in the tonal structure of the Organ, the less it will satisfy the musical sense when used alone in harmony. A melodic succession of single notes will, on the other hand, be pleasing so far as it goes. Like single tones produced by tuning-forks, the single notes will not strike the ear with any feeling of incompleteness: their near approach to simplicity now becomes an element of beauty. But it is foreign to the true office of the OPEN DIAPASON to be used or considered as a solo stop: to all intents and purposes it is the foundation of the tonal structure of the Organ, incomplete without its appropriate superstructure, just as the foundation of a building is incomplete or valueless without the walls and roof which are destined to give it purpose and the reason for being.

The combination of 16 ft. and 8 ft. stops only, as alluded to in the remarks under review, is altogether out of place in the manual department, simply because the unison pitch (8 feet) is, in the natural order of things, disturbed by the sub-octave pitch, and also by the probable generation of the 16 ft. series of harmonics. The unison tone no longer strikes the ear as the undisputed prime or fundamental tone, but rather as the first upper partial of the new harmonic series—unduly pronounced, of course, and struggling for the mastery over what the ear naturally recognizes as the fundamental tone. The addition of a single properly-proportioned stop of 16 ft. tone to two or more stops of 8 ft. tone and the entire 8 ft. harmonic series which belongs to them, gives gravity and volume to the entire compound tone without impairing its true 8 ft. pitch.

In the foregoing remarks we have briefly treated of the acoustical theory on which the tonal structure of the Organ is based, and have pointed out the only method, in strict accordance with the phenomena of sound, by which a satisfactory compound tone can be given to a series of organ pipes. It now becomes expedient to enter on the consideration of the subject of the present Chapter in a more extended manner. Hitherto, in speaking of the harmonic series of stops, we have confined it to its relation to the fundamental OPEN

DIAPASON, yielding the prime tone. This has been done purposely with the view of impressing the reader with the fact that the harmonic series of stops yielding the upper partial tones of the prime must be schemed with reference to the tonal strength of the *one stop*, producing the prime tone, *which is the foundation of the true organ-tone* in whatever division of the Organ it may be located.

It is a very common impression, shared, as has been shown, by the writer of the remarks above quoted, that the harmonic-corroborating stops of the Organ can and should only be used when something approaching the full organ is drawn in combination. This has evidently been a hard and fast conviction among organ builders for a long period, hence the screaming and unduly-pronounced character of all their harmonic-corroborating stops, simple and compound. We hold a widely different view to this, and unhesitatingly affirm that, while the harmonic-corroborating stops should be proportioned with direct reference to the fundamental unison of the division in which they appear, they should be so far independent of that unison as to be available in combination with one or more of the other unison stops also. Many valuable tonal effects can be obtained by the judicious and artistic combination of such stops, when they are scientifically schemed; while similar combinations of such stops as are commonly met with in Organs of the ordinary class are practically valueless for musical purposes. It must be obvious to every one who gives the subject consideration, that if four or five stops (probably embracing eight or ten ranks of pipes) are placed in any division of an Organ, which can only be properly used when the full division is drawn, their utility is, to say the least of it, undesirably circumscribed; and, accordingly, an absence of variety and flexibility becomes apparent in the tonal structure of the entire division.

It may be asked at this point: If all the harmonic series of stops, yielding the upper partial tones, is calculated from the OPEN DIAPASON alone, and is so scaled and voiced as to be perfectly satisfactory when drawn with that stop only, what is the state of affairs when the same series is employed with the full power or resources of the division of the instrument which contains it? In answering this question it is, perhaps, desirable to recapitulate a little of what has been already said so as to clearly define the point we have now to start from. It has been pointed out that, generally speaking, the tones of organ pipes are somewhat deficient in upper partials, but that there are certain classes of pipes which are richer in upper partial tones than others. Of the pipes that are markedly deficient, the most important are those which yield what may be correctly considered pure organ-tone; that is, tone essentially belonging to, and characteristic of, organ pipes that are strictly unimitative in their tonality. The pipes of the true OPEN DIAPASON furnish the best examples of this class. The pipes which yield tones more or less compound in their nature, that is, enriched by the presence of certain of the upper partials, are those which, in their sounds, approach the tones produced by the stringed and bowed instruments and certain other instruments of the orchestra. These pipes are employed to form all stops of the VIOL, or so-called GAMBA, type, the HARMONIC FLUTES, and the lingual stops. Particulars respecting all these are given elsewhere.

Such being the case, it can be readily realized that the stops which produce sounds deficient in upper partial tones require, for the production of that varied, rich, compound quality which is the glory of the Organ, the addition of other ranks of pipes calculated to reinforce such upper partials as may be present, in too weak a state, in the foundation sounds, and to introduce the higher range of upper partial tones which the unaided ear fails to hear in those foundation sounds: and it must also be obvious that those brighter-voiced stops which produce sounds more or less rich in harmonics do not require, to anything like the same extent as the preceding stops, the assistance of the series of harmonic-corroborating stops. The most important section of the pipe-work—that yielding pure, unimitative, organ-tone—is, therefore, dependent on, while the other sections—yielding tones more or less imitative of certain orchestral instruments—are practically independent of, the stops which introduce artificially the series of upper partial tones.

Now, the section which is dependent on these harmonic-corroborating stops is that yielding, as we have already pointed out, pure organ-tone, represented by the OPEN DIAPASONS of 16 FT. in the Pedal Organ and 8 FT. in the manual divisions, and such other stops as strictly belong to the same family. Accordingly, it is essential that each series of harmonic-corroborating stops should be accurately calculated and adjusted to these all-important stops, without any regard to such solo and imitative stops, of the same pitch as the DIAPASONS, as may be introduced. By such a mode of procedure each complete harmonic series of stops is available with its fundamental DIAPASON, producing along with it a compound tone of a complete and satisfactory character.

We have now to enter upon the consideration of what takes place when further unison stops (8 ft. pitch) are added to the above combination in a manual division. It may not have been observed by the student of organ-building that softly-voiced harmonic-corroborating stops have the singular property of meeting, acoustically, almost any demands made upon them through the addition of what might, theoretically, be considered an overwhelming volume of prime tone; and that there is no necessity for making the harmonic-corroborating series any louder than has been above recommended. Our attention was first directed to these facts about thirty years ago, in observing the conduct of a MIXTURE, of five ranks, in our own Chamber Organ.* This compound stop is of very small scale, and so delicately voiced that it forms a perfectly agreeable combination with a single soft unison stop of the DULCIANA class: while, on the other hand, it is equally satisfactory, as a harmonic-corroborating stop, when used with the entire resources of the division—thirteen speaking stops, nine of which are of eight feet pitch. The reason for this accommodating property in the harmonic-corroborating series appears to be that its artificial harmonic tones unite with many upper partial tones which are present, naturally, in the compound sounds of several of the unison stops; and that the ear recognizes this, and realizes a corre-

* Mr. Clarence Eddy, the distinguished organist, writing of this Organ, in 1889, says: "Mention must certainly be made of the extraordinary five-rank MIXTURE, which is quite after my own heart in its delicacy of voicing."

sponding increase in the volume of harmonic upper partials sufficient to satisfy its musical sense. Under such favorable conditions the compound tones become full and rich, but entirely devoid of that screaming and ear-splitting character which has unfortunately marred the full effects of so many otherwise satisfactory Organs. We are aware that this ear-splitting character of tone has had, and probably still has, its advocates and admirers; but we venture to think that to the refined and cultivated musical ear it must be about as agreeable as the sound of breaking glass. It may have, what its advocates have claimed for it, a value in dominating, and accordingly leading, a number of mixed voices, but *per se* it is neither musical nor agreeable. Much of the appreciation extended to this exaggerated tonality is due, we feel convinced, to a vitiated taste—a taste essentially different from that which experiences its greatest delight in the marvelous compound tones of the string quartet or vocal quartet, in which the most perfect relations exist between the prime and upper partial tones.

It is not now unusual to find Organs from which all harmonic-corroborating stops higher in pitch than the Octave have been omitted; and in some cases the full effects of such Organs are far from being unsatisfactory. This is caused by the liberal and judicious introduction of certain unison stops whose voices are naturally rich, up to a certain point, in upper partial tones; and also by the firm corroboration of the first and most important upper partial by the Octave stop or stops. This observation goes far to prove that the introduction of *powerful* harmonic-corroborating stops of high pitch are not absolutely necessary for the production of a satisfactory compound organ-tone; but, on the contrary, that only slight aid is required from the corroborating stops to introduce the substantiating effect which gives life to all the timid harmonics which Nature provides in the sounds of organ pipes. It must never be forgotten that when loud, screaming harmonic-corroborating stops are used, we subject the natural laws of sound to little short of a gross outrage, and our ears suffer the penalty of our musical philistinism. It should also be borne in mind that we cannot err if we humbly follow the teaching of Nature in her immutable laws of sound.

We have just alluded to Organs, of course small in size, in the tonal structure of which unison and octave-sounding stops are alone used; and it now becomes expedient to enlarge somewhat on the rôle played by the Octave in the acoustics of the Organ. It may be accepted as having three important offices in the tonal structure of the instrument. First, it introduces the most necessary upper partial tone of the prime organ-tone. Secondly, it corroborates the same upper partial which exists, in a weak condition, in the compound tones of certain unison stops. Thirdly, it very decidedly augments and enriches, by the production of the *differential tone*, the prime tone with which it is associated. Of the first and second offices we have already spoken to some length; of the third we have still to speak.

It has long been observed by those engaged in the investigation of the properties of musical sounds, that when two loud tones of different pitches are sounded simultaneously there is heard a combinational tone distinct from both the generating tones. The pitch of this combinational tone is, as a rule, different from that of the generating tones and their upper partials. There is a notable exception, however, to this rule in the combinational tone produced by the simultaneous sounding of a prime tone and its first upper partial or octave.

Sorge discovered that when two tones of different vibrational numbers are sounded together a third is produced, whose vibrational number is exactly the sum of the difference of the vibrational numbers of the two generating tones. This third tone has, accordingly, been appropriately designated the *differential tone* of the two tones which create it. In addition to this differential tone there is another tone generated by the simultaneous and prolonged sounding of two musical tones of different pitches. This combinational tone was first discovered by Helmholtz, and called by him the *summational tone*, because the number of its vibrations is the sum of the vibrations of both the generating tones. With this latter combinational tone we do not profess to have much to do in our present essay; but we are not prepared to say that it is not a somewhat important factor in the tonal structure of a well-balanced Organ. To the differential tones and their obvious influence on the tonal structure of the Organ we have to devote considerable attention.

Let us first investigate the differential tone of two tones which stand in the relationship of a perfect octave to each other. Under these conditions the differential tone has the same vibrational number as the lower of the two generating tones, thus:—

Generating Tones.			Differential Tone.
CC 8 ft.	— C 4 ft.	. . .	CC 8 ft. tone
64	128		64 vibrations

The bearing of this acoustical phenomenon on the tonality of the Organ cannot be disputed; for it must be recognized that the differential tone has an existence outside the generating tone of its own pitch, and that it does not lose itself in that generating tone, but is added to it and proportionately enriches or augments its volume. This fact is proved by analogy. The great value of the Octave stops, in their dual office in the tonal structure of the Organ, is thus made evident.

Helmholtz remarks: "On investigating the combinational tones of two compound musical tones, we find that the primary and upper partial tones may give rise to both differential and summational tones. In such cases the number of combinational tones is very great. But it must be observed that generally the differential are stronger than the summational tones, and that the stronger generating simple tones produce stronger combinational tones. The combinational tones, indeed, increase in a much greater ratio than the generating tones, and diminish also more rapidly. Now since in musical compound tones the prime generally predominates over the partials, the differential tones of the two primes are generally heard more loudly than all the rest, and were consequently first discovered. They are most easily heard when the generating tones are less than an octave apart, because in that case the differential is deeper than either of the two generating tones." *

The most striking proof of this latter fact that can be given, in connection with the tonal structure of the Organ, is the creation of the so-called "acoustic bass," of 32 ft. pitch, by the simultaneous sounding of two pipes of 16 ft. and 10⅔ feet speaking length respectively. It will be found that the differential tone is an octave lower in pitch than the deeper of the two generating tones, thus :—

Generating Tones.			Differential Tone.
CCC 16 ft. — GGG 10⅔ ft.		. . .	CCCC 32 ft. tone
32	48		16 vibrations

Considerable use has been made of this differential tone in the appointment of the pedal department of Organs ; and although the deep bass tone so produced cannot be compared to that yielded by an independent stop of 32 ft. pitch, it is of some value in its power of enriching and adding gravity to the tonality of the Pedal Organ.

In speaking of the differential tone in connection with the manual stops, we pointed out the importance of the Octaves, or stops of 4 ft. pitch : let us now see what good office is fulfilled by those harmonic-corroborating stops which stand at the interval of a perfect fifth apart. At the outset, we find that the two ranks of pipes which corroborate the two most important upper partials of the fundamental unison prime are the Octave and Twelfth, a perfect fifth apart. The differential tone produced in this case is, as in that above given, an octave below the deeper of the two generating tones, and, accordingly, in unison with the prime tone, thus :—

Prime Tone.		Generating Tones.			Differential Tone.
CC 8 ft.	. . .	C 4 ft. — G 2⅔ ft.		. . .	CC 8 ft. tone
64		128	192		64 vibrations

Carrying our investigations just one step farther, we come to the differential tone produced by the simultaneous sounding of the ranks which represent the second and third upper partials of the unison prime ; namely, the Twelfth and Super-octave or Fifteenth. These ranks of pipes stand at the interval of a perfect fourth apart ; and their differential tone is precisely the same as that produced by both the pairs of ranks previously spoken of, and which stand, respectively, at the intervals of a perfect octave and a perfect fifth apart. Accordingly we find the differential tone of the Twelfth and Fifteenth is in unison with the prime tone, thus :—

Prime Tone.		Generating Tones.			Differential Tone.
CC 8 ft.	. . .	G 2⅔ ft.— c[1] 2 ft.		. . .	CC 8 ft. tone
64		192	256		64 vibrations

* "On the Sensations of Tone." London, 1875. p. 230.

It is, perhaps, unnecessary to go much farther with this analysis, interesting as it is from the scientific point of view. Although there is no doubt that the differential tones of all the stops of different pitch exert an influence on the general tonality of the Organ, more or less appreciable to the cultivated ear, those which we have above noted are of the greatest importance from a practical point of view. We have directed attention to the fact that the ranks of pipes which yield the unison or prime tone, and the first, second, and third upper partials of that tone, and which stand toward each other, respectively, in couples, at the intervals of a perfect octave, a perfect fifth, and a perfect fourth, produce differential tones which are all alike so far as their vibrational numbers are concerned, and which go to the improvement of the prime or foundation tone. It only remains for us to direct attention to the fact that the entire series of differential tones, resulting from the simultaneous sounding of any couple of ranks, standing respectively at the intervals of a third, fourth, fifth, octave, twelfth, fifteenth, nineteenth, and twenty-second, either accentuate the foundation tone or one or other of its upper partial tones.

The following table, given for ready reference, explains and summarizes what has been said. The letters following those which indicate the pitch or position of the notes in the musical scale signify: foundation or prime tone [P. T.]; first upper partial [1, U.P.]; second upper partial [2, U.P.]; third upper partial [3, U.P.]; fourth upper partial [4, U.P.]; fifth upper partial [5, U.P.]; sixth upper partial [6, U.P.]; seventh upper partial [7, U.P.].

TABLE OF DIFFERENTIAL TONES GENERATED BY THE PRIME AND UPPER PARTIAL TONES, REPRESENTED BY THE DIAPASON, 8 FEET, AND THE HARMONIC-CORROBORATING STOPS OF THE ORGAN.

Generating Tones.				Differential Tones.
CC [P. T.] 64 vibrations	——	C [1, U. P.] 128 vibrations	. . .	CC [P. T.] 64 vibrations
CC [P. T.] 64 "	——	G [2, U. P.] 192 "	. . .	C [1, U. P.] 128 "
CC [P. T.] 64 "	——	c^1 [3, U. P.] 256 "	. . .	G [2, U. P.] 192 "
CC [P. T.] 64 "	——	e^1 [4, U. P.] 320 "	. . .	c^1 [3, U. P.] 256 "
CC [P. T.] 64 "	——	g^1 [5, U. P.] 384 "	. . .	e^1 [4, U. P.] 320 "
CC [P. T.] 64 "	——	c^2 [7, U. P.] 512 "	. . .	Septième [6, U. P.] 448 "
C [1, U.P.] 128 "	——	G [2, U. P.] 192 "	. . .	CC [P. T.] 64 "
C [1, U.P.] 128 "	——	c^1 [3, U. P.] 256 "	. . .	C [1, U. P.] 128 "

Generating Tones.			Differential Tones.
C [1, U. P.] —	e^1 [4, U. P.]	. . .	G [2, U. P.]
128 vibrations	320 vibrations		192 vibrations
C [1, U. P.] —	g^1 [5, U. P.]	. . .	c^1 [3, U. P.]
128 "	384 "		256 "
C [1, U. P.] —	c^2 [7, U. P.]	. . .	g^1 [5, U. P.]
128 "	512 "		384 "
G [2, U. P.] —	c^1 [3, U. P.]	. . .	CC [P. T.]
192 "	256 "		64 "
G [2, U. P.] —	e^1 [4, U. P.]	. . .	C [1, U. P.]
192 "	320 "		128 "
G [2, U. P.] —	g^1 [5, U. P.]	. . .	G [2, U. P.]
192 "	384 "		192 "
G [2, U. P.] —	c^2 [7, U. P.]	. . .	e^1 [4, U. P.]
192 "	512 "		320 "
c^1 [3, U. P.] —	e^1 [4, U. P.]	. . .	CC [P. T.]
256 "	320 "		64 "
c^1 [3, U. P.] —	g^1 [5, U. P.]	. . .	C [1, U. P.]
256 "	384 "		128 "
c^1 [3, U. P.] —	c^2 [7, U. P.]	. . .	c^1 [3, U. P.]
256 "	512 "		256 "
e^1 [4, U. P.] —	g^1 [5, U. P.]	. . .	CC [P. T.]
320 "	384 "		64 "
e^1 [4, U. P.] —	c^2 [7, U. P.]	. . .	G [2, U. P.
320 "	512 "		192 "
g^1 [5, U. P.] —	c^2 [7, U. P.]	. . .	C [1, U. P.]
384 "	512 "		128 "

In the above table no notice has been taken of the sixth upper partial, represented in the tonal structure of the Organ by the SEPTIÈME, beyond the fact that it appears as the differential tone of the prime and its seventh upper partial (c^2). When the SEPTIÈME is inserted as a stop in the Organ it enters into the general scheme in the same favorable manner as do all the other harmonic-corroborating stops. This will be realized from the subjoined table:

TABLE OF DIFFERENTIAL TONES GENERATED BY THE PRIME AND SEVERAL UPPER PARTIAL TONES AND THE SIXTH UPPER PARTIAL TONE REPRESENTED BY THE SEPTIÈME, $1\frac{1}{7}$ FEET.

Generating Tones.			Differential Tones.
CC [P. T.] ——	[Septième]	. . .	g^1 [5, U. P.]
64 vibrations	448 vibrations		384 vibrations
C [1, U. P.] ——	[Septième]	. . .	e^1 [4, U. P.]
128 "	448 "		320 "
G [2, U. P.] ——	[Septième]	. . .	c^1 [3, U. P.]
192 "	448 "		256 "
c^1 [3, U. P.] ——	[Septième]	. . .	G [2, U. P.]
256 "	448 "		192 "
e^1 [4, U. P.] ——	[Septième)	. . .	C [1, U. P.]
320 "	448 "		128 "
g^1 [5, U. P.] ——	[Septième]	. . .	CC [P. T.]
384 "	448 "		64 "
[Septième] ——	c^2 [7, U. P.]	. . .	CC [P. T.]
448 "	512 "		64 "

It must surely be realized, on a careful consideration of all the foregoing data, that the tonal structure of the Organ is a matter of great importance both in its theoretical and practical aspects; and that it is one the organ builder who desires to become an artist in his calling cannot afford to ignore or even neglect. There can be no doubt, as has already been said, that the short-comings and self-evident crudities in the tonality of too many Organs are due to the ignorance or wilful neglect of the acoustical principles or laws which should govern their stop appointment and all matters relating thereto. M. Cavaillé-Coll was the only organ builder known to us who systematically approached the stop appointment of the Organ from the scientific side; and his tonal schemes, though not invariably perfect, may be studied with great advantage.

In the present Chapter, in giving the vibrational numbers of the different tones, we have used the scale adopted by the French physicists, and in accordance with which the beautiful acoustical apparatus constructed by Dr. Kœnig, of Paris, is adjusted. This physical and untempered scale gives middle c^1 512 single vibrations per second according to the French method of counting the forward motion of a swinging body as one vibration, and the backward as another. English acousticians count the backward and forward motion as a single vibration. We have, accordingly, adopted the latter method, giving middle c^1 256 vibrations per second. The pitch of the scale adopted by the German physicists, at the suggestion of Scheibler, in 1834, gives 440 double vibrations to the note a^1, and to middle c^1 264. This pitch is the one followed by Prof. Helmholtz throughout his work "On the Sensations of Tone." In the following table we give the German physical scale, according to Helmholtz, and the French physical scale, according to Kœnig; to which we add the equally tempered scale, in which a^1 has 440 double or 880 single vibrations, also according to Kœnig.

TABLE OF THE VIBRATIONAL NUMBERS OF THE DIATONIC NOTES OF THE GERMAN AND FRENCH PHYSICAL SCALES; WITH THE EQUALLY TEMPERED SCALE GIVING a[1] 880 SINGLE VIBRATIONS PER SECOND.

NAMES OF NOTES	FRENCH PHYSICAL SCALE—KŒNIG	GERMAN PHYSICAL SCALE—HELMHOLTZ	EQUALLY TEMPERED SCALE—KŒNIG
CCCC [32 FT.]	32 *s. v.*	16·5 *d. v.*	32·703 *s. v.*
DDDD . . .	36	18·562	36·708
EEEE . . .	40	20·62	41·203
FFFF . . .	42·66	22	43·653
GGGG . . .	48	24·75	48·999
AAAA . . .	53·33	27·5	55
BBBB . . .	60	30·937	61·735
CCC [16 FT.]	64	33	65·406
DDD . . .	72	37·125	73·416
EEE . . .	80	41·25	82·406
FFF . . .	85·33	44	87·307
GGG . . .	96	49·5	97·998
AAA . . .	106·66	55	110
BBB	120	61·875	123·470
CC . [8 FT.]	128	66	130·812
DD	144	74·25	146·832
EE	160	82·5	164·813
FF	170·66	88	174·614
GG	192	99	195·997
AA	213·33	110	220
BB	240	123·75	246·941
C . [4 FT.]	256	132	261·625
D	288	148·5	293·664
E	320	165	329·627
F	341·33	176	349·228
G	384	198	391·995
A	426·66	220	440
B	480	247·5	493·883
c^1 . [2 FT.]	512	264	523·251
d^1	576	297	587·329
e^1	640	330	659·255
f^1	682·66	352	698·457
g^1	768	396	783·991
a^1	853·33	440	880
b^1	960	495	987·767
c^2 . [1 FT.]	1024	528	1046·502
d^2	1152	594	1174·658

NAMES OF NOTES	FRENCH PHYSICAL SCALE—KŒNIG	GERMAN PHYSICAL SCALE—HELMHOLTZ	EQUALLY TEMPERED SCALE—KŒNIG
e^2	1280 *s. v.*	660 *d. v.*	1318·510 *s. v.*
f^2	1365·33	704	1396·913
g^2	1536	792	1567·982
a^2	1706·66	880	1760
b^2	1920	990	1975·534
c^3 . [½ FT.]	2048	1056	2093·005
d^3	2304	1188	2349·316
e^3	2560	1320	2637·020
f^3	2730·66	1408	2793·826
g^3	3072	1584	3135·964
a^3	3413·33	1760	3520
b^3	3840	1980	3951·068
c^4 . [¼ FT.]	4096	2112	4186·010
d^4	4608	2376	4698·632
e^4	5120	2640	5274·040
f^4	5461·33	2816	5587·652
g^4	6144	3168	6271·928
a^4	6826·66	3520	7040
b^4	7680	3960	7902·136
c^5	8192	4224	8372·020

Before concluding the present brief dissertation, a few words may appropriately be said on the limits of the human ear with reference to musical sounds. It is somewhat difficult to determine the point, in the downward range, at which the musical character of sounds may be said to cease. Helmholtz, whose accuracy of observation, so far as the phenomena of sound is concerned, can hardly be called in question, places the point about the lowest note of the four-stringed Double Bass of the orchestra; namely, EEE of 41·25 vibrations per second. He remarks that the musical character of all tones below this note "is imperfect, because we are here near the limit of the power of the ear to combine vibrations into musical tones. These lower tones cannot therefore be used musically except in connection with their higher octaves, to which they impart a character of greater depth without rendering the conception of the pitch indeterminate." The common impression, among persons interested in organ matters, is that musical sounds of determinate character descend to the 32 ft. note,—CCCC of 16·5 vibrations per second,—and some go so far, in direct opposition to known facts, as to believe that certain notes in the 64 ft. octave can be appreciated by the ear as musical sounds. It is difficult to understand on what grounds, theoretical or practical, such a monster as the 64 ft. reed stop in the pedal department of the Organ in the Centennial Hall, Sydney, was ever constructed: it is in its lower octave as devoid of musical tone as the rattling of a Venetian shutter.

That the sound yielded by an open pipe of 32 ft. speaking length can be heard as a low rumbling we freely admit; but that it has *per se* a determinate musical character we unhesitatingly deny, and we are supported in this firm opinion by all the weight of Helmholtz's investigations.* We have no intention of advocating, on these grounds, the disuse of the 32 ft. octave in the Organ, but we must impress upon all interested in the science and art of organ-building the absolute necessity of associating with the DOUBLE OPEN DIAPASON, 32 FT., a fairly complete harmonic series, so that its grave sounds may be helped and enriched. But, in the name of science and common sense, let there be no groping amidst the sound tombs of the 64 ft. Octave, where nothing more musical can be heard than the rhythmical rattling of the bones of skeletons. There is quite enough to be done, in more fertile fields, to improve the tonal structure of the Organ, to render it advisable to neglect the production therein of unmusical noise.

The ear can appreciate sounds very much higher in pitch than any producible by organ pipes. Despretz has asserted that he has heard the sound of d^8 of 38016 vibrations in a second. This extremely high sound he produced from a tuning-fork excited by a violin bow. Helmholtz remarks: "The musical tones which can be used with advantage, and have clearly distinguishable pitch, have therefore between 40 and 4000 vibrations in a second, extending over seven Octaves. Those which are audible at all have from 20 to 38000 vibrations, extending over eleven Octaves. This shows what a great variety of different vibrational numbers can be perceived and distinguished by the ear."

* "In order, then, to discover the limit of deepest tones, it is necessary not only to produce very violent agitations in the air, but to give these the form of simple pendular vibrations. Until this last condition is fulfilled we cannot possibly say whether the deep tones we hear belong to the prime tone or to an upper partial tone of the motion of the air. [This is according to the wave theory, which we do not indorse.] Among the instruments hitherto employed the wide-stopped organ pipes are the most suitable for this purpose. Their upper partial tones are at least extremely weak, if not quite absent. Here we find that even the lower tones of the sixteen-foot octave, $C_{\prime}$ to $E_{\prime}$ [CCC to EEE], begin to pass over into a droning noise, so that it becomes difficult for even a practiced musical ear to assign their pitch with certainty; and, indeed, they cannot be tuned by the ear alone, but only indirectly by means of the beats which they make with the tones of the upper octaves. We observe a similar effect on the same deep tones of a piano or physharmonica; they form drones and seem out of tune, although their musical character is on the whole better established than in the pipes, because of their accompanying upper partial tones. In music, as artistically applied in an orchestra, the deepest tone used is, therefore, the $E_{\prime}$ of the Double Bass, with 41·25 vibrations in a second, and I think I may predict with certainty that all efforts of modern art applied to produce good musical tones of a lower pitch must fail, not because proper means of agitating the air cannot be discovered, but because the human ear cannot hear them. The sixteen-foot $C_{\prime}$ of the Organ, with 33 vibrations in a second, certainly gives a tolerably continuous sensation of drone, but does not allow us to give it a definite position in the musical scale. We almost begin to observe the separate pulses of air, notwithstanding the regular form of the motion. In the upper half of the 32-foot octave the perception of the separate pulses becomes still clearer, and the continuous part of the sensation, which may be compared with a sensation of tone, continually weaker, and in the lower half of the 32-foot octave we can scarcely be said to hear anything but the individual pulses, or if anything else is really heard, it can only be weak upper partial tones, from which the musical tones of stopped pipes are not quite free. . . . We are then justified in asserting," says Helmholtz, "that sensation of musical tone begins at about 30 vibrations in a second, but that a determinate musical pitch is not perceived till about 40 vibrations are performed in a second."—"On the Sensations of Tone." pp. 266, 268.

CHAPTER XI.

THE COMPOUND STOPS OF THE ORGAN.

HAVING in the preceding Chapter treated at as great a length as necessary the interesting subject of compound musical sounds; and having directed the reader's attention to the legitimate means for their production in the tonal structure of the Organ; we may, in the present Chapter, practically complete this branch of our subject by giving some particulars respecting the Compound Harmonic-corroborating Stops of the Organ, which have been devised for the purpose of carrying, in practical organ appointment, the series of upper partial tones to higher pitches than those possible to be reached by complete or unbroken ranks of pipes—ranks extending throughout the manual compass of 61 notes.

It is quite unnecessary to again enlarge on the reasons for the introduction of harmonic-corroborating stops in the Organ; but we may remark that all the statements made respecting the complete stops or ranks of pipes which represent the chief upper partial tones of the foundation or prime tone of the OPEN DIAPASON, 8 FT., apply, in every particular, to the ranks composing the compound stops described in the present Chapter.

The compound stops, as the term implies, consist of two or more ranks of pipes which yield certain upper partial tones of the prime tone. The numbers of ranks most commonly met with in both old and modern Organs vary from three to eight, but MIXTURES having a greater number of ranks have been frequently made by German builders. The greatest number we have found in a British Organ is fourteen,—in the "HARMONIC MIXTURE" in the Organ of the Edinburgh University. It is quite a common thing to meet with compound stops in which the numbers of the ranks vary in different portions of the compass; and in certain classes of MIXTURES this treatment is advantageous and to be recommended.

Both the number and pitch of the ranks will, in scientific tonal appointment, depend upon the number and pitch of the independent and complete harmonic-corroborating stops inserted in the same division of the Organ. Probably in no branch of stop appointment can the organ builder of to-day display scientific knowledge and true musical sense more clearly than in the correct composition and tonal adjustment of his compound stops. Is this self-evident fact generally or properly realized? The old builders who, in many cases, appear to have looked upon MIXTURES as a legitimate means of obtaining power at any price, introduced into their instruments an excess of compound-work, both in number of ranks and loudness of intonation. In proof of this statement we may refer to the Great and Choir divisions of the Organ in the Old Church at Amsterdam, finished in 1686. The Great, which contains sixteen stops, has three stops of 16 ft. pitch and only three of 8 ft., while there are three compound stops having, collectively, eighteen ranks; namely, a SESQUIALTERA of IV. ranks, a MIXTURE of VI., VII., and VIII. ranks, and a SCHARF of VI. ranks. The Choir Organ contains twelve stops, including five stops of 8 ft. pitch, and has also eighteen ranks in its three compound stops; namely, a SESQUIALTERA of IV. ranks, a MIXTURE of VII. and VIII. ranks, and a SCHARF of VI. ranks. These stops, comprising thirty-six ranks of pipes, are, as in all old Dutch and German Organs, made of comparatively large-scaled pipes, and loudly voiced, in defiance of the teaching of the phenomena which attend, and the natural laws which govern, the production of compound musical sounds: their effect is, accordingly, unduly assertive and somewhat screaming in character. Probably observing the objectionable results attending the excessive use of such assertive stops, modern organ builders have, when left to their own devices, sought to omit compound stops from their smaller Organs, inserting only one, or two at most, in those of important dimensions. For instance, in the Specification now before us of a Church Organ, of 32 speaking stops, built by the late Mr. Roosevelt, of New York, there is a single MIXTURE of III. and IV. ranks in the Great, and a CORNET of III. ranks in the Swell division. This is fairly representative of modern practice among the best builders in England and America. It may be said, to account for the absence of the proper proportion of compound-work in modern Organs, that organ builders are always glad to avoid the introduction of many-ranked compound stops, especially if they are called upon to construct them in a scientific manner; because, apart from the expense and trouble attending their manufacture, the voicing, regulating, and fine tuning, combined with the delicate and sensitive nature, of so many hundreds of small pipes, are attended with an apparently unprofitable expenditure of much thought, time, and labor, to say nothing of the unwonted exercise of patience. Such builders should remember that the Organ proper, from its foundation upward, is, or should be, *one grand* MIXTURE, in which every constituent is of equal importance in the eye of science, and should receive equal justice at the hands of art. In scheming a compound harmonic-corroborating stop for any division of the Organ it is essential, if a successful result is aimed at, to look upon the foundation work and its superstructure as a MIXTURE; first carefully tabulating all the through ranks, and then completing the tonal structure by the addition of the higher upper partials in the ranks of the compound stop or stops. No other mode of procedure can be attended with a satisfactory result.

The compound stops of the Organ are designated by several names, only a few of which have any direct reference to their constitution or to their special tonal character. The most common name is MIXTURE, under which, strictly speaking, all the compound stops may be included. The following are the names commonly found in English and American Organs: MIXTURE, SESQUIALTERA, CORNET, FURNITURE, and ACUTA. In German and Dutch Organs we find the names MIXTUR, MIXTUUR, CORNET, SESQUIALTERA, CYMBEL, SCHARF, SCHERP, RAUSCHQUINTE, and GLOCKENSPIEL. In French Organs the following names occur: CORNET, SESQUIALTERA, FOURNITURE, CYMBALE, PLEIN-JEU, and CARILLON. In Italian Organs the general name for the compound stops is RIPIENO; and in Spanish instruments, LLENO.

Compound stops may be divided into three classes: 1. Those which extend throughout the compass of the clavier without any break. 2. Those which extend through the treble octaves of the manual compass only, also without a break. 3. Those which extend throughout the compass of the clavier, having two or more breaks.

The first class of compound stops finds but a very secondary place in the manual divisions of the Organ; while in the Pedal Organ it is the proper class to adopt, unless some special tonal effect is aimed at—the large size of the pipes representing the proper upper partial tones of the prime (16 ft.) tone of the pedal department, combined with the short compass of that department, rendering it altogether unnecessary to have breaks in the MIXTURE. This fact has apparently done much to discourage the introduction of the harmonic-corroborating ranks in the form of compound stops, preference being usually shown for them as separate stops. Accordingly, it is only in instruments of the first magnitude that compound stops appear in the Pedal Organ, as in the Organ in St. George's Hall, Liverpool, in the pedal department of which there is a MIXTURE, of III. ranks and FOURNITURE, of V. ranks. The pedal departments of many of the large German Organs are richly furnished with compound stops. The Organ in the Church at Mühlhausen has a Pedal Organ MIXTURE, of X. ranks.

The largest pedal compound stops which have hitherto been made are to be found in the Organs in the Votive Church, at Vienna, and the Cathedral of Riga: the stop in the latter instrument is labeled "GRAND BOURDON." This important compound stop represents the first, second, third, fourth, and seventh upper partial tones of the 32 ft. harmonic series. It is composed of five complete ranks, as follows:—

I. PEDAL ORGAN MIXTURE—GRAND BOURDON—V. RANKS.

PRINCIPAL, 16 FT.—QUINT, 10⅔ FT.—OCTAVE, 8 FT.—TIERCE, 6⅖ FT.—SUPER-OCTAVE, 4 FT.

These ranks are planted on a special wind-chest. Gottschalg, speaking of the Vienna example, says that the ranks are finely proportioned and voiced so that the compound tone is characterized by fulness and clearness, leaving nothing to be desired. We regret not having had an opportunity, while in Vienna, of examining and measuring this important stop. Although there is little probability of such a stop, in an independent form, being introduced in English or American Organs, there should be no difficulty of having the ranks which compose it introduced as separate stops, building up the full tonal structure of the pedal department; all being scaled and voiced in accordance with the laws set forth in the preceding Chapter. It is hardly necessary, however, to have a MIXTURE corroborating the upper partials of the 32 ft. prime, because, as has been pointed out, it is more than doubtful if the lower notes of a 32 ft. stop really exist as determinate musical sounds. On the other hand, a MIXTURE corroborating the upper partials of the Pedal Organ unison (16 ft. prime) would be a most desirable addition to any otherwise properly-appointed pedal department. Such a MIXTURE, to be agreeable to the ear and generally useful in varied combinations, should be formed of pipes of medium scales carefully graduated in strength of tone. Its composition should be as follows:—

II. PEDAL ORGAN MIXTURE—VI. RANKS.

CCC to G. . . OCTAVE, 8 FT.—TWELFTH, 5⅓ FT.—FIFTEENTH, 4 FT.—SEVENTEENTH, 3⅕ FT.—NINETEENTH, 2⅔ FT.—TWENTY-SECOND, 2 FT.

The effect of a compound stop of this class, provided it be scientifically scaled and artistically voiced, would be extremely beautiful with the OPEN DIAPASON, 16 FT., or with a full-toned VIOLONE, 16 FT.; producing therewith a compound tone of a richness absolutely unknown in English and American Organs to-day: and, owing to the accommodating nature of properly-proportioned harmonic-corroborating stops, it would prove sufficient for the full strength of the largest pedal department ever likely to be provided in an Organ. It may be added that in a Pedal Organ which is provided with a *softly-voiced* OCTAVE, 8 FT., it may be unnecessary to duplicate it in the MIXTURE. Before leaving this branch of the present subject it may be useful to say a few words respecting the tonal character of the several ranks included in the MIXTURE above suggested. Four perfectly legitimate courses are open to the artistic builder: 1. The ranks may be made of full-scaled metal pipes of the DULCIANA class, whose refined and singing tones will blend admirably with the voice of the foundation OPEN DIAPASON, 16 FT., adding richness and clearness of articulation to its normal tone, naturally weak in higher harmonics. 2. The ranks may be made of softly-voiced metal pipes of the VIOL or string-toned family, yielding a fuller or more complex quality of tone which will form a brilliant combination with the solid voice of the OPEN DIAPASON, 16 FT.; and will assimilate perfectly with the kindred tone of the VIOLONE, 16 FT., adding greatly to its imitative character. Such a MIXTURE will also add a remarkable richness and volume to any reed stops that may be in the department. 3. The ranks may be formed throughout of wood and metal pipes of the LIEBLICHGEDECKT family, producing a magnificent superstructure of sympathetic flute-tone which will combine well with every other quality in the department. 4. The ranks may be varied in tonal character by the introduction of pipes of different classes,—wood or metal, open or stopped,—according to the judgment or artistic aim of the organ builder, who will, or should, be guided in his selection by the general stop appointment of the department. Here, as in all other matters connected with the tonal appointment of the Organ, the true artist can display consummate knowledge and taste.

The following particulars and measurements of the CCC pipes of the GRAND BOURDON, of V. ranks, in the Organ of Riga Cathedral will be interesting to the student of organ-building. They have been kindly furnished by the distinguished builders, Messrs. E. F. Walcker & Company, of Ludwigsburg. The pipes are of wood throughout; the TIERCE, $6\frac{2}{5}$ FT., being formed of conical pipes, doubtless for the purpose of securing a somewhat light and bright quality in this assertive upper partial tone.

MEASUREMENTS OF THE CCC PIPES OF THE GRAND BOURDON—V. RANKS, IN THE ORGAN OF RIGA CATHEDRAL.

PRINCIPAL, 16 FT.	. . .	Width,	220	mm.	Depth, 280	mm.
QUINT, $10\frac{2}{3}$ FT.	. . .	"	110	"	" 153	"
OCTAVE, 8 FT.	. . .	"	108	"	" 131	"
TIERCE, $6\frac{2}{5}$ FT. At mouth,	. .	"	74	"	" 106	"
" " At top,	. .	"	48	"	" 64	"
SUPER-OCTAVE, 4 FT.	. .	"	65	"	" 80	"

Under certain circumstances, and notably in large Pedal Organs in which there are two or more independent OCTAVES and single harmonic-corroborating stops belonging to the 16 ft. harmonic series, it may be found desirable to insert one or two compound stops carrying the upper partial tones still higher: but the consideration of these, as well as the other compound stops which are suitable for insertion in the pedal department, may be left until farther on in the present Chapter.

Before proceeding to consider, in a practical manner, the subject of the compound stops which are required in the manual department of the Organ, it may not be uninteresting to glance at what has been done in this direction by the celebrated old builders—the fathers of the art of organ-building.

However much the old builders may have erred in the way they scaled and voiced their MIXTURES, and, indeed, all their harmonic-corroborating stops, in relation to their foundation stops, they were clearly right in the importance they attributed to them in the tonal structure of the Organ. That we find too great an importance accorded them in numerous cases must, however, be admitted; for we may notice in many old Specifications an undue prominence given to them. For instance, Father Smith inserted in his Organ in Temple Church, London (built in 1684), which contained in all only twenty-three speaking stops, no fewer than one QUINT and four MIXTURES. These comprised 687 pipes out of the total number of 1715 which the instrument contained. Again, in the Great division of the Organ built by Renatus Harris, in 1670, for the Church of St. Sepulchre, Snow Hill, London, a TWELFTH, TIERCE, LARIGOT, and three MIXTURES (eight ranks in all) were introduced—three single and three compound harmonic-corroborating stops—in addition to two PRINCIPALS, 4 FT., and a FIFTEENTH, 2 FT. There were, it seems, in the original scheme only two complete unison labial stops in the Great Organ to furnish the prime tone for this overwhelming superstructure of harmonic-corroborating work. These examples, however, may be looked upon as extraordinary, and not representative of the practice of the early English organ builders.

Turning our attention to old Organs constructed in other countries, what do we find? In the Organ built, in 1738, by Christian Müller for the Cathedral of Haarlem, there is a Great division of sixteen stops, among which (omitting the reed stops) are a QUINT, 5⅓ FT., two OCTAVES, 4 FT., a TWELFTH, 2⅔ FT., a SUPER-OCTAVE, 2 FT., a TERTIAN, of II. ranks, and a MIXTURE, of VI., VIII., and X. ranks, having in all 696 pipes out of a total of 1209 labial pipes. In the Choir Organ there are two OCTAVES, 4 FT., a TWELFTH, 2⅔ FT., a SUPER-OCTAVE, 2 FT., a SESQUIALTERA, of II., III., and IV. ranks, a MIXTURE, of VI., VII., and VIII. ranks, a CYMBEL, of II. ranks, and a CORNET, of V. ranks, having in all 918 pipes out of a total of 1115 labial pipes. In the Echo division there are two OCTAVES, 4 FT., a TWELFTH, 2⅔ FT., a SUPER-OCTAVE, 2 FT., a NINETEENTH, 1⅓ FT., a SESQUIALTERA, of II. ranks, a MIXTURE, of IV., V., and VI. ranks, and a CYMBEL, of IV. ranks, having in all 711 pipes out of a total of 945 labial pipes. Accordingly, there are in the three manual divisions of this noteworthy Organ no fewer than 2325 pipes which may properly be considered as belonging to the harmonic-corroborating system; while the entire number of labial pipes in these divisions outside the above is only 944. In another interesting Organ rebuilt, in 1673, by J. Duyschor Van Goor, of Dordrecht, for the so-called New Church, at Amsterdam, we find a marked example of the excessive use of the compound harmonic-corroborating stops. In the Great division, which presents a list of ten labial stops, there are two MIXTURES composed of thirteen ranks in all. The Choir division of this instrument contains, in addition to other harmonic-corroborating stops, no fewer than five compound stops having an aggregate of twenty ranks. The following is the list of the fourteen stops contained in this division:—

1.	PRESTANT,	8 feet.	8.	FLUIT,	2 feet.
2.	HOLPYP,	8 "	9.*	SIFLET,	1 foot.
3.	QUINTADENA,	8 "	10.*	SESQUIALTERA,	II. ranks.
4.*	OCTAAF,	4 "	11.*	MIXTUR,	III. "
5.	FLUIT,	4 "	12.*	SCHERP,	VI. "
6.*	QUINT-FLUIT,	2⅔ "	13.*	QUARTANE,	IV. "
7.*	OCTAAF,	2 "	14.*	CORNET.	V. "

The nine stops marked with asterisks belong, strictly considered, to the 8 ft. harmonic series, and are all harmonic-corroborating, or, in their excess, harmonic-creating. They greatly exceed the correct proportion in a division containing only three stops yielding unison prime tone, and one of these having a compound voice—the QUINTADENA, 8 FT.*

*The names of the stops in this Organ are given on the authority of Dr. Hopkins, in "The Organ."

In the Great division of fourteen stops in the Organ built by Silbermann for the Protestant Church at Strasbourg, about the middle of the eighteenth century, there are, in addition to four single harmonic-corroborating stops of 4 ft., 2⅔ ft., 2 ft., and 1⅗ ft., three compound stops having eleven ranks in all. In the Organ in the Church of St. Mary, at Berlin, built by Joachim Wagner, about the year 1722, the Great division has twelve stops, comprising in its harmonic structure three single stops of 4 ft., 2⅔ ft., and 2 ft., and three compound stops having an aggregate of thirteen ranks. In the old Organ in the Cathedral of Vienna, the Great division had the four following compound harmonic-corroborating stops: Mixtur, of VIII. ranks, Sesquialtera, of IV. ranks, Cymbel, of VIII. ranks, and Scharf, of IV. ranks—in all, twenty-four ranks. Aloise Moser inserted in the Great division, of sixteen stops, in his Organ in the Cathedral of Fribourg, four compound stops comprising twenty-one ranks. One more example will suffice for our present purpose. The Great division, of sixteen stops, in the noted Organ in the Monastery Church, at Weingarten, constructed in 1750 by J. Gabler, contains, in addition to four stops of 4 ft. and two of 2 ft., a Sesquialtera, of VIII. ranks, a Mixture, of XX. ranks, and a Cornet, of VIII. ranks. In the Choir division, of twelve stops, there are a Mixture, of XXI. ranks, and a Cymbel, of II. ranks; in the Echo division, of thirteen stops, there are a Mixture, of XII. ranks, and a Cornet, of IV. ranks; and in the Positif, of twelve stops, there is a Cornet, of XII. ranks. Accordingly, we find in the manual divisions of this representative Organ, which contain in all fifty-one speaking stops, no fewer than eighty-five ranks of harmonic-corroborating pipes in the compound stops alone. It is worthy of remark that in the tonal appointment of this instrument there is not a single fifth- or third-sounding stop in an independent form.

Surely these few examples tell us that not only were the old builders and their immediate followers fully aware of the compound nature of all rich and effective musical sounds, but that they were also alive to the great importance of reproducing, by artificial means, the structure and musical effects of such rich compound sounds in the Organ. That they rushed into extremes under their somewhat circumscribed knowledge of acoustical phenomena and limited powers of analysis, and that, in their enthusiasm over the glimpse into Nature's workshop they had been able to obtain, they overstepped the bounds which a cooler and more accurate investigation of the natural laws of sound-production would have defined, must be obvious to every student of the earlier schools of organ-building. In addition to all this, one can almost trace in the works of the early German masters a spirit of rivalry, perhaps, as to who should succeed in successfully introducing the greatest number of *harmonic-creating* ranks in their Organs. The view of these early builders seems to have been the construction of instruments for the dominating, supporting, and tying together of great numbers of powerful voices, rather than for the purpose of artistically accompanying them. For the former purpose, loud-voiced Mixtures seemed to the old builders a legitimate means to the desired end.

The most sensitive and refined musical ear may become vitiated, if not absolutely ruined during a lengthened straining toward, or indulgence in, exaggerated musical effects. In the early stages of such an art as that of organ-building a certain unhealthy exaggeration, and a desire to surpass each preceding tentative effort, might reasonably be looked for. Crudities are of necessity an accompaniment of early endeavors in any new direction, the true limits of which have not been defined by scientific investigation and long experience. We do not desire to appear unjust or severe in our remarks on the methods of the old German master-builders, for the organ-building world to-day owes them a deep debt for the manner in which they laid the foundation of the entire art of organ-construction—a foundation upon which the more advanced builders of the present century must erect their most worthy temples of sound. We have the benefit not only of the successes of the old masters but also of their failures, replete with positive and negative teachings of the utmost value if we will only understand them aright. That they viewed the primal office of the compound harmonic-corroborating stops in a light different to that in which we now feel called upon to recognize it, is simply due to their not having had the knowledge and valuable experience which have been gathered, during the many intervening years, for our learning. We have not yet reached the culminating point in that knowledge and experience, and have much to learn respecting the compound stops of the Organ.

Having briefly touched, in our introductory remarks on the MIXTURES introduced in the Pedal Organ, upon those complete compound stops which, on account of their large size and short compass,—never exceeding 32 notes,—do not call for any breaks in their ranks, we may now enter on the consideration of the compound stops which belong to the second class, and which only extend through a portion of the compass of the divisions in which they are inserted. These incomplete stops belong to the manual department of the Organ, and, like the Pedal Organ MIXTURES, do not require to have any broken ranks. They have generally passed under the name of CORNETS—the name now commonly applied to certain compound stops of full compass, having several breaks. The true CORNET, as introduced in old English and German Organs, never extended below tenor C; in English instruments it seldom extended below middle c^1. It was usually formed of open metal pipes, larger in scale than the corresponding pipes of the OPEN DIAPASON or PRINCIPAL, 8 FT., of the division in which it was placed, and voiced to yield a very full and dominating pure organ-tone. As made by the old German masters, the CORNET had several ranks of pipes varying in number from three to eight. In rare instances, as in the Organ at Weingarten, the latter number was exceeded. The representative CORNET consisted of five ranks, thus:—

III. CORNET—V. RANKS.

UNISON, 8 FT.—OCTAVE, 4 FT.—TWELFTH, 2⅔ FT.—FIFTEENTH, 2 FT.—SEVENTEENTH, 1⅗ FT.

As the large-scaled ranks required a considerable space for their accommodation, they were frequently planted on a special wind-chest, elevated above the pipe-work of the main wind-chest, and connected with the grooves of the latter by metal conveyances. When so treated, the stop is known as the MOUNTED CORNET. In the fine interior perspective of a large Organ given in Plate L. of the Work by Dom Bedos, the MOUNTED CORNET is clearly shown occupying a prominent position immediately behind the front displayed pipes. The CORNET was apparently introduced by the German builders for the purpose of imparting great volume to the treble, and for playing out the melody of the Chorales upon, and for the rendition of a kind of church music now practically obsolete. Seidel gives the following particulars respecting this compound stop :—

> "CORNET, or 'CORNETTO,' is a mixture-register of a very wide measure, which begins generally at c^1 or at the G below, and goes through the upper octaves of the manual. It has a strong intonation, and a horn-like tone, which is well adapted for filling out. Sometimes, when hymns are to be sung with a melody which is not familiar to the congregation, this register will be found very efficient for the purpose of making the melody prominent, since the right hand plays the melody upon that manual which contains the CORNET, whilst the left hand plays the accompaniment upon some other manual, for which weaker registers are drawn. This MIXTURE has sometimes five ranks, 8, 4, 2⅔, 2, and 1⅗ feet; sometimes four ranks, 8, 4, 2⅔, and 1⅗ feet; and sometimes three ranks, 4, 2⅔, and 1⅗ feet. In France, the lowest rank of this register is nothing but the ROHRFLÖTE, 8 FT.* Wilke deems it best to construct the CORNET with three ranks only, but so that the lowest of them is a fifth, the next an octave, and the last a third,—5⅓ ft., 4 ft., and 3⅕ ft., or 2⅔ ft., 2 ft., and 1⅗ ft. The latter arrangement is better suited for small Organs, the former for large ones."

Seidel would have spoken more to the purpose had he said that the former composition, which contains ranks which corroborate the second, third, and fourth upper partial tones of the 16 ft. prime, is suitable for the Pedal Organ: it is certainly not suitable for a manual division, however large the Organ may be.

The ECHO CORNET is a stop resembling that just described insomuch that it is commonly of the same compass, number and pitch of the ranks, and mounted. The pipes composing it are of small scale, yielding an echo of the larger CORNET. To further subdue its tone it was sometimes inclosed in a special box placed within the main swell-box. Of other unimportant stops which have, in old Organs, passed under the name of CORNET it is unnecessary to speak here.

The most important class of compound stops in the Organ is that which extends throughout the compass of the manual department, and which, owing to the high pitch and necessarily small size of its pipes, requires to have two or more breaks. Theoretically there should be no breaks in the ranks of the compound harmonic-corroborating stops, any more than in the single mutation stops which corroborate the lower and more important partial tones of the prime (8 ft. tone); but practically there is an almost insuperable difficulty in avoiding breaks in these compound stops, while their presence has been found to be attended by no objectionable results from a musical point of view. That breaks have to be skilfully arranged and covered as much as possible must not, however, be forgotten by the organ builder. On this subject, Dr. Hopkins pertinently remarks: "Moreover, there exists no *necessity* for continuing a compound stop up without a break. The MIXTURES are intended to *corroborate* certain of the higher harmonic sounds. But these sounds are not heard [at all events by the unaided ear] to rise to

* This rank, formed of FLÛTE À CHEMINÉE, or metal ROHRFLÖTE, pipes, is shown in the Plate in Dom Bedos' Work already alluded to.

so great an altitude when the fundamental tone is higher up in the scale, as when it is lower down. So long a series of harmonic sounds will not be traced rising above the middle c^1, as from the CC string of a pianoforte. To continue a compound stop throughout, would be to 'corroborate' what cannot be heard."

No rule for universal acceptance has been formulated as to where, or in how many places, breaks are to occur in the compound stops. As a general rule, however, it is advisable to have as few breaks as possible, so long as the tonal transition from one to another is not too pronounced. MIXTURES of high-pitched ranks always require three or more breaks in their compass, now frequently of five complete octaves—CC to c^4. While no decision has been arrived at by organ experts regarding the notes of the scale on which the breaks should be made, it is agreed by all who have given the stop appointment of the Organ any serious consideration, that when more than one MIXTURE appears in a tonal scheme they should break upon different notes, and in such a manner as to cover each other's breaks as much as possible. This practice should obtain in all cases, whether the MIXTURES are confined to a single division, or distributed throughout the different manual divisions of the Organ. Examples of breaks on different notes of the scale are given in the following compositions.

As the higher-pitched ranks which enter into the composition of the manual compound stops have extremely small pipes, and as these pipes cannot be carried in proper gradation throughout the entire compass of the clavier without causing great practical difficulties in their construction, tuning, and maintenance, breaks become absolutely necessary to prevent such ranks from dying out on reaching the treble octaves. In answer to the question—May not a rank die out instead of presenting breaks? Dr. Hopkins replies: "No. For, in that case, the treble, from having fewer pipes, would sound weaker than the bass, and consequently would be overpowered by it. To prevent this, the same number of ranks should be maintained throughout; and when it becomes advisable to discontinue a rank at its original altitude of pitch above the fundamental sound, a duplication of some larger rank should be introduced in its stead, which, by strengthening one of the most important *remaining* tones, will add fresh energy to that tone, and so compensate for the loss of *extent* in the harmonic series."

The other matters of importance and interest connected with the composition and arrangement of the ranks of the compound stops will be touched upon in the remarks attending the several examples which follow.

When the ranks forming the MIXTURE are not of too high a pitch above the unison it may only be necessary to have one break, thus :—

IV. MIXTURE—III. RANKS.

CC to f^1, ...	15—19—22.
$f\sharp^1$ to top, ...	8—12—15.

For a small Organ this simple MIXTURE is sufficient: in the lower half it will impart brightness to the bass and tenor, and in the upper half fulness and richness to the treble. In the latter the TWELFTH may be voiced softer than the other ranks. A MIXTURE of this composition, which breaks on middle c¹, exists in the Organ in Kinnaird Hall, Dundee, Scotland. In the Swell division of the same instrument is another MIXTURE of a similar class which has a single break on G. The composition, of four ranks, is of a fuller quality than the preceding example:—

V. FULL MIXTURE—IV. RANKS.

CC to F♯, ...	12—15—19—22.
G to top, ...	5— 8—12—15.

In this a grave character is imparted to the upper octaves by the introduction of one member of the sixteen feet harmonic series—the QUINT, 5⅓ FT., corroborating the second upper partial tone of the 16 ft. prime tone. Theoretically, it is incorrect to introduce any ranks corroborating upper partial tones that are not natural accompaniments of the foundation or unison tone of the division; and, accordingly, the above composition, while it of course implies the presence of a stop of 16 ft. tone in the same division of the Organ, is not, strictly considered, correct. When such a QUINT rank is introduced in any portion of the scale, it should be of a much softer intonation than the ranks which belong to the 8 ft. harmonic series. This rule must not be overlooked.

The following two compound stops, used by Roosevelt and called by him CORNETS, are good examples of MIXTURES with a single break. They differ materially from the above Examples, IV. and V., in containing third- as well as fifth-sounding ranks:—

VI. MIXTURE—III. RANKS.

CC to b^2, ...	12—15—17.
c^3 to c^4, ...	10—12—15.

VII. MIXTURE—IV. and V. RANKS.

CC to B, ...	5—8—10—15.
c^1 to c^4, ...	1—5— 8—10—15.

Here, again, we find ranks belonging to the 16 ft. harmonic series; namely, the QUINT and TENTH ranks: all the others belonging to the unison (8 ft.) series. The introduction of third-sounding ranks, even when no independent TIERCE appears in the division, has not found many advocates among modern builders, at all events among those who care little about scientific methods. The fact, however, remains, that as the TIERCE corroborates a very important upper partial tone it should not be omitted, in some form, in the tonal appointment of the more important divisions of the Organ, due care being taken to prevent its being too assertive in tone.

The following examples may be accepted as representative compositions of

MIXTURES having two breaks in their compass. Example VIII. is the MIXTURE, of two, three, and four ranks, included by Edmund Schulze, of Paulinzelle, in the Choir division of his scheme for the Organ for the Cathedral of Cologne. Example IX. will be found suitable for manual divisions of moderate size, especially if

VIII. MIXTURE—II., III., and IV. RANKS.

CC to BB,	. . . . .	12—15.
C to B,	. . . . .	8—12—15.
c^1 to top,	. . . . .	5—8—12—15.

IX. FULL MIXTURE—III. RANKS.

CC to B,	. . . . .	15—19—22.
c^1 to $f\sharp^2$,	. . . . .	8—12—15.
g^2 to c^4,	. . . . .	1—5—8.

they contain a soft open or covered stop of 16 ft. pitch; but if the QUINT (belonging to the 16 ft. harmonic series) in the top break is subdued in tone the MIXTURE will produce a satisfactory effect without a double stop. For the Great Organ, the MIXTURE should be formed of pipes of medium scales, and have a full round tone of a perfect mixing quality; for the Swell Organ, its pipes should be of smaller scales, voiced to yield a bright ringing tone, in correct relation to the foundation tone of the division; and in the Choir Organ, its pipes should be of a DULCIANA scale, voiced to yield a soft singing quality of tone. In the introduction of ranks which produce tones strictly belonging to the 16 ft. harmonic series, in compound stops which are designed to corroborate the upper partial tones of the 8 ft. harmonic series, the greatest care and judgment must be exercised. Their presence is apt to be *timbre-creating*, and, accordingly, may interfere with the desirable regularity of the tone-color throughout the scale. Here science and art come together, and the organ builder must consult them hand in hand.

At this point we may consider the form of compound stop commonly known as the SESQUIALTERA. Correctly composed, this stop should have only two ranks and extend throughout the manual compass without a break, but in this form it seldom appears. The original SESQUIALTERA, as used by the old German masters, and from which the English compound stop of the same name was derived, was of two ranks, composed of a fifth-sounding and a third-sounding rank, the former being the lowest in pitch. The two ranks sounding a major sixth—as G—e^1 on the CC key.* The sizes of the two ranks were usually $2\frac{2}{3}$ ft. and $1\frac{3}{5}$ ft., which,

*The name given to this compound stop does not seem to be entirely satisfactory. The Latin word *sesquialtera* (fem. of *sesquialter*) signifies "one-half more," and on that account it is somewhat difficult to reconcile its use as the name of a stop the ranks of which bear no relation to the ratio $1 : 1\frac{1}{2}$. Reference to different authorities does not clear the way to a comprehension of the matter, as the following extracts will show:

Dr. Hopkins, in "The Organ," tells us that the two ranks which compose the stop sound together a major sixth—"hence the name Sesqui-altera, from Sexta, a sixth."

In "The Century Dictionary" we find the following: "Sesquialtera—In music, an interval having the ratio $1 : 1\frac{1}{2}$ or $2 : 3$—that is, a *perfect fifth*. In organ-building a variety of mixture.

accordingly, correspond with the TWELFTH and TIERCE. When of this size, the stop should be carried throughout the manual compass without a break, the TIERCE being voiced much softer than the TWELFTH, to avoid any tendency toward a harsh effect. Notable examples of this form of SESQUIALTERA obtain in German, Swiss, and Dutch Organs. When the SESQUIALTERA was composed of three ranks the added rank was a FIFTEENTH, 2 FT., the stop sounding G—c^1—e^1 on the CC key; and it was in this form that the stop was introduced by Father Smith and other old English builders in their Organs—commonly as an incomplete or treble stop. Sometimes an octave SESQUIALTERA, of three ranks, sounding g^1—c^2—e^2 on the CC key, was introduced by Harris in his Organs; but such a stop would have to break to prevent its pipes becoming too small, and in all probability it would be a SESQUIALTERA only in a certain portion of its compass.

In manual divisions in which there are both a TWELFTH, 2⅔ FT., and a TIERCE, 1⅗ FT., as through and independent stops, it is unnecessary and undesirable to insert a SESQUIALTERA; but when neither of these complete stops appears in the tonal scheme, a SESQUIALTERA is strongly to be recommended. It is very important that the second and fourth upper partial tones should be corroborated, if a full compound organ-tone is aimed at, as it should be in every Organ worthy of the name. When two compound stops are inserted in any division, one should either be a SESQUIALTERA or a MIXTURE in which there is a third-sounding rank; the other being a MIXTURE composed of octave- and fifth-sounding ranks. The only complete SESQUIALTERAS are those of the original German class, composed throughout of a TWELFTH, 2⅔ FT., and a SEVENTEENTH, 1⅗ FT.; or, better still, of three unbroken ranks—TWELFTH, 2⅔ FT.—FIFTEENTH, 2 FT.—SEVENTEENTH, 1⅗ FT. The Pedal Organ SESQUIALTERA, of three ranks, belonging to the 16 ft. harmonic series, is composed of a TWELFTH, 5⅓ FT., a SUPER-OCTAVE, 4 FT., and a TIERCE, 3⅕ FT. This compound stop may be formed of metal or wood pipes, and the different ranks may be varied in their tonal character: for instance, the TWELFTH may be of LIEBLICHGEDECKT pipes, metal or wood; the SUPER-OCTAVE may be of GEMSHORN pipes, of metal; and the TIERCE may be of ROHRFLÖTE or DOLCE pipes, of metal, or FLAUTO D'AMORE pipes, of wood. In all cases the tonal appointment of the Pedal Organ will dictate the treatment of its SESQUIALTERA.

The so-called SESQUIALTERAS, introduced in old English and Continental Organs, and which were composed of several ranks of pipes, requiring two or more breaks in their compass, were only correct in certain parts of their compass. A representative example is furnished by the stop inserted by Snetzler in the Organ he constructed, in the latter half of the eighteenth century, for

"Sext, sexte—In music the interval of a sixth. In Organ-building a mixture-stop of two ranks separated by a sixth—that is, consisting of a Twelfth and a Seventeenth."

Dr. Baker, in "A Dictionary of Musical Terms," says: "Sesquialtera—A perfect fifth, its ratio to the prime being $1 : 1\frac{1}{2} = 2 : 3$. A mixture-stop in the Organ; the name is properly applied to a mutation-stop a fifth above the fundamental tone or some given octave of the latter, but is ordinarily used to designate a compound stop producing the 3rd, 4th, and 5th partial tones [the 2nd, 3rd, and 4th upper partial tones] or their octaves; it has from 2 to 5 ranks.

"Sext—The interval of the sixth. A compound organ-stop of 2 ranks (a Twelfth and a Seventeenth) a sixth apart."

St. Mary's Church, Nottingham. The composition of this stop is given in Example X.

X. Sesquialtera—IV. ranks.

CC to G, . . .	15 —— 17 —— 19 —— 22.
G♯ to g^1, . . .	12*—— 15 —— 17*—— 19.
g♯^{1} to top, . . .	8 —— 12*—— 15 —— 17*.

XI. Sesquialtera—V. ranks.

CC to c^1, . . .	19*—— 22 —— 24*—— 26 —— 29.
c♯^{1} to top, . . .	8 —— 12*—— 15 —— 17*—— 19.

XII. Sesquialtera—IV. ranks.

CC to B, . . .	12*—— 15 —— 17*—— 22.
c^1 to b^2, . . .	8 —— 12*—— 15 —— 17*.
c^3 to c^4, . . .	8 —— 10 —— 12 —— 15.

XIII. Sesquialtera—IV. ranks.

CC to F, . . .	15 —— 19*—— 22 —— 24*.
F♯ to f^1, . . .	12*—— 15 —— 17*—— 19.
f♯^{1} to c^3, . . .	8 —— 12*—— 15 —— 17*.
c♯^{3} to c^4, . . .	1 —— 5*—— 8 —— 10*.

The above four examples practically cover the Sesquialtera in its many-ranked and broken form, as found in the works of old and modern builders. In each the asterisks mark the sexts. Example XI. gives the composition of a true Sesquialtera throughout, as inserted in the Organ of the old Parish Church of Doncaster, constructed by Harris and Byfield, of London, in 1740. The list of the stops in the Great division of this Organ constructed by builders so celebrated in their day is interesting, as showing how complete old English Organs were in their harmonic-corroborating stops:—

1.	Open Diapason, .	8 feet.	7.	Tierce, ...	$1\frac{3}{5}$ feet.
2.	Open Diapason, .	8 "	8.	Sesquialtera, . .	V. ranks.
3.	Stopped Diapason, .	8 "	9.	Cornet (Middle c^1), .	V. "
4.	Principal, . . .	4 "	10.	Trumpet, . . .	8 feet.
5.	Twelfth, ...	$2\frac{2}{3}$ "	11.	Trumpet, . . .	8 "
6.	Fifteenth, . . .	2 "	12.	Clarion, ...	4 "

The Sesquialtera in Example XI. is given in the modern compass; in the Harris Organ it commenced on GGG and extended upward to d^3. A generally useful stop can be obtained by omitting the fifth, acute rank in both breaks. Example XIV. shows the composition of the MIXTURE introduced by G. P. England in the Organ he constructed in 1809 for High Church, Lancaster, England. It will be observed that it is a SESQUIALTERA only from f^1 to the top note; but it can be carried down to c^1 by substituting a TWELFTH for the OCTAVE in the first rank of the short break at that note. It is, as given, an admirable compound stop, imparting brightness to the bass and tenor octaves and fulness to the treble. The presence of the unbroken TIERCE, $1\frac{3}{5}$ FT., throughout imparts a distinctive character to the composition. To obtain the best effect, the TIERCE should be

XIV. SESQUIALTERA—IV. RANKS.

CC to C,	17—19—22—26.
C♯ to B,	15—17—19—22.
c^1 to e^1,	8—15—17—19.
f^1 to top,	8—12*—15—17*.

so scaled and voiced as to gradually decrease in strength of tone as it becomes less and less covered in the different breaks. This MIXTURE, formed of tin pipes of DULCIANA scale, would be a highly satisfactory stop in the Swell division of a Chamber Organ, or in an expressive Choir division of a Church Organ. Example XII. is a SESQUIALTERA in all save its top octave, where the positions of the fifth- and third-sounding ranks are reversed. In this top octave the TENTH, $3\frac{1}{5}$ FT.,—belonging to the 16 ft. harmonic series,—should be very subdued in tone. This composition was adopted by Roosevelt. In Example XIII. we give the composi-

XV. SESQUIALTERA—VI. RANKS.

CC to F♯,	15—17—19—22—26—29.
G to f♯^{1},	12*—15—17*—19—22—26.
g^1 to f♯^{2},	8—12*—15—17*—19—22.
g^2 to c^4,	1—8—12*—15—17*—19.

tion of a complete SESQUIALTERA, of four ranks, bright in the lower, and full and rich in the upper octaves. This stop is admirably suited for a DULCIANA scale; and it is only necessary to have the octave ranks the most assertive, and the third-sounding ranks softer than the fifth-sounding, to obtain a perfect tonal effect. We give in Example XV. a SESQUIALTERA, of six ranks, admirably suited for a large Swell Organ. In it all the ranks belong to the 8 ft. harmonic series. In Example XVI. is given a SESQUIALTERA, of four ranks, and of full intonation, composed by the late W. T. Best, and recommended by him for the Great Organ, and to be

XVI. SESQUIALTERA—IV. RANKS.

CC to C,	15—17—19—22.
C♯ to B,	17—19—22—26.
c^1 to b♭^{1},	12—15—19*—24*.
b^1 to b^2,	5*—8—10*—15.
c^3 to c^4,	1—5*—8—10*.

specially used when the DOUBLE OPEN DIAPASON, 16 FT., is drawn. It will be observed that the ranks on the two higher breaks—from b^1 to c^4—belong to the 16 ft. harmonic series, imparting breadth and fulness to the treble. It will also be noticed that the intervals peculiar to the SESQUIALTERA appear only in the treble of the stop. The addition of the TWELFTH, 2⅔ FT., in an independent form would create the necessary intervals in the bass and tenor octaves; and Mr. Best certainly contemplated such an addition, covering it, as usual, with the independent SUPER-OCTAVE, 2 FT. We may here remark that the certain or possible addition of complete mutation ranks must always be taken into consideration in the composition or the judging of the compound stops.

The value of the SEVENTEENTH cannot well be overrated, yet this natural and by no means weak harmonic is shunned by organ builders who do not study how to treat it scientifically or proportion it properly in scaling, voicing, and regulating. In the tonal structure of the Pedal Organ the SEVENTEENTH or TIERCE, either in the 32 ft. or 16 ft. harmonic series, is most effective, adding a desirable brightness to the grave and somewhat colorless foundation tones of the department. Two instances of its introduction may be alluded to. In Example XVII. is given the

XVII. PEDAL ORGAN SESQUIALTERA—II. RANKS.

CCC to D, . . . QUINT, 10⅔ FT.—TIERCE, 6⅖ FT.

composition of the SESQUIALTERA belonging to the 32 ft. harmonic series, in the Haupt-Pedal of the Organ in the Cathedral of Riga. Example XVIII. is the composition of the SESQUIALTERA, of five ranks, formed entirely of metal pipes, in the pedal department of the Organ in the Music Hall, at Cincinnati. This stop is labeled CORNET, but it is strictly a SESQUIALTERA, with three added ranks.

XVIII. PEDAL ORGAN SESQUIALTERA—V. RANKS.

CCC to F, ... 12*——15——17*——19——22.

The compound stop which may, in the proper order of things, be considered at this point is that designated the TERTIAN. It is practically an inversion of the SESQUIALTERA, the third-sounding rank being lower in pitch than the fifth-sounding one. The accompanying Example shows the composition of the stop in the 8 ft. harmonic series:—

XIX. TERTIAN—II. RANKS.

CC to c^4, SEVENTEENTH, 1⅗ FT.—NINETEENTH, 1⅓ FT.

In the 16 ft. harmonic series the TERTIAN is composed of a TENTH, 3⅕ FT. and a TWELFTH, 2⅔ FT. In old German Organs it is met with of three ranks, the latter stop having an OCTAVE, 4 FT., added to it. Constructed of small-scaled pipes, voiced and regulated so as to have the third-sounding rank considerably softer than the fifth-sounding rank, the TERTIAN becomes a valuable addition to the tonal appointment of any division of the Organ.

There is another two-rank compound stop less rarely met with than the uncommon TERTIAN; we allude to the QUARTANE. The composition of this stop is given in Example XX.

XX. QUARTANE—II. RANKS.

CC to c^4,	. .	TWELFTH, 2⅔ FT.—FIFTEENTH, 2 FT.

In manual divisions in which a TWELFTH and a SUPER-OCTAVE are inserted as separate stops the QUARTANE may be omitted; but allowing the independent stops are full-toned, and that the SUPER-OCTAVE is in the form of a PICCOLO, 2 FT., the QUARTANE, formed of small-scaled and softly-voiced pipes, will be found a very valuable addition to the tonal forces. It is a good form in which to introduce some *special tone-color*. The name is properly used to designate this compound stop, the two ranks of which stand at the interval of a *quart* or perfect fourth apart; just as the two ranks of the TERTIAN stand at the interval of a third apart. The term QUARTANE has in some instances been applied to a compound stop of *four ranks;* but as there are many four-rank MIXTURES of different compositions, the term is of no significance, from a tonal point of view, when so applied.

We now come to the consideration of the composition of MIXTURES, properly so-called, in which octave- and fifth-sounding ranks are alone introduced, in accordance with the old German practice. The following are representative examples:—

XXI. MIXTURE—III. RANKS.

CC to C,	. . . .	19—22—26.
C♯ to c^1,	. . . .	12—15—19.
$c♯^1$ to c^2,	. . . .	8—12—15.
$c♯^2$ to a^3,	. . . .	1—5—8.

XXII. MIXTURE—III. RANKS.

CC to BB,	. . . .	22—26—29.
C to $f♯^1$,	. . . .	15—19—22.
g^1 to g^3,	. . . .	8—12—15.

XXIII. MIXTURE—IV. RANKS.

CC to B,	. . .	19—22—26—29.
c^1 to f^2,	. . .	12—15—19—22.
$f♯^2$ to b^2,	. . .	8—12—15—19.
c^3 to c^4,	. . .	1—8—12—15.

XXIV. MIXTURE—IV. RANKS.

CC to BB,	. . .	19—22—26—29.
C to B,	. . .	15—19—22—26.
c^1 to b^1,	. . .	12—15—19—22.
c^2 to b^2,	. . .	8—12—15—19.
c^3 to c^4,	. . .	5—8—12—15.

XXV. Mixture—IV. and V. ranks.

CC to b^1,	. . .	5— 8—12—15.
c^2 to a^3,	. . .	1— 5— 8—12—15.

XXVI. Mixture—V. ranks.

CC to BB,	. . .	12—15—19—22—29.
C to B,	. . .	8—12—15—19—22.
c^1 to b^1,	. . .	5— 8—12—15—19.
c^2 to c^4,	. . .	1— 5— 8—12—15.

XXVII. Mixture—V. ranks.

CC to F♯,	. . .	15—19—22—26—29.
G to $f\sharp^1$,	. . .	8—12—15—19—22.
g^1 to c^4,	. . .	1— 5— 8—12—15.

XXVIII. Mixture—V. ranks.

CC to BB,	. . .	15—19—22—26—29.
C to B,	. . .	12—15—19—22—26.
c^1 to b^1,	. . .	8—12—15—19—22.
c^2 to b^2,	. . .	1— 8—12—15—19.
c^3 to c ,	. . .	1— 5— 8—12—15.

Example XXI. is a useful Mixture when properly proportioned, bright in the bass and tenor and full from middle $c\sharp^1$ to the top. Harris inserted one of this composition in his fine Organ in the Church of St. Peter, Mancroft, Norwich, constructed sometime in the second quarter of the eighteenth century. This example has one octave- and two fifth-sounding ranks in its bass and tenor octaves; and one fifth- and two octave-sounding ranks in its first treble break; with one unison-, one fifth-, and one octave-sounding rank in its top break. This last break strictly belongs to the 16 ft. harmonic series, and if skilfully proportioned in its strength of tone will impart great firmness to the top octave of the division. Example XXII. is the Mixture, of three ranks, inserted by John Snetzler in the Organ in the Parish Church of Halifax, Yorkshire, constructed in the year 1766. It was originally labeled Furniture, probably on account of the high-pitched ranks in its lower octave, and its bright and assertive voicing. Example XXVI. is the Mixture, of five ranks, in the Swell division of the Organ in the Cincinnati Music Hall, where it appears along with the Dolce Cornet, of six ranks, Example XXXVI.

By the term Furniture or Fourniture is understood a compound stop in which the pipes are smaller in scale, and the ranks generally higher in pitch, than those of the other Mixtures introduced in the same division of the Organ. Owing to the smallness of the pipes it is usually necessary to break the stop at every octave. The following two examples are good compositions for this compound stop:—

XXIX. FOURNITURE—IV. RANKS.

CC	to BB,	. . .	22—26—29—33.
C	to B,	. . .	19—22—26—29.
c^1	to b^1,	. . .	15—19—22—26.
c^2	to b^2,	. . .	12—15—19—22.
c^3	to a^3,	. . .	8—12—15—19.

XXX. FOURNITURE—V. RANKS.

CC	to BB,	. . .	24—26—29—33—36.
C	to B,	. . .	19—22—24—26—29.
c^1	to b^1,	. . .	15—17—19—22—26.
c^2	to b^2,	. . .	12—15—17—19—22.
c^3	to c^4,	. . .	8—12—15—17—19.

The general effect of this FOURNITURE, Example XXX., is singularly crisp and bright through the introduction of a third-sounding rank in every break.

Another compound stop formed of several ranks of high-pitched pipes is designated the CYMBAL or CYMBEL and is frequently found in old Organs of large size. Example XXXI. is a modern example of a noteworthy character: it appears in the Great division of the Organ in the Cincinnati Music Hall. It comprises no fewer than 427 pipes.

XXXI. CYMBEL—VII. RANKS.

CC	to BB,	. . .	15—19—22—26—29—33—36.
C	to B,	. . .	12—15—19—22—26—29—33.
c^1	to b^1,	. . .	8—12—15—19—22—26—29.
c^2	to b^2,	. . .	1— 5— 8—12—15—19—22.
c^3	to c^4,	. . .	DOUBLE—1— 5— 8—12—15—19.

Returning to the consideration of our series of ordinary MIXTURES: Example XXIII. is another MIXTURE which produces a brightening effect in the lower half and a filling-up effect in the upper half of the manual compass. It belongs, in all its intervals, to the unison (8 ft.) harmonic series; and, accordingly, is suitable, other conditions being favorable, for any division of the Organ in which no stop of 16 ft. tone is inserted. Example XXIV. is a MIXTURE very similar to the preceding. Its breaks are more gradual in their tonal transition, and occur at every octave. One rank—the QUINT—in the highest break belongs to the 16 ft. harmonic series; but, in the absence of a stop of 16 ft. pitch in the division, or if preferred, a unison rank can take its place, as in Example XXIII. Example XXVII. is a MIXTURE, of five ranks, capable of imparting a very full and rich coloring to any well appointed tonal scheme. The top break may be considered as belonging to the 16 ft. harmonic series in all its ranks, although its three higher ranks also belong to the 8 ft. series. This and the following Example XXVIII. are very suitable for leading manual divisions in which stops of 16 ft. pitch are inserted. Example XXV. is a Roosevelt MIXTURE, which entirely belongs to the 16 ft. harmonic series. It is somewhat noteworthy from the fact that it is the only MIXTURE in the Roosevelt standard collection of fourteen compound stops which is purely a QUINT MIXTURE: in all the others third-sounding ranks appear. This fact clearly proves that the late Mr. Hilborne L. Roosevelt and his able expert Mr. Walter F. Crosby fully understood and appreciated the tonal value of the TIERCE, now too much overlooked by organ designers and builders, as has been previously remarked. When an independent and through TIERCE, 1 3/5 FT., is provided in any manual division, it is not necessary, nor perhaps desirable, to duplicate it in any break of the MIXTURE; but if the latter contains an OCTAVE TIERCE, 4/5 FT., in its lower breaks, the effect will be perfectly satisfactory, provided the proper graduation of tonal strength has been observed.

It is now only necessary to add to our list of examples by giving particulars of certain special compound stops, which, under different names, have been introduced by both old and modern organ builders.

Several attempts have been made to produce MIXTURES whose compound tones shall imitate the sounds peculiar to bells. The results have only been moderately successful. Stops of this class are commonly called CARILLONS. The characteristic features of these stops lie in the scales and voicing of their pipes, and in their composition presenting three ranks—octave-, third-, and fifth-sounding. Example XXXII. is a CARILLON of this class; and Example XXXIII. is one specified by the late Mr. W. T. Best. It will be observed that the bell effect

XXXII. CARILLON—III. RANKS.

CC to F, ...	17—19—22.
F♯ to f¹, ...	15—17—19.
f♯¹ to f², ...	12—15—17.
f♯² to c⁴, ...	10—12—15.

XXXIII. CARILLON—III. RANKS.

CC to BB, ...	15—19—22.
C to B, ...	12—17—22.
c¹ to b¹, ...	12—15—17.
c² to a³, ...	8—12—15.

is confined to the tenor and the lower treble octaves, just where it would prove most effective. CARILLONS, of I. and III. ranks, are to be found in the Organ of the Royal Conservatoire, at Brussels, where it is introduced in the Positif Expressif; and in the Organ in the Town Hall, Manchester; both constructed by Cavaillé-Coll. The CARILLON in the latter instrument has a single fifth-sounding rank from CC to F♯; and a fifth-, a third-, and an octave-sounding rank from G to c⁴. All the pipes are of large scale, having wide and low mouths, and languids finely and closely nicked. There is a four-rank stop of this class in the Echo division of the Organ in the Centennial Hall, Sydney, N. S. W., under the

German name, GLOCKENSPIEL. CARILLONS, of II. or III. ranks, are to be found in several Dutch Organs and also in a few German instruments. It must be observed that while these compound stops are, from the nature of the ranks which compose them, harmonic-corroborating, they are chiefly valuable on account of their *timbre-creating* qualities. Of the true GLOCKENSPIEL or CARILLON, formed of bells, steel bars, or metallic tubes, we speak elsewhere.

Compound stops composed of several ranks of very small-scaled and delicately-voiced pipes are of the greatest value and beauty. Of this fact we have had satisfactory proof in our own Chamber Organ, in which is a stop formed of five ranks of DULCIANA pipes, carefully voiced on wind of 2 3/8 inches. Its composition is as follows:—

XXXIV. DULCIANA CORNET—V. RANKS.

CC to BB, . . .	19—22—24—26—29.
C to B, . . .	12—15—17—19—22.
c^1 to b^1, . . .	8—12—17—19—22.
c^2 to g^3, . . .	1—8—10—12—15.

This MIXTURE is so carefully graduated in its tones, and is of so delicate and refined a character, that it can be used with a single DULCIANA, 8 FT., while as a harmonic-corroborating stop it is sufficient when combined with the full strength of the Great Organ of thirteen stops. Speaking of this MIXTURE, Mr. F. E. Robertson, in "A Practical Treatise on Organ-Building," remarks: "Mr. Audsley had a very beautiful Chamber Organ of his own building,* the specification of which was as follows: [The Specification is given]. Wind 2 3/8″. The scale of the OPEN DIAP. is 5 1/4″ dia. A V-rank MIXTURE in an Organ of that size [Nineteen speaking stops] would, in the ordinary acceptation of the word, be a monstrosity, but to DULCIANA scale, and with every pipe [280 in number] regulated and voiced with the utmost care, it has a beautiful effect."

In the Roosevelt standard collection of compound stops we find the following composition for a DOLCE CORNET, which would produce a much broader tonal effect than the preceding:—

XXXV. DOLCE CORNET—V. RANKS.

CC to f^1, . . .	12—15—17—19—22.
$f\sharp^1$ to f^2, . . .	8—12—15—17—19.
$f\sharp^2$ to c^3, . . .	1—8—12—15—17.
$c\sharp^3$ to c^4, . . .	1—8—10—12—15.

In the Swell division of the Organ in the Music Hall, at Cincinnati, built by Messrs. Hook and Hastings, of Boston, Mass., is a DOLCE CORNET, the composition of which is given in Example XXXVI. This composition points to consid-

* This Organ was purchased by the late Lord Dysart, and now stands in Ham House, on the Thames, near Richmond, England.

XXXVI. Dolce Cornet—VI. ranks.

CC to BB, . . .	15—19—22—26—29—36.
C to B, . . .	12—15—19—22—26—29.
c^1 to b^1, . . .	8—12—15—19—22—26.
c^2 to c^4; . . .	1—5—8—10—12—15.

erable brilliancy of tonal effect in the two lower octaves; to richness in the middle octave; and to singular fulness in the two higher octaves. It will be observed that all the ranks in the two higher octaves belong to the 16 ft. harmonic series, corroborating the first, second, third, fourth, fifth, and seventh upper partial tones; and that in these octaves only is a third-sounding rank introduced. The fulness of the tonal effect in the higher octaves of this stop is due to the close relationship of the ranks which are there inserted. A stop of this class demands, beyond pipes of small scale, most artistic voicing and scientific graduation of tone throughout its ranks. Perfect regulation and accurate tuning are essential to its beauty and utility. These remarks, however, apply to all compound harmonic-corroborating stops.

A Mixture of high-pitched ranks, called by the German builders Scharf, and by others Acuta, is sometimes introduced in large divisions in which there

XXXVII. Acuta—III. ranks.

CC to B, . . .	22—24—26.
c^1 to b^1, . . .	17—19—22.
c^2 to b^2, . . .	15—17—19.
c^3 to c^4, . . .	12—15—17.

are other compound stops of graver intonation. The Acuta should be formed of medium- or small-scaled pipes, voiced to yield a bright silvery tone of carefully graduated strength. It is intended to add brilliancy to the general tone of the division in which it is inserted, without being unduly assertive. It is invaluable,

XXXVIII. Acuta—IV. ranks.

CC to BB, . . .	15—19—22—29.
C to B, . . .	12—15—19—22.
c^1 to b^1, . . .	8—12—15—19.
c^2 to c^4, . . .	1—8—12—15.

when scientifically made, in the production of varied tone colorings or *timbres.* The Acuta should invariably comprise a third-sounding rank throughout its compass, for its true character and office depend on its introduction. Example XXXVII. may be accepted as a representative composition, each break comprising an octave-, a third-, and a fifth-sounding rank. The Acuta, of IV. ranks, in the Great division of the Cincinnati Organ, Example XXXVIII., contains no third-sounding rank. It was, in all probability, considered unnecessary to include a Tierce in the Acuta, as one was carried throughout in the Cornet in the same manual division. Its omission was, we venture to think, a mistake on the part of the builders, especially as no independent TIERCE, $1\frac{3}{5}$ FT., was introduced in the Organ.

It is only necessary to particularly notice one other compound stop, called by the French organ builders PLEIN-JEU. A fine example of this stop exists in the Organ in the Town Hall of Manchester, built by Cavaillé-Coll. The composition of this MIXTURE is given in Example XXXIX. It has no special feature to dis-

XXXIX. PLEIN-JEU—VII. RANKS.

CC to E, ...	15—19—22—26—29—33—36.
F to e^1, ...	8—12—15—19—22—26—29.
f^1 to e^2, ...	1—8—12—15—19—22—26.
f^2 to b^2, ...	1—5—8—12—15—19—22.
c^3 to f^3, ...	DOUBLE—1—5—8—12—15—19.
$f\sharp^3$ to c^4, ...	DOUBLE—DOUBLE QUINT—1—5—8—12—15.

tinguish it from an ordinary MIXTURE in which octave- and fifth-sounding ranks only are used, except in its extreme richness of structure, and the introduction of ranks lower in pitch than the unison stops of the manual division (Grand-Orgue) in which it is placed. It may be remarked that this division, of fourteen speaking stops, contains three stops of 16 ft. pitch, which fact accounts for the presence of the DOUBLES and DOUBLE QUINT in the upper breaks of the PLEIN-JEU, as well as the other fifth-sounding ranks in the three higher breaks which strictly belong to the 16 ft. harmonic series.

In the scaling, voicing, and regulating of all the compound stops great knowledge, skill, and taste are demanded; and unless the organ builder is prepared to give both careful study and painstaking attention to all matters connected with their formation and tonal adjustment, he had much better omit them altogether from his organ schemes. It is preferable to have no MIXTURES than to have bad ones, for bad ones will destroy what may in their absence be satisfactory. Proof of this is afforded by too many modern Organs. The chief fault lies in the practice of ignoring the true offices of the compound stops, and this naturally leads to all manner of mistakes, notably the great mistake of making them much too loud and penetrating in their tones. It was the old practice of making such stops loud and screaming that led Seidel, of Breslau, to pen these words: "We find sometimes MIXTURES with from six to eight, and in old Organs even from ten to sixteen, ranks, both in the manual and in the pedal departments. A MIXTURE of so many ranks is a most absurd thing; for by the horrible noise it produces, the other stops lose their gravity and dignity, and the full organ produces nothing but a benumbing, stupefying noise." Seidel was right as regards the effect produced, but he was wrong respecting the cause. It was not the number of the ranks in the old MIXTURES, so much as their large scales and coarse, unscientific voicing and adjustment, that produced the "horrible noise" he wrote about. He utterly failed to grasp the true facts of the case; for he says, in his definition of a MIXTURE,—in his treatise on the Organ,—that it is "a stop of tin or metal having the same scale as the PRINCIPAL, repeating generally in the two upper octaves." How he could expect a simple harmonic-corroborating stop, formed of several ranks of pipes of the same large scale as the pipes of the foundation unison (8 ft.), to produce anything "but a benumbing, stupefying noise," in combination with the other stops of the Organ, is difficult to divine. Without giving one the slightest information respecting the proper method of constructing a compound stop, he adds: "On the other hand, a well-constructed MIXTURE is a very useful stop, since it unites in itself several stops, as it were, neither of which could be used by itself, and thereby saves a deal of space. Besides, it gives to the tone of the Organ, especially the full organ, fulness and power; distinctness and sharpness to the lower tones, more especially distinctness; and to the whole mass of tone a silver-like quality. In the repetition of a MIXTURE, fifths and octaves must be used alternately." A "*well-constructed* MIXTURE" does all that is above claimed, and more; but such a stop is rarely to be found in any Organ, old or new.

It must be borne in mind by all connected with the scheming and construction of Organs, that all compound stops should be scientifically proportioned with respect to the general tonal structure or appointment of the divisions in which they are to be placed. A MIXTURE that may be perfectly satisfactory in one Organ will, in all probability, be quite unsuitable in another. Under these circumstances it is obvious that every MIXTURE must be recognized as a distinct problem, to be solved only on scientific and artistic lines.

The composition of compound stops along artistic lines has not hitherto received proper study and attention. Much remains to be done to invest such stops with special tonal colorings, by the introduction of different classes of pipes in their separate ranks, and, under special circumstances, in their several breaks. Some tentative essays have been made in this direction with fair success. For instance, in the Swell division of the Concert-room Organ in the Public Halls, at Glasgow, is an ECHO DULCIANA CORNET, of six ranks, in which wood and metal, and open and stopped, pipes are associated together artistically. In compound stops in which the ranks are carried throughout the manual compass without a break, such as MIXTURES composed of a TWELFTH and SEVENTEENTH; TWELFTH, FIFTEENTH and SEVENTEENTH; OCTAVE, TWELFTH, FIFTEENTH, and SEVENTEENTH; or any other combination of such ranks, favorable opportunities are afforded for the production of varied tonal colorings, each rank having a special tonal tint.

While the office of the compound stops in corroborating the naturally weak harmonic upper partial tones of the foundation stops of the Organ has been commonly recognized, and may be said to be fairly well understood, among students of the art of organ-building, their equally important office as tone-creating or *timbre-creating* stops seems to have been overlooked, or, at best, only very partially realized. It is quite certain that up to the present time no systematic essays have been made to impart varied tonal coloring to the voices of the Organ through the agency of the compound stops; yet a fertile field for scientific investigation and practical skill lies in this direction.

It is a well-known fact that unison stops of any tone can be modified or altered in tonal coloring by their combination with harmonic-corroborating stops;

and, such being the case, it becomes obvious that such tonal coloring depends largely on the composition of the compound stops and on the tonal character of the pipes of which they are formed. MIXTURES formed of the same number of ranks and of the same intervals will produce different tonal colorings if their pipes are of different classes. For instance, a MIXTURE formed of the ordinary pipes, derived from the OPEN DIAPASON, will produce a widely different tonal effect in combination with any unison stop than will a similar MIXTURE formed of DULCIANA, DOLCE, SALICIONAL, VOX ANGELICA, VIOL, GEMSHORN, SPITZFLÖTE, or LIEBLICHFLÖTE pipes, or of a combination of any or all these pipes.

How far it is desirable to introduce compound stops extending through only a portion of the compass of the pedal and the manual claviers remains a question to be solved. There can be no doubt, however, that favorable results would attend their introduction if carried out in a thoroughly scientific and artistic manner. The first important essay in this direction appears to have been made by Musikdirektor Wilke, of Neu-Ruppin, who invented the compound stop called the COMPENSATIONSMIXTUR, and had it inserted in the pedal department of the Organ in the Church of St. Catherine, at Salzwedel, constructed by F. Turley, in 1838. Seidel, in his work on the Organ, describing this compound stop, says: "Its purpose is to give to the lower notes of the Pedal Organ the promptest and most distinct intonation possible; and to impart to the pedal department throughout such an even power of tone that rapid passages can be rendered thereon, with an equal roundness and distinctness from the lowest to the highest notes of the compass. According to the opinion of all competent judges, this register fully attains the end for which it was designed. Moreover, this MIXTURE has the advantage of not interfering with the gravity essential in the Pedal Organ, as is the case with an ordinary pedal MIXTURE, the small ranks of which have an objectionable effect. It consists of:—1. A TIERCE, 3⅕ FT., beginning on CCC and going up to GGG, thus consisting of only eight pipes, the intonation of which from DDD is gradually reduced in strength until on GGG it is so faint as to be almost inaudible. 2. A QUINT, 2⅔ FT., from CCC to AAA, having ten pipes, the tone of which diminishes from EEE, as before. 3. A PRINCIPAL, 2 FT., from CCC to GGG♯, nine pipes, the tone of which decreases from DDD in like manner. 4. A QUINT, 1⅓ FT., from CCC to FFF♯, seven pipes, diminishing in tone from CCC♯, and having a wide measure to render the tone as mellow as possible. 5. A SIFFLÖTE, 1 FT., from CCC to FFF, six pipes, scaled and voiced like the QUINT, 1⅓ FT.

The MIXTURE above described is remarkable on account of its very short compass, and the manner in which the pipes of its several ranks terminate on different notes, and their tones diminish in strength as they ascend in the scale. Although Seidel affirms that the stop, according to the opinion of competent judges, was found to fully attain the end for which it was designed, it may be said that its introduction did not meet with support among the conservative and generally slow-going organ builders of Germany. Whatever the tonal effect of this unique MIXTURE, as originally constructed, may have been, its scheme and the idea which prompted its formation are deserving of careful consideration. On both scientific and esthetic grounds, harmonic-corroborating compound stops, formed on lines similar to those above described, but extending much higher, and in one or two ranks throughout the compass of the Pedal Organ, are to be strongly recommended; for, while they may be made so as to greatly enrich and impart distinct coloring to the lower tones of the unison and double stops, they will, on account of their diminishing voices, add no disagreeable shrillness to the higher tones. We are of opinion that similar principles of construction and tonal treatment might with advantage be followed in certain classes of compound stops suitable for the manual divisions of the Organ. At this point the following extract may be read with advantage. Prof. Helmholtz, after an instructive analysis of the tones produced by the strings of the Pianoforte, says:—

"In many other instruments, where their construction does not admit of such absolute control over the quality of tone as on the Pianoforte, attempts have been made to produce similar varieties of quality in the high notes, by other means. In the bowed instruments this purpose is served by the resonance box, the proper tones of which lie within the deepest Octaves of the scale of the instrument. Since the partial tones of the resonant strings are reinforced in proportion to their proximity to the partial tones of the resonance box, this resonance will assist the prime tones of the higher notes as contrasted with their upper partials, much more than it will do so for the deep notes. On the contrary, the deepest notes of the Violin will have not only their prime tones, but also their Octaves and Fifths favored by the resonance; for the deeper proper tone of the resonance box lies between the prime and second partial, and its higher proper tone between the second and third partials. *A similar effect is attained in the* COMPOUND STOPS *of the Organ, by making the series of upper partial tones, which are represented by distinct pipes, less extensive for the higher than for the lower notes in the stop. Thus each digital opens six pipes for the lower octaves, answering to the first six partial tones of its note; but in the two upper octaves, the digital opens only three or even two pipes, which give the Octave and Twelfth, or merely the Octave, in addition to the prime.*"

We offer, for the consideration of the organ expert, the following composition for a COMPENSATIONSMIXTUR or what may be designated a COMPENSATING MIXTURE, one rank of which extends throughout the compass of the Pedal Organ:—

PEDAL ORGAN COMPENSATING MIXTURE—VI. RANKS.

CCC to G,	SUPER-OCTAVE, 4 FT.	32 notes.	CCC to GG,	TWENTY-SECOND, 2 FT.	20 notes.
CCC to D,	TIERCE, $3\frac{1}{5}$ FT. . .	27 "	CCC to EE,	TWENTY-SIXTH, $1\frac{1}{3}$ FT.	17 "
CCC to BB,	OCTAVE QUINT, $2\frac{2}{3}$ FT.	24 "	CCC to CC,	TWENTY-NINTH, 1 FT.	13 "

The scales of the several ranks should be relatively smaller as they rise in pitch; and their ratio should be such as to place the half diameter on the thirteenth pipe. In addition to this quick reduction in scale, it is essential to the true office of the stop that the voice of each rank be gradually reduced in strength as it ascends the scale, so as to render its cessation practically imperceptible to the ear. As the sole purpose of this compound stop is to corroborate the higher upper partials of the 16 ft. prime, and by that means impart a certain degree of life and distinctness to the grave and somewhat droning tones of the foundation unisons of the pedal department, the several ranks should be formed of metal pipes, preferably of the GEMSHORN class. Should a fuller and rounder tone be desired, cylindrical metal pipes may be adopted.

Under certain circumstances, and especially in a large and richly-appointed pedal department, in which there is a practically complete series of independent stops corroborating the lower and more important upper partials of the 16 ft. prime, it may be found desirable to add a FURNITURE, formed of small-scaled metal pipes, carefully graduated in tone, corroborating the higher upper partials. If artistically scaled and voiced, a compound stop of this description would impart a rare beauty of tonal coloring to the numerous combinations of both the labial and lingual stops of the department. Its usefulness and charm would be greatly increased if it were inclosed in the manner set forth in the Chapter on the Concert-room Organ. The FURNITURE may be composed as follows:—

PEDAL ORGAN FURNITURE—VI. RANKS.

CCC to G, . . 15——19——22——24——26——29.

Certain individuals who claim to be authorities in organ-building matters have pronounced an opinion that, under the modern or their special manner of stop appointment, MIXTURES are unnecessary and undesirable. It is practically a waste of words to discuss the arguments, if arguments they can be called, that these persons have advanced; for, after the researches of Prof. Helmholtz, the value of the harmonic-corroborating stops cannot well be questioned, even if one is disposed to forget all that past experience has proved, and to ignore the opinions of the many musicians who have advocated their introduction and recognized their importance in the tonal appointment of the Organ. We are disposed to believe that those who dispute the importance and utility of the harmonic-corroborating stops in tone-creation have given very little, if any, serious attention to the acoustical phenomena involved. That a certain class of organ builders should be willing to meet the wishes of those who object to the introduction of MIXTURES is not to be wondered at. However many ranks a MIXTURE may comprise, it appears in an Organ Specification as a single stop; and this, when a builder is estimating for an Organ on the many-stop basis, is a decided drawback in his estimation. Besides this, an organ builder, unless he is a consummate artist, looks upon MIXTURES unfavorably, because they are usually unsatisfactory in their tonal effects through unscientific treatment; and because they are expensive and troublesome to make, and still more troublesome to regulate, tune correctly, and keep in order. Such considerations, however, should not influence the musician who realizes the proper office and true value of the harmonic-corroborating stops.

There is a growing impression in certain quarters that the introduction of labial and lingual stops of unison pitch, the tones of which are rich in harmonic upper partials, renders the introduction of harmonic-corroborating stops unnecessary. All that need be said with respect to the pungent string-toned and imitative stops is that they do not call, in their more important office in a tonal scheme, for direct aid from mixture-work, except under special circumstances, as already pointed out in the Chapter on the Concert-room Organ. It must not be forgotten, however, that there are numerous stops, and among them the foundation stops of the Organ, the normal tones of which are essentially weak in harmonics; and that, for the production of many beautiful and valuable varieties of *timbre* or tone-color, these important stops have to be associated with the different harmonic-corroborating or *timbre-creating* stops. For the successful production of these valuable varieties of *timbre*, it is absolutely necessary that the compound stops be, in the first place, scientifically composed, scaled, voiced, and regulated; and, in the second place, be under control as regards their strength of tone. We put these matters to a crucial test in our own Chamber Organ, in which we introduced in one of the two expressive sections of the Great Organ the five-rank DULCIANA CORNET already alluded to, and the composition of which is given in Example XXXIV. This stop, under the peculiar conditions of its tonal character and its extreme flexibility, was available in combination with every unison and octave stop in the instrument, producing an endless variety of beautiful tonal effects. It was sufficient for the full organ; while with the softest unison in the Organ it produced a quality of tone that was the admiration of every musician that sat at the keys. It also combined in a perfectly satisfactory manner with such solo stops as the VIOLA D'AMORE, CLARINET, OBOE, and VOX HUMANA.

Another objection has been advanced in connection with the use of mixture-work; namely, that it "clashes with equal temperament": but this objection hardly deserves serious consideration in the face of the scientific demonstrations of Helmholtz; and the approval of many great musicians who have studied the Organ, from the time of the greatest advocate of equal temperament—the immortal Johann Sebastian Bach. We freely acknowledge, however, that there are innumerable old and modern MIXTURES that not only "clash with equal temperament," but are of such a character as to clash with themselves and every stop that can be drawn with them. Such MIXTURES are the results of ignorance of the fundamental principles that should guide the formation of harmonic-corroborating stops, and, accordingly, are of no value in an argument against the introduction of scientifically constructed mixture-work.

Among the great modern masters of the Organ, no one devoted more study and attention to the subject of the compound harmonic-corroborating stops than the late Mr. W. T. Best; and we venture to say no one understood the scientific composition and the musical value of such stops better than he did. Having enjoyed his friendship during a period of more than a quarter of a century, and having many times discussed with him the problems connected with the tonal structure of the Organ,—not the least in importance being those presented by the harmonic-corroborating stops,—we feel that we can speak with some authority respecting his views on the subject now under consideration. Mr. Best not only condemned the omission of MIXTURES from Organs of all classes as wrong from every point of view, but did everything in his power to secure their retention in modern organ-building by giving their scientific composition and treatment serious study, and by devising and introducing several MIXTURES of singular tonal beauty and value. Among the countless striking tonal effects we have heard this consummate master of the Organ produce on the grand instrument in St. George's

Hall, Liverpool, none struck us as more remarkable than those due to the masterly combination of the single and compound harmonic-corroborating stops with unison and double stops of different tonalities. Mr. Best strongly advocated the introduction of third-sounding ranks in the composition of MIXTURES; namely, those which corroborate the fourth, ninth, and nineteenth upper partial tones. In this we are strictly in accord with him. That such ranks are commonly eschewed by English and American builders only goes to prove want of proper appreciation on their part. They have not found the few instances of the introduction of these ranks in their own works altogether satisfactory, simply because they were not scientifically and artistically treated. Such examples are replete with negative teaching, and they go no way to support the belief that third-sounding ranks should be omitted in the harmonic-corroborating stops of the Organ. These third-sounding ranks are, unfortunately, not the only ones that have been and are being unscientifically and inartistically treated.

The prevailing treatment of the compound stops, throughout all the schools of organ-building, is extremely faulty. For proof of this, in the German school, we have only to refer to the writings of Prof. Helmholtz. He says: "Very piercing qualities of tone are produced by the reed pipes and compound stops on the Organ. The latter are artificial imitations of the natural composition of all musical tones, each key bringing a series of pipes into action, which correspond to the first three or first six partial tones of the corresponding note. They can be used only to accompany congregational singing. *When employed alone they produce insupportable noise and horrible confusion.* But when the singing of the congregation gives overpowering force to the prime tones in the notes of the melody, the proper relation of quality of tone is restored, and the result is a powerful, well-proportioned mass of sound. Without the assistance of these compound stops it would be impossible to control a vast body of sound produced by unpracticed voices, such as we hear in churches." These remarks, from the pen of so great an authority on matters of tone-production, give us a clear insight into the methods and purposes of the German builders of Church Organs. Noise, not music, is their path to fame. It is but right to say that there are MIXTURES and MIXTURES; while it is true that there are few to be found in Organs to-day which fulfil their proper and legitimate office in the tonal structure of the Organ in an artistic and perfectly satisfactory manner.

We may, at the risk of repeating what has already been remarked, say that no section of the tonal forces of the Organ calls for more scientific knowledge, more painstaking investigation, more careful experimentation, and a more highly cultivated musical sense, than the section which embraces the harmonic-corroborating voices: yet at the present time the tendency, even among those who profess to be artistic organ builders, is to pay very slight attention to these invaluable voices. By some they are held to be of little importance and may be dispensed with,—surely here the wish is father to the thought,—while the truth is they are of great importance and value, affecting to a marked degree the entire tonal character of the Organ. They are factors of immense influence in the production of varied *timbres* and rich compound tones, which would simply be unobtainable without them. The influence of MIXTURES, for good or bad, cannot be overestimated; and, accordingly, all matters connected with their composition and artistic treatment claim very serious attention. It has been thoughtlessly asserted that modern organ appointment is independent of their aid; and had the imitative stops of to-day been known to the old organ builders, they would have abandoned to a large extent, if not entirely, the insertion of mixture-work in their Organs. There is absolutely no authority for such an assumption; but we are disposed to believe that had the results of modern skill been at the disposal of the old masters, they would have handed down to us compound stops of a class widely different from that met with in their representative Organs. Viewed from a scientific stand-point, and even an artistic one, there is little doubt that old Organs, generally, were overcharged with MIXTURES of too assertive a character; but in this matter one must not forget the work such Organs were designed to accomplish. While such is unquestionably the case, we must acknowledge that the best mixture-work of the old school is to be found in German Organs; and even while one questions its scientific treatment, one cannot help being struck with the marvelous brilliancy with which, when judiciously used, it sometimes clothes the full foundation tones of certain grand old instruments.

Notwithstanding all that has been done during the last two centuries, we are strongly of opinion that the making of mixture-work is in its infancy. Surely much more can be done than has yet been achieved; and, directed by the results of the researches conducted by Professor Helmholtz in the realms of tone, the organ experts of to-day are in a position altogether superior to that occupied by the old pioneers of the art of organ-building. But seeing the little that has been attempted of a truly scientific and artistic character, it is difficult to divine what may be accomplished in the future, when highly educated and thoroughly trained organ builders realize the necessity of giving their undivided attention to the development of the tonal resources of the Organ.

TIMBRE-CREATING COMPOUND STOPS.

In the foregoing remarks we have touched upon a subject which deserves the careful consideration of the student of the art of organ-building. We have pointed out that much remains to be done to invest the compound stops of the Organ with special and varied tonal colorings, by the introduction of different classes of pipes in their separate ranks, and, under special circumstances, in their several breaks. While a few tentative essays in this direction have been made by certain builders, no noteworthy results of systematic methods have as yet appeared in important Organs. The field is practically a virgin one, offering a wide scope for study and experiment: and it is to be hoped that the musicians and the students of organ construction of the twentieth century will give this important branch of tonal appointment the attention it deserves. When it is fully recognized that the compound stops are not merely harmonic-corroborating, but that they are also, under certain conditions, *timbre-creating*, it is not difficult to realize that much can be done, under the inspiration of acoustical science and musical art, which has never been attempted under the methods adopted by the old builders, and followed, more or less blindly, by their successors.

It may be safely said that no stop of the Organ affords so wide a field for the display of acoustical knowledge and refined musical sense as the MIXTURE; and, under usual conditions, no single stop exerts so potent an influence for good or ill on the general tone of the instrument. We have already pointed out how the compound stops can be improved by constructing them more closely in accordance with the teaching of acoustical science and the phenomena of musical sounds; and it only remains for us to close this Chapter by offering a few suggestions for their further development.

While we maintain that all the harmonic-corroborating stops of the Organ should be so voiced and regulated as to yield tones in strict accordance with the natural laws of sound, we do not say that they should all be constructed alike. On the contrary, we go so far as to say that no two MIXTURES in the same Organ should be similar in their tonal character or office. In a large instrument, having three, four, or more separate manual divisions or subdivisions, every one of its several compound stops should be entirely different from the others; its predominant pitch, the number of its ranks, the number and positions of its breaks, and the tonal character of each of its ranks, being dictated by the tonal appointment of the division or subdivision in which it is placed, and the office it has to fulfil therein. Speaking broadly, the compound stops may be grouped under two classifications; namely, *harmonic-corroborating* and *timbre-creating*. The former properly belong to the foundation-work, represented by the OPEN DIAPASONS, and find their proper place and office in the division in which the principal pure organ-toned stops are congregated—that commonly called the Great Organ. Here the compound stops, in their correct treatment, are of normal organ-tone, corroborating, and to a considerable extent introducing, the upper partial tones of the DIAPASON prime, to which they impart fulness and richness without changing its pure organ-tone. The *timbre-creating* compound stops, as the term implies, are those which have a distinctive and varied tonality, and which introduce a special tonal coloring into every combination of which they form a constituent. These compound stops have a dual office. In the first place, they enrich the harmonic structure of the divisions in which they are placed, by introducing the higher upper partial tones of the unison prime. In the second place, they create in combination with the several unison labial and lingual stops important and striking changes in tonal coloring,—imparting to certain stops or combinations an element of intense brilliancy; to others rich and vivid coloring; to others solidity of tone,—apparently altering their own tonal character with every change of the prime tones and their combinations.

The timbre-creating compound stops may be formed according to two methods, which may now be briefly described. In the first method of construction, all the ranks employed are of the same class of pipes, yielding the same quality of tone, and graduated in strength in accordance with the laws which govern the natural harmonic upper partial tones, as already dwelt upon. The pipes forming a timbre-creating compound stop, of the form now under consideration, may be all of metal or all of wood, and all open or all covered; and they may be of any tonality possible in labial pipes. Accordingly, we can have compound stops composed of pipes belonging to any of the following classes: LIEBLICHGEDECKT, ROHRFLÖTE, SPITZFLÖTE, HARMONIC FLUTE, ZAUBERFLÖTE, ZARTFLÖTE, GEMSHORN, DULCIANA, VOX ANGELICA, ÆOLINE, VIOLA DA GAMBA, VIOLA D'AMORE, VIOL, DOLCAN, and several others that will suggest themselves to the artist in quest of tone-colors. Compound stops constructed under this method have been introduced to some extent by certain builders, and invariably with encouraging results; but it is open to the artistic builders of the present century to carry their construction to the highest point of excellence, and to introduce them into the expressive divisions of their Organs. That the timbre-creating value of compound stops of different tonalities will ultimately be recognized by musicians we have very little doubt: and the general introduction of such stops, in scientifically and artistically appointed instruments, can only be retarded by the reluctance of organ builders to depart from the old-fashioned and time-honored manner of tonal appointment.

When we approach the consideration of the compound stops constructed according to the second method, we enter upon ground all but unexplored,—at best, only pressed by the hesitating footsteps of those whose musical sense and artistic perception lead to a desire for better things than are commonly served up by the average organ builder, or are dreamt of by the average organist. This second method of constructing the timbre-creating compound stops consists in forming their ranks of pipes of different tonalities. This method, as may be readily realized, opens up a wide and fertile field for study and experiment on the part of the organ builder who will for a time forget the modern craze for mechanical complexity, and deign to turn his attention to the far more important matters of scientific and artistic tone-production and tonal appointment. As we have already remarked, at the present time too little interest is being evinced in the branch of organ-building which makes, or should make, the Organ a *musical instrument.* Simplicity of mechanical structure and complexity of tonal structure are what are called for in the perfect Organ of the Future, which shall be the delight of the musical *virtuoso*, and the obedient servant of the ordinary performer.

While it is imperative, from a scientific point of view, that the different ranks of a compound stop be graduated in strength of tone, it is by no means necessary, from an artistic point of view, that the same tonal character should pervade all its ranks. Indeed, when we realize the importance of the compound stops as timbre-creators, and not merely as harmonic-corroborators, we can surely see the musical value certain to accrue from a well-considered and artistic introduction of different tone-colors in their several ranks. We will suppose a MIXTURE, of five ranks, to be introduced in an expressive division of an Organ, each rank of which is formed of pipes having a distinct and contrasting tonality; and that unison stops of similar tonalities are present in the same division, or, perhaps, in other divisions which are capable of being coupled with that containing the MIXTURE. Now, any one well versed in the subject of tonal combinations can easily imagine the immense variety of *timbres* that would result from the combination of such a MIXTURE with the several unison stops, individually or in varied groups. Each unison stop would find only one rank in the MIXTURE yielding tones strictly belonging to its own family of harmonics; while the tones of all the other ranks, falling in—in pitch only—with the sequence of the harmonic upper partials of the prime unison tone, would create special, and frequently remarkable and beautiful, effects of tonal coloring—effects absolutely impossible to obtain in the Organ by any other expedients. Such effects—which may be compared to the wonderful hues produced by the painter on his many-tinted palette—would be practically inexhaustible in Organs of moderate dimensions, while in Concert-room Organs of the first magnitude they would be absolutely inexhaustible.

It is not practicable to formulate any rules for the tonal structure of these timbre-creating compound stops, simply because it depends upon the tonal appointment of the divisions of the Organ in which they are placed and the peculiar tonal coloring aimed at. In deciding the treatment to be adopted, the following matters have to be taken into careful consideration: First, the number of ranks have to be decided on. Secondly, the pitches of the ranks have to be selected, with respect to the general tonal appointment of the division in which the stop is to be placed. Thirdly, the different tones to be congregated have to be selected, in accordance with the special purposes of the stop. Fourthly,—and this is a question of great moment,—the apportionment of the selected tones to the different ranks. In the case of a MIXTURE of five ranks this apportionment can be varied to almost any extent, each one producing a distinct tonal coloring. For instance, in the case of a MIXTURE of five ranks, in which a different quality of tone is given to each rank, the following table shows the number of tonal combinations of which it is capable, while the same tone is retained throughout in the first rank. The Roman numerals indicate the several ranks; while the letters under them indicate the tones that may be apportioned to them. The letter L represents a tone such as is produced by the LIEBLICHGEDECKT; O a normal organ-tone; V a string-tone such as is produced by a VIOL stop; F an open flute-tone; and G a tone such as that yielded by the GEMSHORN:—

	I.	II.	III.	IV.	V.		I.	II.	III.	IV.	V.		I.	II.	III.	IV.	V.		I.	II.	III.	IV.	V.
1.	L.	O.	V.	F.	G.	7.	L.	V.	O.	F.	G.	13.	L.	F.	V.	O.	G.	19.	L.	G.	V.	F.	O.
2.	L.	O.	V.	G.	F.	8.	L.	V.	F.	G.	O.	14.	L.	F.	O.	G.	V.	20.	L.	G.	F.	O.	V.
3.	L.	O.	F.	G.	V.	9.	L.	V.	G.	O.	F.	15.	L.	F.	G.	V.	O.	21.	L.	G.	O.	V.	F.
4.	L.	O.	G.	F.	V.	10.	L.	V.	O.	G.	F.	16.	L.	F.	V.	G.	O.	22.	L.	G.	V.	O.	F.
5.	L.	O.	G.	V.	F.	11.	L.	V.	G.	F.	O.	17.	L.	F.	G.	O.	V.	23.	L.	G.	O.	F.	V.
6.	L.	O.	F.	V.	G.	12.	L.	V.	F.	O.	G.	18.	L.	F.	O.	V.	G.	24.	L.	G.	F.	V.	O.

The above table shows twenty-four different combinations, each rank representing a special harmonic upper partial; and the arrangements of the different tones on these would of necessity produce varied qualities of compound tone, which would be essentially timbre-creating when combined with any of the prime or unison tones in the Organ. Other tables can be formed by changing the tones of the first and second ranks, as can be readily seen. The production of varied qualities of tone, in a compound stop so appointed, is greatly favored by the natural law which governs the decreasing strength of the upper partial tones as they rise in pitch. Accordingly, the tone which is required to be the most assertive should be apportioned to the first rank, or that which corroborates or represents the lowest upper partial tone of the series.

After the few hints we have ventured to give on a very complex subject, it is advisable to remark that only a comparatively limited use can be made of the timbre-creating compound stops. Their proper place is in those divisions of the Concert-room Organ in which the principal solo and imitative voices are congregated. In the First Organ, or that division which may be designated the Organ proper, the ordinary harmonic-corroborating stops are unquestionably the most suitable. Here a rich, full, and properly-balanced volume of pure organ-tone is an artistic necessity, while variety of timbre or extreme changes of tonality may be safely pronounced out of place. The true and grand office of the First Organ should never be sacrificed for the sake of varied tonal effects, however fascinating they may be. The full meaning of these concluding remarks will be realized on referring to our Chapter on the Concert-room Organ.

CHAPTER XII.

THE TONAL APPOINTMENT OF THE ORGAN.

IN Chapter X., on The Tonal Structure of the Organ, we deal chiefly with the different pitches of organ pipes, and the acoustical phenomena and laws relating to them, both in their association with, and their relation to, each other. In the present Chapter we treat of the Tonal Appointment of the Organ, or the grouping of stops, chiefly with reference to their individual and distinctive qualities of tone. The correct and artistic appointment of an Organ is a matter of the greatest importance, and is one that calls for the exercise of some scientific knowledge and considerable judgment and musical taste.

We are entering on the consideration of a subject somewhat complicated in character, and one that deserves to be treated at great length and in the fullest possible manner; but in the present treatise only a very limited space can be devoted to it: indeed, the following notes must be looked upon as little more than introductory, and valuable only for their suggestiveness.

While the voices of the Organ are numerous and varied in their character and strength of tone, they seem naturally to group themselves into more or less sharply defined and distinctive classes. We have found it convenient and satisfactory to divide the entire range of the tonal forces at the disposal of the modern organ builder into two primary groups, subdividing each into four secondary groups. By so doing we obtain the following:—

FIRST GROUP.
Organ-Tone.
Unimitative Quality.

1. PURE ORGAN-TONE.
2. FREE ORGAN-TONE.
3. FLUTE ORGAN-TONE.
4. VIOL ORGAN-TONE.

SECOND GROUP.
Orchestral-Tone.
Imitative Quality.

1. ORCHESTRAL FLUTE-TONE.
2. ORCHESTRAL STRING-TONE.
3. ORCHESTRAL REED-TONE.
4. ORCHESTRAL BRASS-TONE.

Although all the tones just given must be adequately represented in the appointment of a complete and perfect modern Organ, devised for the rendition of both organ and orchestral music, the four tones forming the first group are the only ones that are essential to the constitution of the Organ proper. The purely imitative voices are, however, of the greatest value, and should be introduced to some extent in instruments of every class. In the properly-appointed Concert-room Organ the orchestral-tones are indispensable, and should be represented to the fullest extent called for by the size of the instrument. In the Chamber Organ, which in all cases should be schemed on the Concert-room model, the imitative voices are also indispensable up to a certain point, and care must be taken to give them a refined character suitable for chamber music. In the true, and properly appointed, Church Organ, the imitations of orchestral instruments are of less importance, and may be sparingly introduced. They are not so well adapted as the several organ-tones for the support and accompaniment of the voices of a choir, or for the production of the solemn, refined, and dignified tones which should characterize the music of the Church.

Pure organ-tone is essentially unimitative in character, and is that which is peculiar to the Organ. It is produced by open cylindrical metal pipes, commonly of large scale, copiously blown by wind of moderate pressure. Such pipes when properly voiced yield singularly full and round tones that are practically simple in their nature; for, under proper and usual conditions, no harmonic upper partial tones are pronounced in them: indeed, the only upper partial tones that produce any sensible effect are the first and second. It is from the stops formed of such pipes that the Organ derives its distinctive character and the chief elements of its grandeur. Of such stops, those commonly known as the OPEN DIAPASONS are the most important; and they form the true foundation of every properly-appointed Organ. As Helmholtz correctly remarks: "Wide pipes, having larger masses of vibrating air and admitting of being much more strongly blown [than smaller-scaled, open cylindrical pipes] without jumping up into an harmonic, are used for the great body of sound on the Organ, and are hence called *Principal-stimmen* [principal voices]. For the above reasons they produce the prime tone alone strongly and fully, with a much weaker retinue of secondary tones."

These principal or foundation stops are of 16 ft. pitch in the pedal and 8 ft. pitch in the manual departments. The tones of such stops, pure and full as they are, produce, if massed together and depended upon entirely, too cloying and heavy an effect to be perfectly acceptable to the musical sense. As before stated, these foundation voices are essentially deficient and weak in harmonic upper partial tones; therefore it is found desirable, in accordance with the phenomena of compound musical sounds, to associate with them other and higher voices, calculated to create a perfectly satisfactory compound tone, rich, bright, and jubilant in its quality. The higher tones so introduced corroborate and supply a desirable number of the upper partials of the prime tones.

The harmonic-corroborating stops associated with the OPEN DIAPASONS are, like them, formed of open cylindrical metal pipes, yielding pure organ-tone. These stops must be properly scaled with reference to the OPEN DIAPASONS, and voiced so as to combine with, or be absorbed in, the prime tones without asserting any undue prominence. On this subject we have dwelt at sufficient length in the preceding Chapter, so need not enlarge upon it here.

The more important associated harmonic-corroborating stops are the OCTAVE, TWELFTH, FIFTEENTH, SEVENTEENTH, NINETEENTH, and TWENTY-SECOND. These corroborate the 1st, 2nd, 3rd, 4th, 5th, and 7th upper partial tones of the unisons. In addition to these, other open cylindrical metal stops, yielding pure organ-tone, and belonging to the foundation-work, bear the following names in English Organs: DOUBLE OPEN DIAPASON, 32 FT. (in the Pedal Organ), DOUBLE OPEN DIAPASON, 16 FT. (in manual divisions), "SHARP TWENTIETH," TWENTY-FOURTH, TWENTY-SIXTH, TWENTY-NINTH, THIRTY-THIRD, and THIRTY-SIXTH. The SHARP TWENTIETH which corroborates the 6th upper partial of the unison, is very rare in English Organs; but, under the name of SEPTIÈME, it appears in the form of a complete stop in certain French Organs. All the other harmonic-corroborating ranks above the FIFTEENTH commonly appear in the several breaks of the compound stops or MIXTURES; but the SEVENTEENTH, NINETEENTH, and TWENTY-SECOND sometimes appear as complete stops. In the Pedal Organ they should always be inserted complete, as they would belong to the 16 ft. harmonic series and be of short compass.

We have in the above list a practically complete series of stops and ranks of pipes yielding pure organ-tone, from which a great variety of more or less satisfactory Pedal and Great Organ appointments can be made; but the only perfect appointment is that in which every member of the series is represented in due relation and subordination to the prime or foundation unisons. The importance of having a complete tonal structure and appointment in at least the pedal department and one manual division of the Organ cannot be overestimated, for such an appointment gives the performer a limitless range and variety of compound organ-tones. As Helmholtz remarks: "In this respect the Organ has an advantage over all other instruments, as the player is able to mix and alter the qualities of tone at pleasure, and make them suitable to the character of the piece he has to perform."

We have stated that pure organ-tone is that produced by open, cylindrical metal pipes, of large scale, copiously blown by wind of moderate pressure. This is strictly true, for the purest organ-tone is yielded by the true English OPEN DIAPASON, formed of cylindrical metal pipes of a scale ranging between 6 inches and 7 inches in diameter at the CC, or 8 ft., pipe,* and blown by wind of from 3 inches to 4 inches pressure. It is never desirable for the production of pure organ-tone to exceed the latter pressure, for when it is exceeded the purity or character of the tone suffers. The CC pipe of the fine OPEN DIAPASON, 8 FT., by Father Smith, in the Organ of Trinity College Chapel, at Cambridge, measures 6 inches in diameter; while the large OPEN DIAPASON, 8 FT., by Schulze, in the

* Stops ostensibly of the OPEN DIAPASON class have been made of much larger scales than those here advocated; and, doubtless, their voices are extremely grand when heard under the acoustical advantages which obtain in spacious cathedrals and vaulted churches: but, at the same time, it is questionable if such large-scaled stops can be strictly said to belong to the true diapason-work, for their tones, properly analyzed, are more likely to place them in the flute-work of the Organ.

Organ of the Parish Church of Leeds, probably the grandest stop of its class in existence, has its CC pipe 6¼ inches in diameter. This latter stop is very copiously blown by wind of 3¾ inches pressure.

Although both scale and wind pressure are factors of great importance, the art of the voicer is a factor of almost more influence than either; and it is through its skilful and painstaking exercise that we must look for the perfection of pure organ-tone. This fact is exemplified to a remarkable extent in the work of the great Schulze. We find in his notable Organ, now in the Church of St. Bartholomew, at Armley, near Leeds, the bass octaves of the SUB-PRINCIPAL, 16 FT. (DOUBLE OPEN DIAPASON), MAJOR PRINCIPAL, 8 FT. (Great OPEN DIAPASON), and MINOR PRINCIPAL, 8 FT. (Choir OPEN DIAPASON), all formed of quadrangular wood pipes, voiced so skilfully that the beautiful tones of the metal pipes of their higher octaves are carried down in the most perfect manner; so much so, that while one cannot help admiring the richness of the tones of the bass octaves of these stops, one would not readily suspect their being produced by wood pipes.

In practice it is extremely difficult to define the boundary lines between the several divisions of organ-tone; and in written description it is practically impossible to define them. Between pure organ-tone and what we mean by free organ-tone there is a very fine line of demarkation; indeed, one may be said to flow imperceptibly into the other. On the boundary line between the stops producing pure organ-tone and those yielding free organ-tone stands the true DULCIANA, the tone of which is only distinguishable from pure organ-tone by its extreme softness and delicacy. This stop is formed of small-scaled open cylindrical metal pipes, voiced in a similar manner to the OPEN DIAPASON, and blown by a small supply of wind at a moderate pressure, preferably from 2½ inches to 3 inches. Like the OPEN DIAPASON, the DULCIANA, 8 FT., may be properly attended by its family of harmonic-corroborating stops, producing very lovely compound tones of the greatest value in the appointment of the Choir Organ, or any other softly-voiced manual division. The members of the family most useful are the OCTAVE DULCIANA, 4 FT., DULCIANA TWELFTH, 2⅔ FT., SUPER-OCTAVE DULCIANA, 2 FT., and the DULCIANA CORNET or MIXTURE, of V. ranks, in which octave-, third-, and fifth-sounding ranks are introduced. (See Chapter on The Compound Stops of the Organ.) In the appointment of the Pedal Organ a DULCIANA, 16 FT., should in all possible cases be included. The value of a stop of this class, to furnish an appropriate bass to soft manual stops and combinations, cannot be overrated. For the sub-octave tone in the Choir Organ no stop can supersede the DOUBLE DULCIANA, 16 FT. Still more delicate in tone than the DULCIANA is the so-called VOX ANGELICA, 8 FT.; and much more assertive than the DULCIANA are the SALICIONAL and KERAULOPHON, both stops of unison pitch. It is somewhat difficult to class these latter stops, because their tones vary considerably under different systems of voicing. Notwithstanding the fact that the SALICIONAL has sometimes a pronounced string-tone, and the KERAULOPHON yields a horn-like quality of voice, they may be classed among the stops producing free organ-tone. They are formed of cylindrical metal pipes; those of the KERAULOPHON having a tuning slide at top, perforated with a circular hole. The KERAULOPHON is invariably a manual stop of unison pitch ; but the SALICIONAL is introduced both as a unison and an octave stop, the latter being called a SALICET when both appear together. These stops require a medium supply of wind of the same pressure as that adopted for the OPEN DIAPASON. The DOLCAN, 8 FT., formed of open inverted conical pipes of either metal or wood, and the DOLCE, 8 FT., formed either of small-scaled cylindrical or inverted conical metal pipes, are stops yielding free organ-tone of a quiet and somewhat plaintive character. Among the few wood stops which produce free organ-tones of valuable and distinctive qualities are the MELODIA, 8 FT., and the HARMONICA, 8 FT. These voices are of considerable importance on account of their special character and good mixing properties. Of loudly-voiced stops yielding free organ-tones of great assertiveness may be mentioned the so-called HORN DIAPASON, 8 FT., the FLÛTE À PAVILLON, 8 FT., and the STENTORPHONE, 8 FT. The last named, when blown by wind of about 10 inches pressure, is the most powerful labial stop in the Organ, and is properly included in the stops suitable for the appointment of the Solo Organ. Other varieties of free organ-tone are produced by conical metal pipes, such as those which form the GEMSHORN series of stops, and also the stops which stand on the boundary line between free organ-tone and flute organ-tone, known as the SPITZFLÖTES, of 8 ft., 4 ft., and 2 ft. pitch. The examples above given are sufficient to indicate the wide range of free organ-tone, and to show the number and importance of the stops producing its several varieties. In the tonal appointment of the Organ the great value of such voices must not be overlooked, for they supply qualities that the pure organ-tone is deficient in, as well as add desirable varieties of tone by combination. Certain stops yielding free organ-tone have their voices comparatively rich in the higher upper partial tones ; and these are very effective in combination with the OPEN DIAPASONS, adding fire and brightness to their dignified voices. Alluding to the SALICIONAL, GEMSHORN, and SPITZFLÖTE stops, Helmholtz says : "These pipes have, I find, the property of rendering some higher partial tones, from the fifth to the seventh,* comparatively stronger than the lower. The quality of tone is consequently poor, but peculiarly bright." Such facts as these show the great importance of a scientific as well as an artistic tonal appointment.

By almost imperceptible gradations the voices of the Organ pass from what we have designated free organ-tone into flute organ-tone. The stops which produce the latter are very numerous and valuable. They are formed of both metal and wood pipes of different shapes and proportions, and are either open, half-covered, or stopped. All these stops, as well as all the others alluded to in this Chapter, are described in the Chapters on the Names and General Particulars of Organ Stops, and on the Construction of Metal and Wood Pipes ; it is, therefore, only necessary to allude to the representative examples here.

When one considers the construction of the labial pipes of the Organ, and the manner in which they are blown, one might reasonably expect to find all their tones partaking strongly of the tones of the Flûte à bec and Flageolet. The skill

*These are the sixth to the eighth *upper* partial tones. When the term *partial tones* is used the fundamental tone is included, it being the *prime partial tone* of the compound tone. All the partials above and exclusive of the prime are, correctly speaking, *upper partial tones.*

and ingenuity of the pipe maker and the voicer have saved us from monotony in this direction, and have created an almost endless variety of tones, from those of the ancient Pandean pipes and the primitive whistle up to the complex sounds imitative of the tones of the most perfect orchestral instruments; and recent additions to the long list of stops go to show that the limit of tone-production has not yet been reached. One has only to remember the beautiful imitative string-toned stops produced by the late Edmund Schulze and William Thynne, and the equally noteworthy reed-toned stops introduced by Mr. W. E. Haskell which imitate in so remarkable a manner the voices of the orchestral Oboe and Saxophone, to be assured that the tonal powers of wood and metal labial pipes have by no means been exhausted. As we have remarked elsewhere, had more attention been paid to the development of the tonal department and less to the mechanical appliances of the Organ, we should have a higher class of *musical* instruments in our churches, concert-rooms, and private music-rooms to-day.

By the term flute organ-tone we signify that wide and varied range of fluty tone, produced by organ pipes, which is not strictly imitative of the clear tones of the orchestral Flutes. The pipes which yield flute organ-tone may be classified into seven groups, as follows: 1. Open cylindrical metal pipes, of ample scales and of standard speaking lengths. 2. Open cylindrical metal and wood pipes, of medium scales and double the standard speaking lengths: these are known as harmonic pipes, producing tones proper to half their lengths by being perforated near their centers and overblown. 3. Half-covered cylindrical metal pipes, of large and medium scales. 4. Stopped cylindrical metal pipes, of large and medium scales. 5. Open quadrangular and triangular wood pipes, of large, medium, and small scales. 6. Half-covered quadrangular wood pipes, of medium and small scales. 7. Stopped quadrangular wood pipes, of large, medium, and small scales. With all these forms of pipes, and with the further differences created by the various styles and proportions of mouths, methods of voicing, the varied wind supply, and different pressures of wind, it is not difficult to realize the production of an immense range of tones in this single division.

Generally speaking, the flute organ-tones are weak in upper partials, and are, accordingly, somewhat dull; but in certain varieties, yielded by open pipes, and especially by those rendered harmonic, the upper partial tones are more distinct, numerous, and assertive, producing brighter qualities of tone. The following particulars given by Helmholtz, who carefully investigated the sounds produced by the principal classes of organ pipes, may be studied with advantage:—

"When flute stops of the Organ, and the German Flute are blown softly, the upper partials lose strength at a greater rate than the prime tone, and hence the musical quality becomes weak and soft.

"The *narrower stopped cylindrical pipes* have proper tones corresponding to the uneven partials of the prime, that is, the third partial or Twelfth, the fifth partial or higher major Third, and so on. For the *wider* stopped pipes, as for the wide open pipes, the next adjacent proper tones of the mass of air are distinctly higher than the corresponding upper partials of the prime, and consequently these upper partials are very slightly, if at all, reinforced. Hence wide stopped pipes, especially when gently blown, give the prime tone almost alone. Narrow stopped pipes, on the other hand, let the Twelfth be very distinctly heard at the same time with the prime tone ; and have hence been called QUINTATEN (*quintam tenentes*). When these pipes are strongly blown they also give the fifth partial [fourth upper partial tone], or higher major Third, very distinctly.

"Another variety of quality is produced by the ROHRFLÖTE. Here a tube, open at both ends, is inserted in the cover of a stopped pipe, and in the examples I examined its length was that of an open pipe giving the fifth partial tone of the prime tone of the stopped pipe. The fifth partial tone is thus proportionably stronger than the rather weak third partial of these pipes, and the quality of tone becomes peculiarly bright. Compared with open pipes the quality of tone in stopped pipes, where the even partial tones are absent, is somewhat hollow ; the wider stopped pipes have a dull quality of tone, especially when deep, and are soft and powerless. But their softness offers a very effective contrast to the more cutting qualities of the narrower open pipes and the noisy *compound stops*.

"Wooden pipes do not produce such a cutting wind rush as metal pipes. Wooden sides also do not resist the agitation of the waves of sound so well as metal ones, and hence the vibrations of higher pitch seem to be destroyed by friction. For these reasons wood gives a softer, but duller, less penetrating quality than metal."

Professor Helmholtz wrote prior to the year 1862, and his investigations were apparently, in this latter direction, confined to the tones produced by such wood pipes as were to be found in German Organs at the time. Great advances have been made since then in the formation and voicing of wood pipes; and through them several new voices have been added to the Organ. Had he been acquainted with these, he would, in all probability, have materially altered the statements made respecting the tones of wooden pipes.

Of all the stops which produce flute organ-tone, the least important are those formed of open cylindrical metal pipes, of standard speaking lengths. Their fluty tones are forced, by the necessary system of voicing and blowing, and have very little to recommend them. Pipes of this class are chiefly useful in forming the lower portion of the metal harmonic stops.

The HARMONIC FLUTES, invented and first introduced by MM. Cavaillé-Coll, of Paris, and which are formed of medium-scaled open cylindrical metal pipes, of double the standard speaking lengths, furnish most valuable voices in the Organ. Their tones are singularly clear and penetrating, owing to the presence of the higher upper partials. They can be voiced to produce tones strongly imitative of those of the orchestral Flute and Piccolo. HARMONIC FLUTES are made of 8 ft. and 4 ft. pitch, and the HARMONIC PICCOLO of 2 ft. pitch. There is a FLAGEOLET HARMONIQUE, 2 FT., in the Organ in the Royal Church of Saint-Denis, near Paris. These valuable voices should not be overlooked in the tonal appointment of important Organs, for they are highly suitable for the Swell or chief expressive division.

The stops formed of half-covered cylindrical metal pipes produce bright fluty tones, owing to the presence of the fourth upper partial tone, or the higher major third of the prime tone, in a comparatively strong state. The principal stops of this class are the German ROHRFLÖTE and the French FLÛTE À CHEMINÉE. The former is made of either cylindrical metal or quadrangular wood pipes, the stoppers of which are pierced through in a vertical direction. The stop is usually of 8 ft. and 4 ft. pitch, but sometimes appears of 2 ft. pitch. The FLÛTE À CHEMINÉE is made of large-scaled cylindrical pipes covered with a sliding cap, from the center of which rises a small tube communicating with the internal air-column. Pipes of this form are occasionally used for the higher octaves of the BOURDON, 16 FT., as in the Great division of the Organ in the Manchester Town Hall, where the stop has half-covered pipes from the c^2 key to the top. By difference of scale, variation in the length and diameter of the small tube or *cheminée*, variety in the form and proportions of the mouth, special styles of voicing, and the adoption of different pressures of wind, many beautiful qualities of flute organ-tone can be obtained from half-stopped metal pipes. When not too powerful they supply valuable voices for the Choir division of a Church Organ.

Stopped cylindrical metal pipes were frequently used for the treble octaves of the STOPPED DIAPASON, 8 FT., by the old English organ builders. Sometimes they formed the entire stop of metal, as in the fine work by Harris and Byfield in the old Organ in Doncaster Parish Church. In modern French Organs the BOURDON, 8 FT., is formed of metal pipes, of large scale, covered with sliding metal caps. The twelve notes c^1 to b^1 of the BOURDON, 16 FT., in the Organ in the Manchester Town Hall, have pipes of this description. Stopped metal pipes of medium and small scales, voiced on moderate and low pressures of wind, yield charming qualities of flute organ-tone. Stops formed of such pipes are commonly called LIEBLICHGEDECKTS, and are made of 8 ft., 4 ft., and 2 ft. pitch. It is usual to make the bass octave of the unison stop of covered wood pipes. In the tonal appointment of the Organ this family of "lovely-toned" stops should invariably be introduced. When a very bright treble is desired, the higher octaves of the LIEBLICHGEDECKT, 8 FT., may have half-covered pipes instead of fully stopped ones.

In the wood stops which yield flute organ-tone we have a most valuable series of voices—a series that has not been properly recognized by French and English builders, apparently for reasons that have no reference to its tonal value. German and American builders have paid more attention to the claims of wood stops, and the tonal characters of their Organs have gained accordingly.

There are several very important stops formed of open wood pipes which yield flute organ-tones, and these deserve to be carefully considered in the tonal appointment of the Organ. They are specially valuable on account of their good mixing qualities, and for the fulness and solidity they impart to the somewhat thin and piercing voices of both the reed stops and the metal labial stops whose tones are rich in the higher upper partial tones. As representative stops of this class may be named the GROSSFLÖTE, CLARABELLA, HOHLFLÖTE, WALDFLÖTE, and the so-called PHILOMELA. The GROSSFLÖTE and CLARABELLA, formed of medium-scaled quadrangular pipes, produce fluty tones of a full and agreeable character and perfect mixing quality. They are valuable in combination with string-toned stops and reeds. The CLARABELLA, 8 FT., should be carried throughout the manual compass in open pipes, although it usually has its bass octave of stopped pipes for the sake of economy. An octave stop of this class—the CLARABEL FLUTE, 4 FT.—would be a very valuable voice in the same division of the Organ. The BASS FLUTE, 8 FT., of the Pedal Organ is, in its best form, a large-scaled CLARABELLA. The HOHLFLÖTE, of 8 ft., 4 ft., and 2 ft. pitch, is formed of either quadrangular or triangular pipes. Its tones are of a powerful, hollow, and somewhat dull character, owing to the weakness or absence of the higher upper partial tones. This stop, on account of its filling-up and good mixing qualities, has always been a favorite with German organ builders; and these valuable qualities should be carefully taken into account in appointing it, in either of its pitches, to any division of the Organ. The WALDFLÖTE, 4 FT., is preferably an open wood stop of medium scale, the pipes of which have inverted mouths and sunk blocks. Its tone is full and clear, in good examples approaching an imitative quality. This stop is specially valuable where the presence of an octave voice of a clear flute organ-tone is required. A WALDFLÖTE, 8 FT., having the bass octave in LIEBLICHGEDECKT pipes, would be a desirable stop in many instances, especially if associated with the WALDFLÖTE, 4 FT. The German organ builders construct the WALDFLÖTE of 8 ft., 4 ft., and 2 ft. pitch, wisely forming what is practically a complete family of valuable voices. The importance of introducing special families of stops in the different manual divisions of the Organ has not been sufficiently recognized by organ designers. PHILOMELA is the name given to two open wood stops of widely different tonalities. In one case the stop is formed of small-scaled pipes, producing an extremely delicate flute-tone; while in the other case it is formed of large-scaled pipes, having double mouths, and yielding the most powerful and dominating voice of all the flute-toned stops. In the former case it is suitable for the Choir or Echo Organ, and in the latter case for the Solo Organ. An example appears in the Solo of the Cincinnati Music Hall Organ. The stop has hitherto been made of 8 ft. pitch, although one of 16 ft. pitch would be most effective in the Pedal Organ of a large Concert-room instrument.

There are very few half-covered wood stops to be found in existing Organs; but, judging from the beautiful tonal quality of those with which we are acquainted, it is to be regretted that pipe makers and voicers have not given this class of stops more attention. The most important stop at present introduced is the ROHRFLÖTE, 8 FT., which, as already mentioned, is also, and very frequently, made of metal. When made by a master hand, the wooden ROHRFLÖTE yields a tone of a pure singing quality, which mixes well with all the medium and softer voices of the Organ. The brightness of the tone is due, as we have before explained in speaking of the metal ROHRFLÖTE, to the presence, in a comparatively strong state, of the fourth upper partial tone, or the higher major third of the prime tone. When two ROHRFLÖTES are inserted in an Organ, one of them should certainly be of wood. An octave stop, having a voice of singular delicacy and beauty, is made of small-scaled wood pipes with perforated stoppers. This has been called the FLAUTO D'AMORE, 4 FT. It is a valuable voice in the Choir or Echo Organ, especially when these divisions are on light wind. There is no reason why a stop of this variety should not be made of 8 ft. pitch; and, judging by the beautiful and delicate flute-tone of the octave stop, there can be no question as to the value of such a unison voice. It would be an admirable companion to the DULCIANA, 8 FT.

There is at the present time a decided deficiency of soft and refined voices, of distinct tonalities, in the Organ; indeed, the tendency on the part of the organ builders of to-day, and also on the part of a large majority of organists who prepare organ specifications, is toward the production of as much loud sound as there is money to pay for. This is a grave mistake, and especially so in instruments designed to accompany the human voice, and for chamber music. The student of organ-building should never overlook the value of the delicately-toned stops in the appointment of Organs of all sizes and classes. We have invariably found, among educated persons and those of refined musical taste, that the softly-voiced stops of the Organ have been those most admired. In the loud stops power of tone goes far to destroy that individuality and variety so essential in an instrument like the Organ, in which musical expression is largely dependent on the varied qualities and strengths of its voices.

We now come to the consideration of the valuable qualities of tone produced by wholly stopped wooden pipes. When such pipes are of large scale, and are blown by wind of low or medium pressure, they yield prime tones almost entirely free from upper partials: but when they are of smaller scales, and are blown by wind of higher pressure, or are copiously blown, they yield tones in which the second upper partial, or twelfth, of the prime is present to a pronounced degree; so much so that the name QUINTATEN has been employed to distinguish the stops formed of such small-scaled pipes so blown. With wind of still higher pressure these pipes give, as Helmholtz has correctly observed, the fourth upper partial, or higher major third, in addition to the prime and second upper partial tones. As has been explained in our Chapter on Acoustical Matters connected with Organ Pipes, stopped pipes cannot produce the *uneven* upper partial tones, such as the first or octave, the third or super-octave, etc. Even with such passing remarks as these, the student of organ-building must surely realize that there is much more to be considered, in the tonal appointment of an Organ, than merely inserting the names of some familiar stops in his Specifications, simply as a matter of taste or fancy. The tonal appointment of an Organ is a problem in science as well as in art. The instant an instrument is constructed with more than one rank of pipes, science asserts itself and must be recognized.

The most important covered wood stops inserted in modern Organs are the STOPPED DIAPASON, BOURDON, DOPPELFLÖTE, LIEBLICHGEDECKT, and QUINTATEN (or QUINTATÖN as it is frequently and incorrectly rendered). When made and voiced by a master hand, the STOPPED DIAPASON, 8 FT., has a quiet fluty voice of a beautiful singing quality. Its best tone is produced from pipes of medium scale, blown by wind not exceeding 4 inches pressure; and under these favorable conditions it forms a stop very suitable for the Choir Organ, while in rather a more assertive character it forms a good voice in the Swell division. In all cases it is valuable on account of its rare mixing property, imparting fulness and roundness to the more assertive open metal stops and the delicate reeds. It must be borne in mind, in tonal appointment, that while the STOPPED DIAPASON may produce a tone as free from upper partials as the OPEN DIAPASON, it has a distinct quality which holds its own in combination, chiefly from the absence of acoustical sympathy. The STOPPED DIAPASON can be carried down to the CCC note (16 ft.), when the stop becomes suitable for the Pedal Organ. In the year

1824, Smith, of Bristol, introduced, for the first time in England, a "DOUBLE STOPPED DIAPASON," 32 FT., in the Organ he constructed for the Church of St. James, at Bristol.

The BOURDON, in English and American Organs, is usually a Pedal Organ stop of 16 ft. pitch, formed of large-scaled wooden pipes in all essentials similar to those of the STOPPED DIAPASON, 16 FT., but which, on account of their larger scale and the different proportions of their mouths, produce a heavier and duller quality of tone. In the true BOURDON the second upper partial tone is distinctly produced along with the prime, and in this respect it approximates to the characteristic *timbre* of the QUINTATEN, while it is more drone-like. The manual BOURDON, 16 FT., is in its best form simply a DOUBLE STOPPED DIAPASON, slightly larger in scale than the unison STOPPED DIAPASON, and accordingly fuller in tone. These variations in tonal character should be carefully considered in the appointment of the Organ. Under the name of SUB-BOURDON, 32 FT., a wood stop is found in certain Organs. Although properly a Pedal Organ stop, it appears in the Great division of the Organ, constructed by Schulze, in the Parish Church of Doncaster, where it is carried down to tenor C.

Perhaps the most valuable and beautiful flute organ-tone produced by stopped pipes is that of the DOPPELFLÖTE, 8 FT. This stop, on account of its fine and remarkably solid tone, should be inserted in every Great Organ of any pretensions; and it is also very valuable in the Solo division, where its filling-up quality is most effective in combination with the reed stops usually inserted there. When of moderate strength of tone it produces striking orchestral effects in combination with such stops as the CLARINET and the BASSOON. The true quality of the DOPPELFLÖTE rarely extends below tenor C, at which the double-mouthed pipes commence. The bass pipes have single mouths and are loudly voiced. When space in the Organ is ample, this fine stop should be carried throughout the manual compass in double-mouthed pipes. It is always desirable, in the tonal appointment of the Organ, to avoid having broken or short stops; but when such are unavoidable, and two or more are introduced in the same instrument, care must be taken to break or commence them on different notes. The reason for this is obvious and need not be enlarged upon. Under the name of DOPPELFLÖTENBASS, a DOPPELFLÖTE, of 16 ft. pitch, is inserted in Schulze's fine Organ in the Marienkirche, at Lübeck. It appears in the Choir Pedal Organ, forming the true bass to the manual stop. The DOPPELFLÖTE has rarely been used by English organ builders; indeed, we believe that the first time it was introduced in England was when we inserted one in our own Chamber Organ, in the year 1883.

We now come to the very beautiful family of flute organ-toned stops known as the LIEBLICHGEDECKTS. These stops, in their most refined and characteristic tonal character, are composed of small-scaled wood pipes, although their treble octaves are frequently formed of metal pipes because they are more easy to make and voice. The average organ builder always seeks to save time and trouble, even at the sacrifice of tonal beauty. He is prone to do this because he is hardly ever properly remunerated for his work. In the LIEBLICHGEDECKTS, of 16 ft. and 8 ft. pitch, wood pipes should alone be used; but in those of higher pitches metal pipes become imperative on account of their small size. The stops commonly introduced are those of 16 ft., 8 ft., and 4 ft. pitch; but we strongly advocate, on tonal grounds, the extension of the family, so as to form a more complete harmonic series; and we also advocate the insertion of the family in one division of the Organ, as shown in our suggested scheme for the Concert-room Organ. The tones of LIEBLICHGEDECKT pipes vary considerably, being largely affected by scale, form of mouth, pressure of wind, and style of voicing. There is no acknowledged standard, but the best qualities are those in which the second and fourth upper partial tones are just sufficiently strong to brighten and enrich the delicate prime tone. The compound voice so produced is extremely beautiful, hence the name LIEBLICHGEDECKT. The LIEBLICHGEDECKTS mix perfectly with all the other stops of the Organ; and even with the VOX HUMANA, one of unison pitch adds greatly to the imitative character of the stop, imparting to its tones fulness and depth without interfering with their characteristic quality. The LIEBLICHGEDECKT, 16 FT., forms a valuable Double stop in the Choir Organ, and also in a small Swell Organ, where it will not have power sufficient to disturb the proper balance and prominence of the unison tone. It is likewise a valuable stop in any Pedal Organ, and should be considered indispensable in that of a properly-appointed Chamber Organ. For such a position it should be of larger scale than is desirable in the manual stop, and may be voiced so as to produce the second upper partial tone, or twelfth, of the prime tone somewhat distinctly. It may be remarked that a much freer use may advantageously be made of the complete LIEBLICHGEDECKT family than has yet been made in even the best specimens of modern organ appointment.

The stop known as the QUINTATEN differs only from the LIEBLICHGEDECKT in its tone having the second upper partial more distinct, so much so that in good examples of the QUINTATEN it approaches the strength of the prime tone. The QUINTATEN has been made of 32 ft., 16 ft., and 8 ft. pitch; the last being the stop suitable for general introduction in the manual divisions of the Organ. In certain cases, however, the QUINTATEN, 16 FT., forms an effective Double on the manuals. The QUINTATEN, 8 FT., is specially valuable in a division in which there is no TWELFTH, 2⅔ FT., to corroborate the second upper partial of the unison tone: in this case it supplies a want in the tonal structure of the division, and imparts fulness and richness to the general tone. It is also extremely valuable in a manual division which contains several stops of string-tone, even when there is a separate TWELFTH, 2⅔ FT., present. In such a case it is highly effective in the softer combinations, giving solidity to the imitative voices, and affording means of producing a great variety of tonal effects with stops of different classes and colorings. In the appointment of Pedal Organs the QUINTATEN should receive careful consideration. It is found, of both 16 ft. and 8 ft. pitch, in the pedal departments of many German Organs; and an example, of 32 ft. pitch, is inserted in the Pédale of the Grand Organ in the Madeleine, at Paris. It is impossible to form any rule, of general application, respecting the introduction of the unison QUINTATEN in the Pedal Organ, for it will depend almost entirely on the size and stop appointment of the department. The student of organ-building will have to take into consideration the complete tonal structure of the Pedal Organ, and decide how far the peculiar compound voice of the QUINTATEN is necessary or desirable therein. If the second upper partial of the unison (16 ft.) tone is to be corroborated by the voice of an independent stop of 5⅓ ft. pitch, the QUINTATEN, 16 FT., will probably be altogether superfluous; but there is always the provision of suitable and effective basses for the numerous representative manual combinations to be carefully considered; and the compound tone of the QUINTATEN may prove a valuable element in such basses. Even when the unison stop is not considered necessary, the QUINTATEN, 8 FT.,—a small and inexpensive stop,—will prove a serviceable addition to the Pedal Organ, and especially so when no MIXTURE appears in the tonal scheme.

There are several stops introduced in the Organ which yield tones partaking more or less of the character of those produced by bowed instruments; and when not strictly imitative these voices fall into the First Group, as organ-tones. We have used the term viol organ-tone to distinguish the voices of these useful stops from the other organ-tones, and from the voices of the purely imitative string-toned stops which belong to the Second Group. This quality of organ-tone is commonly known as *gamba*-tone; but, as we explain in our Chapter on a Systematic Organ Stop Nomenclature, we do not consider this term a very appropriate one, and have accordingly adopted the term *viol* as both more expressive and more suitable.

The most important stop yielding viol organ-tone is that known as the GEIGENPRINCIPAL, or VIOLIN DIAPASON, 8 FT. This stop produces the second upper partial tone in so pronounced a manner, in combination with its fine prime tone and the first upper partial, that a decided string-tone is the result. When a true GEIGENPRINCIPAL pipe is quickly sounded, by a sharply struck key, the twelfth, or second upper partial tone, is quite as prominent as, if not more prominent than, the prime tone of the pipe. When this stop is appointed in place of an OPEN DIAPASON, 8 FT., in any manual division of the Organ, its crisp string-tone may with advantage be subdued in favor of a more pronounced prime tone; but, on the other hand, when there is also a true unison PRINCIPAL or OPEN DIAPASON present, the full character of the GEIGENPRINCIPAL should be retained. In combination these stops produce a magnificent compound tone. The GEIGENPRINCIPAL is made of 16 ft., 8 ft., and 4 ft. pitch, and all the stops are valuable. In the Second Manual of the Organ in the Cathedral of Riga there is a GEIGENPRINCIPAL, 16 FT., and in the Third Manual there are others of 8 ft. and 4 ft. pitch. Alluding to the GEIGENPRINCIPAL, Helmholtz remarks:—

"Open organ pipes afford a favorable means of meeting the harmonic requirements of polyphonic music, and consequently form the *Principal* stops. They make the lower partials distinctly audible, the wide pipes up to the third [second upper partial], the narrow ones (*Geigenprincipal*) up to the sixth partial tone [fifth upper partial]. The wider pipes have more power of tone than the narrower; to give them more brightness the 8-foot stops, which contain the 'principal work,' are connected with the 4-foot stops which add the Octave to each note; or the *Principal* is connected with the *Geigenprincipal*, so that the first gives power and the second brightness. By this means qualities of tone are produced which contain the first six partial tones in moderate force, decreasing as the pitch ascends. These give a very distinct feeling for the purity of the consonant intervals, enabling us to distinguish clearly between consonance and dissonance, and preventing the unavoidable but weak dissonances resulting from the higher upper partials in the imperfect consonances from becoming too marked, but at the same time not allowing the hearer's appreciation of the progression of the parts to be disturbed by a multitude of loud accessory tones. In this respect the Organ has an advantage over all other instruments, as the player is able to mix and alter the qualities of tone at pleasure, and make them suitable to the character of the piece he has to perform."

Next in importance to the GEIGENPRINCIPAL is the stop commonly known as the GAMBA, composed of medium-scaled cylindrical metal pipes. When properly made and artistically voiced, this stop yields a full tone in which the first five upper partial tones are commonly audible. The strength of these, in relation to the prime tone, varies considerably in different examples of the stop; and it is, accordingly, possible to adapt the tone to the special requirements of any division of the Organ. When the upper partial tones are of moderate strength, and decrease considerably as they ascend in pitch, the compound tone of the GAMBA is full and rich; but when the upper partials are relatively strong, and are distinctly heard up to the fifth, or octave twelfth of the prime tone, the compound tone becomes somewhat more harsh and cutting. As Helmholtz correctly says:—

"In reality, on forcibly blowing the narrow cylindrical pipes of an Organ (in the *Geigenprincipal*, *Violoncell*, *Violonbass*, *Viola da Gamba* stops) we hear a series of upper partials distinctly and powerfully accompany the prime tone, giving them a more cutting quality, resembling a Violin. By using resonators I find that on narrow pipes of this kind the partial tones may be clearly heard up to the sixth* [the fifth upper partial tone, or octave twelfth of the prime]. For wide open pipes, on the other hand, the adjacent proper tones of the tube are all somewhat sharper than the corresponding harmonic tones of the prime, and hence these tones will be much less reinforced by the resonance of the tube."

There are several stops of different forms and scales which belong to the family yielding viol organ-tone, and some of these have voices so strongly imitative in character that it is sometimes difficult to classify them as belonging to one group more than to the other. This is the case with such characteristic stops as the VIOLA DA GAMBA and VIOLA D'AMORE, especially when voiced by the hands of a master. These may fairly be considered imitative stops, and their place would seem to be among those yielding orchestral string-tone; but even when the best of them are compared with the modern stops that imitate so closely the pungent and complex tones of the orchestral Violin, Violoncello, and Contra-Basso, their timid voices fall back into what may be correctly considered organ-tone. Several

* In reading the quotations from "The Sensations of Tone," given in the present Chapter, the student must carefully observe that Helmholtz uses both the terms "partial tones" and "upper partial tones"; and he must not confuse them. He must bear in mind that when the former term is employed, the prime tone is understood to be included, and is the first partial tone of the series; and when the latter term is used, the prime tone is not understood to be included, and the first upper partial tone is the octave of the prime. Accordingly, it must be understood that the second partial tone and the first upper partial tone are one and the same tone. To prevent confusion where it is likely to arise in the minds of the inexperienced in such matters, we have in some instances added explanatory words within brackets.

names have been introduced to distinguish different forms of GAMBAS, and to indirectly convey some ideas respecting their tonal character. Among these names we find CONE GAMBA, BELL GAMBA, and GERMAN GAMBA. The first and second names are obviously derived from the peculiar shapes of the pipes forming the respective stops. It is well known that the shape of a pipe has a great influence on its tonal character, chiefly by altering the number and relative intensity of the upper partials which, in combination with the prime, go to create its compound tone. Such being the case, we find that each of the above-named GAMBAS have voices of a more or less distinctive tonality; and this obtains even when all are voiced in a similar manner on wind of the same pressure. Of course further differences of tone are created by changes in the manner of voicing, and blowing by wind of different pressures. The true GERMAN GAMBA is a somewhat powerful string-toned stop, unpleasantly slow in speech, and is, accordingly, seldom, if ever, used alone: in combination with a flute-toned stop, which has been called its "helper," it speaks with sufficient promptness for all ordinary requirements. The GAMBA is made of 16 ft., 8 ft., and 4 ft. pitch; and sometimes stops of all these pitches are introduced in the same division, keeping the family together in a manner to be commended. We find this to be the case in the First Manual of Walcker's large Organ in Riga Cathedral. The softest stop yielding viol organ-tone is the ÆOLINE, 8 FT. This is frequently found in German and Swiss Organs, and is a valuable voice in all classes of instruments in which delicately-toned stops are desirable. It is especially suitable for the Chamber Organ and the expressive Choir division of the Church Organ. Walcker has placed it, in the proper position, in the Fourth Manual of the Riga Organ, where it is associated with several stops of a soft and refined character, such as the BOURDON DOUX, 8 FT., VOIX CÉLESTE, 8 FT., VOX ANGELICA, 4 FT., and HARMONIA ÆTHERIA.

In the appointment of the Organ the tonal value of the stops yielding viol organ-tone should be fully recognized; but they must, on account of their cutting and penetrating voices, be introduced with great care and judgment. They must be selected with due reference to their strength of tone and the nature of their compound voices, so as to harmonize with the complete tonal scheme of the division of the Organ in which they are placed. It is not too much to say that a badly proportioned or unsuitable GAMBA will entirely destroy the tonal balance of a division. In all delicate matters of this kind scientific knowledge, experience, and a refined musical sense can alone guide the organ builder and expert. How often are these acquirements exercised in the tonal appointment of the Organ?

We have now to briefly consider the organ stops which belong to the Second Group, the pipes of which are constructed and voiced with the aim of producing tones imitating, as closely as possible, those of the principal string and wind instruments of the orchestra.

The old builders were satisfied with very few and indifferent imitative stops; and, indeed, it is only within the last fifty years, or since the inception of the Concert-room Organ, that leading organ builders have given serious attention to the production of organ equivalents of the principal voices of the orchestra. Every step made in this direction has been a substantial gain; and to-day the tonal resources at the disposal of the builder and expert are extensive and very varied. What is now chiefly needed is scientific knowledge combined with artistic taste, to so dispose these tonal forces in the different divisions of the Organ that their fullest powers, both separately and in combination, may be placed at the ready disposal of the performer. Opinions differ respecting the liberal introduction of the purely imitative voices into the Organ; and those who are adverse to their holding a prominent place in the tonal economy of the instrument point, in support of the objection, to the works of the older masters, notably those of Germany and Holland. Reference to old Organs, however, carries no weight, simply because only a very few isolated stops of an imitative character were known at the time of their construction; and even the best of these stops, as the existing examples show, fell far short of being satisfactory. Such being the case, the old builders did wisely in confining themselves to the stops with which they were familiar, and which proved sufficient for all the demands made by the organ music of the period. The old Church Organ had its own special office to fulfil, and did not call for the introduction of orchestral-toned stops; and we are willing to admit (much as we admire the results of modern ingenuity and skill) that the average Church Organ of to-day requires but little aid in that direction, just as we are prepared to assert that until true organ-tone is adequately represented in its tonal appointment no attention need be paid to the introduction of imitative voices. Countless Church Organs have been spoiled by the unreasoning desire on the part of the writers of their Specifications to have some ear-tickling or favorite stops inserted, at the expense of the correct tonal structure and the general utility, dignity, and beauty of the instruments. The old German masters were not guilty of this folly, although even they did some ridiculous things in connection with the Organ. The orchestral-toned stops are of the highest value, and should never be neglected in the tonal appointment of large instruments; but it must be borne in mind that they are only a means to a special end, and that, in all save perhaps the grand Concert-room Organ, they are of secondary importance to the true organ-toned stops.

Notwithstanding the fact that the stringed instruments have always formed the foundation of the orchestra, the orchestral string-toned stops of the Organ have, until very recently, received comparatively little attention; indeed, it was not until such masterly voicers as the late Edmund Schulze, of Paulinzelle, and William Thynne, of London, demonstrated what could be done in the direction of imitative string-toned stops, that one fully realized their importance and could form some conception of the place they are destined to occupy in the Concert-room Organ of the future, and of the valuable tonal resources they will place at the command of the organ virtuoso in years to come, when the scientific and artistic tonal appointment of the "King of Instruments" is better understood.

The stringed instruments whose complex tones have been successfully imitated by the voicers above named are the Violin, Violoncello, and Contra-Basso. Under the name of VIOLE D'ORCHESTRE, the late Mr. Thynne produced small-scaled open metal stops, the tones of which exactly imitated those of the orchestral Violin. In the Organ in Tewkesbury Abbey the Solo VIOLONCELLO, 8 FT., voiced by the same master hand, reproduces in a marvelous manner the characteristic tones of the true Violoncello. This fine stop is of metal and wood. Of the many imitative string-toned stops voiced by the renowned Schulze we know of none that surpasses the Pedal VIOLONE, 16 FT., of the Organ in the Church of St. Peter, Hindley, Lancashire. Knowing that such stops are possible and can be created by clever voicers at will,—for that which has been done can surely be accomplished again,—it is greatly to be regretted that the many important Concert-room Organs in England and elsewhere are so lamentably deficient in imitative string-toned stops. In this direction their tonal appointments are most imperfect; for in those instruments in which attempts have been made to introduce something in the nature of string-tone, the few stops are so aimlessly distributed as to render effective massing a practical impossibility. If we glance at the Specification of the large Concert Organ in St. George's Hall, Liverpool, as it was reconstructed in the year 1867, we find in the Great Organ a VIOLONCELLO, 8 FT., and a VIOLA, 4 FT.; in the Choir Organ a VIOLA DA GAMBA, 8 FT., and a GAMBA, 4 FT.; and in the Pedal Organ a VIOLONE, 16 FT. We have here only five string-toned stops in an instrument comprising one hundred speaking stops, and none of them can lay claim to be considered imitative voices. At the recent restoration of this instrument matters were only slightly improved by the addition of a VIOLA DA GAMBA, 8 FT., and OCTAVE VIOLA, 4 FT., in the Swell Organ, and another VIOLA DA GAMBA, 8 FT., in the Solo Organ. It will be seen from the above that without coupling, and practically crippling two manual divisions, it is impossible to form a combination of even two unison string-toned stops in this immense instrument. Further comment is unnecessary. Turning now to the largest Concert Organ in existence (1903),—that in the Centennial Hall, at Sydney, N. S. W.,—we find matters to be only very little better. In the Great Organ there are two unimitative string-toned stops, a VIOLA, 8 FT., and a GAMBA, 8 FT.; in the Choir Organ a GAMBA, 8 FT., and a VIOLINO, 4 FT.; in the Swell Organ a VIOLA DA GAMBA, 8 FT.; in the Solo Organ a VIOLA, 8 FT.; and in the Echo Organ a VIOLE D'AMOUR, 8 FT., and a VIOLE D'AMOUR, 4 FT. In this instrument it is only in the Great division that two unison string-toned stops can be sounded in combination without resorting to objectionable coupling. Again further comment is unnecessary. Continuing our hasty survey, we may glance at the tonal appointment of the most important Concert-room Organ at present (1903) existing on the Continent of America,—the instrument in the Auditorium, at Chicago,—in which, so far as imitative string-toned stops are concerned, a most unsatisfactory state of affairs obtains. In the Great Organ we find a VIOLA DA GAMBA, 8 FT., a VIOLA D'AMORE, 8 FT., and a GAMBETTE, 4 FT.; and in the Solo Organ a VIOLONCELLO, 8 FT., and VIOLA, 4 FT. Neither of the other four manual divisions contains any stops of a pronounced string-tone; but the Pedal Organ has a VIOLONE, 16 FT., and a VIOLONCELLO, 8 FT. Surely this is a miserable provision of string-tone in an instrument of the first rank, comprising one hundred and seven speaking stops and the most complete series of mechanical appliances as yet introduced in an Organ. At this point the reader may glance at the suggestive scheme of tonal appointment given in our Chapter on The Concert-room Organ.

The tones of the organ stops that so closely imitate the Violin, Violoncello, and Double-Bass of the orchestra are due to the presence of an extended series of upper partials—a more extended series than is to be found in the compound voices of any other labial stops. In the tones of the bowed instruments the upper partials are distinctly audible up to the ninth or tenth, while by the aid of properly-constructed resonators higher ones can be realized by the ear. Helmholtz remarks: "The prime in the compound tones of bowed instruments is comparatively more powerful than in those produced on a pianoforte or guitar by striking or plucking the strings near to their extremities; the first upper partials are comparatively weaker; but the higher upper partials, from the sixth to about the tenth, are much more distinct, and give these tones their cutting character." In the compound voices of the ordinary string-toned stops of the Organ, Helmholtz found upper partial tones as high as the fifth; as he says: "On forcibly blowing the narrow cylindrical pipes of an Organ we hear a series of upper partials distinctly and powerfully accompany the prime tone, giving them a more cutting quality, resembling a Violin." This investigator does not appear to have had any opportunity of examining such imitative string-toned pipes as those produced by Schulze and Thynne subsequently to the appearance of his "Sensations of Tone." Had such pipes come before his observation, he would have found a higher series of upper partials in their compound tones than those he discovered, by the aid of resonators, in the ordinary string-toned pipes he used in his investigations.

The imitative tones of the VIOLE D'ORCHESTRE or ORCHESTRAL VIOLIN, 8 FT., the ORCHESTRAL VIOLONCELLO, 8 FT., and the ORCHESTRAL DOUBLE-BASS, 16 FT., are produced by metal and wood pipes of small scale, the mouths of which are furnished with the harmonic-bridge or some form of the *frein harmonique.* The VIOLONE, 16 FT., in Schulze's Organ, at Hindley, has its CCC pipe only 5½ inches square internally. Pipes of this imitative class speak best on wind of 3½ inches to 4 inches pressure, although for solo stops of brilliant intonation wind of 6 inches may be employed. The dimensions and acoustical properties of the room or hall in which the Organ is to be placed will to a large extent dictate the wind-pressures for these and other important stops. Stops of less powerful and cutting intonation than those just named, which imitate the singing and somewhat plaintive tones of the old Viola da Gamba and Viola d'Amore, are most valuable in the tonal appointment of the Organ. They are suitable for the Chamber Organ and for the softer manual divisions of Church and Concert-room Organs. There is a beautiful VIOLA, 8 FT., formed of small-scaled wood and metal pipes, in the Choir division of Schulze's Organ in St. Peter's Church, Hindley; and there is also, in the same division, a fine VIOLE D'AMOUR, 4 FT. Stops of this delicate character produce their most beautiful tones on wind of about 2½ inches—a pressure favored by Schulze for his Choir Organ stops, as in his fine Organ in the Church of St. Bartholomew, Armley.

In the tonal appointment of a Concert-room Organ of any importance the provision of a sufficient volume of orchestral string-tone to meet all demands in the rendition of the largest orchestral compositions must not be neglected; and it is essential that this volume, scientifically built up, be immediately, and at all times, available in one division of the instrument; so that all the other divisions are free for the other necessary tonal effects and combinations. It is a somewhat remarkable fact, as we have already shown, that in even the largest Concert-room Organ at present in existence it is impossible to mass together string-tone to any impressive extent, even by coupling three or four manual divisions together and completely crippling the other tonal forces of the divisions. We have, during the public recitals given throughout a period of a quarter of a century, observed the late Mr. W. T. Best's futile attempts to obtain sufficient combinations of string-tone on the Organ in St. George's Hall, Liverpool, for the orchestral compositions he so frequently performed; and have noted how unsatisfactory the instrument proved in this direction even under his consummate manipulation; yet as much can be done on this Organ as on any other hitherto constructed. Although the voices of the orchestral string-toned stops of unison pitch contain the extended series of harmonic upper partials sufficient to create their individual imitative tones, such unison stops are not alone sufficient, even when multiplied, to produce the extremely rich and complex musical effect of the string division of the grand orchestra. Such being the case, it is desirable to associate along with the unison stops other and higher-pitched ranks of pipes, preferably of soft viol-tone, to corroborate the upper partials of the unison tones and generate those of still higher pitch, so as to build up the required volume of characteristic musical sound and form a complete string-toned subdivision of the Organ, as suggested in our Chapter on the Concert-room Organ.

Little requires to be said on the subject of orchestral flute-tone, because there are only three stops of a strictly imitative character that furnish it satisfactorily; namely, the ORCHESTRAL FLUTE or FLAUTO TRAVERSO, 8 FT., the FLAUTO TRAVERSO, 4 FT., and the ORCHESTRAL PICCOLO, 2 FT. The pipes of these stops are made of both wood and metal, but the former material is preferable and should always be used for the unison and octave stops. The finest examples of the ORCHESTRAL FLUTES have the pipes in their middle and higher octaves made of hardwood, turned out of the solid and bored, and furnished with circular mouths resembling those of the true orchestral Flutes. These cylindrical pipes are harmonic; that is, they are made double the standard speaking lengths, and are perforated near the center of their tubes, in the usual fashion, and as described and illustrated in our Chapter devoted to the Construction of Wood Pipes. The tones produced by these cylindrical pipes are highly satisfactory imitations of those produced by the orchestral instruments, and ably represent them in the tonal appointment of the Organ. Schulze and other German builders have been very successful with stops of this imitative form. Very satisfactory ORCHESTRAL FLUTES have been made with quadrangular wooden pipes, harmonic from about f^1 in the unison, and an octave lower in the stops of 4 ft. pitch; the lower pipes being of open wood of the standard speaking lengths. The ORCHESTRAL FLUTES, of 8 ft. and 4 ft. pitch, and the ORCHESTRAL PICCOLO, 2 FT., are stops of the first importance in organ appointment, representing as they do an effective section of the wood-wind of the orchestra. While in the Concert-room Organ the above-named three stops should find a place in the manual division devoted to the stops which represent the wood-wind forces of the orchestra, it is desirable to place Orchestral Flutes, preferably of powerful intonation, in the division specially reserved for solo voices, so that Flute passages can be rendered at any moment without crippling the important tonal combinations or effects that may be provided in the other divisions of the instrument. All such matters as these must be carefully considered in the tonal appointment of the Organ.

The instruments of the orchestra that are more or less successfully imitated by the stops of the Organ yielding orchestral reed-tone are the Oboe, Fagotto, Corno Inglese, Clarinet, Corno di Bassetto, and the Saxophones. All the stops which bear these names yield, when artistically made and voiced, tones of great beauty and value. The Oboe, 8 ft., is made in two forms: one yielding a tone somewhat fuller than that of the orchestral instrument, and not closely imitative; while the other, called the Orchestral Oboe, is voiced to produce a tone of a strictly imitative character. In the tonal appointment of the Concert-room Organ the Orchestral Oboe, 8 ft., should be inserted in the division specially devoted to the wood-wind, it being understood that this division is expressive. In an instrument of the first magnitude a second Orchestral Oboe may, with advantage, be inserted in the division reserved for solo voices. This second stop should have a voice somewhat stronger than the one in the wood-wind division, for it is never desirable to have two stops exactly alike in the same Organ. The Oboe as usually made and voiced is very desirable in the Church Organ, where a soft reed-tone of a distinctive character is particularly useful in combinations, and occasionally in solo passages of a plaintive character. This reed is also well suited for a small Chamber Organ, where, on account of its admirable mixing quality, it is most valuable at all times; but in a large Chamber Organ, appointed on the model of the Concert-room Organ, the preference should certainly be given to the Orchestral Oboe, 8 ft. Up to very recently the Orchestral Oboe has invariably been a small-scaled metal reed stop, but lately an open wood labial stop has been invented by Mr. Haskell, of Philadelphia, the tone of which is a faithful imitation of that of the orchestral instrument when properly played. This stop is a very valuable addition to the tonal forces of the Organ, both on account of its beautiful voice and the fact that it is not a reed, with its many disadvantages. A description of this new stop is given in our Chapter on Wood Pipes.

An Octave Oboe, 4 ft., has been introduced in certain modern Organs. It appears in both the Choir and Solo divisions of the Concert-room Organ in the Centennial Hall, Sydney, N. S. W., and another is to be found in the Second Manual of the Organ in the Cathedral of Riga. When not of the strictly orchestral character, this stop will form a very suitable octave reed in the softer divisions of the Organ. Although there is no authority from the orchestra for the introduction of a Contra-Oboe, 16 ft., yet, as the tone of the unison stop is so satisfactory, there can be no good reason why a similarly-toned stop of 16 ft. pitch should not be introduced in an important Organ. Under the name of Contra-Hautboy, 16 ft., a fine example is to be found in the Swell division of the Concert Organ in St. George's Hall, Liverpool. According to the above particulars it is shown that there are four OBOE stops available for the tonal appointment of the Organ; namely, the ORCHESTRAL OBOE, 8 FT., having a strictly imitative and solo voice, and the CONTRA-OBOE, 16 FT., OBOE, 8 FT., and OCTAVE OBOE, 4 FT., having voices of a slightly imitative character and good mixing qualities. As we strongly advocate the association of the different families of stops in the different manual divisions of the Organ, we suggest the desirability of keeping these three OBOES together in any division it may be considered advisable to place them. This appointment would, in all probability, be practicable only in Concert-room Organs of the first magnitude.

The Corno Inglese, or Cor Anglais, is an orchestral instrument of the Oboe class; it is, so to speak, the Alto of the Oboe. Speaking of the Corno Inglese, Berlioz says: "Its quality of tone, less piercing, more veiled, and deeper than that of the Hautboy, does not so well as the latter lend itself to the gaiety of rustic strains . . . It is a melancholy, dreamy, and rather noble voice." The organ stop which has been designed to imitate this orchestral instrument, and which bears its name, may in its best form be accepted as sufficiently successful to be included in the tonal appointment of a large Organ. The stop is usually a free reed, furnished with resonant tubes of peculiar form. Its tone is distinct from that of the OBOE, and has valuable mixing and coloring properties. The CORNO INGLESE is, correctly, a stop of 8 ft. pitch. A good example is to be found in the Solo division of the Concert Organ in the Auditorium, at Chicago; and another, originally labeled COR ANGLAIS & BASSOON, 8 FT., is inserted in the Solo division of the Concert-room Organ in the Town Hall of Leeds. A stop of 16 ft. pitch, labeled COR ANGLAIS, is placed in the Choir division of the Organ in the Cincinnati Music Hall; but this stop is neither imitative in tone nor pitch.

The orchestral Fagotto or Bassoon is the true Bass of the Oboe; and the value of a good imitation of its characteristic voice, in the Concert-room Organ, may be realized from the following remarks by Berlioz: "The Bassoon is of the greatest use in the orchestra on numerous occasions. Its sonorousness is not very great, and its quality of tone, absolutely devoid of brilliancy or nobleness, has a tendency toward the grotesque—which should be always kept in mind when bringing it forward into prominence. Its low notes form excellent basses to the whole group of wooden wind instruments. . . The character of its high notes is somewhat painful, suffering,—even, I may say, miserable,—which may be sometimes introduced into either a slow melody, or passages of accompaniment, with most surprising effect." The FAGOTTO, 8 FT., as made by a master hand, is a very satisfactory stop, but it is only moderately imitative. As the orchestral instrument extends, in its upward range, to e^2, the FAGOTTO proper ceases at that note and is theoretically carried up by an OBOE. If such is recognized, the stop may be properly labeled OBOE & FAGOTTO (or BASSOON), 8 FT.

The Contrafagotto or Double Bassoon of the orchestra is to the Fagotto or Bassoon what the Contra-Basso is to the Violoncello. The compass of the orchestral Contrafagotto is BBBB♭ to F=32 notes, and, accordingly, the stop which represents it in the Organ properly belongs to the pedal department, the compass of which simply cuts two notes from its downward range. When the

CONTRAFAGOTTO, 16 FT., is inserted in a manual division it properly extends upward to f^1, being carried to e^3 in FAGOTTO pipes, and thence to the top by pipes that theoretically belong to the OBOE, 8 FT. The stop is practically carried throughout in pipes of one formation so as to secure perfect uniformity of tonal character; and the same should be the case with the unison FAGOTTO, 8 FT., when properly made. There is nothing more objectionable in the tonal appointment of an Organ than stops which have different intonations in different portions of their compass. The CONTRAFAGOTTO, 16 FT., appears in different divisions in important Organs, and, except as regards its correct position in the pedal department, apparently without any special reference to the general tonal appointment of the divisions. In the Sydney Organ it appears in the Choir, Swell, Solo, and Pedal Organs; in the Organs in Doncaster Parish Church and the Auditorium, Chicago, it is placed in the Swell and Pedal Organs; in the Organs in York Minster and St. George's Hall, Liverpool, it now appears in the Solo and Pedal Organs; in the Organ in Woolsey Hall, Yale University, it is inserted in the Choir and Pedal Organs; in the Organ in Saint-Sulpice, Paris, it is placed in the Grand-Chœur and Pédale; in the Organ in Notre-Dame, Paris, it appears in the Grand-Orgue and Pédale; and in the Organ in the Cathedral of Riga it appears only in the First Manual division. The CONTRAFAGOTTO is *par excellence* a Pedal Organ stop, and should be inserted in that department in every important instrument. Its position in the manual department will be, or should be, dictated by the special tonal appointment. In the average Church Organ it need not appear in a manual division; but when it does, it certainly should be in an expressive one. In the properly-appointed Concert-room Organ its proper place is in the wood-wind division, and, of course, also in the Pedal Organ to aid in furnishing suitable orchestral bass effects when required, and to carry down the FAGOTTO, 8 FT.

Of all the stops of the Organ which imitate the tones of the orchestral reed instruments, the CLARINET, 8 FT., may be said to be the most satisfactory. When made by a master hand, and used in combination with a soft-toned covered wood stop, such as the LIEBLICHGEDECKT, 8 FT., it produces an almost perfect imitation of the orchestral instrument in its best registers. The tubes of the CLARINET are, like the tube of the orchestral instrument, cylindrical. The tube of the orchestral Clarinet is of the nature of a stopped pipe, producing, in addition to the prime, the second, fourth, and higher even upper partial tones. Such being the case, the CLARINET of the Organ naturally derives considerable benefit by having associated with it a covered stop which has in its voice the same progression of upper partial tones. We accordingly strongly recommend that the ORCHESTRAL CLARINET, 8 FT., in the Concert-room Organ, be composed of two ranks; namely, the reed stop and a small-scaled covered stop, preferably a QUINTATEN, 8 FT. The characteristic voice of the Clarinet is closely imitated by this combination of organ pipes. The Clarinets of the orchestra cover a compass extending from DD to e^4, and accordingly go four notes above the manual compass of the Organ, while they are only two notes short of it downward. The organ stop can, therefore, be correctly labeled CLARINET, 8 FT. The stop has been labeled CLARINET & BASSOON, under the impression, we presume, that the Bassoon belongs to the

Clarinet family in the orchestra. Speaking of the Clarinet, Berlioz suggestively remarks: "The Clarinet has four registers; each of these registers has also a distinct quality of tone. That of the high register is somewhat tearing, which should be used only in the *fortissimo* of the orchestra, or in the bold passages of a brilliant solo. Those of the chalumeau and medium registers are suited to melodies, to arpeggios, and to smooth passages; and the low register is appropriate—particularly in the holding notes—to those *coldly threatening* effects, those dark accents of *motionless rage*, which Weber so ingeniously invented." Again: "It is the one of all the wind instruments which can best breathe forth, swell, diminish, and die away its sound. Thence the precious faculty of producing *distance*, echo, an echo of *echo*, and a *twilight* sound. What more admirable example could I quote, of the application of some of these shadowings, than the dreamy phrase of the Clarinet, accompanied by a tremolo of stringed instruments, in the midst of the Allegro of the Overture to *Freischütz*." And yet, in spite of these remarkable properties of the orchestral instrument, we find the thoughtless organ builders and framers of organ specifications perpetually placing the CLARINET in an exposed Choir or some other uninclosed and *unexpressive* division of the Organ. Could anything be more inartistic and absurd than this practice? Alluding to the Bass Clarinet of the orchestra, Berlioz says that, according to the manner the composer writes for it, "and the talent of the performer, this instrument may borrow that wild quality of tone which distinguishes the bass notes of the ordinary Clarinet, or that calm, solemn, and sacerdotal accent belonging to certain registers of the Organ. It is therefore of frequent and fine application."

In the tonal appointment of a Concert-room Organ of the first magnitude two ORCHESTRAL CLARINETS should, at least, be introduced: one occupying a place in the manual division chiefly devoted to the "wood-wind"; and the other being placed in the division devoted to the principal solo voices. The latter stop should be composed of two ranks, as above suggested, because as a solo stop it will be comparatively seldom used in combination.

The Corno di Bassetto is another fine orchestral instrument that is closely imitated by the organ stop of the same name. Its compass is from FF to c^3; so the organ CORNO DI BASSETTO, 8 FT., has its top octave beyond the upward range of the orchestral instrument. The tone of the Corno di Bassetto is somewhat similar to, but richer than, that of the Alto Clarinet: its finest notes are in its lowest register. Mozart, realizing the value of this fine instrument, used it in two parts for darkening the coloring of his harmonies in his *Requiem*, and has assigned to it some important solos in his Opera *La Clemenza di Tito*. The imitative CORNO DI BASSETTO, 8 FT., is by no means a common stop, and perhaps the finest in existence is that in the Solo Organ of the instrument in St. George's Hall, Liverpool. Another example is to be found in the Solo division of the Organ in the Centennial Hall, Sydney. No example appears in the three important American Organs at Chicago, Cincinnati, and Yale University. In the Solo Organ of the Chicago instrument there is a BASSET HORN, of 16 ft. pitch; but this cannot be considered representative of the orchestral Corno di Bassetto or Basset Horn, while it is, so far as our knowledge extends, a unique stop. The CORNO DI BAS-

SETTO, 8 FT., very rarely appears in the Church Organ; but we find one in the Schwell-Pedal of the Organ in Riga Cathedral, and one in the Second Pedal of the Organ in the Cathedral of Ulm. As the proper voice of the CORNO DI BASSETTO closely resembles that of the ORCHESTRAL CLARINET, it should be placed in a manual division which does not contain the latter stop. This separation is desirable for several obvious reasons that need not be entered on here.

We have now to mention, in concluding our necessarily brief remarks on the organ stops yielding orchestral reed-tone, the beautiful family of orchestral single-reed instruments known as the Saxophones. They are six in number,—the High, Soprano, Alto, Tenor, Baritone, and Bass,—collectively covering a compass from BBB to f^3; practically the compass of the ordinary claviers of the Organ, being one note below the CC downward limit of all modern claviers, and only seven notes short of the upward limit of the five-octave clavier now commonly adopted for the majority of large Organs. The Organ SAXOPHONE, 8 FT., must in all cases be a complete stop, the fact that it extends a few notes—two, four, or seven—above the High Saxophone of the orchestra being a matter of no moment. The lowest note of the Bass Saxophone has unfortunately to be omitted, as above shown.

Up to the present time few serious attempts have been made by organ builders to produce stops having voices imitative of the orchestral Saxophones; and in the case of certain free reed stops, whose tones resemble those of the orchestral instruments, only a very limited success has been attained. Unquestionably the best, and we may say the only satisfactory, organ stop yet made, that yields tones strictly imitative of the Saxophones, is the one invented and first introduced by Mr. W. E. Haskell. This beautiful and invaluable stop is described and illustrated in the Chapter on Wood Pipes. Strange to relate, it is not a reed, but a small-scaled open wood labial stop, furnished with cylindrical harmonic-bridges. This stop opens up possibilities in tone-production that point to further advances in the Organ as a *musical* instrument.

Although there does not appear to be a Double-bass Saxophone in present use in the orchestra, we are informed by Berlioz that M. Sax contemplated the construction of one, and in all probability he carried out his intention. That such an instrument was practical, in the renowned instrument-maker's mind, is sufficient to guarantee our strongly recommending the construction of a CONTRA-SAXOPHONE, 16 FT., for insertion either in the Pedal Organ or in one of the expressive manual divisions of the Concert-room Organ. It is probable that the most satisfactory stop of this pitch, suitable for the Pedal Organ, would be a free-reed, having resonant tubes of the form best adapted to produce a powerful imitative tone; but there is little doubt that Mr. Haskell could carry his present SAXOPHONE, 8 FT., down another octave and produce a most satisfactory stop.

While the tubes of the orchestral Saxophones are of brass, their reeds are, like those of the Clarinets, constructed of wood; accordingly the Saxophones belong to the reed forces and the wood-wind division of the orchestra. These facts should influence the appointing of the SAXOPHONES to the divisions of the Concert-room Organ most appropriate for their reception.

The organ reed stops which represent the brass-wind of the orchestra are not so successful in their imitative voices as the reed stops previously mentioned. The orchestral brass instruments whose tones are more or less closely imitated are the Trumpet, Trombone, Ophicleide, and Bass Tuba. Others, such as the Horn, Euphonium, and Cornopean or Cornet à pistons, have not been nearly so successfully imitated in the Organ; indeed, it seems a hopeless task to imitate the tones of the Horn by any kind of reed pipes. We are convinced that if these tones are ever successfully imitated, labial pipes will be employed for the purpose. The beautiful and smooth tones of the Euphonium are certainly difficult to imitate, and they seem to be more closely allied to the tones produced by free reed pipes than those yielded by the more generally used striking reeds. The difficulty attending the satisfactory imitation of the characteristic and not altogether pleasing tones of the Cornopean is also great; and it is not too much to say that the CORNOPEAN, 8 FT., as commonly met with in the Organ, is by no means a satisfactory imitative stop. One of the commonest and most generally useful reed stops is the TRUMPET, 8 FT., and this is to be found in the tonal appointment of every Organ of any pretensions, while in large instruments it appears in two or more divisions: for instance, in the Organ in the Centennial Hall, Sydney, it is introduced in four divisions—the Great, Swell, Solo, and Pedal Organs. This stop appears in some large Organs under two names; namely, TRUMPET and TROMBA, as in the instrument in the Auditorium, at Chicago, where there are TRUMPETS in the Great and Stage, and a TROMBA in the Choir Organ. When two or more TRUMPETS are introduced in the same instrument, they should be made of different scales, and voiced to yield distinctive tones, suitable for the divisions in which they are placed. The ORCHESTRAL TRUMPET, 8 FT., the tone of which resembles, as closely as practicable, that of the Trumpet of the orchestra, finds its proper place in the division which contains the principal solo stops, or in that devoted to the stops which represent the brass-wind of the orchestra. The other TRUMPETS, whose tones are of the usual organ character, may be placed in the Great, Swell, and Pedal Organs, according to the demands of the general tonal appointment of the instrument. There is a manual stop of 16 ft. pitch, known as the DOUBLE TRUMPET, formed of pipes similar in form to, but smaller in scale than, the corresponding pipes of the unison TRUMPET. The tone of this double stop should be lighter than that of the TRUMPET, 8 FT., when both stops are placed in the same division, as in the Great division of the Organ in the Parish Church of Doncaster. TRUMPETS of powerful intonation are frequently introduced in large Organs, and are very effective when placed, as they always should be, in expressive divisions. The powerful intonation is chiefly due to the high pressure wind employed, the scale of the pipes and the mode of forming and voicing the reeds being adapted to the requirements. The HARMONIC TRUMPET, 8 FT., when properly scaled and voiced, is perhaps the finest of the loud-toned TRUMPETS, and is accordingly highly to be recommended for insertion in the expressive Solo Organ. There is a TRUMPET, 8 FT., on wind of 22 inches, in the Solo division of the Organ in St. George's Hall, Liverpool; but unfortunately this magnificent stop has lost much of its value, from a true musical point of view, by being placed outside the swell-box which contains the greater number of the stops of the division. As we have said elsewhere, it is astonishing that the very common practice of placing the high-pressure reed stops beyond control and powers of expression was not long ago condemned by men of cultivated and refined musical taste. These men advocate the appointment of the most delicately- and softly-voiced stops known to expressive divisions of the Organ, while they advocate, in a thoroughly inconsistent manner, the placing of the loudest and coarsest stops in an exposed position, where it is impossible to modify or impart any light and shade to their voices. As they roar at first, so must they roar for all time. There is no authority in the orchestra for such unmusical treatment, nor is the slightest authority furnished by any musical instrument outside the Organ. Every orchestral instrument, and, indeed, every musical instrument of any value, is capable of producing a *crescendo* and *diminuendo*, at the will of the performer. Why, then, in the name of common sense, should the assertive stops of the Organ which are designed to represent important orchestral instruments be denied, by the illogical builder, these all-important powers of expression? The question is difficult to answer.

The TROMBONES of the Organ, while they cannot be said to successfully imitate in their tones the fine Trombones of the orchestra, are majestic and most valuable stops. The compass covered by the Trombones of the orchestra extends from AAA to f♯^{2}; accordingly the TROMBONE, 8 FT., can be accepted as imitative only up to the latter note; above that it is strictly a full-toned TRUMPET, to which no exception need be taken. The unimitative TROMBONES, of 16 ft. and 32 ft. pitch, are very important stops in the modern Organ, and when voiced by a master hand produce tones of singular grandeur and dignity. Under the name of CONTRA-POSAUNE, we find the stop of 16 ft. pitch in both the Great and Pedal Organs of the instrument in the Centennial Hall, at Sydney. TROMBONES, 16 FT., are to be found in the Great and Swell divisions of the Organ in St. George's Hall, Liverpool; and a POSAUNE, 32 FT., is inserted in the pedal department of the same instrument. A TROMBONE, 16 FT., is placed in the pedal department of the Organ in the Auditorium, at Chicago; but no TROMBONE, 8 FT., is to be found in its manual divisions. In the Liverpool Organ, unison TROMBONES are inserted in both the Great and Solo divisions; accordingly, there are two TROMBONES of 8 ft., two of 16 ft., and one of 32 ft. pitch in this instrument. The stops above mentioned are also introduced in important Church Organs, as in the large instrument in the Parish Church of Doncaster, where we find a POSAUNE, 8 FT., in the Great Organ, and a POSAUNE, 16 FT., and a CONTRA-POSAUNE, 32 FT., in the Pedal Organ.

The TROMBONES are represented in French Organs by the BOMBARDES, and these stops appear in almost every instrument of any importance. In the Grand Organ in the Church of Saint-Sulpice, Paris, there are BOMBARDES of 16 ft. pitch in the Grand Chœur, the Clavier de Bombardes, and the Récit expressif; and in the Clavier de Pédale there are a BOMBARDE of 16 ft. and a CONTRE-BOMBARDE of 32 ft. pitch. In his scheme for the Grand Organ for the Basilica of St. Peter, at Rome, M. Cavaillé-Coll has introduced in the pedal department a QUINTE BOM-

BARDE, 10⅔ FT., in addition to the BOMBARDE, 16 FT., and the CONTRE-BOMBARDE, 32 FT. The tones of the French BOMBARDES are much softer than those of the English TROMBONES, and on this account are more generally useful in varied combinations. TROMBONES of an intonation, in strength, between the voices of the BASSOONS and the loud TROMBONES at present introduced, would be valuable in all modern Organs.

The Ophicleides of the orchestra cover a compass extending from GGG to f^2; accordingly the Pedal Organ OPHICLEIDE, 16 FT., is only extended downward seven notes below the Bass Ophicleide. There is the Double-Bass Ophicleide which goes down to DDD, but this monster instrument is little known and rarely used. The manual OPHICLEIDE, 8 FT., exceeds the upward range of the Alto Ophicleide in F about an octave and a half. While the tones of the OPHICLEIDES of the Organ are not strictly imitative, they are, in good examples, superior in musical quality and evenness to the tones of the orchestral instruments. In the Organ in St. George's Hall, Liverpool, there are four fine OPHICLEIDES. Three of 8 ft. pitch occupy places in the Great, Swell, and Solo Organs; that in the last-named division speaking on wind of 22 inches, and being placed outside the swell-box. The fourth OPHICLEIDE, which is of 16 ft. pitch, is placed in the pedal department. In the Organ in the Auditorium, at Chicago, there is only one OPHICLEIDE, 16 FT., and this is placed in the Great Organ. The OPHICLEIDE is not commonly introduced in German and French Organs. An example is to be found in the Second Manual of the Organ in the Cathedral of Riga, built by Walcker, of Ludwigsburg; and one is inserted in the Clavier de Pédale of the Organ in the Church of Saint-Sulpice, at Paris, by Cavaillé-Coll. In the latter builder's scheme for the Grand Organ for the Basilica of St. Peter, at Rome, no OPHICLEIDE appears.

There is really no necessity to consider the claims of the OPHICLEIDE in the appointment of the Church Organ, even when of the first magnitude; but in that of the Concert-room Organ its value should be acknowledged. In large instruments a unison OPHICLEIDE should be inserted in the expressive division in which the brass wind instruments of the orchestra are properly represented, while an OPHICLEIDE, 16 FT., may with advantage be placed in the Pedal Organ. The multiplication, as met with in the Liverpool instrument, is not to be recommended, on several grounds. In short, the lesson taught by the use of the Ophicleide in the orchestra should be recognized in the tonal appointment of the Organ.

Speaking of the Bass Tuba, Berlioz correctly says: "The Bass Tuba possesses an immense advantage over all other low wind instruments. Its quality of tone, incomparably more noble than that of Ophicleides, Bombardons, and Serpents, has something of the vibration and quality of tone of Trombones. It has less agility than the Ophicleides; but its sonorousness is more powerful than theirs, and its low compass is the largest existing in the orchestra." The Bass Tuba, of M. Sax, has a compass of from AAA♭ to $a♭^1$. This majestic instrument deserves to be carefully studied with the view of its tones being imitated closely in the Organ. The BASS TUBA of the Organ is of course a reed stop of 16 ft. pitch, and its proper place, on account of the short compass upward, would appear to be the Pedal Organ, especially as the finest tones of the orchestral instrument lie within the compass of the Pedal; but where it has been introduced it occupies a place in one of the manual divisions. Under the name of TUBA MAJOR, 16 FT., the stop appears in the Solo division of the Organ in the Auditorium, at Chicago; and under the name of CONTRA-TUBA, 16 FT., it is to be found in the same division in the Organ in the Centennial Hall, at Sydney. The correct place for the imitative BASS TUBA, 16 FT., when not included in the appointment of the Pedal Organ, is in the manual division specially devoted to the assertive stops which represent the brass wind instruments of the orchestra. When introduced in this division, the notes above a♭^{1}, which do not belong to the orchestral Bass Tuba, may be accepted as imitative of the tones of the Sax-Tubas or the Sax-Horns, according to their intonation and quality.

The stops of 8 ft. pitch called TUBAS, apparently intended as organ representatives of the Sax-Tubas, vary very much in their qualities and strengths of tone, according to their scales, modes of voicing, and the pressures of wind on which they speak. These effective stops find their culmination in the high-pressure reed commonly designated the TUBA MIRABILIS, of which several fine specimens exist in English Organs. The TUBA, 8 FT., of moderate intonation may be inserted in either the Swell or Solo divisions; but when of powerful intonation its proper place is in the latter division, where it certainly should be inclosed and rendered flexible and expressive. There is a TUBA MIRABILIS, 8 FT., in the Solo division of the Organ in the Auditorium, at Chicago, which, according to the late Mr. Roosevelt's sensible treatment, is inclosed in the special swell-box of the division. There are others in the Solo Organs of the instruments in the Royal Albert Hall, Kensington, and Westminster Abbey; but neither of these is expressive, while both are on high-pressure wind. The TUBAS in the Solo division of the Organ in York Minster are unwisely placed outside the swell-box.

In addition to the TUBAS, of 16 ft. and 8 ft. pitch, above mentioned, there is a stop of 4 ft. pitch called the TUBA CLARION. This is usually a high-pressure reed of brilliant intonation. Examples are to be found in the Solo divisions of the Organs in the Royal Albert Hall, and the Centennial Hall, Sydney. In the same division of the Organ in St. George's Hall, Liverpool, there are two high-pressure reeds of this class and pitch, an unnecessary and undesirable duplication, especially as they are both uninclosed, like the TUBA CLARIONS, 4 FT., in the preceding two Organs.

As we have already said, no satisfactory imitation of the peculiar and beautiful tones of the orchestral Horn have been accomplished through the medium of organ pipes. Indeed, the voice of this "noble and melancholy instrument," as Berlioz calls it, seems foreign to the sounds characteristic of all reed pipes. The nearest approach to the voice of the Horn, that we have ever heard in the Organ, was produced in the tenor and middle octaves of a labial stop of the KERAULOPHON species. Notwithstanding the unimitative character of the organ stop commonly labeled the HORN, 8 FT., there is no question that it is, when artistically voiced, a valuable voice in the Organ—even if we accept it as little more than a soft and smooth-toned TRUMPET. Reed stops of soft and smooth tones are so rare in modern Organs that their introduction should always be encouraged by the musician. There are some very satisfactory examples of the so-called HORN to be found in the works of the leading organ builders, and especially in instruments built by those who have made a special study of the voicing of reed pipes. In a HORN of a satisfactory character all brassy quality must be eliminated, and a smooth velvety tone must be produced in which there is no trace of reed vibration. These desirable conditions are by no means fulfilled by reed pipes of the ordinary construction. How far the adoption of free reeds would solve the problem has not yet been properly tried. Both English and American organ builders have a decided objection to the introduction of free reed stops, and perhaps this is not altogether to be wondered at.

While the correct position for the HORN in an Organ may vary according to its tonal character and assertiveness, it is certainly proper that it should be placed in an expressive division. When of the smooth and soft tone, as closely imitative as can be arrived at by the present style of reed voicing, we recommend its being placed in the division of the Concert-room Organ in which are located the stops that represent the wood wind instruments of the orchestra. When introduced in the Church Organ, the HORN finds its most appropriate place in the expressive Choir division, or in the Swell division when the Choir is unexpressive. Probably the best example of the stop, under the name of FRENCH HORN, 8 FT., is to be found in the Solo division of the Organ in the Royal Albert Hall, London, where it is properly rendered expressive by being inclosed, along with certain other solo stops, in a special swell-box. HORNS also appear in the Swell divisions of the Organs in St. George's Hall, Liverpool, the Centennial Hall, Sydney, and the Parish Church of Doncaster. In the last it is also introduced (of 8 ft. pitch) in the pedal department. In the Organ of the Auditorium, at Chicago, the HORN appears in the expressive Echo division. The HORN has never been introduced in any important French or German Organs, so far as we are aware. The stop is evidently of English origin, and is believed to have been invented by Richard Bridge and introduced for the first time in the Organ he built, in 1730, for Christ Church, Spitalfields, London. In 1732 Byfield added a Swell division to the Organ in the Temple Church, London, in which he placed a HORN, 8 FT.

Attempts have apparently been made by several builders to produce a stop, the tones of which shall imitate those of the orchestral Euphonium; but, as in the case of the Horn, the task seems almost hopeless. Under the names of EUPHONIUM and EUPHONE, free-reed stops of soft and pleasing intonation have been introduced in several Organs. A EUPHONE, 16 FT., is introduced in the Positif of the Organ in the Church of Saint-Sulpice, at Paris, and one of 8 ft. pitch is inserted in the First Manual division of the Organ in the Cathedral of Riga. Representative examples of this stop, of 16 ft. pitch, are to be found in the Choir divisions of the Roosevelt Organs in the Cathedral of Garden City, Long Island, and the Auditorium, at Chicago. In the last instance the Choir Organ is expressive, and the value of the stop therein is greatly increased.

When the EUPHONE is simply a soft-toned reed of an unimitative character, it may be placed in any manual division of the Organ where its voice would be suitable for combination; but when its tone is rich, full, and imitative of that of the orchestral instrument, it may properly take its place, under the name of EUPHONIUM, in the Solo Organ. When of 16 ft. pitch, its most useful place, we are of opinion, is in the Pedal Organ, where the presence of a soft-toned reed of distinctive and good mixing character is invaluable. The provision of voices of soft and medium intonation in the appointment of the Pedal Organ has been much too often neglected.

The CORNOPEAN, 8 FT., of the Organ, as usually made, cannot be considered an imitative stop in the strict sense of the term. There is great scope for improvement in the voicing and intonation of this stop; for the existing examples are far from satisfactory in comparison with the effects produced by the orchestral Cornopean, played by a master. The proper tones of the CORNOPEAN lie between the brassy tones of the TRUMPET and the smooth round tones of the HORN; and on this account they are desirable in a large Organ, imparting variety of tonal coloring. When the CORNOPEAN is distinctive and approaches an imitative character, its correct place is in the Solo Organ or in the manual division specially devoted to the stops which represent the brass wind instruments of the orchestra. Examples are to be found in the Swell divisions of the Organs in the Auditorium, at Chicago; the Albert Hall, Kensington, London; the Crystal Palace, Sydenham; the Centennial Hall, Sydney; the Town Hall, Leeds; and in a great number of English churches. As in all these instances, the CORNOPEAN should invariably be placed in an expressive division of the Organ.

Such, then, are the more important tonal forces at the disposal of the organ designer and builder; and it is in their selection for the different classes of Organs, and in their apportionment to the several divisions of an Organ, that the scientific knowledge, musical taste, and constructive skill of the designer and builder are displayed.

We have already shown, in the Chapters specially devoted to them, that there are three classes of Organs—the Church Organ, the Concert-room Organ, and the Chamber Organ—and have endeavored to prove that each of these, having a different office to fulfil, should be designed on special lines, so far, at least, as its tonal appointment is concerned. We do not hesitate to say that very many of the failures in modern organ-building are directly due to the fact that those interested in the art failed to fully realize the nature of the problems submitted to them. There is many a Church Organ that would be more properly placed in a concert-room; many a Concert-room Organ that would be more useful if placed in a church; while the majority of Chamber Organs are merely small instruments, on the ordinary Church Organ model, very much out of place in private residences. Such a state of affairs would not obtain if organ designers and builders realized the obvious fact that in each case the Organ should be schemed from a different starting point, and developed on special lines.

It must never be forgotten that in the tonal appointment of the Organ two equally important matters demand careful study and consideration; namely, the selection of the complete series of speaking stops suitable for the special class of instrument and the chief work it has to do; and the proper disposition of the stops, so selected, in the different divisions of the instrument, so as to enable the performer to separate or combine the several varieties of tone, in the most convenient and effective manner, without having to resort to an undesirable and perplexing use of mechanical helps or appliances; and likewise enable him to control the entire tonal forces at his disposal in the most direct and musicianly manner.

In disposing the stops in the different divisions of the Organ, due attention must be paid to the separation of those which demand powers of expression and flexibility * from those which may properly be planted on exposed or uninclosed wind-chests. And this necessary separation should exercise a decided influence on the selection of the entire series of stops. In a scientifically schemed instrument, having full powers of expression, the series of speaking stops will vary considerably from the series proper and desirable for an instrument with very limited expressive powers, or which may only have one division—the Swell Organ—inclosed in a swell-box. This self-evident fact appears, however, to be very generally unknown or ignored.

The division of the Organ commonly called the Great Organ, which is usually entirely uninclosed, may, with great advantage from a musical or artistic point of view, have a portion of its speaking stops rendered tonally flexible by being inclosed in a swell-box. The great advantage of such an arrangement has been fully considered in preceding Chapters; and it was thoroughly realized by the celebrated American builders, the late Hilborne and Frank Roosevelt. And it must be quite obvious to every one who has studied the tonal structure of the Organ, that the same stop appointment would not be equally appropriate for an entirely uninclosed and for a partly inclosed Great Organ. In the latter a much greater latitude obtains in the selection of the stops, and a much more satisfactory harmonic structure may be introduced. This is due to the great tonal flexibility imparted to the stops which properly form the inclosed section of the division. In short, the stops that would be proper for the inclosed section, in combination with the usual uninclosed stops, such as the DIAPASONS and other full-toned labial stops of unison pitch, would not be altogether suitable for an entirely exposed division. In the former case the great variations in strength of tone in, and the flexible character of, the Great Organ, secured by its inclosed section, multiply ten-fold the tonal effects that are both possible and desirable from a strictly musical point of view.

While in the case of the Great Organ, or that manual division of the instrument which is its equivalent, it is clearly unnecessary and undesirable to inclose the double and unison labial stops which form the foundation of the entire Organ, it is, both on scientific and artistic grounds, most desirable to render flexible the stops which strictly belong to the harmonic-corroborating series. The inclosing of these stops renders the introduction of a practically complete tonal structure not only possible but highly desirable. The harmonic-corroborating series, including the octave stops, mutation stops, and compound stops, under the controlling influence of the swell-box becomes so flexible as to be of value in almost every combination of the unison and double stops of the division. It is no longer

*See the Chapter on The Swell in the Organ.

necessary to confine the use of the mutation and compound stops to full or loud tonal effects: on the contrary, they may be most effectively used with the softest combinations possible in the division, or even with a single unison stop. The advantage of such an arrangement must surely be obvious to the musician. Both artistic skill and musical taste can be displayed in the proper gradation of the harmonic-corroborating tone in all the possible combinations; and brilliant flashes of tonal coloring may be produced by the powers of expression the swell supplies. As this subject has been fully treated in other Chapters, it is unnecessary to do more than allude to it here.

The speaking stops which strictly belong to the Great Organ are those which yield pure organ-tone—the OPEN DIAPASONS and the stops derived therefrom; and in instruments of moderate dimensions which comprise three manual divisions it is unnecessary to add materially to these, beyond, perhaps, two or three unisons of varied qualities of tone. These may be a full-toned covered stop, a stop of viol organ-tone, and an effective reed, such as the DOPPELFLÖTE, 8 FT., the GAMBA, 8 FT., and the TRUMPET, 8 FT. While it may not be generally desirable to inclose the labial stops, the TRUMPET should certainly be placed in the swell-box. If an OCTAVE of either of these stops should be introduced, it ought to be inclosed so as to place its strength of tone under control.

The characteristic qualities which should mark the stop appointment of the Great Organ are grandeur, dignity, and solidity of tone; and these can only be secured by accurately proportioned scales, artistic voicing, and a copious wind supply at a moderate pressure—a scientifically schemed harmonic structure being understood. The importance of the inclosed harmonic-corroborating series of stops is not confined to the Great Organ; for it will prove of the greatest value, in numerous combinations, when coupled to the other divisions of the instrument which, in the usual order of things, are not furnished with anything approaching a complete harmonic structure. The value of the Great Organ flexible harmonic-corroborating series, in conjunction with combinations in the other divisions of the Organ, cannot well be realized by the ordinary performer who has had experience only with instruments of the usual old-fashioned description, in which only one flexible and expressive division—the Swell Organ—is introduced. Both in the construction and playing of the Organ there are possibilities hardly dreamt of at the present time. The organist of the twentieth century has a fertile field before him.

The second division of the Organ, or that very commonly termed, by English and American organ builders, the Choir Organ, calls for a tonal appointment widely different from that of the Great Organ. The tonal character of this second division should be distinctive, and present a decided contrast to that of the first division. While in the first division grandeur, dignity, and solidity should, as we have said, be the characteristic qualities of tone, in the Choir Organ stop appointment moderate strength of tone, variety of character, and extreme refinement of intonation should obtain throughout. In the Church Organ this is essentially an accompanimental division, and this fact must be steadily held in view while scheming its tonal appointment. The Choir Organ is at the present time almost invariably uninclosed, while as an accompanimental division it certainly should have powers of flexibility and expression imparted to it. There is a strong prejudice, as we have pointed out elsewhere, against the multiplication of the swell in the Organ; and even accomplished organists object, we venture to say, illogically, to the inclosure of the Choir Organ in a swell-box. We met with notable examples of this illogical objection on the occasion when we brought the subject of 'The Swell in the Organ' before the Royal College of Organists. In the organ-building world no builders have realized the artistic necessity of imparting expressive powers to the Choir Organ so fully as did the late Roosevelts, of New York, and their practical advocacy forms a valuable page in Organ history.

In the Concert-room Organ the second manual division can hardly be pronounced an accompanimental one. It simply consists of a series of stops, softer and more varied in tonal character than those forming the first division. It groups, under easy control by means of a special clavier, certain tonal forces, which are selected from the entire stop appointment of the instrument for a well-conceived purpose, and with a definite aim. The second division of the Concert-room Organ should certainly be rendered expressive, as in the case of the Organ in the Auditorium, at Chicago, and in the Organ in the Albert Hall, at Sheffield. In the large majority of existing Concert-room Organs the second, or so-called Choir, divisions are uninclosed. Accordingly in both Church and Concert-room Organs there are two classes of Choir divisions,—the uninclosed and inclosed,—and these call for different stop appointments or, at the least, for stops of different strengths of tone. Much greater liberty may be exercised in the selection of the stops for an inclosed or expressive division than one that has to be heard, at all times, at its full strength of tone; and this is especially the case when the Choir Organ is schemed for accompanimental purposes. Under no circumstances should the Choir be treated as a miniature Great Organ; for duplication of any of the Great Organ stops, even though they be OPEN DIAPASONS of softer intonation, leads to an undesirable narrowing of tonal variety. In the case of very large instruments, however, this rule against duplication of similar qualities of tone may be to some extent relaxed in favor of the foundation stops of pure organ-tone, but no farther. In small instruments no trace of duplication should appear. It may be remarked that in certain cases the Choir Organ may be only partly inclosed; and this arrangement should certainly be adopted when there are any stops of a strictly solo character, and when there is a strong prejudice against rendering the entire division expressive. The CLARINET, 8 FT., is very frequently inserted in the uninclosed Choir Organ; but this should never obtain in a properly schemed and appointed instrument. Whenever the CLARINET is inserted, it should either be in an expressive division or be inclosed in a special swell-box, which, of course, may be shared with any other stop or stops demanding powers of expression. It may be said that, in a properly appointed Organ, no stop of a strictly solo character should be inserted in an unexpressive division or in an uninclosed condition.

Beyond the directions above given no hard and fast rules, of general application, can be given for the stop appointment of the Second or Choir Organ; for in this, as in all the other divisions, the appointment entirely depends on the size, number of manual divisions, and the tonal appointment of the entire instrument. For further particulars respecting the stops suitable for the Choir division of the Church Organ and the corresponding manual division of the Concert-room Organ we must direct our readers to the Chapters on the Church and Concert-room Organs. The Chapter on the Chamber Organ may also be consulted.

In the tonal appointment of the third division of the Organ—that commonly designated the Swell Organ, from the fact that in old and in the large majority of modern Organs it is the only division inclosed in a swell-box—considerable latitude obtains. In every instrument which has only one expressive division the Swell Organ should be both the largest and, tonally, the most varied division; and it should also be the most brilliant in its tonal effects. It becomes in this case the chief accompanimental division, simply because it alone is flexible and expressive. It is difficult, we venture to say, for the true musician to imagine any instrument suitable for the accompaniment of the human voice that is not endowed with powers of expression. If an accompaniment is to be of any artistic value it must follow, and in all instances accentuate, the tonal expression of the vocal music; and in an instrument of great strength of tone, like the Organ, flexibility and expression are absolutely essential properties. We lay great stress on these facts because they must never be lost sight of in scheming the tonal appointment of the Swell Organ.

In addition to its being the chief accompanimental division in an Organ which has only a single swell-box, the Swell Organ is, or should be, the most important division for the production of solo effects; and this simply because it is essential that all purely solo voices should be endowed with powers of expression. But when an Organ has a fourth or Solo division, inclosed in a swell-box, the so-called Swell Organ should be appointed as a full accompanimental division, and that not only with reference to the human voice, but also with reference to the solo voices of the Solo Organ. The Swell Organ, in what may be considered its proper form, strictly belongs to the Church Organ; and as we have treated its appointment at considerable length in the Chapter on the Church Organ, it is only necessary to pass a few remarks in addition here. Whether the Swell Organ is schemed as an accompanimental division only, or as both an accompanimental and a solo division, it should have a fairly complete tonal structure, founded on an OPEN DIAPASON, 8 FT., of a bright quality; or a GEIGENPRINCIPAL, 8 FT., of rich intonation, as dictated by the general tonal appointment of the Organ. This structure may in all favorable cases be richer in harmonic-corroborating stops than even that of the Great Organ; for, as we have already said, brilliancy should characterize the tonal effects of the Swell Organ; and this desirable brilliancy cannot easily be secured without the introduction of special mutation and compound harmonic-corroborating and timbre-creating stops. Further richness and brilliancy of tonal effect, combined with a general increase of body and weight, can be secured by the judicious introduction of unison stops which are in themselves rich in harmonic over-tones. In Organs of small dimensions every expedient, consistent with general tonal excellence, should be resorted to to enrich the unison tone without the undue introduction of small stops. There are many solo stops, as mentioned in the earlier portion of the present Chapter and described in the Chapter on the Names and General Particulars of Organ Stops, which are comparatively rich in certain natural harmonic upper partial tones: and the introduction of such stops goes far to render, especially in small instruments and in certain divisions of large Organs, the addition of medium-pitched mutation stops unnecessary; but as such unison stops are somewhat weak in the higher upper partial tones, it is not generally desirable to depend upon them for the compound tonal effects the MIXTURES are constructed to produce. As we have fully treated the subject of compound harmonic-corroborating stops in the preceding Chapter it is unnecessary to enlarge on it here. The remarks made in this and the foregoing paragraph have special reference to the appointment of the Church Organ.

The third division of a properly appointed Concert-room Organ is a very important one, furnishing effective accompaniments to the prominent solo voices of the fourth division, or so-called Solo Organ, and independent solo voices required for special orchestral effects and tonal combinations. The full appointment of this division of the Concert-room Organ is considered in the Chapter specially devoted to that instrument; but several other satisfactory tonal appointments may be schemed, on similar lines, for instruments of lesser size. As a general rule it is always desirable to scheme the stop appointment of this division so that it may not only be distinctly marked from that of every other division, but that it may fill a clearly defined and special office in the tonal economy of the instrument. While in the ordinary Church Organ it is desirable, if not absolutely necessary, to have the Swell division complete in itself and practically independent, so that it may fulfil its accompanimental office in the most efficient manner; in the Concert-room Organ, which has two or more of its manual divisions wholly or partly inclosed and expressive, the corresponding division does not call for a similar treatment. On the contrary, it should be tonally appointed with strict reference to every other division of the instrument, taking its place as simply a part of the grand tonal scheme; just as a division of the orchestra, organized for the production of special musical effects, is a portion of, and is dependent on, the entire tonal fabric of the orchestra.

In the case of a large Concert-room Organ, having only four manual claviers, it is well worth serious consideration whether or not the third division, commanded by the third clavier, should be subdivided and given double expression; for the decision in this matter will materially influence the tonal appointment of the division. This will be clearly seen on reference to our dissertation on the appointment of the Third Organ, in the Chapter on the Concert-room Organ. When the division is subdivided, each part should have a distinct tonal character, chiefly with the view of aiding the performer to easily produce special orchestral effects and masses of distinct tonal coloring, without the objectionable resort to coupling, and without stultifying any other manual division for the time. It is essential that each subdivision be inclosed in a separate swell-box, and very remarkable effects are obtainable by this system of compound expression.

In the properly-appointed Concert-room Organ the third division, whether it be subdivided or not, should be strongly orchestral in its tonal character; and it appears, to our mind, to be the proper division in which to represent the string forces of the orchestra. String-toned stops should here be massed together, forming a rich harmonic structure, always ready at the command of the organist without drawing upon the resources of the other divisions in the slightest degree; and, when coupled to the other divisions, imparting to them a vast increase of brilliancy and variety, aided by the compound powers of expression. If the reader will turn to the tonal scheme given in our Chapter on the Concert-room Organ, and imagine the Third Clavier coupled to the First Clavier, he will perhaps be able to form some conception of the absolutely inexhaustible series of tonal effects at his disposal while performing on the First Clavier, with the three different tonal sources to draw upon, and the three distinct means of expression at his command—tonal effects practically impossible on any Organ at present in existence, and, indeed, on any Organ constructed and appointed on the old lines. A similar inexhaustible series of fine tonal effects are furnished when the divided Third Organ is coupled to the expressive Second Organ.

The stops which may be accepted as most suitable for the appointment of the third division of the Concert-room Organ are the imitative string-toned stops, as before mentioned, and their derivatives; the family of HARMONIC FLUTES; and the labial and reed stops which represent the wood wind instruments of the orchestra. To these should be added a few stops of organ-tone, including, in instruments of the first magnitude, a PRINCIPAL or OPEN DIAPASON, 8 FT., an OCTAVE, 4 FT., and a compound harmonic-corroborating stop, of four or five ranks, of medium strength of tone. The most appropriate double stops are a QUINTATEN, 16 FT., and a DOUBLE BASS VIOL or CONTRA-BASSO, 16 FT. To these may be added, in the reed section, a CONTRAFAGOTTO, 16 FT., and a CONTRA-OBOE, 16 FT.

The fourth division in all Organs having four manual claviers, and the fifth division in instruments having five manual claviers, may be considered, as the name commonly given to it implies, to be the division devoted to the stops of a decidedly solo character, and to those of a specially powerful intonation which are more suitable for pronounced solo effects and dominating musical passages than for the purpose of combination. Except in Concert-room Organs of the first magnitude, the Solo Organ need not contain many stops; but in all cases the stops must be carefully selected, so as to supply what may be markedly deficient in the other manual divisions of the instrument, and to furnish voices of an orchestral character, strongly imitative and assertive in their tonality. In a small Solo Organ there should be no duplication of stops that appear elsewhere in the instrument; while in large Solo Organs duplication is only admissible under very special tonal appointments, and for the necessary production of well-defined tonal effects. When a stop of any class is duplicated, care must be taken to give individuality to the voice of that inserted in the Solo Organ, so that it may have due prominence over the stop of the same name which is inserted in any other division. All the more important stops of the Solo Organ should be, as we have already remarked, of an imitative and orchestral character; and this division is the most appropriate one for the reception of those assertive stops which represent the brass-wind of the orchestra, and which speak on wind of high pressures. The above remarks will be more clearly understood on reference being made to the stop appointment of this division in our scheme given in the Chapter on the Concert-room Organ.

The Solo Organ should invariably be rendered entirely expressive by being inclosed in a special swell-box; and, notwithstanding the present objectionable practice of certain organ builders, which places the high-pressure reed stops in an uninclosed position, such powerful and dominating voices should never, in truly artistic tonal appointment, be placed beyond proper control or without powers of of expression. On this important subject we have spoken fully elsewhere.

We have brought the matter of the swell somewhat prominently forward in the present Chapter, simply because its introduction or omission very materially affects the tonal appointment of the Organ. It is not too much to say that between an exposed and an inclosed division of the Organ a wide difference of tonal appointment should obtain; and not only should this difference be in the class of stops selected, but also in their scaling and voicing, and in the pressures of wind on which they speak. In the scientific and artistic tonal appointment of an Organ not a single thing affecting the tonality of the stops should be overlooked. It must never be forgotten that a stop perfectly suitable for one position, or in one tonal scheme, may be out of place in another; and it is in such a case that scientific knowledge and cultivated musical sense are required and display themselves. How many organ builders or organists, while they prepare the tonal schemes of Organs, give heed to the teachings of science, or seek the guidance of cultivated musical sense?

The present Chapter would be markedly incomplete without some allusion to one other manual division, sometimes introduced in large modern Organs, but which is of comparatively little importance, and is only useful for the production of certain effects rarely called for in legitimate organ music or in the rendition of orchestral scores. We allude to the so-called Echo Organ, or the small division usually located at some distance from the main portion of the instrument, and in a position calculated to impart to its tone the effect of great distance and a somewhat mysterious character.

A manual division called the Echo appears in the works of the old European builders, which is simply a softly-toned division occupying the place later taken by the Swell Organ. In the celebrated Organ in the Cathedral at Haarlem, built in the year 1738, the Echo comprises fifteen stops and 1098 pipes. It presents a very complete tonal structure, having two mutation stops and three compound stops, in all fourteen ranks of pipes. Its reed stops are the SCHALMEI, 8 FT., DULCIAN, 8 FT., and VOX HUMANA, 8 FT. The last stop usually found a place in the old Echo Organs. In many instances, in old Dutch and German instruments, the Echo was larger and more complete in its tonal appointment than the Choir Organ. With these old examples, however, we have nothing to do in the present Chapter, for the Echo division in modern organ-building is a widely different thing when properly treated.

Perhaps the most noteworthy Echo Organ, in a modern instrument, is that of the large Organ in the Auditorium, at Chicago. It is placed in an elevated locality, above the hall, more than one hundred feet from the console, is inclosed in a swell-box, and played from the fourth or Solo Organ clavier. The following is a list of its stops :—

ECHO ORGAN.

1.	Quintaten, ...	16 feet.	7.	Flauto Traverso, .	4 feet.
2.	Keraulophon, . .	8 "	8.	Harmonia Ætheria,	IV. ranks.
3.	Dolcissimo, . . .	8 "	9.	Horn, ...	8 feet.
4.	Unda Maris, . .	8 "	10.	Oboe, ...	8 "
5.	Fernflöte, . . .	8 "	11.	Vox Humana, . .	8 "
6.	Dulcet, . . .	4 "	—	Tremolant.	

The chief conditions required for a successful Echo Organ obtain in this example; namely, considerable distance from the player and audience, and inclosure in a swell-box. The tonal appointment, in relation to the rest of the instrument, may be accepted as fairly satisfactory: it is certainly capable of producing many charming tonal effects.

Turning now to the larger modern Organ in the Centennial Hall, at Sydney, N. S. W., we find an expressionless Echo Organ, having the following rather peculiar stop appointment :—

ECHO ORGAN.

1.	Viole d'Amour, . .	8 feet.	5.	Flageolet, ...	2 feet.
2.	Unda Maris, (II. ranks)	8 "	6.	Echo Dulciana Cornet,	IV. ranks.
3.	Lieblichgedeckt, . .	8 "	7.	Glockenspiel, .	IV. "
4.	Viole d'Amour, . .	4 "	8.	Basset Horn, . .	8 feet.

It is somewhat remarkable that this Echo division is not inclosed in a swell-box. To leave such a division without powers of expression, and beyond control so far as strength of tone is concerned, is surely an error of judgment.

In deciding the tonal appointment of the Echo Organ, the office of the division should, at the outset, be clearly defined. The Echo Organ may either be independent of all the other manual divisions and be tonally complete in itself, or a dependent division schemed with the view of furnishing echo effects to several of the special solo stops in other manual divisions. In the latter case it is, strictly speaking, an Echo Organ. In all cases it should be inclosed in a swell-box and located in a position favorable to the production of distant effects. Unless the Echo Organ can be properly treated, so as to yield artistic results, it should be entirely omitted. It is by no means necessary in the tonal appointment of any instrument.

As the tonal appointment of the Pedal Organ, when correctly schemed, depends entirely on the appointment of the manual divisions of the instrument, nothing beyond a single rule need be given here. Let the Pedal Organ stops carry down as many as practicable of the more important stops of the manual divisions, with due regard to variety of character and strength of tone, and by this means provide suitable basses for the most useful and effective manual combinations and solo voices. As the Pedal Organ has to furnish basses for *all* the manual divisions, separate and combined, it is obvious that its tonal appointment, so far as unison (16 ft.) stops are concerned, must have a considerable range in tonal strength. It must not be forgotten that a soft bass is as valuable as a loud one; yet we find very few modern Church Organs, of medium size, provided with adequate Pedal Organs, or with those which contain soft unison stops. On this important branch of our subject further remarks will be found in the Chapters on the Church and Concert-room Organs. We desire the reader's special attention to what we say on the subject of the expressive Pedal Organ in the Chapters on the Concert-room Organ and the Swell in the Organ. The adoption of an expressive division will materially alter the desirable tonal appointment.

The student of organ-building may obtain many valuable hints on organ appointment by studying the annotated Specifications of representative Organs, given in the concluding part of this treatise. We have briefly criticised them, under the principles of construction and tonal appointment advocated throughout this work, with the view of making the Specifications means of instruction. The collection of Specifications may be accepted as an appendix to the present Chapter, and should be carefully studied by those interested in the scientific and artistic tonal appointment of the Organ.

CHAPTER XIII.

NAMES AND GENERAL PARTICULARS OF ORGAN STOPS—ANCIENT AND MODERN.

IN this Chapter an attempt is made to give the names and leading characteristics or peculiarities of all the more important speaking stops that have been introduced in the Organ, since the fifteenth century, in the different organ-building countries of the world; and which have existed or still exist in European and American instruments. The observations on each stop are necessarily brief; but this is a matter of no great moment, seeing that all the important speaking stops introduced in the modern Organ are more or less fully described elsewhere in this treatise. Special attention is paid to the correct orthography of each term, according to the language or languages in which it properly appears; and any modifications or corruptions are pointed out, so that, being undesirable, they may be avoided in modern stop nomenclature. This is a matter of considerable importance, for at present there is a lack of uniformity and accuracy in the nomenclature of organ stops, probably springing more from carelessness than positive ignorance. It is now most desirable that this irregularity should cease; and we have written the present Chapter, in the form of a Glossary for easy reference, in the hopes of establishing an orthographic standard which will be adopted by English and American organ builders and experts.

ACUTA or VOX ACUTA (from Lat. *acutus*—sharp).—A compound, labial, harmonic-corroborating stop, formed of three, four, or more ranks of metal pipes, having a keen, bright quality of tone. When correctly composed it has a third-sounding rank. Accordingly, it commences in a three-rank stop with c^2—e^2—g^2; in a four-rank stop with c^2—e^2—g^2—c^3, or with c^3—e^3—g^3—c^4; and in a five-rank stop with g^2—c^3—e^3—g^3—c^4. As the several ranks are required to be acute or high in pitch, the stop will have to break three or four times in the manual compass of five octaves. The ACUTA is sometimes composed of octave- and fifth-sounding ranks only, as in the example in the Organ of the Music Hall, Cincinnati; but this composition is not to be recommended. The ACUTA strictly belongs to the Great Organ, where it should appear with other compound stops of graver pitch. It appears in numerous German Organs labeled SCHARF and sometimes AKUTA, and in Dutch instruments it is commonly designated SCHERP.

ÆOLINE.—This name has been employed to designate extremely soft-toned stops of both lingual and labial forms. Seidel describes it as a reed stop voiced in imitation of the Æolian Harp, and this definition is supported by Hamel.* Locher says: "This stop is sometimes met with as an 8 ft. or 16 ft. reed, either like the PHYSHARMONICA, or with a small bell." Allihn also describes it as a delicate free reed stop. In its more modern form it is a labial stop of extremely small scale, producing the softest string-tone in the Organ. Locher, describing the labial ÆOLINE or ÆOLINA, says: "It is of a soft string-toned character, and is found in almost all recently built German and Swiss Organs as an 8 ft. solo stop." The true ÆOLINE is to be found in numerous Organs by American builders. It is properly formed of tin; the pipes being of a very small scale, slotted, and having mouths furnished with small curved beards which aid the production of the delicate string-tone. When skilfully voiced it is an extremely beautiful stop, peculiarly adapted for Chamber Organs. The corresponding names for this stop in other languages are:—Lat., ÆOLINA. Ger., ÄOLINE. Fr., ÉOLINE. Ital., EOLINA.

ÆOLODICON, Grk.—The name originally given to a keyboard instrument and the precursor of the Harmonium, and subsequently used by Walcker to designate a soft-toned reed stop of 16 ft. pitch, placed in the Second Manual division of the Grand Organ in the Cathedral of Riga.

ÄQUALPRINCIPAL, Ger.—The term which has occasionally been used by German builders to designate the principal manual unison stop—the PRINCIPAL, 8 FT. In early times of the art the simple term ÄQUAL was deemed sufficient. The term has been applied to other stops to denote their unison pitch.

AMOROSA, Lat.—The name sometimes used by Steinmeyer and other builders to designate a small-scaled wood FLUTE, of 8 ft. pitch, resembling the FLAUTO D'AMORE. The extended term VOX AMOROSA has occasionally been used.

ANGENEHMGEDECKT, Ger.—The term that has occasionally been substituted for LIEBLICHGEDECKT by German organ builders. It is formed from the word *angenehm*—pleasant.

ANTHROPOGLOSSA, Grk.—The term that has been sometimes used by the old German organ builders to designate the stop now known as the VOX HUMANA.

APFELREGAL, Ger. Eng., APPLE-REGAL.—An obsolete reed stop which derived its peculiar name from the shape of its resonant tubes; which were formed of short cylindrical portions surmounted by apple-shaped heads, perforated with

*C'est un jeu d'anches libres qui, ainsi que son nom l'indique, doit imiter le murmure de la harpe æolienne, et qui, par conséquent, doit avoir une intonation extrêmement tendre et aérienne. Les corps des tuyaux qui sonnent quelquefois le seize pieds, sont très-petits et d'un diapason très-étroit. On trouve ce jeu disposé avec des huit pieds dans le nouvel orgue de Sainte-Marie à Wismar."—"Manuel Complet du Facteur d'Orgues."

numerous small holes for the emission of the wind and sound. Hamel tells us that the cylindrical body of the largest pipe was only four inches long. The APFELREGAL must be classed among the curiosities of German organ-building.

BARDONE, Ital.—The name that has occasionally been employed to designate the stop commonly known as the BOURDON. The more correct Italian rendering is BORDONE. There was an old bass instrument called Viola di Bardone.

BAREM, Ger.—According to Hamel, this name was given to a covered stop of 8 ft. and 16 ft. pitch, voiced to yield a soft tone. The term is from the old German word *baren*—to sing. This stop appears to have been identical with that now known as the STILLGEDECKT.

BÄRPFEIFE, Ger. Dtch., BAARPIJP.—An old lingual stop, having pipes of a very peculiar shape, resembling two cones joined together at their bases, and both truncated. The illustration given by Seidel shows these two cones surmounted by a third truncated cone, forming a small bell to the pipe. The tone is described by Wolfram as of "a soft growling character," hence the name of the stop. The BAARPIJP is to be found, of 8 ft. pitch, in the Echo division of the celebrated old Organ in the Cathedral of St. Bavon, at Haarlem, and in certain other old Organs in Holland.

BARYTONE (Grk. *βαρύτονος*—deep-toned). Ital., BARITONO.—The name given by certain builders to a reed stop, of 8 ft. pitch, producing a singularly rich and full tone on moderate wind pressure. Under the name BARITONE, a stop of this class exists in the Solo division of the Organ, by Roosevelt, in the Cathedral of the Incarnation, Garden City, Long Island, U. S. A.

BASSET-HORN. Fr., COR DE BASSET. Ger., BASSETTHORN. Ital., CORNO DI BASSETTO.—A stop voiced to yield a tone resembling that of the orchestral instrument of the same name. In its proper and imitative form it is a reed stop of 8 ft. pitch. See CORNO DI BASSETTO.

BASS FLUTE. Ger., BASSFLÖTE.—An open labial stop, of 8 ft. pitch, constructed of either wood or metal, and yielding a pronounced flute-tone. This stop properly belongs to the Pedal Organ. It is frequently borrowed from the OPEN DIAPASON, 16 FT., by means of an Octave coupler.

BASSONELL.—Described by Wolfram as a lingual stop, of 8 ft. or 4 ft. pitch, made of tin or metal. It was probably of a soft Bassoon quality. The name appears to be obsolete. This is probably the stop described by Hamel under the Italian name BASSANELLO.*

BASSOON. Fr., BASSON. Ger., FAGOTT. Ital., FAGOTTO.—A small-scaled reed stop voiced to imitate the tone of the orchestral instrument bearing the same name. As a manual stop, of 8 ft. pitch, it is sometimes, and correctly, associated with the HAUTBOY or OBOE, being labeled HAUTBOY & BASSOON or OBOE & FAGOTTO, 8 FT. The orchestral Bassoon furnishes the true bass to the Hautboy. As a stop of 16 ft. pitch, the BASSOON frequently appears in the Pedal Organ, and sometimes in a manual division. When of this grave pitch it is more correctly called DOUBLE BASSOON or CONTRAFAGOTTO. A BASSON, 16 FT., appears in the

*"BASSANELLI. Ce sont des instruments à vent du siècle dernier [XVIIIe] ; ils ressemblent beaucoup au chalumeau. Dans l'orgue, ils ont été imités par des jeux d'anches particuliers de huit et de quatre pieds."

pedal department of the Grand Organ in the Church of Saint-Sulpice, Paris; and a CONTRAFAGOTTO, 16 FT., is placed in both the Pedal and Solo Organs of the instrument in St. George's Hall, Liverpool.

The tubes of the BASSOON, when in its best form as a striking reed, are of inverted conical form, small-scaled, and made of either metal or wood. Continental organ builders have made the BASSOON with free reeds, having comparatively short tubes formed of two cones, joined at their bases, the upper one of which is truncated so as to leave a small opening for the emission of the sound. Seidel, however, gives an illustration of a BASSOON pipe having a slender cylindrical tube similar to that which is now used for the CLARINET pipe. See ORCHESTRAL BASSOON. This stop appears in Spanish Organs under the name BAJON.

BASSPOSAUNE, Ger. Eng., BASS TROMBONE.—The Pedal Organ reed stop, of 32 ft. pitch, in all respects similar to the CONTRAPOSAUNE, an example of which appears in the pedal department of the large Organ in Christ Church, at Hirschberg. Stops of the same class and pitch are to be found in numerous other important Organs. The name is sometimes given to a POSAUNE of 16 ft. pitch.

BASS TUBA. Ger., BASSTUBA.—A powerful reed stop of 16 ft. pitch, the tones of which are supposed to imitate those of the brass instrument of the same name. See CONTRA-TUBA.

BASS VIOL.—The name that may be appropriately given to a string-toned labial stop which has a voice less pronounced than the VIOLONCELLO, 8 FT., and which may be accepted as imitative of the old Bass Viol, the largest and deepest of the "chest of Viols." This instrument had six strings, tuned DD, GG, C, E, A, d^1; but this *accordatura* varied according to the requirements of the music to be played.

BAUERNFLÖTE, BAUERNPFEIFE, Ger.—Literally *Peasant Flute*. A small-scaled covered stop, of 4 ft. or 2 ft. pitch, producing a tone somewhat resembling the whistling of the human mouth. It has sometimes been labeled BAUERFLÖTE and BÄUERLEIN in old German Organs. This stop has been made in a half-covered form, after the fashion of the ROHRFLÖTE, and called BAUERNROHRFLÖTE.

BAXONCILLO or BAJONCILLO, Span.—The name employed by the Spanish organ builders to designate the equivalent of the German PRINCIPAL or the English OPEN DIAPASON. Under the name BAJONCILLO the stop appears in the Organ in Burgos Cathedral.

BAZUIN, Dtch.—The name given by Dutch builders to a powerful reed stop, commonly of 32 ft. and 16 ft. pitch. Examples of this stop in both pitches exist in the pedal department of the celebrated Organ in the Cathedral of Haarlem. It appears, of 16 ft. pitch, in several other important instruments in Holland. The stop is practically identical with the POSAUNE of other builders.

BEARDED GAMBA.—An open metal labial stop, of 8 ft. pitch, producing a string-tone. The peculiarity of this stop obtains in its pipes having their mouths furnished with projecting beards in addition to their ears. The beards exert a decided influence on the tone of the pipes.

BELL DIAPASON.—A large-scaled open metal labial stop, the pipes of which have their cylindrical bodies surmounted by conical bells similar to those of the

French FLÛTE À PAVILLON. The stop is of 8 ft. pitch, and its tone is more reedy or horn-like and more powerful than the ordinary OPEN DIAPASON, 8 FT.

BELL GAMBA. Ger., GLOCKENGAMBA.—A labial stop, of 8 ft. pitch, of metal, and of medium scale, the pipes of which have their bodies of a tapering or conical form surmounted by a bell ; hence the name BELL GAMBA, which is used to distinguish this stop from the ordinary German GAMBA, which has pipes with plain cylindrical bodies. This stop is rarely carried down below tenor C in its true form. As the peculiar form of the BELL GAMBA pipe does not permit of its being tuned at top in the usual manner, its mouth is furnished with large, projecting, flexible ears, which flatten or sharpen the tone according to the position they hold in relation to the mouth. This stop should be made of tin or very high-class metal. When skilfully voiced, the tone of the BELL GAMBA is extremely delicate, stringy, and beautiful, strongly resembling that of the old orchestral Viola da Gamba. It is a valuable stop for the Choir division of the Church Organ, and for any manual division of the Chamber Organ.

BIFARA, Ger. Lat., TIBIA BIFARIS.—This name has been employed by German organ builders to designate two entirely different labial stops, both of which are double-voiced. Seidel describes it as a fine but rare manual stop of large scale, of 8 ft. and 4 ft. pitch. The pipes are of metal, open, and have two mouths, one of which is cut up a little higher than the other, causing a slight and agreeable *vibrato*. The name has also been given to a stop composed of two ranks of pipes, one of which is slightly sharpened in the process of tuning. The "BIFRA" in Walcker's Organ in the Church of St. Peter, at St. Petersburg, consists of a rank of stopped pipes of 8 ft. pitch, and a second rank of open pipes of 4 ft. pitch and soft intonation. Wolfram speaks of both the above forms of the stop, and the tones they produce as resembling that of the UNDA MARIS. He gives the following corrupt names for this stop: BIFFARO, BIFFURA, PIFFARO, and PIFFARA, showing that the organ builders up to his time were as careless in the matter of orthography as is the average organ builder of to-day.

BLOCKFLÖTE, or BLOCKPFEIFE, Ger. Lat., TIBIA VULGARIS.—An open metal labial stop of ordinary form, and usually of 4 ft. pitch. The tone of this stop is of a normal flute character, full and round, and possessing a pronounced filling-up property. Wolfram, who may be accepted as an authority on the subject of the old stops introduced in German Organs, says: "the BLOCKFLÖTE is sometimes open and sometimes stopped, of 4 ft., 8 ft., and 16 ft. pitch; and occasionally its pipes resembled in form those of the SPITZFLÖTE." From this it would appear that the name was given to any flute-toned stop for which a more expressive name was not forthcoming. The BLOCKFLÖTE was introduced by Father Smith in both his St. Paul's and Durham Cathedral Organs. These were open metal stops, of large scale, and 2 ft. pitch.

BOCKFLÖTE, Ger.—This term has been given, though very seldom, to an open metal stop resembling the GEMSHORN. The term is evidently derived from *Gemsbock*—the male of the Gemse or Chamois. The name of this stop is peculiar; and it is very difficult to understand how it came to be applied to an organ FLUTE, unless its tone resembled some rude instrument fabricated from a horn of the animal named. The only instance of its insertion in an organ Specification which has come under our observation occurs in that issued by the Town Clerk of Sydney, N. S. W., for the Organ in the Centennial Hall. Directions are given in this original Specification for a BOCKFLÖTE to be directly associated with the VOX HUMANA.

BOMBARDE, Fr.—A reed stop of 16 ft. pitch and powerful intonation. The BOMBARDE is commonly found in important French Organs: for instance, in the Grand Organ in the Church of Saint-Sulpice, at Paris, constructed by Cavaillé-Coll, there are no fewer than four BOMBARDES; and in the same builder's Organ in the Cathedral of Notre-Dame there are three BOMBARDES of 16 ft. pitch. This important stop gives a name to a manual division in large French Organs; namely, "Clavier des Bombardes." The tubes or resonators of this stop are of inverted conical form, similar to those of the TRUMPET and POSAUNE.

A stop of similar construction and tonality, and of 32 ft. pitch, under the appropriate name of CONTRE-BOMBARDE, is to be found in the pedal department of certain large French Organs; notably in that of the Organs in the Cathedral of Notre-Dame, and the Churches of Saint-Sulpice and Saint-Eustache, at Paris. The Concert-room Organ in the Albert Hall, Sheffield, built by Cavaillé-Coll, has a CONTRE-BOMBARDE, 32 FT., in its pedal department. Hamel says: "The BOMBARDE is the largest of all the reed stops."

There was an old stop occasionally called BOMBARD, but more frequently BOMMER or BÄRBOMMER, evidently deriving its name from *Bombardo*—a mediæval reed instrument of large size and coarse intonation, and apparently the precursor of the Fagotto and Oboe. The old instrument was occasionally named Pommer, but this name is evidently a corruption. According to Wolfram the old BOMMER, BOMBARD or BÄRBOMMER, was a Pedal Organ reed stop, of 8 ft. and 16 ft. pitch, having wooden tubes, which were sometimes partly covered so as to soften the tones produced. These corruptions have long and properly been disused.

BOMBARDON, Fr. Ital., BOMBARDONE.—A full-toned Pedal Organ reed stop, of 16 ft. and 32 ft. pitch. It derives its appellation from the brass instrument of the same name, the powerful and grave tones of which it is supposed to imitate so far as its compass extends. The available compass of the Bombardon is from FFF to d^1, but five notes lower can, with difficulty, be produced. A BOMBARDON, 32 FT., exists in Walcker's Organ in the Cathedral of Ulm. This stop, owing to its grave pitch, which extends more than an octave below the compass of the brass instrument, should have been labeled CONTRA-BOMBARDON, 32 FT.

BOURDON, Fr. Ital., BORDONE. Ger., BOURDON, BRUMMBASS, BASSBRUMMER.—In English and American Organs the BOURDON almost invariably assumes the form of a covered wood stop of large scale and 16 ft. pitch. Its normal tone has a somewhat dull droning quality, which is well expressed by the German synonyms BRUMMBASS or BRUMMER (from *brummen*—to hum, to drone). We may here remark that the term BORDUN, which is sometimes used, is evidently an old corruption, and should not be retained in modern nomenclature.

The BOURDON most frequently appears, in English and American instruments of moderate dimensions, in the pedal department; indeed, in small Organs it is frequently the only pedal stop, but in large instruments it is introduced in one or more of the manual divisions. In the Concert-room Organ in Leeds Town Hall the BOURDON, 16 FT., is introduced in the Great, Swell, and Echo divisions. As might reasonably be expected, the manual BOURDONS are made of a much smaller scale than those introduced in the Pedal Organ. In German Organs the BOURDON, 16 FT., may be said to be confined to the manual divisions. In French Organs the BOURDON appears in the manual divisions of 16 ft. and 8 ft. pitch. In the Organ in the Cathedral of Notre-Dame, Paris, there are no fewer than five manual BOURDONS—two of 16 ft. and three of 8 ft. pitch. It rarely appears in the pedal department, and when it does it is usually of 8 ft. pitch, as in the Grand Organ in the Church of Saint-Ouen, at Rouen. In some rare instances the French organ builders have applied the name BOURDON to a covered metal stop of large scale and of only 4 ft. pitch. In the price list of metal pipes manufactured by Zimmermann, of Paris, we find BOURDONS of 16 ft., 8 ft., and 4 ft. pitch mentioned.

In modern English and in American Organs the BOURDON, 16 FT., is invariably made of wood; but we learn from Dr. Burney's "History of Music" that the old English builders constructed it of metal. Speaking of Snetzler's Organ in St. Margaret's Church, Lynn Regis, he says: "One of the metal Stops of this instrument, [built in 1754] called the Bourdon, is an octave below the Open Diapason, and has the effect of a double bass in the chorus." Both the French and German organ builders use metal pipes largely in their manual BOURDONS, wood pipes appearing chiefly in their bass octaves. In the Great division of the celebrated Organ at Haarlem the BOURDON, 16 FT., is of metal throughout the compass of the manual.

The tone of the BOURDON varies considerably, according to the scale and voicing of its pipes; but in almost all the varieties of the stop the tone is thick and characterized by the presence of the second upper partial tone (the twelfth), in more or less prominence, in combination with the ground tone. In numerous instances this upper partial is so pronounced that the stop becomes practically a QUINTATEN. It is to this combination that is due the peculiar drone-like, filling-up quality of the true BOURDON. Stops of this class of 32 ft. pitch have been constructed by English and other organ builders. See CONTRA-BOURDON.

BOURDONALFLÖTE, Ger.—A flute-toned labial stop, of 8 ft. and 4 ft. pitch, the pipes of which are constructed on lines similar to those of the BOURDON. The tone of this stop should, however, approach that of the English STOPPED DIAPASON, but have greater power and volume. The stop has commonly been labeled BORDUNALFLÖTE, but this is evidently a corruption, like BORDUN, above mentioned.

BOURDONECHO, Ger.—According to Locher, the name which has been used to designate an exceedingly soft, flute-toned stop, the pipes of which are covered and of medium scale. This stop has been usually placed in a swell-box located some distance from the main body of the Organ.

The French employ the term BOURDON DOUX to designate a soft-toned covered stop somewhat similar to the German LIEBLICHGEDECKT.

BUCCINA, Lat.—The name given by certain Italian organ builders to the reed stop commonly known as the POSAUNE.

CARILLON, Fr.—The name used to designate a compound stop formed of two, three, or four ranks of open metal pipes, the combined tones of which somewhat resemble the sounds of bells. Examples exist in several important Organs built by A. Cavaillé-Coll. See Chapter on The Compound Stops of the Organ. The term would be more correctly applied to a series of bells, metal tubes, or steel bars struck with hammers. See GLOCKENSPIEL.

CHALUMEAU, Fr. Ger., SCHALMEI. Ital., SCIALUMÒ. Eng., SHAWM—A soft-toned reed stop of 8 ft. pitch, somewhat resembling the CLARINET in its tonal coloring. It is supposed to imitate the tone of the obsolete instrument called the Schalmei or Shawm, the precursor of the orchestral Clarinet. An example is to be found in the Choir division of Silbermann's Organ in the Royal Church, at Dresden. Seidel says the SCHALMEI appears both in the manual and pedal departments of 4 ft., 8 ft., and 16 ft. pitch. The last is designated SCHALMEIBASS. "The bodies of the pipes are generally funnel-shaped, and are sometimes covered, with the exception of a few sound-holes."

CHORALBASSETT, Ger.—According to Wolfram, an open metal stop of 2 ft. pitch introduced in the Pedal Organ. Seldom used.

CLAIRON, Fr.—A striking reed stop of 4 ft. pitch. See CLARION.

CLARABEL FLUTE.—An open wood stop of 4 ft. pitch, formed in all essentials similar to the CLARABELLA, 8 FT., to which it is the true octave stop.

CLARABELLA. Ger., OFFENFLÖTE.—An open wood stop of medium scale and 8 ft. pitch. When skilfully voiced it has a flute-tone of a full and agreeable character and good mixing quality. This stop has been held in great favor by English builders, and has reached its highest perfection in their hands. The stop in its original English form was invented by Mr. Bishop, an eminent London organ builder. Its pipes are quadrangular in form, rather deeper than wide, and have the ordinary direct English mouth, cut up from one-fourth to one-third its width in height. The stop is seldom carried throughout the entire manual compass in open pipes, generally having its bass octave of stopped pipes. It should, however, on all possible occasions be carried down in true CLARABELLA pipes.

CLARINA, Ital.—An open metal stop, of large scale, and 2 ft. pitch. It has a loud intonation, and is introduced in the Pedal Organ to impart clearness and crispness to the fuller combinations.

CLARINET. Fr., CLARINETTE. Ger., CLARINETTE. Ital., CLARINETTO.—A reed stop, of 8 ft. pitch, voiced in imitation of the orchestral Clarinet. When made by the hand of a master it is one of the most successful imitative voices of the Organ. Apart from its tone, the chief peculiarity of this stop exists in the shape of its resonant tubes, which are cylindrical and connected to the reed blocks by short conical pieces. Unlike the generality of open stops, the CLARINET produces the 8 ft. tone from pipes about half the standard speaking lengths. It is mainly due to this fact, in combination with the cylindrical form of the tubes, that the distinctive tone-color of the stop is produced. The CLARINET frequently commences at tenor C, probably because the orchestral Clarinet in A does not go lower than tenor C♯; but, as the Bass Clarinet goes about an octave lower, the CLARINET of the Organ should in all cases extend throughout the manual compass. In English and French Organs the CLARINET is, in all important instances, a striking reed;

but in German and Swiss instruments it frequently appears as a free reed, having resonant tubes of different forms. The tubes of CLARINET pipes are usually made of tin or spotted metal, but cylindrical tubes of wood have been used with good results. The term CLARIONET has been commonly employed by English organ builders, but we agree with Mr. E. Prout in condemning its use as incorrect.*

CLARINET FLUTE.—The inappropriate name sometimes given to a half-covered wood stop of 8 ft. pitch. It is a species of ROHRFLÖTE, differing from the true ROHRFLÖTE only in having larger perforations in its stoppers and lower mouths, a treatment which imparts a slight reedy quality to its fluty tone. This peculiar tonality is the only apology for the use of the above inappropriate name.

CLARION. Fr., CLAIRON. Ital., CLARINO.—A reed stop of metal, of 4 ft. pitch, and bright intonation. It may be considered an OCTAVE TRUMPET, having reeds and tubes similar to those of the unison TRUMPET. Its voice imparts richness and brilliancy to the double and unison reed stops, without unduly asserting itself. As an octave stop it is, or should be, of smaller scale and softer tone than the unison TRUMPET, or other unison reed stop, which accompanies it. Owing to the difficulty of constructing reed pipes of very high pitch, the top octave of the CLARION is usually inserted in loudly-voiced labial pipes. In French Organs the top octave is frequently of unison or TRUMPET pipes, and the result is perfectly satisfactory.†

In the Grand Organ in the Church of Saint-Sulpice, Paris, there is an OCTAVE CLARION, 2 FT., under the name of CLAIRON-DOUBLETTE; and in the Clavier des Bombardes of the Grand Organ in the Abbey Church of St. Denis, near Paris, there is a CLAIRON HARMONIQUE, 4 FT., accompanying the TROMPETTE HARMONIQUE, 8 FT. The tubes of these stops are double the standard speaking lengths.

CLAVÄOLINE, Ger.—In the year 1830 Beyer, an organ builder of Nürnberg, invented a manual reed stop to which he gave the name CLAVÄOLINE or KLAVÄOLINE, for the word is rendered in both forms in German. From the unsatisfactory description given by Seidel, this stop would appear to have been something in the nature of the PHYSHARMONICA (*q. v.*). The free reeds were placed in small blocks of wood, standing on the upper-board of the wind-chest, and were devoid of resonant tubes. Stops of this name are given in the Specifications of the Organs in the Church of St. Wenzel, at Naumburg, and the Town Church of Fulda. The CLAVÄOLINE in the former Organ was inserted by its inventor. Both stops are of 8 ft. pitch.

CLEAR FLUTE. Ger., HELLFLÖTE.—An open wood stop, of 4 ft. pitch, pro-

*In this talented musician's work on "The Orchestra" we find the following note: "The author desires here to enter an emphatic protest against the common but quite indefensible spelling of the instrument as 'clarionet.' It has nothing whatever to do with the English word 'clarion.'" We most heartily join Mr. Prout in his "emphatic protest," and hope to see the word *Clarionet* entirely abandoned even by those who attempt to apologize for its retention in organ-stop nomenclature.

†"En France, le CLAIRON a toujours quatre-pieds; en Allemagne, quatre et huit. C'est un régistre d'harmonie mordante et claire, comme l'indique son nom, et destiné à donner de la pointe aux huit-pieds d'anches. Cependant on peut le faire chanter seul, ou mélangé avec les fonds; mais dans ce dernier cas il est bon de ne pas le toucher sur les notes les plus hautes, où il devient d'une grande aigreur. On fait ce régistre d'étain fin et de forme conique. Comme ces tuyaux extrêmes sont fort exigus, on lui donne ordinairement une reprise à la dernière octave; et pour le toucher, on y joint le PRESTANT et la DOUBLETTE, qui dissimulent la reprise en suivant la marche ascendante qu'est censé suivre le CLAIRON."—Regnier.

ducing a full and clear tone. Its pipes are quadrangular, have inverted mouths, and are copiously winded. See Chapter on Wood Pipes. The CLEAR FLUTE is said to have been first introduced in English organ-building by Kirtland & Jardine, of Manchester.

CŒLESTINA, Lat.—An open metal stop, of 4 ft. pitch, of small scale and delicate intonation. It may be looked upon as an OCTAVE DULCIANA. An example occurs in the Choir division of the Concert-room Organ in the Centennial Hall, Sydney, N. S. W. This stop is often, but less correctly, labeled CELESTINA or CELESTIANA.

COMPENSATIONSMIXTUR, Ger.—A Pedal Organ harmonic-corroborating stop, invented by Musikdirektor Wilke, of Neu-Ruppin, and first introduced, in 1838, in the Organ in St. Catherine's Church, Salzwedel. It is a compound stop of five ranks and very short compass, the longest rank (all the ranks vary in length) extending only from CCC to AAA=10 pipes. The stop was designed with the view of imparting to the graver notes of the Pedal Organ a prompt and decisive intonation, and to the whole pedal department a uniform distinctness of articulation favorable to the production of rapid passages. This invention of Wilke did not receive the consideration it deserved by the conservative and slow-going organ builders of Germany; and, indeed, it was attacked in a narrow-minded manner, in a *brochure* on the Organ in the Marienkirche, Wismar, written in 1846 by Ferdinand Baake, an organist in Halberstadt. There is more in Wilke's idea than it has yet been credited with. For the composition of the COMPENSATIONSMIXTUR, and our suggestion for a similar stop, of an extended form, which we term the COMPENSATING MIXTURE, see the Chapter on the Compound Stops of the Organ.

CONCERT FLUTE. Ger., CONCERTFLÖTE.—The name occasionally given to the open labial stop which closely imitates the tone of the Flute of the orchestra. See ORCHESTRAL FLUTE.

CONE GAMBA.—An open metal labial stop, of 8 ft. pitch, the pipes of which have bodies smaller at the top than at the mouth line. The mouth is, in width, about one-third of the larger circumference of the pipe, and is furnished with ears and a harmonic bridge. In some rare instances the stop has been fitted with the *frein harmonique*. Certain builders have formed this stop with inverted conical pipes, similar to those of the DOLCAN, having the properly bridged GAMBA mouths. When artistically voiced, the tone of the stop is delicate, refined, and very pleasing. A CONE GAMBA OCTAVE, 4 FT., would be a valuable addition to the timbre-creating stops.

CONTRA-BASSO, Ital. Ger., CONTRABASS. Fr., CONTRE-BASSE. Eng., DOUBLE BASS.—The name correctly given to an open labial stop, of 16 ft. pitch, constructed of wood or metal, and voiced to yield a tone more or less closely resembling that of the orchestral Double Bass. In strength of tone it properly occupies an intermediate place between the Pedal Organ PRINCIPAL, 16 FT., and the VIOLONE, 16 FT. The CONTRE-BASSE, 16 FT., is invariably a Pedal Organ stop, as found in the majority of large French instruments, notably in those of the Cathedrals of Paris, Amiens, Orléans, Autun, and Senlis, and the Churches of Saint-Sulpice, Saint-Eustache, and the Madeleine, Paris. The organ builder of to-day should apply the name CONTRA-BASSO or DOUBLE BASS to a stop that produces a full string-tone imitative of that of the orchestral instrument. In the Concert-room Organ it may properly appear in the manual department.

CONTRA-BOURDON or SUB-BOURDON. Ger., UNTERSATZ. Fr., SOUBASSE.—A covered stop of wood, of 32 ft. pitch, properly belonging to the Pedal Organ, but occasionally appearing, in an incomplete form, in the Great Organ. It is commonly resorted to, as a pedal stop, when either space or funds prevent the introduction of the DOUBLE OPEN DIAPASON or SUB-PRINCIPAL, 32 FT. The CONTRA-BOURDON is to be found in the Organ in the Church of St. Olave, Southwark; in the Concert instrument in the Town Hall, Leeds; and in the large Organ in the Centennial Hall, Sydney, N. S. W. Under the name SUB-BOURDON, 32 FT., this grave stop appears, in the usual incomplete state, in the Great division of the Organ in the Parish Church of Doncaster; as SUBBASS, 32 FT., it occurs in the pedal department of the Organ in the Church of St. Michael, Hamburg; as GRAND BOURDON, 32 FT., in the Organ in the Church of Saint-Vincent de Paul, Paris; as GROSSUNTERSATZ, 32 FT., in the Organ in the Church of Waltershausen, Gotha; and as UNTERSATZ, 32 FT., in the Organ in the Royal Catholic Church, at Dresden.

When the UNTERSATZ, 32 FT., or SUB-BOURDON, 32 FT., is introduced in the manual department, it invariably is of short compass, starting at tenor C, as in the Parish Churches of Doncaster and Leeds.

CONTRA-DULCIANA.—An open labial stop, of 16 ft. pitch, the pipes of which are of metal, cylindrical in form, and of small scale; yielding a soft and singing organ-tone. It is a valuable manual stop, although very rarely introduced. An example is to be found in the Choir division of the Organ in the Centennial Hall, Sydney, N. S. W. This stop is the same as the DOUBLE DULCIANA (*q. v.*).

CONTRAFAGOTTO, Ital. Ger., CONTRAFAGOTT.—A reed stop, of 16 ft. pitch, the resonant tubes of which are either of wood or metal and of small scale. Its tone is imitative of that of the orchestral instrument of the same name. Although usually and correctly placed in the Pedal Organ, where it furnishes the true bass for the manual OBOE & FAGOTTO, 8 FT., it has sometimes been inserted in a manual division. The English name for this stop is DOUBLE BASSOON. See BASSOON.

CONTRA-GAMBA, Ital.—A labial stop, of 16 ft. pitch, the pipes of which are open, cylindrical, and of medium scale. It is introduced in both the manual and pedal departments of the Organ; when in the latter it furnishes the true bass to the unimitative manual GAMBA, 8 FT. In its normal form, the CONTRA-GAMBA has a full, string-like tone, but not strongly imitative. An example appears in the Great division of the Roosevelt Organ in the Cathedral of the Incarnation, Garden City, Long Island. When inserted in the Pedal Organ, this stop, being a unison one, may be labeled GAMBA, 16 FT., as in the Organ in the Centennial Hall, Sydney, N. S. W. See GAMBENBASS.

CONTRA-OBOE, Ital. Eng., CONTRA-HAUTBOY.—A very uncommon reed stop of 16 ft. pitch, the tone of which resembles that of the ordinary OBOE, 8 FT. A remarkably fine example is to be found, labeled CONTRA-HAUTBOY, 16 FT., in the Swell division of the Grand Organ in St. George's Hall, Liverpool.

CONTRAPOSAUNE, Ger.—A powerfully-voiced reed stop, of 16 ft. pitch in the manual department, and 32 ft. pitch in the Pedal Organ. Its pipes are of the inverted conical form and of large scale. Its tone is supposed to imitate those of the orchestral Trombones at their loudest effect. Inverted pyramidal pipes of wood are sometimes used, but metal pipes are to be preferred. An example of the CONTRAPOSAUNE, 16 FT., exists in the Great division of the Organ in the Centennial Hall, Sydney, N. S. W.; and a CONTRAPOSAUNE, 32 FT., is placed in the pedal department of the same instrument, and in the pedal department of the Organ in the Parish Church of Doncaster.

CONTRAPRINCIPAL, Ger.—The name occasionally employed to designate the DOUBLE OPEN DIAPASON, 16 FT., in the manual department; and the DOUBLE OPEN DIAPASON, 32 FT., when of metal, in the Pedal Organ.

CONTRA-SALICIONAL or DOUBLE SALICIONAL.—As the name implies, this is a SALICIONAL of 16 ft. pitch. In the material and form of its pipes and in its peculiar voice it is similar to the manual unison stop. See SALICIONAL.

CONTRA-SAXOPHONE.—A stop of 16 ft. pitch, the voice of which carries down, in its lower octave, that of the manual SAXOPHONE, 8 FT. This stop may be formed of either free reed or labial pipes. Up to the present time the most satisfactory imitation of the tones of the orchestral Saxophones has been produced by labial pipes. See SAXOPHONE.

CONTRA-TROMBONE.—A reed stop having a tone of the quality characteristic of the Bass Trombone of the orchestra. While similar to the CONTRAPOSAUNE in this respect, its voice should not be so brassy and powerful. The CONTRA-TROMBONE is of 16 ft. pitch on the manuals and of 32 ft. pitch in the Pedal Organ. Its pipes are similar in shape to those of the CONTRAPOSAUNE, but not of so large a scale. A CONTRA-TROMBONE, 16 FT., occurs in the Great division of the Organ in the Town Hall, Leeds. Under the name of CONTRA-TROMBONE, Messrs. Hill & Son, of London, have inserted a monster reed stop, of 64 ft. pitch (if such a grave pitch can be accepted as obtaining in the range of audible or determinate musical sounds), in the pedal department of their Concert Organ in the Centennial Hall, Sydney, N. S. W.

CONTRA-TUBA.—The most powerfully-voiced reed stop of 16 ft. pitch introduced in the Organ. It speaks on wind ranging in pressure between 10 inches and 30 inches. The resonant tubes of the CONTRA-TUBA, 16 FT., are inverted conical in form, are made of thick metal to withstand the extreme vibration, and are usually of large scale. The tone of this powerful stop is singularly grand and impressive, and, while it is rarely so provided, it calls aloud for control and powers of expression. An example is to be found in the Solo division of the Organ in the Centennial Hall, Sydney, N. S. W.

CONTRA-VIOLONE, Ital.—A labial stop, of 16 ft. pitch, formed of medium-scaled open pipes of either metal or wood, or of both wood and metal. In its proper voice it imitates the tone of the orchestral instrument of the same name. The CONTRA-VIOLONE, 16 FT., is strictly a manual stop; the corresponding stop in the Pedal Organ being commonly labeled VIOLONE, 16 FT. A very beautiful stop of this class, from the master hand of Edmund Schulze, is to be found in the Great division of the Organ in the Church of St. Peter, Hindley, Lancashire. It is formed of wood pipes from CC to B, and of metal pipes from middle c^1 to the top note.

CONTRE-BOMBARDE, Fr.—A reed stop of large scale and powerful intonation. It is of 32 ft. pitch, and is usually to be found in the pedal department of important French Organs. See BOMBARDE.

COR ANGLAIS, Fr. Ital., CORNO INGLESE.—A reed stop, of 8 ft. pitch, voiced to imitate the tone of the orchestral instrument of the same name, which Berlioz describes as "a melancholy, dreamy, and rather noble voice." The stop has been made both as a striking and a free reed, and probably the most successful examples are of the latter form. The tubes are of a peculiar shape, being very slender, inverted conical, and surmounted by resonant chambers formed of two attached truncated cones. An example of a free reed COR ANGLAIS, 8 FT., exists in the Solo division of the Organ in the Leeds Town Hall. There is a fine COR ANGLAIS, 8 FT., in the Claviers des Bombardes of the Grand Organ in the Church of Saint-Eustache, Paris; and a very fine one, of 16 ft. pitch, in the Récit expressif of the Concert Organ in the Albert Hall, Sheffield.

COR DE BASSET, Fr.—The name employed by French organ builders to designate the reed stop more commonly known as the CORNO DI BASSETTO (*q. v.*).

CORDELAIN.—A small-scaled open metal stop, of 4 ft. pitch, producing a bright flute-tone. An example occurs in the Echo division of the Organ in St. Thomas' Church, Strasbourg. The stop was probably made by the great Silbermann, in 1740.

COR DE NUIT, Fr.—The German NACHTHORN or NACHTSCHALL (*q. v.*).

CORMORNE, Fr.—The name which has occasionally been employed to designate a reed stop of 8 ft. pitch. It is probably formed from *cor*—horn, and *morne*—sombre, or mournful; but, as it is commonly met with in the Cavaillé-Coll Organs as CROMORNE, the term may be a corruption of the German name KRUMMHORN. See CROMORNE.

CORNAMUSA, Ital. Fr., CORNEMUSE.—This name, which signifies a Bagpipe, is used by Italian and French organ builders to designate a labial stop of 16 ft. pitch. An example exists in the second manual division of the Organ in the Church of Santissimo Crocifisso, at Como. It probably derived its name from the drone-like character of its tone.

CORNET. A compound stop of short compass, which was a great favorite of the old German and English organ builders. It usually consisted of three, four, or five ranks of large-scaled open metal pipes. In compass, the stop never descended below tenor C, while it usually, and especially in English Organs, commenced at middle c^1. It appears to have been introduced by the German builders chiefly for the purpose of playing out the melodies of the Chorales, its powerful and dominating voice rendering it highly effective for such simple melodic passages.* Sometimes, as the CORNET required considerable space for its accom-

* "Le CORNET, jeu bruyant, clair et dominateur de l'harmonie entière de l'orgue. Un *Cornet* complet dans sa facture a par note cinq tuyaux de grosse taille, dont chacun porte un nom et un caractère différents. Le premier tuyau est un *Bourdon* de huit; le second un *Prestant;* le troisième un *Nasard*, quinte supérieure du *Prestant;* le quatrième une *Quarte de Nasard*, octave du *Prestant;* le cinquième enfin est une *Tierce* au-dessus de cette octave.

modation, its pipes were planted on a special wind-chest, elevated above the main wind-chest, and connected thereto by a series of conveyances—one for each note of the CORNET. When treated in this manner, the stop was designated MOUNTED CORNET. See Chapter on the Compound Stops of the Organ.

In modern Organs the stop called a CORNET is simply a MIXTURE of three, four, or five ranks, one of which is a third-sounding rank. This class of CORNET is invariably a complete stop, having the necessary breaks. When composed of small-scaled pipes, and delicately voiced, this stop is called a DULCIANA CORNET or DOLCE CORNET.

CORNO DI BASSETTO, Ital. Ger., BASSETTHORN. Fr., COR DE BASSET.—The orchestral instrument called the Corno di Bassetto is of the Clarinet family. Its construction resembles that of the Clarinet, having a long tube with a curved and bell-shaped end. The tone is of a rich and beautiful quality. The CORNO DI BASSETTO of the Organ is a stop of 8 ft. pitch, and has been made of both labial and reed pipes. Töpfer describes it as made of the former; but English organ builders have invariably made it of reed pipes, similar in form to those of the CLARINET. A fine example exists in the Solo division of the Concert Organ in St. George's Hall, Liverpool. The CORNO DI BASSETTO should be voiced to have a fuller and rounder tone than is usually produced by the CLARINET or ORCHESTRAL CLARINET, 8 FT. While the CORNO DI BASSETTO, 8 FT., is correctly a manual stop, it has been inserted in the Pedal Organ. It appears, under the name "BASSETTHORN," 8 FT., in the Second Pedal of the Organ in the Cathedral of Ulm, and in the Schwell-Pedal of the Organ in the Cathedral of Riga, both constructed by Walcker, of Ludwigsburg. The CORNO DI BASSETTO is invariably made as a striking reed by English builders; but it appears in a free reed form in certain Continental Organs. Locher speaks of it as a free reed stop only, as a rule without tubes or resonators, like a PHYSHARMONICA.

CORNO INGLESE, Ital.—A reed stop, of 8 ft. pitch, yielding a tone resembling that of the orchestral instrument of the same name. See COR ANGLAIS.

"Ainsi, l'*ut* du *Cornet* est à la fois *ut* de huit-pieds en *Bourdon*, *ut* de quatre en *Prestant*, *sol* de trois en *Nasard*, *ut* de deux en *Quarte*, enfin *mi* d'un-pied cinq-septièmes. Le *ré* suivra les mêmes proportions: $ré^1$, $ré^2$, la^2, $ré^3$, fa^3.

"Ainsi, dans toute sa longueur, le *Cornet* appuie chacune de ses notes ou de ses marches, comme on dit, sur cinq notes à la fois; il y a donc cinq tuyaux *sur marche*. Son régistre est donc un ensemble de cinq régistres, cinq rangées de tuyaux au lieu d'une, comme les jeux simples. Mais le *Cornet* n'a pas toujours toute la longueur du clavier; quoique ces cinq rangées soient à l'unisson du *Bourdon*, du *Prestant*, etc., cependant elles en diffèrent par la taille, qui est plus grosse et l'harmonie plus forte. L'étendue de ce régistre empêche qu'on ne le place sur le grand sommier; aussi le transporte-t-on toujours sur un ou deux petits sommiers supplémentaires, que l'on nomme pièces gravées; ce ne sont, en effet, que des pièces et non des totalités de sommier, car le vent leur vient toujours du sommier principal par des conduits de plomb, qu'on fait serpenter jusqu'à l'orifice inférieur des tuyaux posés, ou, comme on dit, *postés* sur ces pièces, de sorte que les tuyaux obéissent tout de même à l'action des soupapes et des régistres du grand sommier. . .

"Autrefois, on mettait un *Cornet* à chaque clavier; celui du grand orgue s'appelle encore le *grand Cornet;* il est de plus forte taille et sonne huit-pieds; il en est même de seize. Celui du positif, le *petit Cornet*, est un quatre-pieds. Le *Cornet de récit* a d'ordinaire la même mesure. Le *Cornet d'écho* peut être de moindre taille que celui de récit, mais toujours sonnant quatre-pieds. Ces deux derniers cornets n'ont pas toujours cinq tuyaux sur marche; en Allemagne même, le *grand Cornet* est souvent de quatre, de trois tuyaux. Dans certaines orgues, où la *Bombarde* (le plus fort des jeux d'anches) se trouve séparée, on met encore un *Cornet de Bombarde;* c'est à celui-là qu'on peut le mieux assigner pour premier tuyau un *Bourdon* de seize, mais c'est généralement le *Bourdon* de huit."—Regnier.

CORNOPEAN.—A reed stop, of 8 ft. pitch, the tubes of which are of inverted conical form, resembling those of the TRUMPET, but larger in scale, and properly of tin or spotted metal. The tone of the CORNOPEAN should be full and smooth, being free from the brassy clang of the ORCHESTRAL TRUMPET, 8 FT. Locher describes it as "an 8 ft. labial stop of horn-like tone." Allihn describes it in the following words: "CORNOPEAN (ital.), Päanshorn, eine veraltete Labialstimme von hornartigem Ton. Zu deutsch etwa: Jubelhorn."

CREMONA.—This very inappropriate name for a reed stop is evidently a corruption. Hawkins, in his "History of Music," says: "The names and descriptions of several instruments instruct us as to the nature and design of many Stops in the Organ, and what they are intended to imitate. For instance, in the Krummhorn, the tone of it originally resembled that of a small Cornet, though many organ-makers have corrupted the word into Cremona, supposing it to be an imitation of the Cremona Violin." See CRÒMORNE.

Max Allihn gives a more correct usage of the term in the following words: "CREMONA bedeutet eine Labialstimme von streichendem Ton. Die Cremonesergeige wird in Frankreich kurzweg Cremona genannt." The term should be abandoned in modern nomenclature.

CROMORNE, Fr. Ger., KRUMMHORN.—A reed stop, of 8 ft. pitch, having a tone somewhat resembling that of the CLARINET, but smoother and of a mournful character. Seidel says of the name KRUMMHORN: "Properly 'CORMORNE,' from *cor* 'horn,' and *morne* 'mournful, still, soft,' meaning a soft, quiet horn, is a reed stop of a delicate intonation, of 8 ft. or 4 ft. pitch, of tin or metal, open or partly covered, and sometimes formed of small-scaled cylindrical pipes. This stop has been constructed in imitation of an old instrument, called the Krummhorn (crooked horn), which had six holes, and was, at its lower end, bent in form of a half-circle."

The CROMORNE is a favorite stop of French organ-builders. It appears in the Positif divisions of the Organs in the Cathedrals of Paris and Amiens, and the Church of St. Ouen, at Rouen; in the Concert Organ in Albert Hall, Sheffield; and in all instruments built by Cavaillé-Coll, of Paris. Its voice is distinct from that of the Clarinet, for in the last-named Organ, and in the Grand Organ in the Church of Saint-Eustache, built by J. Merklin, of Paris, both a CROMORNE, 8 FT., and a CLARINETTE, 8 FT., appear. In the price list of stops issued by Henri Zimmermann, of Paris, this stop is written CROMHORNE and given as distinct from the CLARINETTE.*

CYMBAL. Fr., CYMBALE. Ger., CYMBEL or ZYMBEL. Ital., CIMBALO.—A compound harmonic-corroborating stop, usually composed of from two to eight ranks of pipes of high pitch, and breaking at every octave. The ranks are alternately

* "Le CROMORNE (de l'allemand *Krumm-Horn*, Corne torse), est encore un quatre-pieds qui en forme huit, en raison de sa forte languette. On conçoit que, n'ayant pas la hauteur de tuyaux que comporte son ton, il rende des sons nécessairement moins forts que la *Trompette*, où la hauteur et le ton se trouvent d'accord. C'est néanmoins le meilleur des jeux d'anches accessoires. Il a le timbre clair, plus nourri que le *Hautbois*, tenant du *Cor anglais* et de la *Clarinette* avec une teinte plus métallique et une certaine *mollesse gutturale* qui n'est pas sans grâce et qu'on nomme *cruchement*. La difficulté est d'obtenir cet effet à son point: avec trop de mollesse, le *Cromorne* râle; avec trop de raideur, au lieu de crucher, il crache.

octave- and fifth-sounding. The stop frequently appears in large French Organs. There are a GROSSE CYMBALE, of VI. ranks, and a CYMBALE, of V. ranks, in the Organ in the Church of Saint-Sulpice, Paris.

CYMBELREGAL, Ger.—An obsolete reed stop, of either 4 ft. or 2 ft. pitch, the tone of which was peculiarly bright and ringing in character.

CYMBELSTERN, Ger.—Literally, *Cymbal-star*. This so-called organ-stop has been properly classed among the several puerilities of old German organ-building. It is a mechanical device in the form of a star, to the points of which small bells or metallic "jingles" are attached. When the star revolves, at the will of the performer, a confused tinkling sound is produced. An example exists, or recently existed, in the Organ in the Cathedral of Merseburg.

DECIMA, Ital.—The term used by Italian organ builders to designate the TENTH, 3⅕ FT. The following terms are also employed by them for other harmonic-corroborating ranks: DECIMA QUINTA—the FIFTEENTH, 2 FT.; DECIMA SETTIMA—the SEVENTEENTH, 1⅗ FT.; and DECIMA NONA—the NINETEENTH, 1⅓ FT.

DIAPASON, Grk.—Literally, *an Octave*. Used by the French to signify the compass of a voice or musical instrument. A rule or scale employed by the makers of various wind instruments. Used by English organ builders to designate the foundation unison stops of the Organ. See OPEN DIAPASON.

DIAPASON PHONON.—A name recently given to an open metal stop similar to, but more powerful in tone than, the standard OPEN DIAPASON. It is made of 16 ft. and 8 ft. pitch.

DIAPHONE.—A stop of peculiar construction, patented by Mr. R. Hope-Jones. The vibrations within its resonators are generated by pallets actuated by the wind that enters the mechanical portions of the pipes. The pallets open and close the holes at the lower ends of the resonant tubes, acting much in the same manner as the striking tongues in ordinary reed pipes. As the vibrating column of air in the resonant tube, or resonator, controls the action of the pallet, the pitch of the pipe is not affected by a change of wind-pressure, while its strength and character of tone are altered. The tone is in good examples smooth and majestic. Further particulars of the DIAPHONE are given elsewhere in this treatise.

DIEZMONOVENA, Span.—The term that has been used (in rare instances) by Spanish organ builders to designate the NINETEENTH, 1⅓ FT.

DIVINARE.—The name which has sometimes been given to a covered stop of 4 ft. pitch, yielding a peculiarly sweet and refined tone, which fact has doubtless suggested the rather inappropriate name, derived from the Latin word *divinus*. Regnier says: "DIVINARE, flûte de bourdon de quatre-pieds, *flûte divine*,

"On fait ce régistre de forme cylindrique et basé sur un cône, à la pointe duquel se soude le noyau qui retient le système de l'anche."—Regnier.

"Le CROMORNE se traitera à-peu-près comme la Trompette; mais ce Jeu est plus délicat pour la juste longueur des Tuyaux: une ligne de plus ou de moins y est bien sensible, pour la qualité de l'harmonie. Le Cromorne, surtout dans les Basses, est difficile à bien traiter & à faire bien parler. La courbe des languettes doit être un peu plus basse que pour la Trompette; mais c'est de très-peu. Plus le Cromorne est anché grand, plus il est difficile à bien traiter. On en vient plus aisément à bout, lorsqu'il est anché un peu plus petit; mais son son a moins de corps. Il ne s'agit pas de chercher un grand éclat dans ce Jeu, mais beaucoup de tendre, & de moëlleux. Il est essentiel qu'il parle bien promptement & bien nettement."—Dom Bedos de Celles.

est une singulière traduction de ce mot, et c'est la seule indiquée pour exprimer la qualité divinement supérieure de cette flûte . . . . à peu près inconnue."

Dolcan.—A labial stop, of 8 ft. pitch, the pipes of which are of metal, having a larger diameter at the top than at the mouth. The tone of this stop is clear and sweet, and its speech is prompt. Although the true Dolcan is made of metal, imitations have been essayed in wood with some success.

Dolce, Ital.—The name is given to stops of different formation, but which are alike insomuch that they yield tones of great delicacy and sweetness. Its pipes are sometimes made like those of the Dolcan—larger at the top than at the mouth. It is of 8 ft. pitch, and in its intonation inclines toward a stringy character. The Dolce, when carefully voiced on a light wind, is a valuable stop for a Chamber Organ. A very fine example exists in the Echo division of the Organ in the Parish Church of Leeds. It is of inverted conical pipes of metal, and has a tone of a quiet nasal quality; and, being on wind of 1½ inches pressure, has a tendency to be slow, which imparts a peculiar intonation to its speech.

Dolce Cornet.—A compound stop, formed of several ranks of very small-scaled metal pipes, and yielding a sweet, singing quality of compound tone. See the Chapter on the Compound Stops of the Organ.

Dolcette.—The term which may appropriately be employed to designate the true Octave Dolce, 4 ft. This is a valuable stop for the Chamber Organ.

Dolcissimo, Ital.—The softest flute-toned stop made, and one highly suitable for the true Chamber Organ. In its best form it is of 8 ft. pitch, constructed of small-scaled wood pipes having very narrow mouths, voiced on wind of 1½ inches.

Doppelflöte, Ger.—A covered wood stop, of 8 ft. pitch, the pipes of which have double mouths placed directly opposite each other. See the Chapter on Wood Pipes. The tone of the Doppelflöte is remarkably full and round, and mixes well with almost every other tone of the Organ. These properties make it one of the most valuable flute-toned stops at the disposal of the organ builder to-day. It has, however, been practically ignored by English builders, partly because they are unacquainted with its tonal value, and partly because it is a somewhat troublesome stop to make and voice. The double-mouthed pipes are very rarely carried below tenor C, the bass octave being supplied by large-scaled Lieblichgedeckt pipes of full intonation. In large Organs the stop should be completed with double-mouthed pipes. Fine examples of the Doppelflöte are to be found in American Organs, notably those built by Roosevelt. The older German name for this stop is Duiflöte.

Doppelflötenbass, Ger.—A Doppelflöte, of 16 ft. pitch, and true bass to the manual Doppelflöte, 8 ft. It is placed in the Pedal Organ, where its grand voice is of the greatest value. A fine example exists in the Second Pedal Organ in Schulze's important instrument in the Marienkirche, at Lübeck.

Doppelgedeckt, Ger.—A covered wood stop, of 8 ft. or 16 ft. pitch, the pipes of which are of large scale and furnished with two mouths. In construction it is similar to the Doppelflöte, but in tone it should be thicker and more assertive.

Doppelrohrflöte, Ger.—As the name implies, this stop is a Rohrflöte, the pipes of which have double mouths. It is made of 8 ft. and 4 ft. pitch; and, owing to the perforation in the stoppers of its pipes, its tone is brighter and lighter than that of the wholly-stopped DOPPELFLÖTE. Examples of the DOPPELROHRFLÖTE, in both pitches, are inserted in the Great division of Müller's Organ in the Catholic Church at Katscher. Another pair appears in the Echo division of the Grand Organ in the Cathedral of Breslau.

DOPPELROHRGEDECKT, Ger.—A half-covered wood and metal stop of a larger scale and fuller intonation than the DOPPELROHRFLÖTE. It is commonly made of 8 ft. pitch.

DOPPELSPITZFLÖTE, Ger.—As the name implies, this stop is a SPITZFLÖTE (*q. v.*), the pipes of which have two mouths. An example is to be found in the Echo division of the Organ in the Church of St. Mary Magdalen, at Breslau.

DOUBLE BASSOON.—The reed stop of 16 ft. pitch whose voice imitates that of the Double Bassoon of the orchestra, the compass of which extends from BBB♭ to F, and accordingly covers the entire compass of the Pedal Organ, to which department the stop properly belongs. See BASSOON.

DOUBLE DULCIANA.—A manual stop, of 16 ft. pitch, formed in all respects similar to the unison DULCIANA. When made by a master hand, it yields a pure organ-tone of exquisite character and pathos. It is to be regretted that this very beautiful voice is so much neglected by organ builders; but this neglect may be accounted for by the modern craze for powerful tones and high wind-pressures. Purity and delicacy of intonation seem to be at a discount in the organ-building of to-day. The DOUBLE DULCIANA forms a perfect Double for the Choir Organ, especially if it is uninclosed; and it is the most beautiful open stop of 16 ft. pitch for the true Chamber Organ. When inserted in the Pedal Organ it is properly labeled DULCIANA, 16 FT., being simply a unison stop in that department. A Pedal Organ DOUBLE DULCIANA would be a small-scaled open metal stop, of 32 ft. pitch. See CONTRA-DULCIANA and DULCIANA.

DOUBLE MELODIA.—A wood stop, of medium scale and 16 ft. pitch, belonging to the manual department. It is usually formed of open pipes from tenor C to the top note, the bass octave being in LIEBLICHGEDECKT or some soft-toned covered pipes. The open pipes, like the unison MELODIA, have inverted mouths. A fine example of the DOUBLE MELODIA, 16 FT., exists in the Great division (tower section) of the Organ in the Cathedral of the Incarnation, Garden City, Long Island, U. S. A. See MELODIA.

DOUBLE OPEN DIAPASON. Ger., DOPPELPRINCIPAL.—A stop formed of large-scaled open cylindrical metal, or quadrangular wood, pipes. When introduced in the manual divisions it is of 16 ft. pitch, and when placed in the Pedal Organ it is of 32 ft. pitch. In almost all good examples of the manual stop the pipes are carried throughout the compass in metal, the bass octave being effectively displayed in the case, forming towers or other important features. A notable exception to this general rule obtains in the remarkably fine stop labeled SUB-PRINCIPAL, 16 FT., in the Great division of the Organ in St. Bartholomew's Church, Armley, which is formed of open wood pipes in the two lower octaves, and of metal from middle c^1. Such a method should, however, not be ventured upon by any builder less skilled than the master who made and voiced the Armley stop.

When introduced in the Pedal Organ, the DOUBLE OPEN DIAPASON, 32 FT., is either of metal or wood; but on account of its great cost metal is comparatively seldom used. In Organs of the first magnitude, however, the stop is found in both materials complete, as in the pedal departments of the Organs in St. George's Hall, Liverpool, and the Centennial Hall, Sydney, N. S. W. A magnificent example of this stop, under the name of CONTRA-BASS, 32 FT., adorns the front of the imposing Organ in the Church of the Monastery at Weingarten. This stop, the largest pipe of which is about 16 inches in diameter, is constructed of tin. Other fine examples exist in the Organs in the Cathedral of Haarlem, and the Royal Albert Hall, London.

The manual DOUBLE OPEN DIAPASON, 16 FT., is formed in all respects similar to the manual OPEN DIAPASON, 8 FT., while in scale it should be smaller; its tenor C pipe being from two to four pipes less than the CC pipe of the unison stop. In German Organs the DOUBLE OPEN DIAPASONS bear the more appropriate names of PRINCIPAL, 16 FT., PRINCIPALBASS, 16 FT., and PRINCIPALBASS, 32 FT., as in the Organ in the Grand Hall of the Liederhalle, at Stuttgart. In the Pedal Organ the 32 ft. stop is properly labeled GROSSPRINCIPAL or GROSSPRINCIPALBASS. In French Organs the stops appear as MONTRE, 16 FT. (when mounted in the case), PRINCIPAL-BASSE, 16 FT., PRINCIPAL-BASSE, 32 FT., etc.

DOUBLE STOPPED DIAPASON.—The name that has been given to a manual wood, or wood and metal, covered stop of 16 ft. pitch. Its pipes are constructed like those of the unison STOPPED DIAPASON. Such a stop if placed in the Pedal Organ would be properly labeled STOPPED DIAPASON, 16 FT.

DOUBLE TROMBONE.—The Pedal Organ reed stop, of 32 ft. pitch, similar in all respects to the CONTRA-TROMBONE, 32 FT. (*q. v.*).

DOUBLE TRUMPET.—A manual reed stop, of 16 ft. pitch, formed of metal pipes and voiced in every respect similar to the unison TRUMPET, 8 FT. There is a DOUBLE TRUMPET, 16 FT., made by Greenwood, in the Great division of the Organ in the Parish Church of Leeds; and another, made by Edmund Schulze, in the Great division of the Parish Church of Doncaster.

DOUBLETTE, Fr.—In French Organs this stop is formed of open metal pipes of 2 ft. pitch, properly yielding pure organ-tone.* In English and German instruments the term has been used to designate stops formed of two ranks of pipes. In the Grand Organs in the Cathedral of Notre-Dame, and in the Church of Saint-Sulpice, at Paris, the DOUBLETTE appears as a single rank of 2 ft. pitch; while in the Organ in the Cathedral of Merseburg it is formed of two ranks, of 4 ft. and 2 ft. pitch. Compound DOUBLETTES have been made of the following ranks: 2 ft. and 1 ft.; 2 ft. and 1⅓ ft.; and 2⅔ and 2 ft. pitch.

DUIFLÖTE.—The old and obsolete name for the double-mouthed covered stop now known as the DOPPELFLÖTE.

DULCET.—An open metal stop of 4 ft. pitch. It is in reality a DULCIANA

* "La DOUBLETTE, ou simplement le *deux-pieds*, car c'est le ton de son plus grand tuyau, est par cette raison même la *double octave* de huit-pieds pris pour base générale du ton d'orgue, puisque le huit-pieds, avons-nous dit, est à l'unisson de la voix commune de l'homme. La DOUBLETTE est donc l'octave du PRESTANT, ouvert comme lui, de taille médiocre comme lui, et comme lui d'étain fin."—Regnier.

OCTAVE, and is sometimes called DULCIANA PRINCIPAL in English organ nomenclature. It is formed of small-scaled open metal pipes, in all respects similar to those of the unison DULCIANA, 8 FT. When inserted along with the DULCIANA in any one manual division its scale should be two or three pipes less; accordingly, the CC pipe of the DULCET, 4 FT., would be the same diameter as the D or D♯ pipe of the DULCIANA, 8 FT. The best material for the DULCET is tin, which lends itself to the delicate manipulation necessary for the production of the light "silvery tone" characteristic of the stop. The DULCET, 4 FT., was introduced by Samuel Green (probably between 1780 and 1790), and was used by him, along with the DULCIANA, in certain of his Swell Organs, and labeled DULCIANA PRINCIPAL.

DULCIAN or DOLCIAN, Ger. Ital., DOLCIANO.—A soft-toned reed stop of both 16 ft. and 8 ft. pitch. Its tone closely resembles that of the FAGOTTO. Examples are to be found in the Echo division of the celebrated Organ at Haarlem, and in the Rückpositiv of the Organ in St. Catherine's Church, Hamburg.

DULCIANA, 8 FT.—A manual stop formed of open cylindrical metal pipes of small scale, and voiced to yield a delicate and "silvery tone." It appears to have been first introduced by John Snetzler in the Organ he built, under Dr. Burney's direction, in the year 1754, for the Church of St. Margaret, Lynn Regis, Norfolk. The DULCIANA is one of the most beautiful and valuable soft stops made. It is highly desirable in the chief accompanimental division of an Organ, and is indispensable in Church and Chamber Organs of any pretensions to completeness.

When properly made, with *unslotted* pipes, the DULCIANA yields a pure and refined organ-tone which may be considered the diminutive of the normal diapason-tone. Under no conditions whatever should its pipes be slotted or perforated at top, because such a treatment is totally destructive of the gentle and characteristic voice of the stop. This stop has been too often, and always unwisely, inserted in an incomplete form, grooved, in the lower octave, into some soft stopped bass; but this practice should never be followed in good work. The bass octave of the DULCIANA is most beautiful, and of great value in accompanimental music. The DULCIANA should always be made of high-class metal.

The Pedal Organ DULCIANA is an open metal stop, of 16 ft. pitch, forming the true bass of the manual DULCIANA, 8 FT. Its pipes are in all respects similar in form and treatment to those of the manual stop. The DULCIANA, 16 FT., should occupy a place in every Pedal Organ of any importance. See DOUBLE DULCIANA.

DULCIANA CORNET.—A compound stop of five or more ranks of DULCIANA pipes, producing a delicate, silvery, compound tone, corroborating the harmonic upper partial tones of the softer unison stops of the Organ. This stop should find a place in the manual department of every good Organ. See Chapter on the Compound Stops of the Organ.

DULCIANA PRINCIPAL.—The name given by Samuel Green (1780–1790) to what may more correctly be called the DULCIANA OCTAVE, 4 FT. He probably introduced this stop. See DULCET.

DULZFLÖTE, Ger. Ital., FLAUTO DOLCE.—An open wood stop, of either 8 ft. or 4 ft. pitch, the pipes of which are of small scale, voiced to yield a very soft and sweet flute-tone.

Echo Dulciana.—A small-scaled, cylindrical, open stop, of 8 ft. pitch, the pipes of which are properly of 90% tin. The mouths of the pipes are narrow and cut up to about a quarter their width. The tone of the stop resembles that of the Dulciana, 8 ft., but in strength is intermediate between the tone of the latter stop (as usually voiced) and that of the Vox Angelica, 8 ft. The Echo Dulciana is a valuable stop for the true Chamber Organ.

Echoflöte, Ger.—An extremely soft flute-toned stop, of 8 ft. or 4 ft. pitch, suitable for the softest manual division of the Church Organ, and for the manual department of the true Chamber Organ. Sometimes this is simply labeled Echo. Locher says: "When this word alone appears on a draw-stop knob, it indicates an exceedingly soft, flute-like stop, which is often placed in a swell-box, separate from the main body of the Organ. It is sometimes labeled Bourdon-echo."

Echo Oboe.—The name given by Edmund Schulze, the celebrated organ builder, of Paulinzelle, to an open wood stop, of 8 ft. pitch, the pipes of which are of small scale and about twice their width in depth. See Chapter on Wood Pipes. The tone of this stop is a combination of string- and reed-tone, and is singularly delicate and beautiful. A fine example, made by Schulze, exists in the Echo division of the Organ in the Church of St. Bartholomew, at Armley, Yorkshire. This stop is of tenor C compass, being grooved into the bass of the Vox Angelica, 8 ft. Another example exists in the Echo division of the Organ in the Parish Church of Leeds. This Echo Oboe was accurately copied from the Armley stop by Abbott, of Leeds. Both these stops speak on wind of 1½ inches pressure.

Engelstimme, Ger.—The name that has been occasionally employed by German organ builders to designate the Vox Angelica (*q. v.*).

English Horn. Ger., Englisch Horn.—The orchestral instrument from which this organ stop derives its name is a reed of the Oboe family, its compass extending two octaves and a fifth from tenor E. The stop, accordingly, need not be carried below tenor C; but it is usually, as a stop of 8 ft. pitch, carried throughout the manual compass. It has even been made of 16 ft. pitch. See Cor Anglais.

Engprincipal, Ger. (from *eng*—narrow).—The name which has sometimes been used to designate a Principal, 8 ft., of small scale and soft intonation, so as to distinguish it from the Principal of full scale and loud voice.

Euphone or Euphonium.—The name derived from the Greek word *εὔφωνος*, and employed to designate a free reed stop of 16 ft. and 8 ft. pitch, the resonators or tubes of which are similar to those of the Trumpet in form, but smaller in scale. Its tone is supposed to imitate that of the Euphonium; but a successful imitation has not yet been achieved, so far, at least, as our observation extends. The Euphones of both pitches are valuable and very agreeable stops; and, on account of the richness and smoothness of their voices, should be more frequently introduced in Organs than they have hitherto been. English organ builders have always had a prejudice against the use of free reed stops; first, on account of their great success in the voicing of striking reeds; and, secondly, because of the great labor attending the production of equally good free reed stops. A fine example of the Euphone, 16 ft., exists in the Choir Organ of the large Roosevelt instrument in the Cathedral of the Incarnation, Garden City, Long Island, U. S. A.

Another, of the same pitch, is to be found in the Positif of the Grand Organ in the Church of Saint-Sulpice, at Paris. A EUPHONE, 8 FT., exists in the First Manual division of Walcker's Grand Organ in the Cathedral of Riga, Russia, where it is labeled EUPHON, 8 FT.

FAGOTTO, Ital.—A small-scaled reed stop, of 8 ft. pitch, voiced in imitation of the tone of the orchestral instrument of the same name. See BASSOON.

FAGOTTONE, Ital.—This word, which has the Italian augmentative ending, is employed to designate a reed stop of the FAGOTTO family, of 32 ft. pitch, and of impressive voice. It is a Pedal Organ stop, and carries the characteristic voice of the CONTRAFAGOTTO, 16 FT., an octave lower. It has, of course, no equivalent in the orchestra.

FELDFLÖTE or FELDPFEIFE, Ger. Lat., FISTULA MILITARIS.—An open metal stop, of pungent and penetrating flute- or fife-tone; hence its name. It is usually of 2 ft. pitch, but has sometimes been introduced as a stop of 1 ft. pitch.

FERNFLÖTE, Ger.—Literally *Distant* or *Echo Flute*. A small-scaled labial stop, of 8 ft. or 4 ft. pitch, yielding the softest flute-tone produced by organ pipes. It differs in no essentials from the ECHOFLÖTE (*q. v.*).

FIFE. Fr., FIFRE. Ger., PFEIFE.—An open metal stop, of 2 ft. or 1 ft. pitch, yielding a shrill flute-tone, an imitation of the military Fife, the compass of which extends from d^2 about two octaves. As an organ stop of 2 ft. pitch the FIFE differs from the PICCOLO, 2 FT., only in the loudness of its tone. It is an undesirable voice, and should only be introduced in very large Organs as a SUPER-OCTAVE in association with high-pressure reed- and labial-work. An example of the FIFRE, 1 FT., as made by the French builders, and of comparatively soft tone, exists in the Positif of the Grand Organ in the Cathedral of Abbeville.

FIFTEENTH or SUPER-OCTAVE.—The name given to organ-toned open metal stops sounding two octaves above the unisons; accordingly, in the manual divisions it is of 2 ft. pitch, and in the Pedal Organ of 4 ft. pitch. The scale of the FIFTEENTH varies in different Organs, being, properly, calculated from that of the foundation unison or OPEN DIAPASON, 8 FT. It is now usually made two or three pipes less in scale; but the old builders, including Bernard Smith and John Harris, made their FIFTEENTHS only one pipe less in scale than their OPEN DIAPASONS, simply voicing them somewhat softer than the intermediate OCTAVES, 4 FT. As a rule, in modern Organs, the FIFTEENTH, 2 FT., is made of too large a scale and voiced of too assertive a tone, builders overlooking the fact that it is, in its proper office, only a harmonic-corroborating stop, and that it should be treated as such in the tonal structure of the Organ. In divisions in which there is no OPEN DIAPASON, the SUPER-OCTAVE, when not imitative, should be modified to suit the principal unison stop both in power and character of tone. In all cases it should be bright without undue assertiveness.

FIFTH.—The English synonym of the Fr. and Ger. QUINTE, and the Lat. and Ital. QUINTA. It is only properly applied to a stop the voice of which is at the interval of a perfect fifth above the unison. In the Pedal Organ the FIFTH is of 10⅔ ft. pitch, and in the manual divisions the FIFTH is of 5⅓ ft. pitch. These stops may be either of wood or metal, and open, covered, or half-covered.

FLACHFLÖTE, Ger.—A stop, of 8 ft., 4 ft., or 2 ft. pitch, the pipes of which are either cylindrical or conical according to the fancy of the maker and the character of the flute-tone desired. According to Wolfram the stop resembles the GEMSHORN or SPITZFLÖTE; and Seidel describes its tone as somewhat thin but not disagreeable. His illustration shows a pipe having a cylindrical body surmounted by a truncated cone. Although this stop seems to have been usually made of metal, there is one, of 4 ft. pitch, made of pear-tree, in the Organ in the Church of St. Boniface, at Langensalza. It would seem likely, from the name, which signifies *Flat Flute*, that the original FLACHFLÖTE was made of wood, its pipes being flat in form with their mouths on the wider way. If such was the case, the stop would have a full and distinctive intonation. Under other circumstances the name would be meaningless; and German organ builders had usually some reasons for naming their stops.

FLAGEOLET. Ger., FLAGEOLETT. Ital., FLAGEOLETTA. Span., FLAUTIM. — A metal labial stop of 2 ft. or 1 ft. pitch, the pipes of which are cylindrical and of medium scale. The tone is liquid and penetrating, in imitation of the old English Flageolet, the instrument for which Handel wrote the *obbligato* in the song, "O ruddier than the cherry" ("Acis and Galatea"). In some English Organs the FLAGEOLET, 2 FT., is a small-scaled wood stop. The stop appears in several Dutch Organs. In the Grand Organ in the Cathedral of Haarlem it appears in the Echo division as a stop of 1⅓ ft. pitch. In the Organ, by Druyschot, in the Old Church at Amsterdam, it is introduced in the Great division as a stop of 1 ft. pitch.

FLAGEOLET HARMONIQUE, Fr.—A medium-scaled labial stop, yielding a bright tone closely resembling that of the true Flageolet (*q. v.*). Its pipes are of double the standard speaking lengths and have the harmonic perforation in their bodies, as usual in harmonic pipes. A FLAGEOLET HARMONIQUE, 2 FT., appears in the Positif of the Grand Organ in the Royal Church of Saint-Denis, near Paris, built by MM. Cavaillé-Coll in 1841.

FLAUTADA DE 52, Span. Ital., CONTRABASSO DOPPIO.—The stop belonging to the pedal department, in all essentials similar to the English DOUBLE OPEN DIAPASON, 32 FT. FLAUTADA DE 13 signifies an open FLUTE, 8 FT., while FLAUTADA DE 26 signifies an open FLUTE, or DOUBLE OPEN DIAPASON, 16 FT. Examples are to be found in the Organs in the Cathedrals of Burgos and Valladolid, and in other Spanish instruments.

FLAUTINO, Ital.—This word, terminating in the Italian diminutive, *ino*, is used to designate a flute-toned stop of small size. It is usually an open metal stop, of 2 ft. pitch, formed of small-scaled cylindrical pipes yielding a bright flute-tone of medium strength. A stop of this name and pitch exists in the Choir division of the interesting Organ in the Church of Santa Maria in Capitolio, at Cologne; and in the Choir division of the Organ in the Jesuits' Church, in the same city, is a FLAUTINO, 4 FT. In modern Organs the name should be confined to the smaller stop. This stop has been frequently and incorrectly labeled FLAUTINA.

FLAUTO AMABILE, Ital.—A small-scaled labial stop, properly constructed of wood pipes, of either 8 ft. or 4 ft. pitch, yielding an extremely delicate and refined flute-tone. Examples occur in the Organs in the German Church, at Montreux, and the Church of Saint-Martin, at Vevey. This stop, when made of slender open wood pipes, with narrow inverted mouths, furnishes an admirable voice for the true Chamber Organ.

FLAUTO AMOROSO, Ital.—This name has been used to designate an open metal stop, of 4 ft. pitch and small scale, voiced to yield an extremely soft and sweet quality of flute-tone. It is a suitable stop for the softest manual division of the Church Organ, and a desirable one for the Chamber Organ. A fine FLAUTO AMOROSO, 4 FT., is to be found in the Echo division of the Organ in the Church of SS. Peter and Paul, at Liegnitz, in Silesia.

FLAUTO D'AMORE, Ital. Fr., FLÛTE D'AMOUR.—The name given to certain small-scaled wood stops, producing a delicate and fascinating quality of flute-tone. This stop is generally of 4 ft. pitch; but is sometimes found of 8 ft. pitch. Its pipes are, in the most satisfactory examples, half covered, as described and illustrated in the Chapter on Wood Pipes. An example of the FLÛTE D'AMOUR, 4 FT., is to be found in the Choir division of Buckow's Organ, in the Frauenkirche, at Görlitz.

FLAUTO DOLCE, Ital. Fr., FLÛTE DOUCE. Ger., DULZFLÖTE.—An open labial stop, of small scale, and of either 8 ft. or 4 ft. pitch. The pipes are made of metal or wood. The proper tone of this stop is soft, resembling that of the orchestral Flute in *piano* passages.* This stop is suitable in every way for introduction in the Chamber Organ; or in the Choir or Echo division of larger Organs when delicacy and refinement of intonation are specially desired. A fine example, of 4 ft. pitch, exists in the Echo division of the Organ in the Parish Church of Leeds, where it speaks on the appropriate wind-pressure of 1½ inches. This beautiful stop was made by Edmund Schulze, of Paulinzelle.

FLAUTO MAGGIORE, Ital.—The name appropriately given to the most important flute-toned stop in any division of the Organ—the stop holding the same commanding position in the flute-work as the OPEN DIAPASON holds in the foundation-work of the instrument. The FLAUTO MAGGIORE is properly an open wood, or wood and metal stop, of large scale, of 8 ft. pitch, and yielding a normal flute-tone of considerable volume and intensity. We find the principal flute-toned stop, of 8 ft. pitch, in the Great division of the Organ in the Cathedral of Breslau, labeled MAJORFLÖTE; and the same name is applied to the corresponding stop in the Choir division. This term has also been used by German builders to designate a full-toned, covered stop of wood, as in the Grand Organ in the Church of St. Elizabeth, at Breslau.

FLAUTO MINORE, Ital. — The appropriate name for a flute-toned stop of secondary importance as regards strength of tone, placed in any division of the Organ in which a powerful flute-toned stop labeled FLAUTO MAGGIORE is inserted. The German equivalent—MINORFLÖTE—has been used to designate a flute-toned stop of 4 ft. pitch, as in the Organ in the choir of the Cathedral of Breslau.

FLAUTONE, Ital.—The name given by the Italian organ builders to a large-

* "FLAUTO DOLCE, la flûte douce, *Dulzflöte*, que les facteurs de France ont eu tort de confondre avec la flûte allemande beaucoup plus fine et vive, est un régistre également ouvert et de très-menue taille, mais d'un ton plus rond et éminemment doux."—Regnier.

scaled stop of 8 ft. pitch, yielding a round and somewhat subdued flute-tone. The pipes of this stop are made either open or covered. The FLAUTONE in the North Organ in the Cathedral of Milan is formed of covered pipes; while that in the Choir division of the Organ in the Church of St. Gaetano, at Florence, is a metal stop, of 8 ft. pitch, the pipes of which are apparently open.*

FLAUTO TEDESCO, Ital.—The name employed by Italian organ builders to designate an open wood stop, of medium scale, and 8 ft. pitch. This stop resembles, both in the form and tone of its pipes, the English CLARABELLA, 8 FT. Examples are to be found in numerous Italian Organs; as in the North Organ in the Cathedral of Milan, and the Organ in the Church of Santa Maria di Carignano, at Genoa.

FLAUTO TRAVERSO, Ital. Fr., FLÛTE TRAVERSIÈRE. Ger., QUERFLÖTE or TRAVERSFLÖTE.—The names frequently used to designate the open stop, properly of wood and harmonic, which imitates the tone of the orchestral Flute. Ever since the invention of harmonic pipes, this important stop has been a great favorite, and many fine examples are to be found in important Organs, notably in those of the great German builders. See ORCHESTRAL FLUTE.

FLÖTENBASS, Ger.—An open wood stop, of 8 ft. pitch, and powerful flute-tone, properly introduced in the Pedal Organ. An example occurs in the Organ in the Cathedral of Bremen, built by Schulze. This stop is the same as the BASS FLUTE (*q. v.*).

FLÖTENPRINCIPAL, Ger.—The name given by Walcker to the principal unison and its attendant octave stop in the Fourth (Echo) division of the Grand Organ in the Cathedral of Riga, Russia. The stops are of open pipes, yielding flute organ-tone, and are labeled FLÖTENPRINCIPAL, 8 FT., and FLÖTENPRINCIPAL, 4 FT., respectively.

FLÛTE À BEC, Fr.—A flute-toned stop of ordinary form supposed to imitate the voice of the old Flûte à bec, which was played with a mouthpiece after the fashion of the Flageolet. Speaking of this instrument, Engel says: "The most common *flûte à bec* was made with six finger-holes, and its compass embraced somewhat more than two octaves. . . . There was often a key on this instrument in addition to the finger-holes. This flute was much in favor in England; hence it was called in France 'Flûte d'Angleterre.' It has gradually been supplanted by the 'Flûte traversière,' or 'German Flute.' The *flageolet*, the smallest *flûte à bec*, was formerly played in England even by ladies." The Italians appear to have called this instrument Flauto suabile or Flauto a becco.

FLÛTE À CHEMINÉE, Fr.—In its correct form, as constructed by the French organ builders, this stop is composed of large-scaled pipes of metal. The pipes have covers or lids of metal, from the center of which rise small tubes, or so-called chimneys, from which the stop derives its peculiar name. See Chapter on Metal Pipes. The FLÛTE À CHEMINÉE appears in French Organs of both 8 ft. and 4 ft.

* "A la pédale, les Italiens l'emploient sous le nom de *Flautone*, Flûton, ou grosse flûte douce. Celle de huit-pieds, qui est la plus usitée, chante admirablement les adagios en solo ou en chœur, mais seule à la main; il ne faut pourtant pas trop augmenter le nombre des parties, la confusion s'y jetterait, et adieu l'effet instrumental."—Regnier.

pitch, although it is properly a unison stop. An example of the octave pitch exists in the Choir division of the Organ in the Cathedral of Abbeville.

FLÛTE À FUSEAU, Fr.—A flute-toned labial stop, of 8 ft. and 4 ft. pitch, the metal pipes of which somewhat resemble the form of the spindle used in spinning, hence its name. An example occurs in the Fourth Clavier of the Organ of the Church of Saint-Nicholas, at Blois. The FLÛTE À FUSEAU is practically the same as the German SPINDELFLÖTE (*q. v.*).

FLÛTE À PAVILLON, Fr.—A large-scaled open metal stop, properly of 8 ft. pitch, the pipes of which have cylindrical bodies surmounted with sliding bells of inverted conical form. Hence the distinctive name of the stop. Owing, perhaps, to the difficulty of finding the necessary standing room for the pipes on wind-chests of ordinary dimensions this fine and commanding stop has been seldom used. The spreading bells (which prevent the larger pipes being planted closely) increase the strength and impart a peculiar character to the tone of the stop. Examples exist in the Great division of the Grand Organ in the Church of Saint-Sulpice, and in the same division of the Organ in the Church of Saint-Eustache, at Paris. The stop also appears in the Great Organ of the Concert-room instrument in the Town Hall, Leeds. See BELL DIAPASON.

FLÛTE À PYRAMIDE, Fr.—The name properly employed to designate an open wood stop of 8 ft. or 4 ft. pitch, the pipes of which are quadrangular and inverted pyramidal in form; that is, larger at top than at the mouth; in this respect resembling the pipes of the DOLCAN (*q. v.*). The tone of the FLÛTE À PYRAMIDE varies according to the scale, and treatment of the mouth, but, properly, it should be of a light and singing fluty quality.

FLÛTE ALLEMANDE, Fr.—The name employed by French organ builders to designate the GERMAN FLUTE or FLAUTO TRAVERSO. The French also apply the name FLÛTE TRAVERSIÈRE to this imitative stop. See FLAUTO TRAVERSO.

FLÛTE CREUSE, Fr.—The name given by the French organ builders to a full-toned stop, which is in all essentials, as its name implies, similar to the German HOHLFLÖTE (*q. v.*).

FLÛTE DOUCE, Fr.—An open labial stop, of small scale, yielding a soft and pure flute-tone. An example exists in the Positif of the Grand Organ in the Church of Saint-Sulpice, Paris. See FLAUTO DOLCE.

FLÛTE HARMONIQUE, Fr. HARMONIC FLUTE.—The principle of construction which obtains in the harmonic stops was first applied by MM. Cavaillé-Coll to the series of stops inserted by them in the Grand Organ in the Royal Church at Saint-Denis, near Paris, constructed in the year 1841. This series of HARMONIC FLUTES is so noteworthy that the stops which belong to it deserve enumeration here. In the Clavier du Grand Orgue—FLÛTE TRAVERSIÈRE HARMONIQUE, 8 FT., and FLÛTE OCTAVIANTE HARMONIQUE, 4 FT. In the Clavier du Positif—FLÛTE HARMONIQUE, 8 FT., and FLAGEOLET HARMONIQUE, 2 FT. In the Clavier de Récit-Echo expressif—FLÛTE HARMONIQUE, 8 FT., FLÛTE OCTAVIANTE HARMONIQUE, 4 FT., and OCTAVIN HARMONIQUE, 2 FT.

The FLÛTE HARMONIQUE, properly so called, is an open stop, of either metal or wood, and of 8 ft. pitch. From about f^1 the pipes are of twice the standard speaking lengths, and are so treated and voiced as to speak the octave, or first harmonic upper partial tone, instead of the ground tone; hence the name given to this important stop. The stop is sometimes of 4 ft. pitch, when the harmonic pipes commence at tenor F or at middle c^1. The non-harmonic portion of the stop is properly formed of large-scaled open pipes; but in the larger stop the bass octave is frequently inserted in covered pipes. The stops whose tones imitate most closely those of the orchestral Flute are formed with harmonic pipes. See Chapter on Wood Pipes.

FLÛTE OCTAVIANTE, Fr.—An open flute-toned stop, of either metal or wood, and of octave or 4 ft. pitch. This stop in its most effective form is constructed of harmonic pipes from tenor F or middle c^1, the lower pipes being of the standard speaking length. In this form it is called FLÛTE OCTAVIANTE HARMONIQUE.

FLÛTE ORCHESTRALE, Fr.—The name sometimes given by French organ builders to the open labial stop, usually harmonic, the tone of which imitates, as closely as possible in organ pipes, the beautiful intonation of the Flute of the orchestra. The name seems to have been given to stops whose imitative tones were exceptionally good. For further particulars anent this stop, see ORCHESTRAL FLUTE.

FLÛTE OUVERTE, Fr.—The general name given by French organ builders to large-scaled open stops, of metal or wood, yielding normal organ-tone. The FLÛTE OUVERTE is of 32 ft., 16 ft., 8 ft., and 4 ft. pitch, as shown by the pedal department of the Organ in the Royal Church, at Saint-Denis, near Paris, in which examples of all these pitches appear under that name. In English nomenclature, these four pedal stops would be labeled DOUBLE OPEN DIAPASON, 32 FT., OPEN DIAPASON, 16 FT., OCTAVE, 8 FT., and SUPER-OCTAVE, 4 FT.

FLÛTE POINTUE or FLÛTE À POINT, Fr.—A metal open labial stop, of 8 ft. and 4 ft. pitch, the pipes of which are conical in form, like those of the German SPITZFLÖTE. A flute-toned stop of 4 ft. pitch bearing this uncommon name is to be found in the Great division of the Organ in the Church of Saint-Martin, at Liège, built by M. Clerinex.

FLUTTUAN, Ger.—A Pedal Organ labial stop, of 16 ft. pitch. The name is rarely met with, and may be said to be obsolete so far as modern Organs are concerned.

FOURNITURE, Fr. Eng., FURNITURE.—A compound harmonic-corroborating stop, composed of three or more ranks of open metal pipes of medium scale; the ranks usually being alternately octave- and fifth-sounding. Third-sounding ranks are, however, sometimes introduced. The FOURNITURE or FURNITURE is properly of higher pitch than the other compound stops associated with it.

FRENCH HORN.—The name that has in some rare instances been used to designate a reed stop, the voice of which is supposed to imitate that of the orchestral instrument of the same name.

FUGARA.—A metal stop, of 8 ft. and 4 ft. pitch, of small scale, and yielding a string-tone of a cutting character.* According to Locher, the tone characteristic

* "LA FUGARA est une variété de la longue et incisive famille des régistres étroits et fermes de métal. Elle a plus de clarté et non moins de mordant que la Viole. Malgré sa douceur de voix, elle rappelle plus aussi le son de Violon que la Gambe de huit-pieds. La *Fugara* se fait généralement de huit et de quatre, rarement de seize."—Regnier.

of the FUGARA, as met with in German and Swiss Organs, stands between the tones of the GAMBA and GEIGENPRINCIPAL. According to Seidel, the FUGARA is of either metal or wood, of small scale, and slow intonation, the tone of which is brighter than that of the GAMBA, as known to him. An example of the FUGARA, 8 FT., in tin, exists in the Rückpositiv of the Organ in the Cathedral of Merseburg, Province of Saxony; and one of 4 ft. is in the Choir division of the Organ in the Garrison Church, at Berlin.

FÜLLQUINTE, Ger.—The name used by certain German builders to designate the manual QUINT, 5⅓ FT., which strictly belongs to the 16 ft. harmonic series. Drawn with the PRINCIPAL, 8 FT., it produces the differential tone of 16 ft. pitch.

GAMBA, Ital. Fr., GAMBE. Ger., GAMBE.—This name, which is simply an abbreviation of the full name VIOLA DA GAMBA or VIOLE DE GAMBE, is used to designate an open metal stop, the pipes of which are usually cylindrical and of small scale, producing a refined string-tone more or less imitative of that of the old orchestral Viola da Gamba. The GAMBA in the manual department of the Organ is invariably of 8 ft. pitch. When it appears of 16 ft. pitch it is correctly called CONTRA-GAMBA. The GAMBA of the Pedal Organ is of 16 ft. pitch. See VIOLA DA GAMBA.

GAMBENBASS, Ger.—The Pedal Organ GAMBA, 16 FT., the true bass to the manual GAMBA, 8 FT. It is properly of larger scale than the manual CONTRA-GAMBA, 16 FT. (*q. v.*).

GAMBETTE, Fr.—A manual stop of the GAMBA family, of 4 ft. pitch, the pipes of which are of the same form as those of the unison GAMBA, but, correctly, of softer intonation. An example of the GAMBETTE, 4 FT., exists in the Great division of the Organ in the Marienkirche, at Lübeck. It is also to be found in the larger Organs built by Roosevelt, of New York. In Organs of any pretensions the GAMBETTE, 4 FT., should accompany the GAMBA, 8 FT., to which it is the true octave.

GEDÄMPFTREGAL, Ger.—An old reed stop, so called on account of its subdued, muted, or muffled tone. Both the stop and its name are obsolete.

GEDECKT, Ger.—This term is here given in its correct form (participle past of *decken*—to cover). The term GEDACKT is an undesirable form, notwithstanding its very frequent use by organ builders, and should be abandoned in stop nomenclature. GEDECKT is applied generally to a covered stop of wood or metal of any scale. As Wolfram tells us, it is made sometimes of large and sometimes of small scale pipes, the mouths of which are cut to various heights, thereby producing several qualities of tone. To distinguish the several GEDECKTS, which vary in form and in the qualities of tone they produce, German builders have introduced such compound names as the following: ANGENEHMGEDECKT, DOPPELGEDECKT, GELINDGEDECKT, GROBGEDECKT, GROSSGEDECKT, HUMANGEDECKT, KLEINGEDECKT, LIEBLICHGEDECKT, MUSICIERGEDECKT, ROHRGEDECKT, STARKGEDECKT, STILLGEDECKT, and WEITGEDECKT. See these names. The GEDECKTS are made of all pitches, from 32 ft. to 2 ft., inclusive.

GEDECKTFLÖTE, Ger.—A covered wood or metal stop of medium scale and 8 ft. or 4 ft. pitch. Its tone is of a hollow, fluty quality, resembling, but not so full as, that of the DOPPELFLÖTE.

GEDECKTQUINTE, Ger.—A covered wood or metal stop of $5\frac{1}{3}$ ft. pitch in the manual, and $10\frac{2}{3}$ ft. pitch in the pedal department. The latter stop is usually made of wood. Its harmonic-corroborating character is greatly extended when it is made of the QUINTATEN class.

GEIGENPRINCIPAL, Ger. VIOLIN DIAPASON.—As both these names imply, this stop produces a tone in which organ-tone and string-tone are combined, the former predominating in a decided manner. This beautiful stop is formed of open, cylindrical pipes, of medium scale, and preferably of tin or best spotted metal. The tone of a really good GEIGENPRINCIPAL is full and brilliant, without the cutting intonation of the GAMBA, holding a place in the foundation-work, and yet affording a contrast to the voice of the true OPEN DIAPASON.

The scale of the GEIGENPRINCIPAL, 8 FT., varies; but when introduced along with the OPEN DIAPASON it should be made four or five pipes smaller than the latter. The GEIGENPRINCIPAL is usually a manual stop of 8 ft. pitch, but it occasionally appears also of 16 ft. pitch, as in the Organ in the Cathedral of Riga, where a GEIGENPRINCIPAL, 16 FT., is placed on the Second Manual, while on the Third Manual it appears of both 8 ft. and 4 ft. pitch. It would be more correct to name the 4 ft. stop GEIGENOCTAVE. The bass octave of the GEIGENPRINCIPAL, 16 FT., may be effectively made of wood, as there is no difficulty of obtaining the necessary string-tone from small-scaled open wood pipes. The mouths of these wood pipes should be furnished with harmonic-bridges so as to carry down the characteristic voice of the manual stop.

GEIGENREGAL, Ger.—An obsolete reed stop, the tone of which somewhat resembled that of the Geige or Violin.

GELINDGEDECKT, Ger. (from *gelind*—mild).—A covered stop, of 16 ft. or 8 ft. pitch, the pipes of which, constructed of wood, or wood and metal, are of small scale, voiced to yield a soft and refined tone, less assertive than that of the normal LIEBLICHGEDECKT.

GEMSHORN, Ger. Fr., COR DE CHAMOIS.—An open stop, generally of metal but sometimes of wood, the pipes of which are tapered so as to have their openings at top about one-third the diameter of their bodies at the mouth line. The tone of this stop is clear and penetrating, with a quality which may be placed between a reed-tone and a string-tone.* As a manual stop, the GEMSHORN appears of 8 ft., 4 ft., and 2 ft. pitch; and as a Pedal Organ stop it is of 16 ft., properly called GEMSHORNBASS. In the Choir division of the Organ in the Town Church of Fulda it appears as an 8 ft. stop, the bass and tenor octaves of which are of wood and the remainder of tin. In the Great division of the Organ in the chief Protestant Church of Utrecht, GEMSHORNS of both 4 ft. and 2 ft. are introduced.

*"Le COR DE CHAMOIS ou *Gemshorn* est une des jolies flûtes étroites et ouvertes dont l'harmonie suit celle du *Salicional*, mais plus délicate encore. Ses tuyaux, plus pointus que ceux de la *Spitzflöte*, les sons clairs mais lointains qui s'échappent de ses lèvres serrées, lui ont sans doute valu le nom qu'il porte. On le fait d'étain ou d'étoffe tant qu'il ne descend pas plus bas que huit-pieds. A seize on peut employer le bois. On le confond, mais à tort, avec deux régistres d'assez semblable timbre, mais à tuyaux bouchés, *Koppelflöte*, *Spielflöte*; enfin, il ne dédaigne pas de figurer comme quinte (*Gemshorn-Quinte* ou *Cylinder-Quinte*) et de produire alors sur une masse de violes un assez curieux effet. Le *Gemshorn* chantant se mélange volontiers avec la *Hohlflöte*, qui lui donne beaucoup de force par son harmonie violée, mais profonde."—Regnier.

GEMSHORNBASS or GROSSGEMSHORN, Ger.—The Pedal Organ stop, of 16 ft. pitch, which furnishes the true bass to the manual GEMSHORN, 8 FT. The pipes are of metal, or wood and metal, tapering in form like those of the manual stop. See GEMSHORN.

GEMSHORNQUINTE, Ger.—An open stop of metal, or wood and metal, the pipes of which are formed and voiced like those of the GEMSHORN (*q. v.*). This stop is fifth-sounding, and accordingly is found of 10⅔ ft., 5⅓ ft., 2⅔ ft., and 1⅓ ft. pitch. A GEMSHORNQUINT, 10⅔ FT., exists in the pedal department of the most important Organ in the Church of St. John, at Breslau; and in the pedal department of the Organ in St. Elizabeth's Church, in the same city, is a GEMSHORNQUINT, 5⅓ FT., of metal.

GERMAN GAMBA. Ger., GAMBE.—The stop so called, and as made by the old German organ builders, is formed of cylindrical pipes, usually of tin, of medium scale, and voiced to yield a full, unimitative, string-tone. In its original form it is decidedly slow in speech, and on that account it is invariably used in combination with other stops of prompt speech. In its old form the stop is very rarely inserted in modern Organs, even in conservative Germany.

GLOCKENSPIEL, Ger. Fr., CARILLON. Ital., CAMPANELLA or CAMPANETTA.—Correctly considered this is a mechanical or percussion stop, formed of dish-shaped bells, steel bars, or spiral rods, and a hammer-action resembling that of the pianoforte. Examples exist in several old German Organs, as in those in the Churches of St. Catherine, St. Nicholas, and St. Jacobi, at Hamburg. These bell accessories may be looked upon as among the curiosities of old organ-building,* although, in the shape of steel bars or long tubes of bell-metal, the appliance has been introduced in several large modern organs, notably in America. The bars or tubes are struck with hammers actuated by simple pneumatic mechanism.

The compound labial stop called GLOCKENSPIEL or CARILLON, inserted in modern Organs, is composed of two or more ranks of open metal pipes of high pitch, producing bell-like tones by the peculiar clang of their combined sounds. See CARILLON.

GLOCKENTON, Ger.—According to Wolfram, a soft-voiced, open metal stop, of 2 ft. pitch, the tone of which has a ringing quality suggestive of bells.

GRAND BOURDON or GROS BOURDON, Fr.—A large-scaled covered stop of wood, of 32 ft. pitch. It appears in the pedal department of the Organ in the Church of St. Vincent de Paul, Paris, constructed by A. Cavaillé-Coll. See

* "GLOCKENSPIEL. Carillon. C'est chez les Allemands un jeu composé de clochettes au lieu de l'être de tuyaux. Ordinairement, on le place dans l'intérieur derrière le principal en montre ; quelquefois il est à l'extérieur où l'on voit des anges placés dans une gloire tenant d'une main une clochette sur laquelle ils frappent avec un marteau qu'ils portent dans l'autre main. . . . Les carillons ne s'étendent ordinairement que dans les deux octaves supérieures du clavier ; cependant, il paraît qu'il s'en trouve de quatre octaves, et que celui de l'église Saint-Michel à Ohrdruff a cette étendue. Il en existe aussi à la pédale. Au lieu de timbres en forme de cloche, on emploie quelquefois des tiges métalliques tournées en spirales et assujéties sur une caisse sonore qui augmente l'intensité de leurs sons. Un des inconvénients des carillons, est de n'être presque jamais d'accord avec l'orgue dont la température fait varier continuellement les jeux de fond dans des proportions qui ne sont point dans le même rapport que celles des variations des métaux. Les marteaux qui frappent les timbres ou les tiges métalliques sont repoussés par un ressort après les avoir mis en vibration, afin de n'en pas arrêter le son."—Hamel.

CONTRA-BOURDON. The term GRAND BOURDON has been employed by Walcker to designate an important compound harmonic-corroborating stop, of five ranks, an example of which appears in the pedal department of the Cathedral of Riga. For the composition of this stop, see Chapter XI., p. 433.

GRAND PRINCIPAL, Fr.—The name which has been used by French Organ builders to designate an open metal labial stop, of 16 ft. pitch, resembling the English DOUBLE OPEN DIAPASON.

GRAVISSIMA, Lat.—Although this term appears in certain modern tonal schemes, it must not be understood to designate an independent stop. It simply signifies the differential tone or the harmonic effect produced by the combination of tones of 32 ft. and 21⅓ ft. pitch, standing at the interval of a perfect fifth apart. There are four ways of producing the so-called GRAVISSIMA, 64 FT.: 1. By associating with the DOUBLE OPEN DIAPASON, 32 FT., an independent DOUBLE QUINT, 21⅓ FT. 2. By extending the compass of the DOUBLE OPEN DIAPASON, 32 FT., seven notes, and introducing a QUINT coupler, acting on the same stop, and sounding its notes in perfect fifths. 3. By extending another stop, of 32 ft. pitch, the necessary seven notes, and coupling it, by a Quint coupler, to the DOUBLE OPEN DIAPASON, 32 FT. 4. By producing the said acoustical or harmonic effect in the lower twelve notes of the Pedal Organ compass, through the agency of an independent stop, of 32 ft. pitch, and the Quint coupler (as set forth in No. 3), and then, by means of a Sub-octave coupler, bringing the 32 ft. pitch, in a simple form, on the CC key of the pedal clavier, and continuing it to the top F or G. There has not been sufficient experience gained respecting the acoustical effect of the so-called GRAVISSIMA to enable one to pronounce a decided opinion upon the ways above outlined; but we strongly favor the first way, because it allows the independent DOUBLE QUINT or GROSSQUINTENBASS, 21⅓ FT. (*q. v.*), to be used in combination with any other stops of 32 ft pitch in the Organ. This arrangement obtains in the Organ in the Cathedral of Bremen. In the Organ recently erected by the Hutchings-Votey Organ Company, in Woolsey Hall, Yale University, the GRAVISSIMA is produced by the combination of the open wood "DIAPASON," 32 FT., with a DOUBLE QUINT, 21⅓ FT., derived from the CONTRA-BOURDON, 32 FT. The combination certainly produces a remarkable acoustic effect, evidently due to the generation of a great volume of harmonic over-tones. It is quite evident that it can have no connection with the supposed tones of the 64 ft. octave, which are inaudible as musical sounds. When, as Helmholtz states, the determinate musical tones cease at that produced by 41·25 vibrations, what can be said of the 64 ft. tone, having only about 8 vibrations per second? The term is, correctly rendered, VOX GRAVISSIMA.

GROBGEDECKT or GROSSGEDECKT, Ger. Lat., PILEATA MAGNA.—The terms signifying "great covered stop," and given by German organ builders to a manual covered labial stop, of 16 ft. pitch, as in the Great division of the Organ in the Church of St. Dominick, at Prague. When the terms are applied to a Pedal Organ stop, a large-scaled covered stop, of 32 ft. pitch, is signified, which is the GROS BOURDON of the French, and the DOUBLE STOPPED DIAPASON or SUB-BOURDON of the English builders.

GROSSDOPPELGEDECKT, Ger.—A covered wood stop of 16 ft. pitch in the manual department. Its pipes are properly of large scale, deep in proportion to their width, and have two mouths. Its tone is bold and of good mixing quality, giving great fulness and dignity to the division in which it is placed. It is the sub-octave of the DOPPELFLÖTE or DOPPELGEDECKT, 8 FT.; and is highly suitable for a division which contains powerful labial and lingual stops of unison (8 ft.) pitch.

GROSSFLÖTE, Ger. Fr., GROSSE FLÛTE.—An open wood stop of medium scale, and properly of 8 ft. pitch. In the form of its pipes it resembles the true English CLARABELLA; but it is voiced to produce a fuller and richer tone. This valuable stop, when artistically voiced, may be introduced instead of a second OPEN DIAPASON, 8 FT., as it combines admirably with a large OPEN DIAPASON.

GROSSHOHLFLÖTE, Ger.—The Pedal Organ stop, of 16 ft. pitch, the pipes of which are of wood and formed in all respects similar to those of the HOHLFLÖTE, 8 FT. See HOHLFLÖTE.

GROSSNASAT, Ger. Fr., GROS NASARD or GROSSE QUINTE.—This stop, which is of 5⅓ FT. pitch in the manual divisions and 10⅔ FT. pitch in the Pedal Organ, is made both in open and covered forms. It appears as an open stop of 10⅔ ft. in the pedal department of the large Organ in the Cathedral of Halberstadt. It appears as GROSSE QUINTE, 10⅔ FT., in the Pédale, and as GROSSE QUINTE, 5⅓ FT., in the Clavier des Bombardes, in the Grand Organ in the Cathedral of Notre-Dame, at Paris.

GROSSPOSAUNE, Ger.—The name given by German organ builders to the powerful reed stop, of 32 ft. pitch, belonging to the Pedal Organ. It is, as its name implies, similar to the CONTRA-TROMBONE, 32 FT. (*q. v.*).

GROSSPRINCIPAL, Ger. Fr., GROS PRINCIPAL.—The name appropriately given to an open foundation stop of 16 ft. pitch in the manual divisions and 32 ft. pitch in the Pedal Organ. It appears of the latter pitch in the pedal department of the Organ in the Marienkirche, at Lübeck. It also appears, constructed of English tin and of 16 ft. pitch, in the Organ in the Church of Waltershausen. These stops are practically the same as the English DOUBLE OPEN DIAPASONS of corresponding pitches.

GROSSQUINTENBASS, Ger.—This name appears in the stop list of the Organ in the Cathedral of Bremen, designating a Pedal Organ covered stop of 21⅓ FT. pitch, strictly belonging to the 64 ft. harmonic series. It has evidently been inserted in this pedal department with the view of producing, in combination with the PRINCIPALBASS, 32 FT., of the same department, the acoustical effect which is now understood by the term GRAVISSIMA (*q. v.*). This fine Organ, of 59 speaking stops, was built by Schulze, of Paulinzelle.

GROSSTERZ, Ger. Fr., GROSSE TIERCE.—This stop, which is properly of 3⅕ ft. pitch in the manual department and 6⅖ ft. in the Pedal Organ, may be constructed of either open or covered metal pipes. Its tone should be clear and of medium strength. In the manual department it belongs to the 16 ft. harmonic series, and in the Pedal Organ it belongs to the 32 ft. harmonic series—in each case corroborating the fourth upper partial tone of the prime of the corresponding series. Examples in both pitches exist in the Grand Organ in the Cathedral of Notre-Dame, Paris. Under the simple name of TERZ, $3\frac{1}{5}$ FT., this stop appears in the First Manual, and as TERZBASS, $6\frac{2}{5}$ FT., in the Haupt-Pedal of the Organ in the Cathedral of Riga.

GROSSUNTERSATZ, Ger.—A large-scaled covered stop of wood, and of 32 ft. pitch, belonging to the Pedal Organ. An example obtains in the appointment of the pedal department of the Organ built by Trost for the Church at Waltershausen. When of medium scale the stop has been frequently labeled UNTERSATZ, 32 FT., as in the pedal department of the Organ in the Town Church at Fulda. A stop of the same nature and pitch, but of smaller scale, appears in the Great division of Walcker's large Organ in the Church of St. Paul, Frankfurt, where it is labeled MANUALUNTERSATZ, 32 FT.

HALBPRINCIPAL, Ger.—The name sometimes used by the old German organ builders to designate the half-length PRINCIPAL; namely, the ordinary OCTAVE, 4 FT. The old English builders abbreviated the term, and called the stop, simply and illogically, PRINCIPAL, 4 FT.

HARFENPRINCIPAL, Ger.—A manual labial stop, of 8 ft. pitch, the pipes of which are cylindrical and of small scale. Its tones are delicate, and in quick *arpeggio* passages bear a faint resemblance to those of the orchestral Harp. The effect is secured by the presence of certain upper partial tones which are prominent in sounds produced by plucked gut strings. The term is practically obsolete.

HARFENREGAL, Ger.—A soft-toned reed stop, the tones of which bore a remote likeness to the twang of Harp strings when roughly plucked. The stop and its name are both obsolete.

HARMONIA ÆTHERIA, Grk.—A compound harmonic-corroborating stop, composed of two or more ranks of small-scaled and very delicately-voiced metal pipes. It appears, of two ranks, in the Echo division of the Organ built by Edmund Schulze for the Parish Church of Doncaster; and it appears, of three ranks, in the Fourth Manual division of Walcker's Organ in the Cathedral of Riga. It is composed of a TWELFTH, $2\frac{2}{3}$ FT., FIFTEENTH, 2 FT., and SEVENTEENTH, $1\frac{3}{5}$ FT. The octave-sounding rank is formed of pipes of very small scale.

HARMONICA, Ger.—An open wood stop, of small scale, voiced to yield a combination of flute- and string-tone of a soft and beautiful quality. For the description and illustration of the pipes forming this stop, see the Chapter on Wood Pipes. The HARMONICA, 8 FT., is a favorite stop of the German organ builders, while it is practically unknown by those of other countries; indeed, in the design and construction of wood stops generally the Germans have always taken the lead. Fine examples of the HARMONICA exist in Walcker's celebrated Organs in the Cathedrals of Ulm and Riga, and also in his Organ in the Gewandhaus, at Leipzig, where it appears in the Third Manual or Echo division in each instance. Equally good examples are to be found in Schulze's Organs in the Parish Church of Doncaster and the Church of St. Bartholomew, at Armley, near Leeds. All these stops are of 8 ft. pitch.

HARMONICABASS, Ger.—A pedal stop, of 16 ft. pitch, formed of small-scaled pipes of wood, yielding (like the HARMONICA, 8 FT., to which it is the true bass) a tone in which both delicate flute- and string-tones are combined. A fine example of this rather uncommon stop exists in the Organ in the Catholic Church, at Berne, Switzerland. The HARMONICABASS, 16 FT., would prove a valuable voice in the true Chamber Organ.

HARMONIC CLARION.—This stop is the true Octave of the HARMONIC TRUMPET, 8 FT. It is accordingly of 4 ft. pitch. The pipes are formed in all respects similar to those of the unison stop, being double the normal speaking lengths. This powerful stop should only be introduced in a manual division which contains a HARMONIC TRUMPET or some other very loud-toned lingual stop.

HARMONIC FLUTE. Fr., FLÛTE HARMONIQUE.—This stop is formed, in its middle and upper octaves when of 8 ft. pitch, of open pipes which are of double the usual speaking lengths; and which are so voiced and overblown as to speak the octaves of the normal tones belonging to the full lengths of the pipes so treated. A small perforation made near the middle of each pipe aids the production of the octave, by preventing the ready formation of a node there, while the pipe is only slightly overblown. See FLÛTE HARMONIQUE.

HARMONIC PICCOLO. Fr., PICCOLO HARMONIQUE.—A cylindrical metal stop, of 2 ft. pitch, formed of pipes of double the normal speaking lengths. The pipes are constructed and voiced in all respects similar to those of the FLÛTE HARMONIQUE. The stop is sometimes called by the French organ builders OCTAVIN HARMONIQUE, 2 FT. See FLÛTE HARMONIQUE.

HARMONIC TRUMPET. Ger., HARMONIETROMPETE. Fr., TROMPETTE HARMONIQUE.—A striking reed stop formed with inverted conical tubes which are greater in length than those required for the ordinary TRUMPET. The reeds are overblown, producing powerful tones, which are the octaves of those which naturally belong to the lengths of the tubes. Accordingly, the tube of eight feet in length in the HARMONIC TRUMPET yields a note of the same pitch as that produced by the tube of four feet in the ordinary TRUMPET, both stops being of 8 ft. pitch. The HARMONIC TRUMPET was first used in the Grand Organ in the Royal Church of Saint-Denis, constructed by MM. Cavaillé-Coll, in the year 1841. In this instrument there are no fewer than five HARMONIC TRUMPETS of 8 ft. pitch.

HARMONIC TUBA.—The most powerful reed stop, of 8 ft. pitch, introduced in the Organ. It is formed of large-scaled pipes, of thick metal, and of the usual inverted conical shape. They are of double the normal speaking lengths. The stop is voiced on wind of 20 inches and upward. The reeds should have double tongues. This commanding stop is usually and very unwisely planted on an uninclosed wind-chest, and is, accordingly, under no proper control and devoid of powers of flexibility and expression.

HARMONIEFLÖTE, Ger.—An open stop, of 8 ft. pitch, yielding a very delicate flute-tone. In the best examples the tone is, in character, between the voices of the MELODIA and the HARMONICA, while it is softer than either. This beautiful stop is highly suitable for the true Chamber Organ.

HAUTBOIS D'AMOUR, Fr. Ital., OBOE D'AMORE.—A reed stop of the OBOE species, having its resonant tubes partly covered so as to impart to its tone a singular softness and refinement. This stop seems to be no longer made; but, for introduction in the true Chamber Organ, it might with advantage be revived.

HAUTBOY. Fr., HAUTBOIS. Ital. and Ger., OBOE.—A reed stop, of 8 ft. pitch, the tone of which imitates, more or less closely, that of the orchestral instrument which bears the same name. The tubes of the HAUTBOY are very slender and surmounted by long bells; while those of the variety of the stop called the ORCHESTRAL OBOE are slender, have, in some examples, no bells, and are sometimes half-covered. In England and America the HAUTBOY is invariably a striking reed; but in France it has been frequently made as a free reed, the tone of which is not satisfactory. See OBOE.

HELLFLÖTE, HELLPFEIFE, Ger.—An open labial stop, of 4 ft. pitch, yielding a full and bright flute-tone. See CLEAR FLUTE.

HOHLFLÖTE, Ger. Fr., FLÛTE CREUSE.—This name, which means *Hollow-toned Flute*, is applied to a wood stop, of 8 ft., 4 ft., and, sometimes, 2 ft. pitch, the pipes of which are made quadrangular or triangular, according to the fancy of the organ builder and the character of tone desired. In general, the voice of this stop is a powerful, hollow, and somewhat dull flute-tone, suitable for giving body to combinations into which it enters. The HOHLFLÖTE has sometimes been made of metal; but it is not the true stop when of that material. The different forms of the HOHLFLÖTE are illustrated and described in the Chapter on Wood Pipes.

In certain Dutch Organs this stop appears under the names of HOLFLUIT and HOLPIJP, 8 FT.; and it appears under the name HOHLPFEIFE, 4 FT., in the Solo division of the Organ in the Music Hall, Cincinnati, U. S. A. In the Second Pedal division of the Organ in the Cathedral of Ulm there is a HOHLFLÖTE, 2 FT. Speaking of this stop, Locher says: "As a particularly rare specimen, I found this stop in Ulm Münsterkirche as a 2 ft. Pedal Organ stop, where, combined with other stops on the Upper Pedal, it gives, without need of any coupler, a power of expression belonging almost exclusively to the manuals."

HOHLFLÖTENBASS or GROSSHOHLFLÖTE, Ger.—An open wood stop, of 16 ft. pitch, the pipes of which are in all respects similar to those of the HOHLFLÖTE, 8 FT. It furnishes the proper bass to the HOHLFLÖTE, and is accordingly a Pedal Organ stop. It is, however, seldom introduced in modern instruments.

HORN.—A manual reed stop of 8 ft. pitch, the tone of which is full and round, devoid of the clang characteristic of the TRUMPET. The tone of the HORN is good in proportion as it approaches that of the orchestral Horn; but it must be acknowledged that no satisfactory imitation has been achieved in an organ stop. Should it ever be achieved, it will be by a labial stop and not by a lingual one.

The tubes of the HORN, 8 FT., are of metal, of inverted conical form, and are usually of larger diameter at the top than those of the TRUMPET. In voicing the HORN, every attempt is made to obtain a smooth and somewhat wailing quality of intonation. Experiments have been made to obtain this peculiar quality by different systems of muting the tubes, but they have not been attended with noteworthy success. The HORN is met with in several English Organs. In the large instrument in Doncaster Parish Church there are two HORNS,—in the Swell and Pedal Organs,—the one in the Solo Organ being borrowed from the Swell. There was originally a third HORN, in the Great Organ, but that has been removed.

HORN DIAPASON.—A manual stop of 8 ft. pitch, formed of metal labial pipes, of large scale, and inverted conical bodies. When properly voiced and copiously winded, this stop yields a full horn-like tone.

HÖRNLEIN, Ger.—According to Seidel, this name has been used to designate the GEMSHORN FIFTEENTH, or *Small Horn;* but in an Organ constructed by John Geissler, for the Cathedral of Lucerne, the HÖRNLEIN was a soft reed stop of 8 ft. pitch.

HUMANGEDECKT, Ger.—A covered stop of wood, or wood and metal, in all essentials similar to the LIEBLICHGEDECKT (*q. v.*).

JEU ÉRARD, Fr.—The name which has been used to designate a free reed stop, invented by Érard, of Paris, and introduced by him in the Organ of the Tuileries, now destroyed. Like all properly-constructed free reed stops, the JEU ÉRARD had very large boots. The resonating bodies were in the form of a short inverted cone surmounted by a hemisphere, having a perforation, where the two forms joined, for the escape of the condensed air and the emission of sound. The tone of this stop is said to have been agreeable but somewhat muffled, doubtless owing to the covered form of the resonators.

JUBALFLÖTE, Ger.—An open stop of 8 ft. and 4 ft. pitch, the pipes of which have double mouths.* An example exists in the Great division of the large Organ built by Walcker, in 1833, for the Church of St. Paul, Frankfurt am Main. The Organ in the Church of SS. Peter and Paul, at Görlitz, contains in its pedal department three stops of this class, of 8 ft., 4 ft., and 2 ft., all of which are incorrectly labeled TUBALFLÖTE.

JUNGFERNREGAL, Ger.—The name given to an old reed stop of delicate intonation. An example occurs in the Choir division of the Organ in the Church of St. Dominick, at Prague, labeled JUNGFERNREGAL, 16 FT. See REGAL.

JUNGFERNSTIMME, Ger.—The name which has occasionally been employed by German organ builders to designate a manual unison stop of extremely delicate intonation. It is formed of small-scaled cylindrical labial pipes, properly of tin. In all these particulars it is practically a VOX ANGELICA, 8 FT.

KERAULOPHON.—This name, derived from the Greek words κέρας—a horn, αὐλός—a pipe or flute, and φωνή—voice or sound, is used to designate an open metal stop, of 8 ft. pitch, yielding a beautiful horn-like tone, which, in certain examples of the stop, and in certain portions of its compass, is the nearest approach yet made to the soft tone of the orchestral Horn. This stop was invented by Gray & Davison, organ builders, of London; and was introduced for the first time in the Organ built by them, in 1843, for the Church of St. Paul, Knightsbridge, London.

The pipes forming the KERAULOPHON are cylindrical, of medium scale, and have sliding tops, each of which is pierced with a good-sized circular hole, placed about the diameter of the slide from the top edge of the same. For further particulars, see the Chapter on Metal Pipes. Though the KERAULOPHON may be carried, in its correct form, throughout the manual compass, it usually starts with

* "JUBALFLÖTE, eine Bezeichnung für ein offenes Flötenwerk 8′ oder 4′, auch mit doppelter Labiierung, kommt im deutschen und amerikanischen Orgelbau vor. Der Name ist entnommen aus 1. Mos. 4, 21."—Töpfer–Allihn.

pierced pipes at tenor C. The stop is common in English organs, and an example appears in the Positif of Merklin's Organ in the Church of Saint-Eustache, at Paris. It has been introduced in other Continental Organs.

Although the name under consideration has invariably been rendered KERAULOPHON, it seems to us that, as its last syllable is derived from the Greek word φωνή, it should be rendered KERAULOPHONE. In this form it would accord with the many other terms which derive their terminations from the same Greek word —such as EUPHONE, STENTORPHONE, DIAPHONE, sarrusophone, telephone, graphophone, and microphone.

KLEINGEDECKT, Ger.—The name given to a small-scaled covered stop, of 8 ft. and 4 ft. pitch, yielding a delicate flute-tone. This stop, according to Regnier, is of metal and only of the latter pitch, but this is not correct, for in the Choir division of the Organ in the Church of St. Michael, Hamburg, there is a KLEINGEDECKT, 8 FT., of wood. Examples of 4 ft. pitch exist in the Organs in the Cathedral of Ulm and the Town Church of Fulda.

KLEINPRINCIPAL, Ger.—Literally, *Small Principal.* The term which has occasionally been employed by German organ builders to designate the OCTAVE, 4 FT., derived from the scale of the MAJORPRINCIPAL, 8 FT. This stop is identical with the English PRINCIPAL, 4 FT., and the German HALBPRINCIPAL, 4 FT.

KNOPFREGAL, Ger.—Literally, *Knob-Regal.* An obsolete reed stop, which, as in the case of several other old REGALS, derived its name from the peculiar shape of the resonators of its pipes. The resonator consisted of a short cylindrical body surmounted by a globular head, across which a narrow slit or opening is cut for the emission of the sound. The head sometimes assumed a pear-shape or other ornamental form, according to the fancy of the organ builder.

KOPFREGAL, Ger.—One of the obsolete reed stops, which derived its name from the form of the resonators of its pipes. These consisted of a short body surmounted by a headpiece usually in the shape of two truncated cones joined together at their bases. The form of the head (*Kopf*) varied in different examples of the stop.

KOPPEL, Ger.—Literally, *Coupler.* The name used by old German organ builders to designate a flute-toned stop, of different pitches, peculiarly suitable, on account of its unpronounced tonality, for combination or coupling with almost any other stop in the Organ. This useful filling-up stop was sometimes called a KOPPELFLÖTE when of unison pitch, and a KOPPELOCTAVE when of 4 ft. pitch. Seidel says: "It is a common labial stop, covered, of 4 ft., 8 ft., or 16 ft. pitch, and in some very few cases it is open, like the HOHLFLÖTE. It belongs to the manual department, and has a very agreeable tone. Some call the GEMSHORN a KOPPELFLÖTE. The KOPPEL is sometimes also a description of QUINT, 5⅓ ft., 2⅔ ft., or 1⅓ ft., and in this case it is open, like the HOHLFLÖTE. KOPPEL means also a kind of MIXTURE, of two or three ranks. There is a KOPPEL of three ranks in the pedal department of the Organ in the Church of St. Dominick, Prague, composed of a TWELFTH, 2⅔ FT., a FIFTEENTH, 2 FT., and a SEVENTEENTH, 1⅗ FT." The term has frequently been rendered "Coppel" by old organ authorities, but should be entirely abandoned in modern nomenclature.

KURZFLÖTE, Ger. Fr., FLÛTE COURTE.—A metal cylindrical stop, of 4 ft. pitch, and agreeable intonation. It does not possess any very distinctive character. An example exists in the Echo division of the Organ in the Cathedral of Lund, in Sweden.

KÜTZIALFLÖTE, Ger.—This, according to Wolfram, is a small-scaled, flute-toned stop, of 4 ft. and 2 ft. pitch; and, according to Seidel, it is an open stop, of 4 ft., 2 ft., and 1 ft. pitch, while it is sometimes met with of 1⅓ ft. pitch. Hamel gives the same description.

LARIGOT, Fr.* Eng., NINETEENTH.—An open metal mutation stop, of 1⅓ ft. pitch in the manual department, and 2⅔ ft. pitch in the Pedal Organ. The tone of this stop is bright and, as a general rule, much too loud and piercing. The LARIGOT, 1⅓ FT., seldom appears as a separate stop, but examples are to be found in the Positif divisions of the Grand Organs in the Cathedral of Notre-Dame and the Church of Saint-Sulpice, at Paris. There is much to be said in favor of the LARIGOT as a separate stop.† See NINETEENTH.

LIEBLICHFLÖTE, Ger.—The name sometimes employed to designate a small-scaled and delicately-voiced stop yielding flute organ-tone, but in fine examples approaching an imitative quality. As the name refers to the tone only, no special form of pipe is implied. The stop has usually been made of 4 ft. pitch. A stop of this class is most suitable for the true Chamber Organ.

LIEBLICHGEDECKT, Ger.—A covered stop of small scale, and of 16 ft., 8 ft., and 4 ft. pitch. The largest stop is commonly, and properly, formed throughout of wood pipes, invariably so when introduced in the Pedal Organ; while the stops of higher pitch are frequently formed of metal pipes in their higher octaves, or entirely of metal. The tone of the true LIEBLICHGEDECKT is of medium strength and extremely sweet and pure in quality; it is flute organ-tone. As a stop of 16 ft. pitch, it is admirably suited for the Choir and Swell divisions of the Organ, both on account of its beautiful tonal character and the moderate space required for its accommodation on the wind-chest. LIEBLICHGEDECKTS of both 16 ft. and 8 ft. pitch, constructed of wood, are inserted in the Brustwerk of the Organ in the Cathedral of Merseburg; and similar stops are to be found in the softer divisions of numerous German Organs. As a stop of 4 ft. pitch it often appears under the shorter name GEDECKT. Although the LIEBLICHGEDECKT, 16 FT., is rarely found in the pedal department of large Organs, its presence there would

* "LARIGOT (from an old French word *l'arigot*, for a small flute or flageolet, now obsolete), the old name for a rank of small open metal pipes, the longest of which is only 1⅓ ft. speaking length. . . It is first met with, in English Organs, in those made by Harris, who passed many years in France, and who placed one in his instrument in St. Sepulchre's Snow Hill [London], erected in 1670."—E. J. H., in "A Dictionary of Music and Musicians."

† "Le LARIGOT est la quinte de la *Doublette*, par conséquent l'octave supérieure du *Nasard*, et la superoctave du *Gros-Nasard*. On le fait, ou plutôt on le faisait de grosse taille et d'étoffe : seize pouces, ou quarante-trois centimètres, à son premier tuyau. On le plaçait d'ordinaire au positif, à cause de son peu de hauteur ; mais il est tombé en désuétude dans la facture française où l'on ne s'est pas suffisamment pénétré de la nécessité d'assembler toujours les trois degrés de l'harmonie pour l'avoir complète, quatre, huit et seize-pieds, et dans ceux-ci, les deux et demi, cinq et dix-pieds. Quand les trois degrés de quinte étaient tirés avec les trois, quatre et cinq degrés de sons toniques, l'effet à ce qu'il paraît en était si perçant qu'on a encore gardé dans la conversation l'expression vulgaire de jouer à *Tire-Larigot*, pour signifier un vacarme solennel."—Regnier.

be extremely valuable for soft combinations. It is a most desirable pedal stop in the true Chamber Organ. The complete family of the LIEBLICHGEDECKTS deserves more attention by modern organ builders than it receives.

LLENO, Span.—The name used by Spanish organ builders, as a general appellation for all compound harmonic-corroborating stops, or MIXTURES.

MAJORBASS, Ger.—The name occasionally used to designate the Pedal Organ UNTERSATZ, or covered wood stop of 32 ft. pitch. It is applied to this stop in the Organ in the Church of St. Elizabeth, at Breslau.

MANUALUNTERSATZ, Ger.—The appropriate name, found in certain important Organs built by Walcker, of Ludwigsburg, designating a manual covered stop of 32 ft. pitch. The stop is never carried below the tenor octave, chiefly on account of the great size of its graver pipes, but also to avoid giving undesirable dullness and gravity to the manual bass. Examples of the MANUALUNTERSATZ, 32 FT., under that name, are to be found in the Great divisions of the Grand Organs in the Münsterkirche of Ulm, the Cathedral of St. Stephen, at Vienna, and the Church of St. Paul, Frankfurt am Main.

MEERFLÖTE, Ger.—This stop is commonly known as UNDA MARIS (*q. v.*).

MELODIA.—An open wood stop, of 8 ft. pitch, having an extremely pleasing tone, somewhat horn-like in fine examples. The pipes of this stop are of medium scale, and usually have inverted mouths and sunk blocks. See Chapter on Wood Pipes. The MELODIA, 8 FT., appears more frequently in American than in European Organs; but it is to be hoped that, notwithstanding it is a wood stop, its value will become more generally recognized by English organ builders. A good example exists in the Choir division of the Organ in the Music Hall, Cincinnati, the tone of which is properly described as "round, rich, and mellow." A MELODIA, 8 FT., of pure and beautiful tone, exists in the Choir division of the Organ in Woolsey Hall, Yale University, constructed by the Hutchings-Votey Organ Company, of Boston. The stop appears, under its French name MÉLODIE, in the Positif of the Grand Organ in the Church of Notre-Dame, Montreal, Canada, built by MM. Casavant Frères of St. Hyacinthe, P. Q. And another example, under the name MELODICA, 8 FT., exists in the Fourth Manual division of the Organ in the Cathedral of Riga, built by Walcker in 1883.

MENSCHENSTIMME, Ger.—The term employed by the old German organ builders to designate the reed stop which, in its peculiar tone, imitated to some extent the human voice. See VOX HUMANA.

MESSINGREGAL, Ger.—An obsolete reed stop, the tone of which was suggestive of the brazen clang of certain brass wind instruments.

MITTELFLÖTE, Ger.—This name, which has no reference either to the form or special tone-color, has been employed to designate a FLUTE of 4 ft. pitch, simply because it occupied a middle position between FLUTES of 8 ft. and 2 ft. pitch in the same division of the Organ. This name is a good example of the vagueness and worthlessness one too often meets with in organ-stop nomenclature.

MIXTURE. Lat., MISCELLA. Ger. MIXTUR. Dtch., MIXTUUR. Ital., RIPIENO. Span., LLENO.—The generic name for all compound harmonic-corroborating stops, and applied generally to all such stops as are composed of octave- and fifth-sounding ranks of ordinary open metal pipes, and to such stops as do not call for any special name indicative of peculiar intonation, composition, or form. The MIXTURE may be composed of two or more ranks, according to the tonal structure of the division of the Organ in which it is placed. The pitch of the different ranks is also dictated by that tonal structure, and the number and nature of the other harmonic-corroborating stops that are included in the stop appointment. For the composition and all other particulars of MIXTURES, see Chapter on the Compound Stops of the Organ.

MONTRE, Fr.—The name commonly applied by the French organ builders to such foundation and organ-toned metal stops as may be mounted or displayed in the *buffet* or case of an Organ; accordingly, the MONTRES, which are usually of burnished tin, may be of 32 ft., 16 ft., and 8 ft. speaking lengths, as in the Organ in the Royal Church at Saint-Denis, near Paris. Sometimes the name is applied to the PRESTANT, 4 FT., when its pipes are mounted. All the MONTRES are most carefully fashioned and finished, producing, when of tin brightly burnished, a beautiful effect in combination with the dark wood-work of the case.*

MOUNTED CORNET.—The name given by English organ builders to a compound stop, of short compass, which was mounted, above the main wind-chest, on a small wind-chest designed for its reception alone. The MOUNTED CORNET consisted usually of five ranks of very large-scaled open metal pipes, yielding a full, dominating tone, though sometimes the unison rank was in covered pipes. Its ranks comprised an OPEN DIAPASON or a FLÛTE À CHEMINÉE, and an OCTAVE, TWELFTH, FIFTEENTH, and SEVENTEENTH. In old English Organs its compass never extended below middle c^1; but in German Organs, in which the stop held a more important office, it usually was carried down to tenor C. Herr Schulze introduced a MOUNTED CORNET of four ranks and tenor C compass in both the Great and Swell divisions of the Organ in Doncaster Parish Church. Hopkins says the MOUNTED CORNET "was chiefly used for playing out the melody of the chorales upon, and for the performance of an obsolete kind of voluntary: but it is of great use in large Organs in hiding the breaks in the several compound stops, as it proceeds itself without any 'repetitions.' In Father Smith's Organs the CORNET was never 'mounted,' but stood on the sound-board. It was afterwards raised, probably to economize room." See Chapter on the Compound Stops of the Organ.

MUSETTE, Fr. Ger., SACKPFEIFE.—The Musette was a small bagpipe much

* "La MONTRE. Jeu labial ouvert, le plus ordinairement de moyenne taille, dont tous les tuyaux ou la plupart sont en évidence, en *montre*, comme les plus brillants et les plus parfaits. Le métal, qui est ou doit être d'étain fin, revêt un poli digne de rivaliser avec les métaux d'Ulm ou de l'Escurial. Les bouches de montre sont ordinairement écussonnées, c'est-à-dire que leurs lèvres, au lieu d'être simplement pliées comme dans le tuyau commun, sont formées de deux pièces rapportées, courbées et terminées en forme d'écusson. . . .

"Nos montres françaises ont les trois degrés de ton, seize, huit, et quatre-pieds: à cette dernière dimension, elles prennent le nom de *prestant;* elles vont rarement à trente-deux ou même vingt-quatre-pieds, à cause de la quantité de vent, de métal, et d'espace nécessaire; souvent même la montre de seize n'exhibe pas ses plus gros tuyaux, qui, simplement en bois, cachent leur humble costume à l'intérieur du buffet. D'autres fois, on aperçoit en montre de magnifiques vingt-quatre et trente-deux-pieds qui n'appartiennent qu'à la pédale de l'orgue; mais *la montre s'entend toujours des tuyaux correspondant aux claviers manuels.*"—Regnier.

used in olden times by the people of different European countries;* and the MUSETTE of the Organ is supposed to imitate the characteristic tone of that old instrument. The MUSETTE is properly a free reed stop, of 8 ft. pitch, having resonant tubes of an inverted conical form, made of tin, and yielding a light and pleasing tone, such as one might expect to be produced by a small and weak species of bagpipe.† The MUSETTE is a valuable voice in the properly-appointed Concert-room Organ, being peculiarly useful in music of a pastoral character.

MUSICIERGEDECKT, Ger.—A name sometimes employed by the old German organ builders to designate a covered stop yielding a very pure and beautiful tone. The stop closely resembles that known as the LIEBLICHGEDECKT (*q. v.*).

NACHTHORN, Ger. Fr., COR DE NUIT. Ital., PASTORITA.—In addition to the name first given, German organ builders have sometimes used the term NACHTSCHALL, which signifies *Night Sound.* The stop known by these names is formed of covered or open pipes, usually of metal but sometimes of wood. It is found of 8 ft. and 4 ft. pitch, and rarely of 2 ft. pitch. According to Wolfram, the covered NACHTHORN resembles the QUINTATEN both in form and tone, but its pipes are of larger scale. The open stop has pipes resembling those of the HOHLFLÖTE. The tone of the NACHTHORN is soft and agreeable, and in fine examples has a slightly horn-like *timbre.* A representative example of the covered NACHTHORN, 8 FT., of large scale, exists in the Positif expressif division of the Organ in the Albert Hall, Sheffield, built by Cavaillé-Coll. One of 4 ft. pitch appears in the pedal department of the Organ in the Garrison Church, at Berlin; and one of 2 ft. pitch exists in the Echo division of the celebrated Haarlem Organ. A sub-octave stop, NACHTHORNBASS, 16 FT., has occasionally been introduced.

NASARD, Fr. Ger., NASAT. Ital. and Span., NASARDO.—The name given to a manual labial stop, of 2⅔ ft. pitch, the pipes of which are either open or covered. It is the equivalent of the TWELFTH, 2⅔ FT., of the English builders, when in the open form, although it differs in tone according to circumstances. When inserted in a soft-toned division, it frequently assumes the form of a FLÛTE À CHEMINÉE. Examples exist in numerous French Organs. The stop of 5⅓ ft. pitch is called the GROS NASARD, and properly belongs to the Pedal Organ as a member of the 16 ft. harmonic series. This stop appears in the Organ, built by Schulze, in the Cathedral of Halberstadt.

NASON.—A name used by the old English organ builders for a covered stop of

* The following particulars may not be uninteresting: "According to Mersenne, who lived in the beginning of the seventeenth century, the *musette* had at his time attained to a somewhat high degree of perfection in France, and the sweetness of its sound is warmly commended by him. He gives a drawing of a *musette* with only one chamber; which had apertures for twelve tones, besides some double apertures, and valves opened by keys. The *musette*, as it was constructed in France more than a century ago, consists of a bag made of sheep's skin, of two chanters (French, *chalumeaux*), which are of different lengths, and are supplied with keys; of a drone (French, *bourdon*) with several reeds; and a pair of bellows. It is, properly speaking, a combination of four drones, since four reeds are contained in a barrel."—Carl Engel.

† "LA MUSETTE, le CHALUMEAU (*Sackpfeife, Schalmey*). Jeu d'anche de forme pyramidale, en étain fin comme la plupart des timbres effilés. La *Musette* a quatre-pieds de hauteur et huit de ton. Le timbre, plus faible que celui du *Cromorne*, imite assez bien le chétif instrument dont on lui a donné le nom. Dom Bedos disait de la *Musette*: 'Ce jeu est encore peu connu, dans le royaume.' Il y est tous les jours moins connu, et si dans certaines mélodies populaires et rares, tolérées par l'Église qui se fait toute à tous, il peut paraître utile, il n'est jamais nécessaire."—Regnier.

wood, of 4 ft. pitch, yielding a soft flute-tone of a good mixing quality. The stop was practically an OCTAVE STOPPED DIAPASON. The name has entirely disappeared from modern nomenclature.

NINETEENTH. Fr., LARIGOT. Ital., DECIMA NONA.—A mutation harmonic-corroborating stop, of 1⅓ ft. pitch in the manual department, and 2⅔ ft. pitch in the Pedal Organ. It corroborates the fifth upper partial of the foundation or unison tone of the department in which it is placed. The NINETEENTH is invariably formed of open metal pipes, scaled in proportion to the scale of the OPEN DIAPASON or principal unison stop. Under the French name LARIGOT, 1⅓ FT., it appears in the Grand Chœur of the Organ in the Cathedral of Notre-Dame, and in the Positif of the Organ in the Church of Saint-Sulpice, at Paris. The NINETEENTH appears to have been seldom introduced by English organ builders as an independent stop, while it has frequently formed a rank in the compound stops. In the Specification of the Organ in Christ Church, Newgate Street, London, we find the term LARIGOT MIXTURE. The LARIGOT, 1⅓ FT., appeared as an independent stop in the Great division of the Organ built by Harris, in 1670, for the Church of St. Sepulchre, Snow Hill, London. Harris also introduced one in the Organ he built for the Church of St. Peter, Mancroft, Norwich.

OBOE, Ital. Fr., HAUTBOIS. Ger., OBOE. Eng., HAUTBOY.—A manual reed stop, of 8 ft. pitch, the tone of which, in the finest examples, closely resembles that of the orchestral instrument of the same name. The stop which is most strictly imitative in its voice is that designated the ORCHESTRAL OBOE. The OBOE, in its more common form, is a small-scaled striking reed, the resonant tubes of which are about the standard speaking lengths, and formed of slender tapered bodies, carrying at their upper and larger ends long conical bells; which bells are sometimes open, and at other times constructed with shades, which can be partly raised or lowered for the purpose of regulating and modifying the tones of the pipes. The OBOE for the Chamber Organ should invariably be shaded. The OBOE is justly one of the most favored reed stops, and it appears in every Organ having any pretension toward completeness.

As the Oboe of the orchestra does not go below tenor B♭, and as the Fagotto of the orchestra furnishes the true bass to the Oboe, it is a correct practice to label the stop, especially when of the imitative class, which extends throughout the manual compass of the Organ, OBOE & FAGOTTO, 8 FT., or HAUTBOY & BASSOON, 8 FT. See BASSOON and ORCHESTRAL OBOE.

OCARINA, Ital.—A rare open metal labial stop, of 4 ft. pitch, the pipes of which, from tenor C upward, have cylindrical bodies surmounted by slotted bells of inverted conical form. The stop produces a hollow, fluty tone, closely resembling that of the terra cotta instrument of the same name. An example of this stop, made by Ch. Anneessens, the Belgian organ builder, is to be found in the Choir division of the Organ in the Church of St. Mary, East Parade, Bradford, Yorkshire. For further particulars see the Chapter on Metal Pipes.

OCTAVE. Ger., OCTAVE. Ital., OTTAVA. Dtch., OCTAAF. Span., OCTAVA.—The name properly used by German, Italian, Dutch, Spanish, and, to some extent, by French organ builders, to distinguish the chief stop of octave or 4 ft. pitch in a manual division, and of 8 ft. pitch in the pedal department of the Organ. The French builders frequently use the term PRESTANT instead of OCTAVE; while English builders continue to prefer the illogical appellation PRINCIPAL to the only correct one. At the present time American builders wisely and almost invariably use the term OCTAVE.

In English work, the OCTAVE, or so-called PRINCIPAL, 4 FT., is formed of cylindrical metal pipes, the scale of which is calculated from that of the OPEN DIAPASON, 8 FT. The old builders usually made their OCTAVES one pipe less in size than the corresponding pipes in the OPEN DIAPASONS. In modern work they are made one or two pipes smaller in scale. The OCTAVE should never be larger than the latter derived scale, while it may with advantage be made still smaller. It must never be forgotten that the OCTAVE is not introduced for the purpose of dominating or disturbing the fundamental unison tone of the division in which it is placed; but, on the contrary, primarily for the purpose of establishing and enriching the fundamental tone, by corroborating its first and most important upper partial tone. See Chapter on the Tonal Structure of the Organ.

As the OCTAVE is the leading stop of medium pitch in a manual division, it is the one first tuned, the other stops below and above it in pitch being tuned from it. It is probably on this account that the English builders gave the name PRINCIPAL to the stop. There seems to be no other apology possible for so illogical an appellation.

In a division of the Organ in which there is no OPEN DIAPASON, the OCTAVE should partake of the character of the principal unison, or be suitable for combination with it. In this case the OCTAVE may serve as a solo stop as well as a harmonic-corroborating one.

The term Octave has been frequently employed, in combination with the names of stops, to clearly indicate their pitch with relation to the unison pitch of the divisions in which they are placed, or with relation to some established musical interval calculated from that unison. Accordingly, we have stops bearing the compound names: OCTAVE DULCIANA, OCTAVE FIFTEENTH, 1 FT., OCTAVE FLUTE, OCTAVE GAMBA, OCTAVE QUINT, 2⅔ FT., OCTAVE TWELFTH, 1⅓ FT., OCTAVE VIOLA, etc.

OCTAVE CLARION. Fr., CLAIRON-DOUBLETTE.—A full-toned reed stop of 2 ft. pitch. An example exists in the Grand Chœur of the Organ in the Church of Saint-Sulpice, Paris. As this high-pitched stop cannot well be carried above c^2, its two upper octaves are properly formed of CLARION, 4 FT., and TRUMPET, 8 FT., pipes; or these octaves may be of large-scaled and loudly-voiced labial pipes. See CLARION.

OCTAVE OBOE.—An OCTAVE OBOE, 4 FT., has been inserted in certain important modern Organs. An example is to be found in the Second Manual of the Organ in the Cathedral of Riga; and others exist in the Organ in the Centennial Hall, Sydney, N. S. W. As we have remarked in the preceding Chapter, when the OCTAVE OBOE is not of a strictly orchestral character, it will form a valuable octave reed in the softer manual divisions of the Organ.

OCTAVE VIOLA.—A labial stop, of 4 ft. pitch, the tone of which imitates that of the orchestral Viola. An example exists in the Swell division of the Organ in St. George's Hall, Liverpool. As a harmonic-corroborating and timbre-creating stop the OCTAVE VIOLA, 4 FT., is extremely valuable in the Concert-room Organ.

OCTAVIN, Fr.—The name sometimes used by French organ builders to designate a medium-scaled metal stop of 2 ft. pitch. Examples are to be found in the Récit expressif divisions of the Organs in the Cathedral of Notre-Dame and the Church of Saint-Sulpice, and in three manual divisions of the Grand Organ in the Madeleine, at Paris. In the Organ in the Church of Saint-Vincent de Paul, Paris, it appears as a harmonic stop under the name OCTAVIN HARMONIQUE.

OFFENBASS, Ger.—The name that has been used by certain German organ builders to designate an open bass stop in contradistinction to the covered stop called GEDECKTBASS. We find the German word *offen* used in other compound names, as OFFENFLÖTENQUINTE, meaning *Open flute-toned Quint*.

OPEN DIAPASON.—The term employed by English organ builders from the middle of the seventeenth century to designate the chief foundation stops both in the manual and pedal departments of the Organ. In the former it is invariably of 8 ft., and in the latter of 16 ft. pitch; these being the true unison pitches of the respective departments. As properly constructed, the English OPEN DIAPASON, 8 FT., is an open metal stop extending throughout the compass of the manual clavier, the pipes of which are cylindrical and of large scale. The tone of the OPEN DIAPASON is that which is accepted as pure organ-tone, being unlike that produced by any other musical instrument. It is rich, full, and majestic; simple, insomuch that it is practically free from harmonic upper partial tones of a prominent character; and pure, insomuch that it receives other tones in combination without destroying their value or color. The true English OPEN DIAPASON holds about the same position among wind instruments that the tuning-fork holds among vibrating sound-producing bodies. The tones of innumerable OPEN DIAPASONS of recent construction have been seriously injured by the modern practice of slotting their pipes for tuning purposes, and by voicing them on wind of inordinate pressures. The results are that the stops have lost much of the true and pure organ-tone which was justly the delight of the old masters, and have acquired a hard and undesirable horn- or gamba-like intonation—loud, harsh, and unsympathetic. The recently-introduced practice of leathering the lips of DIAPASON pipes has led to an improvement in tone. For further particulars see the Chapter on Metal Pipes.

The OPEN DIAPASON, 16 FT., of the Pedal Organ is a large-scaled stop of either metal or wood. As the true bass to the manual OPEN DIAPASON, 8 FT., it is properly a metal stop, but in a large majority of modern Organs it is constructed of wood. In large Organs, however, two OPEN DIAPASONS are introduced in the Pedal Organ, one formed of metal and the other of wood. The tones of the two stops are different in volume and character. For particulars respecting the OPEN DIAPASON, 16 FT., of wood, see the Chapter on Wood Pipes.

The important stops above described are correctly and logically designated PRINCIPALS by German and Italian organ builders. See PRINCIPAL.

OPHICLEIDE. Fr., OPHICLÉIDE. Ger., OPHICLEÏD. Ital., OFFICLEIDE.—The name derived from ὄφις—a serpent, and κλείς—a key, and given to a brass instrument of extensive compass and powerful voice. The organ stop to which the name is applied is supposed to imitate the tone of the orchestral instrument. It is a striking reed of large scale and powerful intonation, of 8 ft. pitch in the manual divisions, and 16 ft. in the Pedal Organ. The pipes have resonant tubes of inverted conical form constructed of thick spotted metal or zinc, and the reeds are so made as to withstand the action of wind of high pressures, sometimes exceeding 20 inches, as in the case of the OPHICLEIDE, 8 FT., in the Solo division of the Organ in St. George's Hall, Liverpool. The OPHICLEIDE was first introduced by Mr. Hill, of London, in the Organ he constructed for the Town Hall of Birmingham. In the Organ in St. George's Hall, Liverpool, there are three OPHICLEIDES, of 8 ft. pitch, in the Great, Swell, and Solo divisions, and one, of 16 ft. pitch, in the Pedal Organ. The OPHICLEIDE, 8 FT., in the Solo division speaks on wind of 22 inches pressure. It is a superb stop, but its value is unfortunately circumscribed through its tone being beyond artistic control. and devoid of powers of expression.

ORCHESTRAL BASSOON.—The name properly given to the reed stop, of 8 ft. pitch, which is voiced to imitate as closely as practicable the characteristic tones of the Bassoon or Fagotto of the orchestra. The resonant tubes, in the most satisfactory examples of this stop, are of wood, pyramidal (inverted) in form, and of very small scale. When extreme refinement of tone is desired, the tubes may be half-covered or shaded, as in the ORCHESTRAL OBOE. The true compass of the Bassoon does not extend beyond e♭²; so above this note the stop is practically continued in ORCHESTRAL OBOE pipes (see ORCHESTRAL OBOE). The tone of the ORCHESTRAL BASSOON should be of greater body or volume than that which characterizes the ORCHESTRAL OBOE, 8 FT., so as to give a marked individuality to the voice of the stop throughout all its octaves.

ORCHESTRAL CLARINET.—The term properly employed to designate the solo reed stop which is voiced in strict imitation of the tones of the Clarinets of the orchestra. For general particulars of the CLARINET, 8 FT., of the Organ, see CLARINET. As it has been found that the CLARINET is greatly improved, in its imitative character, by having a soft-toned covered wood stop drawn with it, we suggest that the term ORCHESTRAL CLARINET be confined to the stop formed of the reed and a rank of unison flute-toned pipes. In our own experience we have found a soft-toned DOPPELFLÖTE, 8 FT., an admirable companion to the CLARINET; but a LIEBLICHGEDECKT or a stop of the QUINTATEN class would, in all probability, be equally suitable. It is in the imitation of the chalameau register of the Clarinet of the orchestra that the organ builder will find the greatest difficulty; it can, however, be successfully accomplished by an artistic combination.

ORCHESTRAL FLUTE or CONCERT FLUTE. Ger., CONCERTFLÖTE.—The stop to which these names are correctly applied yields tones as closely imitative of the tones of the Flute of the orchestra as are practicable in a rank of organ pipes. Several forms of pipes have been devised by different organ builders for this effective stop, and the most successful of these are fully described and illustrated in the Chapter on Wood Pipes. The stop has also been formed of harmonic metal pipes; but the tones produced by them are not so refined or so markedly imitative as those of the harmonic wood pipes.

Although the Flute of the orchestra does not descend below middle c^1,* the ORCHESTRAL FLUTE, 8 FT., is carried two octaves lower, and, accordingly, extends throughout the manual compass of the Organ. In this unison stop the harmonic pipes are never carried below c^1,—the lowest note of the Flute proper,—the lower octaves being furnished in open, or open and stopped, pipes of the standard speaking lengths. The ORCHESTRAL FLUTE, of 4 ft. pitch, is frequently introduced, the harmonic pipes of which go down to tenor C; and, taking into consideration the compass of the Bass Flute mentioned in the note, this stop may be accepted as fully representing the Flutes of the orchestra. Under all these conditions of pitch, compass, and tone, the stops become essentially solo ones. In large Concert-room Organs, ORCHESTRAL FLUTES of both 8 ft. and 4 ft. pitch should be inserted.

ORCHESTRAL OBOE.—This is a striking reed, voiced to imitate the tone of the Oboe of the orchestra. It differs from the ordinary OBOE stop, as found in the generality of Organs, both in the treatment of its reeds and in the form and proportions of its resonant tubes. The most successful examples of the ORCHESTRAL OBOE, 8 FT., we have met with are those constructed by Willis, and introduced in several of his Organs, including those in St. George's Hall, Liverpool, the Town Hall of Huddersfield, and in the Cathedrals of Durham and Glasgow. These stops have very small reeds. Their resonant tubes are of inverted conical shape, very slender, and without the bells of the ordinary OBOE, closed at top, and have long narrow slots, cut near their closed ends, through which the sound finds egress. As the tubes are constructed in the manner described, they are, of course, much shorter than the standard lengths of open tubes. All the above-mentioned peculiarities combine in producing the peculiar tone of the orchestral Oboe, which, as Berlioz correctly remarks, "is especially a melodial instrument, having a pastoral character, full of tenderness—nay, I would even say, of timidity." Reed voicers would do well to remember these words.

It has been a firm conviction among all European organ builders that the orchestral Oboe could only be imitated by a reed stop; and, notwithstanding the fact that Edmund Schulze saw some indications of a possibility in another direction when he constructed his ECHO OBOE (*q. v.*), it has been left to an American expert, himself an oboist, to prove that a remarkable imitation of the tone of the orchestral instrument can be obtained from wood labial pipes. For particulars respecting this labial OBOE, see the Chapter on Wood Pipes.

ORCHESTRAL PICCOLO.—An open metal or wood stop, of 2 ft. pitch, formed, in the best examples, of harmonic pipes. It is voiced to yield the bright and piercing tones characteristic of the Flauto Piccolo of the orchestra. See PICCOLO.

ORLO or CRO ORLO, Span.—A reed stop, of 8 ft. pitch, of the MUSETTE or CHALUMEAU character. It is found in certain large Spanish Organs, including those in the Cathedrals of Valladolid and Burgos. In the North Organ in the latter Cathedral there are two ORLOS on the Lower Clavier, probably of different

*A Bass Flute, extending an octave lower, has recently been made by a celebrated London firm; and notwithstanding the difficulty attending its intonation, it will doubtless be added to the voices of the orchestra. Its tone is extremely fine and full.

pitches; and on the Upper Clavier there are two stops labeled CRO ORLO. We may remark that the number of reed stops introduced in the Spanish Organs is remarkable.

PANFLÖTE, Ger. Ital., FLAUTO DI PAN.—The name that has been given to a very rare Pedal Organ stop of 1 ft. pitch. It is formed of open metal pipes. An example exists in the pedal department of the Grand Organ in the Cathedral of Lund, in Sweden.

PASTORITA, Ital.—The name that has sometimes been given to the stop which is now commonly known as the NACHTHORN (*q. v.*).

PAUKE, Ger.—The stop so called by German organ builders was one of the curiosities met with in old Organs. It consisted of two large-scaled covered pipes, sounding the notes G and C, or the pitches of the Pauken or Kettle-drums of the orchestra, placed in the Pedal Organ. The loud and thumping sounds produced by these pipes, when played *staccato*, were supposed to imitate those of the Kettle-drums.

PERDUNA.—The name which has sometimes been used by German organ builders to designate the BOURDON.

PFEIFE, Ger.—This term when used alone properly designates a bright flute-toned metal stop of 2 ft. pitch. It is practically identical with the stop called FIFE or FIFRE (*q. v.*). In certain compound names, used by German organ builders, the terms *Pfeife* and *Flöte* seem to be synonymous.

PHILOMELA. Ital., FILOMELA.—This name, which signifies the *Nightingale* (*Daulias philomela*), has been used to designate two distinctly different stops. In the first place, it has been applied to a small-scaled wood stop, voiced to yield an extremely sweet and soft flute-tone, probably suggestive of the voice of the nightingale. In the second place, it has been used to designate a double-mouthed open wood stop, of 8 ft. pitch, yielding powerful tones which are anything but imitative. If the name is to be retained in modern stop nomenclature, let it be confined to the stop which most closely imitates the tones of the nightingale's song.

PHYSHARMONICA, Ger.—A soft-voiced free reed stop, of 16 ft. and 8 ft. pitch, to be found in several German and Swiss Organs. In the well-known Organ in the Cathedral of Lucerne, the PHYSHARMONICA appears in the Swell division. The reeds are attached directly to a small wind-chest, having no resonant tubes, but furnished with tuning-clips and wires. All are inclosed in a small, special swell-box, in one side of which heart-shaped openings are cut for the egress of sound; and these are commanded by a sliding shutter in which corresponding perforations are made. The to-and-fro motions of the shutter produce a perfect and gradual *crescendo* and *diminuendo*. In the Organ in the Cathedral of Fribourg, in Switzerland, there are two PHYSHARMONICAS of 16 ft. and 8 ft. pitch. These are furnished with short resonators, which add greatly to the effect of the reeds. They are inclosed in the same manner as in the Lucerne instrument. These fine PHYSHARMONICAS were made by J. & P. Schiedmayer, of Stuttgart, for F. Haas, who inserted them in the Organs named. In the Organ in the Cathedral of Magdeburg there is an 8 ft. stop of a similar description, labeled HARMONIUM.

The musical effect of the PHYSHARMONICA in combination with soft-toned labial stops is singularly pleasing, and is greatly enhanced by the powers of expression provided for the former.

PICCOLO or FLAUTO PICCOLO, Ital.—A labial stop, of 2 ft. pitch, formed of open pipes of wood or metal. When in its best form it is made of harmonic pipes, the lower and middle octaves being of wood and the upper octaves of metal. The stop should be harmonic throughout. The PICCOLO sometimes appears as a stop of 1 ft. pitch, and entirely of metal, as in the Positif of the Organ in the Church of Saint-Sulpice, at Paris. Under the name of HARMONIC PICCOLO a stop, of 4 ft. pitch, is inserted in the Solo division of the Organ in the Town Hall of Leeds, while in the Great division we find a PICCOLO, 2 FT. In the case of a stop like this, which is, or should be, imitative of the orchestral Piccolo, it is desirable that organ builders should adopt a uniform pitch. When voiced in close imitation of the true Flauto Piccolo, it is appropriately called ORCHESTRAL PICCOLO; when formed throughout of harmonic pipes, French builders label it PICCOLO HARMONIQUE.

PICCOLO D'AMORE, Ital.—The true Octave of the FLAUTO D'AMORE, 4 FT. It is a softly-voiced flute-toned stop, of 2 ft. pitch, formed of half-covered wood pipes from CC to c^2, and thence to top of small-scaled open metal pipes. The PICCOLO D'AMORE, 2 FT., is a valuable SUPER-OCTAVE for the true Chamber Organ.

PIFFERO, Ital.—The name that has been employed by Italian organ builders to designate a stop in all essentials similar to the French CHALUMEAU (*q. v.*).

PILEATA, Lat.—Literally, *Hooded.* A generic name for labial covered stops.* When used alone it signifies a GEDECKT. Then we have PILEATA MAXIMA, a GROSSUNTERSATZ, 32 FT.; PILEATA MAGNA, a GROBGEDECKT, 16 FT.; PILEATA MAJOR, a MITTELGEDECKT, 8 FT.; and PILEATA MINOR, a KLEINGEDECKT, 4 FT.

PLEIN-JEU, Fr.—The name given by French organ builders to a compound harmonic-corroborating stop of several ranks of open metal pipes; as a rule it is a MIXTURE composed of alternating octave- and fifth-sounding ranks, as in the PLEIN-JEU, of VII. ranks, in the Organ built by Cavaillé-Coll for the Town Hall of Manchester. See Chapter on the Compound Stops of the Organ. A PLEIN-JEU of X. ranks is the only compound stop introduced in the Great division of the Grand Organ in the Madeleine, at Paris; and in the Positif of the Organ in the Church of Saint-Sulpice is a PLEIN-JEU HARMONIQUE, of III. and IV. ranks. Further particulars respecting the PLEIN-JEU may be gathered from the appended note.†

* "VOX-PILEATA, ou simplement PILEATA. C'est encore un de ces noms génériques de jeu bouché, dont la facture allemande abonde même par tradition, puisque les premiers traités de facture furent écrits en latin. Cela veut dire *voix couverte*, ou, mot à mot, *coiffée;* la coiffe est ce que l'on nomme aujourd'hui *calotte* dans les bourdons de métal, et tampon ou bouchon dans ceux de bois. La qualification de *Pileata* se modifie selon la grandeur du régistre; de tous petits régistres bouchés, tels que la *Bauer-Flöte* d'un pied s'appelleront *Pileata-Minima*. Un bourdon de seize, façonné de manière à prendre un nom quelconque de flûte, ajoutera à ce nom de fantaisie la qualification de *Pileata-Magna* qui empêche l'organiste de l'employer comme jeu ouvert. Enfin *Pileata-Maxima* désignera les bourdons gigantesques de la pédale."—Regnier.

† "Le PLEIN-JEU. Les modernes ont souvent donné le même nom à toute espèce de mixtures; c'est une de ces petites erreurs de détail qui entrainent après elles l'oubli des principes en facture. Ainsi ai-je rencontré souvent dans de petites orgues un régistre appelé *Plein-jeu*, qui n'avait rien de plein, et qui n'était un jeu que dans le sens ridicule du mot. Il y avait de quoi faire prendre en horreur toute espèce de mixture; et j'attribue à ce vol, fait aux vraies conditions du *Plein-jeu* par les facteurs charlatans, la réaction qu'on voit se prononcer contre la vénérable antiquité de cette harmonie. 'Dans un seize-pieds,' dit Dom Bedos, 'le moindre *Plein-jeu* est de neuf tuyaux *sur marche* (ou par note). . . . Si c'est un huit-pieds, le

PORTUNAL. PORTUNALFLÖTE, Ger.—An open wood stop of medium scale and of 8 ft. and 4 ft. pitch. Its pipes are properly of inverted pyramidal form, after the fashion of the DOLCAN. The tone of the PORTUNAL partakes of a Clarinet quality, and, in the best examples, is extremely pleasing. A fine example of the PORTUNALFLÖTE, 8 FT., exists in the Second Clavier division of the Grand Organ in the Marienkirche, at Lübeck, constructed by J. F. Schulze and Son.

POSAUNE, Ger.—A striking reed stop of powerful intonation, imitating more or less closely the tone of the orchestral Trombone when played *forte*. It is of 8 ft. pitch in the manual department, and 16 ft. pitch in the Pedal Organ. The POSAUNE is a stop belonging to the TRUMPET family, and its tubes are of large scale and inverted conical form, like those of the TRUMPET. In the manual stop the resonant tubes are properly of metal, but in the pedal stop they are constructed of either metal or wood. Examples of the POSAUNE, 8 FT., exist in the Great divisions of the Organs in Westminster Abbey, Doncaster Parish Church, and the Royal Albert Hall, London. Examples of the POSAUNE, 16 FT., are to be found in the Pedal Organs of the instruments in the above-named churches, and in the Centennial Hall, at Sydney, N. S. W. See CONTRA-POSAUNE.

PRESTANT, Fr.—The name employed by French organ builders to designate the chief OCTAVE, 4 FT., of a manual division. Its scale is derived from that of the MONTRE, 8 FT., or chief unison of the division. It occupies the same position in a French Organ as the so-called PRINCIPAL, 4 FT., does in an English instrument.

PRINCIPAL, Ger. Ital., PRINCIPALE.—The name correctly given by the German and Italian organ builders to the *principal* unison stop in both the manual and pedal departments—that which is called the OPEN DIAPASON by English builders. In the manual divisions the PRINCIPAL is correctly of 8 ft. pitch, and in the Pedal Organ of 16 ft. pitch; but in many German Organs, as in those in the Marienkirche, at Lübeck, and the Cathedral of Bremen, we find PRINCIPALS of both 16 ft. and 8 ft. pitch in the chief manual division (Hauptwerk), while the chief unison stop in the Pedal Organ is labeled PRINCIPALBASS, 16 FT.

Plein-jeu est (au moins) de sept tuyaux sur marche ; si l'orgue est un trente-deux-pieds ouvert avec bourdon de trente-deux, on doit mettre *Fourniture* entière et *Cymbale* entière (c'est-à-dire que chacun de ces régistres doit avoir sa plus grande force connue). Pour un positif, si c'est un huit-pieds en montre, on met le *Plein-jeu* de sept tuyaux sur marche. S'il n'y a point de huit-pieds ouverts, le *Plein-jeu* ne sera que de cinq tuyaux sur marche, c'est-à-dire composé des trois dernières rangées de la *Fourniture* et des deux dernières de la *Cymbale*.' (Parce qu'alors un *Plein-jeu* plus fort serait trop dur, n'étant pas soutenu par la force des huit-pieds ouverts.) Dom Bedos donne encore les règles pour un *Plein-jeu* de quatre tuyaux sur marche, mais dans ce cas la maigreur du régistre doit le faire rejeter, car il est déjà trop grinçant, même avec cinq tuyaux seulement. 'Si le *Plein-jeu* est de huit ou de six tuyaux sur marche, on prend la moitié dans la *Fourniture*, et l'autre moitié dans la *Cymbale* : voilà les règles ordinaires. . . .' Dom Bedos ajoute: 'Je ne ferai point remarquer ici toutes les variations de quelques facteurs dans la composition et l'arrangement du *Plein-jeu* (il paraît que dès ce temps-là on cherchait à économiser sur la peine et la dépense qu'occasionne la facture du vrai *Plein-jeu*) ; mais tous s'accordent à ne mettre que des quintes et des octaves, et jamais de tierces.' Je ne puis omettre ici la citation de l'éloge du *Plein-jeu* par le grand artiste bénédictin ; il donne trop d'autorité à ce que nous avons déjà dit : 'Tout ce qu'il y a de plus harmonieux dans l'orgue, au jugement des connaisseurs et de ceux qui ont du goût pour la vraie harmonie, c'est le *Plein-jeu*, lorsqu'il est mélangé avec tous les fonds qui le nourrissent dans une juste proportion ; et la raison pour laquelle on met toujours ensemble les fonds de l'orgue avec la *Fourniture* et la *Cymbale*, est que si l'on employait celles-ci seules dans les différentes combinaisons d'accords que fait un organiste, elles formeraient des sons désagréables, qui disparaissent à l'oreille, lorsque le mélange des sons fondamentaux les mettent au rang des sons harmoniques.'"—Regnier.

In English Organs the PRINCIPAL is an open metal stop, of large scale, and of 4 ft. pitch, being the true OCTAVE to the OPEN DIAPASON. The term is in this case both illogical and undesirable. See OCTAVE.

PRINCIPALDISCANT or DISCANTPRINCIPAL, Ger.—A PRINCIPAL or OPEN DIAPASON, 8 FT., which extends throughout the treble octaves of the manual compass, or from middle c^1 to the top note. The stop has sometimes been carried down to tenor C.

PRINCIPALE DOPPIO, Ital.—The name given by Italian organ builders to the stop which in English Organs is called the DOUBLE OPEN DIAPASON.

PROGRESSIO HARMONICA.—A compound harmonic-corroborating stop, the ranks of which increase in number as the stop progresses upward through the manual compass. According to Seidel, the PROGRESSIO HARMONICA is a stop invented by Musikdirektor Wilke, of Neu-Ruppin, and recommended by him especially for small Organs. The stop begins with two ranks of 1⅗ ft. and 1 ft. pitch, and at tenor C a third rank of 2 ft. pitch is added. There are no breaks in this stop. The PROGRESSIO HARMONICA in the Brustwerk of the Organ in the Cathedral of Merseburg, in Saxony, built by Fr. Ladegast, in 1855, commences with two ranks in the bass and finishes with four ranks in the treble. That in the Unterwerk of the Organ in St. Petrikirche, Berlin, commences with three ranks and finishes with five ranks.

PYRAMIDFLÖTE, Ger. Eng., PYRAMIDAL FLUTE.—A wood stop, of 8 ft. pitch, the pipes of which are square and smaller at the top than at the mouth. The tone is light and bright, resembling that of the metal GEMSHORN. A fine example exists in the Choir division of the Organ in the Church of SS. Peter and Paul, at Liegnitz, in Silesia, built by Buckow in 1839.

PYRAMIDON.—The name given to a grave Pedal Organ stop invented by the late Rev. Sir Frederick A. Gore Ouseley, and made by Mr. Flight. The peculiarities of the stop, as stated by Hopkins, "consist, first, in the shape of the pipes, which are more than four times the size at the top that they are at the mouth; and secondly, in their producing sounds of remarkable gravity for their size. From a pipe, measuring only 2 feet 9 inches in length, 2 feet 3 inches square at the top, and 8 inches square at the block, the CCC or 16 feet sound is obtained. The quality of the tone bears some resemblance to that of a stopped pipe." The pipes were covered at top with flat boards. This stop may fairly be classed among the curiosities of organ-building.*

QUARTANE.—This term has been used to designate two different compound stops: 1. A MIXTURE simply comprising *four* ranks of pipes. 2. A compound stop formed of two ranks of pipes which stand at the interval of a *quart* or perfect fourth apart. See Chapter on the Compound Stops of the Organ, p. 447.

QUARTE DE NASARD, Fr.—The term sometimes used by French organ builders to designate the open metal stop, of 2 ft. pitch, belonging to the 8 ft. harmonic

*In reply to a letter written by the author, the late Rev. Sir Frederick A. Gore Ouseley wrote in 1887: "As regards the Pyramidon, it is a *failure*. I have long since had the pipes taken out of my Organ. I found that although the pipes sounded well individually *when apart*, the moment they were planted in juxtaposition they silenced each other, except the pipes at each end of the row. . . The CCC pipe was 2½ feet high only. Let the Pyramidon be forgotten." This stop presents a very interesting acoustical problem.

series. It is similar to the English SUPER-OCTAVE or FIFTEENTH, 2 FT. It derives its name from the fact that its pitch is at the interval of a fourth above the NASARD, 2⅔ FT.*

QUERFLÖTE, Ger.—This name, which is formed of the words *quer*—cross or athwart—and *Flöte*—Flute, has been frequently used by German organ builders to designate the stop which, in its voice, imitates as closely as possible the tone of the Flute of the orchestra. Under the heading of QUERFLÖTE, Seidel gives the following particulars:

"QUERFLÖTE is a labial stop of a particularly fine tone, imitative of that of the real Flute. Organ builders, in their endeavor to make this imitation as striking as possible, have essayed with this stop all sorts of shapes and proportions. The pipes are usually made of oak, pear-tree, or maple; and they are either cylindrical or quadrangular, open or stopped. Some organ builders make the pipes twice as long as they usually appear, and overblow them so as to make them sound the octave higher. Other organ builders bore out the bodies of the pipes, and provide them with mouths of an oval form, like the embouchure of the real Flute. The QUERFLÖTE made by Müller, of Breslau, for his Organ in the Cathedral of his city, has oval mouths in its pipes, against which the wind is directed sidewise, imitating the method of blowing the real Flute."

A QUERFLÖTE, 8 FT., of the compass of the orchestral instrument, appears in the Specification of the Organ of the Cathedral of Cologne, as reconstructed by Engelbert Maas in 1821.

QUINT. Ger. and Fr., QUINTE. Ital. and Lat., QUINTA.—The stop, correctly named, which speaks a fifth above the unison tone of the division of the Organ in which it is placed; it is, accordingly, of 5⅓ ft. pitch in the manual department, and 10⅔ ft. pitch in the Pedal Organ. As the manual QUINT, 5⅓ FT., is a mutation or harmonic-corroborating stop belonging to the 16 ft. harmonic series, it should never be introduced in any division in which there is no open stop of 16 ft. pitch. Strictly considered, the same rule holds good for the Pedal Organ, in which the QUINT, 10⅔ FT., belongs to the 32 ft. harmonic series. It is, however, sometimes introduced, when there is no stop of 32 ft. pitch present, for the purpose of generating, in combination with the OPEN DIAPASON, 16 FT., the differential tone of 32 ft. pitch. See Chapter on the Tonal Structure of the Organ.

The manual QUINT, 5⅓ FT., should be of open metal pipes of medium scale and comparatively soft intonation; for it can never be legitimately used except when the DOUBLE OPEN DIAPASON, 16 FT., is drawn; or in combination with the OPEN DIAPASON, 8 FT., with the view of generating the differential tones of the 16 ft. scale. The QUINT, 10⅔ FT., of the Pedal Organ may be either of wood or metal, and either open or stopped, according to the general stop appointment of the department. In the Organ built by J. F. Schulze, in 1850, for the Cathedral of Bremen, there is a stop labeled QUINTENBASS, 10⅔ FT., and another labeled GROSSQUINTENBASS, 21⅓ FT. The former is legitimate, corroborating the second upper partial of the 32 ft. prime; while the latter could have been introduced

* "QUARTE. Jeu de l'orgue. Quoique ce jeu soit à l'unisson de la doublette, on lui a donné le nom de quarte, parce qu'en suivant la progression ascendante des jeux du cornet dont il est une des parties constituantes, il se trouve à la quarte au-dessus du nasard. Aussi l'appelle-t-on réellement *quarte de nasard*, et ce n'est que par abréviation qu'on dit simplement *quarte*."—Hamel.

solely with the view of generating the differential tones of the 64 ft. scale. For further remarks on this subject, see GRAVISSIMA. The only Organ in existence in which such a stop could find its proper place in the tonal structure is the instrument in the Centennial Hall, Sydney, N. S. W., in which a reed stop of reputed 64 ft. pitch is inserted; but here the GROSSQUINTENBASS, 21⅓ FT., is not introduced.

QUINTADENA.—Stops bearing this name are to be found in numerous Organs, notably in the Choir and Echo divisions of the Organ in the Cathedral of Haarlem. In the former it is of 8 ft., and in the latter division it is of 16 ft. pitch. It also appears of both the above pitches in the Choir division of the Organ in the Cathedral of St. Lawrence, at Rotterdam. The QUINTADENA is in all essentials similar to the covered stop correctly designated QUINTATEN (*q. v.*), yielding a compound tone in which the twelfth, or second upper partial tone, is present in a pronounced manner along with the prime or fundamental tone. We find some variations of the term; namely, QUINTADEN, QUINTADENE, and QUINTADEMA. Under the last name, the stop appears in the Swell division of the Organ in the Music Hall, Cincinnati. It is formed of stopped pipes of pure tin.

QUINTATEN.—The name derived from the Latin words *quintam tenentes*, and properly applied to covered stops which yield compound tones, in which the second upper partial is almost as prominent as the ground tone. Helmholtz correctly remarks: "Narrow stopped pipes let the twelfth be very distinctly heard at the same time with the prime tone; and have hence been called *Quintaten* (*quintam tenentes*)."*

The term QUINTATEN has seldom appeared in organ specifications, several corruptions having taken its place, according to the caprice of different organ builders. We give these corruptions, so that they may be known and avoided in the stop nomenclature of to-day: QUINTATON, QUINTATÖN, QUINTADÈNE, QUINTADINER, QUINTADÖN, and QUINTGETÖN.

QUINTENBASS, Ger.—The QUINT, 10⅔ FT.; the mutation or harmonic-corroborating stop belonging to the 32 ft. harmonic series, and properly introduced in the Pedal Organ along with the DOUBLE OPEN DIAPASON, 32 FT.; or, in the absence of that stop, with the view of producing in combination with the OPEN DIAPASON, 16 FT., the differential tone of 32 ft. pitch, sometimes designated "acoustic bass." A stop labeled QUINTENBASS it to be found in the pedal department of the Organ in the Cathedral of Bremen; and a similar stop, labeled MAJOR-QUINTE, 10⅔ FT., exists in the same department of the Organ in the Marienkirche, at Lübeck.

QUINTFLÖTE, Ger.—A flute-toned stop of 5⅓ ft. and 2⅔ ft. pitch. An example of a covered QUINTFLÖTE, 5⅓ FT., exists in the Choir division of the Organ in St. Paul's Church, Frankfurt; and one of 2⅔ ft. pitch is inserted in the Choir division of the Concert Organ in the Music Hall of Cincinnati. This latter stop is formed of open metal pipes yielding a flute-tone which combines well with the unison and octave flute-work in the division.

RANKET or RANQUET, Ger.—An old reed stop, of 16 ft. pitch, the resonators of which were very short, and closed with the exception of certain perforations provided for egress of sound and wind, after the fashion of certain REGALS. Under

*"On the Sensations of Tone," by Hermann L. F. Helmholtz, M.D. Translated by A. J. Ellis, B.A., 1875.

these conditions, the tone of the RANKET must have been of a buzzing character. Both the stop and its name are now obsolete.

RAUSCHFLÖTE or RAUSCHPFEIFE, Ger.—Literally, *Rustling Flute.* A stop commonly formed, according to Wolfram, of two ranks of pipes yielding flute-tones of 2 ft. and 1⅓ ft. pitch. This stop appears to have been entirely abandoned by the German organ builders; but it furnishes a suggestion for the formation of compound timbre-creating stops which would be of great value in large Concert-room Organs. See Chapter on the Compound Stops of the Organ.

RAUSCHQUINTE, Ger.—Literally, *Rustling Quint.* The stop frequently found in German Organs, usually composed of two ranks of open metal pipes, of 2⅔ ft. and 2 ft. pitch respectively, or at the interval of a fourth apart. The RAUSCHQUINTE of higher pitch consists of two ranks, of 1⅓ ft. and 1 ft. pitch respectively, as in the stop in the Great division of the Organ in Christ Church, at Hirschberg. A RAUSCHQUINTE, of 2⅔ ft. and 2 ft. pitch, is found in the Great division of the important instrument in the Church of St. Mary Magdalen, at Breslau. As the interval between the ranks of the RAUSCHQUINTE is a fourth, the name QUARTE or QUARTA has been given to it by old German builders. See QUARTANE.

REGAL, Ger. Fr., RÉGAL. Eng., REGAL.—The generic name for a large family of ancient reed stops,* which in their original forms are practically obsolete. The name, however, still appears in old German Organs, as in those in certain Lübeck churches. A REGAL, 8 FT., occupies a place in the Choir division of the celebrated Haarlem Organ; and in the same division of the Organ in the Church of St. Dominick, at Prague, there is a REGAL, 8 FT., and also a JUNGFERNREGAL, 16 FT.

The term "Regal" was originally applied to a portable reed organ, or "Portative," used in court ceremonies, from which fact it is said to have derived its dignified name. Subsequently the term was extended to certain reed stops, introduced in large, or "Positive Organs," which in their nature more or less resembled the stops of the earlier Regal. A fine old Regal is in the possession of our valued friend, A. J. Hipkins, Esq., F. S. A., of London, the well-known authority on musical instruments.

From the old writers on the Organ we learn the following names: APFELREGAL, BIBELREGAL, CYMBELREGAL, GEDÄMPFTREGAL, GEDECKTREGAL, GEIGENREGAL, HARFENREGAL, JUNGFERNREGAL, KÄLBERREGAL, KNOPFREGAL, KOPFLINREGAL, KOPFREGAL, MESSINGREGAL, SCHARFREGAL, SINGENDREGAL, SORDUNREGAL, SUBTILREGAL, and TRICHTERREGAL.

*"La RÉGALE, le plus ancien et le plus oublié des jeux d'anches, qui doit, selon Bedos, son nom à l'effet merveilleux que produisait son premier emploi. On proclama cette harmonie royale ou régale (de *Regalis*). C'est une anche dont le pied n'est pas surmonté d'un tuyau. Privée de ce moyen de propager ses vibrations au dehors, l'anche a donc très-peu de puissance, mais assez de finesse. Les Allemands ont conservé ce qu'ils appellent la *Régale à pomme* (*Apfel-Regal*), dont tout le corps se borne à un petit tube cylindrique couronné d'une pomme d'arrosoir. Elle sonne quatre et huit-pieds; le timbre étant d'une grande délicatesse et donnant trop de peine aux facteurs pour le peu d'effet qu'il produit, cet instrument, dans l'orgue, tombe en désuétude, à ce que dit Werner. *Geigen-Regal*, le Violon Régale, *Harfen-Regal*, la Régale de harpe, *Jungfern-Regal*, *Jungfern-Stimme*, la Voix ou Régale virginale, sont un seul ou même régistre depuis longtemps abandonné, qui devait son nom à la finesse de son timbre. A quatre et huit-pieds, il chantait au manuel, à seize à la pédale, sous le nom de *Jungfern-Regal-Bass*. La sourdine de Régale, *Sordun-Regal*, également abandonnée, avait ses corps en bois. Il paraîtrait, d'après M. Seydel, qu'on se sert encore du *Trichter-Regal*, ou Régale à entonnoir, qui diffère des autres par sa forme et l'éclat assez mince qui en résulte."—Regnier.

REGULA MINIMA, Lat.—The ordinary open metal SUPER-OCTAVE or FIFTEENTH, 2 FT., derived in form and scale from the PRINCIPAL, 8 FT., and corroborating the third upper partial tone of the foundation unison or prime tone.

REGULA MINOR, Lat.—The ordinary open metal OCTAVE, 4 FT., belonging to the foundation work, and corroborating the first upper partial tone of the unison prime tone yielded by the PRINCIPAL, 8 FT.

REGULA MIXTA, Lat.—A MIXTURE or compound harmonic-corroborating stop of several ranks of pipes. See MIXTURE.

REGULA PRIMARIA, Lat.—An open metal stop, of full scale and unison pitch, identical with the English OPEN DIAPASON and the German PRINCIPAL, 8 FT.

REIM, Ger.—The name given to a Pedal Organ reed stop, of 16 ft. pitch, having a good mixing quality. An example is to be found in the pedal department of sixteen stops in the Organ in the Cathedral of Bremen, constructed by Schulze, of Paulinzelle.

RINFORZO A LINGUE, Ital.—A stop, of 16 ft. pitch, formed of free reeds without resonant tubes, resembling the PHYSHARMONICA of the Organ in the Cathedral of Lucerne. The RINFORZO A LINGUE is only used where space is too limited for a proper reed stop, of 16 ft. pitch, furnished with resonant tubes. An example appears in the pedal department of the largest Organ in the Basilica of St. Peter, at Rome.

RIPIENO, Ital.—The name used by Italian organ builders for a MIXTURE. As the term *ripieno* signifies "filling-up," it is appropriately applied to a compound harmonic-corroborating stop of the Organ. MIXTURES of two, three, four, and five ranks are labeled RIPIENO DI DUE, RIPIENO DI TRE, RIPIENO DI QUATTRO, and RIPIENO DI CINQUE.

RIPIENFLÖTE or FÜLLFLÖTE, Ger.—A flute-toned stop, of 8 ft. pitch, used for filling up the volume of unison tone in a manual division, chiefly in the Hauptwerk or Great Organ. The term could be properly applied to the OFFENFLÖTE or CLARABELLA; also to the DOPPELFLÖTE, which possesses remarkable filling-up properties in all combinations in which it is introduced.

ROHRFLÖTE or ROHRSCHELLE, Ger. Dtch., ROERFLUIT.—A half-covered stop of wood or metal and of 8 ft., 4 ft., and 2 ft. pitch. The pipes forming this stop have their stoppers pierced with vertical holes, which so affect the internal air-columns as to produce a brighter intonation than is possible with pipes entirely covered. When the pipes are of metal they have either pierced stoppers of wood, or metal caps, from the center of which rise tubes of small dimensions, proportioned both in diameter and in length to the pipes they surmount.* In this latter form

* "De tous les bourdons métalliques, il est facile de faire une *Rohrflöte* en perçant la calotte et y dressant une cheminée du calibre tracé par le trou qu'on vient d'y faire. 'Elle doit être,' dit Dom Bedos, 'd'autant plus haute qu'on la fait grosse ; et plus elle est menue, plus elle doit être courte.' Il est juste, en effet, de proportionner la taille à la hauteur. 'Les plus grosses, ajoute-t-il, ont la moitié du diamètre du corps de tuyau. En ce cas, elles doivent être presque aussi hautes que le corps de leurs tuyaux.' Les plus petites ont le quart et même le demi-quart du diamètre. Le timbre donc tient à la fois du tuyau ouvert et du bourdon; mais il tient d'autant plus du tuyau ouvert, que la cheminée est plus grande et grosse; et d'autant plus du bourdon, que la cheminée est plus mince et basse. La douceur des *Rohrflöten* est toujours mélangée de finesse, et c'est avec raison que souvent les facteurs les préfèrent aux bourdons dans une grande masse de fonds de grosse taille, parce qu'elles en relèvent la rondeur."—Regnier.

the ROHRFLÖTE differs in no essential from the French FLÛTE À CHEMINÉE (*q. v.*). After speaking of the QUINTATEN, Helmholtz remarks: "Another variety of quality is produced by the *Rohrflöte.* Here a tube, open at both ends, is inserted in the cover of a stopped pipe, and in the examples I examined its length was that of an open pipe giving the fifth partial tone [fourth upper partial tone] of the prime tone of the stopped pipe. The fifth partial tone is thus proportionably stronger than the rather weak third partial [second upper partial tone] on these pipes, and the quality of tone becomes peculiarly bright." This brightness is certainly due to the prominence of the third-sounding upper partial tone in the compound tone of the pipe. The ROHRFLÖTE is occasionally made with two mouths, which greatly increase its power. See DOPPELROHRFLÖTE.

ROHRNASAT, Ger.—A half-covered stop of metal, of 2⅔ ft. pitch, the pipes of which are constructed in all respects similar to those of the metal ROHRFLÖTE (*q. v.*).

ROHRQUINTE, Ger.—A ROHRFLÖTE of wood or metal, of 10⅔ ft., 5⅓ ft., 2⅔ ft., or 1⅓ ft. pitch. The stop of 2⅔ ft. pitch is usually designated ROHRNASAT. The ROHRQUINTE, 5⅓ FT., is to be found in the pedal department of the Organ in the Church of St. Peter, Hamburg. The same stop appears in the Great division of the celebrated Organ at Haarlem; and the ROHRQUINTE, 10⅔ FT., is inserted in the Pedal Organ of the same instrument.

SACKBUT or SACBUT.—The name given to an early form of the orchestral Trombone. In organ nomenclature it appears as the term used to designate a Pedal Organ reed stop of 32 ft. pitch. Until recently a SACKBUT, 32 FT., appeared in the list of the Pedal Organ stops of the instrument in York Minster.

SALICIONAL or SALICET.—An open labial stop of cylindrical metal pipes, of medium scale, producing a string-tone less cutting than that of the GAMBA. It is introduced in English, French, and German Organs, chiefly of 8 ft. pitch; but it also appears of other pitches. Seidel says: "In the manual it is four, eight, or sixteen feet, in the pedal eight or sixteen feet, called SALICET-BASS." In the Third Manual of the Organ in the Cathedral of Riga are placed SALICIONALS of 16 ft. and 8 ft.; in the Second Manual is a SALICET, 4 FT.; and in the Fourth Manual is a SALICET, 2 FT. The last stop is rarely met with. The name of the stop appears in different spellings, but it is desirable to adopt the one which commences this article.* It is also desirable to follow Walcker's lead, as shown in the Riga Organ, applying the term SALICIONAL to the stops of 8 ft. and 16 ft., and the term SALICET to their diminutives of 4 ft. and 2 ft. This method, so far as the 8 ft. and 4 ft. stops are concerned, has been followed by Roosevelt, as in his Organ in the Church of the Incarnation, New York. The name SALICIONAL has occasionally been given to wood stops which imitate in tone the metal stops properly so called. Their pipes are usually square and have small mouths and harmonic bridges.

SAXOPHONE.—An open wood labial stop, of 8 ft. pitch, voiced in imitation of the tone of the Saxophone of the orchestra. This beautiful stop was invented by

*"Le *Salcional*, *Solcional* (on dit aussi *Salicional* et *Solicional*), ou *Salicet*, est un jeu de flûte ouverte dont les tuyaux sont fort étroits et dont les sons ont quelque analogie avec ceux de violoncelle. Ce jeu, qui se trouvait dans beaucoup d'orgues allemandes, s'est introduit depuis peu de temps dans celles de France."—Orgue de l'église royale de Saint-Denis: Rapport par J. Adrien de La Fage, 1844.

W. E. Haskell, organ builder, of Philadelphia, Pa.; and was first introduced in the Organ built by C. S. Haskell for the Church of the Holy Trinity, Philadelphia, in 1897. The imitative quality of this remarkable stop was tested, in our presence, by passages being alternately performed on it, and by a player on the orchestral Saxophone standing, close to the stop, in the interior of the Organ. The result was entirely satisfactory. For the description and illustration of the SAXOPHONE, see the Chapter on Wood Pipes.

SCHALMEI, Ger. Ital., SCIALUMÒ.—A reed stop, of 8 ft. pitch, the tone of which is supposed to imitate that of the old Schalmei or Shawm, the precursor of the modern Clarinet. See CHALUMEAU.

SCHARF, Ger.—A compound stop, composed of three, four, or five ranks of metal pipes, of high pitch, and voiced to produce a sharp and bright tone; hence its name. Wolfram says it is usually a three-rank stop, starting with a 15th, 19th, and 22nd; but this composition is not sufficiently acute. Seidel, on the other hand, says the SCHARF differs from the ordinary MIXTURE by having one of its ranks third-sounding; and gives the composition for the three ranks, 15th, 17th, and 19th; for four ranks, 15th, 17th, 19th, and 22nd; and for five ranks, 12th, 15th, 17th, 19th, and 22nd; The German builders made the SCHARF of pipes of too large a scale, and voiced it too cutting and piercing in tone. For modern work, it should be made of higher pitched pipes than those given above, having small scales, and being voiced a clear ringing tone, free from undue assertiveness. See ACUTA; also Chapter on the Compound Stops of the Organ.

SCHARFFLÖTE, Ger.—A metal labial stop of a sharp and bright flute-tone, and usually of 4 ft. pitch. It is valuable for imparting brightness to the Pedal Organ. It appears, in that department, in the large Organ in the Cathedral of Merseburg.

SCHLANGENROHR, Ger.—An old and now disused name for a reed stop, of 16 ft. pitch, better known as the SERPENT, 16 FT. (*q. v.*).

SCHWEIZERFLÖTE or SCHWEIZERPFEIFE, Ger.—Literally, *Swiss Flute*. An open labial stop of metal, and of 8 ft., 4 ft., and 2 ft. pitch. The pipes are of small scale and have low mouths, producing a tone between a flute- and string-tone, soft and pleasing in character. An example, of 8 ft. pitch, exists in the Echo division of the Organ in the Church of St. Maurice, at Halle.

SCHWIEGEL, Ger.—The name that has been sometimes used by old German builders to designate an open metal labial stop, of 8 ft., 4 ft., and 2 ft. pitch, the pipes of which had cylindrical bodies surmounted by truncated cones, leaving only small openings at top. The tone of this stop was very pleasing, partaking of the character of that of a half-covered, metal stop, but with a rounder intonation. The name (derived from *schweigen*—to be silent) signifies a stop of subdued voice.

SEPTIÈME, Fr.—A mutation or harmonic-corroborating stop, of $4\frac{4}{7}$ ft. pitch in the Pedal Organ, and $2\frac{2}{7}$ ft. and $1\frac{1}{7}$ ft. pitch in the manual divisions. The pipes are of cylindrical form and of medium scale, while the tone is similar to that of the usual mutation stops. The SEPTIÈME represents the sixth upper partial tone of the prime tone, produced by seven times the number of vibrations that belong to the prime tone. Although much higher partial tones are corroborated by stops in the Organ, the sixth upper partial tone has been very seldom corroborated by the introduction of the SEPTIÈME. The only example in an English Organ, with which we are acquainted, is to be found, under the name "SHARP TWENTIETH," in the instrument in the Collegiate Institution, Liverpool, built by Jackson, of that city, in 1850. The Organ in which the SEPTIÈME has been systematically introduced is that built by Cavaillé-Coll, in 1868, for the Cathedral of Notre-Dame, at Paris. In the Pedal Organ it appears of $4\frac{4}{7}$ ft. pitch, belonging to the 32 ft. harmonic series. In the Clavier des Bombardes it appears of $2\frac{2}{7}$ ft. pitch, belonging to the 16 ft. harmonic series; and in the Grand Chœur it appears of $1\frac{1}{7}$ ft. pitch, belonging to the 8 ft. harmonic series. See Chapter on the Tonal Structure of the Organ.

SERPENT.—A reed stop, of 16 ft. pitch, the tone of which is between those of the BASSOON and the TROMBONE, and is supposed to imitate the tone of the bass instrument invented by a Priest of Auxerre in the year 1590, to which, from its peculiar twisted shape, the name Serpent was given. The SERPENT, 16 FT., appears in the Second Pedal division of the Organ in the Münsterkirche of Ulm, and in the Schwell-Pedal division of the Organ in the Cathedral of Riga.

SESQUIALTERA.—A compound harmonic-corroborating stop, of two, three, four, or five ranks of open cylindrical pipes of metal. In every properly composed SESQUIALTERA two of its ranks must stand at the interval of a major sixth apart. This interval is secured by placing a fifth-sounding rank under a third-sounding one, as a 12th and 17th, or a 19th and 24th. Accordingly, a two-rank SESQUIALTERA can be composed, without breaks, of a 12th and 17th; or, with breaks, of a 26th and 31st, 19th and 24th, and a 12th and 17th. Octave- and fifth-sounding ranks can be added. See Chapter on the Compound Stops of the Organ.

SEVENTEENTH. Ital., DECIMA SETTIMA. Fr., TIERCE. Ger., TERZ or TERTIE. —A third-sounding mutation stop, of $1\frac{3}{5}$ ft. pitch in the manual divisions, standing a seventeenth above the unisons, and a major third above the OCTAVE, 4 FT.* The SEVENTEENTH corroborates the fourth upper partial tone of the prime or unison tone. On the Pedal Organ the SEVENTEENTH is of $3\frac{1}{5}$ ft. pitch, belonging to the 16 ft. harmonic series. When a SEVENTEENTH, $3\frac{1}{5}$ FT., appears in a manual division it is termed, by French builders, GROSSE TIERCE,† as in the Clavier des Bombardes of the Organ in the Church of Saint-Sulpice, at Paris. A DOUBLE TIERCE, $6\frac{2}{5}$ FT., under the simple name TERTIA, appears in the pedal department of the Organ in the Church at Perleberg; and another, under the name TERZBASS, $6\frac{2}{5}$ FT., is to be found in the Haupt-Pedal of the Organ in the Cathedral of Riga.

* "La TIERCE, jadis nommée par certains auteurs *Sesqui-Octava* et mieux *Sesqui-Quarta*, est un jeu ouvert de dix-neuf pouces, ou cinquante-un centimètres, de grosse taille, d'étain ou d'étoffe, selon qu'on veut lui donner ou lui ôter du tranchant. Il parle à la *Tierce* de la *Doublette*, par conséquent à la dixième du *Prestant;* c'est pourquoi les Italiens l'appellent quelquefois *Decima*. Au positif, on la désigne par le nom de *Petite-Tierce*, en opposition avec celle du grand orgue qui est de taille plus forte, mais de même degré. Les Allemands l'appellent *Terz* et *Tertia*, et encore *Dez*, abrégé de *Decima*."—Regnier.

† "La GROSSE-TIERCE parle à l'octave inférieure de la *Tierce* ordinaire, c'est-à-dire à la *Tierce* du *Prestant*, et à la dixième du huit-pieds. Elle est grosse taille, tout ouverte et d'étoffe, l'étain serait trop mordant. Pour que ce régistre fasse bon effet, il lui faut associer une grande masse de fonds, surtout en huit-pieds; un bourdon de seize ne nuira point. Le plus grand tuyau de la *Grosse-Tierce* a trois-pieds deux pouces, lorsqu'elle se trouve aux claviers de la main. En Allemagne, on la trouve en pédale de six-pieds, sous le nom de *Decem-Bass*."—Ibid.

SIFFLÖTE, Ger. Fr., SIFFLET.—A small open metal labial stop, of medium scale, and 1 ft. or 2 ft. pitch. It rarely appears as a fifth-sounding stop of 1⅓ ft. Two SIFFLÖTES of 1 ft. pitch are introduced in the Organ of the Church of Mühlhausen; and it appears of 2 ft. in the Organ of one of the Churches in Lübeck.

SINGENDREGAL, Ger.—An old reed stop which derived its appellation on account of the singing character of its voice. Both the stop and name are obsolete.

SPINDELFLÖTE, Ger. Eng., SPINDLE FLUTE.—An open metal flute-toned stop, of 8 ft., 4 ft., and 2 ft. pitch, named from the spindle-like form of its pipes, including their feet. The pipes have cylindrical bodies surmounted by conical portions, truncated, leaving small openings at top, and are tuned by means of large flexible ears. The SPINDELFLÖTE is almost identical with the SCHWIEGEL (*q. v.*).

SPITZFLÖTE, Ger. — Literally, *Spire Flute.* A metal labial stop, of 8 ft., 4 ft., and 2 ft. pitch. This stop derives its name from the tapering or conical form of its pipes, which are usually about one-third less in diameter at top than at the mouth line. These proportions seem to be preferred by English organ builders, while the GEMSHORN pipes (which are also conical in their bodies) are only about one-third the larger diameter at top. According to Seidel these treatments should be reversed. He says: "The pipes of the SPITZFLÖTE are more pointed than those of the GEMSHORN;" and this was probably the practice with old German builders. The tone of the SPITZFLÖTE is singularly pleasing, being of a light fluty quality inclining toward a string-tone. It is extremely valuable for insertion in the softer divisions of the Organ, where it furnishes desirable octave and super-octave stops. See FLÛTE POINTUE.

SPITZQUINTE, Ger.—A SPITZFLÖTE of 2⅔ ft. or 1⅓ ft. pitch. Like the octave-sounding stops, this is a valuable stop for the harmonic-corroborating work of the softer divisions of the Organ.

STARKGEDECKT, Ger.—A large-scaled covered stop, of 16 ft. pitch, the pipes of which are of wood, and voiced to yield a full and round tone of good mixing quality.*

STENTORPHONE.—Derived from the Greek Στέντωρ—Stentor, and φωνή—voice or sound. The term is employed to designate a large-scaled labial stop, of 8 ft. pitch, the pipes of which are cylindrical in form and made of thick metal. This stop is usually voiced on wind between 7 and 10 inches pressure, and yields a tone of great breadth, richness, and majesty. It is the most stentorian labial stop introduced in the Organ, and is highly suitable. for the Solo division, imparting a remarkable fulness to the powerful reeds commonly inserted there. Examples of the STENTORPHONE, 8 FT,. are to be found in the Solo divisions of the Organs in the Cathedral of the Incarnation, Garden City, L. I., and the Music Hall, Cincinnati, O. It is introduced in the Swell division of the Organ in Woolsey Hall, Yale University, where it speaks on wind of 10 inches. We are not aware of this stop, in its proper form, ever having been introduced in an English Organ.

STILLGEDECKT, Ger.—This name, which signifies a *quiet-toned covered stop*, is used by German builders to designate stops which are softer in their intonation

*"STARK-GEDACHT est un bourdon de seize fortement embouché et donnant aux flûtes ouvertes de huit un velouté et une profondeur remarquables."—Regnier.

than the LIEBLICHGEDECKTS. The STILLGEDECKT is usually made of wood, and of 8 ft. and 4 ft. pitch. An example, of 8 ft. pitch, exists in the Choir division of the Organ in the Town Church of Fulda; and one, of 4 ft. pitch, appears in the Echo division of the Organ in the Church of Waltershausen.

STOPPED DIAPASON. Ger., GEDECKT. Fr., BOURDON. Span., TAPADA or TAPADILLO.—A covered labial stop, of 8 ft. pitch in the manual divisions, and of 16 ft. pitch in the Pedal Organ. The pipes of the manual stop are either entirely of wood, or of wood in the bass and tenor octaves and metal in the treble. The Pedal Organ stop may be said to be invariably of wood. As there is no difficulty in carrying wood pipes throughout the manual compass, even when it extends to c^4, it is most undesirable to introduce metal. The old builders in England, and notably Father Smith, made their STOPPED DIAPASONS, 8 FT., of oak, and no better material could be used for the purpose. In the "Schedule" of the Organ constructed by Smith for the Temple Church, London, are mentioned two "GEDACKTS" of "wainescott"—a superior quality of straight-grained oak grown abroad.

SUABE FLUTE.—The name given to a soft and clear flute-toned wood stop, of 4 ft. pitch, invented by Mr. William Hill. The pipes are quadrangular, of medium scale, and have inverted mouths. Its tone lies between the tones of the CLARABELLA and the WALDFLÖTE, but is softer than either. It is difficult to understand the signification of the term *Suabe*, for it seems to have no appropriate derivation. It could be properly called SUAVE FLUTE from the Latin *suavis*—sweet, pleasant.

SUB-BASS. Ger., SUBBASS. Fr., SOUBASSE.—According to Wolfram, German builders used the name SUBBASS to designate pedal GEDECKTS, of 32 ft. and 16 ft. pitch, constructed of wood; and the practice of applying it to Pedal stops of both pitches is supported by the pedal department of the Organ built by Cavaillé-Coll for the Cathedral of Orléans, in which we find SOUBASSE, 32 FT., and SOUBASSE, 16 FT. It also appears as a manual stop, of 16 ft. pitch, in the same builder's Organs in the Cathedral of Notre-Dame, and the Church of Saint-Sulpice, at Paris. The SUBBASS, 16 FT., is to be found in the Pedal Organs of Walcker's large instruments in the Cathedrals of Riga and Ulm; while it appears, of 32 ft. pitch, in the pedal department of the Church of St. Michael, at Hamburg. In English instruments we find the term SUB-BASS used to designate both covered and open stops of 32 ft. pitch. In the pedal department of the Organ in the Temple Church the SUB-BASS, 32 FT., is a covered stop; while the SUB-BASS, 32 FT., in the same department of the Organ in the Town Hall of Leeds is an open stop of metal.

There is in connection with this name a proof of the freedom frequently exercised by organ builders in the terminology of their art; and it is somewhat difficult to decide to what particular form of stop the name SUB-BASS should be given and confined. As the name signifies "Under-Bass," it seems reasonable that it should be used to designate a covered stop of 16 ft. pitch in the manual divisions, and a covered stop of 32 ft. pitch in the Pedal Organ; and not for stops of both pitches in the pedal department, as in the Orléans Organ. It is certainly undesirable to apply the name to an open metal stop of 32 ft. pitch, as in the Leeds instrument. For other names under which the covered stop of 32 pitch appears, see CONTRA-BOURDON and SUB-BOURDON.

SUB-BOURDON.—A large-scaled covered stop, of 32 ft. pitch, commonly introduced in the Pedal Organ. An example appears in the Organ built by Willis for the Alexandra Palace, Muswell Hill, near London. For other names used to designate stops of this class, see CONTRA-BOURDON and SUB-BASS.

SUBPRINCIPAL or GROSSPRINCIPALBASS, Ger.—The open stop, of 32 ft. pitch, belonging to the Pedal Organ, called by English builders the DOUBLE OPEN DIAPASON, 32 FT. Under the name of SUBPRINCIPAL, this important stop is to be found in the pedal department of the celebrated Organ in the Cathedral of St. Bavon, at Haarlem, and in the same department of the Organ in the Parish Church of Doncaster. See DOUBLE OPEN DIAPASON.

SUBTILREGAL, Ger.—A reed stop apparently similar in tone to the GEDÄMPFTREGAL (*q. v.*), its tone being of a subdued character. As in the case of the other varieties of the REGAL, it is obsolete.

SUPER-OCTAVE.—The stop sounding two octaves above the foundation unison tones of the manual and pedal departments of the Organ, being of 2 ft. pitch in the former and of 4 ft. pitch in the latter department. See FIFTEENTH.

TAPADA or TAPADILLO, Span.—The name used by Spanish organ builders for a covered stop, similar to the English STOPPED DIAPASON and the German GEDECKT (*q. v.*).

TENTH, Ital., DECIMA. Fr., GROSSE TIERCE. Ger., TERZ.—A third-sounding mutation or harmonic-corroborating stop, belonging to the 16 ft. harmonic series in the manual divisions, where it is of 3⅕ ft. pitch; and to the 32 ft. harmonic series in the Pedal Organ, where it is of 6⅖ ft. pitch. In both cases it corroborates the fourth upper partial tone of the prime or fundamental tone, as produced by the DOUBLE OPEN DIAPASON, 16 FT., in the manual department, and the DOUBLE OPEN DIAPASON, 32 FT., in the Pedal Organ.

The manual TENTH, 3⅕ FT., is formed of cylindrical metal pipes, and should be of medium scale; but the Pedal Organ TENTH, 6⅖ FT., is more frequently constructed of wood than of metal. In neither department should the stop be voiced to be very assertive in tone.

The stop, under the name TERZBASS, 6⅖ FT., appears in the pedal department of the Organ in the Cathedral of Riga. We agree with Töpfer that BASSTERZ would be the better term. It appears under the name TERTIA, 6⅖ FT., in the same department of the Organ in the Church at Perleberg; under the name GROSSE TIERCE, 3⅕ FT.,* in the Clavier des Bombardes of the Organ in the Church of Saint-Sulpice, at Paris; and under the name of TERZ, 3⅕ FT., in the Hauptwerk of the Organ in the Cathedral of Ulm. The extended term TERZENBASS, 6⅖ FT., has also been used by German builders. See SEVENTEENTH.

TERPODION, Grk.—The musical instrument which has given this name to an organ stop was invented by David Buschmann, of Hamburg, in 1816. It resembled a Piano-forte, but its sounds were produced from bars of wood struck by hammers commanded by a clavier action. The organ stop to which the name of this instrument was originally given is described by Seidel as of metal and of 8 ft. pitch; the example which stands in the Fourth Manual of J. F. Schulze's Organ

* See SEVENTEENTH—Second Note to same.

in the Cathedral of Halberstadt producing, in combination with the LIEBLICH-GEDECKTS, of 16 ft. and 8 ft. pitch, and the HARMONICA, 8 FT., an imitation of the tones of Buschmann's instrument. Examples of the TERPODION, 8 FT., exist in the Swell division of Schulze's Organ in the Cathedral of Bremen, in the Echo division of the same builder's Organ in the Marienkirche of Lübeck, and in the Swell division of the Organ built by the late Edmund Schulze for the Parish Church of Doncaster. As made by the latter master, the stop is of cylindrical metal pipes which have low and wide mouths, and yield tones of a pronounced reedy quality.

TERTIAN, Ger.—A compound harmonic-corroborating stop, formed of two ranks of open metal pipes, which stand at the interval of a third apart. The position is, accordingly, an inversion of that of the SESQUIALTERA, the third-sounding rank being larger, or lower in pitch, than the fifth-sounding one. The TERTIAN is composed of ranks of $1\frac{3}{5}$ ft. and $1\frac{1}{3}$ ft. pitch when it belongs to the 8 ft. harmonic series; and of ranks of $3\frac{1}{5}$ ft. and $2\frac{2}{3}$ ft. pitch when it belongs to the 16 ft. harmonic series. Seidel tells us that in some old Organs the TERTIAN was composed of three ranks; namely, of 4 ft., $3\frac{1}{5}$ ft., and $2\frac{2}{3}$ ft. pitch, respectively.

THIRTY-FIRST. Ital., TRIGESIMA PRIMA.—A third-sounding MIXTURE rank corroborating a high upper partial tone of the super-octave (2 ft. pitch) stops; its extremely acute pitch preventing its being considered, in anything save a purely philosophical sense, as belonging to a lower harmonic series. From the smallness of the pipes forming this rank, it can only be introduced in the bass octave of the manual MIXTURE. While it appears to have been used, in some fashion, by the Italian organ builders, as in one of the Organs in Milan Cathedral, we are not aware of this extremely acute third-sounding rank ever having been introduced in an English MIXTURE.

THIRTY-SIXTH. Ital., TRIGESIMA SESTA.—An octave-sounding MIXTURE rank, corroborating a high upper partial tone of the super-octave stops (2 ft. pitch) in the manual department. It cannot be considered, save in a purely philosophical sense, as belonging to a harmonic series of a lower pitch. From the smallness of the pipes forming this rank, it can only be introduced in the bass octave of a MIXTURE. It appears, as in the case of the THIRTY-FIRST (*q. v.*), in one of the Organs in Milan Cathedral, and also in other Italian instruments; but we have not found the THIRTY-SIXTH mentioned in the composition of any MIXTURE of English, French, or German origin.

THIRTY-THIRD. Ital., TRIGESIMA TERZA.—A fifth-sounding MIXTURE rank, corroborating the fourth upper partial in the 2 ft. harmonic series. Except in a purely philosophical sense, it cannot well be considered as belonging to a lower harmonic series. Harris introduced the THIRTY-THIRD, in conjunction with the TWENTY-NINTH, in the bass octave of his two-rank MIXTURE in the Organ erected by him in the Church of St. Peter, Mancroft, Norwich. It appears, in conjunction with the THIRTY-SIXTH, in the North Organ in Milan Cathedral. It is also to be found in other Italian instruments of note.

TIBIA, Lat. (Signifying a *Pipe* or *Flute*).—This name with certain additions has been used to designate different flute-toned stops of the Organ. For instance: TIBIA MAJOR is a large-scaled covered wood stop, of 16 ft. pitch, similar in all essentials to the BOURDON, 16 FT.; TIBIA ANGUSTA is the German DULZFLÖTE; TIBIA SYLVESTRIS is the WALDFLÖTE; TIBIA VULGARIS is the BLOCKFLÖTE; and TIBIA BIFARIS is a flute-toned stop, the pipes of which have double mouths. See BIFARA.

TRAVERSFLÖTE, Ger. Ital., FLAUTO TRAVERSO.—The stop which closely imitates the tone of the German or orchestral Flute. See FLAUTO TRAVERSO and ORCHESTRAL FLUTE.

TRICHTERREGAL, Ger.—Literally, *Funnel Regal*. A reed stop of the REGAL class furnished with funnel-shaped resonators. A TRICHTERREGAL, 8 FT., is to be found in the Organ built by Schnittker for the Church of St. Jacobi, Hamburg.

TROMBA, Ital.—Italian organ builders have employed this term to designate reed stops of the TRUMPET class, of both 8 ft. and 16 ft. pitch, as in the Organ in the Church of St. Alessandro, at Milan. In Spanish and Portuguese Organs we find stops labeled TROMBA REAL (Royal Trumpet), and TROMBA BATALHA (Battle Trumpet).

TROMBONE.—A powerful reed stop of 8 ft. and 16 ft. pitch in the manual divisions of the Organ, and 16 ft. and 32 ft. pitch in the pedal department. In tone this stop imitates the orchestral Trombones at their full intonation. The tubes of the TROMBONE are of inverted conical form, similar to those of the TRUMPET, and are of large scale. See POSAUNE.

TROMPETTE HARMONIQUE, Fr.—The stop first introduced by Cavaillé-Coll in the Organ of the Royal Church of Saint-Denis, near Paris. The pipes of this stop have longer tubes than those of the ordinary TRUMPET, and are overblown. See HARMONIC TRUMPET.

TRUMPET. Ger., TROMPETE. Fr., TROMPETTE.—This is probably, taken generally, the most important reed stop in the Organ, adding richness and dignity to every combination of stops into which it enters.* So important and useful is a good TRUMPET, 8 FT., that no Organ of any pretension is built without one. The

* "La TROMPETTE est le régistre d'anches le plus pur, le plus rond, le plus fin d'harmonie et de sonorité, quand il est bien fait; le plus désagréable, quand il est manqué. Chose singulière il réussit moins souvent en Allemagne qu'en France; j'ai déjà cherché la raison de cette différence dans la différence d'allures des deux nations: le bruit guerrier, l'éclat, tout ce qui tend à accentuer la musique, et à mieux marquer son rhythme, semble être de notre domaine. De leur côté, les facteurs allemands se vengent de la maigreur de leurs *Trompettes* par la variété, la finesse mélancolique de leurs jeux de fonds.

"Une bonne *Trompette* doit avoir le tuyau un peu plus long que de rigueur, de grosse taille et de solide épaisseur, en étain fin et bien battu, posé sur un-pied inébranlable et bien proportionné en hauteur et en embouchure. La languette, de laiton fortement écroui, médiocrement recourbée à l'entrée de l'anche, s'y posera bien également sans dévier, et sera comme cette anche de largeur et d'épaisseur proportionnées à la vigueur du courant d'air contre lequel elle combat. Le tuyau trop long ferait octavier; trop court, il pourrait donner un son plus tranchant, mais criard. Trop d'épaisseur serait inutile, et la minceur ferait grincer le tuyau. La languette trop lâche fait râler le son, trop ferme ou déviée de son aplomb, courbée trop haut ou trop bas, elle devient capricieuse, raide jusqu'au mutisme. Les justes proportions du tuyau de *Trompette* combinées avec celles du vent doivent donner un son égal, brillant sans trop d'éclat, mais mâle et doux à la fois. C'est cette dernière qualité, si rare que les bons accordeurs distinguent au bourdon qui ressort toujours d'une *Trompette* arrivée à sa juste harmonie. Toutes ces perfections doivent se trouver dans chaque tuyau séparément, et dans tous comparés l'un à l'autre. Il faut y joindre enfin celle d'une grande promptitude et netteté de langage.

"La taille des *Trompettes* doit être en rapport avec leur place; ainsi, la pédale de *Trompette* sera de plus forte taille que celle qui chante à la main; celle du récit, plus délicate que celle du grand orgue. Quoiqu'on joue avantageusement la *Trompette* seule, l'alliance de ces octaves extrêmes avec celles du *Clairon* lui donne une grande vigueur, surtout à la pédale; l'habitude de certains facteurs de loger sur un seul clavier deux *Trompettes* de moyenne taille ne vaut rien, parce qu'elles sont rarement d'accord, et qu'il vaut mieux un seul instrument de forte taille, dont les vibrations aient l'avantage de la clarté et de l'unité."—Regnier.

proper tone of the TRUMPET is imitative of that of the orchestral instrument; and there is almost unlimited scope for the skill of the reed voicer in the production of this stop. The tubes of the TRUMPET are of metal and of inverted conical form and normal speaking lengths.

TUBA or TUBA MIRABILIS.—A reed stop of the TRUMPET class, but distinguished from the ordinary TRUMPET by its powerful and commanding voice. Its pipes have resonant tubes of large scale and normal speaking length, and are voiced on high-pressure wind, varying from 10 inches to 30 inches. Much higher pressures have been proposed for this stop; but, in the name of musical art, if not of common sense, it is to be hoped that such proposals will be condemned by every person possessing musical sense and taste.* The four powerful reed stops in the Solo division of the Concert Organ in St. George's Hall, Liverpool, speak on wind of 22 inches, and their tones dominate those of all the remaining ninety-six speaking stops combined.

Three TUBAS of the following names and pitches are inserted in the Solo division of the Concert Organ in the Centennial Hall, Sydney, N. S.W.: CONTRA-TUBA, 16 FT., TUBA, 8 FT., and TUBA CLARION, 4 FT. Under the name of TUBA MIRABILIS, 8 FT., the stop is to be found in the Solo divisions of the Organs in Westminster Abbey, the Cathedral of the Incarnation, Garden City, L. I., and the Music Hall, Cincinnati, O., U. S. A. It also appears in the First Manual of the Organ in the Cathedral of Riga. A TUBA, 16 FT., is to be found in the Great division of Schulze's Organ in the Town Hall of Düsseldorf; and a TUBA MAGNA, 16 FT., exists in the Grand Chœur of Cavaillé-Coll's Organ in the Cathedral of Notre-Dame, at Paris; and in the Récit expressif of the same builder's Organ in the Church of Saint-Ouen, at Rouen.

TUBA CLARION.—A powerfully-voiced reed stop, of 4 ft. pitch, commonly blown by wind of high pressure. The stop is, in other words, an OCTAVE TUBA, 4 FT., having all the tonal characteristics of the TUBA MIRABILIS, 8 FT. An example of the stop is to be found in the Solo division of the Organ in the Auditorium, at Chicago. See TUBA.

TWELFTH or OCTAVE QUINT. Ital., DUODECIMO.—A fifth-sounding mutation or harmonic-corroborating stop belonging to the 8 ft. harmonic series in the manual divisions, where it is of 2⅔ ft. pitch; and to the 16 ft. harmonic series in the Pedal Organ, where it is of 5⅓ ft. pitch. In both cases it corroborates the second upper partial tone of its prime or fundamental tone, as produced by the OPEN DIAPASON, 8 FT., in the manual department, and the OPEN DIAPASON, 16 FT., in the Pedal Organ. The TWELFTH is formed of cylindrical metal pipes, the scale of which should be smaller than that of the OCTAVE, 4 FT. As a rule, in the older Organs, the TWELFTH, 2⅔ FT., was made of too large a scale, and was much too loudly voiced. The practice of making the TWELFTH of the same scale as the OPEN DIAPASON cannot be too strongly condemned, for with so large a scale it is

* We have a pamphlet before us while we write, in which an apparently serious proposal is made, in connection with a Cathedral Organ, to insert a TUBA MIRABILIS, 8 FT., "voiced on 100 inches wind-pressure." This is even too serious to be treated with the ridicule it deserves. Steam whistles will be the next suggestion; for noise at any price must be the master idea of its proposer.

not possible to obtain the refined singing tone so desirable in this harmonic-corroborating stop. It is necessary to prevent the thickening effect that a badly proportioned stop is almost certain to exercise on the tone of the division in which it is placed, and this can only be accomplished by the adoption of a medium scale and a scientific or artistic adjustment of the strength of voice. See the Chapter on the Tonal Structure of the Organ.

The French builders commonly use the name QUINTE, 2⅔ FT., to designate the TWELFTH, as in the Organ in the Cathedral of Notre-Dame, at Paris. The term NASARD is also applied to a stop of the same pitch, as in the Récit expressif of the Organ in the Church of Saint-Sulpice, Paris. See NASARD.

The TWELFTH frequently enters into the composition of compound harmonic-corroborating stops; and as it requires to be covered by an octave-sounding stop or by the SUPER-OCTAVE, 2 FT., it is sometimes associated with that stop as a two-rank MIXTURE, for the convenience of the performer. See RAUSCHQUINTE.

TWENTY-FOURTH. Ital., VIGESIMA QUARTA.—A third-sounding MIXTURE rank, corroborating the ninth upper partial tone in the 8 ft. harmonic series, and the fourth upper partial tone in the 4 ft. harmonic series. The TWENTY-FOURTH does not often appear in modern MIXTURES, but it should always be introduced in those in which a third-sounding rank is used. The old English builders introduced it, along with the SEVENTEENTH, in many of their MIXTURES. When properly scaled and proportioned in tone, the TWENTY-FOURTH has a very good effect in the bass and tenor octaves. It appears, associated with the SEVENTEENTH (DECIMA SETTIMA), in the North Organ in Milan Cathedral.

TWENTY-NINTH. Ital., VIGESIMA NONA.—An octave-sounding MIXTURE rank, corroborating the seventh upper partial tone in the 4 ft. harmonic series, and, philosophically considered, the fifteenth upper partial tone in the 8 ft. harmonic series. The TWENTY-NINTH was commonly introduced in the acute MIXTURES of the old builders. It appears, associated with the TWENTY-SIXTH (VIGESIMA SESTA), in both the Organs in the Cathedral of Milan.

TWENTY-SECOND. Ital., VIGESIMA SECONDA.—An octave-sounding harmonic-corroborating rank, of 1 ft. pitch, commonly found in MIXTURE work, but sometimes as an independent stop, as in the Grand Chœur of the Organ in the Cathedral of Notre-Dame, and the Positif of the Organ in the Church of Saint-Sulpice, at Paris. In both these noted instruments it appears as a PICCOLO, 1 FT. The extremely small size of the pipes forming the TWENTY-SECOND renders it almost impossible to carry the stop throughout the manual compass. In MIXTURE work it is very seldom carried above the tenor octave. Associated with the NINETEENTH (DECIMA NONA) it appears in the North Organ, and separately in the South Organ, in the Cathedral of Milan.

TWENTY-SIXTH. Ital., VIGESIMA SESTA.—A fifth-sounding MIXTURE rank, corroborating the eleventh upper partial tone in the 8 ft. harmonic series, and the fifth upper partial tone in the 4 ft. harmonic series. The TWENTY-SIXTH appears in the majority of high-pitched MIXTURES, but never above middle $c\sharp^1$, and rarely going so high as that note. Associated with the TWENTY-NINTH (VIGESIMA NONA) it appears in the North Organ in Milan Cathedral.

UNDA MARIS, Lat.—Literally, *Wave of the Sea.* The name used to designate a softly-voiced stop, of 8 ft. pitch, the pipes of which are usually made of metal but sometimes of wood. This stop is properly tuned very slightly flatter than the unison pitch of the Organ, so that when it is drawn along with some soft-toned unison stop it produces a wave-like effect in the resultant tone. When the so-called UNDA MARIS is in its best form, it produces slow undulating beats that may be counted; and not the objectionable hurried flutter which too often characterizes it in Organs constructed by inartistic builders. How far it is desirable to introduce a stop of this class in an Organ is open to question; but it is quite certain it is not required in the performance of dignified organ music. The UNDA MARIS is to be found in numerous Organs by French and German builders, as in Walcker's Organ in the Cathedral of Riga, and in Cavaillé-Coll's Organs in the Cathedral of Notre-Dame, the Church of Saint-Sulpice, and the Palais du Trocadéro, at Paris; and in his Organs in the Town Hall of Manchester, and the Albert Hall, at Sheffield. The UNDA MARIS must not be confounded with the trembling VOIX CÉLESTES, the former being properly flute-toned and the latter string-toned in character.* See VOIX CÉLESTES.

UNTERSATZ, Ger. SUB-BOURDON.—A large-scaled covered stop of wood, of 32 ft. pitch. It appears in both manual and pedal departments. Under the name MANUAL-UNTERSATZ, it is to be found in the Great division of the Organ in St. Paul's Church, Frankfurt-am-Main. See CONTRA-BOURDON and SUB-BOURDON.

VIOLA, Ital.—The name correctly given to an open stop, of 8 ft. pitch, formed of metal or wood pipes of small scale, voiced to yield a string-tone of a fuller and broader character than that of the stop properly called the VIOLIN, 8 FT., while it is about the same strength of intonation. The tone should imitate as closely as practicable that of the orchestral Viola. The following names are found in Organs: In the Second Manual of the Organ in the Cathedral of Riga is a "VIOLA DI ALTA," 8 FT., and in the Fourth Manual is a VIOLA TREMOLO, 8 FT. In the Organ at Weingarten is a VIOLA DOUCE, 8 FT., and in the pedal department of the Riga Organ is a VIOLA of 4 ft. pitch.

VIOLA DA GAMBA, Ital. Fr., VIOLE DE GAMBE.—An open metal stop, of 8 ft. pitch, the pipes of which are of small scale and are usually cylindrical in form. They are sometimes conical, surmounted by a bell. See BELL GAMBA. When skilfully voiced on a moderate pressure of wind, this stop closely imitates the delicate and sympathetic tones of the Viola da Gamba, the precursor of the Violoncello. The Organ VIOLA DA GAMBA should in tone be quite distinct from, and subordinate to, the VIOLONCELLO, 8 FT.; and, accordingly, should be placed in a softer and accompanimental division of the Organ. The VIOLA DA GAMBA is to be found in nearly all German Organs of any importance, but it is rarely of a delicate

*"UNDA-MARIS. Flûte de huit, en bois ou en étoffe. Elle s'accorde une idée plus haut que la montre, avec laquelle ce désaccord doit faire constamment une légère oscillation, un *battement*, comme disent les accordeurs. Les ondulations que produit ce battement sont traduites par son nom latin d'*unda maris*. Son effet. assez bizarre, est plus sensible avec des jeux moins accentués que la montre; et quand ce dernier régistre est fortement embouché, il parle trop haut pour laisser entendre son auxiliaire. Quelquefois, l'*unda maris* est composée de manière à se passer de ses voisins; alors, comme la flûte double, appelée *bifara*, elle a deux bouches a chaque tuyau, mais sa puissance est d'autant moindre que les deux bouches sont alimentées par un seul pied."—Regnier.

or an imitative character of tone. The VIOLE DE GAMBE appears in almost all of Cavaillé-Coll's fine Organs, and in English Organs too numerous to mention.

VIOLA D'AMORE, Ital. Fr., VIOLE D'AMOUR.—A softly-voiced string-toned stop, of 8 ft. and 4 ft. pitch, formed of small-scaled open metal or wood pipes. Its tone when voiced by a master hand closely resembles that of the true Viola d'Amore thus described by Berlioz: "The quality of the Viole d'Amour is faint and sweet; there is something *seraphic* in it—partaking at once of the Viola and the harmonics of the Violin. It is peculiarly suitable to the legato style, to dreamy melodies, and to the expression of ecstatic or religious feelings." This brief description is sufficient to convey some idea of the peculiar tone of the Viola d'Amore to those who have not enjoyed the privilege of hearing the instrument performed upon—the privilege which has been frequently enjoyed by the writer.

The VIOLA D'AMORE of the Organ is the softest and sweetest of the imitative string-toned stops, and deserves a place in every Chamber Organ, and, indeed, in every Organ in which delicacy of intonation is aimed at. When formed of metal, the pipes are cylindrical and of small scale. Their mouths have either harmonic bridges, or the appliance called the *frein harmonique*. See the Chapter on Metal Pipes. Wood pipes may be used for the bass and tenor octaves. They may be made straight and of very small scale, with mouths fitted with harmonic-bridges; or they may be of conical form surmounted by a slotted bell. See the Chapter on Wood Pipes.

A VIOLE D'AMOUR, of 4 ft. pitch, is to be found in the Récit expressif of the Organ in the Church of Saint-Ouen, at Rouen. A stop of the same name, of 8 ft. pitch, in metal, exists in the Great division of the Organ in the Cathedral of Worcester, but it can hardly be classed as an imitative stop.

VIOLE À PAVILLON, Fr.—A string-toned labial stop, of 8 ft. pitch, the pipes of which have a conical body surmounted by a bell (*pavillon*), similar to those of the BELL GAMBA, and, like them, tuned by means of large flexible ears. The pipes are properly made of tin, and yield a delicate string-tone.

VIOLE D'ORCHESTRE, Fr.—The name given by the late William Thynne, organ builder, of London, to the stop constructed by him, which is, in our opinion, the most satisfactory imitation, as regards tone, of the orchestral Violin that has yet been produced. The stop is of unison or 8 ft. pitch, the pipes of which are of tin or fine spotted metal, of very small scale, slotted, and have their mouths fitted with metal harmonic-bridges. See the Chapter on Metal Pipes. In the formation of the VIOLE D'ORCHESTRE, Mr. Thynne followed the teaching of Edmund Schulze, but surpassed that great master of voicing in the perfection of his imitative tone.

VIOLE SOURDINE, Fr.—The name given by the late William Thynne, of London, to a delicately voiced string-toned stop, imitative of the tone of the muted Violin. It was first introduced by Mr. Thynne in the Organ now in Tewkesbury Abbey.

VIOLETTA, Ital.—Literally, *Small Viol*. The name properly used to designate a full string-toned stop, of 4 ft. pitch, the pipes of which are of small scale and made of tin. This stop is very valuable in combination with the unison, imitative string-toned stops, firmly corroborating their first and most important upper partial tone.

VIOLIN. Ital., VIOLINO. Fr., VIOLON. Ger., VIOLINE.—A stop, of 8 ft. pitch, which in its tone more or less closely resembles the characteristic tone of the orchestral Violin. This name appears at an early date, for in Father Smith's "Schedule" of his Organ in the Temple Church, dated 1688, we find "A Violl and Violin, of mettle, 61 pipes, 12 foote tone;" but, notwithstanding the early use of the name, it seems certain that the old builders knew nothing of a highly imitative stop such as we would consider worthy of representing the Violin in the stop appointment of the Organ. Even Seidel gives the name VIOLIN to an open metal stop, of 2 ft. pitch, "similar in tone to the OCTAVE." The modern use of the name appears to be extremely free and meaningless. On the one hand, we find in the pedal department of Schulze's Organ in the Church of St. Bartholomew, at Armley, a VIOLIN, 16 FT.; and then, turning to American organ-building, we find in the Choir division of the Organ in the Music Hall, at Cincinnati, a VIOLIN of 4 ft. pitch. In fact none of these stops can be correctly called a VIOLIN, for none of them is of the proper pitch or of an imitative character. To prevent confusion, it would be desirable to label the imitative stop either ORCHESTRAL VIOLIN or VIOLON D'ORCHESTRE, 8 FT.

The VIOLIN is properly constructed of cylindrical pipes, preferably of tin, of very small scale, slotted, and having mouths fitted with the harmonic-bridge. To produce the cutting tone with the rasping effect of the bow, characteristic of the sounds of the true Violin, a wind pressure of not less than 3½ inches is necessary. For further details, see the Chapter on Metal Pipes. Very satisfactory VIOLINS are made with wood pipes, but they are more difficult to voice than those of metal. As the orchestral Violin does not go below tenor G—commonly called fiddle G—the complete Organ stop may be appropriately labeled VIOLIN & VIOLONCELLO, 8 FT.; when only carried down to tenor C, it may be labeled VIOLIN & VIOLA, 8 FT.

VIOLINO.—An open metal stop, of 4 ft. pitch, which is practically an OCTAVE VIOLIN. The VIOLINO appears in the Swell divisions of the Organs in the Cincinnati Music Hall, and the Cathedral of the Incarnation, Garden City, L. I.; and a VIOLINO is inserted in the Choir division of the Organ in the Centennial Hall, at Sydney, N. S. W.

VIOLONCELLO, Ital. Fr., VIOLONCELLE.—An open stop, of 8 ft. pitch, the pipes of which are cylindrical when of metal and square when of wood, and of small scale. The mouths of the pipes are fitted with harmonic-bridges, and they are voiced in close imitation of the tones of the orchestral Violoncello. The VIOLONCELLO of the Organ, when voiced by a master hand, should be fuller and less cutting in tone than the VIOLON D'ORCHESTRE. A very fine example, voiced by the late William Thynne, of London, exists in the Solo division of the Organ built under his directions, and now in Tewkesbury Abbey. This stop is constructed of wood and metal. Another fine VIOLONCELLO, made by the master hand of the late Edmund Schulze, is to be found in the pedal department of the Organ in the Church of St. Bartholomew, Armley, Yorkshire. This stop is formed of small-scaled wood pipes. Although the VIOLONCELLO appears in almost every Organ of any pretensions to completeness, it is very seldom that one is found in any degree deserving of the name.

VIOLON D'AMOUR, Fr.—Under this name there is a softly-voiced string-toned stop, of 16 ft. pitch, in the Second Pedal division of the large Organ in the Church of St. Paul, Frankfurt-am-Main.

VIOLONE, Ital. Fr., VIOLON-BASSE.—An open stop of 16 ft. pitch, the pipes of which are of small scale and constructed of either wood or metal. It is strictly a Pedal Organ stop, and is accepted as the Organ equivalent to the orchestral Contra-Basso; and its excellence is judged in proportion to the closeness of its imitation of the tone of that instrument. Organ builders, accordingly, endeavor to impart to their VIOLONES as much of the harmonic richness of the Contra-Basso as their expedients in construction and skill in voicing can accomplish, aiming also to secure that peculiar rasping intonation which imitates the bow on string, and which is only heard in the finest specimens of the stop.

The usual metal VIOLONES, such as are met with in important English Organs, are of the GAMBA class, and slightly slow in speech, their notes sounding with more or less of a preparatory rasp. Representative examples exist in the Organs in the Royal Albert Hall, London, and the Alexandra Palace, Muswell Hill.

The VIOLONES, or VIOLONS, constructed of wood, and voiced on the German systems, are much more characteristic and effective stops. Fine examples exist in the Organs, built by Schulze, in the Church of St. Peter, Hindley, and the Parish Church of Doncaster. For illustrations and descriptions of these stops, see the Chapter on Wood Stops. The Hindley VIOLONBASS, 16 FT., is the most remarkable imitation, in tone, of the orchestral Contra-Basso we have ever heard. It is certainly the finest stop of its class in England. The VIOLON, 16 FT., in Schulze's Organ in the Marienkirche, at Lübeck, and the VIOLONBASS, 16 FT., in Walcker's Organ in St. Peter's Church, at Hamburg, are also representative examples.

As a rule the VIOLONES of the German builders are somewhat slow in speaking their full tones, and on that account are frequently drawn with another stop or "helper," such as a softly-toned covered FLUTE of 8 ft. pitch. In the pedal department of the Organ in the Stiftskirche, at Stuttgart, the VIOLON is of two ranks of pipes of 16 ft. and 8 ft. pitch—the stop proper and its helper. A VIOLONE, 16 FT., should be inserted in the pedal department of every Organ having any pretensions to completeness. It is, when properly voiced, one of the most beautiful and useful basses in the Organ.

VOIX CÉLESTE, Fr. Lat., VOX CŒLESTIS.—An open metal stop, of 8 ft. pitch, formed of small-scaled cylindrical pipes, either of the GAMBA or DULCIANA class, but preferably of the former. This stop is tuned to a slightly higher pitch than that of the other unison stops of the division in which it is placed. When drawn along with another unison stop, about its own strength of tone, it produces a peculiar tremulous effect, which one may safely pronounce to be a gross libel on the celestial voice. This tremolo is faster or slower, according to the extent the VOIX CÉLESTE it out of tune with its associated stop. The VOIX CÉLESTE was introduced by the French organ builders, and is quite in accord with the light musical taste of their nation. It is very seldom one hears a VOIX CÉLESTE that is agreeable to a musical ear: the one in Cavaillé-Coll's Organ in the Albert Hall, at Sheffield, which one might reasonably expect to be good, is unsatisfactory.

The only case in which we would advocate the introduction of a stop of this class, would be where there were several imitative string-toned stops inserted in any one manual division of an Organ, intended to represent the effect of a number of orchestral stringed instruments played together in unison. In such a case one of the stops might be tuned a beat or two sharp, with the view of imparting to the mass of string-tone a nervous character of intonation. If it is desired to heighten this tonal effect in a string-toned subdivision, a second unison may be tuned a beat or two flat. Nothing, however, approaching a disturbing tremolo should under any circumstances be tolerated. The VOIX CÉLESTE should never be inserted in a non-expressive division of the Organ.

VOIX ÉOLIENNE, Fr.—The name given by M. Cavaillé-Coll to a stop intended to produce an undulating effect in combination with the FLÛTE HARMONIQUE or the FLÛTE TRAVERSIÈRE, 8 FT. An example exists in the Récit expressif of the Grand Organ in the Church of Saint-Ouen, at Rouen.*

VOX ANGELICA, Lat. Fr., VOIX ANGÉLIQUE. Ital., FLAUTO ANGELICO. Ger., ENGELSTIMME.—This name appears to have been given, at the fancy of organ builders, to any description of stop which produced some specially beautiful and delicate quality of tone. It has, accordingly, been applied to both labial and reed stops. When applied to the former it correctly indicates an open metal stop, of 8 ft. pitch, the pipes of which are cylindrical and of very small scale, yielding the softest unison tone in the manual department of the Organ. Fine examples exist in the Echo divisions of Schulze's Organs in the Parish Church of Doncaster and the Church of St. Bartholomew, at Armley. The labial VOX ANGELICA may be either organ-toned or string-toned, according as it is voiced to approach the tones of the DULCIANA or the SALICIONAL or GAMBA.

Both Wolfram and Seidel describe the VOX ANGELICA as an 8 ft. reed stop, but do not give any particulars of its construction. The former writer says its name is the best part of it, which, when one thinks of what reed stops were in his day and country, may be freely accepted as true. Clarke describes the stop as formed of "free reed pipes of the most delicate voicing;" and in this form it appears in the Solo division of the Roosevelt Organ in the Church of St. Thomas, New York; and in the Choir division of the Organ in the Church of St. Paul, at Antwerp. Walcker has introduced a labial VOX ANGELICA, of 4 ft. pitch, in the Fourth Manual of the Organ in the Cathedral of Riga.

VOX HUMANA, Lat. Fr., VOIX HUMAINE. Ital., VOCE UMANA. Ger., MENSCHENSTIMME.—A reed stop, of 8 ft. pitch, the pipes of which, in the most satisfactory

*Alluding to this stop, M. Philbert remarks: "A Saint-Ouen, on rencontre encore un troisième jeu ondulant, la VOIX ÉOLIENNE, destiné à produire l'ondulation avec la FLÛTE HARMONIQUE. Il consiste en une rangée de tuyaux bouchés accordés à battements, et l'effet m'en a paru médiocrement satisfaisant, parce qu'il est un peu lourd. Ce que j'ai vu de mieux comme jeu ondulant destiné à agir sur une FLÛTE on un BOURDON, c'est le suavial de la Suisse allemande, formé de tuyaux ouverts, de taille à peu près identique à celle du SALICIONAL, mais dont le pied n'admet absolument qu'un filet d'air, de façon que le son propre en est extrêmement faible et se perd pour ainsi dire dans celui du jeu auquel on l'associe. La différence d'accord est en même temps très légère, au point que l'ondulation est à peine perceptible comme battement et ne fait qu'imprimer au timbre de la FLÛTE et surtout du BOURDON comme une teinte cristalline un peu vague réellement suave et empreinte de recueillement. Vogt aimait assez ce jeu et s'en servait habilement."—Causerie sur le Grand Orgue à Saint-Ouen de Rouen, p. 30.

examples, have resonators of cylindrical form, half-covered, and much shorter than the standard length of open pipes. Other forms of resonators have been used with varying, but less satisfactory, results. The stop is voiced with the view of producing tones in imitation of the human voice; hence its name: but even the best results that have hitherto been obtained fall far short of what is to be desired. The VOX HUMANA requires the aid of a TREMOLANT to impart the characteristic intonation to its voice; and that is much improved by the addition of a soft unison flute-tone, which imparts to it fulness, roundness, and body. The tonal and imitative effects of the VOX HUMANA depend to a large extent on the position it occupies, and the manner in which it is treated in an Organ; and its imitative quality is also greatly affected by the acoustical properties of the building in which the Organ is located. Of all the stops of the Organ, the VOX HUMANA is the one to which distance lends the greatest charm.

WALDFLÖTE, Ger. Dtch., WOUDFLUIT. Fr., FLÛTE DE BOIS.—Literally, *Forest Flute.* An open stop, properly of 4 ft. pitch, the pipes of which are of large scale, and of either wood or metal, preferably of the former material. In the best examples of the wood stop, the pipes have inverted mouths, and sunk blocks, voiced to produce a full and agreeable flute-tone approaching an imitative quality. The WALDFLÖTE, 4 FT., constructed of wood, is to be found in numerous English Organs, and in several instances is of tenor C compass. As a stop of 4 ft. pitch, it should always be carried throughout the manual compass.

Although the WALDFLÖTE is properly an octave stop, it has been made of other pitches. In the Organ in the Cathedral of Magdeburg it appears as a 4 ft. stop; but Walcker has inserted it of 2 ft. pitch in the Organs in the Cathedrals of Riga and Ulm, and the Marienkirche, at Lübeck. In the last it is of the SPITZFLÖTE form, and of tin.

Seidel describes the WALDFLÖTE (*Tibia sylvestris*) as an open labial stop, of large scale, and of 8 ft., 4 ft., 2 ft., and 1 ft. pitch; and its tone as being rather full and hollow. "As a fifth, 5⅓ ft., 2⅔ ft., or 1⅓ ft., it is called WALDQUINTE."

WIENERFLÖTE, Ger.—Literally, *Vienna Flute.* This appellation, as Locher correctly remarks, "lacks all etymological or historical foundation." The name, whatever its origin may have been, has been employed by certain German organ builders to designate an open stop of 8 ft. and 4 ft. pitch, the pipes of which are properly of wood and of small scale, voiced to imitate the tone of the orchestral Flute. Locher says it may correctly be called CONCERTFLÖTE. A fine example, of 8 ft. pitch, exists in the Third Manual division of the Organ in the Cathedral of Riga; and another appears in the same division of Walcker's Grand Organ in the Cathedral of St. Stephen, at Vienna.

ZARTFLÖTE, Ger.—The stop designated by this name was, according to Seidel, invented by the organ builder Tobias Turley, who first called it a GAMBA; but as its tone was of a tender and delicate fluty quality rather than of a stringy character, Wilke advised its inventor to adopt the more appropriate name ZARTFLÖTE. This stop is formed of small-scaled open pipes, usually of wood, and voiced to yield an extremely tender flute-tone; hence its name. It is made of both 8 ft. and 4 ft. pitch. As a stop of 8 ft. pitch, it appears in the Swell division of the Organ in the Church of St. Mary, at Wismar; and as a wood stop, of 4 ft. pitch, it is to be found in the Echo division of Schulze's fine Organ in the Marienkirche, at Lübeck. In the Echo division of the Organ in the Church of St. Bartholomew, at Armley, near Leeds, built by Edmund Schulze, there is a ZARTFLÖTE, 4 FT., formed of conical metal pipes from tenor C to c^4. The bass octave is of small-scaled wood pipes. This stop speaks on wind of 1½ inches, and has a voice of an extremely refined and soft flute-tone.

The name has been given by Mr. John W. Whiteley, of London, to a beautifully-toned stop invented by him in 1896. This stop, of 8 ft. and 4 ft. pitch, is formed of stopped metal pipes with projecting ears and cylindrical harmonic-bridges. The stop is a modification of QUINTATEN, with every suggestion of coarseness removed. Its voice is a light, bright, flute-tone, with sufficient reedy quality to give it a distinctive character. Full particulars of this stop will be found in the Chapter on Metal Pipes.

ZARTGEDECKT, Ger.—The name given to a covered stop, of small scale and 8 ft. pitch, producing a softer and sweeter tone than the LIEBLICHGEDECKT, 8 FT. The ZARTGEDECKT requires, for the production of its characteristic tone, to be voiced on wind of 1½ inches pressure.

ZAUBERFLÖTE, Ger.—A covered harmonic stop, invented by the late Mr. William Thynne, of London, and first introduced by him in the Organ placed in the Inventions Exhibition, at South Kensington, London, and which is now in Tewksbury Abbey. It is there of 4 ft. pitch, and is placed in the Choir Organ. In the ZAUBERFLÖTE, 4 FT., in the Organ built by Messrs. Beale & Thynne for St. John's Church, Richmond, Surrey—the last one voiced by Mr. Thynne—the harmonic pipes commence at tenor C; and, as they are stopped, they speak their first harmonic, or the second upper partial tone—the Twelfth. To prevent its speaking the ground tone, or that proper to its length, each pipe is pierced with a small hole, as in the case of the open pipes of the HARMONIC FLUTE. The tone of the ZAUBERFLÖTE is exceptional and of a peculiarly refined and sympathetic character, highly appreciated by those endowed with a sensitive ear for tonal coloring. The stop was also made of 8 ft. pitch by its inventor. Full particulars of the ZAUBERFLÖTE, with illustrations, will be found in the Chapter on Metal Pipes.

ZINKEN, Ger.—A reed stop made by the old German organ builders, and intended to imitate the tone of the obsolete wind instrument known as the Zinken,* or by the Italian name Cornetto Curvo. This instrument was a species of Hautboy, of large size, and having a somewhat coarse voice. Examples of the ZINKEN are very rare to-day; but one, of 8 ft. pitch, is to be found in the Great division of the Organ in the Church of Mühlhausen, and is the only reed stop in the division.

*"Although the *Zinken* is blown through a mouth-tube somewhat similar to that of a trumpet, it has finger-holes like a flute. Its sound is harsh, and would be unpleasant in a room, but the *Zinken* was intended for the open air, and for performing chorales on the towers of churches, so that all the people in the town could hear the solemn music. They were, in fact, compelled to hear, for it vibrated through the air over their heads like the church bells themselves. Thus the *Zinken* may have served its purpose well in olden time, notwithstanding its harshness of sound." From these remarks by Carl Engel, the character of the ZINKEN of the old Organs can be better realized.

CHAPTER XIV.

SUGGESTIONS FOR THE INTRODUCTION OF A SYSTEMATIC ORGAN STOP NOMENCLATURE.

IT must be obvious to every one, who has given the Organ and questions connected with it an ordinary amount of thoughtful attention, that there is not only room but also great call for improvement in the matter of its Stop Nomenclature. We venture to say, without much fear of contradiction, that the loose and heterogeneous fashion in which the speaking stops of the Organ are commonly named is unworthy of the present advanced state of the organ builder's art. Our remarks apply especially to the English and American systems—if systems they can be called—of naming the stops; for although the builders of Germany, France, and other Continental countries, generally speaking, show no universally accepted system in their stop nomenclature, they have never shown themselves so whimsical and absolutely unmethodical as English and American builders have always been.

In an interesting article from the pen of the distinguished organist, the late Mr. Frederick Archer, entitled "Uniformity in Organ-Building,"* are the following pertinent remarks: "With respect to the nomenclature of stops much confusion exists, mainly on account of the desire of some builders to differ from their contemporaries in this particular. The system, indeed, whereby the English and American builders distinguish the various classes of organ registers is radically wrong in principle, having no logical foundation, and much of the evil referred to may be primarily attributed to this circumstance." These words form a fitting text for the present Chapter.

In the course of the following remarks we shall be compelled to repeat to some extent what has been said in certain preceding Chapters. This repetition

* In the *Keynote*, New York, July 26, 1884.

is necessary to prevent many references,—always annoying and distracting to the reader,—and to secure clearness and connectedness throughout the course of our argument.

The nearest approach to a systematic stop nomenclature known to us is that met with in the largest Organ in the Basilica of St. Peter, at Rome. The following is a list of its stops; the left-hand column giving the Italian names, to which special attention is directed for our immediate purpose, while the English equivalents appear in the right-hand column:—

GREAT ORGAN.

1.	Principale Doppio, Soprano e Basso	Double Diapason, Treble and Bass.
2.	Principale Primo, Soprano	First Open Diapason, Treble.
	Principale Primo, Basso	First Open Diapason, Bass.
3.	Principale Secondo, Soprano	Second Open Diapason, Treble.
	Principale Secondo, Basso	Second Open Diapason, Bass.
4.	Principale Terzo, Soprano	Third Open Diapason, Treble.
5.	Flauto Traverso, Soprano e Basso	Orchestral Flute, Treble and Bass.
6.	Flauto Tedesco, Soprano	German Flute, Treble.
7.	Ottava, Soprano	Principal, Treble.
	Ottava, Basso	Principal, Bass.
8.	Duodecima	Twelfth.
9.	Decima quinta	Fifteenth.
10.	Ottavini, Basso e Soprano	Super-octave.
11.	Decima nona	Nineteenth.
12.	Vigesima seconda	Twenty-second.
13.	Vigesima nona	Twenty-ninth.
14.	Ripieno di quattro	Mixture, IV. ranks.
15.	Cornetto di cinque, Soprano	Cornet, V. ranks, Soprano.
16.	Tromba, Soprano	Trumpet, Treble.
	Tromba, Basso	Trumpet, Bass.
17.	Corno Inglese, Soprano	English Horn, Soprano.
	Fagotto, Basso	Bassoon, Bass.

SWELL ORGAN.

1.	Principale, Soprano	Open Diapason, Treble.
	Principale, Basso	Open Diapason, Bass.
2.	Ottava	Principal.
3.	Decima quinta	Fifteenth.
4.	Ripieno di cinque	Mixture, V. ranks.
5.	Oboe, Soprano	Hautboy, Treble.
6.	Tromba, Soprano	Trumpet, Treble
	Corno, Basso	Horn, Bass.

PEDAL ORGAN.

1.	PRINCIPALE, di 16	OPEN DIAPASON, 16 FT. (Metal).
2.	CONTRA-BASSO, di 16	OPEN DIAPASON, 16 FT. (Wood).
3.	PRINCIPALE, di 8	PRINCIPAL, 8 FT.
4.	RINFORZO A LINGUE	PHYSHARMONICA (Free reed).

While it might be somewhat difficult to extend such a system of Italian nomenclature to meet the demands of a modern Organ of the first magnitude, yet it certainly furnishes a satisfactory basis to work upon in formulating a system of stop nomenclature suitable for general adoption, as will be shown in the subsequent remarks.

The ordinary German system of stop nomenclature, though certainly better in some respects than our present heterogeneous and fanciful mode, is far from satisfactory. We can, however, learn something from it, especially in those directions in which it coincides with the more consistent and expressive Italian nomenclature. The same may be said of the French system as it appears in the representative type of French Organs.

In arranging a stop nomenclature which shall commend itself for general adoption, it is obvious that it must be formulated on a connected and intelligible system. It is essential that it should be capable of conveying to the mind a tolerably clear idea of the sounds produced by the respective stops; namely, their tonal qualities, their strength of voice, and their relationship to the fundamental unison sounds of the instrument. In the nomenclature we have nothing whatever to do with the *forms of pipes*, or with any of the many expedients resorted to by the organ builder to produce this or that variety of tone: it is with the *resultant sounds* we have to deal, and with them alone. Let this be steadily held in view. It seems remarkable that so self-evident a fact as this should have been so persistently overlooked or ignored by those interested in organ-building or organ playing; but that such has been the case the most superficial inspection of the representative Organs by the different English and American builders (leaving Continental builders out of the question) will be sufficient to prove. Unless the fact had been wilfully ignored, all the names which directly allude to the forms of pipes, and such fanciful and ambiguous names as AMOROSA, MELODIA, HARMONICA, DIVINARE, CŒLESTINA, DOLCAN, CLAVÄOLINE, TERPODION, and PHILOMELA, would never have been inscribed on the stop-handles of Organs. The last name may have been introduced by some conceited organ builder who thought he had produced an imitation of the notes of the nightingale; but what is one to think when one finds it in a Roosevelt Organ, given to a powerfully-voiced open wood stop, of 8 ft. pitch, the pipes of which require double mouths to give them the desired strength of tone? Clarke describes the PHILOMELA as of "small scale stopped wood pipes, voiced with the sweetest and most delicate quality." So much for the consistency and uniformity of modern stop nomenclature. The introduction of meaningless names can only have been the result of "the desire of some builders to differ from their contemporaries," as Mr. Archer correctly puts it; and their continued use evinces about as much sense as gave them birth. This remark induces us to mention the fact that, instead of displaying a sensible and modest desire to aid the simplification of an already embarrassing stop nomenclature, we find, in one quarter at least, a conceited desire to "differ from contemporaries," and to add further new-fangled names to the list. Why such names as HEDEIAPHON, TIBIA PLENA, TIBIA CLAUSA, TIBIA MOLLIS, TIBIA DURA, KALLIOPE, PHONEUMA, KINURA, etc., should at this time be introduced into English stop nomenclature is past reasonable comprehension; especially as they fail to convey to the mind any clear idea of the tones produced by the stops, allowing that they differ slightly from those produced by the stops constructed and voiced by other and more humble-minded builders. It is to be hoped that purchasers of Organs will object, sooner or later, to this stupid jumbling of half a dozen languages in the stop nomenclature of their instruments.

If a thoroughly consistent and expressive stop nomenclature could be arranged on some defined lines, and be generally adopted by English and American builders, the advantage to organists would be considerable; and a new Organ would not (as under present conditions it almost invariably does) require a special study and a somewhat prolonged trial before its tonal character is realized. The nomenclature of its stops, formulated on a definite and accepted system, would, at a glance, be practically sufficient to enable the skilled organist to form a correct conception of the tonal structure and musical capabilities of the instrument. Surely this would be an immense boon to organists, especially as they are now so frequently called upon to inaugurate new Organs, or to perform on large ones, of the tonal character and capabilities of which they have had little or no opportunity of acquiring a knowledge.

The first and most necessary proceeding, in approaching the consideration of a new stop nomenclature, is to carefully analyze the constitution of the Organ, so far as its tonal structure and appointment are concerned. Let us take for this purpose a large Concert-room Organ, which may be accepted as the highest essay of the organ builder's art. We must shut our eyes to the inscriptions at present on the draw-stop knobs or touches, and proceed to make ourselves acquainted with the different voices of the tonal forces of the instrument. The first result of our analysis is the separation of the voices into two grand groups, which may be set forth thus:—

FIRST GROUP,	SECOND GROUP,
Embracing Voices of Unimitative or Organ-Tone.	Embracing Voices of Imitative or Orchestral-Tone.

The first group embraces all those stops which produce tones essentially characteristic of organ pipes pure and simple; the second group embraces all the stops which yield tones resembling, to a greater or lesser degree, those which are characteristic of orchestral and other musical instruments. The perfection of these two groups or classes of stops depends, in the first case, on absolute individuality of voice, and, in the second case, on direct imitation of tone. In other words, the farther the organ-tone separates itself from any resemblance to the sounds producible by the instruments of the orchestra the more satisfactory it becomes. Take the voice of the finest type of English OPEN DIAPASON as an illustration of our meaning. On the other hand, the more perfectly the imitative voices, embraced in the second group, resemble in *timbre* and intonation the orchestral instruments they are intended to represent, the more beautiful and valuable they are deemed to be. The voices of the CLARINET, OBOE, FAGOTTO, and TRUMPET may be taken as examples. No musician or organist of the advanced school will, we venture to think, disagree with these simple propositions.

It is advisable to point out here, as has been stated in a preceding Chapter, and before further progress is made with the subject under consideration, that the line of demarkation between the organ-toned and orchestral-toned groups and their subdivisions is extremely difficult to define. There are certain stops which combine characteristics belonging to both the organ and orchestral qualities of tone, sometimes to a marked degree. Certain FLUTES and so-called GAMBAS furnish examples of this fact. The classification of all such stops, and consequently their nomenclature, will present difficulties which can only be met by a compromise. They are what may be called frontier stops, with an undecided tonal nationality.

Continuing our analysis, we find that the two grand groups into which the differently-toned voices are divided admit of subdivision, which materially aids the development of a satisfactory nomenclature. The subdivisions are as follows:—

FIRST GROUP.	SECOND GROUP.
Unimitative Voices.	*Imitative Voices.*
I. PURE ORGAN-TONE.	V. ORCHESTRAL FLUTE-TONE.
II. FREE ORGAN-TONE.	VI. ORCHESTRAL STRING-TONE.
III. FLUTE ORGAN-TONE.	VII. ORCHESTRAL REED-TONE.
IV. VIOL ORGAN-TONE.	VIII. ORCHESTRAL BRASS-TONE.

I. PURE ORGAN-TONE.—The first subdivision of the stops yielding pure organ-tone is certainly, and beyond all others, the most important; for from it the Organ derives its unique character, as a musical instrument, and the chief constituents of its grandeur and beauty. The stops comprised in this subdivision are, as we have already said, essentially unimitative in their voices; and, accordingly, their nomenclature should be special and connected, devoid of any tendency to divert the mind from their true nature and office. The most important stops, both in the manual and pedal departments, are those commonly known in English nomenclature as the OPEN DIAPASONS. These are unquestionably the *principal* stops of the Organ, from whatever point of view they may be considered, forming, as they do, the foundation of the entire tonal structure and appointment of the instrument.

At this point we enter directly on the subject of the present Chapter. The term *Diapason*, which has obtained in English organ nomenclature since the seventeenth century, is allowed by almost all good authorities to be anything but an expressive and satisfactory appellation with reference to the complete and all-important stops to which it has been, and continues to be, applied. The word *Diapason*, according to the Greek *διαπασῶν*, signifies *the Octave.* The word is further treated thus: "Gr. *διαπασῶν*, the concord of the first and last tones, more correctly written separately, *ἡ διὰ πασῶν*, an abbreviation of the phrase *ἡ διὰ πασῶν χορδῶν συμφωνία*, a concord through all the tones—that is, a concord of the two tones obtained by passing through all the tones."* It can only by a complete disregard of the true signification of the term be considered suitable for the designation of a stop or rank of pipes which invariably extends, in an unbroken form, throughout the entire compass of the Organ. The inappropriateness of the term, as applied to an organ stop, has been recognized by the German, Dutch, French, Italian, and Spanish organ builders, for in none of their stop nomenclatures does it appear. The French apply the term to the rule or scale used by the makers of wind instruments in determining the dimensions or proportions of the latter. They also use it in relation to musical pitch designating their standard pitch "*Diapason normal.*"

There have been arguments advanced in some quarters in favor of the retention of "the meaningless (but universally understood) 'Diapason,'" as the late Mr. F. Archer terms it in one of his articles on organ stop nomenclature, but we are strongly of opinion that this "meaningless" term should be discontinued, and a more expressive and appropriate one adopted in its stead. Indeed, it is impossible to imagine a satisfactory organ stop nomenclature to be possible without a new point of departure, or a proper base on which to build it up.

The stop to which the name OPEN DIAPASON has been given is invariably the chief or fundamental stop in all properly-appointed English and American Organs, both in their manual and pedal departments; and, such being the case, a name should be selected expressive of its position and office in the tonal scheme of the Organ. Reference to the Italian and German systems of stop nomenclature points directly to the proper term for our adoption. With their usual consistency in musical matters, the Italians have designated the chief foundation stop in their Organs by the obviously correct and common-sense name PRINCIPALE. The philosophical Germans have followed their lead in this matter. Can we do better than follow it also? That the so-called OPEN DIAPASON is the *principal stop* in all English and American Organs there can be no question.

In the article from the pen of Mr. Archer, above alluded to, we find the following remarks: "The German plan of substituting the word *Principal* for *Diapason* is much better, but it is inapplicable to English or American instruments, as builders of these nationalities use the term to designate an *octave* stop." † Now,

* "The Century Dictionary," p. 1594.

† This article, entitled "Organ Stop Nomenclature," was written by Mr. Archer, in 1886, as a review of previously published articles on the same subject by the author of the present treatise. Since then American organ builders have shown a disposition to abandon the term PRINCIPAL, 4 FT., in favor of the logical and correct term OCTAVE, 4 FT.; but they have not yet ventured so far as to abandon the "meaningless DIAPASON" in favor of the logical term PRINCIPALE or PRINCIPAL.

with all due deference to the opinion of one who was so great a master of the instrument he loved above all others, we cannot accept his dictum in the matter under consideration. Indeed, we will go farther and say, in direct opposition to his argument, that the very best reason why we should correctly and persistently apply the name PRINCIPAL to the fundamental and all-important unison stop * lies in the very fact that English and American organ builders and organists, at the present time, wrongly and illogically employ the term to designate an essentially subordinate octave and harmonic-corroborating stop. Do away with the inappropriate name DIAPASON altogether, use the perfectly appropriate term PRINCIPAL, or the Italian PRINCIPALE, in its place, and then find a consistent and expressive name for the stop now improperly designated PRINCIPAL, 4 FT., in English Organs. The new name is not difficult to find; for as this subordinate stop is simply an *octave* in pitch above that of the foundation unison stop, and an important member of the harmonic series of the foundation-work, it should be placed in its true relation to what we shall now designate the PRINCIPAL, 8 FT., under the simple and expressive name OCTAVE, 4 FT. These terms are supported by both Italian and German usage. So far the arrangement stands thus :—

Suggested Nomenclature.	*Italian.*	*Old English.*
PRINCIPAL	PRINCIPALE	OPEN DIAPASON.
OCTAVE	OTTAVA	PRINCIPAL.

Now, as all the other stops of the present subdivision are related to the PRINCIPAL in a definite harmonic series, their names should distinctly express that relationship ; accordingly the nomenclature extends itself in a perfectly sequential manner, as follows :—

Suggested Nomenclature.	*Italian.*	*Old English*
PRINCIPAL	PRINCIPALE	OPEN DIAPASON.
OCTAVE	OTTAVA	PRINCIPAL.
TWELFTH	DUODECIMA	TWELFTH.
SUPER-OCTAVE	DECIMA QUINTA	FIFTEENTH.
SEVENTEENTH	DECIMA SETTIMA	TIERCE.
NINETEENTH	DECIMA NONA	LARIGOT.
TWENTY-SECOND . . .	VIGESIMA SECONDA . . .	TWENTY-SECOND.

In inscribing the above names on the draw-stop knobs or touches, it would, of course, be desirable to add the standard lengths or pitches of the stops in plain figures. This proceeding would prevent any confusion arising between the stops of the same names in the manual and pedal departments. The standard length of the manual unison stops being 8 ft., the PRINCIPAL should be named accordingly. The pedal unisons are an octave below those of the manual in pitch, so the PRIN-

* In the stop nomenclature of the "Apollonicon Organ," erected (about the year 1850) by Bevington and Sons, in the Cyclorama, Colosseum, Regent's Park, London, we find, in the manual divisions, the term "UNISON" used instead of DIAPASON ; and the proper term OCTAVE instead of the term PRINCIPAL, 4 FT.

CIPAL of the Pedal Organ must be labeled 16 ft. When a stop, of 16 ft. pitch, of the PRINCIPAL class is inserted in any manual division (the stop now called DOUBLE OPEN DIAPASON, 16 FT.) it should, in our suggested nomenclature, be designated DOUBLE PRINCIPAL, 16 FT., or simply SUB-OCTAVE, 16 FT.; and in Italian, PRINCIPALE DOPPIO, 16 FT. In the Pedal Organ the same names will be applied to kindred stops of 32 ft. pitch.

So far as we have gone, the suggested nomenclature for the first subdivision, or stops of pure organ-tone, stands thus:—

Manual Department.	*Pedal Department.*
DOUBLE PRINCIPAL, 16 FT.	DOUBLE PRINCIPAL, 32 FT.
PRINCIPAL, 8 FT.	PRINCIPAL, 16 FT.
FIFTH, 5⅓ FT.*	FIFTH, 10⅔ FT.*
OCTAVE, 4 FT.	OCTAVE, 8 FT,
TENTH, 3⅕ FT.†	TENTH, 6⅖ FT.†
TWELFTH, 2⅔ FT.	TWELFTH, 5⅓ FT.
SUPER-OCTAVE, 2 FT.	SUPER-OCTAVE, 4 FT.
SEVENTEENTH, 1⅗ FT.	SEVENTEENTH, 3⅕ FT.
NINETEENTH, 1⅓ FT.	NINETEENTH, 2⅔ FT.
TWENTY-SECOND, 1 FT.	TWENTY-SECOND, 2 FT.

We have in this list employed English terms only, but Italian equivalents may be used if preferred. We may say that we are disposed to favor the adoption of a nomenclature entirely in the latter tongue. Italian is *par excellence* the language of music, just as it is the most musical of languages; and as such it is, we venture to think, better adapted for a stop nomenclature for international adoption than any other. Although Germany has from early times been the nursery of the Organ, and its stop nomenclature is extensive and to a considerable extent expressive, it is questionable if a stop nomenclature entirely in German would be favorably received outside the "Fatherland." Confining ourselves to England and America, we are of opinion, bearing in mind the names of many important stops now commonly used, that there would be less difficulty in procuring a general acceptance of a complete nomenclature in Italian than in our own mixed language. We need not enlarge on the fact that the terms used are much more euphonious in Italian than in English.

In the article already alluded to, from the pen of the late Frederick Archer, we

* The FIFTH, 5⅓ FT., belongs to the 16 ft. harmonic series; being the *Twelfth* above the SUB-OCTAVE or DOUBLE PRINCIPAL, 16 FT. To use the term TWELFTH, 5⅓ FT., here would cause some confusion where simplicity should reign supreme. It is expedient to calculate and name all intervals from the unison, represented by the PRINCIPAL, 8 FT. Should, however, the term FIFTH be objected to, as conveying the idea of an impossible harmonic upper partial tone, the name SUB-OCTAVE TWELFTH, 5⅓ FT., may be adopted.

The FIFTH, 10⅔ FT., belongs to the 32 ft. harmonic series; and, accordingly, the preceding remarks respecting the manual FIFTH, 5⅓ FT., apply in this case also.

† The TENTH, 3⅕ FT., belongs to the 16 ft. harmonic series, being the *Seventeenth* above the DOUBLE PRINCIPAL, 16 FT. It is a mutation stop corroborating the fourth upper partial tone of the 16 ft. prime tone.

The TENTH, 6⅖ FT., belongs to the 32 ft. harmonic series. It is the *Seventeenth* above the DOUBLE PRINCIPAL, 32 FT., of the Pedal Organ, corroborating its fourth upper partial tone.

find the following: "Registers of a foreign origin should certainly be permitted to retain their nationality so far as names are concerned, but all familiar stops are most easily recognized by a familiar name." We positively disagree with this proposition; for it is this thoughtless retention of the names which foreign organ builders have chosen to give their stops that has made our commonly-used stop nomenclature the jumble of names it is to-day. Glance at the stop handles or the stop lists of ninety-nine out of every hundred Organs existing in England and America, and you will find a heterogeneous collection of English, German, French, and Italian names, without method or order. And you may be glad if, out of the ninety-nine stop lists, you find a single collection in which the names in the different languages are orthographically correct.

To blindly and freely accept the name given by any organ builder who has devised, or may devise, some modification of a previously-existing stop, is, in the wide interests of art, paying too high a compliment to the ingenuity displayed. It must be allowed that a change in the usual mode of voicing, or an alteration in the shape or scale of a pipe, even though it results in a novel quality of tone, cannot be dignified by being pronounced *an invention;* and, until we do meet with a perfectly original work in this direction, we are in nowise bound to accept the name given by a German, Frenchman, Englishman, or American, to a stop he may lay claim to having introduced in his own Organs. He may have discovered, by accident or experiment, that some ordinary form of pipe, by being made larger or smaller in scale, by having a wider or narrower or higher or lower mouth, by having a perforation of a certain shape and size in some part of its body, by being subjected to some peculiar treatment in the process of voicing, or by being blown by a heavier or a lighter wind, produces an improved or new quality of tone; but surely he cannot under any of these circumstances lay claim to having *invented* a new stop. Modesty should prevent his giving a crack-jaw or new-fangled name to his foundling, and common sense should induce him to seek some simple name calculated to convey to the mind of the organist the exact place such a new voice occupies in the tonal scheme of the Organ. Surely this course would be more seemly than the searching of the Greek lexicon for a compound word which not one in ten thousand can understand. This is a matter we commend to the best consideration of musicians and all interested in the art of organ-building. So long as there exists "the desire of some builders to differ from their contemporaries in this particular," we cannot hope for the initiative to be taken voluntarily by them.

To return to the nomenclature of the important subdivision under review. A question presents itself for consideration at this point; namely, in the event of there being a duplication of the PRINCIPAL, 8 FT., in any manual division, how should the second one be named, so that its position in the tonal appointment of the division can be distinctly set forth? When two unison PRINCIPALS are thus introduced, one is invariably smaller in scale, and, accordingly, subordinate to the other. Such being the case, it is obvious that their respective names should be so qualified as to clearly indicate their relation to each other. In English nomenclature this may be done by designating the stops, respectively, FIRST PRINCIPAL, 8 FT., and SECOND PRINCIPAL, 8 FT.; LARGE PRINCIPAL, 8 FT., and SMALL PRINCIPAL,

8 FT.; or MAJOR PRINCIPAL, 8 FT., and MINOR PRINCIPAL, 8 FT. In Italian, the same stops may be individualized by the following names: PRINCIPALE PRIMO and PRINCIPALE SECONDO (as in the Organ in St. Peter's, at Rome, already alluded to); PRINCIPALE GRANDE and PRINCIPALE DOLCE; or PRINCIPALE MAGGIORE and PRINCIPALE MINORE. Unless two PRINCIPALS are introduced in one manual division, it is, of course, unnecessary to add any qualification to the single term; and, whatever differences in strength of tone may obtain between the PRINCIPALS in the different manual divisions of the Organ, they are simply PRINCIPALS of their respective divisions, and (so long as they all yield pure organ-tone) call for no qualifying terms.

The question now arises respecting the names most appropriate for those PRINCIPALS, of unison pitch, which yield free organ-tones, such as the stops to which the German organ builders have given the names GEIGENPRINCIPAL and HARFENPRINCIPAL; and the English organ builders the names VIOLIN DIAPASON, HORN DIAPASON, and BELL DIAPASON. As we maintain, as a standard rule, that the names of organ stops should, in all possible cases, give a more or less expressive idea of the tonal character and pitch of their voices, there would seem good reasons for the adoption of such compound terms as will convey information respecting such voices. Accordingly, when the chief unison stop in a manual division has a viol organ-tone it may properly be designated VIOL PRINCIPAL, 8 FT.; while that which yields an organ-tone inclining toward a horn-like *timbre* may be named HORN PRINCIPAL, 8 FT. No name should ever be given to the PRINCIPAL which merely alludes to the form of the pipes composing it. The musician, it must be remembered, has nothing to do (save as a matter of curiosity or interest in the art of pipe-making) with the forms of pipes or their modes of construction: it is with tones and tonal coloring alone that his art is concerned. The German organ builders do not seem to have fully grasped this self-evident fact, for a great number of their stops are named without any reference to their tones, and with direct reference to the forms and construction of their pipes. This fact will be realized on reference to the many German names given in our Chapter on the Names of Organ Stops.

So far as the important subdivision now under consideration is concerned, it only remains for us to add a few words respecting the nomenclature of the compound or harmonic-corroborating stops. In English and American Organs of late date fewer stops of this class are met with than in older instruments; accordingly less difficulty besets their nomenclature. As simplicity is all-important, we recommend the discontinuance of such names as SESQUIALTERA, CORNET, ACUTA, FURNITURE, CYMBAL, etc., and the adoption of the single term MIXTURE for all compound stops. But as this term is quite as vague, so far as the composition of the stop and its position in the harmonic series are concerned, we suggest that in addition to the word MIXTURE, the draw-stop knob or touch should present Roman numerals indicating the number of ranks composing the stop, and figures defining their grade or relative positions in the harmonic scheme. Under this simple system the draw-stop contrivances of three- and five-rank compound stops would present such inscriptions as the following:—

III.	V.
MIXTURE	MIXTURE
15 – 19 – 22	19 – 22 – 24 26 – 29

Such inscriptions give, at a glance, both the number of ranks and the initial compositions (on the CC note) or harmonic intervals of the stops—all the information the most exacting musician requires for his guidance. The Italian equivalent for the English term MIXTURE is RIPIENO (literally, *filling up*), a perfectly expressive name for a compound filling-up or harmonic-corroborating stop. If the term is used, it is only necessary to place it in the position of the word MIXTURE in the above stop-labels; or, if preferred, to employ the full Italian names for compound stops of two, three, four, and five ranks—RIPIENO DI DUE, RIPIENO DI TRE, RIPIENO DI QUATTRO, and RIPIENO DI CINQUE.

II. FREE ORGAN-TONE.—The second subdivision of the first group embraces stops which yield organ-tones of a more or less modified character. As we have said in our Chapter on the Tonal Appointment of the Organ, it is difficult to define the boundary line between pure organ-tone and free organ-tone; but in attempting to formulate a systematic stop nomenclature, we must place all those stops which yield tones differing in the slightest degree from that we define as pure organ-tone, in the second subdivision of unimitative voices. Chief among the few stops yielding free organ-tone are the DULCIANA, DOLCE, DOLCAN, VOX ANGELICA, SALICIONAL, MELODIA, FLÛTE À PAVILLON, KERAULOPHONE, and STENTORPHONE. The consistent nomenclature of such stops presents some difficulties both in the English and Italian languages; but as they are comparatively few in number and of minor importance, the renaming of them need not be laid much stress upon. The term SALICIONAL, derived from the Latin words *Salicis fistula*—a willow pipe, is commonly used to designate a medium-scaled metal stop yielding a bright tone inclining toward the viol character. It is difficult to associate it in any way with a willow pipe or whistle; and the term SALICIONAL has no expressive signification so far as quality of tone is concerned. As the name has been long established it is doubtful if any attempt should be made to find a more appropriate one—one directly expressive of the tonal character of the stop. In an Italian nomenclature the probable rendering would be SALCIONALE.

The term DULCIANA, derived from the Latin word *dulcis*—sweet, is fairly expressive of the sweet voice of the small-scaled metal stop to which it is usually given. The term deserves to be retained in English nomenclature, having been first introduced by an English organ builder in the year 1754. In an Italian nomenclature the term DOLCIATO (sweet) may be employed, if used as a substantive, or associated with some appropriate substantive. The term DOLCIANO, which would be appropriate, is at present used to designate a soft-toned reed stop, called by the German builders DULCIAN. See page 524.

The term DOLCE is Italian, and is indicative of the sweet tonal character of the small-scaled stop to which it has been given. As an adjective it is ambiguous when used alone, as if it was a substantive, but is expressive when used in conjunction with substantives, as in the names PRINCIPALE DOLCE, CORNO DOLCE, and

FLAUTO DOLCE. As the stop commonly labeled DOLCE, 8 FT., yields a free organ-tone, tinged with a slight stringy or nasal quality, the application of an expressive English name seems impossible; accordingly, the Italian term, now well understood, may be retained.

The term DOLCAN, derived from the Italian word *dolco*—mild, pleasant, is applied by German organ builders to a metal stop which is practically a variant of the so-called DOLCE. The general character of the stop, in its representative treatment, so closely resembles the DOLCE, that we suggest the general rejection of the term DOLCAN in favor of the Italian term. The multiplication of terms meaning the same thing is creative of confusion. There is not more difference in tonal character between the DOLCE and DOLCAN of one builder than there is between the DOLCE of one builder and the stop of the same name made by another builder. Under such circumstances, names would seem to be valueless, as, indeed, they very frequently are in inartistic work.

When we approach such a high-flown term as VOX ANGELICA, originally used to designate the softest and least important labial stop in the Organ, we may pause and question the propriety of retaining it. But as we have never had the pleasure of hearing the "voice angelical," or are never likely to hear it on this sublunary world, there is no fear of odious comparisons being drawn; and, as a fanciful name for a purely fancy stop, VOX ANGELICA may be retained in English nomenclature. In Italian the corresponding term is VOCE ANGELICA. We imagine the absurdity of the whole thing would be too evident were we straightforward enough to label the stop, in English and American Organs, ANGELIC VOICE. We have to resort to foreign languages to avoid ridicule.

The name VOX ANGELICA has, according to Clarke, been given to a reed stop of delicate intonation, but we know of no instance of this application. The name has also been incorrectly used to designate the compound stop usually labeled VOX CŒLESTIS or VOIX CÉLESTE, which is composed of, or which involves, two ranks of open metal pipes, one of which is tuned slightly sharper than the other, producing a compound tone of a tremulous character. This stop, in its tonal character, cannot be said to be complimentary to the "celestial voices," at least if it implies that they, like so many badly-trained human voices one so frequently hears in the concert-room, are affected with an everlasting wobble, politely called *vibrato*,* or that they can never sing together in perfect accord. However this may be, as the so-called VOX CŒLESTIS furnishes a specimen of organ trickery, in a mild form, the name may be accepted as a mild piece of sarcasm. The true absurdity of the term is only realized when one translates it into English, and labels the stop CELESTIAL VOICE, 8 FT. The term UNDA MARIS, signifying "wave of the sea," employed to designate a stop producing a wavy effect, is not quite so high-flown as the preceding terms, but is not a whit more correct or expressive, and accordingly its use is optional.

* "When the vibrato is really an emotional thrill it can be highly effective, as also the tremolo in extreme cases; but when, as is too often the case, it degenerates into a mannerism, its effect is either painful, ridiculous, or nauseous, entirely opposed to good taste and common sense, and to be severely reprehended in all students, whether of vocal or instrumental music."—Art. VIBRATO, in "A Dictionary of Music and Musicians."—Grove.

The term KERAULOPHON, or, more correctly, KERAULOPHONE, derived from the Greek words κέρος—a horn, αὐλός—a pipe or flute, φωνή—sound, employed to designate a stop yielding a horn-like tone, may be retained in English nomenclature, in which it first appeared, and in which numerous other terms derived, in the same manner, from Greek words are in common use. In Italian nomenclature the KERAULOPHONE may be labeled CORNO DOLCE. A stop so labeled exists in the Organ in St. George's Hall, Liverpool.

The French term FLÛTE À PAVILLON, along with the English equivalent BELL DIAPASON, should not be used in a consistent nomenclature; the stops so named are simply variants of the PRINCIPAL, 8 FT., and should be called PRINCIPALS, with such qualifying terms as will convey a clear idea of their special tonalities. As we have already said, in an expressive stop nomenclature we have nothing to do with the forms of the pipe-work, and this fact should never be forgotten.

The term STENTORPHONE, derived from the Greek words Στέντωρ—Stentor, and φωνή—sound, is expressive of the stentorian voice of the large-scaled and heavily-blown stop which it designates; and, accordingly, there is no reason for its rejection in the compilation of a systematic organ stop nomenclature.

III. FLUTE ORGAN-TONE.—Under the third subdivision numerous stops are embraced which yield tones having, more or less, a resemblance to the tonal character of the orchestral Flute. To these stops, formed either of wood or metal, different names have been given by English, German, French, Italian, and other European builders. The greater number of flute-toned stops are, in their true and original forms, constructed of wood, and owe their origin to German ingenuity, and, accordingly, bear at the present time German names. If we accept Mr. Frederick Archer's dictum that "registers of foreign origin should retain their nationality so far as names are concerned," then our English stop nomenclature should comprise such German, Italian and French names as the following: ANGENEHMGEDECKT, BLOCKFLÖTE, BOURDONALFLÖTE, DOPPELFLÖTE, DOPPELGEDECKT, DOPPELROHRFLÖTE, DOPPELSPITZFLÖTE, DULZFLÖTE, FELDFLÖTE, FERNFLÖTE, FLACHFLÖTE, FLAUTO AMABILE, FLAUTO AMOROSO, FLAUTO D'AMORE, FLAUTO DOLCE, FLAUTO TEDESCO, FLÖTENPRINCIPAL, FLÛTE À CHEMINÉE, FLÛTE À FUSEAU, FLÛTE À PYRAMIDE, FLÛTE POINTUE, GEDECKTFLÖTE, GROBGEDECKT, GROSSFLÖTE, HARMONIEFLÖTE, HELLFLÖTE, HOHLFLÖTE, LIEBLICHFLÖTE, LIEBLICHGEDECKT, RAUSCHFLÖTE, ROHRFLÖTE, SCHARFFLÖTE, SPITZFLÖTE, WALDFLÖTE, ZARTFLÖTE, etc.

We do not consider it either necessary or desirable to employ names which are, for the most part, of so ambiguous and fanciful a character; and until some more reasonable and expressive names are adopted, suitable for general acceptance, it will be impossible to secure the simplicity and clearness in stop nomenclature which are acknowledged, on all sides, as being most desirable in the present epoch of English and American organ-building.* In the note given below is

* On this branch of the present subject the following remarks, from Stainer and Barrett's "Dictionary of Musical Terms," are instructive: "As all open organ pipes of the *flue* class are made on the same principle as the *Flûte à bec*, it will be easily understood that *flutes* are one of the most essential class of organ stops. They are of two kinds—open and stopped, and are equally common in metal and wood. The construction of the stopped flute, so far as the mouthpiece (foot) and *lips* are concerned, is identical also with that of the *Flûte à bec*, only, of course, its first harmonic will be the twelfth, not the octave, of the primary sound. When organ builders describe

shown very clearly the absurdity of the present heterogeneous style of stop nomenclature, even in the single subdivision now under consideration. We certainly do not join Messrs. Stainer and Barrett in their idea that the names of organ stops should in any way be dictated by the *construction* of their pipes. They say: "If the names so chosen carried with them a hint as to the special construction of each register, it would be unfair to complain of their multiplication." We have said, in the earlier part of the present Chapter, that in the naming of organ stops we have nothing to do with their forms, materials, or peculiarities of construction: it is with their *tones*, and their *places in, and relations to, the general tonal structure of the Organ or any division of the Organ*, that we are directly concerned. This is a truth which appears to have always been overlooked or ignored by organ builders, especially in Germany, Holland, France, and England.

The first step to be taken toward a more satisfactory nomenclature for this subdivision is to throw aside every name which has no reference to the tones produced by the respective stops. This weeding-out must be done regardless of questions of nationality, or the conceit of accredited inventors. The few names which will remain in hand deserve due consideration.

Two facts assist in the simplification of the nomenclature. First, that distinctive qualities of flute organ-tone are very few in number; and, secondly, that only two or three of these qualities are introduced in any one division of the Organ at one time. Such being the case, it is unquestionably undesirable to retain in use so embarrassing a list of practically synonymous names as that now obtaining. To arrive at the simplest result, we would suggest the adoption, for all the stops yielding flute organ-tone, the simple term FLUTE, qualifying it, as required, to clearly indicate the position of each stop in, and its relation to, the tonal structure of the division in which it is placed. The organ builder, if he is an artist, introduces one or more stops of this class in each manual division of an Organ with a definite and well-considered aim. He apportions their tones with due reference to

some of their flute-stops as *Flauto traverso*, or *Flûte douce* (another name for the cross-flute), it must be understood that they have only imitated the quality of tone, not the construction of that instrument. By slight modifications of the shape of the different parts of a flute pipe, an almost endless variety of tone may be produced, and organ builders avail themselves of this fact to coin an endless variety of names. If the names so chosen carried with them a hint as to the special construction of each register, it would be unfair to complain of their multiplication; but, with a very few exceptions, this is not the case."

Here we join issue with the authors of the "Dictionary;" for it must be self-evident to every musician that it is with the *tone-color* and not "*the special construction*" of organ stops that one has to deal in forming an intelligible and useful stop nomenclature. What has an organist to do with the "*construction*" of organ pipes? It is surely with their voices, and their positions in the tonal appointment of his instrument, that he has to deal. But to resume the quotation:

"The following are some of the titles appended to flute-stops on English and foreign organs:

"(1) Describing their material, as Wood flute; *Woud*, and *Woude-fluit* (in Holland); Metal flute,

"(2) Stating whether the pipes are open or closed, as Open flute, *Flûte ouverte* (Fr.); Stopped flute; *Gedackt-flöte* (Ger.).

"(3) Showing the pitch of the stop, as Bass flute (16 ft. and 8 ft.); *Flautone* (16 ft.); *Flauto grave* (16 ft.); *Flute principal* (8 ft.); *Flute major* (8 ft.); *Unison flute* (8 ft.); *Flute minor* (4 ft.); *Flûte Octaviante* (4 ft.); *Quint-flöte* (5⅓ ft.); *Quintaton* (sounding unison and twelfth); Piccolo flute (2 ft.); Flautino (2 ft.); *Klein-flöte* (2 ft.); *Terz-flöte* (1⅗ ft.); *Flute discant; Flûte dessus* (treble flute).

"(4) Describing the shape of the pipes, as *Doppel-flöte* (with two mouths); Pyramid flute (having pipes larger at the top than at the mouth) [?]; *Flag fluit* (Dutch), *Flach-flöte* (Ger.) (having flat lips); *Spitz-flöte*

the general scheme of the instrument; and so that they may impart fulness to the complete tonal effect, variety to the numerous combinations, and furnish useful and pleasing solo and accompanimental qualities of tone. He cares, or should care, little about variety of shape in the pipes, still less about telling, on the stop knobs, that one stop has tapered pipes, another double mouths, or a third has stopped pipes: but he does care about their tones, and desires to record on the stop knobs such facts as are required by the performer; namely, that one FLUTE is a unison and another is an octave stop; and that one FLUTE is loud and assertive in tone, whilst another is soft or less prominent in the tonal scheme. It must be recognized that whatever descriptions of these stops he places in the Great, Swell, or Choir Organs, they are simply the FLUTES of the respective divisions: and it may be presumed, if an artistic conception has placed them there, that they are the proper FLUTES for their divisions and for the offices they have to fill therein.

We may now briefly allude to some of the more important unimitative flute-toned stops and the names under which they are at present known. One of the earliest introduced in English Organs is the STOPPED DIAPASON, a full-scaled covered unison, which, probably on account of its prominence among the covered stops, was dignified by this inappropriate name. It appears, so early as the year 1683, in Bernard Smith's agreement for the Durham Cathedral Organ. The name "GEDACKT" takes its place in the same builder's agreement for the Temple Church instrument, dated 1688. It occurs four times in this specification, all the stops so named being of wood. Early usage does not go sufficiently far to recommend the former name; while the latter German name (properly *Gedeckt*), which simply means *covered* or *stopped*,—alluding to the formation of the pipes of the stop and having no reference to the tone it produces,—is not desirable for an expressive nomenclature for present use.

Other flute-toned stops, apparently of German origin, bear names which are to be rejected, not only on account of their nationality, but also by reason of their

(Ger.), and *Flûte pointue* (Fr.) (having pipes smaller at the top than at the mouth); *Rohr-flöte* (Ger.), and *Flûte à Cheminée* (Fr.) (having a chimney in the stopper).

"(5) Intimating their quality of tone, as Full flute, *Hohl-flöte* (Ger.), and *Flûte creuse* (Fr.) (hollow-toned); Clear flute, *Hell-flöte* (Ger.); *Lieblich-flöte* (Ger.) (lovely-toned); *Zart-flöte* (Ger.) (delicately-voiced); *Flûte douce* (Fr.); Dulcet, *Flauto dolce* (It.) (sweet-toned); Oboe-flute; Clarinet-flute (slightly reedy in tone); *Sifflöte* (1 ft.) (whistle-flute).

"(6) After their supposed nationality, as German flute; *Flauto tedesca*, or *allemande; Flûte à bec*, or English flute; *Suabe flute; Schweizer-flöte* (Swiss flute, the German name for what was called in England the German flute); *Flauto Francese; Flute Ravena; Czakan flute.*

"(7) Implying that the quality of tone is similar to the modern flute, more powerful than the *Flûte à bec*, as Orchestral flute; *Flauto traverso* (It.); *Flûte traversière* (Fr.); and *Travers-flöte; Quer-flöte* (Ger.) (cross-flute); Concert flute.

"(8) Names which are merely *fancy* titles, as *Flûte d'amour; Jubal flute; Portunal flute;* Old flute, recorder (*Flûte à bec*), *Wald* and *Bauer-flöte* (Ger.) (pastoral pipe), Echo flute (soft-toned), *Flute tacet, Cordedain*, etc.

"It would be an advantage alike to organ builders and organists if some definite system of nomenclature of flute stops could be devised and universally adhered to."

With respect to the advantage alluded to in the last sentence, there can, we venture to think, be no diversity of opinion among organists; for to them the present confused and inexpressive nomenclature is perplexing, to say the least of it. We have, in the above quotation, taken some liberty with the punctuation of the original, which is very capricious and irregular. Imperfect as the orthography of the stop names is in several instances, we have, beyond a consistent use of capital letters, not made any corrections.

ambiguity. At the present time the names appear to be applied according to the whim or fancy of the organ builder. The HOHLFLÖTE may be taken as an illustration: the stop so called and made by so great an artist as the late Edmund Schulze, and one made by an ordinary English organ builder, bear so little resemblance to each other, *in tone*, that it is absurd and misleading to designate them by the same name. Similar remarks hold good with reference to the other German named stops of the flute-toned class. With reference to the few English and American names, such as CLARABELLA, CLARIBEL FLUTE, CLARINET FLUTE, MELODIA, NASON, OBOE FLUTE, PHILOMELA, SUABE FLUTE, etc., little need be said here, for it is to be hoped that ere long their place will know them no more.

For M. Cavaillé-Coll's clever introduction,—perhaps in this case we may say invention,—the so-called FLÛTE HARMONIQUE, some plea may reasonably be advanced for the retention of its name, especially as it can be correctly Anglicized in the term HARMONIC FLUTE. But is it really necessary to complicate our stop nomenclature with any such term? Let this valuable voice be introduced when the tonal scheme of an Organ requires a flute-tone of powerful and penetrating quality; but let it be labeled simply FLUTE, with the necessary qualification to indicate its position in the tonal scheme. Of qualifying terms we may now briefly speak.

As has already been remarked, in an artistically schemed Organ it is usual and desirable to place one or two flute-toned stops, of unison pitch, in each of its manual divisions. The stops will, of course, be selected on account of the value and variety of their tones, without any reference to, or regard for, the structural forms of their pipes, or the means adopted to produce their tones. Each division of the Organ will be of different power and tonal coloring; so, of necessity, no two FLUTES in the instrument will be of precisely the same form, scale, or intonation. In each division, the unison FLUTE will be proportioned to the office it holds and the work it has to do in connection with the other stops, and requires only to be named FLUTE, 8 FT. If two unison FLUTES, of unimitative character, are introduced in any one division, they will certainly be of different strengths of tone as well as of different tonal qualities. Under these circumstances it will be only necessary to call the one most prominent in tone FIRST FLUTE, LOUD FLUTE, or MAJOR FLUTE; or, in Italian, FLAUTO PRIMO, FLAUTO GRANDE, or FLAUTO MAGGIORE. The stop subordinate in tone will then be appropriately called SECOND FLUTE, SOFT FLUTE, or MINOR FLUTE; or, in Italian, FLAUTO SECONDO, FLAUTO DOLCE, or FLAUTO MINORE. The pitch of the stops should in all cases be added. In our opinion such names give all the information required by the organist, even should he be unacquainted with the instrument; but we can, in imagination, hear a chorus of objections to a nomenclature of so simple a character by those who profess to know a great deal about organ stops, and who urge that they require to know, when they draw a FLUTE, whether it is a HOHLFLÖTE, a ROHRFLÖTE, a STOPPED DIAPASON, or a HARMONIC FLUTE. Now if all the stops which pass under these names were respectively made and voiced to yield precisely the same tone, such demands would be deserving of all attention; but as there is as great a difference between the tones of the HOHLFLÖTES, ROHRFLÖTES, STOPPED DIAPASONS, and HARMONIC FLUTES of *different* makers as there commonly is between the tones of the HOHLFLÖTE and ROHRFLÖTE, or the STOPPED DIAPASON and HARMONIC FLUTE of any *one* maker, it must be allowed that such names are as valueless as they are confusing. At their best they give no reliable or direct information respecting their tones, not even as to their voices being loud or soft.

Flute-toned stops of 4 ft. pitch only require the addition of the word OCTAVE, or 4 ft. to the name FLUTE to clearly indicate, at a glance, their position in the tonal scheme of any division of the Organ. In like manner the word SUPER-OCTAVE, or 2 FT., may be used when necessary.

IV. VIOL ORGAN-TONE.—This peculiar quality of organ-tone is commonly known as *gamba-tone;* but it is difficult to imagine a more inappropriate term, the literal translation being *leg-tone.* Gamba is simply part of Viola da Gamba, the Italian name given to one of the larger instruments included in a "chest of Viols." This instrument may be accepted as the precursor of the Violoncello, and was, like the latter instrument, held between the knees of the player; hence its name Viola da Gamba—literally, *Leg-* or *Knee-Fiddle.* It may be argued that the widespread use of the term Gamba, and its acceptance as the general name for a certain class of organ stops, should plead for its retention in our stop nomenclature; but this we are not prepared to admit, chiefly because the wrong portion of the full name, from which it has been taken, has been selected. If, instead of using the meaningless word (so far as organ-tone is concerned), we use the perfectly appropriate term Viola (or viol organ-tone) no breach of consistency is perpetrated, and a clear idea is conveyed to the mind of the musician with reference to tonal character.

The Viola da Gamba is a six-stringed instrument played with a bow, having a soft, singing quality of string-tone, but devoid of the assertive and penetrating character of that of the Violoncello; accordingly the term Viol serves admirably to designate the quality of string-like organ-tone which cannot be properly classed as imitative of the present stringed instruments of the orchestra. It will be found amply sufficient for all purposes, and will render unnecessary several fanciful and meaningless names, such as ÆOLINE, FUGARA, KALOPHONE, SICILIENNE, etc.; and the compound names more commonly used, and wrongly devised from their allusion to the forms of pipes; namely, BEARDED GAMBA, BELL GAMBA, CONE GAMBA, GERMAN GAMBA, PIERCED GAMBA, and the like. It is only necessary to substitute the English words, *leg* or *knee*, to realize the absurdity of the above terms in organ nomenclature. The name VIOL lends itself, as in the case of the term FLUTE, to any qualification necessary to convey to the organist's mind the position in, or relation to, the tonal scheme of the Organ the stop so designated occupies. Examples of a consistent nomenclature for VIOL stops will be found in the Chapter on the Concert-room Organ.

The nomenclature appropriate for the orchestral-toned or *imitative* stops, embraced in the second group of our analytical scheme, does not present any noteworthy difficulties; and we venture to think that little, if any, diversity of opinion will obtain with respect to its simplicity and clearness.

The organ stops now to be named are all of a directly imitative character. In their formation and voicing, the organ builder has one aim and ambition; namely, to make them yield tones resembling, as closely as practicable, the sounds produced by the orchestral instruments they are designed to represent in the tonal appointment of the Organ.

In Organs of the first magnitude, and, indeed, in all Concert-room instruments, the imitative stops are of great importance. In fact, to so great a perfection have several of them been carried of late years by the skill of artistic builders, and to so great an extent have they been introduced, that they may be said to form a distinctive feature of the Concert-room Organ of to-day. The tendency of the advanced modern school of organ-playing is in a direction which will foster, rather than retard, the development and multiplication of imitative orchestral-toned stops; and the organ builder who distinguishes himself in artistic work of this class will rank high among the honored men of his craft. As such is the state of affairs, it is highly desirable that an expressive nomenclature for all the imitative stops should be clearly defined for general adoption. The following notes may aid in establishing a simple and satisfactory nomenclature.

V. Orchestral String-Tone.—The first subdivision of our second group comprises all those stops which are voiced in as close an imitation as possible of the tones of the orchestral stringed instruments—the Violin, Viola, Violoncello, and Double Bass. Many ingenious expedients have been resorted to, as will be seen on reference to our Chapters on the Construction of Wood and Metal Pipes, by different organ builders to produce qualities of tone, rich in harmonic upper partials, and having much of the crispness of intonation and the characteristic rasping effect of the bowed instruments; and it must be allowed that their efforts have in several cases been eminently successful. We have heard stops, voiced by the late Edmund Schulze, of Paulinzelle, so closely imitating the tones of the Violoncello and Contra-Basso as to be, under certain treatment on the part of the player, absolutely deceptive. An almost matchless Violoncello, 8 ft., exists in the Solo division of the Organ in Tewkesbury Abbey, voiced by the late William Thynne. This lamented artist made several Orchestral Violin stops of remarkable tonal character; and it is not too much to say that they have never yet been surpassed by any other voicer.

The nomenclature of the imitative string-toned stops should clearly indicate their nature and office. The term Violin should be strictly confined to a unison stop, imitating and having, to the greatest possible degree, the penetrating and brilliant intonation of the true Violin. As an organ stop it should be carried throughout the compass of the manuals, or nineteen notes below the range of the Violin. In certain cases it may be sufficient, for all practical purposes, to commence the stop at fiddle G. In Italian, this stop would be called Violino or Violino Principale, 8 ft. (Solo Violin). In small Organs, where only one stop of this class is inserted, it is desirable to label it Violin & Violoncello, as more accurately giving its downward range.

The single name Violoncello, 8 ft., may be correctly given to a stop, of full compass, having a bolder and less cutting tone than the Violin. The Violoncello retains its 8 ft. pitch when introduced in the Pedal Organ.

It is questionable if it is advisable to employ the name Viola in organ stop nomenclature; but it may be used to indicate a stop, of tenor C compass, having a somewhat fuller tone than the VIOLIN. In large Concert-room Organs, in which several unison imitative string-toned stops are inserted, the name VIOLA will doubtless be found useful to indicate a special tone-color between those of the VIOLIN and VIOLONCELLO.

The stops, of 16 ft. pitch, voiced in imitation of the tones of the orchestral Double Bass should most certainly bear that distinctive name, either in the English form of DOUBLE BASS, or the Italian forms of CONTRA-BASSO or VIOLONE.

The names of the older, and now disused, orchestral stringed and bowed instruments (namely, the Viola d'Amore,* Viola da Gamba, Viola Pomposa,† and Viola di Bardone‡) may certainly be retained for use in stop nomenclature; and if judiciously employed to designate imitative string-toned stops of a peculiarly delicate intonation, rich in harmonics, no objection can be urged against them, especially after the peculiar qualities of tone which they respectively represent are fixed, and recognized by the organ-playing world.

VI. ORCHESTRAL FLUTE-TONE.—This subdivision embraces only two stops, namely, the ORCHESTRAL FLUTE, CONCERT FLUTE, or FLAUTO TRAVERSO, and the PICCOLO or FLAUTO PICCOLO. The stops so named should in all cases be close imitations, in their tones, of the orchestral instruments they represent in the tonal scheme of the Organ; and when properly made and voiced by the hand of a master, such stops are very satisfactory in this respect. Their tones are pure and of a penetrating quality, distinct from the fuller and rounder sounds yielded by the majority of the stops which group themselves under the third subdivision of the unimitative group; namely, flute organ-tone.

We must not omit to mention in this place the term FLAGEOLET. The instrument bearing that name is not now used in the orchestra, although it was written for in old English scores. The obbligato in the song, "O ruddier than the cherry," was scored by Handel for the Flageolet. The name may appropriately be used to designate a soft stop, of 2 ft. pitch, of a lighter intonation than the PICCOLO.

VII. ORCHESTRAL REED-TONE.—This subdivision is more important in the number and variety of its pipes than that immediately preceding. The names of the orchestral instruments—all of which are more or less closely imitated by the reed stops of the Organ—are Hautboy or Oboe, Bassoon or Fagotto, Double Bassoon or Contrafagotto, Clarinet or Clarinetto, English Horn or Corno Inglese, Basset-Horn or Corno di Bassetto, Saxophone, and Contra-Saxophone.

* The Viola d'Amore is an instrument of the Viol family, having two sets of strings; seven of catgut which were sounded by the bow, and others of metal, stretched below, which sounded by sympathy. The tones produced are of a delicate and singing character. Meyerbeer introduced an obbligato part for it in the first act of the "Huguenots."

† The Viola Pomposa was a species of Viola da Gamba, invented by John Sebastian Bach. It had five catgut strings played by the bow. Its tones were sonorous and very dignified, closely approaching those of the Violoncello.

‡ The Viola di Bardone had six or seven catgut strings sounded by the bow, beneath which were stretched sympathetic metal strings, varying in number from sixteen to thirty-five or forty. The metal strings sounded very faintly in sympathy with the varied tones of the bowed strings, producing a mysterious compound intonation of great sweetness and richness.

The organ stops called by the above names are usually through or complete stops; but they of course imitate the respective orchestral instruments only in those portions of their compass which agree with the compass of the instruments. It cannot be denied, however, that the Organ gains immensely in grandeur and richness of effect by the increased range or compass of all the different tones.

The orchestral Oboe only goes one note or so below middle c^1; accordingly, the two lower octaves of the organ stop cannot be considered as imitative, fine as their tenor and bass tones are in good examples. As the Fagotto furnishes the true bass to the Oboe in the orchestra, the complete organ stop may be labeled OBOE & FAGOTTO or HAUTBOY & BASSOON, 8 FT. But when an independent BASSOON is introduced, the term ORCHESTRAL OBOE is desirable, the organ builder doing his best to carry the low range down in pipes of the same intonation as the imitative section of the stop. It is but right to remark that stops, labeled OBOE, or HAUTBOY, are commonly met with in Organs, the tones of which bear no resemblance to those of the orchestral instrument: it is, therefore, always advisable to label the imitative stop ORCHESTRAL OBOE.

The Clarinets of the orchestra, including the Bass Clarinet, may be accepted as covering the compass of the manual claviers of the Organ. The Bass Clarinet descends to DD, while the small Clarinet in E♭ practically covers the usual limits of the claviers upward. Some builders have the habit of labeling the organ stop CLARINET & BASSOON, apparently under the impression that the Bassoon gives the true bass to the Clarinet, or that the orchestral Clarinets do not descend to the bass octave. This practice, founded on a misconception, should be discontinued. The stop should in all cases be named CLARINET,* with or without the indication of pitch; it is invariably a unison stop. Such fanciful and incorrect names as CORMORNE, CREMONA, CROMORNE, KRUMMHORN, and SCHALMEI, which have been used to designate the stop, should unhesitatingly be swept into oblivion.

The Orchestral Corno di Bassetto yields notes extending from FF to c^3, and is, accordingly, somewhat short in compass both downward and upward with respect to the usual compass of the manual divisions of the Organ. The organ stop imitating this effective instrument is invariably a complete one, the few additional notes being decidedly a gain. Several very satisfactory examples of the CORNO DI BASSETTO, 8 FT., appear in English Organs built by Willis; one notable example being in the Solo division of the Organ in St. George's Hall, Liverpool. The tones of the orchestral Corno di Bassetto are fuller and richer than those of the Clarinets. Mozart, as Berlioz says, "has used this fine instrument in two parts for darkening the coloring of his harmonies in his 'Requiem'; and has assigned to it some important solos in his opera of 'La Clemenza di Tito.'"

The orchestral Fagotto has a compass, from BBB♭, of three octaves and five semitones: it is, accordingly, two semitones below the accepted manual range of

* Some few persons favor the term CLARIONET; and, although the stop certainly cannot be said to be a diminutive of the CLARION, it can be used if preferred. The following extract from the celebrated "Century Dictionary" may help in deciding the more correct spelling: "CLARINET (klar'i-net or klar-i-net'), *n.* Also *clarionet* (resting on *clarion*); = D. Dan. *klarinet* = G. *clarinet* [correctly Clarinette or Klarinette] = Sw. *klarinett*, < Fr. *clarinette*, < It. *clarinetto* (= Sp. *clarinete* = Pg. *clarineta*), dim. of *clarino*." This favors the adoption of the term CLARINET in preference to CLARIONET. See foot note on page 513.

the Organ, but considerably short of it upward. Notwithstanding this fact, there is no valid objection to the name FAGOTTO or BASSOON being applied to a complete manual stop, which, within the true limits, imitates the orchestral instrument as closely as the skill of the pipe voicer can accomplish.

The orchestral Contrafagotto or Double Bassoon has a compass from BBBB♭ to F, two octaves and seven semitones. The organ stop of the same name is accordingly perfectly suitable for the Pedal Organ, the compass of which is only two semitones less than that of the orchestral instrument. A fine stop, labeled CONTRAFAGOTTO, is to be found in the Solo division of the Organ in St. George's Hall, Liverpool. This is, of course, of 16 ft. pitch; and is imitative of the orchestral instrument so far as its compass extends, being carried up in imitation of the Fagotto. Its original compass was from GGG to a^3; but its present compass is from CC to c^4. (Altered in 1898.) A CONTRAFAGOTTO, 16 FT., also appears in the Pedal Organ of this instrument, furnishing the true bass to the FAGOTTO, 8 FT.

The Corno Inglese has the same compass as the orchestral Oboe, but is a fifth below it in pitch; it extends from tenor E to b^2. The CORNO INGLESE of the Organ may be introduced either as a complete or a tenor C stop; in both cases it will exceed the compass of the orchestral instrument both downward and upward.

The quality of the tone of the orchestral Corno Inglese is somewhat similar to that of the Oboe, but of a more sombre and grave character. Berlioz says: "It is a melancholy, dreamy, and rather noble voice." Let organ builders "look to it" when they take the name of this "noble voice" in vain; for it is reasonable to expect when one sees its name on a stop handle that there is something of a refined and characteristic nature behind it.

We are not aware of the name SAXOPHONE having been applied to an organ stop save in one instance (see SAXOPHONE, page 559); but it is quite at the disposal of the artistic voicer who can produce a labial or reed stop worthy of the name, and imitative of the orchestral instrument. Speaking of the Saxophones, Berlioz remarks: "These new voices given to the orchestra possess most rare and precious qualities. Soft and penetrating in the higher part, full and rich in the lower part, their medium has something profoundly expressive. It is, in short, a quality of tone *sui generis*, presenting vague analogies with the sounds of the Violoncello, of the Clarinet and Corno Inglese, and invested with a brazen tinge which imparts a quite peculiar accent." Here, then, is a problem for the skill of the reed voicer; but, in the name of Art, let him use the name SAXOPHONE only when he has produced a stop worthy of it. The Bass Saxophone goes down to BBB, while the high Saxophone, in E♭, extends upward to f^3; accordingly this fine family of instruments practically covers the manual compass of the Organ. We understand there is a Contra-Saxophone; therefore it is open to the organ builder to enrich the resources of the Pedal Organ by adding a characteristic reed of 16 ft. pitch, carrying down the tone of the manual SAXOPHONE, 8 FT. Its name should be, as above, CONTRA-SAXOPHONE* or DOUBLE BASS SAXOPHONE.

* The Author gave the name CONTRA-SAXOPHONE to a remarkably fine *free reed* stop of 16 ft. pitch, specially made for him by the late Mr. Hilborne L. Roosevelt, of New York, and inserted in the pedal department of his Chamber Organ. In tone it followed Berlioz's description, and very closely resembled the Bass Saxophone in its higher register.

VIII. ORCHESTRAL BRASS-TONE.—The orchestral brass instruments which are more or less closely imitated by the organ stops which are comprised under this important subdivision are the Trumpet or Tromba, Horn or Corno, Cornopean, Trombone, Ophicleide, Bombardon, and Bass Tuba. All these instruments, with the exception of the Horn, can be fairly well represented in the Organ by reed stops; but the hand of the artist is everywhere required in their fabrication before such stops become worthy of bearing the names of the orchestral instruments.

The manual organ stop which imitates the orchestral Trumpet, in the limited number of notes possible on the instrument, is invariably a complete one. The bass is accordingly unimitative unless it be accepted as representing Trombone tone. Notwithstanding this, we do not suggest any departure from the present mode of naming the complete stop. How far we are guaranteed in using the name DOUBLE TRUMPET is open to question, for there is no such instrument as a Double Trumpet or Contra-Tromba invented for the orchestra. But it may be accepted as a fairly expressive appellation for a bright-toned stop of 16 ft. pitch, resembling the TRUMPET in its higher register. When the stop is full-toned and inclined to be brassy in character, the term TROMBONE is certainly more satisfactory and, indeed, more correct.

The TROMBONE in the Pedal Organ is invariably a stop of 16 ft. pitch; and notwithstanding that the orchestral Bass Trombone (rarely used on account of its great strain on the performer) does not cover entirely, even with its so-called "pedal notes," the 16 ft. octave, the name TROMBONE, 16 FT., or, more expressively, BASS TROMBONE, may be used in the most strict stop nomenclature. The reed stops of 32 ft. pitch, commonly designated by the following names: POSAUNE, 32 FT., or CONTRAPOSAUNE, and BOMBARDE, 32 FT., may, in accordance with our suggested system of nomenclature, be better distinguished by the name DOUBLE BASS TROMBONE, 32 FT., or TROMBONE CONTRA-BASSO, 32 FT. Although such names are not found applied to orchestral instruments, they are quite legitimate when used to designate organ stops, clearly defining their true nature and position in the general tonal appointment of the Organ. Nothing more can reasonably be expected of a name, when we bear in mind how very few names of organ stops define anything clearly.

We may here suggest that the powerful reed stops of the Organ, on wind of high pressures, of the TROMBONE, TRUMPET, or any other class, be distinguished from the ordinary stops of the same names by the addition of the term *Grand*, thus: GRAND TROMBONE, GRAND TRUMPET; or in Italian, TROMBONE GRANDE, TROMBA GRANDE.

The orchestral Ophicleides are three in number; namely, the Double Bass, Bass, and Alto, covering a compass extending from DDD to f^2*. It is quite rea-

*Although for our present purpose, relating to imitative organ stops, we speak of the three Ophicleides as orchestral instruments, it is right to remark that only the Bass Ophicleide is used in the true orchestra, and even that is now commonly superseded by the Bass Tuba. Berlioz says: "The Double Bass Ophicleides are very little known. They may be useful in very large orchestras." Of the Alto Ophicleides, he remarks: "They are employed in some kinds of military music to fill up the harmony, and even to execute certain phrases of melody."

sonable that both 16 ft. and 8 ft. organ stops should be made in imitation of this family, and named DOUBLE BASS OPHICLEIDE, 16 FT., and OPHICLEIDE, 8 FT., respectively. The former may also be named CONTRA-BASS OPHICLEIDE, 16 FT.

The names BOMBARDON and BASS TUBA should be applied to stops, of 16 ft. pitch, imitating as closely as possible the tones of the brass instruments so called. When stops of a similar tonal character, of 32 ft. pitch, are introduced, they may properly be named DOUBLE BOMBARDON or CONTRA-BOMBARDON, and DOUBLE BASS TUBA or CONTRA-BASS TUBA.

The orchestral Corno or Horn yields a quality of tone replete with pathos and beauty, and one which it seems hopeless to obtain from organ pipes. In organ nomenclature the name HORN is commonly given to a full-toned and somewhat powerful unison manual stop, which fails, however, to represent the orchestral instrument to any satisfactory degree. The HORN, although when skilfully made and artistically voiced is rounder and smoother than the TRUMPET, produces too much of the characteristic clang of the orchestral Trumpet and Trombone. We despair of ever hearing a good imitation of the Horn by a stop with the usual form of striking reed; but there may be possibilities in the direction of free reed and labial pipes, either separately or in combination, not yet fully tested by artistic voicers.* At the present time organ builders do not seem to aim at a close imitation; and this is to be regretted, for no more valuable quality of tone could be added to the Concert-room Organ.

The orchestral Cornopean, or Cornet à pistons, is supposed to be imitated in the Organ by the stop called the CORNOPEAN, 8 FT. The imitation is, however, far from being satisfactory; indeed, like the Horn, the Cornopean, played by a master, yields tones beyond the powers of organ pipes, at least, as they are at present fashioned. Of course the term CORNOPEAN may be retained; but it is to be hoped a little more discrimination will be exercised, as regards its application, by organ builders. Let it not be given, as in too many cases it is, to a stop which turns out to be too bad to be called either TRUMPET or HORN, although perhaps it was originally intended for one or the other. There is something about the name CORNOPEAN which goes far to disarm criticism; and, accordingly, a stop so called will pass, while even a much better one, designated TRUMPET or HORN, will be condemned. The chief charm of the Cornopean, when not used instead of the Trumpet in the orchestra, is its peculiar flexibility and expression—virtues to which no imitation hitherto introduced in the Organ can lay claim.

The term EUPHONIUM may, appropriately, be used to designate a stop, of 16 ft. pitch, of a rich and refined character, resembling the magnificent tones of the brass instrument which bears that name. The Organ EUPHONIUM, if formed of free reed pipes and blown by a wind of six or seven inches pressure, would be a very valuable addition to either the manual divisions or the pedal department of the Concert-room Organ. It would be effective in both solo passages and in com-

*The closest approach to the tone of the Orchestral Horn which has come under our observation was produced by a medium-scaled labial stop, perforated like the KERAULOPHONE. It only required a powerful intonation to be a satisfactory imitation. We are of opinion that such a stop in association with a full-toned free reed would produce a good HORN.

bination. The name Euphone is at present used to designate a stop (properly a free reed of 16 ft. pitch) of a soft and rich tonal character.

There can be no objection raised to the term Clarion, or Clarino, for an assertive octave stop of the Trumpet species, especially as the name is now so well understood; but the term Octave Trumpet, or in Italian Tromba Alta or Tromba all' Ottava, would fit in better with our suggested nomenclature. It would distinctly indicate its tonal character, and could not possibly be misunderstood by the organist.

We leave this brief survey of a somewhat difficult subject to the consideration of our readers interested in the advancement of all matters connected with the Organ; and we may conclude this Chapter with the late Mr. Frederick Archer's apposite words: "The importance of a well defined system of universal application is abundantly obvious, but it cannot be denied that there are formidable obstacles in the way of the reformer."